AMERICAN GOVERNMENT

Freedom and Power

BRIEF 2006 EDITION

Theodore J. Lowi
CORNELL UNIVERSITY

Benjamin Ginsberg
THE JOHNS HOPKINS UNIVERSITY

Kenneth A. Shepsle
HARVARD UNIVERSITY

 W. W. Norton & Company New York • London

W. W. Norton & Company has been independent since its founding in 1923, when William Warder Norton and Mary D. Herter Norton first published lectures delivered at the People's Institute, the adult education division of New York City's Cooper Union. The Nortons soon expanded their program beyond the Institute, publishing books by celebrated academics from America and abroad. By mid-century, the two major pillars of Norton's publishing program—trade books and college texts—were firmly established. In the 1950s, the Norton family transferred control of the company to its employees, and today—with a staff of four hundred and a comparable number of trade, college, and professional titles published each year—W. W. Norton & Company stands as the largest and oldest publishing house owned wholly by its employees.

Editor: Stephen Dunn
Copy Editors: Andy Saff and Patterson Lamb
Project Editor: Sarah Mann
Production Manager: Diane O'Connor
Book design by JoAnn Simony
Composition by Matrix Publishing Services
Manufacturing by: Quebecor World

Library of Congress Cataloging-in-Publication Data
Lowi, Theodore J.
  American government : freedom and power / Theodore J. Lowi, Benjamin Ginsberg, Kenneth A. Shepsie — Brief 2006 ed.
    p.   cm.
  Includes bibliographical references and index.
  ISBN 0-393-92484-X (pbk.)
    1. United States—Politics and government—Textbooks   I. Ginsberg, Benjamin
  II. Shepsie, Kenneth A.   III. Title

JK276I.69 2005c
320 473–dc22   2005049880

W. W. Norton & Company, Inc., 500 Fifth Avenue, New York, N.Y. 10110
www.wwnorton.com

W. W. Norton & Company Ltd., Castle House, 75/76 Wells St., London W1T 3QT

1 2 3 4 5 6 7 8 9 0

CONTENTS

Preface   ix

PART I

Foundations

1 Freedom and Power:
  An Introduction to the Problem   3

  HOW DOES AMERICAN GOVERNMENT
  WORK?   3

  MAKING SENSE OF GOVERNMENT
  AND POLITICS   5
    Foundations of Government   5
    Forms of Government   7
    Influencing the Government: Politics   8

  FROM COERCION TO CONSENT   9
    Limits and Democratization   9
    The Great Transformation: Tying Democracy
      to Strong Government   11

  DOES AMERICAN DEMOCRACY WORK?   12
    Delegating Authority in a Representative
      Democracy   12
    The Trade-off between Freedom and
      Order   12
    The Instability of Majority Rule   13

  KEY TERMS   13

  FOR FURTHER READING   14

2 Constructing a Government:
  The Founding and the
  Constitution   15

  THE FIRST FOUNDING: INTERESTS
  AND CONFLICTS   17
    Political Strife and the Radicalizing
      of the Colonists   17
    The Declaration of Independence   17
    The Articles of Confederation   18

  THE SECOND FOUNDING: FROM
  COMPROMISE TO CONSTITUTION   18
    International Standing and Balance
      of Power   19
    The Constitutional Convention   19

  THE CONSTITUTION   21
    The Legislative Branch   23
    The Executive Branch   26
    The Judicial Branch   26
    National Unity and Power   27
    Amending the Constitution   29
    Ratifying the Constitution   29
    Constitutional Limitations on the
      National Government's Power   29

  THE FIGHT FOR RATIFICATION   32

  CHANGING THE FRAMEWORK:
  CONSTITUTIONAL AMENDMENT   33
    Amendments: Many Are Called,
      Few Are Chosen   33
    The Twenty-seven Amendments   35

  DOES THE CONSTITUTION WORK?   38
    To Whose Benefit?   39
    To What Ends?   40

  CHAPTER REVIEW   40

  KEY TERMS   41

  FOR FURTHER READING   42

3 The Constitutional Framework: Federalism and the Separation of Powers   43

HOW DO FEDERALISM AND THE SEPARATION OF POWERS WORK AS POLITICAL INSTITUTIONS?   43

THE FIRST PRINCIPLE: FEDERALISM   44

Federalism in the Constitution   45

The Slow Growth of the National Government's Power   48

Cooperative Federalism and Grants-in-Aid   51

THE SECOND PRINCIPLE: THE SEPARATION OF POWERS   59

Checks and Balances   60

Legislative Supremacy   60

The Role of the Supreme Court   60

DO FEDERALISM AND THE SEPARATION OF POWERS WORK?   62

CHAPTER REVIEW   64

KEY TERMS   65

FOR FURTHER READING   66

4 The Constitution and the Individual: The Bill of Rights, Civil Liberties, and Civil Rights   67

CIVIL LIBERTIES: NATIONALIZING THE BILL OF RIGHTS   69

Dual Citizenship   69

The Fourteenth Amendment   71

The Constitutional Revolution in Civil Liberties   74

CIVIL RIGHTS   77

Plessy v. Ferguson: "Separate but Equal"   78

Racial Discrimination after World War II   79

Civil Rights after Brown v. Board of Education   80

The Rise of the Politics of Rights   81

CHAPTER REVIEW   90

KEY TERMS   91

FOR FURTHER READING   91

PART 2

Institutions

5 Congress: The First Branch   95

HOW DOES CONGRESS WORK?   95

THE ORGANIZATION OF CONGRESS   96

Bicameralism: House and Senate   96

Political Parties: Congress's Oldest Hierarchy   98

The Committee System: The Core of Congress   101

The Staff System: Staffers and Agencies   103

Informal Organization: The Caucuses   103

RULES OF LAWMAKING: HOW A BILL BECOMES A LAW   104

Committee Deliberation   104

Debate   105

Conference Committee: Reconciling House and Senate Versions of a Bill   105

Presidential Action   107

HOW CONGRESS DECIDES   107

Constituency   108

Interest Groups   108

Party Discipline   109

Weighing Diverse Influences   113

BEYOND LEGISLATION: ADDITIONAL CONGRESSIONAL POWERS   114

Oversight   114

Advice and Consent: Special Senate Powers   115

Impeachment   116

Direct Patronage   116

DOES CONGRESS WORK?   117

CHAPTER REVIEW   120

KEY TERMS   121

FOR FURTHER READING   122

6 The President   124

HOW DOES THE PRESIDENCY WORK?   124

THE CONSTITUTIONAL BASIS OF THE PRESIDENCY   126

THE CONSTITUTIONAL POWERS OF THE PRESIDENT   126

Expressed Powers   127

THE RISE OF PRESIDENTIAL
GOVERNMENT   132
   The Legislative Epoch, 1800–1933   134
   The New Deal and the Presidency   135

PRESIDENTIAL GOVERNMENT   137
   Formal Resources of Presidential Power   137
   Informal Resources of Presidential
     Power   141

IS THE PRESIDENCY STRONG OR WEAK?   148

CHAPTER REVIEW   150

KEY TERMS   150

FOR FURTHER READING   151

7 The Executive Branch: Bureaucracy
   in a Democracy   152

WHY BUREAUCRACY?   153
   Bureaucratic Organization Enhances
     Efficiency   155
   Bureaucracies Allow Governments to
     Operate   155
   Bureaucrats Fulfill Important Roles   156

HOW IS THE EXECUTIVE BRANCH
ORGANIZED?   158
   Clientele Agencies Serve Particular
     Interests   160
   Agencies for Maintenance of the Union
     Keep the Government Going   160
   Regulatory Agencies Guide Individual
     Conduct   162
   Agencies for Redistribution Implement
     Fiscal/Monetary and Welfare
     Policies   162

WHO CONTROLS THE BUREAUCRACY?   163
   The President as Chief Executive Can Direct
     Agencies   164
   Congress Promotes Responsible
     Bureacracy   165

HOW CAN BUREAUCRACY BE REDUCED?   167
   Termination   167
   Devolution   170

DOES BUREAUCRACY WORK?   171

CHAPTER REVIEW   173

KEY TERMS   174

FOR FURTHER READING   174

8 The Federal Courts:
   Least Dangerous Branch
   or Imperial Judiciary?   175

HOW COURTS WORK?   175
   Courts as Political Institutions   175
   Cases and the Law   179
   Types of Courts   180

FEDERAL JURISDICTION   182
   Federal Trial Courts   183
   Federal Appellate Courts   183
   The Supreme Court   183
   How Judges Are Appointed   184

JUDICIAL REVIEW   187
   Judicial Review of Acts of Congress   188
   Judicial Review of State Actions   188
   Judicial Review of Federal Agency
     Actions   188
   Judicial Review and Presidential Power   189
   Judicial Review and Lawmaking   190

THE SUPREME COURT IN ACTION   191
   How Cases Reach the Supreme Court   191
   Controlling the Flow of Cases: The Role
     of the Solicitor General   194
   The Supreme Court's Procedures   195
   Judicial Decision Making   197
   Other Institutions of Government   199

JUDICIAL POWER AND POLITICS   200
   Traditional Limitations on the Federal
     Courts   200
   Two Judicial Revolutions   201

CHAPTER REVIEW   204

KEY TERMS   205

FOR FURTHER READING   206

PART 3

Politics and Policy

9 Public Opinion and the Media   209

WHAT ARE THE ORIGINS OF PUBLIC
OPINION?   212
   Political Socialization   213
   Political Ideology   220

How Are Political Opinions Formed? 222
  Knowledge and Information 222
  Government and Political Leaders 224
  Private Groups 226
The Media 227
  Shaping Events 227
  The Sources of Media Power 228
  The Rise of Adversarial Journalism 230
Measuring Public Opinion 232
  Constructing Public Opinion from
    Surveys 233
Public Opinion and Government
Policy 237
Chapter Review 238
Key Terms 239
For Further Reading 240

10 Elections 241
How Elections Work 241
Regulating the Electoral Process 244
  Electoral Composition 244
  Translating Voters' Choices into Electoral
    Outcomes 248
  Insulating Decision-Making Processes 251
  Direct Democracy: The Referendum and
    Recall 254
How Voters Decide 255
  The Bases of Electoral Choices 255
The 2004 Elections 258
  Democratic Opportunities 259
  Republican Strategies 260
  The End Game 260
Campaign Finance 261
  Sources of Campaign Funds 262
  Implications for Democracy 266
Do Elections Matter? 267
  Why Is There a Decline in Voter
    Turnout? 267
  Why Do Elections Matter as Political
    Institutions? 270
Chapter Review 271
Key Terms 272
For Further Reading 273

11 Political Parties 274
How Parties Work 274
Functions of the Parties 276
  Recruiting Candidates 277
  Nominations 277
  Getting Out the Vote 278
  Facilitations of Mass Electoral Choice 278
  Influence on National Government 278
  President and Party 280
The Two-Party System in America 281
  The Democrats 281
  The Republicans 283
  Electoral Alignments and Realignments 284
  Third Parties 287
How Strong Are Political Parties
Today? 289
  High-Tech Politics 290
  Contemporary Party Organizations 293
  The Role of the Parties in Contemporary
    Politics 296
Chapter Review 297
Key Terms 298
For Further Reading 299

12 Groups and Interests 300
How Do Interest Groups Work? 300
The Character of Interest Groups 302
  What Interests Are Represented 304
  Organizational Components 305
  The "Free Rider" Problem 306
  The Characteristics of Members 307
The Proliferation of Groups 308
  The Expansion of Government 308
  The New Politics Movement and Public
    Interest Groups 308
Strategies: The Quest for Political
Power 309
  Lobbying 310
  Cultivating Access 313
  Using the Courts (Litigation) 315
  Mobilizing Public Opinion 316
  Using Electoral Politics 317

Do Interest Groups Work? 321
  Do Interest Groups Foster or Impede
    Democracy? 322
Chapter Review 323
Key Terms 323
For Further Reading 324

13 Introduction to Public Policy 325
How Does Public Policy Work? 325
Substantive Uses of Public Policies 326
  Managing the Economy 326
  Maintaining a Capitalist Economy 329
  The Welfare System as Fiscal and Social
    Policy 332
Implementing Public Policies: The
Techniques of Control 339
  Promotional Techniques 339
  Regulatory Techniques 342
  Redistributive Techniques 345
Chapter Review 346
Key Terms 348
For Further Reading 349

14 Foreign Policy and Democracy 350
How Does Foreign Policy Work? 350
  Who Makes Foreign Policy? 350
  Who Shapes Foreign Policy? 353
  Putting It Together 355
The Values in American Foreign
Policy 356
  Legacies of the Traditional System 357
  The Great Leap to World Power 357
The Instruments of Modern American
Foreign Policy 358
  Diplomacy 359

  The United Nations 360
  The International Monetary Structure 362
  Economic Aid 363
  Collective Security 364
  Military Deterrence 366
Roles Nations Play 368
  Choosing a Role 369
  Roles for America Today 370
Does Foreign Policy Work? 375
Chapter Review 376
Key Terms 377
For Further Reading 378

Epilogue: Governance 379
Big Government 379
Can the Government Govern? 381
  The Eisenhower Administration 382
  The Kennedy and Johnson Years 384
  Presidents Nixon and Ford 385
  Jimmy Carter 386
  Ronald Reagan and George H. W. Bush 387
  William Jefferson Clinton 389
  George W. Bush 392
Doing What Is Right 394

Appendix
  The Declaration of Independence A3
  The Constitution of the United States of
    America A6
  Amendments to the Constitution A15
  The Federalist Papers
    No. 10: Madison A22
    No. 51: Madison A26

Glossary of Terms A29

Index A43

*T*his Brief Edition of *American Government: Freedom and Power* is designed specifically for use in courses whose length or format requires a more concise text. We preserved as much as possible of the narrative style and historic and comparative analysis of the larger text. Though this is a Brief Edition, we have sought to provide a full and detailed discussion of every topic that, in our view, is central to understanding American government and politics. We hope that we have written a book that is physically brief but is not intellectually sketchy.

Someone once asked if it is difficult for scholars to "write down" to introductory students. No. It is difficult to "write up" to them. Introductory students, of whatever age or reading level, need more, require more, and expect more of a book.

A good teaching book, like a good novel or play, is written on two levels. One is the level of the narrative, the story line, the characters in action. The second is the level of character development, of the argument of the book or play. We would not be the first to assert that there is much of the theatrical about politics today, but our book may be unusual to the extent that we took that assertion as a guide. We have packed it full of narrative—with characters and with the facts about the complex situations in which they find themselves. We have been determined not to lose sight of the second level, yet we have tried to avoid making it so prominent as to define us as preachers rather than teachers.

We hope also that we brought over from our teaching experience a full measure of sympathy for all who teach the introductory course, most particularly those who are obliged to teach the course from departmental necessity rather than voluntarily as a desired part of their career. And we hope our book will help them appreciate the course as we do—as an opportunity to make sense of a whole political system. Much can be learned about the system from a reexamination of the innumerable familiar facts, under the still more challenging condition that the facts be somehow interesting, significant, and, above all, linked.

All Americans are to a great extent familiar with the politics and government of their own country. No fact is intrinsically difficult to grasp, and in such an open society, facts abound. In America, many facts are commonplace that are suppressed elsewhere. The ubiquity of political commonplaces is indeed a problem, but it can be turned into a virtue. These very commonplaces give us a vocabulary that is widely shared, and such a vocabulary enables us to communicate effectively at the narrative level of the book, avoiding abstract concepts and professional language (jargon). Reaching beyond the commonplaces to the second, deeper level of development also identifies what is to us the single most important task of the teacher of political science—to confront a million facts and to choose from among them the small number of really significant ones.

We have tried to provide a framework to help teachers make choices among facts and to help students make some of the choices for themselves. This is good political science, and it is good citizenship, which means more than mere obedience and voting; it means participation through constructive criticism, being able to pierce through the information explosion to the core of political reality.

Evaluation makes political science worth doing but also more difficult to do. Academics make a distinction between the hard sciences and the soft sciences, implying that hard science is the only real science: laboratories, people in white coats, precision instruments making measurements to several decimal points, testing hypotheses with "hard data." But as medical scientist Jared Diamond observes, that is a recent and narrow view, considering that science in Latin means knowledge and careful observation. Diamond suggests, and we agree, that a better distinction is between hard (i.e., difficult) science and easy science, with political science fitting into the hard category, precisely because many of the most significant phenomena in the world cannot be put in a test tube and measured to several decimal points. We must nevertheless approach them scientifically. And more: Unlike physical scientists, social scientists have an obligation to judge whether the reality could be better. In trying to meet that obligation, we hope to demonstrate how interesting and challenging political science can be.

THE DESIGN OF THE BOOK

The objective we have taken upon ourselves in writing this book is thus to advance our understanding of freedom and power by exploring in the fullest possible detail the way Americans have tried to balance the two through careful crafting of the rules, through constructing balanced institutions, and by maintaining moderate forms of organized politics. The book is divided into four parts, reflecting the historical process by which freedom and governmental power are (or are not) kept in balance. Part 1, "Foundations," comprises the chapters concerned with the writing of the rules of the contract. The founding of 1787–1789 put it all together, but that was actually a second effort after

a first failure. The original contract, the Articles of Confederation, did not achieve an acceptable balance—too much freedom, and not enough power. The second founding, the Constitution ratified in 1789, was itself an imperfect effort to establish the rules, and within two years new terms were added—the first ten amendments, called the Bill of Rights. And for the next century and a half following their ratification in 1791, the courts played umpire and translator in the struggle to interpret those terms. Chapter 1 introduces our theme. Chapter 2 concentrates on the founding itself. Chapters 3 and 4 chronicle the long struggle to establish what was meant by the three great principles of limited government: *federalism, separation of powers,* and *individual liberties and rights.*

Part 2, "Institutions," includes the chapters sometimes referred to as the "nuts and bolts." But none of these particles of government mean anything except in the larger context of the goals governments must meet and the limits that have been imposed upon them. Chapter 5 is an introduction to the fundamental problem of *representative government* as this has been institutionalized in Congress. Congress, with all its problems, is the most creative legislative body in the world. But how well does Congress provide a meeting ground between consent and governing? How are society's demands taken into account in debates on the floor of Congress and deliberations by its committees? What interests turn out to be most effectively "represented" in Congress? What is the modern Congress's constituency?

Chapter 6 explores the same questions for the presidency. Although Article II of the Constitution provides that the president should see that the laws made by Congress are "faithfully executed," the presidency was always part of our theory of representative government, and the modern presidency has increasingly become a law *maker* rather than merely a law implementor. What, then, does a strong presidency do to the conduct and the consequences of representative government?

Chapter 7 treats the executive branch as an entity separate from the presidency, but ultimately it has to be brought back into the general process of representative government. That, indeed, is the overwhelming problem of what we call "bureaucracy in a democracy." After spelling out the organization and workings of "the bureaucracy" in detail, we then turn to an evaluation of the role of Congress and the president in imposing some political accountability on an executive branch composed of roughly five million civilian and military personnel.

Chapter 8 on the judiciary should not be lost in the shuffle. Referred to by Hamilton as "the least dangerous branch," the judiciary truly has become a co-equal branch, to such an extent that if Hamilton were alive today he would probably eat his words.

Part 3 we entitle "Politics and Policy." Politics encompasses all the efforts by any and all individuals and groups inside as well as outside the government to determine what government will do and on whose behalf it will be done. Our chapters take the order of our conception of how politics developed since the Revolution and how politics works today: Chapter 9, "Public Opinion and the Media"; Chapter 10, "Elections"; Chapter 11, "Political Parties"; and Chapter 12, "Groups and Interests." But we recognize that, although there may be a pattern to American politics, it is not readily predictable.

The last chapters are primarily about public policies, which are the most deliberate and goal-oriented aspects of the still-larger phenomenon of "government in action." Chapter 13 is virtually a handbook of public policy. Since most Americans know far less about policies than they do about institutions and politics, we felt it was necessary to provide a usable, common vocabulary of public policy. Since public policies are most often defined by the goals that the government establishes in broad rhetorical terms and since there can be an uncountable number of goals, we have tried to get beyond and behind goals by looking at the "techniques of control" that any public policy goal must embody if the goal is even partially to be fulfilled. Chapter 14, "Foreign Policy and Democracy," turns to the international realm and America's place in it. Our concern here is to understand American for-eign policies and why we have adopted the policies that we have. Given the traditional American fear of "the state" and the genuine danger of international involvements to domestic democracy, a chapter on foreign policies is essential to a book on American government and also reveals a great deal about America as a culture. We conclude by assessing government's ability to govern.

ACKNOWLEDGMENTS

Our students at Cornell, Johns Hopkins, and Harvard have already been identified as an essential factor in the writing of this book. They have been our most immediate intellectual community, a hospitable one indeed. Another part of our community, perhaps a large suburb, is the discipline of political science itself. Our debt to the scholarship of our colleagues is scientifically measurable, probably to several decimal points, in the footnotes of each chapter. Despite many complaints that the field is too scientific or not scientific enough, political science is alive and well in the United States. It is an aspect of democracy itself, and it has grown and changed in response to the developments in government and politics that we have chronicled in our book.

There have, of course, been individuals on whom we have relied in particular. Of all writers, living and dead, we find ourselves most in debt to the writing of two—James Madison and Alexis de Tocqueville. Many other great authors have shaped us as they have shaped all political scientists. But Madison and Tocqueville have stood for us not only as the bridge to all timeless political problems; they represent the ideal of political science itself—that political science must be steadfastly scientific in the search for what is, yet must keep alive a strong sense of what ought to be, recognizing that democracy is neither natural nor invariably good, and must be fiercely dedicated to constant critical analysis of all political institutions in order to contribute to the maintenance of a favorable balance between individual freedom and public power.

We are pleased to acknowledge our debt to the many colleagues who had a direct and active role in criticism and preparation of the manuscript. We have relied heavily on the thoughtful manuscript reviews we received from David Canon, University of Wisconsin; Russell Hanson, Indiana University; William Keech, University of North Carolina; Donald Kettl, University of Wisconsin; Anne Khademian, University of Wisconsin; William McLauchlan, Purdue University; J. Roger Baker, Wittenburg University; James Lennertz, Lafayette College; Allan McBride, Grambling State University; and Joseph Peek, Jr., Georgia State University. The advice we received from these colleagues was especially welcome because all had used the book in their own classrooms. Other colleagues who offered helpful comments based upon their own experience with the text include Douglas Costain, University of Colorado; Robert Hoffert, Colorado State University; David Marcum, University of Wyoming; Mark Silverstein, Boston University; and Norman Thomas, University of Cincinnati.

We are also extremely grateful to a number of colleagues who were kind enough to lend us their classrooms. During the past eight years, we had the opportunity to lecture at a number of colleges and universities around the country and to benefit from discussing our book with those who know it best—colleagues and students who used it. We appreciate the gracious welcome we received at Austin Community College, Cal State-Fullerton, University of Central Oklahoma, Emory University, Gainesville College, Georgia Southern University, Georgia State University, Golden West College, Grambling State, University of Houston–University Park, University of Illinois–Chicago, University of Illinois–Urbana–Champaign, University of Maryland–College Park, University of Massachusetts–Amherst, Morgan State University, University of North Carolina–Chapel Hill, University of North Texas, University of Oklahoma, Oklahoma State University, Pasadena City College, University of Richmond, Sam Houston State, San Bernadino Valley College, Santa Barbara City College, Santa Monica College, University of Southern California, Temple University, University of Texas–Austin, Texas Tech University, Virginia Commonwealth University, and University of Wisconsin–Madison.

We also are grateful for the talents and hard work of several research assistants, whose contribution can never be adequately compensated: Douglas Dow, Rebecca Fisher, John Forren, Michael Harvey, Doug Harris, Brenda Holzinger, Steve McGovern, Melody Butler, Nancy Johnson, Noah Silverman, David Lytell, Mingus Mapps, Dennis Merryfield, Rachel Reiss, Nandini Sathe, Rob Speel, Jennifer Waterston, and David Wirls. For this edition, Israel Waismel-Manor devoted a great deal of time and energy.

Jacqueline Discenza not only typed several drafts of the manuscript, but also helped to hold the project together. We thank her for her hard work and dedication.

Perhaps above all, we wish to thank those who kept the production and all the loose ends of the book coherent and in focus. Steve Dunn has been an extremely talented editor, continuing to offer numerous suggestions for each new edition. Aaron Javsicas helped keep track of the many details. Sarah Mann has been a superb project editor, following the great tradition of her predecessors. We are grateful for the painstaking care and close reading of copy editors Andy Saff and Patterson Lamb and proofreader Maura Burnett. Diane O'Connor has been an efficient production manager.

We are more than happy, however, to absolve all these contributors from any flaws, errors, and misjudgments that will inevitably be discovered. From that standpoint, a book ought to try to be perfect. But substantively we have not tried to write a flawless book; we have not tried to write a book to please everyone. We have again tried to write an effective book, a book that cannot be taken lightly. Our goal was not to make every reader a political scientist. Our goal was to restore politics as a subject matter of vigorous and enjoyable discourse, recapturing it from the bondage of the thirty-second sound bite and the thirty-page technical briefing. Every person can be knowledgeable because everything about politics is accessible. One does not have to be a television anchor to profit from political events. One does not have to be a philosopher to argue about the requisites of democracy, a lawyer to dispute constitutional interpretations, an economist to debate a public policy. We would be very proud if our book contributes in a small way to the restoration of the ancient art of political controversy.

Theodore J. Lowi
Benjamin Ginsberg
Kenneth A. Shepsle
December 2005

PART I

Foundations

CHAPTER 1

Freedom and Power:
An Introduction to the Problem

HOW DOES AMERICAN GOVERNMENT WORK?

$\mathcal{M}$ost Americans find government and politics to be quite confusing. As we shall see in Chapter 9, on public opinion and the media, many individuals have difficulty making sense of major political issues and know very little about the nation's basic political institutions. But perhaps it is no wonder that Americans are bewildered. American government and politics are confusing!

To begin with, America's institutional arrangements are extraordinarily complex. America has many levels of government—federal, state, county, town and city, to say nothing of a host of special and regional authorities. Each of these levels of government operates under its own rules and statutory authority and is related to the others in complex ways. In many nations, regional and local governments are largely appendages of the national government. This is not true in the United States. America's fifty states possess a considerable measure of sovereign authority. The American Constitution, as it has been interpreted by the courts, protects the states from becoming mere vassals of the federal government. In recent years, as Chapter 3 will illustrate, the U.S. Supreme Court has placed strict limits on the federal government's powers vis-à-vis the states.

CORE OF THE ANALYSIS

- Government has become a powerful and pervasive force in the United States.
- American government is based on democratic electoral institutions and popular representative bodies.
- Once citizens perceive that government can respond to their demands, they become increasingly willing to support its expansion.
- The growth of governmental power can pose a threat because it reduces popular influence over policy making and diminishes the need for citizen cooperation.

Each level of government, moreover, consists of a complex array of departments, agencies, offices, and bureaus, all undertaking what often seems to be overlapping tasks. The framers of the Constitution created a complex national government, apportioning governmental powers among three different sets of institutions (see Chapters 2 and 3). In the more than two centuries since the Constitution's ratification, Congress has added to the national government's complexity by creating fifteen Cabinet Departments, such as Treasury, Defense, and Agriculture, a host of bureaus and agencies in the executive branch (Chapter 7), hundreds of general purpose and specialized courts (Chapter 8), and a staff system and staff agencies within the national legislature (Chapter 5).

Each of the cabinet departments is a gigantic enterprise consisting of hundreds of thousands of workers (the government's civilian employees are colloquially known as "feds") engaged in a myriad of activities. America's oldest cabinet departments, created in 1789, are the departments of State, Treasury, Justice, and Defense, which was originally called the War Department. America's newest cabinet department is the Department of Homeland Security (DHS), which was established in 2002 to coordinate the nation's defenses against terrorism. DHS consists of 22 agencies and 170,000 employees; it is responsible for 2,800 power plants, 800,000 bridges, 190,000 miles of natural gas pipelines, and 20,000 miles of border. To create DHS, Congress and the president combined a number of existing agencies such as the Coast Guard, the Customs Service, and the Federal Emergency Management Agency (FEMA). Many of these agencies have a long history of professional antagonism and are not eager to cooperate with one another—something tragically demonstrated in the fall of 2005 when Hurricane Katrina struck New Orleans and other parts of the Gulf Coast. Bureaucratic rivalries add to the difficulties the government faces in carrying out its tasks and the difficulties the citizen faces in trying to understand what the government is doing.

If America's government seems complex, its politics can be utterly bewildering. Like the nation's governmental structure, its political processes have numerous components. For most Americans, the focal point of the politics is the electoral process. As we will see in Chapter 10, tens of millions of Americans participate in a host of national, state, and local elections in which they listen to thousands of candidates debate what may seem to be a perplexing array of issues. Candidates fill the air with promises, charges, and countercharges while an army of pundits and journalists, which we will discuss in Chapter 9, adds its own clamor to the din.

Politics, however, does not end on Election Day. Indeed, given the growing tendency of losers to challenge election results in the courts, even elections do not end on Election Day. Long after the voters have spoken, political struggles continue in the Congress, the executive branch, and the courts (Chapters 5, 6, 7, and 8) and embroil political parties, interest groups, and the mass media (Chapters 9, 10, 11, and 12). In some instances, the participants in political struggles and their goals seem fairly obvious. For example, it is no secret that business and upper-income wage earners strongly support programs of tax reduction; farmers support maintenance of agricultural price supports; labor unions oppose "outsourcing" of production. Each of these forces has created or joined organized groups to advance its cause. We will examine some of these groups in Chapter 12.

In other instances, though, the participants in political struggles and their goals are not so clear. Sometimes corporate groups hide behind environmental causes to surreptitiously promote economic interests. Sometimes groups claiming to want to help the poor and downtrodden seek only to help themselves. And to make matters worse, many of the government's policies are made behind closed doors, away from the light of publicity. For example, as we will see in Chapter 6, after Congress refused to enact his environmental agenda, President Bill Clinton implemented his goals through executive orders and an obscure technique known as "regulatory review." Recent presidents, including Reagan, Clinton, and Bush, have used regulatory review to circumvent the Congress and achieve their objectives through the bureaucratic rule-making process, a process whose importance we will address in Chapter 7.

Government is a powerful force in the United States.

Ordinary citizens can hardly be blamed for failing to understand bureaucratic rule making and regulatory review. For the most part, these are topics that even experienced journalists fail to fully comprehend. Take, for example, a presidential office called OIRA, the Office of Information and Regu-

CENTRAL QUESTIONS

- **How Does American Government Work?**
- **Making Sense of Government and Politics**
  What are the foundations of government?
  What forms can a government take?
  How can citizens influence what government does?
- **From Coercion to Consent**
  By what broad means were constitutional democracies able to secure the consent of their citizens?
  What were the historic consequences of the expansion of democratic politics during this time?
- **Does American Democracy Work?**
  How can the growth of governmental power become a threat to citizens?

latory Assessment. This office within the White House Office of Management and Budget (OMB) is responsible for the president's regulatory agenda. OIRA has become an important instrument of presidential power but has largely gone unnoticed by the press. Can you recall reading a story about OIRA? Try an online search and see how often the media mention OIRA and its mission. When you have finished the search, read Chapters 6 and 7.

MAKING SENSE OF GOVERNMENT AND POLITICS

Can we find order in the apparent chaos of politics? The answer is that we can, and that is precisely the purpose of our text. In the sections below, we shall offer a number of concepts that we hope will clarify why American government works the way it does. *Government* is the term generally used to describe the formal institutions through which a land and its people are ruled. To govern is to rule. *Government is composed of institutions and processes that rulers establish to strengthen and perpetuate their power or control over a territory and its inhabitants.* A government may be as simple as a tribal council that meets occasionally to advise the chief, or as complex as our own vast establishment with its forms, rules, and bureaucracies.

Foundations of Government

Groups aspire to govern for a variety of reasons. Some have the most high-minded aims, while others are little more than ambitious robbers. But whatever their motives and character, those who aspire to rule must be able to secure obedience and fend off rivals as well as collect the revenues needed to accomplish these tasks.[1] That is why, whatever their makeup, governments historically have included two basic components: a means of coercion, such as an army or police force, and a means of collecting revenue. Some governments, including many in the less developed nations today, have consisted of little more than an army and a tax-collecting agency. Other governments, especially those in the developed nations such as the United States, attempt to provide services as well as to collect taxes in order to secure popular consent for control. For some, power is an end in itself. For most, power is necessary to maintain public order. Concept Map 1.1 should give you an idea of the various governmental controls acting upon a recent college graduate.

---

[1]For an excellent discussion, see Charles Tilly, "Reflections on the History of European State-Making," in *The Formation of National States in Western Europe,* ed. Charles Tilly (Princeton: Princeton University Press, 1975), pp. 3–83. See also Charles Tilly, "War Making and State Making as Organized Crime," in *Bringing the State Back In,* ed. Peter Evans, Dietrich Rueschemeyer, and Theda Skocpol (New York: Cambridge University Press, 1895), pp. 169–91.

CONCEPT MAP 1.1

GOVERNMENTAL CONTROL

GOVERNMENT IS A PERVASIVE FORCE IN THE LIVES OF ALL AMERICANS, ESPECIALLY AT THE STATE AND LOCAL LEVEL. THESE ARE SOME OF THE CONTROLS ON A RECENT COLLEGE GRADUATE.

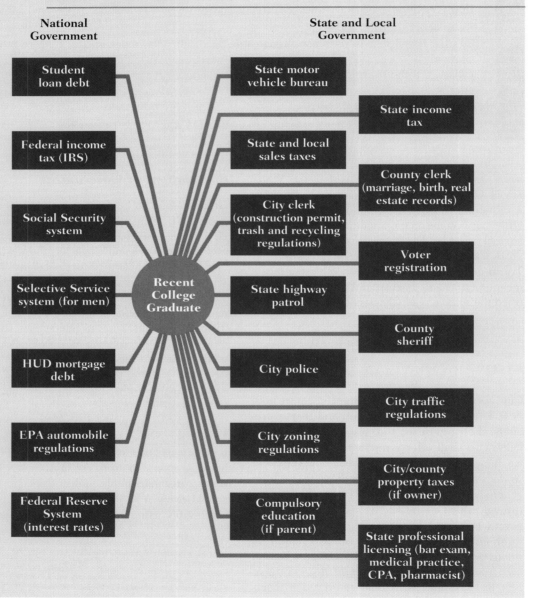

National Government

State and Local Government

Student loan debt

State motor vehicle bureau

State income tax

Federal income tax (IRS)

State and local sales taxes

County clerk (marriage, birth, real estate records)

Social Security system

City clerk (construction permit, trash and recycling regulations)

Voter registration

Selective Service system (for men)

State highway patrol

Recent College Graduate

County sheriff

HUD mortgage debt

City police

City traffic regulations

EPA automobile regulations

City zoning regulations

City/county property taxes (if owner)

Federal Reserve System (interest rates)

Compulsory education (if parent)

State professional licensing (bar exam, medical practice, CPA, pharmacist)

THE MEANS OF COERCION   Government must have the powers to order people around, to get people to obey its laws, and to punish them if they do not. *Coercion* takes many different forms, and each year millions of Americans are subject to one form of government coercion or another. One aspect of coercion is conscription, whereby the government requires certain involuntary services of citizens. The best-known example of conscription is military *conscription*, which is called "the draft." Although there has been no draft since 1974, there were drafts during the Civil War, World War I, World War II, the postwar period, and the wars in Korea and Vietnam. With these drafts, the American government compelled millions of men to serve in the armed forces; one-half million of these soldiers made the ultimate contribution by giving their lives in their nation's service. If the need arose, military conscription would undoubtedly be reinstituted. Eighteen-year-old males are required to register today, just in case. American citizens can also, by law, be compelled to serve on juries; to appear before legal tribunals when summoned; to file a great variety of official reports, including income tax returns; and to attend school or to send their children to school.

Coercion of citizens is necessary for government to maintain order.

THE MEANS OF COLLECTING REVENUE   Each year American governments on every level collect enormous sums from their citizens to support their institutions and programs. Taxation has grown steadily over the years. In 2004, the national government alone collected $809 billion in individual income taxes, $189 billion in corporate income taxes, $733 billion in social insurance taxes, $70 billion in excise taxes, and another $78 billion in miscellaneous revenue. The grand total amounted to almost two trillion dollars, or almost $6,500 from every living soul in the United States. But not everyone benefits equally from programs paid for by their tax dollars. One of the perennial issues in American politics is the distribution of tax burdens versus the distribution of program benefits. Every group would like more of the benefits while passing more of the burdens of taxation onto others.

Forms of Government

Governments vary in their institutional structure, in their size, and in the way they operate. Two questions are of special importance in determining how governments differ from one another: Who governs? How much government control is permitted?

In some nations, a single individual—a monarch or dictator—governs. This is called *autocracy*. Where a small group of landowners, military officers, or wealthy merchants control most of the governing decisions, that government is an *oligarchy*. If many people participate, and if the populace is deemed to have some influence over the leaders' actions, that government is tending toward *democracy*.

Governments also vary considerably in how they govern. In the United States and a small number of other nations, governments are severely limited by law as to *what* they are permitted to control (substantive limits), as well as *how* they go about it (procedural limits). Governments that are so limited are called *constitutional*, or liberal, governments. In other nations, including many in Europe, South America, Asia, and Africa, political and social institutions that the government is unable to control—such as an organized church, organized business groups, or organized labor unions—may help keep the government in check, but the law imposes few real limits. Such governments are called *authoritarian*. In a third group of nations, including the Soviet Union under Joseph Stalin, governments not only are free of legal limits but seek to eliminate those organized social groupings or institutions that might challenge or limit their authority. Because these governments typically attempt to dominate every sphere of political, economic, and social life, they are called *totalitarian*.

IN BRIEF BOX

SCOPE AND LIMITS OF POWER IN CONSTITUTIONAL, AUTHORITARIAN, AND TOTALITARIAN GOVERNMENTS

Constitutional Governments
Scope: power prescribed by a constitution.
Limits: society can challenge government when it oversteps constitutional boundaries.
Examples: United States, France, Canada.

Authoritarian Governments
Scope: answer only to a small number of powerful groups.
Limits: recognize no obligations to limit actions, whether or not such obligations exist.
Examples: Spain (under General Francisco Franco) and Portugal (under Prime Minister Antonio Salazar).

Totalitarian Governments
Scope: government encompasses all important social institutions.
Limits: rivals for power are not tolerated.
Examples: Germany's Third Reich in the 1930s and 1940s (under Adolf Hitler) and the Soviet Union from the 1930s through the 1950s (under Joseph Stalin).

Governments differ in terms of who governs and how much governmental control is permitted.

Influencing the Government: Politics

In its broadest sense, the term **politics** refers to conflicts over the character, membership, and policies of any organizations to which people belong. As Harold Lasswell, a famous political scientist, once put it, politics is the struggle over "who gets what, when, how."[2] Although politics is a phenomenon that can be found in any organization, our concern in this book is more narrow. Here, politics will refer only to conflicts and struggles over the leadership, structure, and policies of *governments*. The goal of politics, as we define it, is to have a share or a say in the composition of the government's leadership, how the government is organized, and what its policies are going to be.

[2]Harold Lasswell, *Politics: Who Gets What, When, How* (New York: Meridian Books, 1958).

Having such a share is called **power** or *influence*. Most people are eager to have some "say" in matters affecting them; witness the willingness of so many individuals over the past two centuries to risk their lives for voting rights and representation. In recent years, of course, Americans have become more skeptical about their actual "say" in government, and many do not bother to vote. This increased skepticism, however, does not mean that Americans no longer want to have a share in the governmental process. Rising levels of skepticism mean, rather, that many Americans doubt the capacity of the political system to provide them with influence.

Politics is the struggle over "who gets what, when, how." The goals of politics are to influence the government's leadership, its organization, and its policies.

As we shall see throughout the book, not only does politics influence government, but the character and actions of government also influence a nation's politics. A constitutional government tries to gain more popular consent by opening channels for political expression. People accept these channels in the hope that they can make the government more responsive to their demands.

FROM COERCION TO CONSENT

Americans have the good fortune to live in a constitutional democracy, with legal limits on what government can do and how it does it. But such democracies are relatively rare in today's world—it is estimated that only twenty or so of the world's nearly two hundred governments could be included in this category. And constitutional democracies were unheard of before the modern era. Prior to the eighteenth and nineteenth centuries, governments seldom sought—and rarely received—the support of their ordinary subjects. History strongly suggests that the ordinary people had little love for the government or for the social order. After all, they had no stake in it. They equated government with the police officer, the bailiff, and the tax collector.[3]

The United States is a constitutional democracy, with legal limits on what government can do and how it does it.

Beginning in the seventeenth century, in a handful of Western nations, two important changes began to take place in the character and conduct of government. First, governments began to acknowledge formal limits on their power. Second, a small number of governments began to provide the ordinary citizen with a formal voice in public affairs through the vote.

Limits and Democratization

Obviously, the desirability of limits on government and the expansion of popular influence on

government were at the heart of the American Revolution of 1776. "No taxation without representation," as we shall see in Chapter 2, was hotly debated, beginning with the American Revolution and continuing through the founding in 1789. But even before the American Revolution, there was a tradition of limiting government and expanding participation in the political process all over western Europe. Thus, to understand how the relationship between rulers and the ruled was transformed, we must broaden our focus to take into account events in Europe as well as those in America. We will divide the transformation into two separate parts. The first is the effort to put limits on government. The second is the effort to expand the influence of the people through politics.

LIMITING GOVERNMENT   The key force behind the imposition of limits on government power was a new social class, the "bourgeoisie." Bourgeois is French for freeman of the city, or bourg. Being part of the bourgeoisie later became associated with being "middle class" and with being in commerce or industry. In order to gain a share of control of government—to join the kings, monarchs, and gentry who had dominated governments for centuries—the bourgeoisie sought to change existing institutions—especially parliaments—into instruments of real political participation. Parliaments had existed for hundreds of years, controlling from the top and not allowing influence from below. The bourgeoisie embraced parliament as the means by which they could use their greater numbers and growing economic advantage against their aristocratic rivals.

Although motivated primarily by self-interest, the bourgeoisie advanced many of the principles that became the central underpinnings of individual freedom for *all* citizens—freedom of speech, of assembly, or conscience, and freedom from arbitrary search and seizure. It is important to note here that the bourgeoisie generally did not favor democracy as such. They were advocates of electoral and representative institutions, but they favored property requirements and other restrictions so as to limit participation to the middle

---

[3]See Eugen Weber, *Peasants into Frenchmen* (Stanford: Stanford University Press, 1976), Chapter 5.

classes. Yet, once the right to engage in politics was established, it was difficult to limit it just to the bourgeoisie. We will see time after time that principles first stated to justify a selfish interest can take on a life of their own, extending beyond those for whom the principles were designed.

The relationship between government and citizen was transformed by a shift in emphasis, which limited governmental power and expanded popular influence through political participation.

THE EXPANSION OF DEMOCRATIC POLITICS
Along with limits on government came an expansion of democratic government. Three factors explain why rulers were force to give ordinary citizens a greater voice in public affairs: internal conflict, external threat, and the promotion of national unity and development.

First, during the eighteenth and nineteenth centuries, every nation was faced with intense conflict among the landed gentry, the bourgeoisie, lower-middle-class shopkeepers and artisans, the urban working class, and farmers. Many governments came to the conclusion that if they did not deal with basic class conflicts in some constructive way, disorder and revolution would result. One of the best ways of dealing with such conflict was to extend the rights of political participation, especially voting, to each new group as it grew more powerful. Such a liberalization was sometimes followed by suppression, as rulers began to fear that their calculated risk was not paying off.

This was true even in the United States. The Federalists, who were securely in control of the government after 1787, began to fear the emergence of a vulgar and dangerous democratic party led by Thomas Jefferson. The Federalist majority in Congress adopted an infamous law, the Alien and Sedition Acts of 1798, which, among other things, declared any opposition to or criticism of the government to be a crime. Alexander Hamilton and other Federalist leaders went so far as to

---

IN BRIEF BOX

THE EXPANSION OF DEMOCRATIC POLITICS

Causes of Expansion
Internal conflict: To quell conflicts between different social groups and economic classes, rulers have found it useful to extend the rights of political participation—to give the masses a bigger stake in the system so that they will be more inclined to support that system.
External conflict: In order to maintain a permanent army as a defense against other nation-states, governments needed popular support for military endeavors. The expansion of participation in government helped ensure enthusiasm for cause and country.
Promotion of national unity: Governments sometimes see local or regional loyalties as an obstacle to national unity; by expanding participation, they hope to tie people more strongly to the central government.

Consequences of Expansion
Citizens might use government for their own benefit (rather than watch it being used for the benefit of others).
The public believes it can control the government and therefore supports the continued expansion of government.

urge that the opposition be eliminated by force, if necessary. The Federalists failed to suppress their Republican opposition, however, in large measure because they lacked the military and political means of doing so. Their inability to crush the opposition eventually led to acceptance of the principle of the "loyal opposition."[4]

Another form of internal threat is social disorder. Thanks to the Industrial Revolution, societies had become much more interdependent and therefore much more vulnerable to disorder. As that occurred, and as more people moved from rural areas to cities, disorder had to be managed, and one important approach to that management was to give the masses a bigger stake in the system itself. As one supporter of electoral reform put it, the alternative to voting was "the spoliation of property and the dissolution of social order."[5] In the modern world, social disorder helped to compel East European regimes and the republics of the former Soviet Union to take steps toward democratic reform.

The second factor that helped expand democratic government was external threat. The main external threat to governments' power is the existence of other nation-states. During the past three centuries, more and more tribes and nations—people tied together by a common culture and language—have formed into separate principalities, or *nation-states*, in order to defend their populations more effectively. But as more nation-states formed, the more likely it was that external conflicts would arise. War and preparation for war became constant rather than intermittent facts of national life, and the size and expense of military forces increased dramatically with the size of the nation-state and the size and number of its adversaries.

The cost of defense forced rulers to seek popular support to maintain military power. It was easier to raise huge permanent armies of citizen-soldiers and induce them to fight more vigorously

and to make greater sacrifices if they were imbued with enthusiasm for cause and country. The turning point was the French Revolution in 1789. The unprecedented size and commitment and the military success of the French citizen-army convinced the rulers of all European nations that military power was forevermore closely linked with mass support. The expansion of participation and representation in government were key tactics used by the European regimes to raise that support. Throughout the nineteenth century, war and the expansion of the suffrage went hand in hand.

Political leaders saw voting rights as a simple means of giving every citizen a stake in the nation.

The third factor often associated with the expansion of democratic politics was the promotion of national unity and development. In some instances, governments seek to subvert local or regional loyalties by linking citizens directly to the central government via the ballot box. America's founders saw direct popular election of members of the House of Representatives as a means through which the new federal government could compete with the states for popular allegiance.

The Great Transformation: Tying Democracy to Strong Government

The expansion of democratic politics had two historic consequences. First, democracies opened up the possibility that citizens might use government for their own benefit rather than simply watching it being used for the benefit of others. This consequence is widely understood. But the second is not so well understood: Once citizens perceived that governments could operate in response to their demands, they *became increasingly willing to support the expansion of government.* The public's belief in its capacity to control the government's action is only one of the many factors responsible for the growth of government. But at the very least, this linkage of democracy and strong government

[4]See Richard Hofstadter, *The Idea of a Party System* (Berkeley: University of California Press, 1969).
[5]Quoted in John Cannon, *Parliamentary Reform, 1640–1832* (Cambridge, England: Cambridge University Press, 1973), p. 216.

set into motion a wave of governmental growth in the West that began in the middle of the nineteenth century and has continued to the present day.

Because citizens saw that government could represent their interests, they became more willing to broaden governmental power.

DOES AMERICAN DEMOCRACY WORK?

The growth of democracy in the United States has led to wider participation, which in turn has fulfilled the democratic ideals of popular sovereignty and majority rule. Thus, democratization creates the possibility that citizens can use government for their own benefit. But given the opportunity, how do citizens create an "ideal" democracy? What are the trade-offs involved in doing so? Are there unintended consequences of too much democracy?[6] The answers to these questions are complex. Despite over two hundred years of development, American democracy has still not worked out the inconsistencies and contradictions woven in its very fiber by the framers of the Constitution. Similarly, despite all that political scientists and political historians know about American government and politics, some of which wisdom we hope we have captured in the pages to follow, puzzles and anomalies reflective of the contradictions within American democracy remain for which we don't

have fully satisfactory answers. We conclude this chapter by examining three of them.

Delegating Authority in a Representative Democracy

For over two centuries, we have expanded popular sovereignty to the point where a citizen, from the time he or she is roughly the age of a college freshman to the time that final breath is taken, can engage in political activity at various levels of government. Yet citizens often find it pragmatic and convenient to delegate many of these activities, sometimes (as when we don't pay attention, or vote, or even register to vote) conceding the field entirely to highly motivated individuals and groups ("special interests"). Popular sovereignty is power *if exercised*. We don't always understand why citizens participate or abstain; this is a puzzle.

Citizens delegate governance to representatives: executives, legislators, regulators, judges—politicians, in a word. Ours is a **representative democracy** for very pragmatic reasons. Most citizens have lives to live and private concerns to attend to, and, therefore, acquiesce in an arrangement enabling them to economize on the effort they must devote to their own governance. This leaves their governance agents on a fairly long leash (or, to continue the metaphor, a leash on which the hands of the more intensely active have considerable pull). This means that citizens don't always get what they want, despite popular sovereignty, because, inadvertently or not, they allow agents to pursue their own purposes or to be influenced unduly by those who care more or who have more at stake. Thus, popular sovereignty is qualified (some would say undermined) by the freedom *not* to exercise it and by our willingness to off-load governance responsibilities onto professional agents.

The Trade-off between Freedom and Order

If the imperfect fit between popular sovereignty and delegation of governance to a "political class" constitutes one anomaly, a second involves the trade-off between liberty and coercion. We have

---

[6]For a review and analysis of the detrimental consequences of the "opening up" of American democracy since the 1960s, see Morris P. Fiorina, "Parties, Participation, and Representation in America: Old Theories Face New Realities," in *Political Science: State of the Discipline,* ed. Ira Katznelson and Helen V. Milner (New York: W.W. Norton, 2002). For a more general and provocative analysis of the detrimental effects of too much democracy, see Fareed Zakaria, *The Future of Freedom: Illiberal Democracy at Home and Abroad* (New York: Norton, 2003).

taken pains to suggest that governments are necessary to maintain order, to protect property, and to provide public goods. All these activities require a degree of coercion. Laws, regulations, and rulings constrain behavior and restrict the uses of property. Taxes include claims on labor income, on gains in the value of capital, and on the transmission of estates from one generation to another. In short, all of these things constitute limits on liberty. The anomaly here is that liberty is one of the very purposes for which the coercion is necessary in the first place. So, a pinch of coercion is one of the ingredients in the stew of liberty. But where to draw the line? And, even if we had an answer to this question, there is another: how to arrange our political life to ensure just the right amount of coercion and no more. As the history of experiments in democratic self-government reveals, and to which the American experience constitutes a significant exception, coercion is a slippery slope. Especially after the events of September 11, 2001 it is clear that a strong desire for public goods like security from terrorism lulls us into accepting extensive limitations on citizens' liberties.

The Instability of Majority Rule

A third anomaly involves the multitude of purposes pursued by different citizens. It is not always easy to add them up into a collective choice without doing damage to the interest of some. Majority rule, as we shall see in subsequent chapters, especially as manifested in the real institutions of constitutional democracies, is vulnerable to the powers of agenda setters, veto players, financial fat cats, and group leaders (political bosses, union heads, corporate CEOs, religious leaders). All democracies struggle with the fact that outcomes, because they entail disproportionate influence by some, are not always fair. In our American democracy, we put a great deal of faith in frequent elections, checks and balances among government institutions, and multiple levels of government. But again we may ask where to draw the line: Elections how frequent? How powerful the checks? How many governmental levels? At what point is something "broke enough" to need fixing? American political history is filled with instances of decisions, followed by reactions, followed by a revisiting of those decisions, followed by further reactions. The disproportionate influence of some would appear inescapable, despite our efforts to control it. We revisit decisions. We reform institutions. We alter political practices. But still perfection eludes us.

In all these puzzles and anomalies, normative principles sometimes clash. Popular sovereignty, individual liberty, delegation, and multiple purposes constitute the circle that cannot quite be squared. The great success of American democracy, we believe, is that at the end of the day our citizens are pragmatic, tolerant, and appear to avoid letting the best be the enemy of the good.

KEY TERMS

authoritarian government A system of rule in which the government recognizes no formal limits but may, nevertheless, be restrained by the power of other social institutions.

autocracy A form of government in which a single individual—a monarch or dictator—rules.

coercion Forcing a person to do something by threats or pressure.

conscription An aspect of coercion whereby the government requires certain involuntary services of citizens, such as compulsory military service, known as "the draft."

constitutional government A system of rule in which formal and effective limits are placed on the powers of the government.

democracy A system of rule that permits citizens to play a significant part in the governmental process, usually through the election of key public officials.

government Institutions and procedures through which a territory and its people are ruled.

nation-state A political entity consisting of a people with some common cultural experience (nation), who also share a common political authority (state), recognized by other sovereignties (nation-states).

oligarchy A form of government in which a small group—landowners, military officers, or wealthy merchants—controls most of the governing decisions.

politics Conflicts over the character, membership, and policies of any organizations to which people belong.

power Influence over a government's leadership, organization, or policies.

representative democracy A system of government that provides the populace with the opportunity to make the government responsive to its views through the selection of representatives, who, in turn, play a significant role in governmental decision making.

totalitarian government A system of rule in which the government recognizes no formal limits on its power and seeks to absorb or eliminate other social institutions that might challenge it.

FOR FURTHER READING

Bendix, Reinhard. *Kings or People: Power and the Mandate to Rule.* Berkeley: University of California Press, 1978.

Bendix, Reinhard. *Nation-Building and Citizenship.* New York: Wiley, 1964.

Dahl, Robert A. *Polyarchy: Participation and Opposition.* New Haven: Yale University Press, 1971.

Grant, Ruth W. *John Locke's Liberalism.* Chicago: University of Chicago Press, 1987.

Hartz, Louis. *The Liberal Tradition in America.* New York: Harcourt, Brace, 1955.

Higgs, Robert. *Crisis and Leviathan: Critical Episodes in the Growth of American Government.* New York: Oxford University Press, 1987.

Huntington, Samuel P. *American Politics: The Promise of Disharmony.* Cambridge: Harvard University Press, 1981.

Keller, Morton. *Affairs of State: Public Life in Late Nineteenth Century America.* Cambridge: Harvard University Press, 1977.

Moore, Barrington. *Social Origins of Dictatorship and Democracy.* Boston: Beacon Press, 1966.

Putnam, Robert. *Making Democracy Work: Civic Traditions in Modern Italy.* Princeton: Princeton University Press, 1993.

Schumpeter, Joseph A. *Capitalism, Socialism, and Democracy.* New York: Harper, 1942.

Skocpol, Theda. *States and Social Revolutions.* New York: Cambridge University Press, 1979.

Strayer, Joseph R. *On the Medieval Origins of the Modern State.* Princeton: Princeton University Press, 1970.

Tilly, Charles, ed. *The Formation of National States in Western Europe.* Princeton: Princeton University Press, 1975.

Tocqueville, Alexis de. *Democracy in America.* Translated by Phillips Bradley. New York: Knopf, Vintage Books, 1945; orig. published 1835.

Weber, Max. *The Theory of Social and Economic Organization.* Translated by Talcott Parsons. New York: Oxford University Press, 1947.

CHAPTER 2

Constructing a Government:
The Founding and the Constitution

$\mathcal{T}$he story of America's Founding and the Constitution is generally presented as something both inevitable and glorious: It was inevitable that the American colonies would break away from England to establish their own country successfully; and it was glorious in that it established the best of all possible forms of government under a new Constitution, which was easily adopted and quickly embraced, even by its critics. In reality, though, America's successful breakaway from England was by no means assured, and the Constitution that we revere today as one of the most brilliant creations of any nation was in fact highly controversial. Moreover, its ratification and durability were often in doubt. George Washington, the man revered as the father of the country and the person chosen to preside over the Constitutional Convention of 1787, thought the document produced that hot summer in Philadelphia would probably last no more than twenty years, at which time leaders would have to convene again to come up with something new.

That Washington's prediction proved wrong is, indeed, a testament to the enduring strength of the Constitution. Nonetheless the Constitution was not carved in stone. It was a product of political bargaining and compromise, formed very much in the same way political decisions are made today. This fact is often overlooked because of what historian Michael Kammen has called the "cult of the Constitution"—a tendency of Americans, going back more than a century, to venerate blindly,

CORE OF THE ANALYSIS

- Both the American Revolution and the Constitution were expressions of competing interests.

- The Constitution laid the groundwork for a government sufficiently powerful to promote commerce and to protect private property.

- The framers sought to prevent the threat posed by "excessive democracy" through internal checks and balances, the indirect selection of the president, and lifetime judicial appointments.

- To secure popular consent for the government, the Constitution provides for the direct popular election of representatives and includes the Bill of Rights.

- To prevent the government from abusing its power, the Constitution incorporates principles such as the separation of powers and federalism.

- The Constitution and its amendments establish a framework within which government and lawmaking can take place.

sometimes to the point of near worship, the founders and the document they created.[1] As this chapter will show, the Constitution reflects polit-

[1] Michael Kammen, *A Machine That Would Go of Itself* (New York: Vintage, 1986), p. 22.

CENTRAL QUESTIONS

- **The First Founding: Interests and Conflicts**
  What conflicts were apparent and what interests prevailed during the American Revolution and the drafting of the Articles of Confederation?

- **The Second Founding: From Compromise to Constitution**
  Why were the Articles of Confederation unable to hold the nation together?
  In what ways is the Constitution a marriage of interest and principle? How did the framers of the Constitution reconcile their competing interests and principles?

- **The Constitution**
  What principles does the Constitution embody? Why did the framers of the Constitution establish the legislative, executive, and judicial branches?
  What limits on the national government's power are embodied in the Constitution?

- **The Fight for Ratification**
  What sides did the Federalists and the Antifederalists represent in the fight over ratification?
  Over what key principles did the Federalists and the Antifederalists disagree?

- **Changing the Framework: Constitutional Amendment**
  Why is the Constitution difficult to amend?
  What purposes do the amendments to the Constitution serve?

ical self-interest, but high principle, too. It also defines the relationship between American citizens and their government.

Often, the story of the Founding and the Constitution is written to emphasize the framers' concerns regarding individual liberty and limits on government. And, of course, the framers had such concerns. It is important to note, however, that the primary goal of the framers was the creation of an *effective* government. They sought a government with the capacity to provide for the nation's safety in a sometimes hostile world: "Among the many objects to which a wise and free people find it necessary to direct their attention," wrote John Jay in *Federalist 3,* "that of providing for their safety seems to be the first." The framers endeavored to create a government with the power to maintain public order, promote prosperity, and secure the nation's independence, powers that the government under the Articles of Confederation lacked. The Constitution begins not with a statement of the limits on government, but with an affirmative statement of the ends a government is designed to achieve—to establish justice, ensure domestic tranquility, and provide for the common defense and general welfare.

To most contemporary Americans, the revolutionary period represents a mythic struggle by a determined and united group of colonists against British oppression. The Boston Tea Party, the battles of Lexington and Concord, the winter at Valley Forge—these are the events that are emphasized in American history. Similarly, the American Constitution—the document establishing the system of government that ultimately emerged from this struggle—is often seen as an inspired, if not divine work, expressing timeless principles of democratic government.

To understand the character of the American Founding and the meaning of the American Constitution, however, it is essential to look beyond the myths and rhetoric and explore the conflicting interests and forces at work during the revolutionary and constitutional periods. Thus, we will first assess the political backdrop of the American Revolution, and then we will examine the Constitution that ultimately emerged as the basis for America's government.

THE FIRST FOUNDING: INTERESTS AND CONFLICTS

Competing ideals and principles often reflect competing interests, and so it was in revolutionary America. The American Revolution and the American Constitution were outgrowths of a struggle among economic and political forces within the colonies. Five sectors of society had interests that were important in colonial politics: (1) the New England merchants; (2) the Southern planters; (3) the "royalists"—holders of royal lands, offices, and patents (licenses to engage in a profession or business activity); (4) shopkeepers, artisans, and laborers; and (5) small farmers. Throughout the eighteenth century, these groups were in conflict over issues of taxation, trade, and commerce. For the most part, however, the Southern planters, the New England merchants, and the royal office and patent holders—groups that together made up the colonial elite—were able to maintain a political alliance that held in check the more radical forces representing shopkeepers, laborers, and small farmers. After 1750, however, British tax and trade policies split the colonial elite, permitting radical forces to expand their political influence and setting into motion a chain of events that culminated in the American Revolution.[2]

The American Constitution reflects a struggle among different economic and political forces.

Political Strife and the Radicalizing of the Colonists

The political strife within the colonies was the background for the events of 1773–1774. In 1773, the British government granted the politically powerful East India Company a monopoly on the export of tea from Britain, eliminating a lucrative form of trade for colonial merchants. Together with their Southern allies, the merchants called upon their radical adversaries—shopkeepers, artisans, laborers, and small farmers—for support. The most dramatic result was the Boston Tea Party of 1773, led by Samuel Adams.

This event was of decisive importance in American history. The merchants had hoped to force the British government to rescind the Tea Act, but they did not support any demands beyond this one. They certainly did not seek independence from Britain. Samuel Adams and the other radicals, however, hoped to provoke the British government to take actions that would alienate its colonial supporters and pave the way for a rebellion. This was precisely the purpose of the Boston Tea Party, and it succeeded. By dumping the East India Company's tea into Boston Harbor, Adams and his followers goaded the British into enacting a number of harsh reprisals. The House of Commons closed the port of Boston to commerce, changed the provincial government of Massachusetts, provided for the removal of accused persons to England for trial, and, most important, restricted movement to the West—further alienating the Southern planters who depended upon access to new western lands. These acts of retaliation confirmed the worst criticisms of England and helped radicalize the American colonists.

Thus, the Boston Tea Party set into motion a cycle of provocation and retaliation that in 1774 resulted in the convening of the First Continental Congress—an assembly consisting of delegates from all parts of the country—that called for a total boycott of British goods and, under the prodding of the radicals, began to consider the possibility of independence from British rule. The result was the Declaration of Independence.

The Declaration of Independence

In 1776, the Second Continental Congress appointed a committee consisting of Thomas Jefferson of Virginia, Benjamin Franklin of Pennsylvania, Roger Sherman of Connecticut, John Adams of Massachusetts, and Robert Livingston of New

---

[2]The social makeup of colonial America and some of the social conflicts that divided colonial society are discussed in Jackson Turner Main, *The Social Structure of Revolutionary America* (Princeton: Princeton University Press, 1965).

York to draft a statement of American independence from British rule. The Declaration of Independence, written by Jefferson and adopted by the Second Continental Congress, was an extraordinary document in both philosophical and political terms. Philosophically, the Declaration was remarkable for its assertion that certain rights, which it called "unalienable rights"—including life, liberty, and the pursuit of happiness—could not be abridged by governments. In the world of 1776, a world in which some kings still claimed to rule by divine right, this was a dramatic statement. The Declaration was remarkable as a political document because it identified and focused on problems, grievances, aspirations, and principles that might unify the various colonial groups. The Declaration was an attempt to identify and articulate a history and set of principles that might help to forge national unity.[3]

The Articles of Confederation

Having declared independence, the colonies needed to establish a government. In November 1777, the Continental Congress adopted the Articles of Confederation and Perpetual Union—the first written constitution of the United States. Although it was not ratified by all the states until 1781, it served as the country's constitution for almost twelve years, until March 1789.

The *Articles of Confederation* was concerned primarily with limiting the powers of the central government. It created no executive branch. Congress constituted the central government, but it had little power. Execution of its laws was to be left to the individual states. Its members were not much more than messengers from the state legislatures. They were chosen by the state legislature, their salaries were paid out of the state treasuries, and they were subject to immediate recall by state authorities. In addition, each state, regardless of its size, had only a single vote.

Congress was given the power to declare war and make peace, to make treaties and alliances, to coin or borrow money, and to regulate trade with Native Americans. It could also appoint the senior officers of the United States Army. But it could not levy taxes or regulate commerce among the states. Moreover, the army officers it appointed had no army to serve in because the nation's armed forces were composed of the state militias. Probably the most unfortunate part of the Articles of Confederation was that the central government could not prevent one state from discriminating against other states in the quest for foreign commerce.

> *The Articles of Confederation was the first written constitution of the United States. The new government it created limited the power of the central government.*

In brief, the relationship between Congress and the states under the Articles of Confederation was much like the contemporary relationship between the United Nations and its member states, a relationship in which the states retain virtually all governmental powers. It was called a *confederation* because, as provided under Article II, "each state retains its sovereignty, freedom and independence, and every Power, Jurisdiction and right, which is not by this confederation expressly delegated to the United States, in Congress assembled." Not only was there no executive, there was also no judicial authority and no other means of enforcing Congress's will. If there was to be any enforcement at all, the states would have to do it.[4]

THE SECOND FOUNDING: FROM COMPROMISE TO CONSTITUTION

The Declaration of Independence and the Articles of Confederation were not sufficient to hold the nation together as an independent and effective

[3]See Carl Becker, *The Declaration of Independence* (New York: Vintage, 1942).

[4]See Merrill Jensen, *The Articles of Confederation* (Madison: University of Wisconsin Press, 1963).

nation-state. From almost the moment of armistice with the British in 1783, moves were afoot to reform and strengthen the Articles.

International Standing and Balance of Power

There was a special concern for the country's international position. Competition among the states for foreign commerce allowed the European powers to play the states against one another, which created confusion on both sides of the Atlantic. At one point during the winter of 1786–1787, John Adams, a leader in the independence struggle, was sent to negotiate a new treaty with the British, one that would cover disputes left over from the war. The British government responded that, since the United States under the Articles of Confederation was unable to enforce existing treaties, it would negotiate with each of the thirteen states separately.

At the same time, well-to-do Americans—in particular the New England merchants and Southern planters—were troubled by the influence that "radical" forces exercised in the Continental Congress and in the governments of several of the states. The colonists' victory in the Revolutionary War had not only meant the end of British rule, but it had also significantly changed the balance of political power within the new states. As a result of the Revolution, one key segment of the colonial elite—the royal land, office, and patent holders—was stripped of its economic and political privileges. In fact, many of these individuals, along with tens of thousands of other colonists who considered themselves loyal British subjects, left for Canada after the British surrender. And while the elite was weakened, the radicals were now better organized than ever before. They controlled such states as Pennsylvania and Rhode Island, where they pursued economic and political policies that struck terror into the hearts of the prerevolutionary political establishment. The central government under the Articles of Confederation was powerless to intervene.

The new nation's weak international position and domestic turmoil led many Americans to con-

sider whether a new version of the Articles might be necessary. In the fall of 1786, delegates from five states met in Annapolis, Maryland, and called on Congress to send commissioners to Philadelphia at a later time to devise adjustments to the constitution. Their resolution took on force as a result of an event that occurred the following winter in Massachusetts: Shays's Rebellion. Daniel Shays led a mob of farmers, who were protesting foreclosures on their land, in a rebellion against the state government. The state militia dispersed the mob within a few days, but the threat posed by the rebels scared Congress into action. The states were asked to send delegates to Philadelphia to discuss constitutional revision, and eventually delegates were sent from every state but Rhode Island.

The United States' weak international position and domestic turmoils helped to promote the idea of a strong national government.

The Constitutional Convention

Twenty-nine of a total of seventy-three delegates selected by the state governments convened in Philadelphia in May 1787, with political strife, international embarrassment, national weakness, and local rebellion fixed in their minds. Recognizing that these issues were symptoms of fundamental flaws in the Articles of Confederation, the delegates soon abandoned the plan to revise the Articles and committed themselves to a second founding—a second, and ultimately successful, attempt to create a legitimate and effective national system. This effort occupied the convention for the next five months.

THE GREAT COMPROMISE The proponents of a new government fired their opening shot on May 29, 1787, when Edmund Randolph of Virginia offered a resolution that proposed corrections and enlargements in the Articles of Confederation. His proposal was not a simple motion. It provided for virtually every aspect of a new government. Randolph later admitted it was intended to be an alternative draft constitution, and it did in fact serve as the framework for what ultimately became the Constitution. (There is no verbatim record of the debates, but James Madison, a Virginia delegate, was present during nearly all of the deliberations and kept full notes on them.[5])

The portion of Randolph's motion that became most controversial was the *Virginia Plan*. This plan provided for a system of representation in the national legislature based upon the population of each state or the proportion of each state's revenue contribution, or both. (Randolph also proposed a second branch of the legislature, but it was to be elected by the members of the first branch.) Since the states varied enormously in size and wealth, the Virginia Plan was thought by many to be heavily biased in favor of the large states.

While the convention was debating the Virginia Plan, additional delegates were arriving in Philadelphia and were beginning to mount opposition to it. In particular, delegates from the less populous states, which included Delaware, New Jersey, Connecticut, and New York, asserted that the more populous states, such as Virginia, Pennsylvania, North Carolina, Massachusetts, and Georgia, would dominate the new government if representation were to be determined by population. The smaller states argued that each state should be equally represented in the new regime regardless of its population. The proposal, called the *New Jersey Plan* (it was introduced by William Paterson of New Jersey), focused on revising the Articles rather than replacing them. Their opposition to the Virginia Plan's system of representation was sufficient to send the proposals back to committee for reworking into a common document.

The outcome was the Connecticut Compromise, also known as the *Great Compromise*. Under the terms of this compromise, in the first

branch of Congress—the House of Representatives—the representatives would be apportioned according to the number of inhabitants in each state. This, of course, was what delegates from the large states had sought. But in the second branch—the Senate—each state would have an equal vote regardless of its size; this was to deal with the concerns of the small states. This compromise was not immediately satisfactory to all the delegates. In the end, however, both sets of forces preferred compromise to the breakup of the union, and the plan was accepted.

The Great Compromise formed a bicameral (two-chambered) legislature to pacify delegates from both populous and small states.

THE QUESTION OF SLAVERY: THE "THREE-FIFTHS" COMPROMISE   The story so far is too neat, too easy, and too anticlimactic. After all, the notion of a bicameral (two-chambered) legislature was very much in the air in 1787. Some of the states had had this for years. The Philadelphia delegates might well have gone straight to the adoption of two chambers based on two different principles of representation even without the dramatic interplay of conflict and compromise. But a far more fundamental issue had to be confronted before the Great Compromise could take place: the issue of slavery.

Many of the conflicts that emerged during the Constitutional Convention were reflections of the fundamental differences between the slave and the nonslave states—differences that pitted the Southern planters and the New England merchants against one another. This was the first premonition of a conflict that was almost to destroy the Republic in later years. In the midst of debate over large versus small states, Madison observed, "The great danger to our general government is the great southern and northern interests of the continent, being opposed to each other. Look to the votes in Congress, and most of them stand divided by the

[5]Madison's notes are included in Max Farrand, ed., *The Records of the Federal Convention of 1787*, 4 vols., rev. ed. (New Haven: Yale University Press, 1966).

geography of the country, not according to the size of the states.[6]

Over 90 percent of all slaves resided in five states—Georgia, Maryland, North Carolina, South Carolina, and Virginia—where they accounted for 30 percent of the total population. In some places, slaves outnumbered nonslaves by as much as ten to one. Were they to be counted in determining how many congressional seats a state should have? Northerners and Southerners eventually reached agreement through the *Three-fifths Compromise*. The seats in the House of Representatives would be apportioned according to a "population" in which five slaves would count as three persons. The slaves would not be allowed to vote, of course, but the number of representatives would be apportioned accordingly. This arrangement was supported by the slave states, which included some of the biggest and some of the smallest states at that time. It was also accepted by delegates from nonslave states who strongly supported the principle of property representation, whether that property was expressed in slaves or in land, money, or stocks.

The Constitutional Convention decided to count slaves as three-fifths of a person when allocating seats to the House of Representatives.

The concern exhibited by most delegates was over how much slaves would count toward a state's representation rather than whether the institution of slavery would continue. The Three-fifths Compromise, in the words of political scientist Donald Robinson, "gave Constitutional sanction to the fact that the United States was composed of some persons who were 'free' and others who were not, and it established the principle, new in republican theory, that a man who lives among slaves had a greater share in the election of representatives than the man who did not. Although the Three-fifths Compromise acknowledged slavery and rewarded slave

owners, nonetheless, it probably kept the South from unanimously rejecting the Constitution."[7]

THE CONSTITUTION

The political significance of the Great Compromise and Three-fifths Compromise was to reinforce the unity of those who sought the creation of a new government. The Great Compromise reassured those who feared that the importance of their own local or regional influence would be reduced by the new governmental framework. The Three-fifths Compromise temporarily defused the rivalry between the merchants and planters. Their unity secured, members of the alliance supporting the establishment of a new government moved to fashion a constitutional framework for this government that would be congruent with their economic and political interests.

In particular, the framers sought a new government that, first, would be strong enough to promote commerce and protect property from radical state legislatures such as Rhode Island's. This became the basis for the establishment in the Constitution of national control over commerce and finance, as well as the establishment of national judicial supremacy and a strong presidency. Second, the framers sought to prevent what they saw as the threat posed by the "excessive democracy" of the state and national governments under the Articles of Confederation (see Concept Map 2.1, page 22). This led to such constitutional principles as *bicameralism* (division of the Congress into two chambers), checks and balances, staggered terms in office, and indirect election (selection of the president by an electoral college rather than by voters directly).

Third, hoping to secure support from the states or the public at large for the new form of government they proposed, the framers provided for direct popular election of representatives and, subsequently, for the addition of the Bill of Rights.

---

[6]Ibid., vol. 1, p. 476.

[7]Donald Robinson, *Slavery in the Structure of American Politics, 1765–1820* (New York: Harcourt Brace Jovanovich, 1971), p. 201.

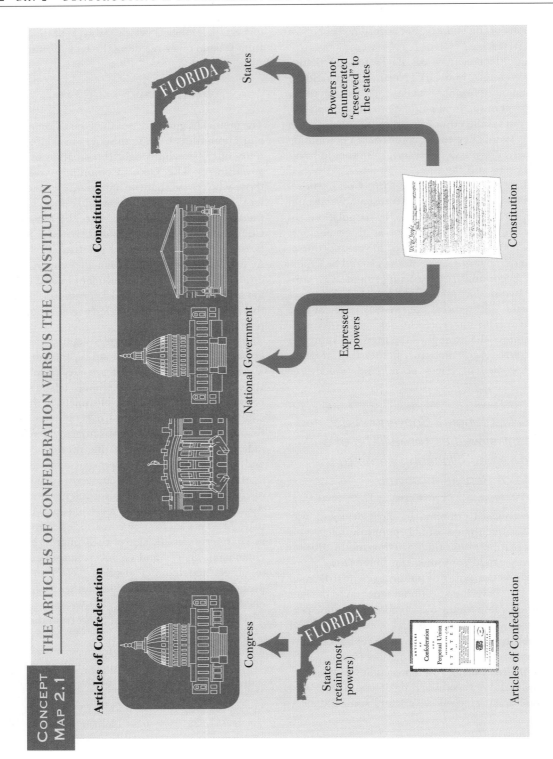

CONCEPT
MAP 2.1

THE ARTICLES OF CONFEDERATION VERSUS THE CONSTITUTION

Articles of Confederation

Constitution

Congress

States
(retain most
powers)

FLORIDA

Articles of Confederation

National Government

Expressed
powers

Constitution

States

Powers not
enumerated
"reserved" to
the states

FLORIDA

Articles of Confederation

Finally, to prevent the new government from abusing its power, the framers incorporated principles such as the separation of powers and federalism into the Constitution. Let us now assess the major provisions of the Constitution's seven articles to see how each relates to these objectives.

The framers of the Constitution had four primary goals: to promote interstate commerce, to prevent "excessive democracy," to promote universal acceptance of the government through popular election of officials and a guarantee of individual rights, and to prevent abuses of power by elected officials.

The Legislative Branch

The first seven sections of Article I of the Constitution provided for a Congress consisting of two chambers—a House of Representatives and a Senate. Members of the House of Representatives were given two-year terms in office and were to be subject to direct popular election—though generally only white males had the right to vote. State legislatures were to appoint members of the Senate (this was changed in 1913 by the Seventeenth Amendment, providing for direct election of senators) for six-year terms. These terms, moreover, were staggered so that the appointments of one-third of the senators would expire every two years. The Constitution assigned somewhat different tasks to the House and Senate. Though the approval of each body was required for the enactment of a law, the Senate alone was given the power to ratify treaties and approve presidential appointments. The House, on the other hand, was given the sole power to originate revenue bills.

The character of the legislative branch was directly related to the framers' major goals. The House of Representatives was designed to be directly responsible to the people in order to encourage popular consent for the new Constitution and, as we saw in Chapter 1, to help enhance the power of the new government. At the same time, to guard against "excessive democracy," the power of the House of Representatives was checked by the Senate, whose members were to be appointed for long terms rather than elected directly by the people for short terms.

Staggered terms of service in the Senate were intended to make that body even more resistant to popular pressure. Since only one-third of the senators would be selected at any given time, the composition of the institution would be protected from changes in popular preferences transmitted by the state legislatures. Thus, the structure of the legislative branch was designed to contribute to governmental power, to promote popular consent for the new government, and at the same time to place limits on the popular political currents that many of the framers saw as a radical threat to the economic and social order.

The framers designed the House of Representatives to be directly responsible to the people, while the Senate was to be resistant to public pressure.

THE POWERS OF CONGRESS AND THE STATES The issues of power and consent were important throughout the Constitution. Section 8 of Article I specifically listed the powers of Congress, which include the authority to collect taxes, to borrow money, to regulate commerce, to declare war, and to maintain an army and navy. By granting it these powers, the framers indicated very clearly that they intended the new government to be far more influential than its predecessor. At the same time, by giving these important powers to Congress, the framers sought to reassure citizens that their views would be fully represented whenever the government exercised its new powers.

As a further guarantee to the people that the new government would pose no threat to them, the

Constitution implied that any powers *not* listed were not granted at all. This is the doctrine of *expressed power*. The Constitution grants only those powers specifically *expressed* in its text. But the framers intended to create an active and powerful government, and so they included the *necessary and proper clause*, sometimes known as the *elastic clause*, which signified that the enumerated powers were meant to be a source of strength to the national government, not a limitation on it. Each power could be used with the utmost vigor, but no new powers could be seized upon by the national government without a constitutional amendment. Any power not enumerated was conceived to be "reserved" to the states (or the people).

The Constitution limited Congress to expressed powers, but the necessary and proper clause (also known as the elastic clause) granted the national government latitude in exercising these powers.

If there had been any doubt at all about the scope of the necessary and proper clause, it was settled by Chief Justice John Marshall in one of the most important constitutional cases in American history, *McCulloch v. Maryland,* which dealt with the question of whether states could tax the federally chartered Bank of the United States.[8] This bank was largely under the control of the Federalist party and was extremely unpopular in the West and South. A number of states, including Maryland, imposed stiff taxes on the bank's operations, hoping to weaken or destroy it. When the bank's Baltimore branch refused to pay state taxes, the state brought a suit that was eventually heard by the U.S. Supreme Court (see also Chapter 3).

Writing for the Court, Chief Justice John Marshall ruled that states had no power to tax national

[8]*McCulloch v. Maryland,* 4 Wheaton 316 (1819).

agencies. Moreover, Marshall took the opportunity to give an expansive interpretation of the necessary and proper clause of the Constitution by asserting that Congress clearly possessed the power to charter a bank even though this was not explicitly mentioned in the Constitution. Marshall argued that so long as Congress was passing acts pursuant to one of the enumerated powers, then any of the means convenient to such an end were also legitimate. As he put it, any government "entrusted with such ample powers . . . must also be entrusted with ample means for their execution." It was through this avenue that the national government could grow in power without necessarily taking on any powers that were not already enumerated.

LIMITS ON THE NATIONAL GOVERNMENT AND THE STATES Section 9 of the Constitution listed a number of important limitations on the national government, which are in the nature of a miniature bill of rights. These included the right of *habeas corpus*, which means, in effect, that the government cannot deprive a person of liberty without explaining the reason to a court. These limitations are part of the reason that most delegates at the Constitutional Convention felt no urgent need to add a full-scale bill of rights to the Constitution. Some provisions were clearly designed to prevent the national government from threatening important property interests. For example, Congress was prohibited from giving preference to the ports of one state over those of another. Furthermore, neither Congress nor the state legislatures could require American vessels to pay duty as they entered the ports of any state, thereby preventing the states from charging tribute. All this was part of the delegates' effort to clear away major obstructions to national commerce.

The framers also included restrictions on the states because of their fear of the capacity of the state legislatures to engage in radical action against property and creditors. There are few absolutes in the Constitution, and most of them are found in Article I, Section 10, among the limitations on state powers in matters of commerce. The states were explicitly and absolutely denied the power to tax imports and exports and to place any regulations or other burdens on commerce outside their own borders. They were also explicitly prohibited from issuing paper money or providing for the payment of debts in any form except gold and silver coin.

The framers of the Constitution, fearing for the liberty of the individual and for the prosperity of the nation, created a federalist government with a balance between state and national power.

IN BRIEF BOX

THE SEVEN ARTICLES OF THE CONSTITUTION

1. **The Legislative Branch**
   House: two-year terms, elected directly by the people.
   Senate: six-year terms (staggered so that only one-third of the Senate changes in any given election), appointed by state legislature (changed in 1913 to direct election).
   Expressed powers of the national government: collecting taxes, borrowing money, regulating commerce, declaring war, and maintaining an army and a navy; all other power belongs to the states, unless deemed otherwise by the elastic (necessary and proper) clause.
   Exclusive powers of the national government: states are expressly forbidden to issue their own paper money, tax imports and exports, regulate trade outside their own borders, and impair the obligation of contracts; these powers are the exclusive domain of the national government.
2. **The Executive Branch**
   Presidency: four-year terms (limited in 1951 to a maximum of two terms), elected indirectly by the electoral college.
   Powers: can recognize other countries, negotiate treaties, grant reprieves and pardons, convene Congress in special sessions, and veto congressional enactments.
3. **The Judicial Branch**
   Supreme Court: lifetime terms, appointed by the president with the approval of the Senate.
   Powers: include resolving conflicts between federal and state laws, determining whether power belongs to national government or the states, and settling controversies between citizens of different states.
4. **National Unity and Power**
   Reciprocity among states: establishes that each state must give "full faith and credit" to official acts of other states, and guarantees citizens of any state the "privileges and immunities" of every other state.
5. **Amending the Constitution**
   Procedures: requires two-thirds approval in Congress and three-fourths adoption by the states.
6. **National Supremacy**
   The Constitution and national law are the supreme law of the land and cannot be overruled by state law.
7. **Ratification**
   The Constitution became effective when approved by nine states.

Finally, and of greatest importance, the states were not allowed to impair the obligation of contracts. This was almost sufficient by itself to reassure commercial interests because it meant that state legislatures would not be able to cancel their contracts to purchase goods and services. Nor would they be able to pass any laws that would seriously alter the terms of contracts between private parties. All the powers that the states were in effect forbidden to exercise came to be known as the *exclusive powers* of the national government.

The Executive Branch

The Constitution provided for the establishment of the presidency in Article II. As Alexander Hamilton put it, the presidential article sought "energy in the Executive." It did so in an effort to overcome the natural stalemate that was built into the bicameral legislature as well as into the separation of powers among the legislative, executive, and judicial branches. The Constitution afforded the president a measure of independence from the people and from the other branches of government—particularly Congress.

In line with the framers' goal of increased power to the national government, the president was granted the unconditional power to accept ambassadors from other countries; this amounted to the power to "recognize" other countries. He was also given the power to negotiate treaties, although their acceptance required the approval of the Senate. The president was given the unconditional right to grant reprieves and pardons, except in cases of impeachment. And he was provided with the power to appoint major departmental personnel, to convene Congress in special session, and to veto congressional enactments. (The veto power is formidable, but it is not absolute, since Congress can override it by a two-thirds vote.)

At the same time, the framers sought to help the president withstand (excessively) democratic pressures by making him subject to indirect rather than direct election (through his selection by a separate electoral college). The extent to which the framers' hopes were actually realized will be the topic of Chapter 6.

The Constitution granted the president specific powers. The Constitution also sought to protect the president from popular pressure by establishing indirect elections.

The Judicial Branch

Article III established the judicial branch. This provision reflects the framers' concern with giving more power to the national government and checking radical democratic impulses, while guarding against abuse of liberty and property by the new national government itself.

The framers created a court that was to be literally a supreme court of the United States, and not merely the highest court of the national government. The Supreme Court was given the power to resolve any conflicts that might emerge between federal and state laws and to determine to which level of government a power belonged. In addition, the Supreme Court was assigned jurisdiction over controversies between citizens of different states. The long-term significance of this was that as the country developed a national economy, it came to rely increasingly on the federal judiciary, rather than on the state courts, for resolution of disputes.

The judicial branch was granted the powers to resolve conflicts among states, the national government, and citizens of different states.

Judges were given lifetime appointments in order to protect them from popular politics and from interference by the other branches. But they would not be totally immune to politics or to the other branches, for the president was to appoint the judges and the Senate was to approve the appointments. Congress would also have the power to create inferior (lower) courts, to change the jurisdiction of the federal courts, to add or subtract federal judges, and even to change the size of the Supreme Court.

No direct mention is made in the Constitution of *judicial review*—the power of the courts to render the final decision when there is a conflict of interpretation of the Constitution or of laws. This conflict could be between the courts and Congress, the courts and the executive branch, or the courts and the states. Scholars generally feel that judicial review is implicit in the very existence of a written Constitution and in the power given directly to the federal courts over "all Cases . . . arising under this Constitution, the Laws of the United States, and Treaties made, or which shall be made, under their Authority" (Article III, Section 2). The Supreme Court eventually assumed the power of judicial review. Its assumption of this power, as we shall see in Chapter 8, was based not on the Constitution itself but on the politics of later decades and the membership of the Court.

National Unity and Power

Various provisions in the Constitution addressed the framers' concern with national unity and power. Article IV's provisions for comity (reciprocity) among states and among citizens of all states were extremely important, for without them there would have been little prospect of unobstructed national movement of persons and goods. Both "comity clauses," the *full faith and credit clause* and the *privileges and immunities clause*, were taken directly from the Articles of Confederation. The first clause provided that each state had to give "full faith and credit" to the official acts of all other states. The second provided that the citizens of any state were guaranteed the "privileges and immunities" of every other state, as though they were citizens of that state. Each state was also prohibited from discriminating against the citizens of other states in favor of its own citizens, with the Supreme Court being the arbiter in each case.

The Constitution also contained the infamous provision that obliged persons living in free states to capture escaped slaves and return them to their owners. This provision, repealed in 1865 by the Thirteenth Amendment, was a promise to the South that it would not have to consider itself an economy isolated from the rest of the country.

The Constitution provided for the admission of new states to the union and guaranteed existing states that no territory would be taken from any of them without their consent. The Constitution provided that the United States "shall guarantee to every State . . . a Republican Form of Government." But this is not an open invitation to the national government to intervene in the affairs of any of the states. A clause states that the federal government can intervene in violent domestic conflicts only when invited to by a state legislature or the state executive when the legislature is not in session or when necessary to enforce a federal court order. This has left the question of national intervention in local disorders almost completely to the discretion of local and state officials.

The framers' concern with national supremacy was also expressed in Article VI, in the *supremacy clause*, which provided that national laws and treaties "shall be the supreme law of the land." This meant that all laws made under the "authority of the United States" would be superior to all laws adopted by any state or any other subdivision, and that the states would be expected to respect all treaties made under that authority. This was a direct effort to keep the states from dealing separately with foreign nations or businesses. The supremacy clause also bound the officials of all state and local as well as federal governments to take an oath of office to support the national Constitution. This meant that every action taken by the U.S. Congress would have to be applied within each state as though the action were in fact state law.

The supremacy clause stipulated that national laws would supercede state laws whenever conflicts between the two occurred.

To found the nation on a solid economic base, the Constitution also provided that all debts entered into under the Articles of Confederation

IN BRIEF BOX

COMPARING THE ARTICLES OF THE CONFEDERATION AND THE CONSTITUTION

	Articles of Confederation	Constitution
Legislative Branch	*Power to:* 　Declare war and make peace. 　Make treaties and alliances. 　Coin or borrow money. 　Regulate trade with Native Americans. 　Appoint senior officers of the United States Army. *Limits on power:* 　Cannot levy taxes, regulate commerce among the states, or create national armed forces.	*Power to:* 　Collect taxes. 　Borrow money. 　Regulate commerce. 　Declare war. 　Maintain an army and navy. *Limits on power:* 　All other powers belong to the states.
Executive Branch	*No executive branch was created.*	*Power to:* 　Recognize other countries. 　Negotiate treaties. 　Grant reprieves and pardons. 　Appoint major departmental personnel. 　Convene special sessions of Congress. 　Veto congressional actions. *Limits on power:* 　Senate must approve treaties. 　Congress can override a veto by a two-thirds vote.
Judicial Branch	*No judiciary branch was created.*	*Power to:* 　Resolve conflicts between state and federal laws. 　Determine to which level of government a power belongs. 　Decide conflicts between citizens of different states. *Limits on power:* 　Judicial appointments are made by the president and approved by the Senate. 　Congress creates lower courts and can change the jurisdiction of the federal courts. 　Congress can add or subtract federal judges and can change the size of the Supreme Court.

were to be continued as valid debts under the new Constitution. The first Congress acted to assume all debts incurred by the states during the Revolution. This action secured the allegiance of the mercantile class within the country, because most of the debts incurred by the national and state governments during and after the Revolution were held by wealthy Americans concerned about the dependability of their government. It was one of the most important assurances to the commercial interests that the Constitution favored commerce. It also assured foreign countries, especially France and England, that the United States could be trusted in matters of trade, treaties, defense, and credit. Repudiation of debts at the very outset would have endangered the country's sovereignty, since sovereignty depends on the credibility a nation enjoys in the eyes of other nations.

Amending the Constitution

The Constitution established procedures for its own revision in Article V. Its provisions are so difficult that Americans have succeeded in the amending process only seventeen times since 1791, when the first ten amendments were adopted. Many other amendments have been proposed in Congress, but fewer than forty of them have even come close to fulfilling the Constitution's requirement of a two-thirds vote in Congress, and only a fraction have gotten anywhere near adoption by three-fourths of the states. (A breakdown of these figures and further discussion of amending the Constitution appear in Chapter 3.) The Constitution could also be amended by a constitutional convention. Occasionally, proponents of particular measures, such as a balanced-budget amendment, have called for a constitutional convention to consider their proposals. Whatever the purpose for which it was called, however, such a convention would presumably have the authority to revise America's entire system of government.

Ratifying the Constitution

The rules for the ratification of the Constitution of 1787 made up Article VII of the Constitution.

This provision actually violated the lawful procedure for constitutional change incorporated in the Articles of Confederation. For one thing, it adopted a nine-state rule in place of the unanimity among the states required by the Articles of Confederation. For another, it provided that ratification would occur in special state conventions called for that purpose rather than in the state legislatures. All the states except Rhode Island eventually did set up state conventions to ratify the Constitution, and none seemed to protest very loudly the extralegal character of the procedure.

Constitutional Limits on the National Government's Power

As we have indicated, though the framers sought to create a powerful national government, they also wanted to guard against possible misuse of that power. To that end, the framers incorporated two key principles into the Constitution—the *separation of powers* and *federalism* (see also Chapter 3). A third set of limitations, in the form of the *Bill of Rights*, was added to the Constitution to help secure its ratification when opponents of the document charged that it paid insufficient attention to citizens' rights.

THE SEPARATION OF POWERS No principle of politics was more widely shared at the time of the 1787 Founding than the principle that power must be used to balance power. The French political theorist Montesquieu (1689–1755) believed that this balance was an indispensable defense against tyranny, and his writings, especially his major work, *The Spirit of the Laws,* "were taken as political gospel" at the Philadelphia Convention.[9] This principle is not stated explicitly in the Constitution, but it is clearly built on Articles I, II, and III, which provide for

1. Three separate branches of government (see Concept Map 2.2, page 30).

---

[9]Max Farrand, *The Framing of the Constitution of the United States* (New Haven: Yale University Press, 1962), p. 49.

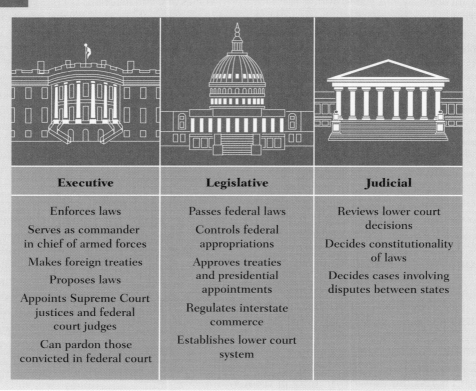

CONCEPT MAP 2.2

THE SEPARATION OF POWERS

Executive	Legislative	Judicial
Enforces laws	Passes federal laws	Reviews lower court decisions
Serves as commander in chief of armed forces	Controls federal appropriations	Decides constitutionality of laws
Makes foreign treaties	Approves treaties and presidential appointments	Decides cases involving disputes between states
Proposes laws	Regulates interstate commerce	
Appoints Supreme Court justices and federal court judges	Establishes lower court system	
Can pardon those convicted in federal court		

2. Different methods of selecting the top personnel, so that each branch is responsible to a different constituency. This is supposed to produce a "mixed regime," in which the personnel of each department will develop very different interests and outlooks on how to govern, and different groups in society will be assured some access to governmental decision making.

3. *Checks and balances*, a system under which each of the branches is given some power over the others. Familiar examples are the presidential veto power over legislation and the power of the Senate to approve high-level presidential appointments (see Concept Map 2.3, page 31).

One clever formulation conceives of this system not as separated powers but as "separated institutions sharing power,"[10] thus diminishing the chance that power will be misused.

The Constitution provided for a separation of powers, such that no branch could obtain supremacy over the others.

[10]Richard E. Neustadt, *Presidential Power* (New York: Wiley, 1960), p. 33.

CONCEPT
MAP 2.3

CHECKS AND BALANCES

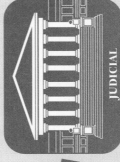
JUDICIAL

LEGISLATIVE

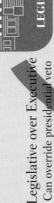

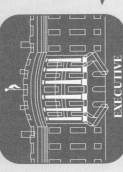
EXECUTIVE

Legislative over Judicial
Can change size of federal court system
and the number of Supreme
Court justices
Can propose constitutional amendments
Can reject Supreme Court nominees
Can impeach and remove federal judges

Judicial over Legislative
Can declare laws
unconstitutional
Chief Justice presides
over Senate during
hearing to impeach
the president

Judicial over Executive
Can declare executive actions
unconstitutional
Can issue warrants
Chief Justice presides over
impeachment of president

Executive over Judicial
Nominates Supreme Court justices
Nominates federal judges
Can pardon those convicted in
federal court
Can refuse to enforce
Court decisions

Executive over Legislative
Can veto acts of Congress
Can call Congress into a special session
Carries out, and thereby interprets,
laws passed by Congress
Vice president casts tie-breaking
vote in the Senate

Legislative over Executive
Can override presidential veto
Can impeach and remove president
Can reject president's appointments and
refuse to ratify treaties
Can conduct investigations into
president's actions
Can refuse to pass laws or to
provide funding that president
requests

FEDERALISM Federalism was actually a step toward greater centralization of power. The delegates agreed that they needed to place more power at the national governmental level, without completely undermining the power of the state governments. Thus, they devised a system of two sovereigns—the states and the nation—with the hope that competition between the two would be an effective limitation on the power of both.

THE BILL OF RIGHTS Late in the Philadelphia Convention, a motion was made to include a bill of rights in the Constitution. After a brief debate in which hardly a word was said in its favor and only one speech was made against it, the motion to include it was almost unanimously turned down. Most delegates sincerely believed that since the federal government was already limited to its expressed powers, further protection of citizens was not needed. The delegates argued that the states should adopt bills of rights because their powers needed more limitations than those of the federal government. But almost immediately after the Constitution was ratified, there was a movement to adopt a national bill of rights. This is why the Bill of Rights, adopted in 1791, comprises the first ten amendments to the Constitution rather than being part of the body of it. We will have a good deal more to say about the Bill of Rights in Chapter 4.

THE FIGHT FOR RATIFICATION

The first hurdle faced by the new Constitution was ratification by state conventions of delegates elected by white, propertied males of each state. This struggle for ratification was carried out in thirteen separate campaigns. Each involved different individuals, moved at a different pace, and was influenced by local as well as national considerations. Two sides faced off throughout all the states, however, taking the names of Federalists and Antifederalists. The *Federalists* supported the Constitution and preferred a strong national government. The *Antifederalists* opposed the Constitution and preferred a more decentralized federal system of government; they took

on their name by default, in reaction to their better-organized opponents. The Federalists were united in their support of the Constitution. The Antifederalists, although opposing this plan, were divided as to what they believed the alternative should be.

The Federalists united behind the new Constitution, while the Antifederalists preferred a more decentralized government.

Under the name of "Publius," Alexander Hamilton, James Madison, and John Jay wrote eighty-five articles in the New York newspapers supporting ratification of the Constitution. These *Federalist Papers*, as they are collectively known today, defended the principles of the Constitution and sought to dispel the fears of a national authority. The Antifederalists, however, such as Richard Henry Lee and Patrick Henry of Virginia and George Clinton of New York argued that the new Constitution betrayed the Revolution and was a step toward monarchy. They accused the Philadelphia Convention of being a "Dark Conclave" that had worked under a "thick veil of secrecy" to overthrow the law and spirit of the Articles of Confederation.

By the end of 1787 and the beginning of 1788, five states had ratified the Constitution. Delaware, New Jersey, and Georgia ratified it unanimously; Connecticut and Pennsylvania ratified by wide margins. Opposition was overcome in Massachusetts by the inclusion of nine recommended amendments to the Constitution to protect human rights. Ratification by Maryland and South Carolina followed. In June 1788, New Hampshire became the ninth state to ratify. That put the Constitution into effect, but for the new national government to have real power, the approval of both Virginia and New York would be needed. After impassioned debate and a great number of recommendations for future amendment of the Constitution, especially for a bill of rights, the Federalists mustered enough votes for approval of the Constitution in June (Virginia) and July (New York) of 1788. North Carolina joined the new government in 1789, after a bill of rights actually was

FEDERALISTS VERSUS ANTIFEDERALISTS

	Federalists	Antifederalists
Who were they?	Property owners, creditors, merchants.	Small farmers, frontiersmen, debtors, shopkeepers.
What did they believe?	Believed that elites were best fit to govern; feared "excessive democracy."	Believed that government should be closer to the people; feared concentration of power in the hands of the elites.
What system of government did they favor?	Favored strong national government; believed in "filtration" so that only elites would obtain governmental power	Favored retention of power by state governments and protection of individual rights.
Who were their leaders?	Alexander Hamilton James Madison George Washington	Patrick Henry George Mason Elbridge Gerry George Clinton

submitted to the states by Congress, and Rhode Island held out until 1790 before finally voting to become part of the new union.

CHANGING THE FRAMEWORK: CONSTITUTIONAL AMENDMENT

The Constitution has endured for two centuries as the framework of government. But it has not endured without change. Without change, the Constitution might have become merely a sacred text, stored under glass.

Amendments: Many Are Called, Few Are Chosen

The framers of the Constitution recognized the need for change. The provisions for amendment incorporated into Article V were thought to be "an easy, regular and Constitutional way" to make changes, which would occasionally be necessary because members of Congress "may abuse their power and refuse their consent on that very account . . . to admit to amendments to correct the source of the abuse."[11] James Madison, again writing in *The Federalist Papers,* made a more balanced defense of the amendment procedures: "It guards equally against the extreme facility, which would render the Constitution two mutable; and that extreme difficulty, which might perpetuate its discovered faults."[12]

[11]Observation by Colonel George Mason, delegate from Virginia, early during the convention period. Quoted in Max Farrand, *The Records of the Federal Convention of 1787,* vol. 1, rev. ed. (New Haven: Yale University Press, 1966), pp. 202–3.
[12]Clinton Rossiter, ed., *The Federalist Papers* (New York: New American Library, 1961), No. 43, p. 278.

Experience since 1789 raises questions even about Madison's more modest claim. The Constitution has proven to be extremely difficult to amend. In the history of efforts to amend the Constitution, the most appropriate characterization is "many are called, few are chosen." Between 1789 and the present, more than eleven thousand amendments were formally offered in Congress. Of these, Congress officially proposed only twenty-nine, and only twenty-seven of these were eventually ratified by the states. But the record is even more severe than that. Since 1791, when the first ten amendments, the Bill of Rights, were added, only seventeen amendments have been adopted. And two of them—prohibition of alcohol (Eighteenth) and its repealer (Twenty-first)—cancel each other out, so that for all practical purposes, only fifteen amendments have been added to the Constitution since 1791. Despite vast changes in American society and its economy, only twelve amendments have been adopted since the Civil War amendments (Thirteenth, Fourteenth, and Fifteenth) in 1868.

As Process Box 2.1 illustrates, Article V provides four methods of amendment:

1. Passage in House and Senate by two-thirds vote; then ratification by majority vote of the legislatures of three-fourths (thirty-eight) of the states.
2. Passage in House and Senate by two-thirds vote; then ratification by conventions called for the purpose in three-fourths of the states.

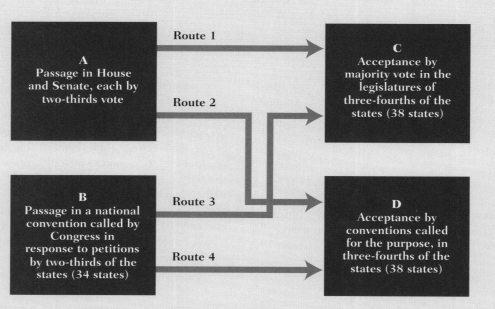

PROCESS BOX 2.1

HOW THE CONSTITUTION IS AMENDED: FOUR POSSIBLE ROUTES

A Passage in House and Senate, each by two-thirds vote

Route 1

Route 2

C Acceptance by majority vote in the legislatures of three-fourths of the states (38 states)

B Passage in a national convention called by Congress in response to petitions by two-thirds of the states (34 states)

Route 3

Route 4

D Acceptance by conventions called for the purpose, in three-fourths of the states (38 states)

*This method of proposal has never been employed. Thus amendment routes 3 and 4 have never been attempted.
†Congress chooses the method of ratification. In each amendment proposal, Congress has the power to provide for the method of ratification, the time limit for consideration by the states, and other conditions of ratification.

3. Passage in a national convention called by Congress in response to petitions by two-thirds of the states; ratification by majority vote of the legislatures of three-fourths of the states.
4. Passage in a national convention, as in method 3; then ratification by conventions called for the purpose in three-fourths of the states.

Since no amendment has ever been proposed by national convention, however, methods 3 and 4 have never been employed. And method 2 has only been employed once (the Twenty-first Amendment, which repealed the Eighteenth, or Prohibition, Amendment). Thus, method 1 has been used for all the others.

The criteria to amend the Constitution are difficult to satisfy. Since the Bill of Rights, only seventeen amendments have been adopted.

It is now clear why it has been so difficult to amend the Constitution. The main reason is the requirement of a two-thirds vote in the House and the Senate, which means that any proposal for an amendment in Congress can be killed by only 34 senators *or* 136 members of the House. The amendment can also be killed by the refusal or inability of only thirteen state legislatures to ratify it. Since each state has an equal vote regardless of its population, the thirteen holdout states may represent a small fraction of the total American population. In the 1970s, the Equal Rights Amendment (ERA), granting protection from denial of rights on account of sex, got the necessary two-thirds vote in Congress but failed by three states to get the necessary three-fourths votes of the

states, even after a three-year extension for its ratification.[13]

Constitutional amendments often fail because two-thirds of the states, representatives, and senators are needed to support an amendment.

If the ERA was a defeat for liberal forces, conservatives have done no better. Constitutional amendments were high on the agenda of the Republican Party from the beginning of its presidential victories in the 1980s and had the blessings of Presidents Ronald Reagan and George H. W. Bush. The school prayer amendment sought to restore power to the states to require selected religious observances, thereby reversing a whole series of earlier Supreme Court decisions.[14] The pro-life amendment sought to reverse *Roe v. Wade* in order to restore to the states the power to outlaw abortions. And President Bush made an effort in 1989 to get Congress to adopt an amendment outlawing the burning or other desecration of the American flag. A gesture to his party's dispirited right wing in the 1988 campaign, it got nowhere in Congress.

The Twenty-seven Amendments

All but two of the Constitution's twenty-seven amendments are concerned with the structure or composition of the government. This is consistent with the concept of a constitution as "higher law," because the whole point and purpose of a higher law is to establish *a framework within which government and the process of making ordinary law can take place.* Even those who would have preferred

---

[13]Marcia Lee, "The Equal Rights Amendment—Public Policy by Means of a Constitutional Amendment," in *The Politics of Policy Making in America,* ed. David Caputo (San Francisco: Freeman, 1977); Gilbert Steiner, *Constitutional Inequality: The Political Fortunes of ERA* (Washington, DC: Brookings Institution, 1985); and Jane Mansbridge, *Why We Lost the ERA* (Chicago: University of Chicago Press, 1986).

[14]For judicial action, see *Engel v. Vitale,* 370 U.S. 421 (1962). For the efforts of states to get around the Supreme Court requirement that public schools be secular, see John A. Murley, "School Prayer: Free Exercise of Religion or Establishment of Religion?" in *Social Regulatory Policy,* ed. Raymond Tatalovich and Byron Daynes (Boulder, CO: Westview Press, 1988), pp. 5–40.

TABLE 2.1

THE BILL OF RIGHTS: AN ANALYSIS OF ITS PROVISIONS

Amendment	Purpose
I	*Limits on Congress:* Congress is not to make any law establishing a religion or abridging the freedom of speech, press, assembly, or the right to petition freedoms.
II, III, IV	*Limits on Executive:* The executive branch is not to infringe on the right of people to keep arms (II), is not to arbitrarily take houses for a militia (III), and is not to engage in the search or seizure of evidence without a court warrant swearing to belief in the probable existence of a crime (IV).
V, VI, VII, VIII	*Limits on Courts:* The courts are not to hold trials for serious offenses without provision for a grand jury (V), a petit (trial) jury (VII), a speedy trial (VI), presentation of charges, confrontation of hostile witnesses (VI), immunity from testimony against oneself (V), and immunity from trial more than once for the same offense (V). Neither bail nor punishment can be excessive (VIII), and no property can be taken without just compensation (V).
IX, X	*Limits on National Government:* All rights not enumerated are reserved to the states or the people.

more changes in the Constitution would have to agree that there is great wisdom in this principle. A constitution ought to *enable* legislation and public policies to take place, but it should not attempt to *determine* what that legislation or those policies ought to be.

The purpose of the ten amendments in the Bill of Rights was basically *to give each of the three branches clearer and more restricted boundaries* (see Table 2.1). The First Amendment clarified Congress's turf. Although the powers of Congress under Article I, Section 8, would not have justified laws regulating religion, speech, and the like, the First Amendment made this limitation explicit: "Congress shall make no law. . . . " The Second, Third, and Fourth Amendments similarly spelled out limits on the executive branch, a necessity given the abuses of executive power Americans had endured under British rule.

The Fifth, Sixth, Seventh, and Eighth Amendments contain some of the most important safeguards for individual citizens against the arbitrary exercise of government power. And these amendments sought to accomplish their goal by defining

the judicial branch more concretely and clearly than had been done in Article III of the Constitution.

Five amendments adopted since 1791 are directly concerned with expansion of the electorate (see Table 2.2).[15] The founders were unable to establish a national electorate with uniform voting qualifications. They decided to evade the issue by providing in the final draft of Article I, Section 2, that eligibility to vote in a national election would be the same as "the Qualification requisite for Elector of the most numerous branch of the state Legislature." Article I, Section 4, added that Congress could alter state regulations as to the "Times, Places and Manner of holding Elections for Senators and Representatives," but this meant that any important *expansion* of the American electorate would almost certainly require a constitutional amendment.

Six more are also electoral in nature, although

---

[15]The Fourteenth Amendment is included in this table as well as in Tables 2.3 and 2.4 because it seeks not only to define citizenship but seems to intend also that this definition of citizenship included, along with the right to vote, all the rights of the Bill of Rights, regardless of the state in which the citizen resided. A great deal more will be said about this in Chapter 4.

TABLE 2.2

AMENDING THE CONSTITUTION TO EXPAND THE ELECTORATE

Amendment	Purpose	Year Proposed	Year Adopted
XIV	Section 1 provided national definition of citizenship*	1866	1868
XV	Extended voting rights to all races	1869	1870
XIX	Extended voting rights to women	1919	1920
XXIII	Extended voting rights to residents of the District of Columbia	1960	1961
XXIV	Extended voting rights to all classes by abolition of poll taxes	1962	1964
XXVI	Extended voting rights to citizens aged 18 and over	1971	1971

*In defining *citizenship,* the Fourteenth Amendment actually provided the constitutional basis for expanding the electorate to include all races, women, and residents of the District of Columbia. Only the "eighteen-year-olds' amendment" should have been necessary, since it changed the definition of citizenship. The fact that additional amendments were required following the Fourteenth suggests that voting is not considered an inherent right of U.S. citizenship. Instead it is viewed as a privilege.

not concerned directly with voting rights and the expansion of the electorate. These six amendments are concerned with the elective offices themselves or with the relationship between elective offices and the electorate (see Table 2.3).

Another five have sought to expand or to limit the powers of the national and state governments (see Table 2.4). The Eleventh Amendment protected the states from suits by private individuals and took away from the federal courts any power to take suits by private individuals of one state (or a foreign country) against another state. The other three amendments in Table 2.4 are obviously designed to reduce state power (Thirteenth), to reduce state power and expand national power (Fourteenth), and to expand national power (Sixteenth). The Twenty-seventh put a moderate limit on Congress's ability to raise its own salary.

TABLE 2.3

AMENDING THE CONSTITUTION TO CHANGE THE RELATIONSHIP BETWEEN ELECTIVE OFFICES AND THE ELECTORATE

Amendment	Purpose	Year Proposed	Year Adopted
XII	Created separate ballot for vice president in the electoral college	1803	1804
XIV	Section 2 eliminated counting of slaves as "three-fifths" citizens for apportionment of House seats	1866	1868
XVII	Provided direct election of senators	1912	1913
XX	Eliminated "lame duck" session of Congress	1932	1933
XXII	Limited presidential term	1947	1951
XXV	Provided presidential succession in case of disability	1965	1967

TABLE 2.4

AMENDING THE CONSTITUTION TO EXPAND OR LIMIT THE POWER OF GOVERNMENT

Amendment	Purpose	Year Proposed	Year Adopted
XI	Limited jurisdiction of federal courts over suits involving the states	1794	1798
XIII	Eliminated slavery and eliminated the right of states to allow property in persons	1865*	1865
XIV	(Part 2) Applied due process of Bill of Rights to the states	1866	1868
XVI	Established national power to tax incomes	1909	1913
XXVII	Limited Congress's power to raise its own salary	1789	1992

*The Thirteenth Amendment was proposed 31 January 1865, and adopted less than a year later, on 18 December 1865.

The Eighteenth, or Prohibition, Amendment underscores the meaning of the rest: This is the only amendment that the country used to try to *legislate*. In other words, it is the only amendment that was designed to deal directly with some substantive social problem. And it was the only amendment ever to have been repealed. Two other amendments—the Thirteenth, which abolished slavery, and the Sixteenth, which established the power to levy an income tax—can be said to have had the effect of legislation. But the purpose of the Thirteenth was to restrict the power of the states by forever forbidding them to treat any human being as property. As for the Sixteenth, it is certainly true that income tax legislation followed immediately; nevertheless, the amendment concerns itself strictly with establishing the power of Congress to enact such legislation. The legislation came later; and if down the line a majority in Congress had wanted to abolish the income tax, they could also have done this by legislation rather than through the arduous path of a constitutional amendment repealing the income tax.

All Constitutional amendments that are still in force deal with the structure or composition of the government.

DOES THE CONSTITUTION WORK?

The final product of the Constitutional Convention would have to be considered an extraordinary victory for those who wanted a new system of government to replace the Articles of Confederation. The new Constitution laid the groundwork for a government that would be sufficiently powerful to promote trade, to protect property, and to check the activities of radical state legislatures. Moreover, this new government was so constructed through internal checks and balances, indirect selection of officeholders, lifetime judicial appointments, and other similar provisions to preclude the "excessive democracy" feared by many of the founders. Some of the framers favored going even further in limiting popular influence, but the general consensus at the convention was that a thoroughly undemocratic document would never receive the popular approval needed to be ratified by the states.[16]

Though the Constitution was the product of a particular set of political forces, the principles of government it established have a significance that

[16]See Farrand, *The Records of the Federal Convention*, vol. 1, p. 132.

goes far beyond the interests of its authors. Two of these principles, federalism and civil liberties, will be discussed in Chapters 3 and 4. A third important constitutional principle that has affected America's government for the past two hundred years is the principle of checks and balances. As we saw earlier, the framers gave each of the three branches of government a means of intervening in and blocking the actions of the others. Often, checks and balances have seemed to prevent the government from getting much done. During the 1960s, for example, liberals were often infuriated as they watched Congress stall presidential initiatives in the area of civil rights. More recently, conservatives were outraged when President Clinton thwarted congressional efforts to enact legislation promised in the Republican "Contract with America." At various times, all sides have vilified the judiciary for invalidating legislation enacted by Congress and signed by the president.

Over time, checks and balances have acted as brakes on the governmental process. Groups hoping to bring about changes in policy or governmental institutions seldom have been able to bring about decisive and dramatic transformations in a short period of time. Instead, checks and balances have slowed the pace of change and increased the need for compromise and accommodation.

Groups able to take control of the White House, for example, must negotiate with their rivals who remain entrenched on Capitol Hill. New forces in Congress must reckon with the influence of other forces in the executive branch and in the courts. Checks and balances inevitably frustrate those who desire change, but they also function as a safeguard against rash action. During the 1950s, for example, Congress was caught up in a quasihysterical effort to unmask subversive activities in the United States, which might have led to a serious erosion of American liberties if not for the checks and balances provided by the executive branch and the courts. Thus, a governmental principle that serves as a frustrating limitation one day may become a vitally important safeguard the next.

Yet, while the Constitution sought to lay the groundwork for a powerful government, the framers struggled to reconcile government power with freedom. The framers surrounded the powerful institutions of the new regime with a variety of safeguards—a continual array of checks and balances—designed to make certain that the power of the national government could not be used to undermine the states' power and their citizens' freedoms. Thus, the framers were the first Americans to confront head on the dilemma of freedom and power. Whether their solutions to this dilemma were successful is the topic of the remainder of our story.

To Whose Benefit?

Of course, the groups whose interests were served by the Constitution in 1789, mainly the merchants and planters, are not the same groups that benefit from the Constitution's provisions today. Once incorporated into the law, political principles often take on lives of their own and have consequences that were never anticipated by their original champions. Indeed, many of the groups that benefit from constitutional provisions today did not even exist in 1789. Who would have thought that the principle of free speech would influence the transmission of data on the Internet? Who would have predicted that commercial interests that once sought a powerful government might come, two centuries later, to denounce governmental activism as "socialistic"? Perhaps one secret of the Constitution's longevity is that it did not confer permanent advantage upon any one set of economic or social forces.

Although they were defeated in 1789, the Antifederalists present us with an important picture of a road not taken and of an America that might have been. Would the country have been worse off if it had been governed by a confederacy of small republics linked by a national administration with severely limited powers? Were the Antifederalists correct in predicting that a government given great power in the hope that it might do good would, through "insensible progress," inevitably turn to evil purposes? Two hundred years of government under the federal Constitution are not necessarily enough to definitively answer these questions. Time must tell.

To What Ends?

The Constitution's framers placed individual liberty ahead of all other political values. Their concern for liberty led many of the framers to distrust both democracy and equality. They feared that democracy could degenerate into a majority tyranny in which the populace, perhaps led by a rabble-rousing demagogue, would trample on liberty. As to equality, the framers were products of their time and place; our contemporary ideas of racial and gender equality would have been foreign to them. The frames were concerned primarily with another manifestation of equality: They feared that those without property or position might be driven by what some called a "leveling spirit" to infringe upon liberty in the name of greater economic or social equality. Indeed, the framers believed that this leveling spirit was most likely to produce demagoguery and majority tyranny. As a result, the basic structure of the Constitution—separated powers, internal checks and balances, and federalism—was designed to safeguard liberty, and the Bill of Rights created further safeguards for liberty. At the same time, however, many of the Constitution's other key provisions, such as indirect election of senators and the president, as well as the appointment of judges for life, were designed to limit democracy and, hence, the threat of majority tyranny.

By championing liberty, however, the framers virtually guaranteed that democracy and even a measure of equality would sooner or later evolve in the United States. For liberty inevitably leads to the growth of political activity and the expansion of political participation. In James Madison's famous phrase, "Liberty is to faction as air is to fire."[17] Where they have liberty, more and more people, groups, and interests will almost inevitably engage in politics and gradually overcome what-

ever restrictions might have been placed upon participation. This is precisely what happened in the early years of the American Republic. During the Jeffersonian period, political parties formed. During the Jacksonian period, many state suffrage restrictions were removed and popular participation greatly expanded. Over time, liberty is conducive to democracy.

Liberty does not guarantee that everyone will be equal. It does, however, reduce the threat of inequality in one very important way. Historically, the greatest inequalities of wealth, power, and privilege have arisen where governments have used their power to allocate status and opportunity among individuals or groups. From the aristocracies of the early modern period to the *nomenklatura* of twentieth-century despotisms, the most extreme cases of inequality are associated with the most tyrannical regimes. In the United States, however, by promoting a democratic politics, over time liberty unleashed forces that militated against inequality. As a result, over the past two hundred years, groups that have learned to use the political process have achieved important economic and social gains.

One limitation of liberty as a political principle, however, is that the idea of limits upon government action can also inhibit effective government. Take one of the basic tasks of government, the protection of citizens' lives and property. A government limited by concerns over the rights of those accused of crimes may be limited in its ability to maintain public order. Currently, the U.S. government is asserting that protecting the nation against terrorists requires law enforcement measures that seem at odds with legal and constitutional formalities. The conflict between liberty and governmental effectiveness is another tension at the heart of the American constitutional system.

CHAPTER REVIEW

Political conflicts between the colonies and England, and among competing groups within the colonies, led to the first Founding as expressed by the Declaration of Independence. The first con-

[17]E. M. Earle, ed., *The Federalist* (New York: Modern Library, 1937), No. 10.

stitution, the Articles of Confederation, was adopted one year later (1777). Under this document, the states retained their sovereignty. The central government, composed solely of Congress, had few powers and no means of enforcing its will. The national government's weakness soon led to the second Founding as expressed by the Constitution of 1787.

In this second Founding, the framers sought, first, to fashion a new government sufficiently powerful to promote commerce and protect property from radical state legislatures. Second, they sought to bring an end to the "excessive democracy" of the state and national governments under the Articles of Confederation. Third, they sought to introduce mechanisms that would secure popular consent for the new government. Finally, the framers sought to make certain that their new government would not itself pose a threat to liberty and property.

The Constitution consists of seven articles. In part, Article I provides for a Congress of two chambers (Sections 1–7), defines the powers of the national government (Section 8), and interprets the national government's powers as a source of strength rather than a limitation (necessary and proper clause). Article II describes the presidency and establishes it as a separate branch of government. Article III is the judiciary article. While there is no direct mention of judicial review in this article, the Supreme Court eventually assumed that power. Article IV addresses reciprocity among states and their citizens. Article V describes the procedures for amending the Constitution. Thousands of amendments have been offered but only twenty-seven have been adopted. With the exception of the two Prohibition amendments, all amendments were oriented toward some change in the framework or structure of government. Article VI establishes that national laws and treaties are "the supreme law of the land." And finally, Article VII specifies the procedure for ratifying the Constitution of 1787.

KEY TERMS

Antifederalists   Those who favored strong state governments and a weak national government and who were opponents of the constitution proposed at the American Constitutional Convention of 1787.

Articles of Confederation   America's first written constitution. Adopted by the Continental Congress in 1777, the Articles of Confederation and Perpetual Union was the formal basis for America's national government until 1789, when it was supplanted by the Constitution.

bicameralism   Division of a legislative body into two houses, chambers, or branches.

Bill of Rights   The first ten amendments to the U.S. Constitution, ratified in 1791. They ensure certain rights and liberties to the people.

checks and balances   Mechanisms through which each branch of government is able to participate in and influence the activities of the other branches. Major examples include the presidential veto power over congressional legislation, the power of the Senate to approve presidential appointments, and judicial review of congressional enactments.

confederation   A system of government in which states retain sovereign authority except for the powers expressly delegated to the national government.

elastic clause   Article I, Section 8, of the Constitution (also known as the necessary and proper clause). It enumerates the powers of Congress and provides Congress with the authority to make all laws "necessary and proper" to carry them out.

exclusive powers   All the powers that the Constitution effectively forbids the states to exercise and which thus rest exclusively with the national government.

expressed power   The notion that the Constitution grants to the federal government only those powers specifically named in its text.

federalism   System of government in which power is divided by a constitution between a central government and regional governments.

Federalists   Those who favored a strong national government and supported the constitution proposed at the American Constitutional Convention of 1787.

full faith and credit clause Article IV, Section 1, of the Constitution. It provides that each state must accord the same respect to the laws and judicial decisions of other states that it accords to its own.

Great Compromise Agreement reached at the Constitutional Convention of 1787 that gave each state an equal number of senators regardless of its population, but linked representation in the House of Representatives to population.

habeas corpus A court order demanding that an individual in custody be brought into court and shown the cause for detention. *Habeas corpus* is guaranteed by the Constitution and can be suspended only in cases of rebellion or invasion.

judicial review Power of the courts to declare actions of the legislative and executive branches invalid or unconstitutional. The Supreme Court asserted this power in *Marbury v. Madison*.

necessary and proper clause Article I, Section 8, of the Constitution, which enumerates the powers of Congress and provides Congress with the authority to make all laws "necessary and proper" to carry them out; also referred to as the "elastic clause."

New Jersey Plan A framework for the Constitution, introduced by William Paterson, which called for equal representation in the national legislature regardless of a state's population.

privileges and immunities clause Article IV of the Constitution, which provides that the citizens of any one state are guaranteed the "privileges and immunities" of every other state, as though they were citizens of that state.

separation of powers The division of governmental power among several institutions that must cooperate in decision making.

supremacy clause Article VI of the Constitution, which states that all laws passed by the national government and all treaties are the supreme laws of the land and superior to all laws adopted by any state or any subdivision.

Three-fifths Compromise Agreement reached at the Constitutional Convention of 1787 that stipulated that for purposes of the appointment of congressional seats, every slave would be counted as three-fifths of a person.

Virginia Plan A framework for the Constitution, introduced by Edmund Randolph, which called for representation in the national legislature based upon the population of each state.

FOR FURTHER READING

Bailyn, Bernard. *The Ideological Origins of the American Revolution.* Cambridge: Harvard University Press, 1967.

Beard, Charles. *An Economic Interpretation of the Constitution of the United States.* New York: Macmillan, 1913.

Becker, Carl L. *The Declaration of Independence.* New York: Vintage, 1942.

Cohler, Anne M. *Montesquieu's Comparative Politics and the Spirit of American Constitutionalism.* Lawrence: University Press of Kansas, 1988.

Farrand, Max, ed. *The Records of the Federal Convention of 1787,* 4 vols., rev. ed. New Haven: Yale University Press, 1966.

McDonald, Forrest. *The Formation of the American Republic.* New York: Penguin, 1967.

Palmer, R. R. *The Age of the Democratic Revolution.* Princeton: Princeton University Press, 1964.

Storing, Herbert, ed. *The Complete Anti-Federalist,* 7 vols. Chicago: University of Chicago Press, 1981.

Walker, Samuel. *In Defense of American Liberties—A History of the ACLU.* New York: Oxford University Press, 1990.

Wills, Garry. *Explaining America.* New York: Penguin, 1982.

Wood, Gordon S. *The Creation of the American Republic.* New York: Norton, 1982.

CHAPTER 3

The Constitutional Framework: Federalism and the Separation of Powers

HOW DO FEDERALISM AND THE SEPARATION OF POWERS WORK AS POLITICAL INSTITUTIONS?

*T*he great achievement of American politics is the fashioning of an effective constitutional structure of political institutions. Although it is an imperfect and continuously evolving "work in progress," this structure of law and political practice has served its people well for more than two centuries by managing conflict, providing inducements for bargaining and cooperation, and facilitating collective action. There has been one enormous failure—the cruel practice of slavery, which ended only after a destructive civil war. But the basic configuration of institutions first formulated in Philadelphia in 1787 survived these debacles, though it was severely scarred by them, and has otherwise stood the test of time.

Institutional arrangements such as federalism and the separation of powers are part *script* and part *scorecard*. As two of the most important features of the constitutional structure, federalism and the separation of powers serve to channel and constrain political agents, first by limiting their jurisdictional authority and second by pitting them against one another as political competitors.

One of the ingenious features of the constitutional design adopted by the framers is the princi-

CORE OF THE ANALYSIS

- Federalism limits national power by creating two sovereigns: the national government and the state governments.

- Under "dual federalism," which lasted from 1789 to 1937, the national government limited itself primarily to promoting commerce, while the state governments directly coerced citizens.

- After 1937, the national government exerted more influence, yet the states maintained more of their traditional powers.

- Checks and balances ensure the sharing of power among separate institutions of government. Within the system of separated powers, the framers of the Constitution provided for legislative supremacy.

ple of dividing and separating. Leaving political authority unobstructed and undivided, it was thought, would invite intense competition of a winner-take-all variety. The winners would then be in a position to tyrannize, while the losers would either submit or, with nothing else to lose, be tempted to violent opposition. By adopting the divide-and-separate principle—implemented as federalism and the separation of powers, and consisting of checks and balances—the framers of the

Constitution created *jurisdictional arrangements*. The Constitution reflects this in two distinct ways. First, it encourages diversity in the political actors occupying the various institutions of government by requiring that they be selected at different times, from different constituencies, by different modes of selection (chiefly various forms of election and appointment). This, it was believed, would prevent a small clique or narrow slice of the political elite from dominating all the institutions of government at the same time. Second, the Constitution allocates the consideration of different aspects of policy to different institutional arenas. Some explicitly mentioned activities, such as the coinage of money or the declaration of war, were assigned to Congress. Matters relating to the execution and implementation of the law were delegated to the president and the executive bureaucracy. Other activities, such as adjudicating disputes between states, were made the preserve of the judicial branch. Those activities not explicitly mentioned in the Constitution were reserved to the states. In short, through a jurisdictional arrangement, the Constitution sought a balance in which there was the capacity for action, but in which power was not so concentrated as to make tyranny likely.

The amazing thing about these American political institutions is that they are not carved in granite (even if the official buildings that house them are!). While the Constitution initially set a broad framework for the division of authority between the national government and the states, and the division of labor among the branches of the national government, much adaptation and innovation took place as these institutions themselves were bent to the purposes of various political players. Politicians are goal-oriented and are constantly exploring the possibilities provided them by their institutional positions and political situations. Another political player that has helped shape the current jurisdictional arrangements and sharing of power is worth remembering as well. This is the United States Supreme Court. As former Supreme Court Justice Charles Evans Hughes once remarked, "We are under a Constitution, but the

Constitution is what the judges say it is."[1] As we shall see in this chapter, the Court has been a central player in settling the ongoing debate over how power should be divided between the national government and the states and between Congress and the president.

THE FIRST PRINCIPLE: FEDERALISM

Federalism can be defined with misleading ease and simplicity as the division of powers and functions between the national government and the state governments.

As we saw in Chapter 2, the states had already existed as former colonies before independence, and for nearly thirteen years they were virtually autonomous units under the Articles of Confederation. In effect, the states had retained too much power under the Articles, a problem that led directly to the Annapolis Convention in 1786 and the Constitutional Convention in 1787. Under the Articles, disorder within states was beyond the reach of the national government (see Shays's Rebellion, Chapter 2), and conflicts of interest between states were not manageable. For example, states were making their own trade agreements with foreign countries and companies that might then play one state against another for special advantages. Some states adopted special trade tariffs, and further barriers to foreign commerce that were contrary to the interests of another state.[2] Tax and other barriers were also being erected between the states.[3] But even after the ratification of the Constitution, the states continued to be more important than the national government. For

[1]Charles Evans Hughes, speech at Elmira, New York, 3 May 1907.
[2]For a good treatment of these conflicts of interests between states, see Forrest McDonald, *E Pluribus Unum—The Formation of the American Republic, 1776–1790* (Boston: Houghton Mifflin, 1965), Chapter 7, especially pp. 319–38.
[3]See David O'Brien, *Constitutional Law and Politics*, vol. 1 (New York: Norton, 1997), pp. 602–3.

CENTRAL QUESTIONS

- **The First Principle: Federalism**
  How does federalism limit the power of the national government?
  How strong a role have the states had traditionally in the federal framework?
  What means does the national government use to control the actions of the states?
  How has the relationship between the national government and the states evolved over the last several decades?
  What methods have been employed to give more control back to the states?
- **The Second Principle: The Separation of Powers**
  How do the separate institutions of government interact with each other? Did the framers intend for one branch of government to be supreme?
- **The Constitution and Limited Government**
  What is the constitutional basis for the United States' system of limited government?

nearly a century and a half, virtually all of the fundamental policies governing the lives of American citizens were made by the state legislatures, not by Congress.

The novelty of this arrangement can be appreciated by noting that each of the major European countries at that time had a *unitary* government: a single national government with national ministries; a national police force; and a single, national code of laws for crimes, commerce, public works, education, and all other areas.

Federalism in the Constitution

The United States was the first nation to adopt federalism as its governing framework. With federalism, the framers sought to limit the national government by creating a second layer of state governments. American federalism recognized two sovereigns in the original Constitution and reinforced the principle in the Bill of Rights by granting a few *expressed powers* to the national government and reserving all the rest to the states.

THE POWERS OF THE NATIONAL GOVERNMENT As we saw in Chapter 2, the expressed powers granted to the national government are found in Article I, Section 8, of the Constitution. These seventeen powers include the power to collect taxes, to coin money, to declare war, and to regulate commerce (which, as we will see, became a very impor-

tant power for the national government). Article I, Section 8, also contains another important source of power for the national government: the *implied powers* that enable Congress "to make all Laws which shall be necessary and proper for carrying into Execution the foregoing Powers." Not until several decades after the founding did the Supreme Court allow Congress to exercise the power granted in this *necessary and proper clause,* but, as we shall see later in this chapter, this doctrine allowed the national government to expand considerably the scope of its authority, although the process was a slow one. In addition to these expressed and implied powers, the Constitution affirmed the power of the national government in the supremacy clause (Article VI), which made all national laws and treaties "the supreme Law of the Land."

THE POWERS OF STATE GOVERNMENT One way in which the framers sought to preserve a strong role for the states was through the Tenth Amendment to the Constitution. The Tenth Amendment states that the powers that the Constitution does not delegate to the national government or prohibit to the states are "reserved to the States respectively, or to the people." The Antifederalists, who feared that a strong central government would encroach on individual liberty, repeatedly pressed for such an amendment as a way of limiting national power. Federalists agreed to the amendment because they did not think it would do much harm, given the powers of the Constitution already granted to the national government. The Tenth Amendment is also called the *reserved powers* amendment because it aims to reserve powers to the states.

The most fundamental power that is retained by the states is that of coercion—the power to develop and enforce criminal codes, to administer health and safety rules, to regulate the family via marriage and divorce laws. The states have the power to regulate individuals' livelihoods; if you're a doctor or a lawyer or a plumber or a barber, you must be licensed by the state. Even more fundamentally, the states have the power to define private property—private property exists because state laws against trespassing define who is and is not entitled to use a piece of property. If you own a car, your ownership isn't worth much unless the state is willing to enforce your right to possession by making it a crime for anyone else to take your car. These are fundamental matters, and the powers of the states regarding these domestic issues are much greater than the powers of the national government, even today.

A state's authority to regulate these fundamental matters is commonly referred to as the *police power* of the state and encompasses the state's power to regulate the health, safety, welfare, and morals of its citizens. Policing is what states do—they coerce you in the name of the community in order to maintain public order. And this was exactly the type of power that the founders intended the states to exercise.

In some areas, the states share *concurrent powers* with the national government, wherein they retain and share some power to regulate commerce and to affect the currency—for example, by being able to charter banks, grant or deny corporate charters, grant or deny licenses to engage in a business or practice a trade, and regulate the quality of products or the conditions of labor. This issue of concurrent versus exclusive power has come up from time to time in our history, but wherever there is a direct conflict of laws between the federal and the state levels, the issue will most likely be resolved in favor of national supremacy.

STATE OBLIGATIONS TO ONE ANOTHER The Constitution also creates obligations among the states. These obligations, spelled out in Article IV, were intended to promote national unity. By requiring the states to recognize actions and decisions taken in other states as legal and proper, the framers aimed to make the states less like independent countries and more like parts of a single nation.

Article IV, Section I, calls for "Full Faith and Credit" among states, meaning that each state is normally expected to honor the "public Acts, Records, and judicial Proceedings" that take place in any other state. So, for example, if a couple is married in Texas—marriage being regulated by state law—Missouri must also recognize that marriage, even though they were not married under Missouri state law.

This *full faith and credit clause* has recently become embroiled in the controversy over gay and lesbian marriage. In 1993, the Hawaii Supreme Court prohibited discrimination against gay and lesbian marriage except in very limited circumstances. Many observers believed that Hawaii would eventually fully legalize gay marriage. In fact, after a long political battle, Hawaii passed a constitutional amendment in 1998 outlawing gay marriage. However, in December 1999, the Vermont Supreme Court ruled that gay and lesbian couples should have the same rights as heterosexuals. The Vermont legislature responded with a new law that allowed gays and lesbians to form "civil unions." Although not legally considered marriages, such unions allow gay and lesbian couples most of the benefits of marriage, such as eligibility for the partner's health insurance, inheritance rights, and the right to transfer property. The Vermont statute could have broad implications for other states. More than thirty states have passed "defense of marriage acts" that define marriage as a union between men and women only. Anxious to show its disapproval of gay marriage, Congress passed the Defense of Marriage Act in

1996, which declared that states will *not* have to recognize a same-sex marriage, even if it is legal in one state. The act also said that the federal government will not recognize gay marriage—even if it is legal under state law—and that gay marriage partners will not be eligible for the federal benefits, such as Medicare and Social Security, normally available to spouses.[4]

In 2004, a presidential election year, Alabama, Georgia, Kentucky, Michigan, Montana, North Dakota, Ohio, Oklahoma, and Utah approved state constitutional amendments strictly defining marriage as between a man and a woman. This large-scale approval of such amendments was probably prompted by a Massachusetts court decision permitting gays and lesbians to wed, which was to go into effect in May 2004. In March 2005 a ruling by the San Francisco Superior Court said that California's state law banning same-sex marriage was a violation of the rights of gays and lesbians. This ruling also nullified the state's Proposition 22, approved by referendum in 2000 (by 61.4 to 38.6 percent), limiting marriage to one man and one woman. This was all the more important because it was California and the judge was a registered Republican appointed in 1996 by a Republican governor. Finally, these developments put fire back into President George W. Bush's pledge to support a constitutional amendment banning same-sex marriage, even though polls have shown substantial majorities favoring some form of same-sex union, whether marriage or "civil union."[5] In effect, although a great many state laws are observed in a normal, routine way in sister states, laws that confront what have come to be called "values" will be exempted from comity—or taken off the table altogether by an amendment to that effect in the U.S. Constitution.

Because of this controversy, the extent and meaning of the full faith and credit clause are sure to be considered by the Supreme Court. In fact, it is not clear that the clause requires states to recognize gay marriage because the Court's past interpretation of the clause has provided exceptions for "public policy" reasons: If states have strong objections to a law, they do not have to honor it. In 1997 the Court took up a case involving the full faith and credit clause. The case concerned a Michigan court order that prevented a former engineer for General Motors from testifying against the company. The engineer, who left the company on bad terms, later testified in a Missouri court about a car accident in which a woman died when her Chevrolet Blazer caught fire. General Motors challenged his right to testify, arguing that Missouri should give "full faith and credit" to the Michigan ruling. The Supreme Court ruled that the engineer could testify and that the court system in one state cannot hinder other state courts in their "search for the truth."[6]

Article IV, Section 2, known as the "comity clause," also seeks to promote national unity. It provides that citizens enjoying the ***"Privileges and Immunities"*** of one state should be entitled to similar treatment in other states. What this has come to mean is that a state cannot discriminate against someone from another state or give special privileges to its own residents. For example, in the 1970s, when Alaska passed a law that gave residents preference over nonresidents in obtaining work on the state's oil and gas pipelines, the Supreme Court ruled the law illegal because it discriminated against citizens of other states.[7] This clause also regulates criminal justice among the states by requiring states to return fugitives to the states from which they have fled. Thus, in 1952, when an inmate escaped from an Alabama prison and sought to avoid being returned to Alabama on the grounds that he was being subjected to "cruel and unusual punishment" there, the Supreme Court ruled that he must be returned according to

[4]Ken I. Kersch, "Full Faith and Credit for Same-Sex Marriages?" *Political Science Quarterly* 112 (Spring 1997): 117–36; Joan Biskupic, "Once Unthinkable, Now under Debate," *Washington Post*, 3 September 1996, p. A1.
[5]This is a peculiar, albeit effective distinction because all marriages are "civil unions"—and nothing else.

[6]Linda Greenhouse, "Supreme Court Weaves Legal Principles from a Tangle of Legislation," *New York Times*, 30 June 1988, p. A20.
[7]*Hicklin v. Orbeck*, 437 U.S. 518 (1978).

Article IV, Section 2.[8] This example highlights the difference between the obligations among states and those among different countries. Recently, France refused to return an American fugitive because he might be subject to the death penalty, which does not exist in France.[9] The Constitution clearly forbids states from doing something similar.

States' relationships to one another are also governed by the interstate compact clause (Article I, Section 10), which states that "No State shall, without the Consent of Congress . . . enter into any Agreement or Compact with another State." The Court has interpreted the clause to mean that states may enter into agreements with one another, subject to congressional approval. Compacts are a way for two or more states to reach a legally binding agreement about how to solve a problem that crosses state lines. In the early years of the Republic, states turned to compacts primarily to settle border disputes. Today they are used for a wide range of issues but are especially important in regulating the distribution of river water, addressing environmental concerns, and operating transportation systems that cross state lines.[10]

LOCAL GOVERNMENT AND THE CONSTITUTION Local government occupies a peculiar but very important place in the American system. In fact, the status of American local government is probably unique in world experience. First, it must be pointed out that local government has no status in the American Constitution. *State* legislatures created local governments, and *state* constitutions and laws permit local governments to take on some of the responsibilities of the state governments. Most states amended their own constitutions to give their larger cities **home rule**—a guarantee of noninterference in various areas of local affairs. But

local governments enjoy no such recognition in the Constitution. Local governments have always been mere conveniences of the states.[11]

Local governments became administratively important in the early years of the Republic because the states possessed little administrative capability. They relied on local governments—cities and counties—to implement the laws of the state. Local government was an alternative to a statewide bureaucracy.

Dual federalism created two sovereigns: the national government and the state governments. Federalism limited the power of the national government to intervene in the economy of the states and allowed the states to differ in many substantial policy issues.

The Slow Growth of the National Government's Power

As we have noted, the Constitution created two layers of government: the national government and the state governments. This two-layer system is called **dual federalism**. The consequences of this dual federalism are fundamental to the American system of government in theory and in practice; they have meant that states have done most of the fundamental governing in this country. For evidence, look at Table 3.1. It lists the major types of public policies by which Americans were governed for the first century and a half under the Consti-

---

[8]*Sweeny v. Woodall,* 344 U.S. 86 (1953).

[9]Marlise Simons, "France Won't Extradite American Convicted of Murder," *New York Times,* 5 December 1997, p. A9.

[10]Patricia S. Florestano, "Past and Present Utilization of Interstate Compacts in the United States," *Publius* 24 (Fall 1994): 13–26.

[11]A good discussion of the constitutional position of local governments is in York Y. Willbern, *The Withering Away of the City* (Bloomington: Indiana University Press, 1971). For more on the structure and theory of federalism, see Thomas R. Dye, *American Federalism: Competition among Governments* (Lexington, MA: Lexington Books, 1990), Chapter 1; and Martha Derthick, "Up-to-Date in Kansas City: Reflections on American Federalism" (the 1992 John Gaus Lecture), *PS: Political Science & Politics* 25 (December 1992): 671–75.

TABLE 3.1

THE FEDERAL SYSTEM: SPECIALIZATION OF GOVERNMENTAL FUNCTIONS IN THE TRADITIONAL SYSTEM (1789–1937)

National Government Policies (Domestic)	State Government Policies	Local Government Policies
Internal improvements	Property laws (including slavery)	Adaptation of state laws to local conditions ("variances")
Subsidies	Estate and inheritance laws	
Tariffs	Commerce laws	Public works
Public lands disposal	Banking and credit laws	Contracts for public works
Patents	Corporate laws	Licensing of public accommodations
Currency	Insurance laws	Assessible improvements
	Family laws	Basic public services
	Morality laws	
	Public health laws	
	Education laws	
	General penal laws	
	Eminent domain laws	
	Construction codes	
	Land-use laws	
	Water and mineral laws	
	Criminal procedure laws	
	Electoral and political parties laws	
	Local government laws	
	Civil service laws	
	Occupations and professions laws	

tution. We call it the "traditional system" because it prevailed for three-quarters of our history and because it closely approximates the intentions of the framers of the Constitution. The contrast between national and state policies, as shown by Table 3.1, demonstrates the difference in the power vested in each. The list of items in column 2 could actually have been made longer. Moreover, each item on the list is a category of law that fills many volumes of statutes and court decisions.

> *Under the traditional system, the national government had little effect on local economies other than to promote interstate commerce.*

Questions about how to divide responsibilities between the states and the national government first arose more than two hundred years ago, when the framers wrote the Constitution to create a stronger union. But they did not solve the issue of who should do what. There is no "right" answer to that question; each generation of Americans has provided its own answer. In recent years, Americans have grown distrustful of the federal government and have supported giving more responsibility to the states.[12] Even so, they still want the federal government to set standards and promote equality.

Political debates about the division of responsibility often take sides: Some people argue for a strong federal role to set national standards, while others say the states should do more. These two goals are not necessarily at odds. The key is to find the right balance. During the first 150 years of American history, that balance favored state power. But the balance began to shift toward Washington in the 1930s. Since the mid-1990s there have been efforts to shift the balance back toward the states.

Since the 1930s, the national government has expanded its influence, but the states continue to be an integral part of American government.

Having created the national government, and recognizing the potential for abuse of power, the states sought through federalism to constrain the national government. The "traditional system" of a weak national government prevailed for over a century despite economic forces favoring its expansion and despite Supreme Court cases giving a pro-national interpretation to Article I, Section 8, of the Constitution.

That article delegates to Congress the power "to regulate commerce with foreign nations, and among the several States and with the Indian tribes." The Supreme Court consistently interpreted this *commerce clause* in favor of national power for most of the nineteenth century. The first

and most important case favoring national power over the economy was *McCulloch v. Maryland* (1819).[13] The case involved the question of whether Congress had the power to charter a national bank, since such an explicit grant of power was nowhere to be found in Article I, Section 8. Chief Justice John Marshall answered that the power could be "implied" from other powers that were expressly delegated to Congress, such as the "powers to lay and collect taxes; to borrow money; to regulate commerce; and to declare and conduct a war."

The constitutional authority for the implied powers doctrine is a clause in Article I, Section 8, which enables Congress "to make all laws which shall be necessary and proper for carrying into Execution the foregoing powers." By allowing Congress to use the necessary and proper clause to interpret its delegated powers expansively, the Supreme Court created the potential for an unprecedented increase in national government power. Marshall also concluded that whenever a state law conflicted with a federal law (as in the case of *McCulloch v. Maryland*), the state law would be deemed invalid since the Constitution states that "the laws of the United States . . . 'shall be the supreme law of the land.' " Both parts of this great case are "pro-national," yet Congress did not immediately seek to expand the policies of the national government.

In McCulloch v. Maryland, *the Supreme Court ruled that the national government was supreme over the states, as implied from the powers delegated to Congress by the Constitution.*

Another major case, *Gibbons v. Ogden* in 1824, reinforced this nationalistic interpretation of the Constitution. The important but relatively narrow issue was whether the state of New York could grant a monopoly to Robert Fulton's steamboat company to operate an exclusive service between

---

[12]See the poll reported in Guy Gugliotta, "Scaling Down the American Dream," *Washington Post,* 19 April 1995, p. A21.

[13]*McCulloch v. Maryland,* 4 Wheaton 316 (1819).

New York and New Jersey. Chief Justice Marshall argued that the state of New York did not have the power to grant this particular monopoly. In order to reach this decision, it was necessary for Marshall to define what Article I, Section 8, meant by "commerce among the several states." He insisted that the definition was "comprehensive," extending to "every species of commercial intercourse." He did say that this comprehensiveness was limited "to that commerce which concerns more states than one," giving rise to what later came to be called "interstate commerce." *Gibbons* is important because it established the supremacy of the national government in all matters affecting interstate commerce.[14] But what would remain uncertain during several decades of constitutional discourse was the precise meaning of interstate commerce.

In Gibbons v. Ogden, *the Court ruled that the national government had a constitutional right to regulate interstate commerce comprehensively.*

Article I, Section 8, backed by the "implied powers" decision in *McCulloch* and by the broad definition of "interstate commerce" in *Gibbons,* was a source of power for the national government as long as Congress sought to facilitate commerce through subsidies, services, and land grants. But later in the nineteenth century, when the national government sought to use those powers to *regulate* the economy rather than merely to promote economic development, the concept of interstate commerce began to operate as a restraint on, rather than a source of, national power.

Any effort of the national government to regulate commerce in such areas as fraud, the production of impure goods, the use of child labor, or the existence of dangerous working conditions or long hours was declared unconstitutional by the Supreme Court as a violation of the concept of interstate commerce. Such legislation meant that the federal government was entering the factory

and workplace—local areas—and was attempting to regulate goods that had not passed into commerce. To enter these local workplaces was to exercise police power—the power reserved to the states for the protection of the health, safety, and morals of their citizens. No one questioned the power of the national government to regulate businesses that intrinsically involved interstate commerce, such as railroads, gas pipelines, and waterway transportation. But well into the twentieth century, the Supreme Court used the concept of interstate commerce as a barrier against most efforts by Congress to expand the national government's power.

After 1937, the Supreme Court threw out the old distinction between interstate and intrastate commerce, converting the commerce clause from a source of limitations to a source of power. The Court began to refuse to review appeals challenging acts of Congress protecting the rights of employees to organize and engage in collective bargaining, regulating the amount of farmland in cultivation, extending low-interest credit to small businesses and farmers, and restricting the activities of corporations dealing in the stock market, and many other laws that contributed to the construction of the "welfare state."

Between the end of the Civil War and the 1930s, entrepreneurs enjoyed minimal government intervention in domestic markets. After 1937, however, the Court threw out the distinction between interstate and intrastate commerce, allowing for greater national power over the economy.

Cooperative Federalism and Grants-in-Aid

If the traditional system of two sovereigns performing highly different functions could be called dual federalism, the system since the 1930s could be called **cooperative federalism**, which generally

---

[14]*Gibbons v. Ogden,* 9 Wheaton 1 (1824).

refers to supportive relations, sometimes partnerships, between national government and the state and local governments. It comes in the form of federal subsidization of special state and local activities; these subsidies are called *grants-in-aid*. But make no mistake about it: Although many of these state and local programs would not exist without the federal grant-in-aid, the grant-in-aid is also an important form of federal influence. (Another form of federal influence, the mandate, will be covered in the next section.)

A grant-in-aid is really a kind of bribe or "carrot"—Congress gives money to state and local governments, but with the condition that the money will be spent for a particular purpose as designed by Congress. Thus, Congress uses grants-in-aid because it recognizes that it does not usually have the political or constitutional power to command the cities to do its bidding directly.

Most national influence over state governments comes through grants-in-aid (monetary incentives to adopt policies).

The principle of grants-in-aid goes back to the nineteenth-century land grants to states for the improvement of agriculture and farm-related education. Since farms were not in "interstate commerce," it was unclear whether the Constitution would permit the national government to provide direct assistance to agriculture. Grants-in-aid to the states, earmarked to go to the farmers, presented a way of avoiding the constitutional problem while pursuing what was recognized in Congress as a national goal.

This same approach was applied to cities beginning in the late 1930s. Congress set national goals such as public housing and assistance to the unemployed and provided grants-in-aid to meet these goals. The value of these *categorical grants-in-aid* increased from $2.3 billion in 1950 to $350 billion in 2002 (see Figure 3.1). Sometimes Congress requires the state or local government to match the national contribution dollar for dollar; but for some

programs, such as the interstate highway system, the congressional grant-in-aid provides 90 percent of the cost of the program.

For the most part, the categorical grants created before the 1960s simply helped the states perform their traditional functions.[15] In the 1960s, however, the national role expanded and the number of categorical grants increased dramatically. For example, during the Eighty-ninth Congress (1965–1966) alone, the number of categorical grant-in-aid programs grew from 221 to 379.[16] The grants authorized during the 1960s announced national purposes much more strongly than did earlier grants. Central to that national purpose was the need to provide opportunities to the poor.

Many of the categorical grants enacted during the 1960s were *project grants,* which require state and local governments to submit proposals to federal agencies. In contrast to the older *formula grants,* which used a formula (composed of such elements as need and state and local capacities) to distribute funds, the new project grants made funding available on a competitive basis. Federal agencies would give grants to the proposals they judged to be the best. In this way, the national government acquired substantial control over which state and local governments got money, how much they got, and how they spent it.

The most important scholar of the history of federalism, Morton Grodzins, characterized this as a move from "layer cake federalism" to "marble cake federalism" in which intergovernmental cooperation and sharing have blurred the line between where the national government ends and the state and local governments begin (see Concept Map 3.1).[17] Figure 3.2 demonstrates the financial basis

---

[15]Kenneth T. Palmer, "The Evolution of Grant Policies," in *The Changing Politics of Federal Grants,* by Lawrence D. Brown, James W. Fossett, and Kenneth T. Palmer (Washington, DC: Brookings Institution, 1984) p. 15.

[16]Ibid., p. 6.

[17]Morton Grodzins, "The Federal System," in *Goals for Americans,* President's Commission on National Goals (Englewood Cliffs, NJ: Prentice Hall, 1960), p. 265. In a marble cake, the white cake is distinguishable from the chocolate cake, but the two are streaked rather than in distinct layers.

FIGURE 3.1

HISTORICAL TREND OF GRANTS-IN-AID, 1950–2006

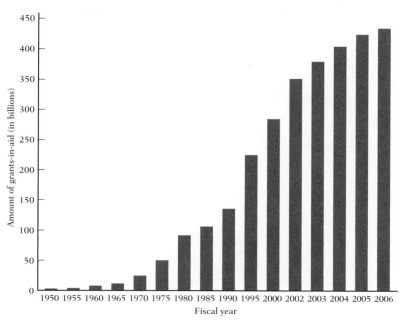

*Excludes outlays for national defense, international affairs, and net interest.
SOURCE: Office of Management and Budget, *Budget of the United States Government, Fiscal Year 2006, Analytical Perspectives* (Washington, DC: Government Printing Office, 2005).

of the marble cake idea. At the high point of grant-in-aid policies in the late 1970s, federal aid contributed about 25–30 percent of the operating budgets of all the state and local governments in the country.

Dual federalism evolved into cooperative federalism, in which intergovernmental cooperation has lessened the distinction between the responsibilities of state and national governments.

REGULATED FEDERALISM AND NATIONAL STANDARDS Developments from the 1960s to the

present have moved well beyond marble cake federalism to what might be called *regulated federalism.*[18] In some areas the national government actually regulates the states by threatening to withhold grant money unless state and local governments conform to national standards. The most notable instances of this regulation are in the areas of civil rights, poverty programs, and environmental protection. In these instances, the national government provides grant-in-aid financing but sets conditions the states must meet in order to keep the grants. The national government refers to these policies as "setting

[18]The concept and the best discussion of this modern phenomenon will be found in Donald F. Kettl, *The Regulation of American Federalism* (Baltimore: Johns Hopkins University Press, 1983 and 1987), especially pp. 33–41.

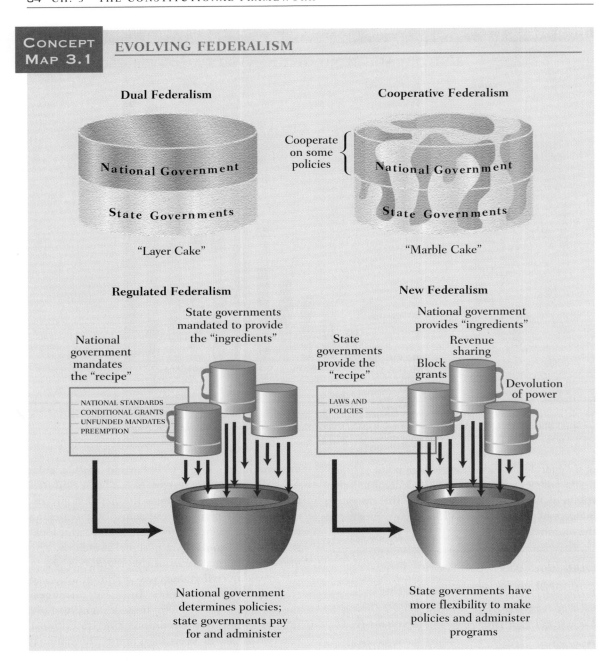

CONCEPT MAP 3.1

EVOLVING FEDERALISM

Dual Federalism

National Government

State Governments

"Layer Cake"

Cooperate on some policies

Cooperative Federalism

National Government

State Governments

"Marble Cake"

Regulated Federalism

National government mandates the "recipe"

State governments mandated to provide the "ingredients"

NATIONAL STANDARDS
CONDITIONAL GRANTS
UNFUNDED MANDATES
PREEMPTION

National government determines policies; state governments pay for and administer

New Federalism

State governments provide the "recipe"

National government provides "ingredients"

Revenue sharing

Block grants

Devolution of power

LAWS AND POLICIES

State governments have more flexibility to make policies and administer programs

national standards." Important cases of such efforts are in interstate highway use, in social services, and in education. The net effect of these national standards is that state and local policies are more uniform from coast to coast. However, there are a number of other programs in which the national government engages in regulated federalism by imposing obligations on

FIGURE 3.2

THE RISE, DECLINE, AND RECOVERY OF FEDERAL AID

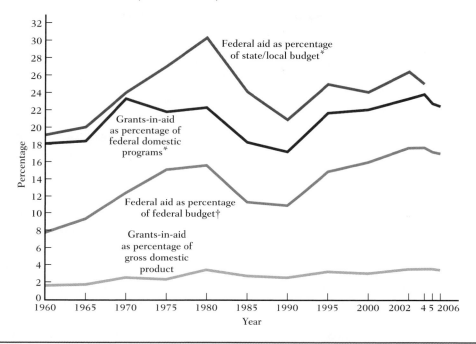

*Federal aid as a percentage of state/local expenditures after transfers.
†Federal aid as a percentage of federal expenditures from own funds.
‡Excludes outlays for national defense, international affairs, and net interest.
SOURCE: Office of Management and Budget, *Budget of the United States Government, Fiscal Year 2006, Analytical Perspectives* (Washington, DC: Government Printing Office, 2005).

the states *without providing any funding at all.* These have come to be called *unfunded mandates.*[19] States complained that mandates took up so much of their budgets that they were not able to set their own priorities.

These burdens became a major part of the rallying cry that produced the famous Republican Congress elected in 1994, with its Contract with America. One of the first measures adopted by the 104th Republican Congress was an act to limit unfunded mandates—the Unfunded Mandates Reform Act (UMRA). This was considered a triumph of lobbying efforts by state and local governments, and it was "hailed as both symbol and substance of a renewed congressional commitment to federalism."[20] Under this law, a point of order raised on the House or Senate floor can stop any mandate with an uncompensated state and local cost estimated at greater than $50 million a year as determined by the Congressional Budget Office (CBO). This was called a "stop, look, and listen"

[19]John DiIulio and Don Kettl report that in 1980 there were thirty-six laws that could be categorized as unfunded mandates. And despite the concerted opposition of the Reagan and Bush administrations, another twenty-seven laws qualifying as unfunded mandates were adopted between 1982 and 1991. See John DiIulio, Jr., and Donald F. Kettl, *Fine Print: The Contract with America, Devolution, and the Administrative Realities of American Federalism* (Washington, DC: Brookings Institution, 1995), p. 41.

[20]Paul Posner, "Unfunded Mandate Reform: How Is It Working?" *Rockefeller Institute Bulletin* (Albany: Nelson A. Rockefeller Institute of Government, 1998): 35.

requirement, forcing Congress to take positive action to own up to the mandate and its potential costs. During 1996, its first full year of operation, only eleven bills included mandates that exceeded the $50 million threshold—from a total of sixty-nine estimates of actions in which mandates were included. Examples included minimum wage increase, parity for mental health and health insurance, mandated use of Social Security numbers on drivers' licenses, and extension of Federal Occupation Safety and Health to state and local employees. Most of them were modified in the House to reduce their costs. However, as one expert put it, "The primary impact of UMRA came not from the affirmative blockage of [mandate] legislation, but rather from its effect as a deterrent to mandates in the drafting and early consideration of legislation."[21]

As indicated by the first year of its operation, the effect of UMRA will not be revolutionary. UMRA does not prevent congressional members from passing unfunded mandates; it only makes them think twice before they do. Moreover, UMRA exempts several areas from coverage. And states must still enforce antidiscrimination laws and meet other requirements to receive federal assistance. But, on the other hand, UMRA does represent a serious effort to shift power in the national–state relationship a bit further toward the state side.

NEW FEDERALISM AND THE NATIONAL STATE TUG OF WAR   There have been countertrends, attempts to reverse this nationalization and reestablish traditional policy making and implementation. Presidents Nixon and Reagan called their efforts the *new federalism,* by which national policies attempted to return more discretion to the states. This was the purpose of Nixon's *revenue sharing* and the goal of Reagan's *block grants,* which consolidated a number of categorical grants into one larger category, leaving the state (or local) government more discretion to decide how to use the money. Presidents Nixon and Reagan, as well as former President Bush,

were sincere in wanting to return somewhat to a traditional notion of freedom of action for the states. They called it new federalism, but their concept and their goal were really much closer to the older, traditional federalism that predated the 1930s.

During the past twenty-five years, cooperative federalism has given way to regulated federalism, in which the national government regulates the states by threatening to withhold money unless the states meet specific obligations. Some states have fought for a reversal of increased national control, calling their revised system the new federalism.

In effect, President Clinton adopted the "new federalism" of Nixon and Reagan even though he gave the appearance of expanding federal government activity. He signed the Unfunded Mandates Reform Act of 1995 as well as the Personal Responsibility and Work Opportunity Reconciliation Act of 1996 (PRA), which goes farther than any other act of Congress in the past sixty years to relieve the states from both funded and unfunded national mandates. The PRA replaced the sixty-one-year-old *Aid to Families with Dependent Children (AFDC)* program with block grants to states for the Temporary Assistance to Needy Families program (TANF). Although some national standards remain, the place of the states in the national welfare system has been virtually revolutionized through *devolution,* the strategy of delegating to the states more and more authority over a range of policies that had been under national government authority, plus providing the states with a substantial portion of the cost of these programs. Since the mid-1990s, devolution has been quite consequential for the national-state tug of war.

One argument in favor of devolution is that states can act as "laboratories of democracy" by

21Ibid., p. 36.

experimenting with many different approaches to find one that best meets the needs of their citizens.[22] As states have altered their welfare programs in the wake of the new law, they have indeed designed diverse approaches. For example, Minnesota has adopted an incentive-based approach that offers extra assistance to families that take low-wage jobs. Other states, such as California, have more "sticks" than "carrots" in their new welfare programs.

President George W. Bush, though sometimes compared to Reagan, has not proven to be an unwavering supporter of new federalism and states' rights. On certain matters dear to his heart, Bush has been closer to the spirit of "regulated federalism." The most visible example of Bush's occasional preference for national standards is the education program known as No Child Left Behind. This program sets standards of accomplishment in reading and math that are to be applied nationally and backed by federal grants that the government withholds if a state fails to meet the standards. The program gives the states "full freedom" to use the federal money, but states are to be held accountable for results, as measured by national standards of performance. This program is an especially significant example of Bush's view of federalism considering that education is the most local of all activities. On certain other matters, historical circumstance has made Bush a proponent of nationalization. Homeland security policies are the prime example. President Bush has sought billions of dollars to pull cities and states into assuming more of their own security measures. He has even supported some "unfunded mandates" on the larger and more vulnerable cities, resulting in demands from such liberal Democratic senators as Charles Schumer and Hillary Clinton of New York, for more federal reimbursement for federally generated local safety measures. Another circumstance that has pushed more responsibility back on the national government is the spate of recent state budget crises. Since many states' constitutions prohibit running budget deficits, the national government has been forced to fill in the gaps.

As these examples from the last decade show, assessments about "the right way" to divide responsibility in the federal system change over time.

THE SUPREME COURT AS REFEREE   For much of the nineteenth century, federal power remained limited. The Tenth Amendment was used to bolster arguments about *states' rights*, which in their extreme version claimed that the states did not have to submit to national laws when they believed the national government had exceeded its authority. These arguments in favor of states' rights were voiced less often after the Civil War. But the Supreme Court continued to use the Tenth Amendment to strike down laws that it thought exceeded national power, including the Civil Rights Act passed in 1875.

In the early twentieth century, however, the Tenth Amendment appeared to lose its force. Reformers began to press for national regulations to limit the power of large corporations and to preserve the health and welfare of citizens. The Supreme Court approved of some of these laws, but it struck others down, including a law combating child labor. The Court stated that the law violated the Tenth Amendment because only states should have the power to regulate conditions of employment. By the late 1930s, however, the Supreme Court had approved such an expansion of federal power that the Tenth Amendment appeared irrelevant. In fact, in 1941, Justice Harlan Fiske Stone declared that the Tenth Amendment was simply a "truism," that it had no real meaning.[23]

Recent years have seen a revival of interest in the Tenth Amendment and important Supreme Court decisions limiting federal power. Much of the interest in the Tenth Amendment stems from conservatives who believe that a strong federal government encroaches on individual liberties.

---

[22]The phrase "laboratories of democracy" was coined by Supreme Court Justice Louis Brandeis in his dissenting opinion in *New State Ice Co. v. Liebman,* 285 U.S. 262 (1932).

[23]*United States v. Darby Lumber Co.,* 312 U.S. 100 (1941).

They believe such freedoms are better protected by returning more power to the states through the process of devolution. In 1996, Republican presidential candidate Bob Dole carried a copy of the Tenth Amendment in his pocket as he campaigned, pulling it out to read at rallies.[24] Around the same time, the Court revived the Eleventh Amendment concept of *state sovereign immunity*. This legal doctrine holds that states are immune from lawsuits by private persons or groups claiming that the state violated a statute enacted by Congress.

The Supreme Court's ruling in *United States v. Lopez* in 1995 fueled further interest in the Tenth Amendment. In that case, the Court, stating that Congress had exceeded its authority under the commerce clause, struck down a federal law that barred handguns near schools. This was the first time since the New Deal that the Court had limited congressional powers in this way. (The New Deal is discussed in Chapter 6.) The Court further limited the power of the federal government over the states in a 1996 ruling based on the Eleventh Amendment that prevented Native Americans from the Seminole tribe from suing the state of Florida in federal court. A 1988 law had given Indian tribes the right to sue a state in federal court if the state did not negotiate in good faith over issues related to gambling casinos on tribal land. The Supreme Court's ruling appeared to signal a much broader limitation on national power by raising new questions about whether individuals can sue a state if it fails to uphold federal law.[25]

Another significant decision involving the relationship between the federal government and state governments was the 1997 case *Printz v. United States* (joined with *Mack v. United States*),[26] in which the Court struck down a key provision of the Brady Bill, enacted by Congress in 1993 to regulate gun sales. Under the terms of the act, state and local law enforcement officers were required

to conduct background checks on prospective gun purchasers. The Court held that the federal government cannot require states to administer or enforce federal regulatory programs. Since the states bear administrative responsibility for a variety of other federal programs, this decision could have far-reaching consequences. Finally, in another major ruling from the 1996–1997 term, in *City of Boerne v. Flores*,[27] the Court ruled that Congress had gone too far in restricting the power of the states to enact regulations they deemed necessary for the protection of public health, safety, or welfare. These rulings signal a move toward a much more restricted federal government.

In 1999, the Court's ruling on another Eleventh Amendment case further strengthened the doctrine of state sovereign immunity, finding that "The federal system established by our Constitution preserves the sovereign status of the States. . . . The generation that designed and adopted our federal system considered immunity from private suits central to sovereign dignity."[28] In 2000 in *United States v. Morrison*, the Supreme Court invalidated an important provision of the 1994 Violence against Women Act, which permitted women to bring private damage suits if their victimization was "gender-motivated." Although the 1994 act did not add any new national laws imposing liability or obligations on the states, the Supreme Court still held the act to be "an unconstitutional exercise" of Congress's power. And, although *Morrison* is a quite narrow federalism decision, when it is coupled with *United States v. Lopez* (1995)—the first modern holding against national authority to use commerce power to reach into the states—there is a definite trend toward strict scrutiny of the federal intervention aspects of all national civil rights, social, labor, and gender laws.[29]

There has clearly been a historical ebb and flow to the federal relationship: The national government's authority grew relative to that of the states

[24]W. John Moore, "Pleading the 10th," *National Journal*, 29 July 1995, p. 1940.
[25]*Seminole Indian Tribe v. Florida*, 116 S. Ct. 1114 (1996).
[26]*Printz* and *Mack*, 521 U.S. 898, 117 S. Ct. 2365 (1997).

[27]*Boerne v. Flores*, 521 U.S. 507, 117 S. Ct. 2157 (1997).
[28]*Alden v. Maine.*
[29]*United States v. Morrison*, 529 U.S. 598 (2000).

FEDERALISM

Consequences of Federalism as Established in the Constitution

Existence of two sovereigns—the national government and the state governments, with state governments wielding more power for the first 150 years after the writing of the Constitution.

Particular restraint on the power of the national government to affect economic policy.

Great variations from state to state in terms of citizens' rights, role of government, and judicial activity.

Evolution of the Federal System

1789–1834	*Nationalization:* The Marshall Court interprets the Constitution broadly so as to expand and consolidate national power.
1835–1930s	*Dual federalism:* The functions of the national government are very specifically enumerated. States do much of the fundamental governing that affects citizens' day-to-day life. There is tension between the two levels of government, and the power of the national government begins to increase.
1930s–70s	*Cooperative federalism:* The national government uses grants-in-aid to encourage states and localities to pursue nationally defined goals.
1970s–	*Regulated federalism:* The national government sets conditions that states and localities must meet in order to keep certain grants. The national government also sets national standards in areas without providing funding to meet them.
	New federalism: The national government attempts to return more power to the states through block grants to the states.

during the middle decades of the twentieth century but moderated as the century drew to a close. As new issues arise, the ongoing debate about what are properly the states' responsibilities and what the federal government should do will surely continue.

Over the last decade, Congress has delegated more power to state governments.

For the moment, the balance seems to be tipped toward the states, though the tug of war between the states and national government will certainly continue. As a result of this ongoing struggle for power, federalism remains a vital part of the American system of government, even as the national government grows larger. States and cities clamor (and lobby) for a larger share of the national budget, but with the help of the Supreme Court, states continue to hold on jealously to their freedom of action.

THE SECOND PRINCIPLE: THE SEPARATION OF POWERS

James Madison is best qualified to speak to Americans about the *separation of powers:*

> There can be no liberty where the legislative and executive powers are united in the same person . . . [or] if the power of judging be not separated from the legislative and executive powers.[30]

Using this same reasoning, many of Madison's contemporaries argued that there was not *enough* separation among the three branches, and Madison had to do some backtracking to insist that the principle did not require complete separation:

> . . . unless these departments [branches] be so far connected and blended as to give each a constitutional control over the others, the degree of separation which the maxim requires, as essential to a free government, can never in practice be duly maintained.[31]

This is the secret of how we have made the separation of powers effective: We made the principle self-enforcing by giving each branch of government the means to participate in and partially or temporarily obstruct the workings of the other branches.

Checks and Balances

The means by which each branch of government interacts with each other branch is known informally as *checks and balances*. The best-known examples are shown in the In Brief box on the next page. The framers sought to guarantee that the three branches would in fact use these checks and balances as weapons against one another by giving each branch a different political constituency and therefore a different perspective on what the government ought to do: direct, popular election for the members of the House; indirect election of senators (until the Seventeenth Amendment, adopted in 1913); indirect election of the president through the electoral college; and appointment of federal judges for life. All things considered, the best characterization of the separation of powers principle in action is "separated institutions sharing power."[32]

The three branches of national government interact with each other through a series of controls known as checks and balances.

[30]Clinton Rossiter, ed., *The Federalist Papers* (New York: New American Library, 1961), No. 47, p. 302.
[31]Ibid., No. 48, p. 308.
[32]Richard E. Neustadt, *Presidential Power* (New York: Wiley, 1960), p. 33.

Legislative Supremacy

Although each branch was to be given adequate means to compete with the other branches, it is also clear that within the system of separated powers the framers provided for *legislative supremacy* by making Congress the preeminent branch. Legislative supremacy made the provision of checks and balances in the other two branches all the more important.

The most important indications of the intentions of the framers were the provisions in Article I, the legislative article, to treat the powers of the national government as powers of Congress and their decision to give Congress the sole power over appropriations.

Although "presidential government" seemed to supplant legislative supremacy after 1937, the relative power of the executive and legislative branches has varied. The power play between the president and Congress is especially intense when one party controls the White House and another controls Capitol Hill, as has been the case almost continuously since 1969. Clinton's impeachment trial at the end of 1998 was a dramatic illustration of the give and take between Congress and president (see also Chapters 5 and 6).

Although the Constitution provides for a system of checks and balances for the branches of government, the legislative branch was designed to be the most powerful.

The Role of the Supreme Court

The role of the judicial branch in the separation of powers has depended upon the power of judicial review, a power not provided for in the Constitution but asserted by Chief Justice Marshall in 1803:

> If a law be in opposition to the Constitution; if both the law and the Constitution apply to a particular case, so that the Court must either

CHECKS AND BALANCES

Legislative Branch

Checks executive:

Controls appropriations. (Neither the executive branch nor the judicial branch can spend any money without an act of Congress appropriating it. Includes salaries, except Congress cannot reduce compensation of president or judges during their terms.)

Controls by statute. (Except for a narrow sphere of national security and emergency operations under executive order of the president, no agency in the executive branch has any authority to act except as provided by statutes delegating such authority to the agency or to the department in which the agency is housed.)

Checks judicial:

Controls appropriations (see above).

Can create inferior courts. (All federal district courts and courts of appeal were created by Congress; so were the tax court, the court of claims, and the U.S. customs court.)

Can add new judges. (Congress can add new judges by expanding the number of judgeships for existing courts, including the Supreme Court, and it can add judges whenever it creates a new court.)

Executive Branch

Checks legislative:

Can call a special session. (The president may call Congress into special session "on extraordinary occasions: to take care of unfinished or new legislative business—e.g., to pass a law without which the president feels he cannot carry out his promises or responsibilities.)

Power to veto legislation.

Checks judicial:

Appoints federal judges.

Judicial Branch

Checks legislative:

Judicial review of legislation. (Any and all legislation can come before the federal courts when there is a dispute over the interpretation of a law or over its constitutionality. It is rare, however, that courts will declare a law unconstitutional, although that is always a possibility.)

Checks executive:

Can issue or refuse to issue warrants. (The police or any other executive officers cannot engage in any searches or arrests without a warrant from a judge showing "probable cause" and specifying the place to be searched and the persons or things to be seized.)

decide that case conformable to the law, disregarding the Constitution, or conformable to the Constitution, disregarding the law; the Court must determine which of these conflicting rules governs the case: This is of the very essence of judicial duty.[33]

[33]*Marbury v. Madison,* 1 Cranch 137 (1803).

Review of the constitutionality of acts of the president or Congress is relatively rare. For example, there were no Supreme Court reviews of congressional acts in the fifty plus years between *Marbury v. Madison* (1803) and *Dred Scott* (1857). In the century or so between the Civil War and 1970, eighty-four acts of Congress were held unconstitutional (in whole or in part), but this includes long periods of complete Supreme Court deference to the Congress, punctuated by flurries of judicial review during periods of social upheaval. The most significant of these was 1935–1936, when twelve acts of Congress were invalidated, blocking virtually the entire New Deal program.[34] Then, after 1937, when the Court made its great reversals, no significant acts were voided until 1983, when the Court declared the legislative veto unconstitutional.[35] The Supreme Court became much more activist (that is, less deferential to Congress) after the elevation of Justice William H. Rehnquist to chief justice (1986–2005), and "a new program of judicial activism"[36] seemed to be in place. Between 1995 and 2002, at least twenty-six acts or parts of acts of Congress were struck down on constitutional grounds.[37]

Since the New Deal period, the Court has been far more deferential toward the president, with only five significant confrontations. One was the so-called *Steel Seizure* case of 1952, in which the Court refused to permit President Truman to use "emergency powers" to force workers back into the steel mills during the Korean War.[38] A second case was *United States v. Nixon*, in which the Court declared unconstitutional President Nixon's refusal to respond to a subpoena to make available the infamous White House tapes as evidence in a criminal prosecution. The Court argued that although *executive privilege* did protect confidentiality of communications to and from the president, this did not extend to data in presidential files or tapes varying upon criminal prosecutions.[39] During the heat of the Clinton scandal, the Supreme Court rejected the claim that the pressures and obligations of the office of president were so demanding that all litigation "but the most exceptional cases" should be deferred until his term ends.[40] The Supreme Court also struck down the Line-Item Veto Act of 1996 on the grounds that it violated Article I, Section 7, which prescribed procedures for congressional enactment and presidential acceptance or veto of statutes. Any such change in the procedures of adopting laws would have to be made by amendment to the Constitution, not by legislation.[41] Most recently, and of far greater importance, the Supreme Court repudiated the Bush administration's claims about the president's authority to detain enemy combatants without giving detainees an opportunity to defend themselves in an open court.[42]

DO FEDERALISM AND THE SEPARATION OF POWERS WORK?

Federalism and the separation of powers are two of the three most important constitutional principles upon which the United States' system of limited government is based. (The third is the principle of individual rights.) As we have seen, federalism limits the power of the national government in numerous ways. By its very existence, federalism recognizes the principle of two sovereigns, the national government and the state governments (hence the term "dual federalism"). In addition, the Constitution specifically restrained the power of the national government to regulate the economy. As a result, the states were free to do most of the fundamental governing for the first century and a half of American government. This began to change during and following the New Deal, as the national government began to exert more influence over the states through grants-in-aid and mandates. But even as the powers of the national government grew, so did the powers of the states. In the last decade, as well, we have noticed a counter-

[34]C. Herman Pritchett, *The American Constitution* (New York: McGraw-Hill, 1959), pp. 180–86.
[35]*Immigration and Naturalization Service v. Chadha*, 462 U.S. 919 (1983). (See Chapter 7.)
[36]Cass R. Sunstein, "Taking Over the Courts," *New York Times*, 9 November 2002, p. A19.
[37]Ibid.
[38]*Youngstown Sheet & Tube Co. v. Sawyer*, 343 U.S. 579 (1952).
[39]*United States v. Nixon*, 418 U.S. 683 (1974).

[40]*Clinton v. Jones*, 117 S. Ct. 1636 (1997).
[41]*Clinton v. City of New York*, 524 U.S. 417 (1998).
[42]*Hamdi v. Rumsfeld*, 124 S. Ct. 2633 (2004).

trend to the growth of national power as Congress has opted to devolve some of its powers to the states. The most recent notable instance of devolution was the welfare reform plan of 1996.

But the problem that arises with devolution is that programs that were once uniform across the country (because they were the national government's responsibility) can become highly variable, with some states providing benefits not available in other states. To a point, variation can be considered one of the virtues of federalism. But there are dangers inherent in large variations and inequalities in the provision of services and benefits in a democracy. For example, the Food and Drug Administration has been under attack in recent years. Could the government address the agency's perceived problems by devolving its regulatory tasks to the states? Would people care if drugs would require "caution" labels in some states but not in others? Would Americans want each state to set its own air and water pollution control policies without regard to the fact that pollution flows across state boundaries? Devolution, as attractive as it may be, is not an approach that can be applied across the board without analyzing carefully the nature of the program and of the problems it is designed to solve. Even the capacity of states to handle "devolved" programs will vary. According to the Washington research organization the Brookings Institution, the level of state and local government employment varies from state to state—from a low of 400 per 10,000 residents in some states to a high of 700 per 10,000 in others. "Such administrative diversity is bound to mediate the course and consequences of any substantial devolution of federal responsibility; no one-size-fits-all devolution [from federal to state and local government] can work."[43]

A key puzzle of federalism is deciding when differences across states represent the proper democratic decisions of the states and when such differences represent inequalities that should not be tolerated. Sometimes a decision to eliminate dif-

ferences is made on the grounds of equality and individual rights, as in the Civil Rights Act of 1964, which outlawed segregation. At other times, a stronger federal role is justified on the grounds of national interest, as in the case of the oil shortage and the institution of a fifty-five mile per hour speed limit in the 1970s. Advocates of a more limited federal role often point to the value of democracy. Public actions can more easily be tailored to fit distinctive local or state desires if states and localities have more power to make policy. Viewed this way, variation across states can be an expression of democratic will.

In recent years, many Americans have grown disillusioned with the federal government and have supported efforts to give the states more responsibilities. A 1997 poll, for example, found that Americans tended to have the most confidence in governments that were closest to them. Thirty-eight percent expressed "a great deal" of confidence in local government, 32 percent in state government, and 22 percent in the federal government. Nearly two-thirds of those polled believed that shifting some responsibility to states and localities would help achieve excellence in government. After the terrorist attacks of September 11, 2001, however, support for the federal government soared. With issues of security topping the list of citizens' concerns, the federal government, which had seemed less important with the waning of the cold war, suddenly reemerged as the central actor in American politics. As one observer put it, "Federalism was a luxury of peaceful times."[44] Yet the newfound respect for the federal government is likely to be contingent on how well the government performs. If the federal government does not appear to be effective in the fight against terrorism, its stature may once again decline in the minds of many Americans.

American federalism remains a work in progress. As public problems shift and as local, state, and federal governments change, questions about the relationship between American values

---

[43]Eliza Newlin Carney, "Power Grab," *National Journal*, 11 April 1998, p. 798.

[44]Linda Greenhouse, "Will the Court Reassert National Authority?" *New York Times*, 30 Sept. 2001, Sect. 4, p. 14.

and federalism naturally emerge. The different views that people bring to this discussion suggest that concerns about federalism will remain a central issue in American democracy.

The second principle of limited government, separation of powers, is manifested in our system of checks and balances, whereby separate institutions of government share power with each other. Even though the Constitution clearly provided for legislative supremacy, checks and balances have functioned well. Some would say this system has worked too well. The last fifty years have witnessed long periods of *divided government*, when one party controls the White House while the other party controls Congress. During these periods, the level of conflict between the executive and legislative branches has been particularly divisive, resulting in what some analysts derisively call *gridlock*. Nevertheless, this is a genuine separation of powers, not so far removed from the intent of the framers. We can complain at length about the inability of divided government to make decisions, and we can criticize it as stalemate or gridlock.[45] But even that is in accord with the theory of the framers that new public policy should be difficult to make.

The purpose of a constitution is to provide a framework. A constitution is good if it produces the *cause of action* that leads to good legislation, good case law, and appropriate police behavior. A constitution cannot eliminate power. But its principles can be a citizen's dependable defense against the abuse of power.

[45]Not everybody will agree that divided government is all that less productive than government in which the same party controls both branches. See David Mayhew, *Divided We Govern: Party Control, Law Making and Investigations, 1946–1990* (New Haven: Yale University Press, 1991). For another good evaluation of divided government, see Charles O. Jones, *Separate but Equal Branches—Congress and the Presidency* (Chatham, NJ: Chatham House, 1995).

CHAPTER REVIEW

In this chapter we have traced the development of two of the three basic principles of the U.S. Constitution: federalism and the separation of powers. Federalism involves a division between two layers of government, national and state. The separation of powers involves the division of the national government into three branches. These principles are limitations on the powers of government; Americans specified these principles as a condition of giving their consent to be governed. And these principles became the framework within which the government operates. The persistence of local government and of reliance of the national government on grants-in-aid to coerce local governments into following national goals demonstrates the continuing vitality of the federal framework. The intense competition among the president, Congress, and the courts dramatizes the continuing vitality of the separation of powers.

The purpose of a constitution is to organize the makeup or the composition of the government, the *framework* within which government and politics, including actual legislation, can take place. A country does not require federalism and the separation of powers to have a real constitutional government. And the country does not have to approach individual rights in the same manner as the American Constitution. But to be a true constitutional government, a government must have some kind of framework that consists of a few principles that cannot be manipulated by people in power merely for their own convenience. This is the essence of constitutionalism—principles that are above the reach of everyday legislatures, executives, bureaucrats, and politicians, yet that are not so far above their reach that these principles cannot sometimes be adapted to changing conditions.

KEY TERMS

Aid to Families with Dependent Children (AFDC) Federal funds, administered by the states, for children living with parents or relatives who fall below state standards of need.

block grants Federal grants-in-aid that allow states considerable discretion in how the funds should be spent.

categorical grants-in-aid Grants by Congress to states and localities, given with the condition that expenditures be limited to a problem or group specified by the national government.

checks and balances Mechanisms through which each branch of government is able to participate in and influence the activities of the other branches. Major examples include the presidential veto power over congressional legislation, the power of the Senate to approve presidential appointments, and judicial review of congressional enactments.

commerce clause Article 1, Section 8 of the Constitution delegates to Congress the power "to regulate commerce with Foreign nations, and among the several States and with the Indian tribes. . . . " The Supreme Court interpreted this clause in favor of national power over the economy.

concurrent powers Authority possessed by *both* state and national governments, such as the power to levy taxes.

cooperative federalism A type of federalism existing since the New Deal era in which grants-in-aid have been used strategically to encourage states and localities (without commanding them) to pursue nationally defined goals. Also known as intergovernmental cooperation.

devolution A strategy in which the national government would grant the states more authority over a range of policies currently under national government authority.

divided government The condition in American government wherein one party controls the presidency while the opposing party controls one or both houses of Congress.

dual federalism The system of government that prevailed in the United States from 1789 to 1937 in which most fundamental governmental powers were shared between the federal and state governments.

executive privilege The claim that confidential communications between a president and close advisers should not be revealed without the consent of the president.

expressed powers (Congress) Specific powers granted to Congress under Article I, Section 8, of the Constitution.

federalism System of government in which power is divided by a constitution between a central government and regional governments (in the United States, between the national government and state governments).

formula grants Grants-in-aid in which a formula is used to determine the amount of federal funds a state or local government will receive.

full faith and credit clause Article IV, Section 1, of the Constitution provides that each state must accord the same respect to the laws and judicial decisions of other states that it accords to its own.

grants-in-aid A general term for funds given by Congress to state and local governments.

gridlock The state of affairs when the executive and legislative branches cannot agree on major legislation and neither side will compromise.

home rule Power delegated by the state to a local unit of government to manage its own affairs.

implied powers Powers derived from the necessary and proper clause of Article I, Section 8, of the Constitution. Such powers are not specifically expressed but are implied through the expansive interpretation of delegated powers.

legislative supremacy The preeminence of Congress among the three branches of government, as established by the Constitution.

necessary and proper clause From Article I, Section 8, of the Constitution, it provides Congress with the authority to make all laws "necessary and proper" to carry out its expressed powers.

new federalism Attempts by Presidents Nixon and Reagan to return power to the states through block grants.

police power Power reserved to the state to regulate the health, safety, and morals of its citizens.

privileges and immunities clause Provision from Article IV, Section 2, of the Constitution that a state cannot discriminate against someone from another state or give its own residents special privileges.

project grants Grant programs in which state and local governments submit proposals to federal agencies and for which funding is provided on a competitive basis.

regulated federalism A form of federalism in which Congress imposes legislation on the states and localities requiring them to meet national standards.

reserved powers Powers, derived from the Tenth Amendment of the Constitution, that are not specifically delegated to the national government or denied to the states.

revenue sharing Provision of money by the national government to state governments.

separation of powers The division of governmental power among several institutions that must cooperate in decision making.

state sovereign immunity Legal doctrine that holds that states cannot be sued for violating an act of Congress.

states' rights The principle that states should oppose increasing authority of the national government. This view was most popular before the Civil War.

unfunded mandates Regulations or conditions for receiving grants that impose costs on state and local governments for which they are not reimbursed by the federal government.

FOR FURTHER READING

Anton, Thomas. *American Federalism and Public Policy*. Philadelphia: Temple University Press, 1989.

Bensel, Richard. *Sectionalism and American Political Development: 1880–1980*. Madison: University of Wisconsin Press, 1984.

Berger, Raoul. *Executive Privilege: A Constitutional Myth*. Cambridge: Harvard University Press, 1974.

Bowman, Ann O'M., and Richard Kearny. *The Resurgence of the States*. Englewood Cliffs, NJ: Prentice Hall, 1986.

Corwin, Edward, and J. W. Peltason. *Corwin & Peltason's Understanding the Constitution*, 13th ed. Fort Worth: Harcourt, Brace, 1994.

Crovitz, L. Gordon, and Jeremy Rabkins, eds. *The Fettered Presidency: Legal Constraints on the Executive Branch*. Washington, DC: American Enterprise Institute, 1989.

Dye, Thomas R. *American Federalism: Competition among Governments*. Lexington, MA: Lexington Books, 1990.

Elazar, Daniel. *American Federalism: A View from the States*. New York: Harper & Row, 1984.

Ginsberg, Benjamin, and Martin Shefter. *Politics by Other Means: Institutional Conflict and the Declining Significance of Elections in America*. New York: Basic Books, 1990.

Grodzins, Morton. *The American System*. Chicago: Rand McNally, 1974.

Kelley, E. Wood. *Policy and Politics in the United States: The Limits of Localism*. Philadelphia: Temple University Press, 1987.

Kettl, Donald. *The Regulation of American Federalism*. Baltimore: Johns Hopkins University Press, 1987.

Palley, Marian Lief, and Howard Palley. *Urban America and Public Policies*. Lexington, MA: D. C. Heath, 1981.

Peterson, Paul, Barry Rabe, and Kenneth K. Wong. *When Federalism Works*. Washington, DC: Brookings Institution, 1986.

Robinson, Donald L. *To the Best of My Ability*. New York: Norton, 1986.

Wright, Deil S. *Understanding Intergovernmental Relations*. Monterey, CA: Brooks/Cole, 1982.

CHAPTER 4

The Constitution and the Individual: The Bill of Rights, Civil Liberties, and Civil Rights

*T*he first ten amendments of the United States Constitution, together called the *Bill of Rights,* are the basis for the freedoms we enjoy as American citizens. The Bill of Rights might well have been entitled the "Bill of Liberties," because the provisions that were incorporated in the Bill of Rights were seen as defining a private sphere of personal liberty, free of governmental restrictions. These freedoms include the right to free speech, the right to the free exercise of religion, prohibitions against unreasonable searches and seizures, guarantees of due process of law, and the right to privacy, including a woman's right to have an abortion.

As Jefferson had put it, a bill of rights "is what people are entitled to against every government on earth. . . . " Note the emphasis—people *against* government. *Civil liberties* are *protections from* improper government action. Thus, the Bill of Rights is a series of restraints imposed upon government. Some of these restraints are *substantive liberties,* which put limits on *what* the government shall and shall not have power to do—such as establishing a religion, quartering troops in private homes without consent, or seizing private property without just compensation. Other restraints are *procedural liberties,* which deal with *how* the government is supposed to act. These procedural liberties are usually grouped under the general category of *due process of law,* which first appears in the Fifth Amendment provision that "no person shall be . . . deprived of life, liberty, or property,

CORE OF THE ANALYSIS

- The rights in the Bill of Rights are called "civil liberties" because they protect citizens from improper government action.

- Not until the 1960s were most of the civil liberties in the Bill of Rights nationalized, or applied to the states as well as the national government.

- Civil rights are obligations, imposed on government by the equal protection clause of the Fourteenth Amendment, to take positive action to protect citizens from the illegal actions of other citizens and government agencies.

- As with civil liberties, there was little advancement in the application of the equal protection clause until after World War II and the breakthrough case of *Brown v. Board of Education.*

- Since the passage of major civil rights legislation in 1964, the civil rights struggle has been expanded and universalized to include women, the disabled, gays and lesbians, and other minority groups.

without due process of law." For example, even though the government has the substantive power to declare certain acts to be crimes and to arrest and imprison persons who violate criminal laws, it may not do so without meticulously observing procedures designed to protect the accused person. The best-known procedural rule is that an accused person is presumed innocent until proven guilty. This rule does not question the government's power to punish someone for committing a crime; it questions only the way the government determines who committed the crime. Substantive and procedural restraints together identify the realm of civil liberties.

Today, we may take the liberties contained within the Bill of Rights for granted. Few citizens of other countries can make such a claim. In fact, few people in recorded history, including American citizens before the 1960s, have enjoyed such protections. For more than 170 years after its passage in 1789, the Bill of Rights meant little to most Americans. As we shall see in this chapter, guaranteeing the liberties articulated in the Bill of Rights to all Americans required a long struggle. As new challenges to the Bill of Rights arise, this struggle will likely continue.

As recently as the early 1960s, many of the freedoms we enjoy today were not guaranteed. At that time, abortion was illegal everywhere in the United States, criminal suspects in state cases did not have to be informed of their rights, some states required daily Bible readings and prayers in their public schools, and some communities regularly censored reading material that they deemed to be obscene. Since the early 1960s, the Supreme Court has expanded the scope of individual freedoms considerably. But since these liberties are constantly subject to judicial interpretation, their provisions are fragile and need to be vigilantly safeguarded, especially during times of war or a threat to national security, such as in the aftermath of September 11, 2001.

While civil liberties are phrased as negatives, *civil rights* are obligations imposed on government to *guarantee equal citizenship and to protect citizens from discrimination by other private citizens and other government agencies*. Civil rights did not become part of the Constitution until 1868 with the adoption of the Fourteenth Amendment, which addressed the issue of who was a citizen and pro-

vided for each citizen "equal protection of the laws." From that point on, we can see more clearly the distinction between civil liberties and civil rights, because civil liberties issues arise under the "due process of law" clause, and civil rights issues arise under the "equal protection of the laws" clause.[1]

The Fourteenth Amendment's guarantee to each citizen of the "equal protection of the laws" launched a century of political movements and legal efforts to press for racial equality. The African American quest for civil rights, in turn, inspired many other groups, including members of other racial and ethnic groups, women, the disabled, and gays and lesbians, to seek new laws and constitutional guarantees of their civil rights.

Congress passed the Fourteenth Amendment, and the states ratified it in the aftermath of the Civil War. Together with the Thirteenth Amendment, which abolished slavery, and the Fifteenth Amendment, which guaranteed voting rights for black men, the Fourteenth Amendment seemed to provide a guarantee of civil rights for the newly freed black slaves. But the general language of the Fourteenth Amendment meant that its support for civil rights could be far-reaching. The very simplicity of the *equal protection clause* of the Fourteenth Amendment left it open to interpretation:

> No State shall make or enforce any law which shall . . . deny to any person within its jurisdiction the equal protection of the laws.

While this clause allowed the government to take an active role in promoting equality, there was little advancement in the interpretation or application of the equal protection clause until after World War II. The major breakthrough came in 1954 with *Brown v. Board of Education*, and advancements came in fits and starts during the

---

[1]For recent scholarship on the Bill of Rights and its development, see Geoffrey Stone, Richard Epstein, and Cass Sunstein, eds. *The Bill of Rights and the Modern State* (Chicago: University of Chicago Press, 1992); and Michael J. Meyer and William A. Parent, eds., *The Constitution of Rights* (Ithaca: Cornell University Press, 1992).

CENTRAL QUESTIONS

- **Civil Liberties: Nationalizing the Bill of Rights**
  Does the Bill of Rights put limits only on the national government or does it limit state governments as well?
  How and when did the Supreme Court nationalize the Bill of Rights?
  What is the likelihood that the current Supreme Court will try to reverse the nationalization of the Bill of Rights?

- **Civil Rights**
  What is the legal basis for civil rights?
  How has the equal protection clause been enforced historically?
  What groups were spurred by the provision of the Civil Rights Act of 1964—that outlawed discrimination in employment practices based on race, religion, and gender—to seek broader protection under the law?
  How does affirmative action contribute to the polarization of the politics of civil rights?

succeeding ten years.

But even today, the question of what is meant by "equal rights" is hardly settled. While most Americans reject the idea that government should create equal outcomes for its citizens, they do widely endorse government action to prohibit public and private discrimination and they support the idea of equality of opportunity. However, even this concept is elusive. When past denial of rights creates unequal starting points for some groups, should government take additional steps to ensure equal opportunity? What kinds of groups should be specially protected against discrimination? Should the disabled receive special protection? Should gays and lesbians? Finally, what kinds of steps are acceptable to remedy discrimination, and who should bear the costs? These questions are at the heart of contemporary debates over civil rights.

CIVIL LIBERTIES: NATIONALIZING THE BILL OF RIGHTS

The First Amendment provides that "Congress shall make no law respecting an establishment of religion . . . or abridging freedom of speech, or of the press; or the right of [assembly and petition]." But this is the only amendment in the Bill of Rights

that addresses itself exclusively to the national government. For example, the Second Amendment provides that "the right of the people to keep and bear Arms shall not be infringed." The Fifth Amendment says, among other things, that "*no person* shall . . . be twice put in jeopardy of life or limb" for the same crime; that *no person* "shall be compelled in any Criminal Case to be a witness against himself"; that *no person* shall "be deprived of life, liberty, or property, without due process of law"; and that private property cannot be taken "without just compensation."[2]

Dual Citizenship

Since the First Amendment is the only part of the Bill of Rights that is explicit in its intention to put limits on the national government, a fundamental question inevitably arises: *Do the remaining amendments of the Bill of Rights put limits on state governments or only on the national government?* This question was settled in 1833 in a way that

---

[2]It would be useful at this point to review all the provisions of the Bill of Rights (in the Appendix) to confirm this distinction between the wording of the First Amendment and the rest of the Bill of Rights. Emphasis in the example quotations was not in the original. For a spirited and enlightening essay on the extent to which the entire Bill of Rights was about equality, see Martha Minow, "Equality and the Bill of Rights," in Meyer and Parent, *The Constitution of Rights*, pp. 118–28.

THE BILL OF RIGHTS

Amendment I: Limits on Congress
Congress cannot make any law establishing a religion or abridging freedoms of religious exercise, speech, assembly, or petition.

Amendments II, III, IV: Limits on the Executive
The executive branch cannot infringe on the right of people to keep arms (II), cannot arbitrarily take houses for militia (III), and cannot search for or seize evidence without a court warrant swearing to the probable existence of a crime (IV).

Amendments V, VI, VII, VIII: Limits on the Judiciary
The courts cannot hold trials for serious offenses without provision for a grand jury (V), a trial jury (VII), a speedy trial (VI), presentation of charges and confrontation by the accused of hostile witnesses (VI), immunity from testimony against oneself and immunity from trial more than once for the same offense (V). Furthermore, neither bail nor punishment can be excessive (VIII), and no property can be taken without "just compensation" (V).

Amendments IX, X: Limits on the National Government
Any rights not enumerated are reserved to the states or the people (X), but the enumeration of certain rights in the Constitution should not be interpreted to mean that those are the only rights the people have (IX).

---

seems odd to Americans today. The case was *Barron v. Baltimore*, and the facts were simple. In paving its streets, the city of Baltimore had disposed of so much sand and gravel in the water near Barron's wharf that the value of the wharf for commercial purposes was virtually destroyed. Barron brought the city into court on the grounds that it had, under the Fifth Amendment, unconstitutionally deprived him of his property without just compensation. Barron had to take his case all the way to the Supreme Court. There Chief Justice Marshall, in one of the most significant Supreme Court decisions ever handed down, disagreed with Barron:

> The Constitution was ordained and established by the people of the United States for themselves, for their own government, and not for the government of the individual States. Each State established a constitution for itself, and in that constitution provided such limitations and restrictions on the powers of its particular government as its judgment dictated. . . .
> If these propositions be correct, *the fifth*

amendment must be understood as restraining the power of the general government, not as applicable to the States. [Emphasis added.][3]

In other words, if an agency of the *national* government had deprived Barron of his property, there would have been little doubt about Barron's winning his case. But if the constitution of the state of Maryland contained no such provision protecting citizens of Maryland from such action, then Barron had no legal leg to stand on against Baltimore, an agency of the state of Maryland.

In Barron v. Baltimore, *the Court ruled that the Bill of Rights put limits only on the national government, not on the states.*

Barron v. Baltimore confirmed dual citizenship—that is, that each American was a citizen of the

[3]*Barron v. Baltimore*, 7 Peters 243 (1833).

national government and *separately* a citizen of one of the states. This meant that the Bill of Rights did not apply to decisions or procedures of state (or local) governments. Even slavery could continue, because the Bill of Rights could not protect anyone from state laws treating people as property. In fact, the Bill of Rights did not become a vital instrument for the extension of civil liberties for anyone until after a bloody Civil War and a revolutionary Fourteenth Amendment intervened. And even so, as we shall see, nearly a second century would pass before the Bill of Rights would truly come into its own.

The Fourteenth Amendment

From a constitutional standpoint, the defeat of the South in the Civil War settled one question and raised another. It probably settled forever the question of whether secession was an option for any state. After 1865, there was more "united" than "states" to the United States. But this left unanswered just how much the states were obliged to obey the Constitution, in particular, the Bill of Rights. Just reading the words of the Fourteenth Amendment, anyone might think it was almost perfectly designed to impose the Bill of Rights on the states and thereby to reverse *Barron v. Baltimore*. The very first words of the Fourteenth Amendment point in that direction:

> All persons born or naturalized in the United States, and subject to the jurisdiction thereof, are citizens of the United States and of the State wherein they reside.

This provides for a *single national citizenship*, and at a minimum that means that civil liberties should not vary drastically from state to state. That would seem to be the spirit of the Fourteenth Amendment: *to nationalize the Bill of Rights by nationalizing the definition of citizenship.*

This interpretation of the Fourteenth Amendment is reinforced by the next clause of the Amendment:

> *No state* shall make or enforce any law which shall abridge the privileges or immunities of citizens of the United States; nor shall any state

deprive any person of life, liberty, or property, without due process of law. [Emphasis added.]

All of this sounds like an effort to extend the Bill of Rights in its *entirety* to citizens *wherever* they might reside.[4] But this was not to be the Supreme Court's interpretation for nearly a hundred years. Within five years of ratification of the Fourteenth Amendment, the Court was making decisions as though it had never been adopted.[5] The shadow of *Barron* grew longer and longer. Table 4.1 outlines the major developments in the history of the Fourteenth Amendment against the backdrop of *Barron*, citing the particular provisions of the Bill of Rights as they were incorporated by Supreme Court decisions into the Fourteenth Amendment as limitations on all the states. This is a measure of the degree of "nationalization" of civil liberties.

The Fourteenth Amendment provided for single national citizenship, in effect, an effort to extend the Bill of Rights to all citizens. The Supreme Court did not adopt this view, however, until more than one hundred years after its ratification.

The only change in civil liberties during the first sixty years after the adoption of the Fourteenth Amendment came in 1897, when the Supreme Court held that the due process clause of the Fourteenth Amendment did in fact prohibit states from taking property for a public use without just compensation.[6] This effectively overruled the specific

---

[4]The Fourteenth Amendment also seems designed to introduce civil rights. The final clause of the all-important Section 1 provides that no state can "deny to any person within its jurisdiction the equal protection of the laws." It is not unreasonable to conclude that the purpose of this provision was to obligate the state governments as well as the national government to take *positive* actions to protect citizens from arbitrary and discriminatory actions, at least those based on race. This will be explored in the second half of the chapter.

[5]The Slaughter-House Cases, 16 Wallace 36 (1873); The Civil Rights Cases, 109 U.S. 3 (1883).

[6]*Chicago, Burlington and Quincy Railroad Company v. Chicago,* 166 U.S. 266 (1897).

TABLE 4.1

INCORPORATION OF THE BILL OF RIGHTS INTO THE FOURTEENTH AMENDMENT

Selected Provisions and Amendments	Year "Incorporated"	Key Case
Eminent domain (V)	1897	*Chicago, Burlington and Quincy Railroad v. Chicago*
Freedom of speech (I)	1925	*Gitlow v. New York*
Freedom of press (I)	1931	*Near v. Minnesota*
Freedom of assembly (I)	1939	*Hague v. C.I.O.*
Freedom from warrantless search and seizure (IV) (exclusionary rule)	1961	*Mapp v. Ohio*
Right to counsel in any criminal trial (VI)	1963	*Gideon v. Wainwright*
Right against self-incrimination and forced confessions (V)	1964	*Malloy v. Hogan* *Escobedo v. Illinois*
Right to counsel and to remain silent (VI)	1966	*Miranda v. Arizona*
Right against double jeopardy (V)	1969	*Benton v. Maryland*
Right to privacy (III, IV, & V)	1973	*Roe v. Wade* *Doe v. Bolton*

holding in *Barron;* henceforth a citizen of Maryland or any state was protected from a "public taking" of property (eminent domain) even if the state constitution did not provide such protection. But in a broader sense, *Barron* still cast a shadow, because the Supreme Court had "incorporated" into the Fourteenth Amendment *only* the property protection provision of the Fifth Amendment, despite the fact that the *due process* clause applied to the taking of life and liberty as well as property.

No further expansion of civil liberties through incorporation occurred until 1925, when the Supreme Court held that freedom of speech is "among the fundamental personal rights and 'liberties' protected by the due process clause of the Fourteenth Amendment from impairment by the states."[7] In 1931, the Supreme Court added freedom of the press to that short list of civil rights

protected by the Bill of Rights from state action; in 1939, it added freedom of assembly.[8]

For the following two decades, this was as far as the Supreme Court was willing to go in the effort to nationalize more of the rights in the Bill of Rights. And it should be made clear at this point that none of the rights in the Bill of Rights is absolute, including the most sacred right of all, freedom of speech. Concept Map 4.1 is a pictorial definition of when free speech is protected and when it is not protected. A similar map could be constructed for each of the rights listed in Table 4.1. The only promise the Supreme Court is willing to make is that it will give "strict scrutiny" to any action taken by a state to limit or abridge a right. Again, no right is absolute; no right is protected at all times, regardless of the circumstances.

[7]*Gitlow v. New York*, 268 U.S. 652 (1925).

[8]*Near v. Minnesota*, 283 U.S. 697 (1931); *Hague v. C.I.O.*, 307 U.S. 496 (1939).

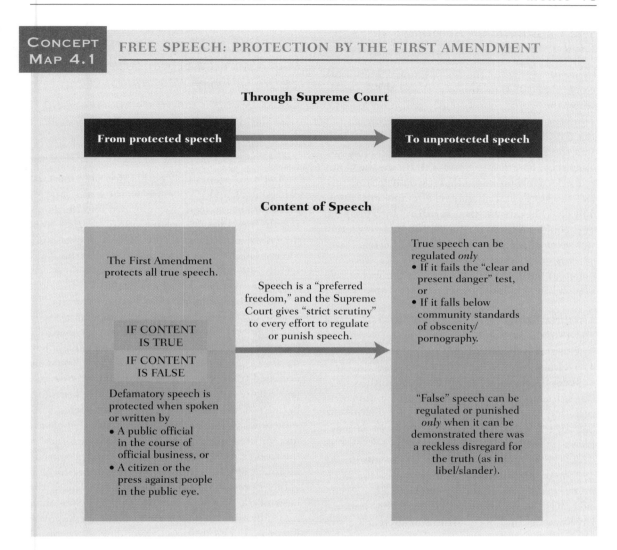

CONCEPT MAP 4.1

FREE SPEECH: PROTECTION BY THE FIRST AMENDMENT

Through Supreme Court

From protected speech → To unprotected speech

Content of Speech

The First Amendment protects all true speech.

IF CONTENT IS TRUE

IF CONTENT IS FALSE

Defamatory speech is protected when spoken or written by
• A public official in the course of official business, or
• A citizen or the press against people in the public eye.

Speech is a "preferred freedom," and the Supreme Court gives "strict scrutiny" to every effort to regulate or punish speech.

True speech can be regulated *only*
• If it fails the "clear and present danger" test, or
• If it falls below community standards of obscenity/ pornography.

"False" speech can be regulated or punished *only* when it can be demonstrated there was a reckless disregard for the truth (as in libel/slander).

The shadow of *Barron* extended into its second century, despite adoption of the Fourteenth Amendment. At the time of World War II, the Constitution, as interpreted by the Supreme Court, left standing the framework in which the states had the power to determine their own law on a number of fundamental issues. It left states with the power to pass laws segregating the races. It also left states with the power to engage in searches and seizures without a warrant, to indict accused persons without benefit of a grand jury, to deprive persons of trial by jury, to force persons to testify against themselves, to deprive accused persons of their right to confront adverse witnesses, and to prosecute accused persons more than once for the same crime.[9] Few states exercised these powers, but the power was there for any state whose legislative majority chose to use it.

[9]All of these were implicitly identified in *Palko v. Connecticut,* 302 U.S. 319 (1937), as "not incorporated" into the Fourteenth Amendment as limitations on the powers of the states.

The Constitutional Revolution in Civil Liberties

Signs of change in the constitutional framework came after 1954, in *Brown v. Board of Education*, when the Court found state segregation laws for schools unconstitutional. Even though *Brown* was not a civil liberties case, it indicated rather clearly that the Supreme Court was going to be expansive about civil liberties, because with *Brown* the Court had effectively promised that it would *actively* subject the states and all actions affecting civil rights and civil liberties to **strict scrutiny**. In retrospect, one could say that this constitutional revolution was given a "jumpstart" in 1954 by *Brown v. Board of Education*, even though the results were not apparent until after 1961, when the number of civil liberties incorporated increased (see Table 4.1).

NATIONALIZING THE BILL OF RIGHTS   The constitutional revolution in federalism, as we saw in Chapter 3, began when the Supreme Court in 1937 interpreted "interstate commerce" in favor of federal government regulation.[10] Both revolutions, then, were movements toward nationalization, but they required opposite motions on the part of the Supreme Court. In the area of commerce (the first revolution), the Court had to decide to assume a *passive* role by not interfering as Congress expanded the meaning of the commerce clause of Article I, Section 8. This expansion has been so extensive that the national government can now constitutionally reach a single farmer growing twenty acres of wheat or a small neighborhood restaurant selling barbecue to local "whites only" without being anywhere near interstate commerce routes. In the second revolution—involving the Bill of Rights and particularly the Fourteenth Amendment—the Court had to assume an *active* role. It required close review of the laws of state legislatures and decisions of state courts in order to apply a single national Fourteenth Amendment standard to the rights and liberties of all citizens.

[10]*NLRB v. Jones & Laughlin Steel Corp.*, 301 U.S. 1 (1937).

The Second Constitutional Revolution began with the Brown *decision in 1954, at which time the Supreme Court became active in incorporating the Bill of Rights into the Fourteenth Amendment.*

Table 4.1 shows that until 1961, only the First Amendment and one clause of the Fifth Amendment had been clearly incorporated into the Fourteenth Amendment.[11] After 1961, several other important provisions of the Bill of Rights were incorporated. Of the cases that expanded the Fourteenth Amendment's reach, the most famous was *Gideon v. Wainwright*, which established the right to counsel in a criminal trial, because it became the subject of a best-selling book and a popular movie.[12] In *Mapp v. Ohio*, the Court held that evidence obtained in violation of the Fourth Amendment ban on unreasonable searches and seizures would be excluded from trial.[13] This **exclusionary rule** was particularly irksome to the police and prosecutors because it meant that patently guilty defendants sometimes go free because the evidence that clearly incriminated them could not be used. In *Miranda*, the Court's ruling required that arrested persons be informed of the right to remain silent and to have counsel present during interrogation.[14] This is the basis of the **Miranda rule** of reading persons their rights. By 1969, in *Benton v. Maryland*, the Supreme Court had come full circle regarding the rights of the criminally accused, explicitly reversing a 1937 ruling and thereby incorporating double jeopardy.

During the 1960s and early 1970s, the Court also expanded another important area of civil lib-

[11]The one exception was the right to public trial (Sixth Amendment), but a 1948 case (*In re Oliver*, 33 U.S. 257) did not actually mention the right to public trial as such; this right was cited in a 1968 case (*Duncan v. Louisiana*, 391 U.S. 145) as a precedent establishing the right to public trial as part of the Fourteenth Amendment.
[12]*Gideon v. Wainwright*, 372 U.S. 335 (1963); Anthony Lewis, *Gideon's Trumpet* (New York: Random House, 1964).
[13]*Mapp v. Ohio*, 367 U.S. 643 (1961).
[14]*Miranda v. Arizona*, 384 U.S. 436 (1966).

erties: rights to privacy. When the Court began to take a more activist role in the mid-1950s and 1960s, the idea of a "right to privacy" was revived. In 1958, the Supreme Court recognized "privacy in one's association" in its decision to prevent the state of Alabama from using the membership list of the National Association for the Advancement of Colored People in the state's investigations.[15]

The sphere of privacy was drawn in earnest in 1965, when the Court ruled that a Connecticut statute forbidding the use of contraceptives violated the right of marital privacy. Estelle Griswold, the executive director of the Planned Parenthood League of Connecticut, was arrested by the state of Connecticut for providing information, instruction, and medical advice about contraception to married couples. She and her associates were found guilty as accessories to the crime and fined $100 each. The Supreme Court reversed the lower court decisions and declared the Connecticut law unconstitutional because it violated "a right of privacy older than the Bill of Rights—older than our political parties, older than our school system."[16] Justice William O. Douglas, author of the majority decision in the *Griswold* case, argued that this right of privacy is also grounded in the Constitution, because it fits into a "zone of privacy" created by a combination of the Third, Fourth, and Fifth Amendments. A concurring opinion, written by Justice Arthur Goldberg, attempted to strengthen Douglas's argument by adding that "the concept of liberty . . . embraces the right of marital privacy though that right is not mentioned explicitly in the Constitution [and] is supported by numerous decisions of this Court . . . and *by the language and history of the Ninth Amendment.* [Emphasis added.]"[17]

The right to privacy was confirmed—and extended—in 1973 in the most important of all privacy decisions, and one of the most important Supreme Court decisions in American history: *Roe*

v. Wade.[18] This decision established a woman's right to have an abortion and prohibited states from making abortion a criminal act. The basis for the Supreme Court's decision in *Roe* was the evolving right to privacy. But it is important to realize that the preference for privacy rights and for their extension to include the rights of women to control their own bodies was not something invented by the Supreme Court in a political vacuum. Most states did not begin to regulate abortions in any fashion until the 1840s (by 1839 only six of the twenty-six existing states had any regulations governing abortion). In addition, many states began to ease their abortion restrictions well before the 1973 Supreme Court decision. In recent years, however, a number of states have reinstated restrictions on abortion, testing the limits of *Roe*.

Like any important principle, once privacy was established as an aspect of civil liberties that was protected by the Bill of Rights through the Fourteenth Amendment, it took on a life all its own. In a number of important decisions, the Supreme Court and the lower federal courts sought to protect rights that could not be found in the text of the Constitution but could be discovered through the study of the philosophic sources of fundamental rights. Through this line of reasoning, the federal courts ruled to protect sexual autonomy, lifestyle choices, sexual preferences, procreational choice, and various forms of intimate association.

Criticism mounted with every extension of this line of reasoning. The federal courts were accused of creating an uncontrollable expansion of rights demands. The Supreme Court, the critics argued, had displaced the judgments of legislatures and state courts with its own judgment of what is reasonable, without regard to public preferences and without regard to specific constitutional provisions. This is virtually the definition of what came to be called "judicial activism," and it was the basis for a more critical label, "the imperial judiciary."[19]

---

[15]*NAACP v. Alabama ex rel. Patterson*, 357 U.S. 449 (1958).
[16]*Griswold v. Connecticut*, 381 U.S. 479 (1965).
[17]*Griswold v. Connecticut,* concurring opinion. In 1972, the Court extended the privacy right to unmarried women: *Eisenstadt v. Baird*, 405 U.S. 438 (1972).

[18]*Roe v. Wade*, 410 U.S. 113 (1973).
[19]A good discussion is found in Paul Brest and Sanford Levinson, *Processes of Constitutional Decisionmaking: Cases and Materials,* 2nd ed. (Boston: Little, Brown, 1983), p. 660. See also Chapter 8.

The history of civil liberties in the United States is evidence that, as a political institution, the Bill of Rights has not been carved in stone. Through subsequent amendments, on the one hand, and the interpretations of the Supreme Court, on the other, the balance between freedom and power has been transformed. Indeed, the framers of the Constitution would be unlikely to recognize their original handiwork. But, as we shall see next, what the Supreme Court gives, the Supreme Court can also take away.

A DENATIONALIZING TREND?   While constitutional developments may be represented as the history of doctrinal disputes and the general evolution of interpretation—and, as the last few pages have made clear, there is nothing linear and straightforward about these developments—it must be recognized that these events are as much *political* as *philosophical*. Judges and justices are, after all, *politicians*. And courts are *political institutions*. The backdrop, therefore, for debates over legal doctrine and constitutional meaning consists of the preferences of politicians, on the one hand, and the tug and pull of maneuvering between the courts and other (separate) institutions of government, on the other.

The preferences of individual Supreme Court justices have certainly been consequential during the first two centuries of our republic, with John Marshall probably casting the longest shadow. Likewise, conflicts between the judiciary, legislature, and executive had ebbed and flowed. Throughout, controversy over judicial power has not diminished. In fact, it intensified under William Rehnquist, who served as chief justice from 1986 to his death in 2005. Although it is difficult to determine just how much influence Chief Justice Rehnquist had, the Court moved in a more conservative, denationalizing direction during his nineteen years in charge.

A good measure of the Court's growing conservatism is the following comparison made by constitutional scholar David M. O'Brien: Between 1961 and 1969, more than 76 percent of the Earl Warren Court's rulings tended to be liberal—that is, tended toward nationalizing the Bill of Rights to protect individuals and minorities mainly against the actions of state government. During the Warren Burger years, 1969–1986, the liberal tendency

dropped on average below 50 percent. During the first four years of the Rehnquist Court (the extent of O'Brien's research), the average liberal "score" dropped to less than 35 percent.[20]

For example, the Supreme Court has moved in a conservative direction regarding the First Amendment's "establishment clause," which prescribed a "wall of separation" between church and state. In the 1995 case of *Rosenberger v. University of Virginia,* the Court seemed to open a new breach in the wall between church and state when it ruled that the university had violated the free speech rights of a Christian student group by refusing to provide student activity funds to the group's magazine, although other student groups had been given funds for their publications. In the 1997 case of *Agostini v. Felton,* the Court again breached the wall between church and state, ruling that states could pay public school teachers to offer remedial courses at religious schools.[21]

The conservative trend has also extended to the burning question of abortion rights. In *Webster v. Reproductive Health Services,* the Court narrowly upheld by a five-to-four majority the constitutionality of restrictions on the use of public medical facilities for abortion.[22] And in 1992, in the most recent

[20]David M. O'Brien, *Supreme Court Watch—1991,* Annual Supplement to *Constitutional Law and Politics* (New York: Norton, 1991), p. 6 and Chapter 4. Each era of the Supreme Court is conventionally given the name of the chief justice. Thus, the Rehnquist Court is the era over which Rehnquist presided (1986–2005). Immediately prior to that was the Burger Court (1969–86), and before that was the Warren Court (1953–69), and so forth.

[21]*Rosenberger v. Rectors and Visitors of the University of Virginia,* 115 S. Ct. 2510 (1995); *Agostini v. Felton,* 117 S. Ct 1997 (1997).

[22]In *Webster v. Reproductive Health Services,* 109 S. Ct. 3040 (1989), Chief Justice Rehnquist's decision upheld a Missouri law that restricted the use of public medical facilities for abortion. The decision opened the way for other states to limit the availability of abortion. The first to act was the Pennsylvania legislature, which in late 1989 adopted a law banning all abortions after pregnancy had passed twenty-four weeks, except to save the life of the pregnant woman or to prevent irreversible impairment of her health. In 1990, the pace of state legislative action increased, with new statutes being passed in South Carolina, Ohio, Minnesota, and Guam. In 1991, the Louisiana legislature adopted, over the governor's veto, the strictest law yet. The Louisiana law prohibits all abortions except when the mother's life is threatened or when rape or incest victims report these crimes immediately.

IN BRIEF BOX

DENATIONALIZATION OF THE BILL OF RIGHTS

Provision/amendment	Year	Case
Abortion rights	1989	*Webster v. Reproductive Health Services*, 5-to-4 ruling that restrictions on the use of public medical facilities for abortion are constitutional.
Writ of *habeas corpus*	1991	*McCleskey v. Zant*, 6-to-3 ruling severely limiting repeated prisoner *habeas corpus* petitions.
Abortion rights	1992	*Planned Parenthood v. Casey*, 5-to-4 ruling upheld but narrowed the scope of *Roe v. Wade*.
Writ of *habeas corpus*	1996	*Felker v. Turpin*, Court unanimously upheld legislation that limits state prisoners' right to file second or successive applications for writs of *habeas corpus* if no new claim is presented.

major decision on abortion, *Planned Parenthood v. Casey,* another five-to-four majority of the Court barely upheld Roe but narrowed its scope, refusing to invalidate a Pennsylvania law that significantly restricts freedom of choice. The decision defined the right to an abortion as a "limited or qualified" right subject to regulation by the states as long as the regulation does not impose an "undue burden."[23]

The Rehnquist Court was less willing to follow the nationalizing role of previous Courts.

With Rehnquist's death and Sandra Day O'Connor's resignation from the Court in 2005, the future of civil liberties is again open to reinterpretation. Will the Supreme Court, led by the Bush appointee John J. Roberts, Jr. and with a majority of conservatives, reverse the nationalization of the Bill of Rights? Possibly, but not necessarily. First of all, the Rehnquist Court did not actually reverse any of the decisions made by the Warren or Burger Courts during the 1960s that nationalized most of

the clauses of the Bill of Rights. As we have seen, the Rehnquist Court gave narrower and more restrictive interpretations of some earlier decisions, but it did not reverse any, not even *Roe v. Wade.* Second, President Clinton's appointments to the Court, Ruth Bader Ginsburg and Stephen Breyer, have helped form a centrist contingent that seems unwilling—for the time being, at least—to sanction any major steps to turn back the nationalization of the Bill of Rights.

Thus we end not very far from where we began. The spirit of *Barron v. Baltimore* has not been entirely put to rest, and its shadow over the Bill of Rights still hovers. A Court with the power to expand the Bill of Rights also has the power to contract it.[24]

CIVIL RIGHTS

The very simplicity of the civil rights clause of the Fourteenth Amendment left its meaning open to interpretation:

---

[23]*Planned Parenthood of Southeastern Pennsylvania v. Casey,* 112 S.Ct. 2791 (1992).

[24]For a lively and readable treatment of the possibilities of restricting provisions of the Bill of Rights, without actually reversing Warren Court decisions, see David G. Savage, *Turning Right: The Making of the Rehnquist Supreme Court* (New York: Wiley, 1992).

No State shall make or enforce any law which shall . . . deny to any person within its jurisdiction the equal protection of the laws.

But in the very first Fourteenth Amendment case to come before the Supreme Court, in 1873, the majority gave it a distinct meaning:

> . . . it is not difficult to give a meaning to this clause ["the equal protection of the laws"]. The existence of laws in the States . . . which discriminated with gross injustice and hardship against [Negroes] as a class, was the evil to be remedied by this clause, and by it such laws are forbidden.[25]

Beyond that, contemporaries of the Fourteenth Amendment understood well that private persons offering conveyances, accommodations, or places of amusement to the public incurred certain obligations to offer them to one and all—in other words, these are *public* accommodations, such that arbitrary discrimination in their use would amount to denial of equal protection of the laws—unless a government took action to overcome the discrimination.[26] This obligated the government to take positive actions to equalize the opportunity for each citizen to enjoy his or her freedom.

Discrimination is the use of unreasonable and unjust exclusion. Of course, all laws discriminate, including some people while excluding others; but some discrimination is considered unreasonable. Now, for example, it is considered reasonable to enforce twenty-one as the legal drinking age; thus the age criterion is considered reasonable discrimination. But is age a reasonable distinction when seventy (or sixty-five or sixty) is selected as the age for compulsory retirement? In the mid-1970s, Congress answered this question by making old age a new civil right; compulsory retirement at seventy is now an unlawful, unreasonable discriminatory use of age.[27]

Plessy v. Ferguson: "Separate but Equal"

Following its initial decision making "equal protection" a right, the Supreme Court was no more ready to enforce the civil rights aspects of the Fourteenth Amendment than it was to enforce the civil liberties provisions. The Court declared the Civil Rights Act of 1875 unconstitutional on the ground that the act sought to protect blacks against discrimination by *private* businesses, while the Fourteenth Amendment, according to the Court's interpretation, was intended to protect individuals only against discrimination by *public* officials of state and local governments.

In 1896, the Court went still further, in the infamous case of *Plessy v. Ferguson*, by upholding a Louisiana statute that *required* segregation of the races on trolleys and other public carriers (and by implication in all public facilities, including schools). The Supreme Court held that the Fourteenth Amendment's "equal protection of the laws" was not violated by racial distinction as long as the facilities were equal.[28] People generally pretended they were equal as long as some accommodation existed. What the Court was saying, in effect, was that it was not unreasonable to use race as a basis of exclusion in public matters. This was the origin of the *"separate but equal" rule* that was not reversed until 1954.

Until 1954, the Supreme Court was unwilling to support the equal protection clause of the Fourteenth Amendment. In Plessy v. Ferguson, *the Court ruled that public facilities separated by race were acceptable as long as they were equal.*

---

[25]The Slaughter-House Cases, 16 Wallace 36 (1873).
[26]See Civil Rights Cases, 109 U.S. 3 (1883).
[27]A superb discussion of age discrimination is found in Lawrence Friedman, *Your Time Will Come—The Law of Age Discrimination and Mandatory Retirement* (New York: Russell Sage, 1984).

[28]*Plessy v. Ferguson*, 163 U.S. 537 (1896).

Racial Discrimination after World War II

The Supreme Court had begun to change its position regarding racial discrimination just before World War II by being stricter about what the states would have to do to provide equal facilities under the "separate but equal" rule. In 1938, the Court rejected Missouri's policy of paying the tuition of qualified blacks to out-of-state law schools rather than admitting them to the University of Missouri Law School.[29] After the war, modest progress resumed. In 1950, the Court rejected Texas's claim that its new "law school for Negroes" afforded education equal to that of the all-white University of Texas Law School; without confronting the "separate but equal" principle itself, the Court's decision anticipated *Brown v. Board* by opening the question of whether *any* segregated facility could be truly equal.[30]

As the Supreme Court was ordering the admission of blacks to all-white state laws schools, it was also striking down the Southern practice of "white primaries," which legally excluded blacks from participation in the nominating process.[31] The most important pre-1954 decision was probably *Shelley v. Kraemer*,[32] in which the Court ruled against the practice of "restrictive convenants," whereby the seller of a home added a clause to the sales contract requiring the buyer to agree not to resell the home to a non-Caucasian, non-Christian, and so on.

Although none of those cases confronted "separate but equal" and the principle of racial discrimination as such, they were extremely significant to black leaders, and gave them encouragement enough to believe that there was at last an opportunity and enough legal precedent to change the constitutional framework itself. By the fall of 1952, the Court had on its docket cases from Kansas, South Carolina, Virginia, Delaware, and the District of Columbia challenging the constitutionality of school segregation. Of these, the Kansas case became the chosen one. It seemed to be ahead of the pack in its district court, and it had the special advantage of being located in a state outside the Deep South.[33]

Oliver Brown, the father of three girls, lived "across the tracks" in a low-income, racially mixed Topeka neighborhood. Every school-day morning, one of his daughters, Linda Brown, took the school bus to the Monroe School for black children about a mile away. In September 1950, Oliver Brown took Linda to the all-white Sumner School, which was actually closer to home, to enter her into the third grade in defiance of state law and local segregation rules. When they were refused, Brown took his case to the NAACP, and soon thereafter *Brown v. Board of Education* was born.

In deciding the case, the Court, to the surprise of many, rejected as inconclusive all the learned arguments about the intent of the Fourteenth Amendment and committed itself to considering only the consequences of segregation:

> Does segregation of children in public schools solely on the basis of race, even though the physical facilities and other "tangible" factors may be equal, deprive the children of the minority group of equal educational opportunities? We believe that it does. . . . We conclude that in the field of public education the doctrine of "separate but equal" has no place. Separate educational facilities are inherently unequal.[34]

The *Brown* decision altered the constitutional framework in two fundamental respects. First, after *Brown*, the states would no longer have the power to use race as a basis of discrimination in law. Second, the national government would from then on have the power (and eventually the obli-

---

[29]*Missouri ex. rel. Gaines v. Canada*, 305 U.S. 337 (1938).
[30]*Sweatt v. Painter*, 339 U.S. 629 (1950).
[31]*Smith v. Allwright*, 321 U.S. 649 (1944).
[32]*Shelley v. Kraemer*, 334 U.S. 1 (1948).

[33]The District of Columbia case came up too, but since the District of Columbia is not a state, it did not directly involve the Fourteenth Amendment and its equal protection clause. It confronted the Court on the same grounds, however—that segregation is inherently unequal. Its victory in effect was "incorporation in reverse," with equal protection moving from the Fourteenth Amendment to become part of the Bill of Rights. See *Bolling v. Sharpe*, 347 U.S. 497 (1954).
[34]*Brown v. Board of Education of Topeka, Kansas*, 347 U.S. 483 (1954).

gation) to intervene with strict regulatory policies against the discriminatory actions of state or local governments, school boards, employers, and others in the private sector.

In Brown v. Board of Education, *the Supreme Court rejected the validity of the "separate but equal" doctrine.*

Civil Rights after Brown v. Board of Education

Although *Brown v. Board of Education* withdrew all constitutional authority to use race as a criterion of exclusion, this historic decision was merely a small opening move. First, most states refused to cooperate until sued, and many ingenious schemes were employed to delay obedience (such as paying the tuition for white students to attend newly created "private" academies). Second, even as Southern school boards began to cooperate by eliminating their legally enforced (*de jure*) school segregation, there remained extensive actual (*de facto*) school segregation in the North as well as the South. *Brown* could not affect *de facto* segregation, which was not legislated but happened as a result of racially segregated housing. Third, *Brown* did not directly touch discrimination in employment, public accommodations, juries, voting, and other areas of social and economic activity.

A decade of frustration following *Brown* made it fairly obvious to all that the goal of "equal protection" required positive, or affirmative, action by Congress and by administrative agencies. And given massive Southern resistance and a generally negative national public opinion toward racial integration, progress would not be made through courts, Congress, *or* agencies without intense, well-organized support.

SCHOOL DESEGREGATION   Although the District of Columbia and some of the school districts in the border states began to respond almost immediately to court-ordered desegregation, the states of the Deep South responded with a well-planned delaying tactic. Southern legislatures passed laws ordering school districts to maintain segregated schools and state superintendents to withhold state funding from racially mixed classrooms. Some Southern states centralized public school authority to give them power to close the schools that might tend to obey the Court and to provide alternative private schooling.

Many states avoided compliance with the Brown *decision.*

Most of these plans of "massive resistance" were tested in the federal courts and were struck down as unconstitutional.[35] But Southern resistance was not confined to legislation. For example, in Arkansas in 1957, Governor Orval Faubus ordered the National Guard to prevent enforcement of a federal court order to integrate Central High School of Little Rock. President Eisenhower was forced to deploy U.S. troops and place the city under martial law. The Supreme Court handed down a unanimous decision requiring desegregation in Little Rock.[36] The end of massive resistance, however, became simply the beginning of still another Southern strategy. "Pupil placement" laws authorized school districts to place each pupil in a school according to a whole variety of academic, personal, and psychological considerations, never mentioning race at all. This put the burden of transferring to an all-white school on the nonwhite children and their parents.[37]

---

[35]The two most important cases were *Cooper v. Aaron*, 358 U.S. 1 (1958), which required Little Rock, Arkansas to desegregate; and *Griffin v. Prince Edward County School Board*, 337 U.S. 218 (1964), which forced all the schools of that Virginia county to reopen after five years of being closed to avoid desegregation.

[36]In *Cooper v. Aaron*, the Supreme Court ordered immediate compliance with the lower court's desegregation order and went beyond that with a stern warning that it is "emphatically the province and duty of the judicial department to say what the law is." The justices also took the unprecedented action of personally signing the decisions.

[37]*Shuttlesworth v. Birmingham Board of Education*, 358 U.S. 101 (1958). This decision upheld a "pupil placement" plan purporting to assign pupils on various bases, with no mention of race. This case interpreted *Brown v. Board of Education* to mean that school districts must stop explicit racial discrimination but were under no obligation to take positive steps to desegregate. For a while, black parents were doomed to case-to-case approaches.

It was thus almost impossible for a single court order to cover a whole district, let alone a whole state. This delayed desegregation a while longer.

As new devices were invented by the Southern states to avoid desegregation, it was becoming unmistakably clear that the federal courts could not do the job alone.[38] The first modern effort to legislate in the field of civil rights was made in 1957, but the law contained only a federal guarantee of voting rights, without any powers of enforcement, although it did create the Civil Rights Commission to study abuses. Much more important legislation for civil rights followed during the 1960s, especially the Civil Rights Act of 1964 (see Process Box 4.1).

In response to the massive resistance to the Brown *decision, Congress passed a series of civil rights bills, the most important being the Civil Rights Act of 1964.*

Further progress in the desegregation of schools came in the form of busing[39] and redistricting, but it was slow and is likely to continue to be slow unless the Supreme Court decides to permit federal action against *de facto* segregation and against the varieties of private schools and academies that have sprung up for the purpose of avoiding integration.[40] A Supreme Court decision handed down in 1995, in which the Court signaled to the lower courts to "disengage from desegregation efforts," dimmed the prospects for further school integration. This is a direct and explicit threat to the main basis of the holding in the original *Brown v. Board* case.

The Rise of the Politics of Rights

OUTLAWING DISCRIMINATION IN EMPLOYMENT Despite the agonizingly slow progress of school desegregation, there was some progress in other areas of civil rights during the 1960s and 1970s. Voting rights were established and fairly quickly began to revolutionize Southern politics. Service on juries was no longer denied to minorities. But progress in the right to participate in politics and government dramatized the relative lack of economic progress, and it was in this area that battles over civil rights were increasingly fought.

The federal courts and the Justice Department entered this area through Title VII of the Civil Rights Act of 1964. Title VII outlawed job discrimination by all private and public employers, including governmental agencies (such as fire and police departments), that employed more than fifteen workers. We have already seen that the Supreme Court gave "interstate commerce" such a broad definition that Congress had the constitutional authority to outlaw discrimination by virtually any local employer.[41] Title VII made it unlawful to discriminate in employment on the basis of color, religion, sex, or national origin, as well as race.

---

[38]For good treatments of that long stretch of the struggle of the federal courts to integrate the schools, see Brest and Levinson, *Processes of Constitutional Decisionmaking*, pp. 471–80; and Alfred Kelly, Winifred Harbison, and Herman Boltz, *The American Constitution: Its Origins and Development*, 7th ed. (New York: Norton, 1991), pp. 610–16.

[39]*Swann v. Charlotte-Mecklenburg Board of Education*, 402 U.S. 1 (1971). See also Bernard Schwartz, *Swann's Way: The School Busing Case and the Supreme Court* (New York: Oxford University Press, 1986).

[40]For a good evaluation, see Gary Orfield, *Must We Bus? Segregated Schools and National Policy* (Washington, DC: Brookings Institution, 1978), pp. 144–46. See also Bob Woodward and Scott Armstrong, *The Brethren: Inside the Supreme Court* (New York: Simon and Schuster, 1979), pp. 426–27; and J. Anthony Lukas, *Common Ground* (New York: Random House, 1986).

[41]See especially *Katzenbach v. McClung*, 379 U.S. 294 (1964). Almost immediately after passage of the Civil Rights Act of 1964, a case was brought challenging the validity of Title II, which covered discrimination in public accommodations. Ollie's Barbecue was a neighborhood restaurant in Birmingham, Alabama. It was located eleven blocks away from an interstate highway and even farther from railroad and bus stations. Its table service was for whites only; there was only a take-out service for blacks. The Supreme Court agreed that Ollie's was strictly an intrastate restaurant, but since a substantial proportion of its food and other supplies were bought from companies outside the state of Alabama, there was sufficient connection to interstate commerce; therefore, racial discrimination at such restaurants would "impose commercial burdens of national magnitude upon interstate commerce." Although this case involved Title II, it had direct bearing on the constitutionality of Title VII.

PROCESS BOX 4.1   CAUSE AND EFFECT IN THE CIVIL RIGHTS MOVEMENT: WHICH CAME FIRST—GOVERNMENT ACTION OR POLITICAL ACTION?

Judicial and Legal Action	Political Action
1954 *Brown v. Board of Education*	
1955 *Brown* II—Implementation of *Brown* I	**1955** Montgomery bus boycott
1956 Federal courts order school integration, especially one ordering Autherine Lucy admitted to University of Alabama, with Governor Wallace officially protesting	
1957 Civil Rights Act creating Civil Rights Commission; President Eisenhower sends National Guard troops to Little Rock, Arkansas, to enforce integration of Central High School	**1957** Southern Christian Leadership Conference (SCLC) formed, with Martin Luther King Jr. as president
1960 First substantive Civil Rights Act, primarily voting rights	**1960** Student Nonviolent Coordinating Committee (SNCC) formed to organize protests, sit-ins, freedom rides
1961 Interstate Commerce Commission orders desegregation on all buses and trains, and in terminals	
1961 JFK favors executive action over civil rights legislation	
1963 JFK shifts, supports strong civil rights law; assassination; LBJ asserts strong support for civil rights	**1963** Nonviolent demonstrations in Birmingham, Alabama, lead to King's arrest and his "Letter from Birmingham Jail"
	1963 March on Washington
1964 Congress passes historic Civil Rights Act covering voting, employment, public accommodations, education	
1965 Voting Rights Act	**1965** King announces drive to register 3 million blacks in the South
1966 War on Poverty in full swing	**1966** Movement dissipates: part toward litigation, part toward community action programs, part toward war protest, part toward more militant "Black Power" actions

Title VII outlawed job discrimination by public and private employers on the basis of color, religion, sex, national origin, and race.

One problem with Title VII was that the complaining party had to show that deliberate discrimination was the cause of the failure to get a job or a training opportunity. Rarely does an employer explicitly admit discrimination on the basis of race, sex, or any other illegal reason. For a time, courts allowed the complaining parties to make their case if they could show that an employer's hiring practices, whether intentional or not, had the *effect* of exclusion. Employers, in effect, had to justify their actions.[42]

GENDER DISCRIMINATION Even before equal employment laws began to have a positive effect on the economic situation of blacks, something far more dramatic began happening—the universalization of civil rights. The right not to be discriminated against was being successfully claimed by the other groups listed in Title VII—those defined by sex, religion, or national origin—and eventually by still other groups defined by age or sexual preference. This ***universalization of rights*** has become the new frontier of the civil rights struggle, and women have emerged with the greatest prominence in this new struggle. The effort to define and end gender discrimination in employment has led to the historic joining of women's rights to the civil rights cause.

Despite its interest in fighting discrimination, the Supreme Court in the 1950s and 1960s paid little attention to gender discrimination. Ironically, it was left to the more conservative Burger Court (1969–1986) to establish gender discrimination as a major and highly visible civil rights issue. In recent years, the Court has furthered the civil rights of women by making it easier for individuals to prove sexual harassment and by ruling in

[42]*Griggs v. Duke Power Company,* 401 U.S. 24 (1971).

favor of the integration of the formerly all-male Virginia Military Institute. The future direction of the Court on gender discrimination may quite possibly be toward an even broader definition and application of civil rights with regard to women.

The development of gender discrimination as an important part of the civil rights struggle has coincided with the rise of women's politics as a discrete movement in American politics. As with the struggle for racial equality, the relationship between government policies and changes in political action suggests that changes in government policies to a great degree produce political action. Today, the existence of a powerful women's movement derives in large measure from the enactment of Title VII of the Civil Rights Act of 1964 and from the Supreme Court's vital steps in applying that law to protect women. The recognition of women's civil rights has become an issue that in many ways transcends the usual distinctions of American political debate. In the heavily partisan debate over the federal crime bill enacted in 1994, for instance, the section of the bill that enjoyed the widest support was the Violence against Women Act, whose most important feature is that it defines gender-biased violent crimes as a matter of civil rights and creates a civil rights remedy for women who have been the victims of such crimes. Since the Supreme Court ruled the act unconstitutional in 2000, the struggle for women's rights will likely remain part of the political debate.

The protections won by the civil rights movements expanded to protect other groups as well, including women, disabled Americans, and gays and lesbians.

DISCRIMINATION AGAINST OTHER GROUPS As gender discrimination began to be seen as an important civil rights issue, other groups arose demanding recognition and active protection of their civil rights. Under Title VII of the 1964 Civil Rights Act, any group or individual can try, and in fact is encouraged to try, to convert his or her goals and grievances into questions of rights and the deprivation of those rights. A plaintiff must only establish that his or her membership in a group is an unreasonable basis for discrimination unless it can be proven to be a "job-related" or otherwise clearly reasonable and relevant decision. In America today, the list of individuals and groups claiming illegal discrimination is lengthy. The disabled, for instance, increasingly press their claim to equal treatment as a civil rights matter, a stance encouraged by the Americans with Disabilities Act of 1990.[43] Deaf Americans increasingly demand social and legal recognition of deafness as a separate culture, not simply as a disability.[44] One of the most familiar of these "new" groups has been the gay and lesbian movement, which in less than thirty years has emerged from invisibility to become one of the largest civil rights movements in contemporary America. Beginning with street protests in the 1960s, the movement has grown into a well-financed and sophisticated lobby. The Human Rights Campaign Fund is the primary national political action committee (PAC) focused on gay rights; it provides campaign financing and volunteers to work for candidates endorsed by the group. The movement has also formed legal rights organizations, including the Lambda Legal Defense and Education Fund.

Gay and lesbian rights drew national attention in 1993, when President Bill Clinton confronted the question of whether gays should be allowed to serve in the military. As a candidate, Clinton had said he favored lifting the ban on homosexuals in the military. The issue set off a huge controversy in the first months of Clinton's presidency. After nearly a year of deliberation, the administration enunciated a compromise: their "Don't ask, don't tell" policy. This policy allows gays and lesbians to serve in the military as long as they do not openly proclaim their sexual orientation or engage in homosexual activity. The administration maintained that the ruling would protect gays and lesbians against witch-hunting investigations, but many gay and lesbian advocates expressed disappointment, charging the president with reneging on his campaign promise.

But until 1996, there was no Supreme Court ruling or national legislation explicitly protecting gays and lesbians from discrimination. The first gay rights case that the Court decided, *Bowers v. Hardwick,* ruled against a right to privacy that would protect consensual homosexual activity.[45] After the *Bowers* decision, the gay and lesbian rights movement sought suitable legal cases to test the constitutionality of discrimination against gays and lesbians, much as the black civil rights movement did in the late 1940s and 1950s. As one advocate put it, "Lesbians and gay men are looking for their *Brown v. Board of Education,*"[46] Among the cases tested were those stemming from local ordinances restricting gay rights (including the right to marry), job discrimination, and family law issues such as adoption and parental rights. In 1996, the Supreme Court, in *Romer v. Evans,* explicitly extended fundamental civil rights protections to gays and lesbians by declaring unconstitutional a 1992 amendment to the Colorado state constitution that prohibited local governments from passing ordinances to protect gay rights.[47] The decision's forceful language highlighted the connection between gay rights and civil rights as it declared discrimination against gay people unconstitutional.

In *Lawrence v. Texas* (2003), the Court overturned *Bowers* and struck down a Texas statute criminalizing certain intimate sexual conduct

---

[43]In 1992, for instance, after pressure from the Justice Department under the terms of the Americans with Disabilities Act, one of the nation's largest rental-car companies agreed to make special hand-controls available to any customer requesting them. See "Avis Agrees to Equip Cars for Disabled," *Los Angeles Times,* 2 September 1994, p. D1.

[44]Thus a distinction has come to be made between "deaf," the pathology, and "Deaf," the culture. See Andrew Solomon, "Defiantly Deaf," *New York Times Magazine,* 28 August 1994, pp. 40ff.

[45]*Bowers v. Hardwick,* 478 U.S. 186 (1986).

[46]Quoted in Joan Biskupic, "Gay Rights Activists Seek a Supreme Court Test Case," *Washington Post,* 19 December 1993, p. A1.

[47]*Romer v. Evans,* 116 S. Ct. 1620 (1996).

between consenting partners of the same sex.[48] A victory for lesbians and gays every bit as significant as *Roe v. Wade* was for women, *Lawrence v. Texas* extends at least one aspect of civil liberties to sexual minorities: the right to privacy. However, this decision by itself does not undo the various exclusions that deprive lesbians and gays full civil rights, including the right to marry, which became a hot-button issue in 2004. In early 2004, the Supreme Judicial Court of Massachusetts ruled that under that state's constitution, gay men and lesbians were entitled to marry. The state senate then asked the court to rule on whether a civil-union statute (avoiding the word "marriage") would, as it did in Vermont, satisfy the court's ruling—to which the court ruled negatively, asserting that civil unions were too much like the "separate but equal" doctrine that maintained legalized racial segregation from 1896 to 1954. Meanwhile, in San Francisco, hundreds of gays and lesbians responded to the opportunity provided by the mayor, who had directed the city clerk to issue marriage licenses to same-sex couples in defiance of California law. At the same time, signs were that Massachusetts might move toward a state constitutional amendment that would ban gay unions by whatever name. Voters in Missouri and Louisiana approved a ban on same-sex marriages, joining Alaska, Hawaii, Nebraska, and Nevada in implementing such a ban. Voters in eleven other states approved similar bans in the November 2004 elections.

AFFIRMATIVE ACTION The relatively narrow goal of equalizing opportunity by eliminating discriminatory barriers had been developing toward the far broader goal of *affirmative action*—compensatory action to overcome the consequences of past discrimination. An affirmative action policy tends to involve two novel approaches: (1) positive or benign discrimination in which race or some other status is actually taken into account, but for compensatory action rather than mistreatment; and (2) compensatory action to favor members of the disadvantaged group who themselves may never have been the victims of discrimination. Quotas may be, but are not necessarily, involved in affirmative action policies.

President Lyndon Johnson inaugurated affirmative action by ordering a policy of minority employment in the federal civil service and in companies doing business with the national government. As the movement spread in the 1970s, it also began to divide civil rights activists and their supporters. Must more highly qualified white candidates have to give way to less qualified minority candidates? Wasn't this a case of "reverse discrimination"? The whole issue was addressed formally in the case of Allan Bakke. Bakke, a white male with no minority affiliation, brought suit against the University of California at Davis Medical School on the grounds that in denying him admission, the school had discriminated against him on the basis of his race (that year the school had reserved sixteen of a hundred available seats for minority applicants). He argued that his grades and test scores had ranked him well above many black or Hispanic students who had been accepted.

Affirmative action has become one of the most contested aspects of the civil rights struggle. Some argue that compensatory action based on race helps traditional victims of discrimination, while others argue that it is reverse discrimination.

In 1978, Bakke won his case before the Supreme Court and was admitted to the medical school, but he did not succeed in getting affirmative action declared unconstitutional. The Court rejected the procedures at the University of California because its medical school had used both a quota *and* a separate admissions system for minorities. The Court held that the method of a rigid quota of student slots assigned on the basis of race was incompatible with the equal protection clause. Thus, the Court permitted universities (and presumably other schools, training programs, and hir-

[48]*Lawrence v. Texas*, 123 S.Ct. 2472 (2003).

DEVELOPMENT OF AFFIRMATIVE ACTION

Regents of the University of California v. Bakke (1978)	Court permitted minority status to be considered in hiring/selection processes, but restricted the use of quotas.
Wards Cove v. Atonio (1989)	Court ruled that the burden of proof for unlawful discrimination should be shifted from the defendant (employer) to the plaintiff (person claiming to be a victim of discrimination).
Martin v. Wilks (1989)	Any affirmative action program already approved by federal courts could be subsequently challenged by white males who alleged that the program discriminated against them.
Civil Rights Act of 1991	Congress put the burden of proof back on the employer to show that standards for employment that favored whites or males were "essential to the job."
St. Mary's Honor Center v. Hicks (1993)	Employees must prove that their employers intended discrimination, once again placing the burden of proof on employees.
Adarand Constructors, Inc. v. Peña (1995)	"Benign" federal racial classifications could be used, like those of the state, but a federal set-aside program violated the "equal protection" clause of the Fourteenth Amendment.

ing authorities) to continue to take minority status into consideration, but restricted the use of quotas to situations in which (1) previous discrimination had been shown, and (2) it was used more as a *guideline* for social diversity than as a mathematically defined ratio.[49]

For nearly a decade after *Bakke,* the Supreme Court was tentative and permissive about efforts by corporations and governments to experiment with affirmative action programs in employment.[50]

But in 1989, the Court returned to the *Bakke* position that any "rigid numerical quota" is suspect. In *Wards Cove v. Atonio,* the Court further weakened affirmative action by easing the way for employers to prefer white males, holding that the burden of proof of unlawful discrimination should be shifted from the defendant (the employer) to the plaintiff (the person claiming to be the victim of discrimination).[51] This decision virtually overruled the Court's prior holding. That same year, the Court ruled that any affirmative action program already

[49]*Regents of the University of California v. Bakke,* 438 U.S. 265 (1978).
[50]*United Steelworkers v. Weber,* 443 U.S. 193 (1979); and *Fullilove v. Klutznick,* 100 S. Ct. 2758 (1980).

[51]*City of Richmond v. J. A. Croson Co.,* 109 S. Ct. 706 (1989); *Wards Cove v. Atonio,* 109 S. Ct. 2115 (1989).

approved by federal courts could be subsequently challenged by white males who alleged that the program discriminated against them.[52]

In 1991, Congress strengthened affirmative action with the Civil Rights Act of 1991, which put the burden of proof back on the employer to show that educational and other standards for employment that favored whites or males were "essential to the job." Despite Congress's actions, however, the federal judiciary will have the last word when cases under the new law reach the courts. In fact, in a five-to-four decision in 1993, the Court ruled that employees had to prove their employers intended discrimination, once again placing the burden of proof on employees.[53]

In 1995, the Supreme Court's ruling in *Adarand Constructors v. Peña* further weakened affirmative action. This decision stated that race-based policies, such as preferences given by the government to minority contractors, must survive strict scrutiny, placing the burden on the government to show that such affirmative action programs serve a compelling government interest and are narrowly tailored to address identifiable past discrimination.[54] President Clinton responded to the *Adarand* decision by ordering a review of all government affirmative action policies and practices. Although many observers suspected that the president would use the review as an opportunity to back away from affirmative action, the conclusions of the task force largely defended existing policies. Reflecting the influence of the Supreme Court's decision in *Adarand,* President Clinton acknowledged that some government policies would need to change. But on the whole, the review found that most affirmative action policies were fair and that they did not "unduly burden nonbeneficiaries."[55]

Although Clinton sought to "mend, not end," affirmative action, developments in the courts and the states continued to restrict affirmative action in important ways. One of the most significant was the *Hopwood* case, in which white students challenged admissions practices in the University of Texas Law School, charging that the school's affirmative action program discriminated against whites. In 1996, a federal court (the U.S. Court of Appeals for the Fifth Circuit) ruling on the case stated that race could never be considered in granting admissions and scholarships at state colleges and universities.[56] This decision effectively rolled back the use of affirmative action permitted by the 1978 *Bakke* case. In *Bakke*, as discussed earlier, the Supreme Court had outlawed quotas but said that race could be used as one factor among many in admissions decisions. Many universities and colleges have since justified affirmative action as a way of promoting racial diversity among their student bodies. What was new in the *Hopwood* decision was the ruling that race could *never* be used as a factor in admissions decisions, even to promote diversity.

In 1996, the Supreme Court refused to hear a challenge to the *Hopwood* case. This meant that its ruling remains in effect in the states covered by the Fifth Circuit—Texas, Louisiana, and Mississippi—but does not apply to the rest of the country. The impact of the *Hopwood* ruling is greatest in Texas because Louisiana and Mississippi are under conflicting court orders to desegregate their universities. In Texas, in the year after the *Hopwood* case, minority applications to Texas universities declined. Concerned about the ability of Texas public universities to serve the state's minority students, the Texas legislature quickly passed a new law granting students who graduate in the top 10 percent of their classes automatic admission to the state's public universities. It is hoped that this measure will ensure a racially diverse student body.[57]

---

[52]*Martin v. Wilks,* 109 S. Ct. 2180 (1989). In this case, Chief Justice Rehnquist held that white firefighters in Birmingham could challenge the legality of a consent decree mandating goals for hiring and promoting blacks, even though they had not been parties to the original litigation.
[53]*St. Mary's Honor Center v. Hicks,* 113 S. Ct. 2742 (1993).
[54]*Adarand Construction, Inc. v. Peña,* 115 S. Ct. 2097 (1995).
[55]Ann Devroy, "Clinton Study Backs Affirmative Action," *Washington Post,* 19 July 1995, p. A1.

[56]*Hopwood v. State of Texas,* 78 F3d 932 (Fifth Circuit, 1996).
[57]See Lydia Lum, "Applications by Minorities Down Sharply," *Houston Chronicle,* 8 April 1997, p. A1; R. G. Ratcliffe, "Senate Approves Bill Designed to Boost Minority Enrollments," *Houston Chronicle,* 8 May 1997, p. A1.

In recent years, the Court has ruled that strict quota systems in affirmative action are incompatible with the equal protection clause of the Fourteenth Amendment. The Court has also held that the burden of proof for unlawful discrimination falls on the plaintiff.

The weakening of affirmative action in the courts was underscored in a case the Supreme Court agreed to hear in 1998. A white schoolteacher in New Jersey who had lost her job sued her school district, charging that her layoff was racially motivated; a black colleague, who had been hired on the same day, was not laid off. Under President George H. W. Bush, the Justice Department had filed a brief on her behalf in 1989, but in 1994 the Clinton administration formally reversed course in a new brief supporting the school districts' right to make distinctions based on race as long as it did not involve the use of quotas. Three years later, the administration, worried that the case was weak and could result in a broad decision against affirmative action, reversed course again. It filed a brief with the Court urging a narrow ruling in favor of the dismissed worker. Because the school board had justified its actions on the grounds of preserving diversity, the administration feared that a broad ruling by the Supreme Court could totally prohibit the use of race in employment decisions, even as one factor among many designed to achieve diversity. But before the Court could issue a ruling, a coalition of civil rights groups brokered and arranged to pay for a settlement. This unusual move reflected the widespread fear of a sweeping negative decision. Cases involving dismissals, as the New Jersey case did, are generally viewed as much more difficult to defend than cases that concern hiring. In addition, the particular facts of the New Jersey case—two equally qualified teachers hired on the same day—were

seen as unusual and unfavorable to affirmative action.[58]

This betwixt and between status of affirmative action was how things stood in 2003, when the Supreme Court took two cases against the University of Michigan that were virtually certain to clarify, if not put closure on, affirmative action. The first suit, *Gratz v. Bollinger* (the university president), was against the University of Michigan's undergraduate admissions policy and practices, alleging that by using a point-based ranking system that automatically awarded 20 points (out of 150) to African American, Latino, and Native American applicants, the university discriminated unconstitutionally against white students of otherwise equal or superior academic qualifications. The Supreme Court agreed, six to three, arguing that something tantamount to a quota was involved because undergraduate admissions lacked the necessary "individualized consideration," employing instead a "mechanical one," based too much on the favorable minority points.[59] The Court's ruling in *Gratz v. Bollinger* was not surprising, given *Bakke*'s (1978) holding against quotas and given recent decisions calling for strict scrutiny of all racial classifications, even those that are intended to remedy past discrimination or promote future equality.

The second case, *Grutter v. Bollinger*, broke new ground. Grutter sued the University of Michigan Law School on the grounds that it had discriminated in a race-conscious way against white applicants with equal or superior grades and law boards. A precarious majority of five to four aligned the majority of the Supreme Court with Justice Powell's lone plurality opinion in *Bakke* for the first time. In *Bakke*, Powell argued that (1) diversity in education is a compelling state interest and (2) race could be constitu-

---

[58]Linda Greenhouse, "Settlement Ends High Court Case on Preferences," *New York Times*, 22 November 1997, p. A1; Barry Bearak, "Rights Groups Ducked a Fight, Opponents Say," *New York Times*, 22 November 1997, p. A1.
[59]*Gratz v. Bollinger*, 123 S. Ct. 2411 (2003).

tionally considered as a plus factor in admissions decisions. In *Grutter*, the Court reiterated Powell's holding and, applying strict scrutiny to the law school's policy, found that the law school's admissions process is narrowly tailored to the school's compelling state interest in diversity because it gives a "highly individualized, holistic review of each applicant's file" in which race counts but is not used in a "mechanical way."[60]

Throughout the 1990s, federal courts, including the Supreme Court, had subjected public affirmative action programs to strict scrutiny in order to invalidate them. *Adarand Constructors, Inc. v. Peña* (1995) definitively established the Supreme Court's view that constitutionally permissible use of race must serve a compelling state interest.[61] Since *Korematsu v. United States* (1944) and until *Grutter,* no consideration of race had survived strict scrutiny.[62] Any affirmative action plans that survived constitutional review did so before 1995 under a lower standard of review reserved for policies intended to remedy racial injustice. For affirmative action to survive under the post-1995 judicial paradigm, the Court needed to find that sometimes racial categories can be deployed to serve a compelling state interest. That the Court found exactly this in *Grutter* puts affirmative action on stronger ground—at least if its specific procedures pass the Supreme Court's muster.

The courts have not been the only center of action: Challenges to affirmative action have also emerged in state and local politics. One of the most significant state actions was the passage in 1996 of the California Civil Rights Initiative, also known as Proposition 209. Proposition 209 outlawed affirmative action programs in the state and local governments of California, thus prohibiting state and local governments from using race or gender pref-

erences in their decisions about hiring and contracting or university admissions. The political battle over Proposition 209 was heated, and supporters and defenders took to the streets as well as the airwaves to make their cases. When the referendum was held, the measure passed with 54 percent of the vote, including 27 percent of the black vote, 30 percent of the Latino vote, and 45 percent of the Asian American vote.[63] In 1997, the Supreme Court refused to hear a challenge to the new law.

Many observers predicted that the success of California's ban on affirmative action would provoke similar movements in states and localities across the country. But the political factors that contributed to the success of Proposition 209 in California may not exist in many other states. Winning a controversial state referendum takes leadership and lots of money. Popular California Republican governor Pete Wilson led with a strong anti-affirmative action stand (favoring Proposition 209) and his campaign had a lot of money for advertising. But those conditions did not exist elsewhere. Few prominent Republican leaders in other states were willing to come forward to lead the anti-affirmative action campaign. Moreover, the outcome of any referendum, especially a complicated and controversial referendum, depends greatly upon how the issue is drafted and placed on the ballot for the voters. California's Proposition 209 was framed as a civil rights initiative: "the state shall not discriminate against, or grant preferential treatment to, any individual or group on the basis of race, sex, color, ethnicity, or national origin." Different wording can produce quite different outcomes, as a 1997 vote in Houston revealed. There, the ballot initiative asked voters whether they wanted to ban affirmative action in city contracting and hiring, not whether they wanted to end preferential treatment. Fifty-five percent of

[60]*Grutter v. Bollinger,* 123 S.Ct. 2325 (2003).
[61]*Adarand v. Peña,* 115 S. Ct. 2097 (1995).
[62]*Korematsu v. United States,* 323 U.S. 214 (1944).

[63]Michael A. Fletcher, "Opponents of Affirmative Action Heartened by Court Decision," *Washington Post,* 13 April 1997, p. A21.

Houston voters decided in favor of affirmative action.[64]

CHAPTER REVIEW

Civil liberties and *civil rights* are two quite different phenomena and have to be treated legally and constitutionally in two quite different ways. We have defined civil liberties as that sphere of individual freedom of choice created by restraints on governmental power. The Bill of Rights explicitly placed an entire series of restraints on government. Some of these restraints were *substantive*, regarding *what* government could do; other restraints were *procedural*, regarding *how* the government was permitted to act. We call the rights listed in the Bill of Rights civil liberties because they are the rights of citizens to be free from arbitrary government interference.

But *which* government? This was settled in the *Barron v. Baltimore* case in 1833 when the Supreme Court held that the restraints in the Bill of Rights were applicable only to the national government and not to the states. The Court was recognizing "dual citizenship." At the time of its adoption in 1868, the Fourteenth Amendment was considered by many observers as a deliberate effort to reverse *Barron*, to put an end to the standard of dual citizenship, and to nationalize the Bill of Rights, applying its restrictions to state governments as well as to the national government. But the post–Civil War Supreme Court interpreted the Fourth Amendment otherwise. Dual citizenship remained almost as it had been before the Civil War, and the shadow of *Barron* extended across the rest of the nineteenth century and well into the twentieth century.

The slow process of nationalizing the Bill of Rights began in the 1920s, when the Court recognized that at least the restraints of the First Amendment had been "incorporated" into the Fourteenth Amendment as restraints on the state governments. But it was not until the 1960s that most of the civil liberties in the Bill of Rights were also incorporated into the Fourteenth Amendment.

The second aspect of protection of the individual, *civil rights*, stresses the expansion of governmental power rather than restraints upon it. If the constitutional base of civil liberties is the due process clause of the Fourteenth Amendment, the constitutional base of civil rights is the equal protection clause. This clause imposes a positive obligation on government to advance civil rights, and its original motivation seems to have been to eliminate the gross injustices suffered by "the newly emancipated Negroes . . . as a class." But as with civil liberties, there was little advancement in the interpretation or application of the equal protection clause until after World War II. The major breakthrough came in 1954 with the case of *Brown v. Board of Education*, and advancements came in fits and starts during the succeeding ten years.

After 1964, Congress finally supported the federal courts with effective civil rights legislation. From that point, civil rights developed in two ways. First, the definition of civil rights was expanded to include victims of discrimination other than blacks. Second, the definition of civil rights became increasingly positive through affirmative action policies. Judicial decisions, congressional statutes, and administrative agency actions all have moved beyond the original goal of eliminating discrimination toward creating opportunities for minorities and, in some areas, compensating present individuals for the consequences of discriminatory actions against members of their group in the past. This kind of compensation has sometimes relied on quotas. The use of quotas, in turn, has given rise to intense debate over the constitutionality as well as the desirability of affirmative action.

The story has not ended and is not likely to end. The politics of rights will remain an important part of American political discourse.

[64]See Sam Howe Verhovek, "Houston Vote Underlined Complexity of Rights Issue," *New York Times,* 6 November 1997, p. A1.

KEY TERMS

affirmative action   A policy or program designed to redress historic injustices against specified groups by actively promoting equal access to educational and employment opportunities.

Bill of Rights   The first ten amendments to the U.S. Constitution.

civil liberties   Areas of personal freedom with which governments are constrained from interfering.

civil rights   Legal or moral claims that citizens are entitled to make upon the government to protect them from the illegal actions of other citizens and government agencies.

de facto **segregation**   Racial segregation that is not a direct result of law or government policy but is, instead, a reflection of residential patterns, income distributions, or other social factors.

de jure **segregation**   Racial segregation that is a direct result of law or official policy.

due process   To proceed according to law and with adequate protection for individual rights.

equal protection clause   A clause in the Fourteenth Amendment that requires that states provide citizens "equal protection of the laws."

exclusionary rule   The ability of the court to exclude evidence obtained in violation of the Fourth Amendment.

Miranda **rule**   Principles developed by the Supreme Court in *Miranda v. Arizona* (1966) requiring those under arrest be informed of their legal rights, including right to counsel, prior to police interrogation.

procedural liberties   Restraints on how the government is supposed to act.

separate but equal rule   Doctrine that public accommodations could be segregated by race but still be equal.

strict scrutiny   Higher standard of judicial protection for speech cases and other civil liberties and civil rights cases, in which the burden of proof shifts from the complainant to the government.

substantive liberties   Restraints on what the government shall and shall not have the power to do.

universalization of rights   The recognition that any group—whether defined by sex, religion, race, ethnicity, or gender—has the right not to be discriminated against.

FOR FURTHER READING

Abraham, Henry. *Freedom and the Court: Civil Rights and Liberties in the United States,* 5th ed. New York: Oxford University Press, 1994.

Baer, Judith A. *Equality under the Constitution: Reclaiming the Fourteenth Amendment*. Ithaca, NY: Cornell University Press, 1983.

Brigham, John. *Civil Liberties and American Democracy*. Washington, DC: Congressional Quarterly Press, 1984.

Eisenstein, Zillah. *The Female Body and the Law*. Berkeley: University of California Press, 1988.

Forer, Lois G. *A Chilling Effect: The Mounting Threat of Libel and Invasion of Privacy Actions to the First Amendment*. New York: Norton, 1987.

Friendly, Fred W. *Minnesota Rag: The Dramatic Story of the Landmark Supreme Court Case That Gave New Meaning to Freedom of the Press*. New York: Vintage, 1982.

Garrow, David J. *Bearing the Cross: Martin Luther King and the Southern Christian Leadership Conference: A Personal Portrait*. New York: William Morrow, 1986.

Hentoff, Nat. *The First Freedom: The Tumultuous History of Free Speech in America*. New York: Delacorte, 1980.

Kelly, Alfred, Winfred A. Harbison, and Herman Beltz. *The American Constitution: Its Origins and Development,* 7th ed. New York: Norton, 1991.

Levy, Leonard. *Freedom of Speech and Press in Early America: Legacy of Suppression*. New York: Harper & Row, 1963.

Lewis, Anthony. *Gideon's Trumpet*. New York: Random House, 1964.

Minow, Martha. *Making All the Difference—Inclusion, Exclusion, and American Law*. Ithaca, NY: Cornell University Press, 1990.

Randall, Richard S. *Censorship of the Movies*. Madison: University of Wisconsin Press, 1970.

Silberman, Charles. *Criminal Violence, Criminal Justice*. New York: Random House, 1978.

Silverstein, Mark. *Constitutional Faiths*. Ithaca, NY: Cornell University Press, 1984.

Thernstorm, Abigail M. *Whose Votes Count? Affirmative Action and Minority Voting Rights*. Cambridge: Harvard University Press, 1987.

PART 2

Institutions

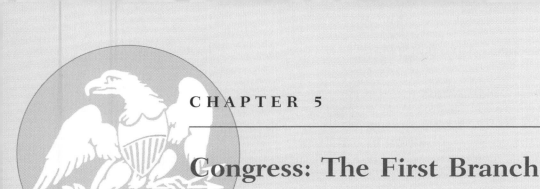

CHAPTER 5

Congress: The First Branch

HOW DOES CONGRESS WORK?

*T*he U.S. Congress is the "first branch" of government under Article I of our Constitution. Congress has vast authority over the two most important powers given to any government: the power of force (control over the nation's military forces) and the power over money. Specifically, in Article I, Section 8, Congress can "lay and collect Taxes," deal with indebtedness and bankruptcy, impose duties, borrow and coin money, and generally control the nation's purse strings. It also may "provide for the common Defense and general welfare," regulate interstate commerce, undertake public works, acquire and control federal lands, promote science and "useful Arts" (pertaining mostly to patents and copyrights), and regulate the militia.

In the realm of foreign policy, Congress has the power to declare war, deal with piracy, regulate foreign commerce, and raise and regulate the armed forces and military installations. These powers over war and the military are supreme—even the president, as commander in chief of the military, must obey the laws and orders of Congress *if* Congress chooses to assert its constitutional authority. (In the past century, Congress has usually surrendered this authority to the president.) Further, the Senate has the power to approve treaties (by a two-thirds vote) and to approve the appointment of ambassadors. Capping these powers, Congress is charged to make laws "which shall be necessary

CORE OF THE ANALYSIS

- Before a bill can become law, it must pass through the legislative process, a complex set of procedures in Congress.

- The legislative process is driven by six sets of political forces: political parties, committees, staffs, caucuses, rules of lawmaking, and the president.

- From the New Deal through the 1960s, the presidency seemed to be the dominant institution in American government; since the 1960s, Congress has sought to reassert its power by effectively representing important new groups and forces in society.

and proper for carrying into Execution the foregoing Powers, and all other Powers vested by this Constitution in the Government of the United States, or in any Department or Officer thereof."

It is extraordinarily difficult for a large, representative assembly to formulate, enact, and implement the laws. The internal complexities of conducting business within Congress—the legislative process—are daunting. In addition, many individuals and institutions have the capacity to influence the legislative process. For example, legislation to raise the salaries of members of the

CENTRAL QUESTIONS

- **How Does Congress Work?**
  What are the basic building blocks of congressional organization? What is the role of each in forming legislation?

- **Rules of Lawmaking: How a Bill Becomes a Law**
  How do the rules of congressional procedure influence the fate of legislation as well as determine the distribution of power in Congress?

- **How Congress Decides**
  What sorts of influences inside and outside of government determine how members of Congress vote on legislation? How do these influences vary according to the type of issue?

- **Beyond Legislation: Additional Congressional Powers**
  Besides the power to pass legislation, what other powers allow Congress to influence the process of government?

- **The Fall and Rise of Congressional Power**
  In recent decades, how has Congress sought to reclaim some of the power it has lost to the presidency?

House of Representatives received input from congressional leaders of both parties, special legislative task forces, the president, the national chairs of the two major parties, public interest lobbyists, the news media, and the mass public before it became law in 1989. Since successful legislation requires the confluence of so many distinct factors, it is little wonder that most of the thousands of bills considered by Congress each year are defeated long before they reach the president.

Before an idea or proposal can become a law, it must pass through a complex set of organizations and procedures in Congress. Collectively, these are called the policy-making process, or the legislative process. Understanding this process is central to understanding why some ideas and proposals eventually become the law of the land while most do not. Although the supporters of legislative proposals often feel that the formal rules of the congressional process are deliberately designed to prevent their own deserving proposals from ever seeing the light of day, these rules allow Congress to play an important role in lawmaking. If it wants to be more than simply a rubber stamp for the executive branch, like so many other representative assemblies around the world, a national legislature such as the Congress must develop a division of labor, set an agenda, maintain order through rules and procedures, and place limits on discussion. Equal-

ity among the members of Congress must give way to hierarchy—ranking people according to their function within the institution.

To exercise its power to make the law, Congress must first bring about something close to an organizational miracle. In this chapter, we will examine the organization of Congress and the legislative process. In particular, we will be concerned with the basic building blocks of congressional organization: bicameralism, political parties, the committee system, congressional staff, the caucuses, and the parliamentary rules of the House and Senate. Each of these factors plays a key role in the organization of Congress and in the process through which Congress formulates and enacts laws. We will also look at other powers Congress has in addition to lawmaking, and we will explore the future role of Congress in relation to the powers of the executive.

THE ORGANIZATION OF CONGRESS

Bicameralism: House and Senate

The framers of the Constitution provided for *bicameralism*—that is, a legislative body consisting of two chambers. As we saw in Chapter 2, the framers intended each of these chambers, the House and Senate, to serve a different constituency. Members of the Senate, appointed by state legislatures for six-year terms, were to represent the elite members of society and to be more attuned to the interests of property than to those of population. Today, members of the House and Senate are elected directly by the people. The 435 members of the House are elected from districts apportioned according to population: the 100 members of the Senate are elected by state, with two senators from each. Senators continue to have much longer terms in office and usually represent much larger and more diverse constituencies than do their counterparts in the House (see the In Brief Box below).

The framers of the Constitution provided for a bicameral legislature to represent different constituencies.

The House and Senate play different roles in the legislative process. In essence, the Senate is the more deliberative of the two bodies—the forum in which any and all ideas can receive a thorough public airing. The House is the more centralized and organized of the two bodies—better equipped to play a routine role in the governmental process. In part, this difference stems from the different rules governing the two bodies. These rules give House leaders more control over the legislative process and provide for House members to specialize in certain legislative areas. The rules of the much-smaller Senate give its leadership relatively little power and discourage specialization.

Both formal and informal factors contribute to differences between the two chambers of Congress. Differences in the length of terms and requirements for holding office specified by the Constitution in turn generate differences in how members of each body develop their constituencies and exercise their powers of office. The result is that members of the House most effectively and frequently serve as the agents of well-organized local interests with specific legislative agendas— used car dealers seeking relief from regulation,

IN BRIEF BOX — MAJOR DIFFERENCES BETWEEN THE HOUSE AND THE SENATE

House	Senate
Larger (435 members)	Smaller (100 members)
Shorter term in office (two years)	Longer term of office (six years)
Less flexible rules	More flexible rules
Narrower constituency	Broader, more varied constituencies
Policy specialists	Policy generalists
Less press and media coverage	More press and media coverage
Power less evenly distributed	Power more evenly distributed
Less prestige	More prestige
More expeditious in floor debate	Less expeditious in floor debate
Less reliance on staffs	More reliance on staffs
Initiates all money bills	Confirms Supreme Court justices, ambassadors, and heads of executive departments
	Confirms treaties

SOURCE: Walter J. Oleszek, *Congressional Procedures and the Policy Process* (Washington, DC: Congressional Quarterly Press, 1978), p. 24.

labor unions seeking more favorable legislation, or farmers looking for higher subsidies. The small size and relative homogeneity of their constituencies and the frequency with which they must seek reelection make House members more attuned to the legislative needs of local interest groups. This, too, was the intent of the Constitution's drafters—that the Senate should provide a balance to the more responsive House with its narrower and more homogenous constituencies. The Senate was said to be "the saucer that cools the tea," bringing deliberation, debate, inclusiveness, calm, and caution to policy formulation.

Senators, on the other hand, serve larger and more heterogeneous constituencies. As a result, they are somewhat better able than members of the House to serve as the agents for groups and interests organized on a statewide or national basis. Moreover, with longer terms in office, senators have the luxury of considering "new ideas" or seeking to bring together new coalitions of interests, rather than simply serving existing ones. This is what the framers intended when they drafted the Constitution—namely, that the House of Representatives would be "the people's house" and that its members would reflect and represent public opinion in a timely manner.

Members of the House tend to emphasize district interests in their representation, while members of the Senate are more able to represent statewide or national interests.

In recent years, the House has exhibited considerably more intense partisanship and ideological division than the Senate. Because of their diverse constituencies, senators are more inclined to seek compromises that will offend as few voters and interest groups as possible. Members of the House, in contrast, typically represent more homogeneous districts in which their own party is dominant. This situation has tended to make House members less inclined to seek compromises and more willing than their Senate counterparts to stick to partisan and ideological guns during the policy debates of the past several decades. In a similar vein, the House divided almost exactly along partisan lines on the 1998 vote to impeach President Clinton. In the Senate, by contrast, some Republicans joined all Democrats in voting to acquit Clinton.[1]

Political Parties: Congress's Oldest Hierarchy

The Constitution makes only one provision for the organization of business in Congress. In Article I, it gives each chamber a presiding officer. In the Senate, this officer is known as the president, and the office is held *ex officio* by the vice president of the United States. The Constitution also allows the Senate to elect a president *pro tempore*—a temporary president—to serve in the absence of the vice president. In the House of Representatives, the presiding officer is known as the speaker and is elected by the entire membership of the House.

Article I of the Constitution gives little guidance for how to conduct congressional business. Even during the first Congress (1789–91), it was the political parties that provided the organization needed by the House and Senate. For the first century or more of the Republic, America had literally a party government in Congress.[2]

PARTY LEADERSHIP IN THE HOUSE AND THE SENATE   Every two years, at the beginning of a new Congress, the members of each party gather to elect their House leaders. This gathering is traditionally called the *party caucus,* or, in the case of Republicans, the conference.

The elected leader of the majority party is later proposed to the whole House and is automatically elected to the position of *speaker of the House,* with voting along straight party lines. The House majority caucus (or conference) then also elects a *majority leader.* The minority party goes through the same process and selects the *minority leader.*

[1]Eric Pianin and Guy Gugliotta, "The Bipartisan Challenge: Senate's Search for Accord Marks Contrast to House," *Washington Post,* 8 January 1999, p. 1.
[2]*Origins and Development of Congress* (Washington, DC: Congressional Quarterly Press, 1982).

Both parties also elect whips to line up party members on important votes and relay voting information to the leaders.

Next in order of importance for each party after the majority and minority whips are the caucus (Democrats) or conference (Republicans) chairs. Next comes the Committee on Committees (called the Steering and Policy Committee by the Democrats), whose tasks are to assign new legislators to committees and to deal with the requests of incumbent members for transfers from one committee to another. The speaker serves as chair of the Republican Committee on Committees, while the minority leader chairs the Democratic Steering and Policy Committee. (The Republicans have a separate Policy Committee.) At one time, party leaders strictly controlled committee assignments, using them to enforce party discipline. Today, representatives expect to receive the assignments they want and resent leadership efforts to control committee assignments. For example, during the 104th Congress (1995–96) the then-chair of the powerful Appropriations Committee, Robert Livingston, sought to remove freshman Mark Neumann (R-Wisc.) from the committee because of his lack of party loyalty. The entire Republican freshman class angrily opposed this move and forced the leadership to back down. Not only did Neumann keep his seat on the Appropriations Committee, but he was given a seat on the Budget Committee, as well, to placate the freshmen.[3] The leadership's best opportunities to use committee assignments as rewards and punishments come when more than one member seeks a seat on the same committee.

Generally, representatives seek assignments that will allow them to influence decisions of special importance to their districts. Representatives from farm districts, for example, may request seats on the Agriculture Committee.[4] Seats on powerful committees such as Ways and Means, which is responsible for tax legislation, and Appropriations are especially popular.

[3]Linda Killian, *The Freshmen: What Happened to the Republican Revolution* (Boulder, CO: Westview, 1998).
[4]Richard Fenno, Jr., *Home Style: House Members in Their Districts* (Boston: Little, Brown, 1978).

Within the Senate, the president pro tempore exercises mainly ceremonial leadership. Usually, the majority party designates a member with the greatest seniority to serve in this capacity. Real power is in the hands of the majority leader and minority leader, each elected by party caucus or conference. The majority and minority leaders, together, control the Senate's calendar or agenda for legislation. In addition, the senators from each party elect a whip. (The whip system is discussed in the Party Discipline section of this chapter.) Each party also selects a Policy Committee, which advises the leadership on legislative priorities. The majority party structures for the House and Senate are shown in Figures 5.1 and 5.2.

The leader of the majority party in the House is the speaker of the House; in the Senate, that distinction belongs to the majority leader. The leadership in each chamber of Congress is important for imposing party discipline and assigning members to committees.

In addition to the tasks of organizing Congress, congressional party leaders may also seek to set the legislative agenda. Since the New Deal, presidents have taken the lead in creating legislative agendas. (This trend will be discussed in the next chapter.) But in recent years, congressional leaders, especially when facing a White House controlled by the opposing party, have attempted to devise their own agendas. Democratic leaders of Congress sought to create a common Democratic perspective in 1981 when Ronald Reagan became president. The Republican Congress elected in 1994 expanded on this idea with its Contract with America. In both cases, the majority party leadership has sought to create a consensus among its congressional members around an overall vision to guide legislative activity and to make individual pieces of legislation part of a bigger picture that is distinct from the agenda of the president.

FIGURE 5.1

MAJORITY PARTY STRUCTURE IN THE HOUSE OF REPRESENTATIVES

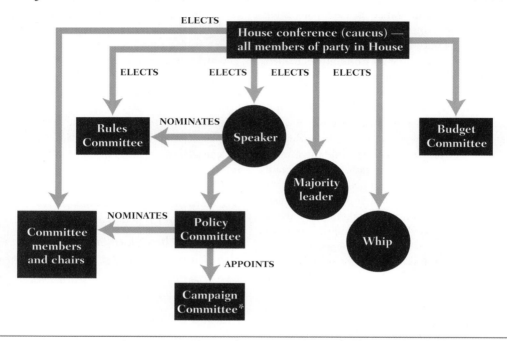

*Includes speaker (chair), majority leader, chief and deputy whips, caucus chair, four members appointed by the speaker, and twelve members elected by regional caucuses.

The leaders of the majority party also devise legislative agendas.

In recent years, party leaders have sought to augment their formal powers by reaching outside Congress for resources that might enhance their influence within Congress. One aspect of this external strategy is the increased use of national communications media, including televised speeches and talk show appearances by party leaders. Former Republican House Speaker Newt Gingrich, for example, used television extensively to generate support for his programs among Republican loyalists.[5] As long as it lasted, Gingrich's sup-

port among the Republican rank-and-file gave him an added measure of influence over Republican members of Congress.

A second external strategy involves fundraising. In recent years, congressional leaders have frequently established their own political action committees. Interest groups are usually eager to contribute to these "leadership PACs" to curry favor with powerful members of Congress. The leaders, in turn, use these funds to support the various campaigns of their party's candidates in order to create a sense of obligation. For example, in the 1998 congressional election, Majority Leader Dick Armey, who was running unopposed, raised more than $6 million, which he distributed to less well-heeled Republican candidates. Armey's generosity served him well in the leadership struggle that erupted after the election.

[5]Douglas Harris, *The Public Speaker* (Ph.D. diss., Johns Hopkins University, 1998).

FIGURE 5.2

MAJORITY PARTY STRUCTURE IN THE SENATE

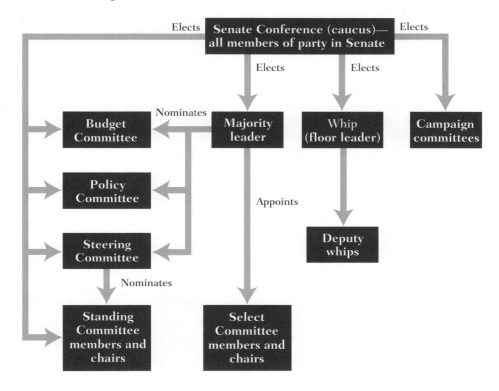

The Committee System: The Core of Congress

The committee system provides Congress with its second organizational structure, but it is more a division of labor than a hierarchy of power. Committee and subcommittee chairs have a number of important powers, but their capacity to discipline committee members is limited. Ultimately, committee members are hired and fired by the voters, not by the leadership. Committee chairs just have to put up with members whose views they might find distasteful.

The committee system is the backbone of Congress, where legislation is proposed and drafted.

Six fundamental characteristics define the congressional committee system:

1. *The official rules give each **standing committee** a permanent status, with a fixed membership, officers, rules, staff, offices, and, above all, a jurisdiction that is recognized by all other committees and usually the leadership as well* (see Table 5.1).
2. *The jurisdiction of each standing committee is defined according to the subject matter of basic legislation.* Except for the House Rules Committee, all the important committees are organized to receive proposals for legislation and to process them into official bills. The House Rules Committee decides the order in which bills come up for a vote and determines the specific rules that govern the length of debate and the opportunity for amendments. Rules can be used to help or hinder particular proposals.

3. *Standing committees' jurisdictions usually parallel those of the major departments or agencies in the executive branch.* There are important exceptions—Appropriations (House and Senate) and Rules (House), for example—but by and large, the division of labor is self-consciously designed to parallel executive branch organization.

4. *Bills are assigned to standing committees on the basis of subject matter, but the speaker of the House and the Senate's presiding officer have some discretion in the allocation of bills to committees.* Most bills "die in committee"—that is, they are not reported out favorably. Ordinarily this ends a bill's life. There is only one way for a legislative proposal to escape committee processing: A bill passed in one chamber may be permitted to go directly on to the calendar of the other chamber. Even here, however, the bill has received the full committee treatment before passage in the first chamber.

5. *Each standing committee is unique.* No effort is made to compose the membership of any committee to be representative of the total House or Senate membership. Members with a special interest in the subject matter of a committee are expected to seek membership on it. In both the House and the Senate, each party has established a Committee on Committees, which determines the committee assignments of new members and of established members who wish to change committees. Ordinarily, members can keep their committee assignments as long as they like.

6. *Each standing committee's hierarchy is based on seniority.* **Seniority** is determined by years of continuous service on a particular committee, not by years of service in the House or Senate.

TABLE 5.1

PERMANENT COMMITTEES OF CONGRESS

House Committees

Agriculture	National Security
Appropriations	Resources
Banking and Financial Services	Rules
Budget	Science
Commerce	Small Business
Economic and Educational Opportunities	Standards of Official Conduct
Government Reform and Oversight	Transportation and Infrastructure
House Oversight	Veterans' Affairs
International Relations	Ways and Means
Judiciary	

Senate Committees

Agriculture, Nutrition, and Forestry	Finance
Appropriations	Foreign Relations
Armed Services	Governmental Affairs
Banking, Housing, and Urban Affairs	Judiciary
Budget	Labor and Human Resources
Commerce, Science, and Transportation	Rules and Administration
Energy and Natural Resources	Small Business
Environment and Public Works	Veterans' Affairs

In general, each committee is chaired by the most senior member of the majority party. Although the power of committee chairs is limited, they play an important role in scheduling hearings, selecting subcommittee members, and appointing committee staff. Because Congress has a large number of subcommittees and has given each representative a larger staff, the power of the committee chairs has been diluted.

The Staff System: Staffers and Agencies

A congressional institution second in importance only to the committee system is the staff system. Every member of Congress employs a large number of staff members, whose tasks include handling constituency requests and, to a large and growing extent, dealing with legislative details and overseeing the activities of administrative agencies. Increasingly, staffers bear the primary responsibility for formulating and drafting proposals, organizing hearings, dealing with administrative agencies, and negotiating with lobbyists. Indeed, legislators typically deal with one another through staff rather than through direct, personal contact. Representatives and senators together employ nearly eleven thousand staffers in their Washington and home offices. Today, staffers even develop policy ideas, draft legislation, and, in some instances, have a good deal of influence over the legislative process.

Each member of Congress has a large staff, whose duties include drafting proposals and dealing with legislation.

In addition to the personal staffs of individual senators and representatives, Congress also employs roughly two thousand committee staffers. These individuals are the permanent staff, who stay regardless of turnover in Congress, attached to every House and Senate committee, and who are responsible for organizing and administering the committee's work, including research, scheduling, organizing hearings, and drafting legislation. Congressional staffers can come to play key roles in the legislative process. One example of the importance of congressional staffers is the so-called Gephardt health care reform bill, introduced in August 1994. Although the bill bore Representative Richard Gephardt's name, it was actually crafted by a small group of staff members of the House Ways and Means Committee. These aides, under the direction of David Abernathy, the staff's leading health care specialist, debated methods of cost control, service delivery, the role of the insurance industry, and the needs of patients, and listened to hundreds of lobbyists before drafting the complex Gephardt bill.[6]

The number of congressional staff members grew rapidly during the 1960s and 1970s, leveled off in the 1980s, and decreased dramatically in 1995. This sudden drop fulfilled the Republican congressional candidates' 1994 campaign promise to reduce the size of committee staffs.

Not only does Congress employ personal and committee staffs, but it has also established three *staff agencies* designed to provide the legislative branch with resources and expertise independent of the executive branch. These agencies enhance Congress's capacity to oversee administrative agencies and to evaluate presidential programs and proposals. They are the Congressional Research Service, which performs research for legislators who wish to know the facts and competing arguments relevant to policy proposals or other legislative business; the General Accounting Office, through which Congress can investigate the financial and administrative affairs of any government agency or program; and the Congressional Budget Office, which assesses the economic implications and likely costs of proposed federal programs, such as health care reform proposals.

Informal Organization: The Caucuses

In addition to the official organization of Congress, there also exists an unofficial organizational structure—the caucuses, formally known as *legislative*

---

[6]Robert Pear, "With Long Hours and Little Fanfare, Staff Members Crafted a Health Bill," *New York Times,* 6 August 1994, p. 7.

service organizations (LSOs). Caucuses are groups of senators or representatives who share certain opinions, interests, or social characteristics. They include ideological caucuses such as the liberal Democratic Study Group, the conservative Democratic Forum (popularly known as the "boll weevils"), and the moderate Republican Wednesday Group. At the same time, there are a large number of caucuses composed of legislators representing particular economic or policy interests, such as the Travel and Tourism Caucus, the Steel Caucus, the Mushroom Caucus, and the Concerned Senators for the Arts. Legislators who share common backgrounds or social characteristics have organized caucuses such as the Congressional Black Caucus, the Congressional Caucus for Women's Issues, and the Hispanic Caucus.

Caucuses are organized groups of senators or representatives with one or more common interests.

All these caucuses seek to advance the interests of the groups they represent by promoting legislation, encouraging Congress to hold hearings, and pressing administrative agencies for favorable treatment.

RULES OF LAWMAKING: HOW A BILL BECOMES A LAW

The institutional structure of Congress is one key factor that helps to shape the legislative process. A second and equally important factor is the rules of congressional procedures. These rules govern everything from the introduction of a bill through its submission to the president for signing. Not only do these regulations influence the fate of each and every bill, they also help to determine the distribution of power in Congress.

Committee Deliberation

Even if a member of Congress, the White House, or a federal agency has spent months developing and drafting a piece of legislation, it does not become a bill until it is submitted officially by a senator or representative to the clerk of the House or Senate and referred to the appropriate committee for deliberation. No floor action on any bill can take place until the committee with jurisdiction over it has taken all the time it needs to deliberate. During the course of its deliberations, the committee typically refers the bill to one of its subcommittees, which may hold hearings, listen to expert testimony, and amend the proposed legislation before referring it to the full committee for its consideration. The full committee may accept the recommendation of the subcommittee or hold its own hearings and prepare its own amendments. Or, even more frequently, the committee and subcommittee may do little or nothing with a bill that has been submitted to them. Many bills are simply allowed to "die in committee" with little or no serious consideration ever given to them. Often, members of Congress introduce legislation that they neither expect nor desire to see enacted into law, merely to please a constituency group. These bills die a quick and painless death. Other pieces of legislation have ardent supporters and die in committee only after a long battle. But in either case, most bills are never reported out of the committees to which they are assigned. In a typical congressional session, 85–90 percent of the roughly eight thousand bills introduced die in committee—an indication of the power of the congressional committee system.

Before the House or Senate floor can vote upon a bill, the appropriate committee must deliberate on its merits. Committees allow most bills to die before reaching a floor vote.

The relative handful of bills that are reported out of the committee to which they were originally referred must, in the House, pass one additional hurdle within the committee system: the Rules Committee. This powerful committee determines the rules that will govern action on the bill on the House floor. In particular, the Rules Committee allots the time for debate and decides to what extent amendments to the bill can be proposed from the floor. A bill's supporters generally prefer what is called a *closed rule,* which severely limits floor debate and amendments. Opponents of a bill usually prefer an *open rule,* which permits potentially damaging floor debate and makes it easier to add amendments that may cripple the bill or weaken its chances for passage. Thus, the outcome of the Rules Committee's deliberations can be extremely important, and the committee's hearings can be an occasion for sharp conflicts.

Debate

Party control of the agenda is reinforced by the rule giving the speaker of the House and the majority leader of the Senate the power of recognition during debate on a bill. Usually the chair knows the purpose for which a member intends to speak well in advance of the occasion. Spontaneous efforts to gain recognition are often foiled. For example, the speaker may ask, "For what purpose does the member rise?" before deciding whether to grant recognition.

In the House, virtually all of the time allotted by the Rules Committee for debate on a given bill is controlled by the bill's sponsor and by its leading opponent. In almost every case, these two people are the committee chair and the ranking minority member of the committee that processed the bill—or those they designate. These two participants are, by rule and tradition, granted the power to allocate most of the debate time in small amounts to members who are seeking to speak for or against the measure. Preference in the allocation of time goes to the members of the committee whose jurisdiction covers the bill.

In the Senate, other than the power of recognition, the leadership has much less control over the floor debate. Indeed, the Senate is unique among the world's legislative bodies for its commitment to unlimited debate. Once given the floor, a senator may speak as long as he or she wishes.

On a number of memorable occasions, senators have used this right to prevent action on legislation that they opposed. Through this tactic, called the *filibuster,* small minorities or even one individual in the Senate can force the majority to give in to their demands. During the 1950s and 1960s, for example, opponents of civil rights legislation often sought to block its passage by adopting the tactic of filibuster. The votes of three-fifths of the Senate, or sixty votes, are needed to end a filibuster. This procedure is called *cloture.*

In the House, the party leadership controls debate on a bill. But in the Senate, once a speaker has been recognized, the member can speak as long as he or she wishes. This tactic, the filibuster, allows senators to prevent a vote on bills that they oppose.

Whereas the filibuster was once an extraordinary tactic used only on rare occasions, in recent decades it has been used increasingly often. In general, the party leadership in the House has total control over debate. In the Senate, each member has substantial power to block debate. This is one reason that the Senate tends to be a less partisan body than the House. A House majority can override opposition, while a majority in the Senate must still accommodate the views of other members.

Conference Committee: Reconciling House and Senate Versions of a Bill

Getting a bill out of committee and through one of the houses of Congress is no guarantee that a bill will be enacted into law. Frequently, bills that began with similar provisions in both chambers emerge with little resemblance to each other. Alternatively, a bill may be passed by one chamber but undergo substantial revision in the other chamber. In such cases, a *conference committee* composed of the senior members of the committees or sub-

PROCESS BOX 5.1   HOW A BILL BECOMES A LAW

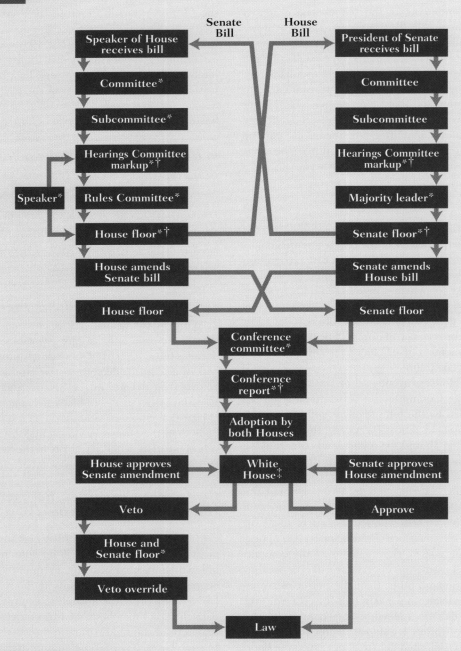

*Points at which bill can be amended.
†Points at which bill can die.
‡If the president neither signs nor vetoes the bill within ten days, it automatically becomes law.

committees that initiated the bills may be required to iron out differences between the two pieces of legislation. Sometimes members or leaders will let objectionable provisions pass on the floor with the idea that they will get the change they want in conference. Usually, conference committees meet behind closed doors. Agreement requires a majority of each of the two delegations. Legislation that emerges from a conference committee is more often a compromise than a clear victory of one set of political forces over another.

The House and the Senate reconcile altered versions of the same bill in a conference committee.

When a bill comes out of conference, it faces one more hurdle. Before a bill can be sent to the president for signing, the House-Senate conference report must be approved on the floor of each chamber. Usually, such approval is given quickly. Occasionally, however, a bill's opponents use approval as one last opportunity to defeat a piece of legislation.

Presidential Action

Once adopted by the House and Senate, a bill goes to the president, who may choose to sign the bill into law or veto it. The *veto* is the president's constitutional power to reject a piece of legislation. To veto a bill, the president returns it within ten days to the house of Congress in which it originated, along with his objections to the bill. If Congress adjourns during the ten-day period, and the president has taken no action, the bill is also considered to be vetoed. This latter method is known as the *pocket veto*. The possibility of a presidential veto affects how willing members of Congress are to push for different pieces of legislation at different times. If they think the president is likely to veto a proposal, they might shelve it for a later time. Alternatively, the sponsors of a popular bill opposed by the president might push for passage in order to force the president to pay the political

costs of vetoing it.[7] For example, in 1996 and 1997, Republicans passed bills outlawing partial-birth abortions though they knew President Clinton would veto them. The GOP calculated that Clinton would be hurt politically by vetoing legislation that most Americans favored.

A presidential veto may be overridden by a two-thirds vote in both the House and the Senate. A veto override says much about the support that a president can expect from Congress, and it can deliver a stinging blow to the executive branch. Presidents will often back down from a veto threat if they believe that Congress will override the veto.

Once a bill has passed both chambers of Congress, the president may sign or veto the bill. Congress may override a veto by a two-thirds vote in each house.

HOW CONGRESS DECIDES

What determines the kinds of legislation that Congress ultimately produces? According to the most simple theories of representation, members of Congress would respond to the views of their *constituency*—the members of the district from which they are elected. In fact, the process of creating a legislative agenda, drawing up a list of possible measures, and deciding among them is very complex, and a variety of influences from inside and outside government play important roles. External influences include a legislator's constituency and various interest groups. Influences from inside government include party leadership, congressional colleagues, and the president. Let us examine each of these influences individually and then consider how they interact to produce congressional policy decisions.

[7]John Gilmour, *Strategic Disagreement* (Pittsburgh: University of Pittsburgh Press, 1995).

Constituency

Because members of Congress, for the most part, want to be reelected, we would expect the views of their constituents to have a key influence on the decisions that legislators make. Yet constituency influence is not so straightforward. In fact, most constituents do not even know what policies their representatives support. The number of citizens who *do* pay attention to such matters—the attentive public—is usually very small. Nonetheless, members of Congress spend a lot of time worrying about what their constituents think, because these representatives realize that the choices they make may be scrutinized in a future election and used as ammunition by an opposing candidate. Because of this possibility, members of Congress try to anticipate their constituents' policy views.[8] In some instances, the results may seem bizarre. For example, in April 2003, Senator Thad Cochran (R-Miss.) was able to insert language into the bill funding the war in Iraq that provided $250 million for "disaster relief" for Southern catfish farmers.[9] Most Americans would never have guessed that driving Saddam Hussein from power would have an effect on catfish farmers in Mississippi. Legislators are more likely to act in accordance with their constituents' views if they think that voters will take them into account during elections. In this way, constituents may affect congressional policy choices even when there is little direct evidence of their influence.

Members of Congress attempt to discern their constituents' views on issues and take them into account when deciding how to vote.

[8]See John W. Kingdon, *Congressman's Voting Decisions* (New York: Harper and Row, 1973), Chapter 3; and R. Douglas Arnold, *The Logic of Congressional Action* (New Haven: Yale University Press, 1990).
[9]Dan Morgan, "War Funding Bill's Extra Riders," *Washington Post,* 8 April 2003, p. A4.

Interest Groups

Interest groups are another important external influence on the policies that Congress produces. When members of Congress are making voting decisions, those interest groups that have some connection to constituents in particular members' districts are most likely to be influential. For this reason, interest groups with the ability to mobilize followers in many congressional districts may be especially influential in Congress. The small-business lobby, for example, played an important role in defeating President Clinton's proposal for comprehensive health care reform in 1993–1994. Because of the mobilization of networks of small businesses across the country, virtually every member of Congress had to take their views into account.

In the 2004 electoral cycle, interest groups and political action committees (PACs) donated many millions of dollars in campaign contributions to incumbent legislators and challengers. What does this money buy? A popular conception is that campaign contributions buy votes. In this view, legislators vote for whichever proposal favors the bulk of their contributors. Although the vote-buying hypothesis makes for good campaign rhetoric, it has little factual support. Empirical studies by political scientists show little evidence that contributions from large PACs influence legislative voting patterns.[10]

If contributions don't buy votes, then what do they buy? Our claim is that campaign contributions influence legislative behavior in ways that are difficult for the public to observe and for political scientists to measure. The institutional structure of Congress provides opportunities for interest groups to influence legislation outside the public eye.

Committee proposal power enables legislators, if they are on the relevant committee, to introduce legislation that favors contributing groups. Gatekeeping power enables committee members to block legislation that harms contributing groups.

[10]See Janet M. Grenke, "PACs and the Congressional Supermarket: The Currency Is Complex," *American Journal of Political Science* 33 (1989): 1–24.

The fact that certain provisions are *excluded* from a bill is as much an indicator of PAC influence as the fact that certain provisions are *included*. The difference is that it is hard to measure what you don't see. Committee oversight powers enable members to intervene in bureaucratic decision making on behalf of contributing groups.

The point here is that voting on the floor, the alleged object of campaign contributions according to the vote-buying hypothesis, is a highly visible, highly public act, one that could get a legislator in trouble with his or her broader electoral constituency. The committee system, on the other hand, provides loads of opportunities for legislators to deliver to PAC contributors and other donors "services" that are more subtle and disguised from broader public view. Thus, we suggest that the most appropriate places to look for traces of campaign contribution influence on the legislative process are in the manner in which committees deliberate, mark up proposals, and block legislation from the floor; outside public view, these are the primary arenas for interest-group influence.

Interest groups often wage lobbying or publicity campaigns in an effort to persuade members of Congress.

Party Discipline

In both the House and the Senate, party leaders have a good deal of influence over the behavior of their party members. This influence, sometimes called "party discipline," was once so powerful that it dominated the lawmaking process. At the turn of the century, because of their control of patronage and the nominating process, party leaders could often command the allegiance of more than 90 percent of their members. A vote on which 50 percent or more of the members of one party take a particular position while at least 50 percent of the members of the other party take the opposing position is called a *party vote.* At the beginning of the twentieth century, most **roll-call votes** in the House of Representatives were party votes. Today, primary elections have deprived party leaders of the power to decide who receives the party's official nomination. The patronage resources available to the leadership, moreover, have become quite limited. As a result, party-line voting happens less often. It is, however, fairly common to find at least a majority of Democrats opposing a majority of Republicans on any given issue.

Party leaders have a strong, but not absolute, influence over the behavior of their members.

Typically, party unity is greater in the House than in the Senate. House rules grant greater procedural control of business to the majority party leaders, which gives them more influence over their members. In the Senate, however, the leadership has few sanctions over its members. Former Senate Minority Leader Tom Daschle once observed that a Senate leader seeking to influence other senators has as incentives "a bushel full of carrots and a few twigs."[11] Party unity has increased in recent sessions of Congress as a consequence of the intense partisan struggles during the 1980s and 1990s (see Figure 5.3). On the whole, there was more party unity in the House during 1995 than in any year since 1954. By 1996, the level of party unity was back to average. In 1997, party unity diminished as House Republicans divided over budget and tax cut negotiations with President Clinton.

In 2001, George W. Bush called for an end to partisan squabbling in Congress. During his 2000 presidential campaign, Bush claimed that, as governor of Texas, he had built effective bipartisan coalitions that should serve as models for congressional activities as well. September 11, 2001, prompted almost every member of Congress to

[11]Holly Idelson, "Signs Point to Greater Loyalty on Both Sides of the Aisle," *Congressional Quarterly Weekly Report,* 19 December 1992, p. 3849.

FIGURE 5.3

PARTY UNITY SCORES BY CHAMBER*

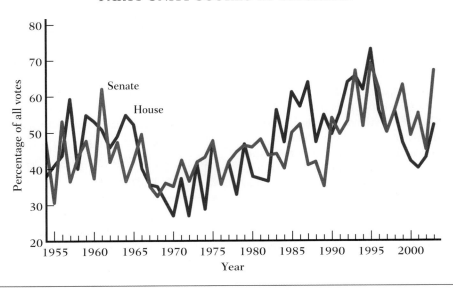

*The percentage of times that members voted with the majority of their party, based on recorded votes on which a majority of one party voted against the majority of the other party.
SOURCE: *Congressional Quarterly Weekly Report,* 3 January 2004, p. 11.

rally behind President Bush's military response. But Democrats and Republicans in the House divided sharply over the issue of airport security. Over the next several years, partisan differences emerged on a variety of issues, including taxation and foreign policy. On the issue of taxation, President Bush had sought to reduce federal taxes by as much as $700 billion over a period of several years. Many Democrats, on the other hand, opposed most or all of Bush's tax-cut proposals and called for increased federal spending on social programs, especially health care. On issues of foreign policy, many Democrats were deeply troubled by the president's willingness to use military force unilaterally when he deemed it necessary to do so. Prior to the 2003 Iraq war, Democratic leaders argued for giving UN weapons inspectors and diplomacy more time. Some Democrats accused the president of undermining America's relations with its allies.

To some extent, party divisions are based on ideology and background. Republican members of Congress are more likely than Democrats to be drawn from rural or suburban areas. Democrats are likely to be more liberal on economic and social questions than their Republican colleagues. This ideological gap has been especially pronounced since 1980 (see Figure 5.4). These differences certainly help to explain roll-call divisions between the two parties. Ideology and background, however, are only part of the explanation of party unity. The other part has to do with organization and leadership.

Although party organization has weakened since the turn of the century, today's party leaders still have some resources at their disposal: (1) committee assignments, (2) access to the floor, (3) the whip system, (4) logrolling, and (5) the presidency. These resources are regularly used and are often very effective in securing the support of party members.

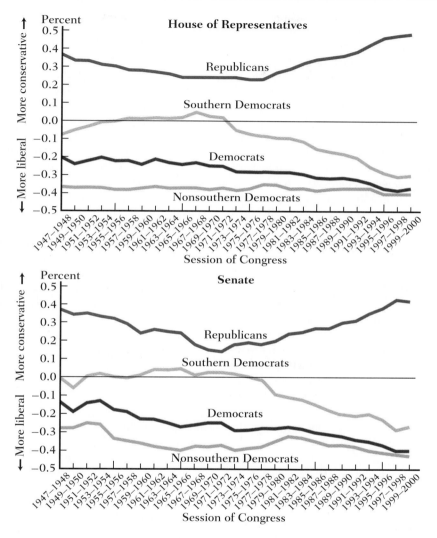

FIGURE 5.4

THE WIDENING IDEOLOGICAL GAP BETWEEN THE PARTIES IN CONGRESS

SOURCES: Data from Keith T. Poole and Howard Rosenthal, computed by Gary Jacobson, and reprinted in Poole and Rosenthal's *Congress: A Political-Economic History of Roll Call Voting* (New York: Oxford University Press, 1997); updates by Keith T. Poole.

COMMITTEE ASSIGNMENTS Leaders can create debts among members by helping them get favorable committee assignments. These assignments are made early in the congressional careers of most members and cannot be taken from them if they later balk at party discipline. Nevertheless, if the leadership goes out of its way to get the right assignment for a member, this effort is likely to create a bond of obligation that can be called upon without any other payments or favors.

ACCESS TO THE FLOOR   The most important everyday resource available to the parties is control over access to the floor. With thousands of bills awaiting passage and most members clamoring for access in order to influence a bill or to publicize themselves, floor time is precious. In the House, the speaker, as head of the majority party (in consultation with the minority leader), allocates large blocks of floor time. More important, the speaker of the House and the majority leader in the Senate possess the power of recognition. Although this power may not appear to be substantial, it is a formidable authority and can be used to block a piece of legislation completely or to frustrate a member's attempts to speak on a particular issue. Because the power is significant, members of Congress usually attempt to stay on good terms with the speaker and the majority leader to ensure that they will continue to be recognized.

THE WHIP SYSTEM   Some influence accrues to party leaders through the *whip system,* which is primarily a communications network. Between twelve and twenty assistant and regional whips are selected by zones to operate at the direction of the majority or minority leader and the whip. They take polls of all the members in order to learn their intentions on specific bills. This tells the leaders whether they have enough support to allow a vote, as well as whether the vote is so close that they need to put pressure on a few swing votes. Leaders also use the whip system to convey their wishes and plans to the members, but only in very close votes do they actually exert pressure on a member. In those instances, the speaker or a lieutenant will go to a few party members who have indicated they will switch if their vote is essential. The whip system helps the leaders limit pressuring members to a few times per session.

Whips work to discover party members' voting inclinations on bills and to line up party votes by pressuring members when necessary.

The whip system helps maintain party unity in both houses of Congress, but it is particularly critical in the House of Representatives because of the large number of legislators whose positions and votes must be accounted for. The majority and minority whips and their assistants must be adept at inducing compromise among legislators who hold widely differing viewpoints. The whips' personal styles and their perception of their function significantly affect the development of legislative coalitions and influence the compromises that emerge.

LOGROLLING   An agreement between two or more members of Congress who have nothing in common except the need for support is called *logrolling.* The agreement states, in effect, "You support me on bill X and I'll support you on another bill of your choice." Since party leaders are the center of the communications networks in the two chambers, they can help members create large logrolling coalitions. Hundreds of logrolling deals are made each year, and while there are no official record-keeping books, it would be a poor party leader whose whips did not know who owed what to whom.

Logrolling occurs when two or more members exchange support for bills.

In some instances, logrolling produces strange alliances. In August 1994, for example, an unlikely coalition of Republicans, conservative Democrats, and members of the Congressional Black Caucus temporarily blocked President Clinton's crime bill in the House of Representatives. The Republicans were interested in undermining Clinton. Conservative Democrats had been mobilized by the National Rifle Association (NRA) to oppose the bill's ban on the sale of several types of assault weapons. Some members of the Congressional Black Caucus were opposed to the bill because it expanded the potential use of the death penalty in federal cases. Many African American representatives demanded a "racial justice" provision, designed to ensure that blacks convicted of capital offenses could not be sentenced to death with greater frequency than whites, as a condition for

PARTY DISCIPLINE

The influence party leaders have over the behavior of their party members is maintained through a number of sources:

Committee assignments—By giving favorable committee assignments to members, party leaders create a sense of debt.

Access to the floor—Ranking committee members in the Senate and the speaker of the House control the allocation of floor time, so House and Senate members want to stay on good terms with these party leaders in order that their bills get time on the floor.

Whip system—The system allows party leaders to keep track of how many votes they have for a given piece of legislation; if the vote is close, they can try to influence members to switch sides.

Logrolling—Members who have nothing in common agree to support one another's legislation because each needs the vote.

Presidency—The president's legislative proposals are often the most important part of Congress's agenda. Party leaders use the president's support to rally members.

supporting the president's anti-crime initiative. This provision, however, had been defeated several weeks earlier by the same Republicans and conservative Democrats who now joined with disgruntled members of the Black Caucus to block the entire bill. Eventually Clinton was able to secure passage of the legislation by making concessions to the Republicans. Another logrolling alliance of strange bedfellows was the 1994 "corn for porn" logroll, in which liberal urbanites supported farm programs in exchange for rural support for National Endowment for the Arts funding.

THE PRESIDENCY Of all the influences that maintain the clarity of party lines in Congress, the influence of the presidency is probably the most important. Indeed, it is a touchstone of party discipline in Congress. Since the late 1940s, under President Truman, presidents each year have identified a number of bills to be considered part of the administration's program. By the mid-1950s, both parties in Congress began to look to the president for these proposals, which became the most significant part of Congress's agenda. The president's support is a criterion for party loyalty, and

party leaders in Congress are able to use it to rally some members.

Weighing Diverse Influences

Clearly, many different factors affect congressional decisions. But at various points in the decision-making process, some factors are likely to be more influential than others. For example, interest groups may be more effective at the committee stage, when their expertise is especially valued and their visibility is less obvious. Because committees play a key role in deciding what legislation actually reaches the floor of the House or Senate, interest groups can often put a halt to bills they dislike, or they can ensure that the options that do reach the floor are those that the group's members support.

Once legislation reaches the floor, and members of Congress are deciding among alternatives, constituent opinion will become more important. Legislators are also influenced very much by other legislators: Many of their assessments about the substance and politics of legislation come from fellow members of Congress.

The influence of the external and internal forces described in the preceding section also varies according to the kind of issue being considered. On policies of great importance to powerful interest groups—farm subsidies, for example—those groups are likely to have considerable influence. On other issues, members of Congress may be less attentive to narrow interest groups and more willing to consider what they see as the general interest.

The influence of individual factors upon legislation varies according to the stage of the legislation and to the issues being considered.

Finally, the mix of influences varies according to the historical moment. The 1994 electoral victory of Republicans allowed their party to control both houses of Congress for the first time in forty years. That fact, combined with an unusually assertive Republican leadership, meant that party leaders became especially important in decision making. The willingness of moderate Republicans to support measures they had once opposed indicated the unusual importance of party leadership in this period. As Former House Minority Leader Richard Gephardt put it, "When you've been in the desert 40 years, your instinct is to help Moses."[12]

BEYOND LEGISLATION: ADDITIONAL CONGRESSIONAL POWERS

In addition to the power to make the law, Congress has at its disposal an array of other instruments through which to influence the process of government. The Constitution gives the Senate the power to approve treaties and appointments. And Congress has drawn to itself a number of other powers through which it can share with the other branches the capacity to administer the laws. The

[12]David Broder, "At 6 Months, House GOP Juggernaut Still Cohesive," *Washington Post,* 17 July 1995, p. A1.

powers of Congress can be called "weapons of control" to emphasize Congress's power to govern and to call attention to what governmental power means.

Oversight

Oversight, as applied to Congress, refers not to something neglected but to the effort to oversee or to supervise how the executive branch carries out legislation. Individual senators and members of the House can engage in a form of oversight simply by calling or visiting administrators, sending out questionnaires, or talking to constituents about programs. But in a more formal sense, oversight is carried out by committees or subcommittees of the Senate or House, which conduct hearings and investigations in order to analyze and evaluate bureaucratic agencies and the effectiveness of their programs. The purpose may be to locate inefficiencies or abuses of power, to explore the relationship between what an agency does and what a law intended, or to change or abolish a program. Most programs and agencies are subject to some oversight every year during the course of hearings on *appropriations,* that is, the funding of agencies and government programs. Committees or subcommittees have the power to subpoena witnesses, take oaths, cross-examine, compel testimony, and bring criminal charges for contempt (refusing to cooperate) and perjury (lying).

Congress has the power to oversee or supervise how the executive branch carries out legislation.

Hearings and investigations resemble each other in many ways, but they differ on one fundamental point. A hearing is usually held on a specific bill, and the questions asked there are usually intended to build a record with regard to that bill. In an investigation, the committee or subcommittee does not begin with a particular bill, but examines a broad area or problem and then concludes its investigation with one or more proposed bills.

One example of an investigation is the Senate hearings on the abuse of prisoners in Iraq's Abu Ghraib prison. Many Democrats and some Republicans complained that congressional oversight of the entire Iraq war had been too lax. Reflecting on the prison abuse scandal, Representative Christopher Shays (R-Conn.) stated, "I believe our failure to do proper oversight has hurt our country and the administration. Maybe they wouldn't have gotten into some of this trouble if our oversight had been better."[13]

Advice and Consent: Special Senate Powers

The Constitution has given the Senate a special power, one that is not based on lawmaking. The president has the power to make treaties and to appoint top executive officers, ambassadors, and federal judges—but only "with the Advice and Consent of the Senate" (Article II, Section 2). For treaties, two-thirds of those present must concur; for appointments, a majority is required.

The power to approve or reject presidential requests also involves the power to set conditions. The Senate only occasionally exercises its power to reject treaties and appointments. The Senate has rejected only nine judicial nominees during the past century, while approving hundreds.

More common than Senate rejection of presidential appointees is a senatorial "hold" on an appointment. By Senate tradition, any member may place an indefinite hold on the confirmation of a mid- or lower-level presidential appointment. The hold is typically used by senators trying to wring concessions from the White House on matters having nothing to do with the appointment in question. Since Bush took office in January 2001, the Democratic minority in the Senate has scrutinized judicial nominations and prevented final confirmation votes on a dozen especially conservative nominees, a matter about which the president frequently complained during the 2004 reelection campaign. Bush resubmitted these nominations to the Senate in February 2005. Not surprisingly, judicial nomination politics have loomed large during Bush's second term.

Most presidents make every effort to take potential Senate opposition into account in treaty negotiations and will frequently resort to *executive agreements* with foreign powers instead of treaties. The Supreme Court has held that such agreements are equivalent to treaties, but they do not need Senate approval.[14] In the past, presidents sometimes concluded secret agreements without informing Congress of the agreements' contents, or even their existence. American involvement in the Vietnam War grew in part out of a series of secret arrangements made between American presidents and the South Vietnamese during the 1950s and 1960s. Congress did not even learn of these agreements until 1969.

The Senate can annul treaties and reject presidential appointments of top officers. Presidents often resort to executive agreements to circumvent the Senate's right to approve or reject policy.

In 1972, Congress passed the Case Act, which requires that the president inform Congress of any executive agreement within sixty days of its having been reached. This provides Congress with the opportunity to cancel agreements that it opposes. In addition, Congress can limit the president's ability to conduct foreign policy through executive agreement by refusing to appropriate the funds needed to implement an agreement. In this way, for example, Congress can modify or even cancel executive agreements to provide American economic or military assistance to foreign governments.

[13]Carl Hulse, "Even Some in G.O.P. Call for More Oversight of Bush," *New York Times*, 31 May 2004, p. A13.

[14]*U.S. v. Pink,* 315 U.S. 203 (1942). For a good discussion of the problem, see James W. Davis, *The American Presidency* (New York: Harper & Row, 1987), Chapter 8.

Impeachment

The Constitution also grants Congress the power of *impeachment* over the president, vice president, and other executive officials. To impeach means to charge a government official (president or otherwise) with "Treason, Bribery, or other high Crimes and Misdemeanors," and bring him or her before Congress to determine guilt. Impeachment is thus like a criminal indictment in which the House of Representatives acts like a grand jury, voting (by simple majority) on whether the accused ought to be impeached. If a majority of the House votes to impeach, the impeachment trial moves to the Senate, which acts like a trial jury by voting whether to convict and forcibly remove the person from office (this vote requires a two-thirds majority of the Senate).

Controversy over Congress's impeachment power has arisen over the grounds for impeachment, especially the meaning of "high Crimes and Misdemeanors." A strict reading of the Constitution suggests that the only impeachable offense is an actual crime. But a more commonly agreed upon definition is that an impeachable offense is whatever the majority of the House of Representatives considers it to be at a particular point in time. In other words, impeachment, especially the impeachment of a president, is a political decision.

Congress has the power to impeach the president or other executive officials.

During the course of American history, only two presidents have been impeached. In 1867, President Andrew Johnson, a Southern Democrat who had battled a congressional Republican majority over Reconstruction, was impeached by the House but saved from conviction by one vote in the Senate. In 1998, President Bill Clinton was impeached by the House for perjury and obstruction of justice arising from his sexual relationship with a former White House intern, Monica Lewinsky. At the conclusion of a Senate trial in 1999, Democrats, joined by a handful of Republicans, acquitted the president of both charges.

The impeachment power is an important one. The framers of the Constitution gave Congress the power to impeach in order to guard against executive tyranny. Congress must make certain that it does not use this power as a mere weapon in partisan warfare. Used wisely, impeachment can be a safeguard against the abuse of power. Used too casually, the power to impeach can destroy the presidency and the entire constitutional system of checks and balances.

Direct Patronage

Another instrument of congressional power is direct *patronage*. Members of Congress often have an opportunity to provide direct benefits for their constituents. The most important of these opportunities for direct patronage is in legislation that has been described half-jokingly as the *"pork barrel."* This type of legislation specifies the projects or other authorizations and the location within a particular district. Many observers of Congress argue that pork-barrel bills are the only ones that some members take seriously because they boost the members' reelection prospects. Often, congressional leaders will use pork-barrel projects in exchange for votes on other matters, and other members seek immortality through pork. The Mark Hatfield Marine Science Center in Oregon was built with funds obtained by Oregon's Senator Mark Hatfield. The Mildred and Claude Pepper fountain is the centerpiece of a Miami park project that had been strongly supported by the late Representative Claude Pepper. Federal dollars secured by Pennsylvania Representative Bud Shuster helped to build the Bud Shuster Byway, a four-lane highway serving Everett, Pennsylvania. The most important rule of pork-barreling is that any member of Congress whose district receives a project as part of a bill must support all the other projects on the bill. This cuts across party and ideological lines.

> *Members of Congress use direct patronage to gain funds and other benefits for their constituents.*

A common form of pork-barreling is the "earmark," the practice through which members of Congress insert into otherwise "pork-free" public laws language that provides special benefits for their own constituents. For example, by one count, the major spending legislation passed in 2004 (which rolled eleven of the annual appropriations bills into a single giant omnibus spending bill) contained seven thousand earmarks and projects worth more than $7.5 billion for House members' districts or senators' states.[15] Highway bills are a favorite vehicle for congressional pork-barrel spending. The 2004 highway bill was full of such items, containing more than three thousand projects earmarked for specific congressional districts. Among them were such things as horse trails in Virginia, and costing $3.5 million, and a $5 million parking garage in downtown Bozeman, Montana. These measures often have little to do with transportation needs, instead serving as evidence that congressional members can bring federal dollars back home. Perhaps the most extravagant item in the 2004 bill was a bridge in Alaska designed to connect a barely populated island to the town of Ketchikan, which has a population just short of eight thousand. At a cost that could soar to $2 billion, the bridge would replace an existing five-minute ferry ride. Representative Don Young (R.) proudly claimed credit for such pork-barrel projects. At the suggestion that Alaska's senior senator, Ted Stevens (R.), chair of the Senate Appropriations Committee, might be the reason that Alaska won these projects, Young pretended to be offended, saying, "If he's the chief porker, I'm upset."[16]

Another form of direct patronage is intervening with federal administrative agencies on behalf of constituents and supporters. Members of the House and Senate spend a great deal of time on the telephone and in administrative offices seeking favorable treatment for constituents. A small but related form of patronage is getting an appointment to one of the military academies for the child of a constituent. Traditionally, these appointments are allocated one to a district.

A different form of patronage is known as the ***private bill***—a proposal to grant some kind of relief, special privilege, or exemption to the person named in the bill. The private bill is a type of legislation, but it is distinguished from a public bill, which is supposed to deal with general rules and categories of behavior, people, and institutions.

As many as 75 percent of all private bills introduced (and one-third of the ones that pass) are concerned with providing relief for foreign nationals who cannot get permanent visas to the United States because the immigration quota for their country is filled or because of something unusual about their situation. Most of the other private bills are introduced to give money to individual citizens for injuries allegedly received from a public action or for a good deed that would have otherwise gone unrewarded. About 20 percent of those bills become law.[17]

Private legislation is a congressional privilege that is often abused, but it is impossible to imagine members of Congress giving it up completely. It is one of the easiest, cheapest, and most effective forms of patronage available to each member.

DOES CONGRESS WORK?

Congress is both a representative assembly and a powerful institution of government. In assessing the effectiveness of Congress, we will focus on both its representative character and the efficiency

[15]Joseph J. Schatz, "GOP Hopeful for Quick Resolution on Spending Omnibus in New Year," *Congressional Quarterly Weekly,* 13 December 2003, p. 3080.
[16]Timothy Eagen, "Built with Steel, Perhaps, But Greased with Pork," *New York Times,* 10 April 2004, p. A1.
[17]Congressional Quarterly, *Guide to the Congress of the United States,* 2nd ed. (Washington, DC: Congressional Quarterly Press, 1976), pp. 229–310.

by which Congress is able to get things done. Congress is the most important representative institution in American government. Each member's primary responsibility is to the district, to his or her constituency, not to the congressional leadership, a party, or even Congress itself. Yet the task of representation is not a simple one. Views about what constitutes fair and effective representation differ, and constituents can make very different kinds of demands on their representatives. Members of Congress must consider these diverse views and demands as they represent their districts (see Concept Map 5.1). A representative claims to act or speak for some other person or group. But how can one person be trusted to speak for another? How do we know that those who call themselves our representatives are actually speaking on our behalf, rather than simply pursuing their own interests?

Legislators generally vary in the weight given to personal priorities and the things desired by campaign contributors and past supporters. Some see themselves as perfect agents of others; they have been elected to do the bidding of those who sent them to the legislature, and they act as **delegates.** Other legislators see themselves as being selected by their fellow citizens to do what the legislator thinks is "right," and they at as **trustees.** Most legislators are mixes of these two types.

One person might be trusted to speak for another if the two are formally bound together so that the representative is in some way accountable to those he or she purports to represent. If representatives can somehow be punished or held to account for failing to speak properly for their constituents, then we know they have an incentive to provide good representation even if their own personal backgrounds, views, and interests differ from those they represent. This principle is called **agency representation**—the sort of representation that takes place when constituents have the power to hire and fire their representatives. Frequent competitive elections constitute an important means by which constituents hold their representatives in account and keep them responsive to constituency views and preferences. Most members of Congress take this electoral check very seriously. They try to anticipate the wishes of their constituents even when they don't know exactly what those interests are, because they know that unpopular decisions can be used against them in the coming election.

Indeed, taking care of constituents explains a lot of the legislation that Congress produces. It is not too much of an exaggeration to suggest the following list of individuals whose support is necessary in order to get a measure through Congress and signed into law:

- A majority of the authorizing subcommittees in House and Senate (probably including the subcommittee chairs)
- A majority of the full authorizing committees in House and Senate (probably including committee chairs)
- A majority of the appropriations subcommittees in House and Senate (probably including the subcommittee chairs)
- A majority of the full appropriations committees in House and Senate (probably including committee chairs)
- A majority of the House Rules Committee (including its chair)
- A majority of the full House
- A majority—possibly as many as sixty votes, if needed to shut off a filibuster—of the Senate
- The speaker and majority leader in the House
- The majority leader in the Senate
- The president

This list constitutes an extraordinarily large number of public officials.

With so many hurdles to clear for a legislative initiative to become a public law, the benefits must be spread broadly. It is as though a bill must travel on a toll road past a number of tollbooths, each one containing a collector with his or her hand out for payment. Frequently, features of the bill are drafted initially or revised so as to be more inclusive, spreading the benefits widely among beneficiaries. This is the **distributive tendency.**

The distributive tendency is part of the Ameri-

CONCEPT
MAP 5.1

CONGRESSIONAL REPRESENTATION

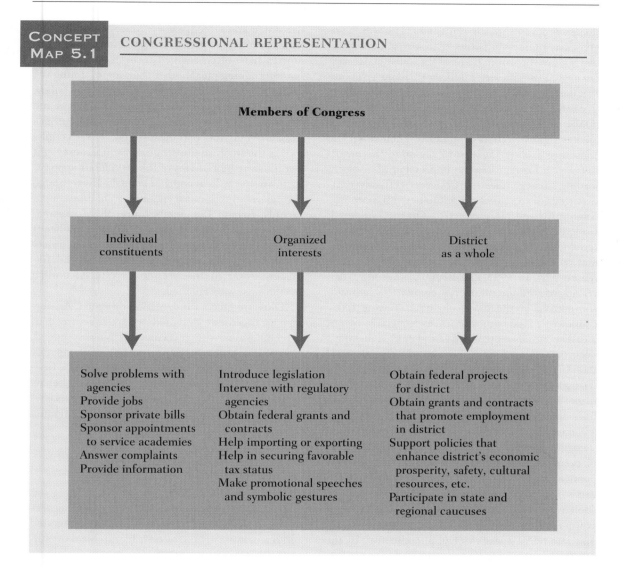

Members of Congress

Individual constituents	Organized interests	District as a whole
Solve problems with agencies Provide jobs Sponsor private bills Sponsor appointments to service academies Answer complaints Provide information	Introduce legislation Intervene with regulatory agencies Obtain federal grants and contracts Help importing or exporting Help in securing favorable tax status Make promotional speeches and symbolic gestures	Obtain federal projects for district Obtain grants and contracts that promote employment in district Support policies that enhance district's economic prosperity, safety, cultural resources, etc. Participate in state and regional caucuses

can system of representative democracy. It is as American as apple pie! Legislators, in advocating the interests of their constituents, are eager to advertise their ability to deliver for their state or district. They maneuver to put themselves in a position to claim credit for good things that happen there and to duck blame for bad things. This is the way they earn trust back home, deter strong challengers in upcoming elections, and defeat those

who run against them. This means that legislators must take advantage of every opportunity that presents itself. In some instances, as in our earlier discussion of the pork barrel, the results may seem bizarre. Nevertheless, the distributive tendency is a consequence of how Congress was designed to work.

Another consequence of Congress's design is almost the opposite of the distributive tendency:

the tendency toward the status quo. The U.S. Congress has more veto points than any other legislative body in the world. If any of the individuals listed on page 118 says no, a bill dies. Some celebrate this design. As a result, the government is unlikely to change in response to superficial fluctuations in public sentiment. Congress's design does mean greater representation of minority interests in the legislative process (at least to say no to the majority). But it also creates the impression of gridlock, leading some to question Congress's effectiveness.

Critics of Congress want it to be both more representative and more effective. On the one hand, Congress is frequently criticized for falling victim to "gridlock" and failing to reach decisions on important issues like Social Security reform. This was one reason why, in 1995, the Republican House leadership reduced the number of committees and subcommittees in the lower chamber. Having fewer committees and subcommittees generally means greater centralization of power and more expeditious decision making. On the other hand, critics demand that Congress become more representative of the changing makeup and values of the American populace. In recent years, for example, some reformers have demanded limits on the number of terms that any member of Congress can serve. Term limits are seen as a device for producing a more rapid turnover of members and, hence, a better chance for new political and social forces to be represented in Congress. The problem, however, is that while reforms such as term limits and greater internal diffusion of power may make Congress more representative, they may also make it less efficient and effective. By the same token, reforms that may make Congress better able to act, such as strong central leadership, reduction of the number of committees and subcommittees, and retention of members with seniority and experience, may make Congress less representative. This is the dilemma of congressional reform. Efficiency and representation are often competing principles in our system of government; we must be wary of gaining one at the expense of the other.

At the same time, however, the constant struggle between Congress and the president can hin-
der stable and effective governance. Over the past three decades in particular, presidents and Congresses have often seemed to be more interested in undermining one another than in promoting the larger public interest. On issues of social policy, economic policy, and foreign policy, Congress and the president have often been at each other's throats while the nation suffered. For example, during the Bush administration, Democrats fought vigorously to block many of the president's appointments to the federal court of appeals. Even though several of the judicial nominees had excellent records, Senate Democrats found them ideologically unpalatable. And even though Republicans held a slim Senate majority, Democratic procedural maneuvers, including the use of the filibuster, thwarted the president's efforts, until a compromise was reached.

Thus, we face a fundamental dilemma. A political arrangement designed to preserve freedom can undermine the government's power. Indeed, it can undermine the government's very capacity to govern. Must we always choose between freedom and power? Can we not have both? Let us turn now to the second branch of American government, the presidency, to view this dilemma from a somewhat different angle.

CHAPTER REVIEW

The legislative process must provide the order necessary for legislation to take place amid competing interests. It is dependent on a hierarchical organizational structure within Congress. Six basic dimensions of Congress affect the legislative process: (1) the parties, (2) the committees, (3) the staff, (4) the caucuses (or conferences), (5) the rules, and (6) the presidency.

Since the Constitution provides only for a presiding officer in each house, some method had to be devised for conducting business. Parties quickly assumed the responsibility for this. In the House, the majority party elects a leader every two years. This individual becomes speaker. In addition, a majority leader and a minority leader (from the minority party) and party whips are elected. Each party has a committee whose job it is to make committee assignments. Party structure in the Senate is similar, except that the vice president of the United States is the president of the Senate.

The committee system surpasses the party system in its importance in Congress. In the early nineteenth century, standing committees became a fundamental aspect of Congress. They have, for the most part, evolved to correspond to executive branch departments or programs and thus reflect and maintain the separation of powers.

The Senate has a tradition of unlimited debate, on which the various cloture rules it has passed have had little effect. Filibusters still occur. The rules of the House restrict talk and support committees; deliberation is recognized as committee business. The House Rules Committee has the power to control debate and floor amendments. The rules prescribe the formal procedure through which bills become law. Generally, the parties control scheduling and agenda, but the committees determine action on the floor. Committees, seniority, and rules all limit the ability of members to represent their constituents. Yet, these factors enable Congress to maintain its role as a major participant in government.

While party voting regularity remains strong, party discipline has declined. Still, parties do have several means of maintaining discipline: (1) Favorable committee assignments create obligations; (2) floor time in the debate on one bill can be allocated in exchange for a specific vote on another; (3) the whip system allows party leaders to assess support for a bill and convey their wishes to members; (4) party leaders can help members create large logrolling coalitions; and (5) presidents, by identifying pieces of legislation as their own, can muster support along party lines. In most cases, party leaders accept constituency obligations as a valid reason for voting against the party position.

This power of the post–New Deal presidency does not necessarily signify the decline of Congress and representative government. During the 1970s, Congress again became the "first branch" of government. During the early years of the Reagan administration, some of the congressional gains of the previous decade were diminished, but in the last two years of Reagan's second term, and in President G. W. Bush's term, Congress reasserted its role. At the start of the Clinton administration, congressional leaders promised to cooperate with the White House rather than confront it. But only two years later, confrontation was once again the order of the day.

KEY TERMS

agency representation   The type of representation by which representatives are held accountable to their constituents if they fail to represent them properly.

appropriations   The amounts of money approved by Congress in statutes (bills) that each unit or agency of government can spend.

bicameralism   Division of a legislative body into two houses, chambers, or branches.

caucus (congressional)   An association of members of Congress based on party, interest, or social group such as gender or race.

closed rule   Provision by the House Rules Committee limiting or prohibiting the introduction of amendments during debate.

cloture   Rule allowing a majority, two-thirds, or three-fifths of the members in a legislative body to set a time limit on debate over a given bill.

conference committee   A joint committee created to work out a compromise on House and Senate versions of a piece of legislation.

constituency   Members of the district from which an official is elected.

delegate   A representative who votes according to the preferences of his or her constituency.

distributive tendency   The tendency of Congress to spread the benefits of a bill over a wide range of members' districts.

executive agreement   Agreement between the president and another country, which has the force of a treaty but does not require the Senate's "advice and consent."

filibuster   A tactic used by members of the Senate to prevent action on legislation they oppose by continuously holding the floor and speaking until the majority backs down. Once given the floor, senators have unlimited time to speak, and it requires a vote of three-fifths of the Senate to end the filibuster.

impeachment   To charge a governmental official (president or otherwise) with "Treason, Bribery, or other high Crimes and Misdemeanors" and bring him or her before Congress to determine guilt.

logrolling   A legislative practice wherein reciprocal agreements are made between legislators, usually in voting for or against a bill. In contrast to bargaining, parties to logrolling have nothing in common but their desire to exchange support.

majority leader   The elected leader of the party holding a majority of the seats in the House of Representatives or in the Senate. In the House, the majority leader is subordinate in the party hierarchy to the speaker.

minority leader   The elected leader of the party holding less than a majority of the seats in the House or Senate.

open rule   Provision by the House Rules Committee that permits floor debate and the addition of amendments to a bill.

oversight   The effort by Congress, through hearings, investigations, and other techniques, to exercise control over the activities of executive agencies.

party vote   A roll-call vote in the House or Senate in which at least 50 percent of the members of one party take a particular position and are opposed by at least 50 percent of the members of the other party. Party votes are rare today, although they were fairly common in the nineteenth century.

patronage   The resources available to higher officials, usually opportunities to make partisan appointments to offices and to confer grants, licenses, or special favors to supporters.

pocket veto   A presidential veto of legislation wherein the president takes no formal action on a bill. If Congress adjourns within ten days of passing a bill, and the president does not sign it, the bill is considered to be vetoed.

pork barrel   Appropriations made by legislative bodies for local projects that are often not needed but that are created so that local representatives can win reelection in their home district.

private bill   A proposal in Congress to provide a specific person with some kind of relief, such as a special exemption from immigration quotas.

roll-call vote   A vote in which each legislator's yes or no vote is recorded as the clerk calls the names of the members alphabetically.

seniority   Priority or status ranking given to an individual on the basis of length of continuous service in a committee in Congress.

speaker of the House   The chief presiding officer of the House of Representatives. The speaker is elected at the beginning of every Congress on a straight party vote. The speaker is the most important party and House leader, and can influence the legislative agenda, the fate of individual pieces of legislation, and members' positions within the House.

standing committee   A permanent committee with the power to propose and write legislation that covers a particular subject such as finance or appropriations.

trustee   A representative who votes based on what he or she thinks is best for his or her constituency.

veto   The president's constitutional power to turn down acts of Congress. A presidential veto may be overridden by a two-thirds vote of each house of Congress.

whip system   Primarily a communications network in each house of Congress, whips take polls of the membership in order to learn their intentions on specific legislative issues and to assist the majority and minority leaders in various tasks.

FOR FURTHER READING

Arnold, R. Douglas. *The Logic of Congressional Action.* New Haven: Yale University Press, 1990.

Baker, Ross K. *House and Senate,* 2nd ed. New York: Norton, 1995.

Davidson, Roger, ed. *The Postreform Congress.* New York: St. Martin's Press, 1991.

Dodd, Lawrence, and Bruce I. Oppenheimer, eds. *Congress Reconsidered,* 5th ed. Washington, DC: Congressional Quarterly Press, 1993.

Fenno, Richard. *Congressmen in Committees.* Boston: Little, Brown, 1973.

Fenno, Richard. *Home Style: House Members in Their Districts.* Boston: Little, Brown, 1978.

Fiorina, Morris. *Congress: Keystone of the Washington Establishment,* 2nd ed. New Haven: Yale University Press, 1989.

Fisher, Louis. *The Politics of Shared Power: Congress and the Executive,* 3rd ed. Washington, DC: Congressional Quarterly Press, 1993.

Fowler, Linda, and Robert McClure. *Political Ambition: Who Decides to Run for Congress?* New Haven: Yale University Press, 1989.

Mayhew, David R. *Congress: The Electoral Connection.* New Haven: Yale University Press, 1974.

Oleszek, Walter J. *Congressional Procedures and the Policy Process,* 3rd ed. Washington, DC: Congressional Quarterly Press, 1989.

Rieselbach, Leroy. *Congressional Reform.* Washington, DC: Congressional Quarterly Press, 1986.

Sinclair, Barbara. *The Transformation of the U.S. Senate.* Baltimore: Johns Hopkins University Press, 1989.

Smith, Steven S., and Christopher Deering. *Committees in Congress,* 2nd ed. Washington, DC: Congressional Quarterly Press, 1990.

Sundquist, James L. *The Decline and Resurgence of Congress.* Washington, DC: Brookings Institution, 1981.

CHAPTER 6

The President

HOW DOES THE PRESIDENCY WORK?

*P*resident Bill Clinton didn't have much going for him, it seemed, when the U.S. Senate failed to remove him from office at the conclusion of his impeachment trial in early 1999. As only the second president in history to be put on trial for impeachable offenses (the first was the hapless Andrew Johnson in 1868), Clinton avoided defeat at the hands of his opponents when the Senate failed to muster the necessary two-thirds vote to remove him from office. Still, how could he hope to govern in the final two years of his presidency when more Americans blamed Clinton for the impeachment mess than blamed his opponents in Congress,[1] when Clinton's personal reputation was caked with mud following his admission of having had an affair with White House intern Monica Lewinsky (after having denied the affair for months), and when the Republicans in Congress who tried to remove him from office were still furious at the Democratic president?

To the surprise of many, Clinton wasted no time getting back to work. Within days of the impeachment vote, Clinton had proposed moving ahead on such domestic policy ideas as raising pay for the

[1]Richard Morin and Claudia Deane, "Public Blames Clinton, Gives Record Support," *Washington Post,* 15 February 1999, p. A1.

CORE OF THE ANALYSIS

- Since the 1930s, the presidency has been the dominant branch of American government.

- Most of the real power of the modern presidency comes from the powers granted by the Constitution and the laws made by Congress. Mass public opinion, however, is the president's most potent resource of power.

- Both the president and Congress attempt to make the bureaucracy accountable to the people—the president through management control, Congress through legislative oversight.

military, fixing the Y2K computer problem, providing financial security for the Medicare and Social Security programs, allowing the states flexibility in their education policy, and developing an antimissile system. In foreign policy, Clinton engaged the United States in a full-scale daily air war over Iraq, followed shortly thereafter by a large-scale military intervention in Kosovo (the former Yugoslavia). Even more surprising than Clinton's flurry of activity was Congress's response: House and Senate Republican leaders said they were anx-

- **The Constitutional Basis of the Presidency**

  What conflicting views over presidential power did the framers of the Constitution have?

  What powers does the Constitution provide to the president as head of state? Have presidents used these powers to make the presidency too powerful or even imperial?

  What powers does the Constitution provide to the president as head of government?

- **The Rise of Presidential Government**

  What factors led to the growth of a more powerful presidency?

- **Presidential Government**

  What formal resources does the president use to manage the executive branch? On which of these resources have presidents increasingly relied?

  What informal resources can the president draw on in exercising the powers of the presidency? Which of these resources is a potential liability? Why?

ious to "pick up the pieces" and "move forward on the people's business."[2]

What is most important about Congress's response is this: The modern American government cannot operate without the active involvement of the president. Even though the Constitution's founders created a system in which Congress was to be the first and most important branch (as we discussed in the last chapter), the political relationship between Congress and the presidency has changed dramatically since the start of the twentieth century, such that the presidency is viewed by most as the center of the national government. That is, we have witnessed the rise of the modern strong presidency. Even though congressional leaders opposed Clinton, they knew that they could not govern without active presidential involvement.

For his part, Clinton realized that the stigma of impeachment would forever tar his presidency, but that the power of his office still gave him the opportunity to move ahead with the business of the country. Indeed, the fact that Clinton continued to govern effectively during and after the impeachment ordeal helps explain why Clinton's job approval rat-

ing stood at an impressive 68 percent at the end of the impeachment trial—8 percentage points *higher* than Clinton's approval rating when the impeachment began![3] This underscores the critical link between presidential power and citizen support.

The modern presidency is indeed a powerful office. But the Clinton example reveals two other facts about the presidency. First, what we expect of presidents is almost always greater than what they can deliver. In Clinton's case, for example, he continued to have little success to the end of his presidency in getting Congress to set aside money to cover the rising costs of Medicare and Social Security, or to pass new, tougher gun laws. And second, not all presidents are equally skilled at using the powers of their office. Even Clinton's opponents agreed that he was one of the most skilled politicians ever to occupy the White House. A less skillful president might not have been able to avoid removal from office, or may have been unable to pick up the pieces after the impeachment effort failed.

In short, (1) the modern strong presidency is a powerful office, but (2) most Americans expect more than any president can deliver, and (3) the most successful presidents are those who know how best to exploit the formal and informal powers available to them. In this chapter, we will see

[2]Eric Pianin, "Clinton, Hill GOP Turn to Agendas," *Washington Post,* 14 February 1999, p. A24; Robert J. Spitzer, "Clinton's Impeachment Will Have Few Consequences for the Presidency," *PS: Political Science and Politics* 32 (September 999): 541–45.

[3]Morin and Deane, "Public Blames Clinton."

how these themes fit together. We begin with the Constitution.

THE CONSTITUTIONAL BASIS OF THE PRESIDENCY

The presidency was established by Article II of the Constitution. Article II begins by asserting, "The executive power shall be vested in a President of the United States of America." It goes on to describe the manner in which the president is to be chosen and defines the basic powers of the presidency. By vesting the executive power in a single president, the framers were emphatically rejecting proposals for various forms of collective leadership. Some delegates to the Constitutional Convention had argued in favor of a multiheaded executive or an "executive council" in order to avoid undue concentration of power in the hands of one individual. Most of the framers, however, were anxious to provide for "energy" in the executive. They hoped to have a president capable of taking quick and aggressive action. They believed that a powerful executive would help to protect the nation's interests vis-à-vis other nations and promote the federal government's interests relative to the states.

Immediately following the first sentence of Section 1, Article II, defines the manner in which the president is to be chosen. This is a very odd sequence, but it does say something about the struggle the delegates were having over how to give power to the executive and at the same time to balance that power with limitations. The struggle was between those delegates who wanted the president to be selected by Congress, and thus responsible to it, and those delegates who preferred that the president be elected directly by the people. Direct popular elections would create a more independent and more powerful presidency. The framers finally agreed on a scheme of indirect election through an *electoral college* in which the electors would be selected by the state legislatures (and close elections would be resolved in the House of Representatives). In this way, the framers hoped to achieve a "republican" solution: a strong president who would be responsible to state and national legislators rather than directly to the electorate.

The Constitution intended the presidency to be both an office of expressed powers and powers delegated by acts of Congress.

THE CONSTITUTIONAL POWERS OF THE PRESIDENCY

While Section 1 of Article II explains how the president is to be chosen. Sections 2 and 3 outline the powers and duties of the president. These two sections identify two sources of presidential power. Some presidential powers are specifically established by the language of the Constitution. For example, the president is authorized to make treaties, grant pardons, and nominate judges and other public officials. These specifically defined powers are called the *expressed powers* of the office and cannot be revoked by the Congress or any other agency without an amendment to the Constitution. Other expressed powers include the power to receive ambassadors and command of the military forces of the United States.

In addition to establishing the president's expressed powers, Article II declares that the president "shall take Care that the Laws be faithfully executed." Since the laws are enacted by Congress, this language implies that Congress is to delegate to the president the power to implement or execute its will. Powers given to the president by Congress are called *delegated powers.* In principle, Congress delegates to the president only the power to identify or develop the means to carry out Congressional decisions. So, for example, if Congress determines that air quality should be improved, it might delegate to the executive branch the power to determine the best means of improvement as well as the power to actually implement the cleanup process. In practice, of course, decisions about how to clean the air are likely to have an enormous impact on businesses, organizations, and individuals throughout the nation. As it delegates power to the executive, Congress substantially enhances the importance of the presidency and the executive branch. In most cases, Congress delegates power to executive agencies rather than to the president. As we shall see, however, contemporary presidents have found ways to capture a good deal of this delegated power for themselves.

Presidents have claimed a third source of power beyond expressed and delegated powers. These are powers not specified in the Constitution or the law but said to stem from "the rights, duties and obligations of the presidency."[4] They are referred to as the *inherent powers* of the presidency and are most often asserted by presidents in times of war or national emergency. For example, after the fall of Fort Sumter and the outbreak of the Civil War, President Abraham Lincoln issued a series of executive orders for which he had no clear legal basis. Without even calling Congress into session, Lincoln combined the state militias into a ninety-day national volunteer force, called for forty thousand new volunteers, enlarged the regular army and navy, diverted $2 million in unspent appropriations to military needs, instituted censorship of the U.S. mails, ordered a blockade of Southern ports, suspended the writ of *habeas corpus* in the border states, and ordered the arrest by military police of individuals whom he deemed to be guilty of engaging in or even contemplating treasonous actions.[5] Lincoln asserted that these extraordinary measures were justified by the president's inherent power to protect the nation.[6] Subsequent presidents, including Franklin D. Roosevelt and George W. Bush, have had similar views.

Expressed Powers

The president's expressed powers, as defined by Sections 2 and 3 of Article II, fall into several categories:

1. *Military.* Article II, Section 2, provides for the power as "Commander in Chief of the Army and Navy of the United States, and of the Militia of the several States, when called in to the actual Service of the United States."
2. *Judicial.* Article II, Section 2, also provides the power to "grant Reprieves and Pardons for Offenses against the United States, except in Cases of Impeachment."
3. *Diplomatic.* Article II, Section 3, provides the power to "receive Ambassadors and other public Ministers."
4. *Executive.* Article II, Section 3, authorizes the president to see to it that all the laws are faithfully executed; Section 2 gives the chief executive the power to appoint, remove, and supervise all executive officers and to appoint all federal judges.
5. *Legislative.* Article I, Section 7, and Article II, Section 3, give the president the power to participate authoritatively in the legislative process.

MILITARY   The president's military powers are among the most important that the chief executive exercises. The position of *commander in chief* makes the president the highest military officer in the United States, with control of the entire military establishment. The president is also the head of the nation's intelligence hierarchy, which includes not only the Central Intelligence Agency (CIA) but also the National Security Council (NSC), the National Security Agency (NSA), the Federal Bureau of Investigation (FBI), and a host of less well-known but very powerful international and domestic security agencies.

The president is commander in chief of all military forces of the United States.

---

[4]*In re Neagle,* 135 U.S. 1 (1890).
[5]James G. Randall, *Constitutional Problems under Lincoln* (New York: Appleton, 1926), Chapter 1.
[6]Edward S. Corwin, *The President: Office and Powers,* 4th rev. ed. (New York: New York University Press, 1957), p. 229.

WAR AND INHERENT PRESIDENTIAL POWER The Constitution, of course, gives Congress the power to declare war. Presidents, however, have gone a long way toward capturing this power for themselves. Congress has not declared war since December 1941, and yet, since then American military forces have engaged in numerous campaigns throughout the world under the orders of the president. When North Korean forces invaded South Korea in June 1950, Congress was actually prepared to declare war but President Harry S. Truman decided not to ask for congressional action. Instead, Truman asserted the principle that the president and not Congress could decide when and where to deploy America's military might. He dispatched American forces to Korea without a congressional declaration, and in the face of the emergency, Congress felt it had to acquiesce. It passed a resolution approving the president's actions, and this became the pattern for future congressional-executive relations in the military realm. The wars in Vietnam, Bosnia, Afghanistan, and Iraq, as well as a host of smaller scale conflicts, were all fought without declarations of war.

In 1973, Congress responded to presidential unilateralism by passing the *War Powers Resolution* over President Nixon's veto. This resolution reasserted the principle of congressional war power, required the president to inform Congress of any planned military campaign, and stipulated that forces must be withdrawn within sixty days in the absence of a specific congressional authorization for their continued deployment. Presidents, however, have generally ignored the War Powers Resolution, claiming inherent executive power to defend the nation. Thus, for example, in 1989, President George H. W. Bush ordered an invasion of Panama without consulting Congress. In 1990 the same President Bush received congressional authorization to attack Iraq but had already made it clear that he was prepared to go to war with or without congressional assent. President Clinton ordered a massive bombing campaign against Serbian forces in the former nation of Yugoslavia without congressional authorization. And, of course, President George W. Bush responded to the 2001 attacks by Islamic terrorists by organizing a major military campaign to overthrow the Taliban regime in Afghanistan, which had sheltered the ter-

rorists. In 2002, Bush ordered a major American campaign against Iraq, which he accused of posing a threat to the United States. U.S. forces overthrew the government of Iraqi dictator Saddam Hussein and occupied the country. In both instances, Congress passed resolutions approving the president's actions, but the president was careful to assert that he did not need congressional authorization. The War Powers Resolution was barely mentioned on Capital Hill and was ignored by the White House.

MILITARY SOURCES OF DOMESTIC POWER The president's military powers extend into the domestic sphere although Article IV, Section 4, provides that the "United States shall [protect] . . . every State . . . against Invasion . . . and . . . domestic Violence," Congress has made this an explicit presidential power through statutes directing the president as commander in chief to discharge these obligations.[7] The Constitution restrains the president's use of domestic force by providing that a state legislature (or governor when the legislature is not in session) must request federal troops before the president can send them into the state to provide public order. Yet, this proviso is not absolute. First, presidents are not obligated to deploy national troops merely because the state legislature or governor makes such a request. And more important, presidents may deploy troops in a state or city without a specific request if they consider it necessary to maintain an essential national service, to enforce a federal judicial order, or to protect federally guaranteed civil rights.

The president may deploy federal troops at the request of a state legislature or when it is necessary to keep order or to enforce a law or court order.

A famous example of the unilateral use of presidential power to protect the states against domestic disorder occurred in 1957 under President

---

[7]These statutes are contained mainly in Title 10 of the United States Code, Sections 331, 332, and 333.

Eisenhower. He decided to send troops into Little Rock, Arkansas, against the wishes of the state of Arkansas, to enforce court orders to integrate Little Rock's Central High School. Arkansas Governor Orval Faubus had actually posted the Arkansas National Guard at the entrance of the school to prevent the court-ordered admission of nine black students. After an effort to negotiate with Governor Faubus failed, President Eisenhower reluctantly sent a thousand paratroopers to Little Rock, who stood watch while the black students took their places in the all-white classrooms. This case makes quite clear that the president does not have to wait for a request by a state legislature or governor before acting as domestic commander in chief.[8] However, in most instances of domestic disorder—whether from human or from natural causes—presidents tend to exercise unilateral power justified by declaring a "state of emergency," thereby making available federal grants, insurance, and direct assistance as well as troops. In 1992, in the aftermath of the riots in Los Angeles and the devastating storms in Florida, American troops were very much in evidence, sent in by the president, but in the role more of Good Samaritan than of military police. Such was also the case after the devastation of 9/11 and, more recently, after hurricanes Katrina and Rita struck the Gulf Coast in the Fall of 2005. President Bush declared a state of emergency, using both state militias and federal troops for rescue operations, the prevention of looting and violence, and the delivery of medical, health, and food services. The Coast Guard and the Army Corps of Engineers were especially evident. The Federal Emergency Management Agency coordinated many of these services.

Military emergencies have typically also led to expansion of the domestic powers of the executive branch. This was true during the First and Second World Wars and has been true in the wake of the "war on terrorism" as well. Within a month of the 9/11 attacks, the White House had drafted and Congress had enacted the USA Patriot Act, expanding the power of government agencies to engage in domestic surveillance activities, including electronic surveillance, and restricting judicial review of such efforts. The act also gave the attorney general greater authority to detain and deport aliens suspected of having terrorist affiliations. The following year, Congress created the Department of Homeland Security, combining offices from twenty-two federal agencies into one huge new cabinet department that would be responsible for protecting the nation from attack. The new agency, with a tentative budget of $40 billion, was to include the Coast Guard, Transportation Safety Administration, Federal Emergency Management Administration, Immigration and Naturalization Service, and offices from the departments of Agriculture, Energy, Transportation, Justice, Health and Human Services, Commerce, and the General Services Administration. The White House drafted the actual reorganization plan, but Congress weighed in to make certain that the new agency's workers had civil service and union protections.

JUDICIAL   The presidential power to grant reprieves, pardons, and amnesties involves the power of life and death over all individuals who may be a threat to the security of the United States. Presidents may use this power on behalf of a particular individual, as did Gerald Ford when he pardoned Richard Nixon in 1974 "for all offenses against the United States which he . . . has committed or may have committed." Or they may use it on a large scale, as did President Andrew Johnson in 1868, when he gave full amnesty to all Southerners who had participated in the "Late Rebellion," and President Carter in 1977, when he declared an amnesty for all the draft evaders of the Vietnam War. President Bush used this power before his retirement in mid-December 1992, when he pardoned former Secretary of Defense Caspar Weinberger and five other participants in the Iran-Contra affair. This power of life and death over others has helped elevate the president to the level of earlier conquerors and kings by establishing the president as the person before whom supplicants might come to make their pleas for mercy.

The president may pardon those who have violated federal laws.

[8]The best study covering all aspects of the domestic use of the military is that of Adam Yarmolinsky, *The Military Establishment* (New York: Harper & Row, 1971).

DIPLOMATIC   The president is America's "head of state"—its chief representative in dealings with other nations. As head of state, the president has the power to make treaties for the United States (with the advice and consent of the Senate). When President George Washington received Edmond Genêt ("Citizen Genêt") as the formal emissary of the revolutionary government of France in 1793, he transformed the power to "receive Ambassadors and other public Ministers" into the power to "recognize" other countries. That power gives the president the almost unconditional authority to review the claims of any new ruling groups to determine whether they indeed control the territory and population of their country, so that they can commit it to treaties and other agreements.

The president has the power to recognize foreign nations and ambassadors from those countries.

In recent years, presidents have expanded the practice of using executive agreements to conduct foreign policy. An *executive agreement* is like a treaty because it is a contract between two countries, but an executive agreement does not require a two-thirds vote of approval by the Senate. Ordinarily, executive agreements are used to carry out commitments already made in treaties, or to arrange for matters well below the level of policy. But when presidents have found it expedient to use an executive agreement in place of a treaty, Congress has typically acquiesced.

EXECUTIVE POWER   The most important basis of the president's power as chief executive is to be found in the sections of Article II, which stipulate that the president must see that all the laws are faithfully executed and which provide that the president will appoint all executive officers and all federal judges. In this manner, the Constitution focuses executive power and legal responsibility upon the president. The famous sign on President Truman's desk, "The buck stops here," was not merely an assertion of Truman's personal sense of responsibility. It acknowledged his acceptance of the constitutional

imposition of that responsibility upon the president. The president is subject to some limitations, because the appointment of all the top officers, including ambassadors and ministers and federal judges, is subject to a majority approval by the Senate. But these appointments are at the discretion of the president. Although the Constitution is silent on the power of the president to remove such officers, the federal courts have filled this silence with a series of decisions that grant the president this power.[9]

The executive power of the president requires that he make sure all laws are faithfully executed and that he appoint all executive officers and federal judges.

Another component of the president's power as chief executive is *executive privilege,* which is the claim that confidential communications between a president and close advisers should not be revealed without the consent of the president. Presidents have made this claim ever since George Washington refused a request from the House of Representatives to deliver documents concerning negotiations of an important treaty. Washington refused (successfully) on the grounds that, first, the House was not constitutionally part of the treaty-making process, and, second, that diplomatic negotiations required secrecy.

Executive privilege became a popular part of the "checks and balances" counterpart between president and Congress, and presidents have usually had the upper hand when invoking it. The expansion of executive privilege into a claim of "uncontrolled discretion" to refuse Congress's request for information came when President Nixon was beginning to get into political trouble over the Vietnam War in

---

[9]*Myers, v. U.S.,* 272 U.S. 52 (1926); modified by *Humphrey's Executor v. U.S.,* 295 U.S. 602 (1935), *Wiener v. U.S.,* 357 U.S. 349 (1958), *Bowsher v. Synar,* 478 U.S. 714 (1986), and *Morrison v. Olson,* 108 S. Ct. 2597 (1988). See also Michael Nelson, ed., "The Removal Power," in *Congressional Quarterly's Guide to the Presidency* (Washington, DC: Congressional Quarterly Press, 1989), pp. 414–15.

1971.[10] During the investigation of the Watergate break-in, it was President Nixon's claim to an almost absolute immunity to congressional inquiry that led to a Supreme Court rejection of the doctrine as a constitutional feature of the presidency in *United States v. Nixon* (418 U.S. 683, 1974). Although succeeding presidents continued to invoke the doctrine, they usually did so when they had something to hide that was of questionable legality (Iran-Contra) or potentially scandalous (Clinton's various scrapes). The exercise of presidential power through the executive-privilege doctrine has been all the more frequent in the past twenty years, when we lived nearly 90 percent of the time under conditions of divided government, where the party not in control of the White House controlled one or both of the chambers of Congress.

THE PRESIDENT'S LEGISLATIVE POWER   The president plays a role not only in the administration of government but also in the legislative process. Two constitutional provisions are the primary sources of the president's power in the legislative arena. Article II, Section 3, provides that the president "shall from time to time give to the Congress Information of the State of the Union, and recommend to their Consideration such Measures as he shall judge necessary and expedient." The second of the president's legislative powers is the "veto power" assigned by Article I, Section 7.[11]

[10]Raoul Berger, *Executive Privilege: A Constitutional Myth* (Cambridge, Mass.: Harvard University Press, 1974), pp. 1–14.

[11]There is a third source of presidential power implied from the provision for "faithful execution of the laws." This is the president's power to impound funds—that is, to refuse to spend money Congress has appropriated for certain purposes. One author referred to this as a "retroactive veto power" (Robert E. Goosetree, "The Power of the President to Impound Appropriated Funds," *American University Law Review*, January 1962). Many modern presidents have used this impoundment power freely and quite effectively, and Congress occasionally delegated such power to the president by statute. But in reaction to the Watergate scandal, Congress adopted the Budget and Impoundment Control Act of 1974, designed to circumscribe the president's ability to impound funds and requiring that the president must spend all appropriated funds unless both houses of Congress consent to an impoundment within forty-five days of a presidential request. Therefore, since 1974, the use of impoundment has declined significantly. Presidents have either had to bite their tongues and accept unwanted appropriations or had to revert to the older and more dependable but politically limited method of vetoing the entire bill.

The first of these powers has been important only since Franklin Delano Roosevelt began to use the provision to initiate proposals for legislative action in Congress. Roosevelt established the presidency as the primary initiator of legislation.

The *veto* power is the president's constitutional power to turn down acts of Congress. This power alone makes the president the most important single legislative leader. No bill vetoed by the president can become law unless both the House and the Senate override the veto by a two-thirds vote. In the case of a *pocket veto,* Congress does not even have the option of overriding the veto, but must reintroduce the bill in the next session. The president may exercise a pocket veto when presented with a bill during the last ten days of a legislative session. Usually, if a president does not sign a bill within ten days, it automatically becomes law. But this is true only while Congress is in session. If a president chooses not to sign a bill within the last ten days that Congress is in session, then the ten-day limit does not expire until Congress is out of session, and instead of becoming law, the bill is vetoed. Process Box. 6.1 illustrates the president's veto option. In 1996, a new power was added— the *line-item veto*—giving the president power to strike specific spending items from appropriations bills passed by Congress, unless reenacted by a two-thirds vote of both the House and Senate. In 1997, President Clinton used this power eleven times to strike eighty-two items from the federal budget. But, as we saw in Chapter 5, in 1998 the Supreme Court ruled that the Constitution does not authorize the line-item veto power. Only a constitutional amendment would restore this power to the president.

The president's legislative power consists of the obligation to recommend policies for Congress's consideration and the power to veto legislation.

The president's initiative does not end with policy making involving Congress and the making of laws in the ordinary sense of the phrase. The president has still another legislative role (in all but name) within the executive branch. This is designated as the power to issue *executive orders*. The executive order is first and foremost simply a management tool, a power possessed by virtually any CEO to make "company policy"—rules setting procedures, etiquette, chains of command, functional responsibilities, and so on. But evolving out of this normal management practice is a recognized presidential power to promulgate rules that have the effect and the formal status of legislation. Most of the executive orders of the president provide for the reorganization of structures and procedures or otherwise direct the affairs of the executive branch—either to be applied across the board to all agencies or applied in some important respect to a single agency or department. One of the most important examples is Executive Order No. 8248, September 8, 1939, establishing the divisions of the Executive Office of the President. Another one of equal importance is President Nixon's executive order establishing the Environmental Protection Agency in 1970–71, which included establishment of the Environmental Impact Statement. President Reagan's Executive Order No. 12291 of 1981 was responsible for a regulatory reform process that brought about more genuine deregulation in the past twenty years than was accomplished by any acts of congressional legislation. President Clinton's important policy toward gays and gay rights in the military took the form of an executive order referred to as "Don't ask, don't tell."

This legislative or policy leadership role of the presidency is an institutionalized feature of the office that exists independent of the occupant of the office. That is to say, anyone duly elected president would possess these powers regardless of his or her individual energy or leadership characteristics.[12]

THE RISE OF PRESIDENTIAL GOVERNMENT

Most of the real influence of the modern presidency derives from the powers granted by the Constitution and the laws made by Congress. Thus, any person properly elected and sworn in as president will possess all of the power held by the strongest presidents in American history. That is true regardless of how large or small a margin of victory a president has. *The popular base of the presidency is important less because it gives the president power than because it gives him consent to use all the powers already granted by the Constitution.* Anyone installed in the office could exercise most of its powers.

But what variables account for a president's success in exercising these powers? Why are some presidents considered to be great successes and others colossal failures? This relates broadly to the very concept of presidential power. Is it a reflection of the attributes of the person or is it more characteristic of the political situations that a president encounters? The personal view of presidential power dominated political scientists' view for several decades,[13] but recent scholars have argued that presidential power should be analyzed in terms of the strategic interactions that a president has with other political actors. The veto, which we reviewed in the last section, is one example of this sort of strategic interaction, but there are many other "games" that presidents play: the Supreme-Court-nomination and treaty-ratification games with the Senate, the executive-order game, the agency-supervision-and-management game with the executive branch. As the political scientist Charles M. Cameron has argued, *"Understanding the presidency means understanding these games."*[14] Success in these "games" translates into presidential power.

We must not forget, however, the tremendous

---

[12]Andrew Taylor, "Clinton Gives Republicans a Gentler Year-End Beating," *Congressional Quarterly Weekly* 13 November 1999, pp. 2698–2700.

[13]Richard Neustadt, *Presidential Power: The Politics of Leadership* (New York: Wiley, 1960).

[14]Charles M. Cameron, "Bargaining and Presidential Power," in Robert Y. Shapiro, Martha Joynt Kumar, and Lawrence R. Jacobs, eds., *Presidential Power: Forging the Presidency for the Twenty-first Century* (New York: Columbia University Press, 2000), p. 47. (Emphasis in original.)

PROCESS
BOX 6.1

THE VETO: HOW A BILL IS BORN, DIES, IS REBORN, AND
BECOMES LAW (OR DOESN'T)

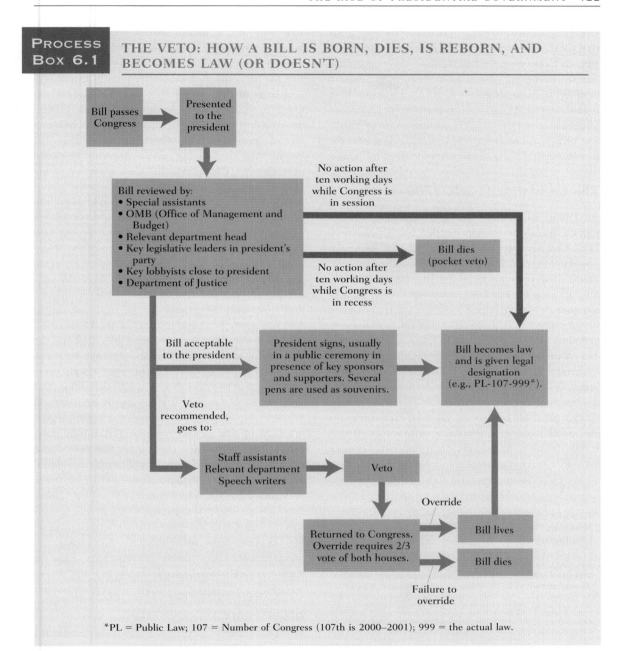

Bill passes Congress → Presented to the president

Bill reviewed by:
• Special assistants
• OMB (Office of Management and Budget)
• Relevant department head
• Key legislative leaders in president's party
• Key lobbyists close to president
• Department of Justice

No action after ten working days while Congress is in session

No action after ten working days while Congress is in recess

Bill dies (pocket veto)

Bill acceptable to the president

President signs, usually in a public ceremony in presence of key sponsors and supporters. Several pens are used as souvenirs.

Bill becomes law and is given legal designation (e.g., PL-107-999*).

Veto recommended, goes to:

Staff assistants
Relevant department
Speech writers

Veto

Override

Returned to Congress. Override requires 2/3 vote of both houses.

Bill lives

Bill dies

Failure to override

*PL = Public Law; 107 = Number of Congress (107th is 2000–2001); 999 = the actual law.

resources that a president can rely on in his strategic interactions with others. Remember that the presidency is a democratic institution with a national constituency. Its broad popular base is a presidential resource that can be deployed strategically in the various bargaining games just discussed; a president's success depends on the qualities of the person in office and the situations that arise. For example, political scientist Samuel Kernell suggests that presidents may rally public opinion and put pressure on Congress by "going public."[15] With the occasional exception, however, it took more than a century, perhaps as much as a century and a half, before presidents came to be seen as consequential players in these strategic encounters. A bit of historical review will be helpful in understanding how the presidency has risen to its current level of influence.

The Legislative Epoch, 1800–1933

In 1885, an obscure political science professor named Woodrow Wilson entitled his general textbook *Congressional Government* because American government was just that, "congressional government." The clear intent of the framers of the Constitution was for *legislative supremacy*. As we saw in Chapter 3, the strongest evidence of this original intent is the fact that the powers of the national government were listed in Article I, the legislative article. Madison had laid it out explicitly in *The Federalist*, No. 51: "In republican government, the legislative authority necessarily predominates."[16]

The first decade of America's government was unique precisely because it was first; everything was precedent making, and nothing was secure. It was a state-building decade in which relations between president and Congress were more cooperative than they would be at any time thereafter. Before the Republic was a decade old, Congress began to develop a strong organization, including its own elected leadership, the first standing committees, and the party hierarchies. Consequently, by the second term of President Jefferson (1805–1809), the executive branch was beginning to play the secondary role anticipated by the Constitution. The quality of presidential performance and then of presidential personality and character declined accordingly. The president was seen by some observers as little more than America's "chief clerk." Of President James Madison, who had been the principal author of the Constitution, it was said that he knew everything about government except how to govern. Indeed, after Jefferson and until the beginning of the twentieth century, most historians agree that Presidents Jackson and Lincoln were the only exceptions to what was the rule of weak presidents; and those two exceptions can be explained, since one was a war hero and founder of the Democratic Party and the other was a wartime president and the first leader of the newly founded Republican Party.

One reason that so few great men became presidents in the nineteenth century is that there was only occasional room for greatness in such a weak office.[17] As Chapter 3 indicated, the national government of that period was not particularly powerful. Another reason is that during this period, the presidency was not closely linked to major national political and social forces. Federalism had taken very good care of this by fragmenting political interests and diverting the energies of interest groups toward state and local governments, where most key decisions were being made.

> During the nineteenth century, Congress dominated the national government.

---

[15]Samuel Kernell, *Going Public: New Strategies of Presidential Leadership*, 3rd ed. (Washington, DC: Congressional Quarterly Press, 1998).

[16]The Library of Congress believes that *Federalist* No. 51 could have been written by Hamilton or by Madison, and it is true that the authorship of certain of the *Federalist Papers* is still in dispute. But we insist on Madison's authorship of *Federalist* No. 51 for two important reasons: First, the style of the essay and the political theory underlying the essay are, to us, clearly Madisonian. Second, Madison's authorship of *Federalist* No. 51 seems to be the consensus among academic political scientists and historians, and we find our strongest support in three of the most esteemed and admirable students of the Founding: historian Forrest McDonald, *Novus Ordo Seclorum—The Intellectual Origins of the Constitution* (Lawrence, KS: University Press of Kansas, 1985), p. 258; political theorist Isaac Kramnick in his edition of *The Federalist Papers* (New York: Viking Penguin, 1987), Editor's Introduction, especially p. 53; and the late Clinton Rossiter, *The Federalist Papers* (New York: New American Library, 1961), pp. xiii–xiv.

[17]For related appraisals, see Jeffrey Tulis, *The Rhetorical Presidency* (Princeton: Princeton University Press, 1988); Stephen Skowronek, *The Politics Presidents Make: Presidential Leadership from John Adams to George Bush* (Cambridge: Harvard University Press, 1993); and Robert Spitzer, *President and Congress: Executive Hegemony at the Crossroads of American Government* (New York: McGraw-Hill, 1993).

The presidency was strengthened somewhat in the 1830s with the introduction of the national convention system of nominating presidential candidates. Until then, presidential candidates had been nominated by their party's congressional delegates. This was the caucus system of nominating candidates, and it was derisively called "King Caucus" because any candidate for president had to defer to the party's leaders in Congress in order to get the party's nomination and the support of the party's congressional delegation in the election. The national nominating convention arose outside Congress in order to provide some representation for a party's voters who lived in districts where they weren't numerous enough to elect a member of Congress. The political party in each state made its own provisions for selecting delegates to attend the presidential nominating convention, and in virtually all states, the selection was dominated by the party leaders (called "bosses" by the opposition party). Only in recent decades have state laws intervened to regularize the selection process and provide (in all but a few instances) for open election of delegates.

In the nineteenth century, the national nominating convention was seen as a victory for democracy against the congressional elite. And the national convention gave the presidency a base of power independent of Congress. Eventually, though more slowly, the presidential selection process began to be further democratized, with the adoption of primary elections through which millions of ordinary citizens were given an opportunity to take part in the presidential nominating process by popular selection of convention delegates.

In the 1830s, a national convention system of nominating presidential candidates emerged. The new system helped presidents develop an independent base of power.

This independence did not immediately transform the presidency into the office we recognize today, because Congress was able to keep tight reins on the president's power. The real turning point came during the administration of Franklin Delano Roosevelt. The New Deal was a response to political forces that had been gathering national strength and focus for fifty years. What is remarkable is not that they gathered but that they were so long gaining influence in Washington.

The New Deal and the Presidency

The "First Hundred Days" of the Roosevelt administration in 1933 have no parallel in U.S. history. But this period was only the beginning. The policies proposed by President Roosevelt and adopted by Congress during the first thousand days of his administration so changed the size and character of the national government that they constitute a moment in American history equivalent to the Founding or to the Civil War. The president's constitutional obligation to see "that the laws be faithfully executed" became, during Roosevelt's presidency, virtually a responsibility to *shape* the laws before executing them.

NEW PROGRAMS EXPAND THE ROLE OF NATIONAL GOVERNMENT   Many of the New Deal programs were extensions of the traditional national government approach, which was described in Chapter 3 (see especially Table 3.1, p. 49). But the New Deal also adopted policies never before tried on a large scale by the national government. It began intervening into economic life in ways that had hitherto been reserved to the states. In other words, the national government discovered that it, too, had "police power" and that it could directly regulate individuals as well as provide roads and other services.

The new programs were such dramatic departures from the traditional policies of the national government that their constitutionality was in doubt. The turning point came in 1937 with *National Labor Relations Board v. Jones & Laughlin Steel Corporation*. At issue was the National Labor Relations Act, or Wagner Act, which prohibited corporations from interfering with the efforts of employees to engage in union activities.

The newly formed National Labor Relations Board (NLRB) had ordered Jones & Laughlin to reinstate workers fired because of their union activities. The appeal reached the Supreme Court because Jones & Laughlin had made a constitutional issue over the fact that its manufacturing activities were local and therefore beyond the national government's reach. The Supreme Court rejected this argument with the response that a big company with subsidiaries and suppliers in many states was innately involved in interstate commerce.[18] Since the end of the New Deal, the Supreme Court has never again seriously questioned the constitutionality of an important act of Congress broadly authorizing the executive branch to intervene into the economy or society.[19]

DELEGATION OF POWER   The most important constitutional effect of Congress's actions and the Supreme Court's approval of those actions during the New Deal was the enhancement of *presidential power*. Most major acts of Congress in this period involved significant exercises of control over the economy. But few programs specified the actual controls to be used. Instead, Congress authorized the president or, in some cases, a new agency to deter-

mine what the controls would be. Some of the new agencies were independent commissions responsible to Congress. But most of the new agencies and programs of the New Deal were placed in the executive branch directly under presidential authority.

This form of congressional act is called the "delegation of power." In theory, the delegation of power works as follows: (1) Congress recognizes a problem; (2) Congress acknowledges that it has neither the time nor the expertise to deal with the problem; and (3) Congress therefore sets the basic policies and then delegates to an agency the power to "fill in the details." But in practice, Congress was delegating not merely the power to "fill in the details," but actual and real *policy-making powers*, that is, real legislative powers, to the executive branch.

No modern government can avoid the delegation of significant legislative powers to the executive branch. But the fact remains that these delegations of power cumulatively produced a fundamental shift in the American constitutional framework. *During the 1930s, the growth of the national government through acts delegating legislative power tilted the American national structure away from a Congress-centered government toward a president-centered government.* Congress continues to be the constitutional source of policy, and Congress can rescind these delegations of power or restrict them with later amendments, committee oversight, or budget costs. But since Congress has continued to enact large new programs involving very broad delegations of legislative power to the executive branch, and since the Court has gone along with such actions,[20] we can say that presidential government has become an established fact of American life.

---

[18]*NLRB v. Jones & Laughlin Steel Corporation*, 301 U.S. 1 (1937). Congress had attempted to regulate the economy before 1933, as with the Interstate Commerce Act and Sherman Antitrust Act of the late nineteenth century and with the Federal Trade Act and the Federal Reserve in the Wilson period. But these were rare attempts, and each was restricted very carefully to a narrow and acceptable definition of "interstate commerce." The big break did not come until after 1933.
[19]Some will argue that there are some exceptions to this statement. One was the 1976 case declaring unconstitutional Congress's effort to supply national minimum wage standards to state and local government employees (*National League of Cities v. Usery*, 426 U.S. 833 [1976]). But the Court reversed itself on this nine years later, in 1985 (*Garcia v. San Antonio Metropolitan Transit Authority*, 469 U.S. 528 [1985]). Another was the 1986 case declaring unconstitutional the part of the Gramm-Rudman law authorizing the comptroller general to make "across the board" budget cuts when total appropriations exceeded legally established ceilings (*Bowsher v. Synar*, 478 U.S. 714 [1986]). In 1999, executive authority was compromised somewhat by the Court's decision to question the Federal Communication Commission's authority to supervise telephone deregulation under the Telecommunications Act of 1996. But cases such as these are few and far between, and they only touch on part of a law, not the constitutionality of an entire program.

[20]The Supreme Court did in fact *disapprove* broad delegations of legislative power by declaring the National Industrial Recovery Act of 1933 unconstitutional on the grounds that Congress did not accompany the broad delegations with sufficient standards or guidelines for presidential discretion (*Panama Refining Co. v. Ryan*, 293 U.S. 388 [1935], and *Schechter Poultry Corp. v. U.S.*, 295 U.S. 495 [1935]). The Supreme Court has never reversed those two decisions, but it has also never really followed them. Thus, broad delegations of legislative power from Congress to the executive branch can be presumed to be constitutional.

During the New Deal, the presidency became the dominant political institution when Congress began to delegate policy-making powers to the executive branch.

PRESIDENTIAL GOVERNMENT

There was no great mystery in the shift from Congress-centered government to president-centered government. Congress simply delegated its own powers to the executive branch. Congressional delegations of power, however, are not the only resources available to the president. Presidents have at their disposal a variety of other formal and informal resources that enable them to govern. Indeed, without these other resources, presidents would lack the tools needed to make much use of the power and responsibility given to them by Congress. Let us first consider the president's formal or official resources (see Figure 6.1). Then, in the section following, we will turn to the more informal resources that affect a president's capacity to govern, in particular the president's popular support.

Formal Resources of Presidential Power

PATRONAGE AS A TOOL OF MANAGEMENT   The first tool of management available to most presidents is a form of *patronage*—the choice of high-level political appointees. These appointments allow presidents to fill top management positions with individuals committed to their agendas and, at the same time, to build links to powerful political and economic interests by giving them representation in the administration.

When President Bush took office in 2001, he had about 4,000 appointments he could make "at the pleasure of the president." At the top are roughly 700 cabinet and high-level White House positions. Next are about 800 Senior Executive

Service (SES) positions that can be appointed from outside the career service.[21] Although 4,000 plums were far too many appointments for President Bush to make personally, he did supervise a large percentage of these appointments.

Presidents use patronage to fill positions with competent people sympathetic to the administration's goals. These people are also chosen because they represent important constituencies.

THE CABINET   In the American system of government, the *cabinet* is the traditional but informal designation for the heads of all the major federal government departments. The cabinet has no constitutional status. Unlike that of England and many other parliamentary countries, where the cabinet *is* the government, the American cabinet is not a collective body. It meets but makes no decisions as a group. Each appointment must be approved by the Senate, but the person appointed is not responsible to the Senate or to Congress at large. Cabinet appointments help build party and popular support, but the cabinet is not a party organ. The cabinet is made up of directors but is not a board of directors.

Presidents tend to develop a burning impatience with and a mild distrust of cabinet members. Presidents seek to make the cabinet a rubber stamp for actions already decided on, demanding results, or the appearance of results, more immediately and more frequently than most department heads can provide. Since cabinet appointees generally come from differing careers, the formation of an effective, governing group out of this motley collection of appointments is very unlikely.

---

[21]For a complete directory of these exempt positions, see Committee on Post Office and Civil Service, House of Representatives, *United States Government, Policy and Supporting Positions* (Washington, DC: Government Printing Office, 1992).

FIGURE 6.1

THE INSTITUTIONAL PRESIDENCY*

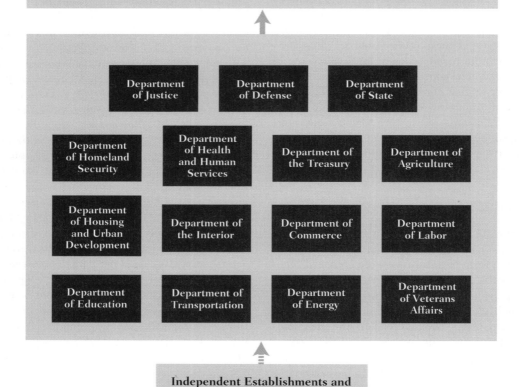

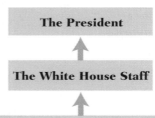

The President

The White House Staff

Executive Office of the President

White House Office
Office of Management and Budget
Council of Economic Advisors
National Security Council
Office of National Drug Control Policy

Office of the U.S. Trade Representative
Council on Environmental Quality
Office of Science and Technology Policy
Office of Policy Development
Office of Administration
Vice President

Department of Justice

Department of Defense

Department of State

Department of Homeland Security

Department of Health and Human Services

Department of the Treasury

Department of Agriculture

Department of Housing and Urban Development

Department of the Interior

Department of Commerce

Department of Labor

Department of Education

Department of Transportation

Department of Energy

Department of Veterans Affairs

Independent Establishments and Government Corporations

*Note: Arrows are used to indicate lines of legal responsibility.
SOURCE: Office of the Federal Register, National Archives and Records Administration, *The United States Government Manual, 1995–96* (Washington, DC: Government Printing Office, 1995), p. 22.

Some presidents have relied heavily on an "inner cabinet," the **National Security Council (NSC)**. The NSC, established by law in 1947, is composed of the president; the vice president; the secretaries of state, defense, and treasury; the attorney general; and other officials invited by the president. It has its own staff of foreign policy specialists run by the special assistant to the president for national security affairs. George W. Bush's "inner cabinet" is composed largely of former and proven senior staffers and cabinet members of former Republican administrations, most particularly Vice President Richard Cheney and Defense Secretary Donald Rumsfeld.

Presidents have obviously been uneven and unpredictable in their reliance on the NSC and other subcabinet bodies, because executive management is inherently a personal matter. However, despite all the personal variations, one generalization can be made: Presidents have increasingly preferred the White House staff to the cabinet as their means of managing the gigantic executive branch.

In American government, the cabinet is a loose collection of department heads that makes no decisions as a group. Presidents tend to rely on the White House staff rather than on the cabinet when formulating policy.

THE WHITE HOUSE STAFF   The White House staff is composed mainly of analysts and advisers. Although many of the top White House staffers are given the title "special assistant" for a particular task or sector, the types of judgments they are expected to make and the kinds of advice they are supposed to give are a good deal broader and more generally political than those that come from the cabinet departments or the Executive Office of the President. For example, the special assistant to the president for intergovernmental affairs advises the president on the functioning of the various branches of government.

From an informal group of fewer than a dozen people (at one time popularly called the "Kitchen Cabinet"), and no more than four dozen at the height of the domestic Roosevelt presidency in 1937, the White House staff has grown substantially (see Table 6.1).[22]

President Clinton promised during the 1992 campaign to reduce the White House staff by 25 percent, and by 1996 had trimmed it by 15 percent. Nevertheless, a large White House staff has become essential. Table 6.1 indicates that President George W. Bush agrees.

The White House staff grew from a small informal group of advisers into a large management institution.

THE EXECUTIVE OFFICE OF THE PRESIDENT   The development of the White House staff can be appreciated only in relation to the still larger Executive Office of the President (EOP). Created in 1939, the EOP is what is often called the "institutional presidency"—the permanent agencies that perform defined management tasks for the president. Somewhere between fifteen hundred and two thousand highly specialized people work for EOP agencies.[23]

The importance of each agency varies according to the personal orientations of each president. For example, the NSC staff was of immense importance under President Nixon because it served essentially as the personal staff of presidential assistant Henry Kissinger. But it was of less importance to former President George H. W. Bush, who looked outside the EOP altogether for military pol-

[22]All the figures since 1967, and probably 1957, are understated; additional White House staff members who were on "detailed" service from the military and other departments are not counted here because they were not on the White House payroll.

[23]The actual number is difficult to estimate because some EOP personnel, especially in national security work, are detailed to EOP from outside agencies.

TABLE 6.1

THE EXPANDING WHITE HOUSE STAFF

Year	President	Full-time Employees	Year	President	Full-time Employees*
1937	Franklin D. Roosevelt	45	1980	Jimmy Carter	488
1947	Harry S. Truman	190	1984	Ronald Reagan	575
1957	Dwight D. Eisenhower	364	1992	George Bush	605**
1967	Lyndon B. Johnson	251	1996	Bill Clinton	511**
1972	Richard M. Nixon	550	2001	George W. Bush	507**
1975	Gerald R. Ford	533			

*The vice president employs over twenty staffers, and there are at least one hundred on the staff of the National Security Council. These people work in and around the White House and Executive Office but are not included in the preceding totals.
**These figures include the staffs of the Office of the President, the Executive Residence, and the Office of the Vice President, according to the Office of Management and Budget (OMB). They don't include the fifty to seventy-five employees temporarily detailed to the White House from outside agencies. While not precisely comparable to previous years, these figures convey a sense of scale.
SOURCES: Thomas E. Cronin, "The Swelling of the Presidency: Can Anyone Reverse the Tide?" in *American Government: Readings and Cases,* 8th ed., ed. Peter Woll (Boston: Little, Brown, 1984), p. 347. Copyright © 1984 by Thomas E. Cronin. Reproduced with the permission of the author. For 1990: U.S. Office of Personnel Management, *Federal Civilian Workforce Statistics, Employment and Trends as of January 1990* (Washington, DC: Government Printing Office, 1990), p. 29. For 1992, 1996, and 2001: OMB and the White House.

icy matters, and much more to the Joint Chiefs of Staff and its chair, General Colin Powell.

The status and power of the Office of Management and Budget (OMB) within the EOP has grown in importance from president to president. Under President Reagan, the budget director was granted cabinet status. Presidents Bush and Clinton continued to increase the director's role, but even if they had not chosen to make the budget director a virtual prime minister, circumstances would have imposed the choice upon them. In 1974, Congress passed the Budget and Impoundment Act, to impose upon itself a more rational approach to the budget. Up until 1974, congressional budget decisions were decentralized, with budget decisions made by the appropriations committees and subcommittees in the House and Senate, and with revenue decisions made independently by the House Ways and Means Committee and by the Senate Finance Committee. The primary purpose of the 1974 act was to impose enough discipline on congressional budget decision making to enable Congress as a whole to confront the presidency more effectively. This centralization of Congress's budget process also centralized the executive budget process, concentrating it more than ever in the OMB.

The Executive Office of the President (EOP), often called the institutional presidency, is larger than the White House staff and comprises the president's permanent management agencies.

Budgeting is no longer "bottom up," with expenditure and program requests passing from the lowest bureaus through the departments to "clearance" in OMB and hence to Congress, where each agency could be called in to reveal what its "original request" had been before OMB got hold of it. Instead the process became "top down," with OMB setting the budget guidelines for agencies as well as for Congress.

THE VICE PRESIDENCY The Constitution created the vice presidency along with the presidency, and the office exists for two purposes only: to succeed the president in the case of a vacancy[24] and to preside over the Senate, casting the tie-breaking vote when necessary.[25] The main value of the vice presidency as a political resource for the president is electoral. Traditionally, a presidential candidate's most important rule for the choice of a running mate is that he or she bring the support of at least one state (preferably a large one) not otherwise likely to support the ticket. Another rule holds that the vice-presidential nominee should come from a region and, where possible, from an ideological or ethnic subsection of the party differing from the presidential nominee's. It is very doubtful that John Kennedy would have won in 1960 without his vice-presidential candidate, Lyndon Johnson, and the contribution Johnson made to carrying Texas. The emphasis has recently shifted away from geographical to ideological balance. George W. Bush's choice of Dick Cheney in 2000 was completely devoid of direct electoral value since Cheney came from one of our least populous states (Wyoming, which casts only three electoral votes). But given Cheney's stalwart right-wing record both in Congress and as President George H. W. Bush's secretary of defense, his inclusion on the Republican ticket was clearly an effort to consolidate the support of the restive right wing of his party. In 2004, John Kerry chose Senator John Edwards of North Carolina as his vice-presidential running mate. Edwards was viewed as an effective campaigner and fund-raiser who might bolster the Democratic ticket's prospects in the South and in rural parts of the Midwest. In the end, the Democrats failed to carry a single Southern state, losing even North Carolina. Edwards also created a controversy with his comments about the sexual orientation of Vice President Cheney's daughter during their nationally televised debate.

As the institutional presidency has grown in size and complexity, most presidents of the past twenty-five years have sought to use their vice presidents as a management resource after the election. George H. W. Bush, as vice president, was "kept within the loop" of decision making because President Reagan delegated so much power. A copy of virtually everything made for Reagan was made for Bush, especially during the first term, when Bush's close friend James Baker was chief of staff. Former President Bush did not take such pains to keep Dan Quayle "in the loop," but President Clinton relied greatly on his vice president, Al Gore, who emerged as one of the most trusted and effective figures in the Clinton White House. Gore's most important task was to oversee the National Performance Review (NPR), an ambitious program to "reinvent" the way the federal government conducts its affairs. The presidency of George W. Bush has resulted in unprecedented power and responsibility for his vice president, Cheney.

The vice president is chosen mainly for electoral reasons; he or she usually represents a large state or a state that the president would have difficulty winning. Some presidential candidates choose running mates to solidify or pacify one wing of the party.

Informal Resources of Presidential Power

ELECTIONS AS A RESOURCE Although we emphasized earlier that even an ordinary citizen, legitimately placed in office, would be a very powerful president, there is no denying that a decisive presidential election translates into a more effective

[24]This provision was clarified by the Twenty-fifth Amendment (1967), which provides that the president (with majority confirmation of House and Senate) must appoint someone to fill the office of vice president if the vice president should die or should fill a vacancy in the presidency. This procedure has been invoked twice—once in 1973 when President Nixon nominated Gerald Ford, and the second time in 1974 when President Ford, having automatically succeeded the resigned President Nixon, filled the vice presidential vacancy with Nelson Rockefeller.

[25]Article I, Section 3, provides that the vice president "shall be President of the Senate, but shall have no Vote, unless they be equally divided."

presidency. Some presidents claim that a landslide victory in an issues-oriented electoral campaign gives them a *mandate,* by which they mean that the electorate approved the programs offered in the campaign and that Congress therefore ought to go along.[26] And Congress is not unmoved by such an appeal. The Johnson and Reagan landslides of 1964 and 1980 gave the presidents real strength during their honeymoon year. In contrast, the close elections of Kennedy in 1960, Nixon in 1968, and Carter in 1976 seriously hampered their effectiveness.

President Clinton, an action-oriented president, was nevertheless seriously hampered by having been elected in 1992 by a minority of the popular vote, a mere 43 percent. Clinton was reelected in 1996 with 49 percent of the vote, a larger percentage of the electorate, but still a minority. His appeals to bipartisanship in 1997 reflected his lack of a mandate from the electorate.

The outcome of the 2000 presidential election indicated a popular-vote deadlock of 48 percent to 48 percent, reflecting a difference of a mere half million votes out of approximately 103 million cast. Given the closeness of the election—as well as the close partisan balance in Congress—initially it mattered little that George W. Bush won since any president possessing such a narrow margin of victory would have little claim to a mandate. The September 11 attacks, however, changed everything and gave Bush the mandate that the election failed to provide.

Presidents use victories in the general election to increase their power by claiming that the election was a mandate to adopt a certain course of action.

INITIATIVE "To initiate" means to originate, and in government that can mean power. The president as an individual is able to initiate decisive action, while Congress as a relatively large assembly must deliberate and debate before it can act.

Over the years, Congress has sometimes deliberately and sometimes inadvertently enhanced the president's power to seize the initiative. Curiously, the most important congressional gift to the president seems the most mundane, namely, the Office of Management and Budget (OMB), known until 1974 as the Bureau of the Budget.

In 1921, Congress provided for an "executive budget" and turned over to a new Bureau of the Budget in the executive branch the responsibility for maintaining the nation's accounts. In 1939, this bureau was moved from the Treasury Department to the newly created Executive Office of the President. The purpose of this move was to enable the president to make better use of the budgeting process as a management tool. In addition, Congress provided for a process called *legislative clearance,* which enables the president to require all agencies of the executive branch to submit through the budget director all requests for new legislation along with estimates of their budgetary needs.[27] Thus, heads of agencies must submit budget requests to the White House so that the requests of all the competing agencies can be balanced. Although there are many violations of this rule, it is usually observed.

Initiative is an important resource of power because the president can propose legislation more quickly and decisively than Congress.

At first, legislative clearance was a defensive weapon, used mainly to allow presidents to avoid the embarrassment of having to oppose or veto legislation originating in their own administrations. But eventually, legislative clearance became far more important. It became the starting point for the devel-

---

[26]Patricia Heidotting Conley, *Presidential Mandates: How Elections Shape the National Agenda* (Chicago: University of Chicago Press, 2001).

[27]Sometimes in appropriations hearings before committees, a member of Congress will attempt to reverse the OMB effort to hold down requests by asking an executive branch witness to reveal "what was your original request." But generally the rule of clearance through OMB and the White House has been observed. The clearance function was formalized in 1940.

RESOURCES OF PRESIDENTIAL POWER

Formal Resources of Presidential Power

Patronage—Presidents fill top management positions with persons committed to their agendas and with individuals who represent powerful political and economic interests.

Cabinet—Another venue where presidents may appoint individuals with important political and economic interests. Presidents want the cabinet to rubber stamp actions already decided on.

National Security Council (NSC)—Some presidents rely heavily on this "inner cabinet" comprised of the president; the vice president; the secretaries of state, defense, and treasury; and the attorney general.

White House staff—Presidents have increasingly preferred to rely on the White House staff, which consists of analysts and advisers, to manage the executive branch.

Executive Office of the President (EOP)—These permanent agencies perform defined tasks for the president. The agencies vary in importance from president to president, but the OMB has been relied upon increasingly by the chief executive.

Vice presidency—The main value of the vice presidency is electoral. Presidential candidates select a running mate who will bring the support of a state whose votes they might not win otherwise.

Informal Resources of Presidential Power

Elections—Some presidents who have won elections by a large percentage feel they have been given a mandate, meaning that the electorate has approved their programs and Congress should therefore go along.

Initiative—Presidents are better able to initiate decisive action than is Congress because the legislative body must get a majority of its members to agree on something before it can move forward.

Media—Press conferences have been the primary avenue for media access to the chief executive, but other forums, such as direct television addresses, radio broadcasts, and now television talk shows, are used.

Party—Party can be a resource in passing legislation because legislators of the president's party will often support legislation put forward by the chief executive.

Groups—Groups organized by regional or ethnic interests, by labor concerns, by big business concerns, or by religious belief can provide core bases of support for presidents.

Mass popularity—Decisive presidential actions, particularly in foreign policy, often increase a president's popularity, but usually only briefly, and the trend is for presidential popularity to decrease throughout a president's term in office.

opment of comprehensive presidential programs.[28] As noted earlier, recent presidents have also used the budget process as a method of gaining tighter "top down" management control. Professed anti-government Republicans, such as Reagan and Bush, as well as allegedly pro-government Democrats, such as Clinton, are alike in their commitment to central management control and program planning. This is precisely why all three recent presidents have given the budget directorship cabinet status.

PRESIDENTIAL USE OF THE MEDIA The president is able to take full advantage of access to the communications media mainly because virtually all the media look to the White House as the chief

[28]Although dated in some respects, the best description and evaluation of budgeting as a management tool and as a tool of program planning is still found in Richard E. Neustadt's two classic articles, "Presidency and Legislation: Planning the President's Program" and "Presidency and Legislation: The Growth of Central Clearance," in *American Political Science Review,* September 1954 and December 1955.

source of news, and they tend to assign their most skillful reporters to the White House "beat." Since news is money, they need the president as much as the president needs them to meet their mutual need to make news.

Presidential personalities affect how each president uses the media. Although Franklin Roosevelt gave several press conferences a month, they were not recorded or broadcast live; direct quotes were not permitted. The model we know today got its start with Eisenhower and was put into final form by Kennedy. Since 1961, the presidential press conference has been a distinctive institution, available whenever the president wants to dominate the news.

Because of the vast amount of proposed policy originating from the White House, the president commands a great deal of media attention.

In addition to the presidential press conference, there are other routes from the White House to news prominence.[29] For example, President Nixon preferred direct television addresses, and President Carter tried to make his initiatives more homey with a television adaptation of President Roosevelt's "fireside chats." President Reagan made unusually good use of prime-time television addresses and also instituted more informal but regular Saturday afternoon radio broadcasts, a tradition that President Clinton continued. Clinton also added various kinds of impromptu press conferences and town meetings.

Walter Mondale, while vice president in 1980, may have summed up the entire media matter with his observation that if he had to choose between the power to get on the nightly news and veto power, he would keep the former and jettison the latter.[30] Modern presidents have learned that they can use the media to mobilize popular support for their programs and to attempt to force Congress to follow their lead.

PARTY   Although on the decline, the president's party is far from insignificant as a political resource, as Figure 6.2 dramatically demonstrates. The figure gives a fifty-year history of the "presidential batting average" in Congress—the percentage of winning roll-call votes in Congress on bills publicly supported by the president. Note, for example, that President Eisenhower's "batting average" started out with a very impressive .900 but declined to .700 by the end of his first term and to little more than half his starting point by the end of his administration. The single most important explanation of this decline was Eisenhower's loss of a Republican Party majority in Congress after 1954, the recapture of some seats in 1956, and then a significant loss of seats to the Democrats after the election of 1958.

The presidential batting average went back up and stayed consistently higher through the Kennedy and Johnson years, mainly because these two presidents enjoyed Democratic Party majorities in the Senate and in the House. Even so, Johnson's batting average in the House dropped significantly during his last two years, following a very large loss of Democratic seats in the 1966 election. Note how much higher Carter's success rate was than that of Ford or Nixon during their last two years in office; this was clearly attributable to the *party* factor: the substantial Democratic Party majorities in the two chambers of Congress.

At the same time, party has its limitations as a resource. The more unified the president's party is behind the president's legislative requests, the more unified the opposition party is also likely to be. Unless the president's party majority is very large, the White House must also appeal to the opposition to make up for the inevitable defectors within the ranks of the president's own party. Consequently, the president often poses as being above partisanship in order to win "bipartisan" support in Congress. Thus, even though President Clinton enjoyed Democratic majorities in the House and the Senate

[29]See George Edwards III, *At the Margins—Presidential Leadership of Congress* (New Haven: Yale University Press, 1989), Chapter 7; and Robert Locander, "The President and the News Media," in *Dimensions of the Modern Presidency,* ed. Edward Kearny (St. Louis: Forum Press, 1981), pp. 49–52.
[30]Reported in Timothy E. Cook, *Governing with the News: The News Media as a Political Institution* (Chicago: University of Chicago Press, 1998), p. 133.

FIGURE 6.2

THE PRESIDENTIAL BATTING AVERAGE: PRESIDENTIAL SUCCESS ON CONGRESSIONAL VOTES* (1953–2003)

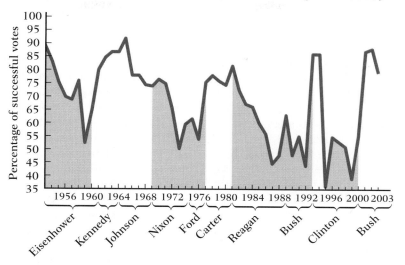

*Percentages based on votes on which presidents took a position.
SOURCE: *Congressional Quarterly Weekly Report*, 3 January 2004, p. 18.

during the first two years of his presidency, he had to be cautious with Republicans because the defection of just four or five Democrats in a close Senate vote could have endangered important but controversial legislation. To the extent that presidents pursue a bipartisan strategy, they cannot afford to throw themselves fully into building their own party discipline, and vice versa.

The president's political party can be an asset when that party controls Congress. However, when the president and the president's party are unified on policy, the opposition is likely to be unified as well.

GROUPS   The classic case in modern times of groups as a resource for the presidency is the New Deal coalition that supported President Franklin

Roosevelt.[31] The New Deal coalition was composed of an inconsistent, indeed contradictory, set of interests. Some of these interests were not organized interest groups, but were regional or ethnic interests, such as Southern whites, residents of large cities in the industrial Northeast and Midwest, or blacks who later succeeded in organizing as an interest group. In addition, there were several large, self-consciously organized interest groups, including organized labor, agriculture, and the financial community.[32] All of the parts were held together by a

[31]A wider range of group phenomena will be covered in Chapter 12. In that chapter, the focus is on the influence of groups *upon* the government and its policy-making processes. Here our concern is more with the relationship of groups to the presidency and the extent to which groups and coalitions become a dependable resource for presidential government.

[32]For updates on the group basis of presidential politics, see Thomas Ferguson, "Money and Politics," in *Handbooks to the Modern World—The United States,* vol. 2, ed. Godfrey Hodgson (New York: Facts on File, 1992), pp. 1060–84; and Lucius J. Barker, ed., "Black Electoral Politics," *National Political Science Review,* vol. 2 (New Brunswick, NJ: Transaction, 1990).

judicious use of patronage—not merely in jobs but also in policies. Many of the groups were virtually permitted to write their own legislation. In exchange, the groups supported President Roosevelt and his Democratic successors in their battles with opposing politicians.

Republicans have had their group coalition base, too, including not only their traditional segments of organized business, upper-income groups, Sun Belt conservatives, and certain ethnic groups but also a very large share of traditionally Democratic Southern whites, many of whom are now part of the Christian Coalition.

The interest bases of the two parties have remained largely unchanged since 1980, when the GOP completed its absorption of most white Southerners and religious conservatives. But whether these coalitions will last remains to be seen.

Groups and interests give their support to a president in exchange for a voice in the legislative process.

PUBLIC OPINION AND MASS POPULARITY AS A RESOURCE (AND A LIABILITY) As presidential government grew, a presidency developed whose power is linked directly to the people.[33] Successful presidents have to be able to mobilize mass opinion.

Public opinion can provide useful information, but it can also lure the president into following public opinion rather than leading it.

Recent presidents, particularly Bill Clinton, have "gone public" by reaching out directly to the American public to gain approval. If successful,

presidents can use this approval as a weapon against Congress. President Clinton's enormously high public profile, as is indicated by the number of public appearances he made (see Figure 6.3), is only the most recent dramatic expression of the presidency as a *permanent campaign* for reelection. A study by political scientist Charles O. Jones shows that President Clinton engaged in campaignlike activity throughout his presidency and was the most-traveled American president in history. In his first twenty months in office, he made 203 appearances outside of Washington, compared with 178 for George Bush and 58 for Ronald Reagan. Clinton's tendency to go around rather than through party organizations is reflected in the fact that while Presidents Bush and Reagan devoted about 25 percent of their appearances to party functions, Clinton's comparable figure is only 8 percent.[34]

President George W. Bush, in his first one hundred days in office, made appearances in twenty-six states—almost as many states as he visited during the entire electoral campaign of 1999–2000. This is the essence of the permanent campaign.

Even with the help of all other institutional and political resources, successful presidents have to be able to mobilize mass opinion in their favor in order to keep Congress in line. But as we shall see, each president tends to *use up* mass resources. Virtually everyone is aware that presidents are constantly making appeals to the public over the heads of Congress and the Washington community. But the mass public does not turn out to be made up of fools. The American people react to presidential actions rather than mere speeches or other image-making devices.

The public's sensitivity to presidential actions can be seen in the tendency of all presidents to lose popular support. This general downward tendency is to be expected if American voters are rational, inasmuch as almost any action taken by the president can be divisive, with some voters

---

[33]For a book-length treatment of this shift, see Theodore J. Lowi, *The Personal President: Power Invested, Promise Unfulfilled* (Ithaca, NY: Cornell University Press, 1985). For an analysis of the character of mass democracy, see Benjamin Ginsberg, *The Captive Public* (New York: Basic Books, 1986).

[34]Study cited in Ann Devroy, "Despite Panetta Pep Talk, White House Aides See Daunting Task," *Washington Post*, 8 January 1995, p. A4.

FIGURE 6.3

PUBLIC APPEARANCES BY PRESIDENTS, 1929–1995

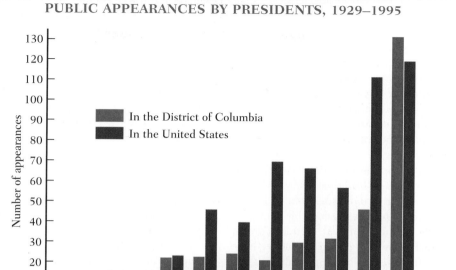

SOURCE: Samuel Kernell, *Going Public*, 3rd ed. (Washington, DC: Congressional Quarterly Press, 1998). p. 118.

approving and other voters disapproving. Public disapproval of specific actions has a cumulative effect on the president's overall performance rating. Thus all presidents are faced with the problem of boosting their approval ratings. And the public generally reacts favorably to presidential actions in foreign policy or, more precisely, to international events associated with the president. For example, President George W. Bush's approval ratings surpassed the 90 percent level as the Taliban fell from power in Afghanistan. Bush also enjoyed a substantial boost in popularity in the Spring of 2003 during the early months of the Iraqi war. Analysts call this the *rallying effect*. Nevertheless, the rallying effect turns out to be only a momentary reversal of the more general tendency

of presidents to lose popular support. In fact, as the conflict in Iraq continued, Bush's performance rating showed a steady decline, resulting from the tepid economy and the slow pace and high cost of establishing a new Iraqi government. The rise and fall of presidential performance ratings are evidence that with power goes vulnerability.

A president's approval rating tends to rise during an international crisis and fall during a domestic dispute, though the "rallying effect" seems to be short-lived.

IS THE PRESIDENCY
STRONG OR WEAK?

The framers of the Constitution, as we saw, created a unitary executive branch because they thought this would make the presidency a more energetic institution. At the same time, they checked the powers of the executive branch by creating a system of separated powers. Did the framers' work make the presidency a strong or weak institution?

At one time, historians and journalists liked to debate the question of strong versus weak presidents. Some presidents, such as Lincoln and FDR, were called "strong" for their leadership and ability to guide the nation's political agenda. Others, like James Buchanan and Calvin Coolidge, were seen as "weak" for failing to develop significant legislative programs and seeming to observe rather than shape political events. Today, the strong versus weak categorization has become moot. *Every president is strong.* This strength is not so much a function of personal charisma as it is a reflection of the increasing powers of the institution of the presidency. Of course, as we noted earlier, political savvy in strategic interactions with other politicians and mobilizing public opinion can account for a president's success in exercising these powers. But contemporary presidents all possess a vast array of resources and powers.

Indeed, presidents seek to dominate the policy-making process and claim the inherent power to lead the nation in time of war. The expansion of presidential power over the past century has not come about by accident but as the result of an ongoing effort by successive presidents to expand the power of the office. Some presidential efforts have succeeded and others have failed. One recent president, Nixon, was forced to resign and others have left office under clouds. Most presidents, nevertheless, have sought to increase the office's power. As the framers of the Constitution predicted, presidential ambition has been a powerful and unrelenting force in American politics. What explains why presidential ambition has gone virtually unchecked? What are the consequences of such a development?

As is often noted by the media and in the academic literature, popular participation in American political life has declined precipitously since its nineteenth-century apogee. Voter turnout in national presidential elections barely exceeds the 50 percent mark, while hardly a third of those eligible participate in off-year congressional races. Turnout in state and local contests is typically even lower. These facts are well known and their implications for the representative character of American government frequently deplored.

The decay of popular political participation, however, also has profoundly important institutional implications that are not often fully appreciated. To put the matter succinctly, the decline of voting and other forms of popular involvement in American political life reduces congressional influence while enhancing the power of the presidency. This is a development with which we should be deeply concerned. For all its faults and foibles, the Congress is the nation's most representative political institution and remains the only entity capable of placing limits on unwise or illegitimate presidential conduct. Certainly, the courts have seldom been capable of thwarting a determined president, especially in the foreign policy realm. Unfortunately, however, in recent decades our nation's undemocratic politics has undermined the Congress while paving the way for aggrandizement of power by the executive and the presidential unilateralism that inevitably follows.

The framers of the Constitution created a system of government in which the Congress and the executive branch were to share power. In recent years, however, the powers of Congress have waned while those of the presidency have expanded dramatically. To begin with a recent instance of congressional retreat in the face of presidential assertiveness, in October 2002, pressed by President George W. Bush, both houses of Congress voted overwhelmingly to authorize the White House to use military force against Iraq. The resolution adopted by Congress allowed the president complete discretion to determine whether, when, and how to attack Iraq. The president had rejected language that might have implied even the slightest limitations on his prerogatives. Indeed, Bush's legal advisers had pointedly declared that the president did not actually need specific congressional authorization to attack Iraq if he deemed such action to be in America's interest. "We don't want to be in the legal position of asking Congress to authorize the use of force when the president already has that full authority," said one senior administration official. Few members of Congress even bothered to object to this apparent rewriting of the U.S. Constitution.

There is no doubt that Congress continues to be able to harass presidents and even, on occasion, to hand the White House a sharp rebuff. In the larger view, however, presidents' occasional defeats—however dramatic—have to be seen as temporary setbacks in a gradual and decisive shift toward increased presidential power in the twenty-first century. Louis Fisher, America's leading authority on the separation of powers, recently observed that in what are arguably the two most important policy arenas, national defense and the federal budget, the powers of Congress have been in "precipitous decline" for at least the past fifty years. The last occasion on which Congress exercised its constitutional power to declare war was 8 December 1941, and yet, since that time, American forces have been committed to numerous battles on every continent by order of the president. The much-hailed 1973 War Powers Resolution, far from limiting presidential power, actually allowed the president considerably more discretionary authority than he was granted by the Constitution. The War Powers Act gave the president the authority to deploy forces abroad without congressional authority for sixty days. The Constitution, though, seems to require congressional authorization before troops can be deployed for even one day.

As to spending powers, the framers of the Constitution conceived the "power of the purse" to be Congress's most fundamental prerogative, and for more than a century this power was jealously guarded by powerful congressional leaders like William Howard Taft–era House Speaker "Uncle" Joe Cannon, who saw congressional control of the budget as a fundamental safeguard against "Prussian-style" militarism and autocracy. Since the New Deal, however, successive Congresses have yielded

to steadily increasing presidential influence over the budget process. In 1939, Congress allowed Franklin D. Roosevelt to take a giant step toward presidential control of the nation's purse strings when it permitted FDR to bring the Bureau of the Budget (BoB) into the newly created Executive Office of the President. Roosevelt and his successors used the BoB (now called the White House Office of Management and Budget) effectively to seize the nation's legislative and budgetary agenda. In 1974, Congress attempted to respond to Richard Nixon's efforts to further enhance presidential control of spending when it enacted the Budget and Impoundment Control Act. This piece of legislation centralized Congress's own budgetary process and seemed to reinforce congressional power. Yet, less than ten years later, Congress watched as President Ronald Reagan essentially seized control over the congressional budget process. Subsequently, as Fisher observes, lacking confidence in its own ability to maintain budgetary discipline, Congress has surrendered more and more power to the president, even attempting to hand the chief executive a line-item veto in 1995.

Representative assemblies like the U.S. Congress derive their influence from the support of groups and forces in civil society that believe these institutions serve their interests. Britain's Parliament ultimately overcame the Crown because it gradually won the confidence and support of the most important forces in civil society. Chief executives such as the president of the United States, on the other hand, fundamentally derive their power from their command of bureaucracies, armies, and the general machinery of the state. Presidents can certainly benefit from popular support. If we imagine, however, a fully demobilized polity in which neither institution could count on much support from forces in civil society, the president would still command the institutions of the state while Congress would be without significant resources. In a fully mobilized polity, on the other hand, Congress might have a chance to counterbalance the president's institutional powers with the support of significant social forces.

A powerful presidency, a weak Congress, and a partially demobilized electorate are a dangerous mix. Presidents have increasingly asserted the right to govern unilaterally and now appear able to overcome most institutional and political constraints. Presidential power, to be sure, can be a force for good. To cite one example from the not-so-distant past, it was President Lyndon Johnson, more than Congress or the judiciary, who faced up to the task of smashing America's segregationist system. Yet, as the framers knew, unchecked power is always dangerous. Americans of the Founding generation feared that unchecked presidential power would lead to *monocracy*—a republican form of monarchy without a king or queen. Have we not taken more than one step in that direction? Inevitably, there is a price to be paid for our undemocratic politics.

CHAPTER REVIEW

The foundations for presidential government were set down in the Constitution, which provided for a unitary executive and made the president head of state as well as head of government. The first section of this chapter reviewed the powers of each: the head of state with its military, judicial, and diplomatic powers; and the head of government with its executive, military, and legislative powers. But the presidency was subordinated to congressional government during the nineteenth century and part of the twentieth, as the national government took part in few domestic functions and was inactive or sporadic in foreign affairs.

The second section of the chapter showed the rise of modern presidential government following the long period of congressional government. There is no mystery in the shift to government centered on the presidency. Congress built the modern presidency essentially in the 1930s by delegating to it not only the power to implement the vast new programs of the New Deal but also by delegating its own legislative power to make policy. The cabinet, the other top presidential appointments, the White House staff, and the Executive Office of the President are some of the impressive formal resources of presidential power.

The third section focused on the president's informal resources, in particular the president's political party, the supportive group coalitions, access to the media, and, through that, access to the millions of Americans who make up the general public. These resources are not cost-free or risk-free. A good relationship with the public is the president's most potent modern resource, but the polls reveal that the public's rating of presidential performance tends to go down with time. Only international actions or events can boost presidential performance ratings, and then only briefly. This means that presidents may be tempted to use foreign policy for domestic purposes.

KEY TERMS

cabinet   The secretaries, or chief administrators, of the major departments of the federal government. Cabinet secretaries are appointed by the president with the consent of the Senate.

commander in chief   The position of the president as commander of the national military and the state National Guard units (when they are called into service).

delegated powers   Constitutional powers that are assigned to one governmental agency but that are exercised by another agency with the express permission of the first.

electoral college   The presidential electors from each state who meet in their respective state capitals after the popular election to cast ballots for president and vice president.

executive agreement   An agreement between the president and another country, which has the force of a treaty but does not require the Senate's "advice and consent."

executive order   A rule or regulation issued by the president that has the effect and formal status of legislation.

executive privilege The claim that confidential communications between a president and close advisers should not be revealed without the consent of the president.

expressed powers (president) Specific powers granted to the president under Article II, Sections 2 and 3, of the Constitution.

inherent powers Powers claimed by a president that are not expressed in the Constitution, but are inferred from it.

legislative clearance A process that enables the president to require all agencies of the executive branch to submit through the budget director all requests for new legislation along with estimates of their budgetary needs.

line-item veto Power that allows a governor (or the president) to strike out specific provisions (lines) of bills that the legislature passes. Without a line-item veto, the governor (or president) must accept or reject an entire bill. The line-item veto is no longer in effect for the president.

mandate (electoral) A claim by a victorious candidate that the electorate has given him or her special authority to carry out promises made during the campaign.

National Security Council (NSC) A presidential foreign policy advisory council composed of the president; the vice president; the secretaries of state, defense, and treasury; the attorney general; and other officials invited by the president. The NSC has a staff of foreign policy specialists.

patronage The resources available to higher officials, usually opportunities to make partisan appointments to offices and to confer grants, licenses, or special favors to supporters.

permanent campaign Description of presidential politics in which all presidential actions are taken with re-election in mind.

pocket veto A presidential veto of legislation wherein the president takes no formal action on a bill. If Congress adjourns within ten days of passing a bill, and the president does not sign it, the bill is considered to be vetoed.

rallying effect The generally favorable reaction of the public to presidential actions taken in foreign policy or, more precisely, decisions made during international crises.

veto The presidents constitutional power to turn down acts of Congress. A presidential veto may be overridden by a two-thirds vote of each house of Congress.

War Powers Resolution A resolution of Congress that the president can send troops into action only by authorization of Congress, or if American troops are already under attack or serious threat.

For Further Reading

Drew, Elizabeth. *On the Edge: The Clinton Presidency.* New York: Simon & Schuster, 1994.

Lowi, Theodore J. *The Personal President: Power Invested, Promise Unfulfilled.* Ithaca, NY: Cornell University Press, 1985.

Milkis, Sidney M. *The President and the Parties: The Transformation of the American Party System since the New Deal.* New York: Oxford University Press, 1993.

Neustadt, Richard E. *Presidential Power: The Politics of Leadership from Roosevelt to Reagan,* rev. ed. New York: Free Press, 1990.

Pfiffner, James P. *The Modern Presidency.* New York: St. Martin's Press, 1994.

Polsby, Nelson, and Aaron Wildavsky. *Presidential Elections,* 10th ed. New York: Free Press, 2000.

Skowronek, Stephen. *The Politics Presidents Make: Presidential Leadership from John Adams to George Bush.* Cambridge, MA: Harvard University Press, 1993.

Spitzer, Robert. *President and Congress: Executive Hegemony at the Crossroads of American Government.* New York: McGraw-Hill, 1993.

CHAPTER 7

The Executive Branch: Bureaucracy in a Democracy

*A*mericans depend on government bureaucracies to accomplish the most spectacular achievements as well as the most mundane. Yet they often do not realize that public bureaucracies are essential for providing the services that they use every day and that they rely on in emergencies. On a typical day, a college student might check the weather forecast, drive on an interstate highway, mail the rent check, drink from a public water fountain, check the calories on the side of a yogurt container, attend a class, log on to the Internet, and meet a relative at the airport. Each of these activities is possible because of the work of a government bureaucracy: the U.S. Weather Service, the U.S. Department of Transportation, the U.S. Postal Service, the Environmental Protection Agency, the Food and Drug Administration, the student loan programs of the U.S. Department of Education, the Advanced Research Projects Agency (which developed the Internet in the 1960s), and the Federal Aviation Administration. Without the ongoing work of these agencies, many of these common activities would be impossible, unreliable, or more expensive. Even though bureaucracies provide essential services that all Americans rely on, they are often disparaged by politicians and the general public alike. Criticized as "big government," many federal bureaucracies come into public view only when they are charged with fraud, waste, and abuse.

In emergencies, the national perspective on bureaucracy and, indeed, on "big government" shifts. After the September 11 terrorist attacks, all

CORE OF THE ANALYSIS

- Despite its problems, the bureaucracy is necessary for the maintenance of order in a large society.
- The size of the federal bureaucracy is large, but it has not been growing any faster than the economy or the population as a whole.
- Government agencies vary in their levels of responsiveness to the president and his political appointees, congressional members and committees, and commercial and private interests.
- Responsible bureaucracy requires more than presidential power and management control.
- Congress has delegated much of its legislative power to the president and the bureaucracy; congressional committees use oversight to make the bureaucracy accountable.

eyes turned to Washington. The federal government responded by strengthening and reorganizing the bureaucracy to undertake a whole new set of responsibilities designed to keep America safe. The president created the new cabinet-level Department of Homeland Security, charged with coordinating all domestic antiterrorism activities. Law-enforcement agencies gained new powers and resources. Reflecting the shift in priorities from crime investigation to terrorism prevention, the Federal Bureau of Investigation (FBI) received new

CENTRAL QUESTIONS

- **Why Bureaucracy?**
  Why do bureaucracies exist? Has the federal bureaucracy grown too large?
  What roles do government bureaucrats perform?
- **How is the Executive Branch Organized?**
  What agencies make up the executive branch?
  How can one classify these agencies according to their missions?
- **Who Controls the Bureaucracy?**
  What popular controls over the bureaucracy exist?
  How do the president and Congress manage and oversee the bureaucracy?
- **How Can Bureaucracy Be Reduced?**
  What methods have been used to reduce the size and the role of the federal bureaucracy?
- **Does Bureaucracy Work?**
  What is the most effective means to guarantee a responsible bureaucracy?

responsibilities for domestic intelligence. Many other agencies assumed new duties associated with the antiterrorism objectives. The Treasury Department, for example, was assigned to create a financial intelligence-gathering system designed to track terrorists' financial transactions. The Centers for Disease Control (CDC) undertook a new set of activities designed to prevent bioterrorism. Congress created a new Transportation Security Administration within the Department of Transportation. Charged with making all forms of travel safe, the new agency presided over a significant expansion of the federal workforce as it hired thousands of workers to screen passengers at airports.

The war on terrorism has highlighted the extensive range of the tasks shouldered by the federal bureaucracy. Both routine and exceptional tasks require the organization, specialization, and expertise found in bureaucracies. Look over the In-Brief Box on page 154, which identifies the basic characteristics of bureaucracy. To provide services, government bureaucracies employ specialists such as meteorologists, doctors, and scientists. To do their jobs effectively, these specialists require resources and tools (ranging from paper to blood samples); they have to coordinate their work with others (for example, the traffic engineers must communicate with construction engineers); and there must be effective outreach to the public (for example, private doctors must be made aware of health warnings). Bureaucracy provides a way to coordinate the many different parts that must work together to provide good services.

In this chapter, we will focus on the federal bureaucracy—the administrative structure that on a day-to-day basis *is* the American government. We will first seek to define and describe bureaucracy as a social and political phenomenon. Second, we will look in detail at American bureaucracy in action by examining the government's major administrative agencies, their role in the governmental process, and their political behavior. These details of administration are the very heart and soul of modern government and will provoke the question of the third and final section of the chapter: "Can bureaucracy be made accountable to the president and Congress? Can bureaucracy and democracy coexist?"

WHY BUREAUCRACY?

Bureaucracies are commonplace because they touch so many aspects of daily life. Government bureaucracies implement the decisions made by the political process. Bureaucracies are full of routine because that assures the regular delivery of services and ensures that each agency fulfills its mandate. Public bureaucracies are powerful because legislatures and chief executives, and indeed the people, delegate to them vast power to make sure a particular job is done—enabling the rest of us to be more free to pursue our private

SIX PRIMARY CHARACTERISTICS OF BUREAUCRACY

Division of Labor
   To increase productivity, workers are specialized.
   Each develops a skill in a particular job and then performs that job routinely.

Allocation of Functions
   Each worker depends on the output of other workers.
   No worker makes an entire product alone.

Allocation of Responsibility
   A task becomes a personal and contractual responsibility.

Supervision
   An unbroken chain of command ties superiors to subordinates from top to bottom to ensure
      orderly communication between workers and levels of the organization.
   Each superior is assigned a limited number of subordinates to supervise—this is the span of
      control.

Purchase of Full-time Employment
   The organization controls all the time the worker is on the job, so each worker can be assigned
      and held to a task.

Identification of Career within the Organization
   Paths of seniority along with pension rights and promotions are all designed to encourage
      workers to identify with the organization.

ends. The public sentiments that emerged after September 11, 2001, revealed this underlying appreciation of public bureaucracies. When faced with the challenge of making air travel safe again, the public strongly supported giving the federal government responsibility for airport security, even though this meant increasing the size of the federal bureaucracy by making the security screeners federal workers. House majority whip Tom DeLay sought to forestall this growth in the federal government, declaring that "the last thing we can afford to do is erect a new bureaucracy that is unaccountable and unable to protect the American public."[1] But the antibureaucratic language that had

been so effective prior to September 11 no longer resonated with a fearful public. Instead, there was a widespread belief that a public bureaucracy would provide more effective protection than the cost-conscious private security companies that had been charged with airport security in the past. Bureaucrats across the federal government felt the new appreciation for their work. As one civil servant at the Pentagon put it, "The whole mood has changed. A couple of months ago we were part of the bloated bureaucracy. Now we're Washington's equivalent of the cops and firemen in New York."[2] How long such sentiments last will depend on the effectiveness of the bureaucracy and on the public's views about whether an expanded bureaucracy

[1]Janet Hook, "U.S. Strikes Back; Political Landscape; GOP Bypasses the Bipartisan Truce," *Los Angeles Times,* 14 October 2001, p. A8.

[2]R. W. Apple, Jr., "White House Letter: Big Government Is Back in Style," *New York Times,* 23 November 2001, p. B2.

is needed when (and if) the immediate threat of terrorism recedes.

Despite the naive tendency to criticize bureaucracy because it is "bureaucratic," most Americans recognize that maintaining order in a large society is impossible without some sort of large governmental apparatus staffed by professionals with some expertise in public administration. When we approve of what a government agency is doing, we give the phenomenon a positive name, *administration;* when we disapprove, we call the phenomenon *bureaucracy.*

Although the terms "administration" and "bureaucracy" are often used interchangeably, it is useful to distinguish between the two. Administration is the more general of the two terms; it refers to all the ways human beings might rationally coordinate their efforts to achieve a common goal. This applies to private as well as public organizations. *Bureaucracy* refers to the actual offices, tasks, and principles of organization that are employed in the most formal and sustained administration. The In Brief Box on the previous page defines bureaucracy by identifying its basic characteristics.

Bureaucratic Organization Enhances Efficiency

The core of bureaucracy is the *division of labor.* The key to bureaucratic effectiveness is the coordination of experts performing complex tasks. If each job is specialized in order to gain efficiencies, then each worker must depend upon the output of other workers, and that requires careful *allocation* of jobs and resources. Inevitably, bureaucracies become hierarchical, often approximating a pyramid in form. At the base of the organization are workers with the fewest skills and specializations; one supervisor can deal with a relatively large number of these workers. At the next level of the organization, where there are more highly specialized workers, the supervision and coordination of work involves fewer workers per supervisor. Toward the top of the organization, a very small number of high-level executives engages in the "management" of the organization, meaning the coordination and

oversight of all the tasks and functions, plus the allocation of the appropriate supplies, and the distribution of the outputs of the organization to the market (if it is a "private sector" organization) or to the public.

Bureaucracies Allow Governments to Operate

The term *bureaucracy,* when used pejoratively, conjures up endless paperwork, red tape, and lazy, uncaring employees. In fact, the term refers to a rather spectacular human achievement. By dividing up tasks, matching tasks to a labor force that develops appropriately specialized skills, routinizing procedures, and providing the incentive structure and oversight arrangements to get large numbers of people to operate in a coordinated, purposeful fashion, bureaucracies accomplish tasks and missions in a manner that would otherwise be unimaginable. The provision of "government goods" as broad as the defense of people, property, and national borders or as narrow as a subsidy to a wheat farmer, beef rancher, or manufacturer of specialty steel requires organization, routines, standards, and, at the end of the day, the authority for someone to cut a check and put it in the mail. Bureaucracies are created to do these things. No large organization would be larger than the sum of its parts, and many would be smaller, without bureaucratizing its activities.

Bureaucracy also consolidates a range of complementary programs and insulates them from the predatory ambitions of out-of-sympathy political forces. Nothing in this world is permanent, but bureaucracies come close. By creating clienteles—in the legislature, the world of interest groups, and public opinion—a bureaucracy establishes a coalition of supporters, some of whom will fight to the end to keep it in place. It is a well-known rule of thumb that everyone in the political world cares deeply and intensely about a subset of policies and the agencies that produce them, and opposes other policies and agencies but not with nearly the same passion. Opponents, to succeed, must clear many hurdles, while proponents, to maintain the status quo, must only marshall their forces at a few veto points. In the final analysis, opponents typically meet obstacle after obstacle and eventually give up their uphill battles and concentrate on protecting and expanding that about which they care most deeply. In a complex political system such as that of the United States, it is much easier to do the latter. Politicians appreciate this fact of life. Consequently, both opponents and proponents of a particular set of government activities wage the fiercest battles at the time programs are enacted and a bureaucracy is created. Once created, these organizations assume a position of relative permanence.

So, in response to the question of how bureaucracy makes government possible, there is an *efficiency* part to the answer and a *credibility* part. The creation of a bureau is a way to deliver government goods efficiently *and* a device by which to "tie one's hands," thereby providing a credible commitment to the long-term existence of a policy.

Bureaucrats Fulfill Important Roles

"Government by offices and desks" conveys to most people a picture of hundreds of office workers shuffling millions of pieces of paper. There is a lot of truth in that image, but we have to look more closely at what papers are being shuffled and why. More than fifty years ago, an astute observer defined bureaucracy as "continuous routine business."[3] Almost any organization succeeds by reducing its work to routines, with each routine being given to a different specialist. But specialization separates people from each other; one worker's output becomes another worker's input. The timing of such relationships is essential, and this requires that these workers stay in communication with each other. Communication is the key. In fact, bureaucracy was the first information net-

work. Routine came first; voluminous routine came as bureaucracies grew and specialized.

BUREAUCRATS IMPLEMENT LAWS Bureaucrats, whether in public or in private organizations, communicate with each other in order to coordinate all the specializations within their organization. This coordination is necessary to carry out the primary task of bureaucracy, which is *implementation,* that is, implementing the objectives of the organization as laid down by its board of directors (if a private company) or by law (if a public agency). In government, the "bosses" are ultimately the legislature and the elected chief executive.

BUREAUCRATS MAKE AND ENFORCE RULES When the bosses—Congress, in particular, when it is making the law—are clear in their instructions to bureaucrats, implementation is a fairly straightforward process. Bureaucrats translate the law into specific routines for each of the employees of an agency. But what happens to routine administrative implementation when there are several bosses who disagree as to what the instructions ought to be? This requires yet a fourth job for bureaucrats: interpretation. Interpretation is a form of implementation, in that the bureaucrats still have to carry out what they believe to be the intentions of their superiors. But when bureaucrats have to interpret a law before implementing it, they are in effect engaging in *lawmaking.*[4] Congress often deliberately delegates to an administrative agency the responsibility of lawmaking. Members of Congress often conclude that some area of industry needs regulating or some area of the environment needs protection, but they are unwilling or unable to specify just how that should

---

[3]Arnold Brecht and Comstock Glaser, *The Art and Techniques of Administration in German Ministries* (Cambridge: Harvard University Press, 1940), p. 6.

[4]When bureaucrats engage in interpretation, the result is what political scientists call bureaucratic drift. Bureaucratic drift occurs because, as we've suggested, the "bosses" (in Congress) and the agents (within the bureaucracy) don't always share the same purposes. Bureaucrats also have their own agendas to fulfill.

be done. In such situations, Congress delegates to the appropriate agency a broad authority within which the bureaucrats have to make law, through the procedures of *rulemaking* and *administrative adjudication.*

Rulemaking is exactly the same as legislation; in fact it is often referred to as "quasi-legislation." The rules issued by government agencies provide more detailed and specific indications of what the policy actually will mean. For example, the Occupational Safety and Health Administration (OSHA) is charged with ensuring that our workplaces are safe. OSHA has regulated the use of chemicals and other well-known health hazards. In recent years, the widespread use of computers in the workplace has been associated with a growing number of cases of repetitive stress injury to hands, arms, and necks. To respond to this new threat to workplace health, OSHA issued a new set of ergonomic rules in November 1999 that tells employers what they must do to prevent and address such injuries among their workers. Such rules only take force after a period of public comment. Reaction from the people or businesses that are subject to the rules may cause an agency to modify the rules they first issue. The rules about ergonomic safety in the workplace, for example, were contested by many businesses, which viewed them as too costly. The rulemaking process is thus a highly political one. Once rules are approved, they are published in the *Federal Register* and have the force of law.

Because laws can often be vague, bureaucrats interpret the intentions of Congress and the president prior to implementation of orders.

BUREAUCRATS SETTLE DISPUTES   Administrative adjudication is very similar to what the judiciary ordinarily does: applying rules and precedents to specific cases in order to settle disputes. In administrative adjudication, the agency

charges the person or business suspected of violating the law. The ruling in an adjudication dispute applies only to the specific case being considered. Many regulatory agencies use administrative adjudication to make decisions about specific products or practices. For example, in December 1999, the Consumer Product Safety Commission held hearings on the safety of bleachers, sparked by concern over the death of children after falls from bleachers. It has issued guidelines about bleacher construction designed to prevent falls. These guidelines have the force of law. Likewise, product recalls are often the result of adjudication.

In sum, government bureaucrats do essentially the same things that bureaucrats in large private organizations do, and neither type deserves the disrespect embodied in the term "bureaucrat." But because of the authoritative, coercive nature of government, far more constraints are imposed on public bureaucrats than on private bureaucrats, even when their jobs are the same. Public bureaucrats are required to maintain a far more thorough paper trail. Public bureaucrats are also subject to a great deal more access from the public. Newspaper reporters, for example, have access to public bureaucrats. Public access has been vastly facilitated in the past thirty years; the adoption of the Freedom of Information Act (FOIA) in 1966 gave ordinary citizens the right of access to agency files and agency data to determine whether derogatory information exists in the file about citizens themselves and to learn about what the agency is doing in general.

And finally, citizens are given far more opportunities to participate in the decision-making processes of public agencies. There are limits of time, money, and expertise to this kind of access, but it does exist, and it occupies a great deal of the time of mid-level and senior public bureaucrats. This public exposure and access serves a purpose, but it also cuts down significantly on the efficiency of public bureaucrats. Thus, much of the lower efficiency of public agencies can be attributed to the political, judicial, legal, and publicity restraints put on public bureaucrats.

How Is the Executive Branch Organized?

Cabinet departments, agencies, and bureaus are the operating parts of the bureaucratic whole. These parts can be separated into four general types: 1) cabinet departments, 2) independent agencies, 3) government corporations, and 4) independent regulatory commissions.

Although Figure 7.1 is an "organizational chart" of the Department of Agriculture, any other department could have been used as an illustration. At the top is the head of the department, who in the United States is called the "secretary" of the department. Below the department head are several top administrators, such as the general counsel and the chief financial officer, whose responsibilities cut across the various departmental functions and enable the secretary to manage the entire organization. Of equal status are the assistant and undersecretaries, each of whom has management responsibilities for a group of operating agencies, which are arranged vertically below each of the assistant secretaries.

The next tier, generally called the "bureau level," is the highest level of responsibility for specialized programs. The names of these "bureau-level agencies" are often very well known to the public: The Forest Service and the Food Safety and Inspection Service are two examples. Sometimes they are officially called bureaus, as in the Federal Bureau of Investigation (FBI), which is a bureau in the Department of Justice. Nevertheless, "bureau" is also the generic term for this level of administrative agency. Within the bureaus, there are divisions, offices, services, and units—sometimes designating agencies of the same status, sometimes designating agencies of lesser status.

Not all government agencies are part of cabinet departments. Some independent agencies are set up by Congress outside the departmental structure

altogether, even though the president appoints and directs the heads of these agencies. Independent agencies usually have broad powers to provide public services that are either too expensive or too important to be left to private initiatives. Some examples of independent agencies are the National Aeronautics and Space Administration (NASA), the Central Intelligence Agency (CIA), and the Environmental Protection Agency (EPA). Government corporations are a third type of government agency, but are more like private businesses performing and charging for a market service, such as delivering the mail (the United States Postal Service) or transporting railroad passengers (Amtrak).

Yet a fourth type of agency is the independent regulatory commission, given broad discretion to make rules. The first regulatory agencies established by Congress, beginning with the Interstate Commerce Commission in 1887, were set up as independent regulatory commissions because Congress recognized that regulatory agencies are "mini-legislatures," whose rules are the same as legislation but require the kind of expertise and full-time attention that is beyond the capacity of Congress. Until the 1960s, most of the regulatory agencies that were set up by Congress, such as the Federal Trade Commission (1914) and the Federal Communications Commission (1934), were independent regulatory commissions. But beginning in the late 1960s and the early 1970s, all new regulatory programs, with two or three exceptions (such as the Federal Election Commission), were placed within existing departments and made directly responsible to the president. Since the 1970s, no major new regulatory programs have been established, independent or otherwise.

There are too many agencies in the executive branch to identify, much less to describe, so a simple classification of agencies will be helpful. Instead of dividing the bureaucracy into four general types, as we did previously, this classification is organized by the mission of each agency, as defined by its jurisdiction: clientele agencies, agencies for maintenance of the Union, regulatory agencies, and redistributive agencies. We shall examine each of these types of agencies, focusing

FIGURE 7.1

ORGANIZATIONAL CHART OF THE DEPARTMENT OF AGRICULTURE

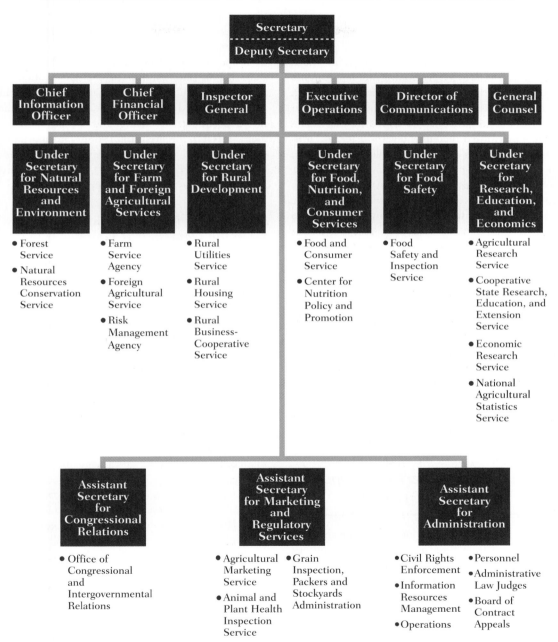

on both their formal structure and their place in the political process.

Clientele Agencies Serve Particular Interests

The entire Department of Agriculture is an example of a **clientele agency.** So are the departments of the Interior, Labor, and Commerce. Although all administrative agencies have clientele, certain agencies are singled out and called by that name because they are directed by law to foster and promote the interests of their clientele. For example, the Department of Commerce and Labor was founded in 1903 as a single department "to foster, promote, and develop the foreign and domestic commerce, the mining, the manufacturing, the shipping, and fishing industries, and the transportation facilities of the United States."[5] It remained a single department until 1913, when the law created the two separate departments of Commerce and Labor, with each statute providing for the same obligation: to support and foster their respective clienteles.[6] The Department of Agriculture serves the many farming interests that, taken together, are the United States' largest economic sector (agriculture accounts for one-fifth of the U.S. total domestic output).

One type of executive agency—the clientele agency—exists to foster the interests of a specific group in society. In turn, that group works to support its agency when it is in jeopardy.

Most clientele agencies locate a relatively large proportion of their total personnel in field offices dealing directly with the clientele. The Extension Service of the Department of Agriculture is among the most familiar, with its numerous local "extension agents" who consult with farmers on farm productivity. These same agencies also seek to foster the interests of their clientele by providing "functional representation"; that is, they try to learn what their clients' interests and needs are and then operate almost as a lobby in Washington on their behalf. In addition to the Department of Agriculture, other clientele agencies include the Department of Interior and the five newest cabinet departments. Housing and Urban Development (HUD), created in 1966; Transportation (DOT), created in 1966; Energy (DOE), created in 1977; and Education (ED) and Health and Human Services (HHS), both created in 1979.[7]

Agencies for Maintenance of the Union Keep the Government Going

These agencies could be called public order agencies were it not for the fact that the Constitution entrusts so many of the vital functions of public order, such as the police, to the state governments. But some agencies vital to maintaining *national* bonds do exist in the national government, and they can be grouped for convenience into three categories: (1) agencies for control of the sources of government revenue, (2) agencies for control of conduct defined as a threat to internal national security, and (3) agencies for defending American security from external threats. The departments of greatest power in these three areas are Treasury, Justice, Defense, State, and Homeland Security.

REVENUE AGENCIES   The Internal Revenue Service (IRS) is the most important revenue agency. The IRS is also one of the federal government's largest bureaucracies. Over one hundred thousand employees are spread through four regions, sixty-three districts, ten service centers, and hundreds of local offices. The IRS is not unresponsive to political influences, given its close working rela-

---

[5]32 Stat. 825; 15 USC 1501.

[6]For a detailed account of the creation of the Department of Commerce and Labor and its split into two separate departments, see Theodore J. Lowi, *The End of Liberalism* (New York: Norton, 1979), pp. 78–84.

[7]The departments of Education and of Health and Human Services until 1979 were joined in a single department, the Department of Health, Education, and Welfare (HEW), which had been established by Congress in 1953.

tionship with Congress through the staffs as well as the members of the House Ways and Means Committee and Senate Finance Committee. But the political patterns of the IRS are virtually opposite to those of a clientele agency; as one expert puts it, "probably no organization in the country, public or private, creates as much clientele *disfavor* as the Internal Revenue Service. The very nature of its work brings it into an adversary relationship with vast numbers of Americans every year."[8]

AGENCIES FOR INTERNAL SECURITY As long as the country is not in a state of insurrection, most of the task of maintaining the Union takes the form of legal work, and the main responsibility for that lies with the Department of Justice. It is indeed a luxury, and rare in the world, when national unity can be maintained by routines of civil law instead of imposed by military force.

A strong connection exists between Justice and Treasury, because a major share of the responsibility for protecting national revenue sources is held by the Tax Division of the Justice Department. This agency handles the litigation arising out of actions taken by the IRS against delinquency, fraud, and disputes over interpretation of the Internal Revenue Code—the source of the tax laws and court interpretations.

Although it looms so very large in American folklore, the FBI is simply another bureau of the Department of Justice. The FBI handles no litigation, but instead serves as the information-gathering agency for all the other divisions. Established in 1908, the FBI expanded and advanced in stature during the 1920s and 1930s under the early direction of J. Edgar Hoover. Although it is only one of the several bureaus and divisions in the department, and although it officially has no higher legal status than any of the others, its political importance is greater than that of the others. It is also the largest, taking

over 40 percent of the appropriations allocated to the Department of Justice.

AGENCIES FOR EXTERNAL NATIONAL SECURITY Two departments occupy center stage here, State and Defense. Although diplomacy is generally considered the primary task of the State Department, diplomatic missions are only one of its organizational dimensions. As of 1996, the State Department comprised nineteen bureau-level units, each under the direction of an assistant secretary. Six of these are geographic or regional bureaus concerned with all problems within a defined region of the world; nine are "functional" bureaus, handling such things as economic and business affairs, intelligence and research, and international organizations. Four are bureaus of internal affairs, which handle such areas as security, finance and management, and legal issues.

Despite the importance of the State Department in foreign affairs, fewer than 20 percent of all U.S. government employees working abroad are directly under its authority. By far the largest number of career government professionals working abroad are under the authority of the Defense Department.

The creation of the Department of Defense by legislation from 1947 to 1949 was an effort to unify the two historic military departments, the War Department and the Navy Department, and to integrate with them a new department, the Air Force Department. Real unification, however, did not occur. Instead, the Defense Department adds more pluralism to national security.

America's primary political problem with its military has not been the historic one of how to keep the military out of the politics of governing—a problem that has plagued so many countries in Europe and Latin America. The American military problem is one of the lower politics of the "pork barrel." President Clinton's long list of proposed military base closings, a major part of his budget-cutting drive for 1993, caused a firestorm of opposition even within his own party, including a number of members of Congress who were otherwise prominently in favor of significant reductions in the Pentagon

[8]George E. Berkley, *The Craft of Public Administration* (Boston: Allyn & Bacon, 1975), p. 417.

budget. Emphasis on local jobs rather than military strategy and policy involves pork barrel politics—and use of military budget issues for political purposes. The Republican desire to increase the amount of defense spending, and President Clinton's willingness to cooperate in such increases by having proposed a $25 billion supplemental increase in the Pentagon budget for 1995, even in the face of tremendous fiscal pressures, had more to do with the domestic pressures of employment in defense and defense-related industries than with military necessity in a post–cold war era. This is why Congress had to create a Base Closing Commission in the late 1980s with authority independent of Congress and the president to decide which military bases could be closed and whether and how to compensate communities for job losses and other sacrifices.

The best way to understand the military in American politics is to study it within the same bureaucratic framework used to explain the domestic agencies. The everyday political efforts of American military personnel seem largely self-interested.

Political considerations have frequently had an impact both on agencies for internal security and on agencies for external national security.

Regulatory Agencies Guide Individual Conduct

The United States has no Department of Regulation but has many **regulatory agencies.** Some of these are bureaus within departments, such as the Food and Drug Administration (FDA) in the Department of Health and Human Services, the Occupational Safety and Health Administration (OSHA) in the Department of Labor, and the Animal and Plant Health and Inspection Service (APHIS) in the Department of Agriculture. Other regulatory agencies are independent regulatory commissions. An example is the Federal Trade Commission (FTC). But whether departmental or independent, an agency or commission is regulatory if Congress delegates to it relatively broad powers over a sector of the economy or a type of commercial activity and authorizes it to make rules governing the conduct of people and businesses within that jurisdiction. Rules made by regulatory agencies have the force and effect of legislation; indeed, the rules they make are referred to as **administrative legislation.** And when these agencies make decisions or orders settling disputes between parties or between the government and a party, they are really acting like courts.

Regulatory agencies in the United States are given the authority to regulate various industries; these agencies often act like courts when making decisions or settling disputes.

Agencies for Redistribution Implement Fiscal/Monetary and Welfare Policies

Welfare agencies and fiscal/monetary agencies are responsible for the transfer of hundreds of billions of dollars annually between the public and the private spheres, and through such transfers these agencies influence how people and corporations spend and invest trillions of dollars annually. We call them agencies of redistribution because they influence the amount of money in the economy and because they directly influence who has money, who has credit, and whether people will want to invest or save their money rather than spend it.

Agencies of redistribution influence the amount of money in the economy and directly influence who has money, who has credit, and whether people will want to invest or spend.

FISCAL AND MONETARY AGENCIES   The best generic term for government activity affecting or relating to money is fiscal policy. However, we choose to make a further distinction, reserving *fis-*

cal for taxing and spending policies and using *monetary* for policies having to do with banks, credit, and currency. And the third, *welfare,* deserves to be treated as an equal member of this redistributive category.

Administration of fiscal policy is primarily performed in the Treasury Department. It is no contradiction to include the Treasury here as well as with the agencies for maintenance of the Union. This indicates that (1) the Treasury is a complex department performing more than one function of government, and (2) traditional controls have had to be adapted to modern economic conditions and new technologies.

Today, in addition to administering and policing income tax and other tax collections, the Treasury is also responsible for managing the enormous federal debt.

The Treasury Department is also responsible for printing the currency that we use, but currency represents only a tiny proportion of the entire money economy. Most of the trillions of dollars used in the transactions that comprise the private and public sectors of the U.S. economy exist on printed accounts and computers, not in currency.

Another important fiscal agency (although for technical reasons it is called an agency of monetary policy) is the **Federal Reserve System,** headed by the Federal Reserve Board. The Federal Reserve System (the Fed) has authority over the credit rates and lending activities of the nation's most important banks. Established by Congress in 1913, the Fed is responsible for adjusting the supply of money to the needs of banks in the different regions and of the commerce and industry in each. The Fed helps shift money from where there is too much to where it is needed. It also ensures that the banks do not overextend themselves by having lending policies that are too liberal, out of fear that if there is a sudden economic scare, a run on a few banks might be contagious and cause another terrible stock market crash like the one in 1929. The Federal Reserve Board sits at the top of the pyramid of twelve district Federal Reserve Banks, which are "bankers' banks," serving the monetary needs of the hundreds of member banks in the national bank system (see also Chapter 13).

WELFARE AGENCIES No single government agency is responsible for all the programs comprising the "welfare state." The largest agency in this field is the Social Security Administration (SSA), which manages the social insurance aspects of Social Security and SSI. Other agencies in the Department of Health and Human Services administer Temporary Assistance to Needy Families (TANF) and Medicaid, and the Department of Agriculture is responsible for the food stamp program. With the exception of Social Security, these are *means-tested* programs, requiring applicants to demonstrate that their total annual cash earnings fall below an officially defined poverty line. These public assistance programs comprise a large administrative burden.

In 1996, Congress adopted the Personal Responsibility and Work Opportunity Reconciliation Act (PRA), which abolished virtually all *national means-tested* public assistance programs, thereby terminating virtually all "entitlements" to welfare benefits to the poor, including single mothers and their children. This was without any question the largest single "devolution" of national power to state governments in U.S. history. However, those who expected revolutionary savings of government expenditures and responsibilities were in for a big disappointment. The national government continues to fund welfare programs, even though the money is allocated to the states in block grants, leaving maximum discretion to the states. Additional costs are involved in the fact that national and state governments are required by law to regulate these grants, because the 1996 law laid down some severe national standards for eligibility—for example, limits on years of eligibility for benefits.

WHO CONTROLS THE BUREAUCRACY?

Two hundred years, millions of employees, and trillions of dollars after the founding, we must return to James Madison's observation that "You must first enable the government to control the

CONCEPT MAP 7.1 CONGRESS, THE PRESIDENT, AND THE EXECUTIVE BRANCH

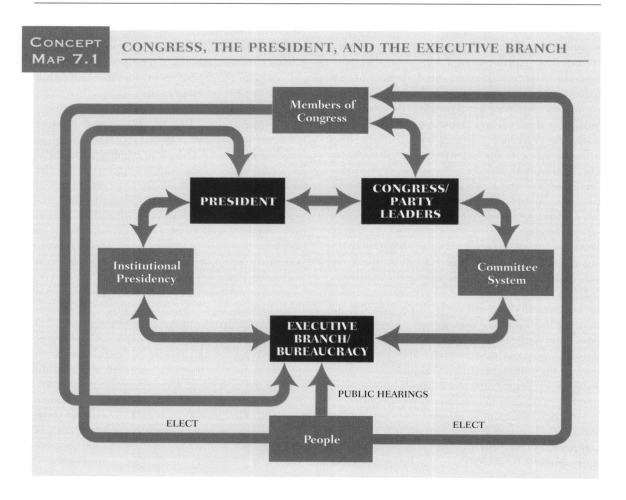

governed; and in the next place oblige it to control itself."[9] Today the problem is the same, but the form has changed. Our problem today is bureaucracy and our inability to keep it accountable to elected political authorities. We conclude this chapter with a review of the presidency and Congress as institutions for keeping the bureaucracy accountable (see Concept Map 7.1). Some of the facts from this and the preceding two chapters are repeated, but in this important context.

[9]Clinton Rossiter, ed., *The Federalist Papers* (New York: New American Library, 1961), No. 51.

The President as Chief Executive Can Direct Agencies

In 1939, President Roosevelt, through his President's Committee on Administrative Management, made the plea that "the president needs help." This is the story of the modern presidency. It can be told largely as a series of responses to the rise of big government: *Each expansion of the national government in the twentieth century has been accompanied by a parallel expansion of presidential management authority.*

FROM CABINET TO WHITE HOUSE STAFF We have already observed that the president's cabinet does not perform as a board of directors. The cabinet is not a constitutionally or historically recognized, collective decision-making body, and only a minority of the members of the cabinet are sufficiently in command of their own respective departments to be able to contribute much to the president's need to be an actual chief executive officer. The vacuum created by the absence of cabinet management has been filled to a certain extent by the White House staff.

Within the White House staff, in the past thirty years, the "special assistants to the president" have been given specialized jurisdictions over one or more executive departments. These staffers have additional power and credibility beyond their access to the president because they also have access to the CIA for international intelligence and to the FBI and the Treasury for knowledge about the agencies themselves. With this information, they can go beyond what the agencies themselves report and gain a great deal of leverage over executive departments.

Each expansion of the national government in the twentieth century has been accompanied by a parallel expansion of presidential management authority.

OMB AS A MANAGEMENT AGENCY It was not accidental that the Bureau of the Budget, established in 1921 and brought into the Executive Office of the Presidency (EOP) in 1939, was reorganized and given a new name (Office of Management and Budget [OMB]) in 1970. President Nixon was deeply committed to making the existing bureaucracy, a product of eight years of growth and commitment under the Democrats, more responsive to Republican programs. OMB was his instrument of choice, and the management power of the director of OMB seems to have increased with each president since Nixon. Some management authority had always been lodged with the director of the budget, but Nixon placed greater

emphasis on planning and budgetary allocations. From President Nixon onward, questions of management became central to the operation of the executive branch, but the need for executive management control goes far beyond what even the boldest of OMB directors can do.

REINVENTING GOVERNMENT President Clinton engaged in the most systematic and probably most successful effort to "change the way the government does business," to borrow a phrase he used to describe the goal of his National Performance Review (NPR). The NPR was one of the more important administrative reforms of the twentieth century. All recent American presidents have decried the size and unmanageability of the federal bureaucracy, but Clinton actually managed to turn proposals for change into real reform. The avowed goal of the NPR was to "reinvent government"—to make the federal bureaucracy more efficient, accountable, and effective. The NPR also focused on cutting red tape, streamlining the way the government purchases goods and services, improving the coordination of federal management, and simplifying federal rules.

The Clinton administration attempted, with some success, to make bureaucracy more efficient, accountable, and effective by creating the National Performance Review (NPR).

Congress Promotes Responsible Bureaucracy

Congress is constitutionally essential to responsible bureaucracy because, in "a government of laws," legislation is the key to government responsibility. When a law is passed and its intent is clear, the president knows what to "faithfully execute," and the agency understands its guidelines. But when Congress enacts vague legislation, everybody, from president to agency to courts to interest groups, gets involved in the interpretation of legislation. In that event, to whom is the agency responsible?

Congress's answer has not been to clarify its legislative intent but to try to supervise agency actions and interpretations through *oversight* (see also Chapter 5). The more legislative power Congress delegates to the executive branch, the more power it seeks to regain through committee and subcommittee oversight of executive branch agencies. The standing committee system of Congress is well-suited for oversight, inasmuch as most congressional committees and subcommittees have jurisdictions roughly parallel to one or more executive departments or agencies. Appropriations committees and authorization committees have oversight powers— and delegate their respective oversight powers to their subcommittees. In addition, there is a committee on government operations both in the House and the Senate, and these committees have oversight powers not limited by departmental jurisdiction.

Committees and subcommittees oversee agencies through public hearings. Representatives from each agency, the White House, major interest groups, and other concerned citizens are called as witnesses to present testimony at these hearings. These are printed in large volumes and are widely circulated. Detailed records of the recent activities and expenditures of each and every agency can be found in these volumes. The number of hearings and equivalent public meetings (sometimes called investigations) has increased dramatically during the past forty years, largely because there is more government to oversee.[10] New questions about the ability of Congress to exercise oversight arose when the Republicans took over Congress in 1995. Reductions in committee staffing and an empha-

sis on using investigative oversight to uncover scandal meant much less time spent on programmatic oversight. Moreover, congressional Republicans complained that they could not get sufficient information about programs from the White House to conduct effective oversight. Congressional records show that in 1991–1992, when Democrats controlled the House, they issued reports on fifty-five federal programs, while in 1997–1998, the Republican Congress issued only fourteen.[11] On issues of major national importance, multiple committees may initiate oversight hearings simultaneously. No less than a dozen congressional committees (along with the Justice Department and the Securities and Exchange Commission) launched investigations into the collapse of the giant energy company Enron. Enron's close ties to the Bush administration and its campaign contributions to hundreds of politicians from both parties aroused intense public interest in the hearings, many of which were televised live. The investigations covered a broad range of issues, including secret partnerships, public utility laws, 401(k) retirement plans, accounting practices, and Enron's political influence.

Although congressional oversight is potent because of Congress's power to make—and, therefore, to change—the law, often the most effective and influential lever over bureaucratic accountability is "the power of the purse"—the ability of the House and Senate committees and subcommittees on appropriations to look at agency performance through the microscope of the annual appropriations process. This annual process makes bureaucrats attentive to Congress because they know that Congress has a chance each year to reduce their funding.[12] A more recent evaluation of the budget and appropriations process by the NPR expressed one serious concern about oversight through appropriation: Pressure to cut appropriations "has put a premium on preserving particular programs, projects, and activities from Executive Branch as

[10]For figures on the frequency and character of oversight, see Lawrence Dodd and Richard Schott, *Congress and the Administrative State* (New York: Wiley, 1979), p. 169. See also Norman Ornstein et al., *Vital Statistics on Congress, 1987–88* (Washington, DC: Congressional Quarterly Press, 1987), pp. 161–62. For a valuable and skeptical assessment of legislative oversight of administration, see James W. Fesler and Donald F. Kettl, *The Politics of the Administrative Process* (Chatham, NJ: Chatham House, 1991), Chapter 11.

[11]Richard E. Cohen, "Crackup of the Committees," *National Journal,* 31 July 1999, p. 2214.
[12]See Aaron Wildavsky, *The New Politics of the Budgetary Process,* 2nd ed. (New York: HarperCollins, 1992), pp. 15–16.

well as congressional action."[13] This may be another explanation for why there may be some downsizing but almost no terminations of federal agencies.

Another form of legislative oversight is conducted by individual members of Congress. This is all part of Congress's "case work," and much of legislative oversight is for individual constituents seeking everything from honest information to favoritism. Some legislation and other good results may come from these acts of oversight by individual representatives and senators, but the greater influence of case work is to particularize the process, bringing the focus of administration away from good policy and responsible management to individual interests.

How Can Bureaucracy Be Reduced?

Americans like to complain about bureaucracy. Americans don't like Big Government because Big Government means Big Bureaucracy, and bureaucracy means *the federal service*—about 2.63 million civilian and 1.46 million military employees.[14] Promises to cut the bureaucracy are popular campaign appeals; "cutting out the fat" with big reductions in the number of federal employees is held out as a sure-fire way of cutting the deficit.

Despite fears of bureaucratic growth getting out of hand, however, the federal service has hardly grown at all during the past thirty years; it reached its peak postwar level in 1968 with 2.9 million civilian employees plus an additional 3.6 million military personnel (a figure swollen by Vietnam). The number of civilian federal executive-branch employees has since remained close to that figure. (In 2002, it was about 2,630,000.[15]) The growth of

the federal service is even less imposing when placed in the context of the total workforce and when compared to the size of state and local public employment which was 18,642,000 in 2002.[16] Figure 7.2 indicates that, since 1950, the ratio of federal service employment to the total workforce has been steady and in fact has declined slightly in the past twenty-five years. Another useful comparison is to be found in Figure 7.3. Although the dollar increase in federal spending shown by the bars looks very impressive, the horizontal line indicates that even here the national government has simply kept pace with the growth of the economy.

In sum, the national government is indeed "very large," but the federal service has not been growing any faster than the economy or the society. The same is roughly true of the growth pattern of state and local public personnel. Bureaucracy keeps pace with our society, despite our seeming dislike for it, because we can't operate the control towers, the prisons, the Social Security system, and other essential elements without bureaucracy. And we certainly could not have gone to war in Iraq without a gigantic military bureaucracy.

The national government is large, but the federal bureaucracy has not been growing any faster than the economy or society has.

Nevertheless some Americans continue to argue that bureaucracy is too big and should be reduced. In the 1990s, Americans seemed particularly enthusiastic about reducing (or to use the popular contemporary word, "downsizing") the federal bureaucracy.

Termination

The only *certain* way to reduce the size of the bureaucracy is to eliminate programs. Variations in the levels of federal personnel and expenditures demonstrate the futility of trying to make perma-

[13]National Performance Review, *From Red Tape to Results: Creating a Government That Works Better and Costs Less* (Washington, DC: U.S. Government Printing Office, 1993), p. 42.
[14]This is just under 99 percent of all national government employees. About 1.4 percent work for the legislative branch and for the federal judiciary. See Office of Management and Budget, *Historical Tables, Budget of the United States Government, Fiscal Year 2004* (Washington, DC: Government Printing Office, 2003), Table 17.5, p. 306.
[15]Ibid.

[16]Ibid.

FIGURE 7.2

EMPLOYEES IN THE FEDERAL SERVICE—AND IN THE FEDERAL WORKFORCE, 1946–2003

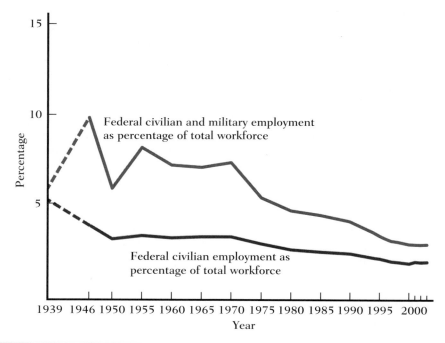

SOURCES: Office of Management and Budget, *Budget of the U.S. Government, Fiscal Year 2005, Historical Tables* (Washington, DC: Government Printing Office, 2004), p. 304, and U.S. Department of Labor, Bureau of Labor Statistics, *Employment and Earnings* (monthly).

nent cuts in existing agencies. Furthermore, most agencies have a supportive constituency that will fight to reinstate any cuts that are made. Termination is the only way to ensure an agency's reduction, and it is a rare occurrence.

The Republican-led 104th Congress (1995–96) was committed to the termination of programs. Newt Gingrich, speaker of the House, took Congress by storm with his promises of a virtual revolution in government. But when the dust had settled at the end of the first session of the first Gingrich-led Congress, no significant progress had been made toward downsizing through termination of agencies and programs.[17] The only two agencies

eliminated were the Office of Technology Assessment, which provided research for Congress, and the Advisory Council on Intergovernmental Relations, which studied the relationship between the federal government and the state. Significantly, neither of these agencies had a strong constituency to defend it.

The overall lack of success in terminating bureaucracy is a reflection of Americans' love/hate relationship with the national government. As antagonistic as Americans may be toward bureaucracy in general, they grow attached to the services being rendered and protections being offered by particular bureaucratic agencies—that is, they fiercely defend their favorite agencies while perceiving no inconsistency between that defense and their antagonistic attitude toward the bureaucracy in general. A good case in point was the agonizing problem of

[17]A thorough review of the first session of the 104th Congress will be found in "Republican's Hopes for 1996 Lie in Unfinished Business," *Congressional Quarterly Weekly Report*, 6 January 1996, pp. 6–18.

FIGURE 7.3

ANNUAL FEDERAL OUTLAYS, 1960–2008

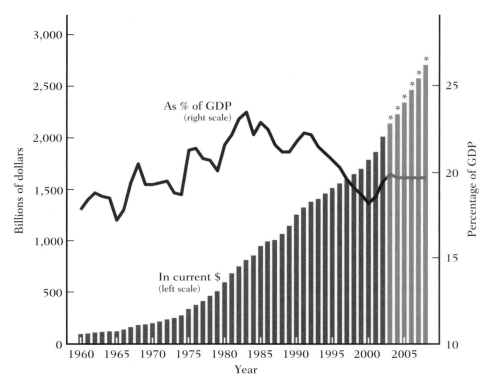

*Data from 1998–2008 are estimated.
SOURCE: Office of Management and Budget, *Historical Tables, Budget of the United States Government, Fiscal Year 2004* (Washington, DC: Government Printing Office, 2003), p. 55.

closing military bases in the wake of the end of the cold war with the former Soviet Union, when the United States no longer needed so many bases. Since every base is in some congressional member's district, it proved impossible for Congress to decide to close any of them. Consequently, between 1988 and 1990, Congress established a Defense Base Closure and Realignment Commission to decide on base closings, taking the matter out of Congress's hands altogether.[18] And even so, the process has been slow and agonizing.

Elected leaders have come to rely on a more incremental approach to downsizing the bureaucracy. Much has been done by budgetary means, reducing the budgets of all agencies across the board by small percentages, and cutting some less-supported agencies by larger amounts. Yet these changes are still incremental, leaving the existence of agencies unaddressed.

An additional approach has been taken to thwart the highly unpopular regulatory agencies, which are so small (relatively) that cutting their budgets contributes virtually nothing to reducing the deficit. This approach is called ***deregulation,*** simply defined as a reduction in the number of

[18]Public Law 101-510, Title XXIX, Sections 2,901 and 2,902 of Part A (Defense Base Closure and Realignment Commission).

rules promulgated by regulatory agencies. But deregulation by rule reduction is still incremental and has certainly not satisfied the hunger of the American public in general and Washington representatives in particular for a genuine reduction of bureaucracy.

Devolution

The next best approach to genuine reduction of the size of the bureaucracy is *devolution*—downsizing the federal bureaucracy by delegating the implementation of programs to state and local governments. Devolution often alters the pattern of who benefits most from government programs. In the early 1990s, a major devolution of transportation policy sought to open up decisions about transportation to a new set of interests. Since the 1920s, transportation policy had been dominated by road-building interests in the federal and state governments. Many advocates for cities and many environmentalists believed that the emphasis on road building hurt cities and harmed the environment. The 1992 reform, initiated by environmentalists, put more power in the hands of metropolitan planning organizations and lifted many federal restrictions on how the money should be spent. Reformers hoped that these changes would open up the decision-making process so those advocating alternatives to road building, such as mass transit, bike paths, and walking, would have more influence over how federal transportation dollars were spent. Although the pace of change has been slow, devolution has indeed brought new voices into decisions about transportation spending, and alternatives to highways have received increasing attention.

Often the central aim of devolution is to provide more efficient and flexible government services. Yet, by its very nature, devolution entails variation across the states. In some states, government services may improve as a consequence of devolution. In other states, services may deteriorate as the states use devolution as an opportunity to cut spending and reduce services. This has been the pattern in the implementation of the welfare reform passed in 1996, the most significant devolution of federal government social programs in many decades. Some states, such as Wisconsin, have used the flexibility of the reform to design innovative programs that respond to clients' needs; other states, such as Idaho, have virtually dismantled their welfare programs. Because the legislation placed a five-year lifetime limit on receiving welfare, the states will take on an even greater role in the future as existing clients lose their eligibility for federal benefits. Welfare reform has been praised by many for reducing welfare rolls and responding to the public desire that welfare be a temporary program. At the same time, it has placed more low-income women and their children at risk for being left with no form of assistance at all, depending on the state in which they live.

This is the dilemma that devolution poses. To a point, variation can be considered one of the virtues of federalism. But there are dangers inherent in large variations in the provisions of services and benefits in a democracy.

Privatization, another downsizing option, seems like a synonym for termination, but that is true only at the extreme. Most of what is called "privatization" is not termination at all but the provision of government goods and services by private contractors under direct government supervision. Except for top-secret strategic materials, virtually all of the production of military hardware, from boats to bullets, is done on a privatized basis by private contractors. Billions of dollars of research services are bought under contract by governments; these private contractors are universities as well as ordinary industrial corporations and private "think tanks." *Privatization* simply means that a formerly public activity is picked up under contract by a private company or companies. But such programs are still very much government programs; they are paid for and supervised by government. Privatization downsizes the government only in that the workers providing the service are no longer counted as part of the government bureaucracy.

The central aim of privatization is to reduce the cost of government. When private contractors can perform a task as well as government but for less money, taxpayers win. Often the losers in such situations are the workers. Government workers are generally unionized and, therefore, receive good pay and benefits. Private sector workers are less likely to be unionized, and private firms often provide lower pay and fewer benefits. For this reason, public sector unions have been one of the strongest voices arguing against privatization. Other critics of privatization observe that private firms may not be more efficient or less costly than government. This is especially likely when there is little competition among private firms and when public bureaucracies are not granted a fair chance to bid in the contracting competition. When private firms have a monopoly on service provision, they may be less efficient than government and more expensive. This problem raises important questions about how private contractors can be held accountable. As one analyst of Pentagon spending put it, "The Pentagon is supposed to be representing the taxpayer and the public interest—its national security. So it's really important to have transparency, to be able to see these competitions and hold people accountable."[19] As security has become the nation's paramount concern, new worries about privatization have surfaced. Some Pentagon officials fear that too many tasks vital to national security may have already been contracted out and that national security might best be served by limiting privatization.

The new demands of domestic security have altered the thrust of bureaucratic reform. The emphasis on reducing the size of government that was so prominent during the previous two decades is gone. Instead, there is an acceptance that the federal government will grow as needed to ensure the safety of American citizens. The administration's effort to focus the entire federal bureaucracy on a single central mission will require unprecedented levels of coordination among federal agencies. Despite the strong agreement on the goal of fighting terrorism, the effort to streamline the bureaucracy around a single purpose is likely to face considerable obstacles along the way. Reform of public bureaucracies is always complex because strong constituencies may attempt to block changes that they believe will harm them. Initiatives that aim to improve coordination among agencies can easily provoke political disputes if the proposed changes threaten to alter the access of groups to the bureaucracy. And groups that oppose bureaucratic changes can appeal to Congress to intervene on their behalf. As respected reform advocate Donald Kettl said of the effort to reinvent government, "Virtually no reform that really matters can be achieved without at least implicit congressional support."[20] In wartime, many obstacles to bureaucratic reform are lifted. But the war on terrorism is an unusual war that will be fought over an extended period of time. Whether the unique features of this war improve or limit the prospects for bureaucratic reform remains to be seen.

DOES BUREAUCRACY WORK?

Our concern in the first two sections of this chapter was to present a picture of bureaucracy, its necessity as well as the particular uses to which the national government puts it. We then explored how the American system of government has tried to accommodate this vast apparatus to the requirements of representative democracy. We then turned this issue on its head and looked at how democratic processes have sought to make this bureaucratic apparatus somewhat smaller. And we now conclude by analyzing whether bureaucracy can work by being both democratic and efficient.

The subtitle of the chapter, "Bureaucracy in a Democracy," was intended to convey the sense that the two are contradictory. We cannot live without bureaucracy—it is the most efficient way to organize people to get a large collective job done. But

[19]Ellen Nakashima, "Defense Balks at Contract Goals; Essential Services Should Not Be Privatized, Pentagon Tells OMB," *Washington Post*, 30 January 2002, p. A21.

[20]Quoted in Stephen Bar, "Midterm Exam for 'Reinvention': Study Cites 'Impressive Results' but Calls for Strategy to Win Congressional Support," *Washington Post*, 19 August 1994, p. A25.

we can't live comfortably with bureaucracy either. Bureaucracy requires hierarchy, appointed authority, and professional expertise. Those requirements make bureaucracy the natural enemy of representation, which requires discussion and reciprocity among equals. Yet the task is not to retreat from bureaucracy but to take advantage of its strengths while trying to make it more accountable to the demands that democratic policies and representative government make upon it.

Indeed, as the president and Congress seek to translate the ideal of democratic accountability into practice, they struggle to find the proper balance between administrative discretion and the public's right to know. An administration whose every move is subject to intense public scrutiny may be hamstrung in its efforts to carry out the public interest. On the other hand, a bureaucracy that is shielded from the public eye may wind up pursuing its own interests rather than those of the public. The last century has seen a double movement toward strengthening the managerial capacity of the presidency and making bureaucratic decision making more transparent. The purpose of these reforms has been to create an effective, responsive bureaucracy. But reforms alone cannot guarantee democratic accountability. Presidential and congressional vigilance in the defense of the public interest is essential.

Although Congress attempts to control the bureaucracy through oversight, a more effective way to ensure accountability may be to clarify legislative intent.

Another approach to bureaucratic accountability is for Congress to spend more of its time clarifying its legislative intent and less of its time on committee or individual oversight. If the intent of the law were clear, Congress could then count on the president to maintain a higher level of bureaucratic responsibility, because bureaucrats are more responsive to clear legislative guidance than to any-

IN BRIEF BOX — HOW THE THREE BRANCHES REGULATE BUREAUCRACY

The president may	appoint and remove agency heads.
	reorganize the bureaucracy (with congressional approval).
	make changes in agencies' budget proposals.
	initiate or adjust policies that would alter the bureaucracy's activities.
Congress may	pass legislation that alters the bureaucracy's activities.
	abolish existing programs.
	investigate bureaucratic activities and force bureaucrats to testify about them.
	influence presidential appointments of agency heads and other officials.
The judiciary may	rule on whether bureaucrats have acted within the law and require policy changes to comply with the law.
	force the bureaucracy to respect the rights of individuals through hearings and other proceedings.
	rule on the constitutionality of all rules and regulations.

thing else. Nevertheless, this is not a neat and sure solution, because Congress and the president can still be at odds, and when they are at odds, bureaucrats have an opportunity to evade responsibility by playing one branch off against the other.

As to the vast apparatus, bureaucracy is here to stay. The administration of myriad government functions and responsibilities in a large, complex society will always require "rule by desks and offices" (the literal meaning of *bureaucracy*). No "reinvention" of government, however well conceived or executed, can alter that basic fact, nor can it resolve the problem of reconciling bureaucracy in a democracy. President Clinton's National Performance Review accomplished some impressive things: The national bureaucracy has become somewhat smaller, and in the next few years, it will become smaller still; government procedures are being streamlined and are under tremendous pressure to become even more efficient. But these efforts are no guarantee that the bureaucracy itself will become more malleable. Congress will not suddenly change its practice of loose and vague legislative draftsmanship. Presidents will not suddenly discover new reserves of power or vision to draw more tightly the reins of responsible management. No deep solution can be found in quick fixes. As with all complex social and political problems, the solution lies mainly in a sober awareness of the nature of the problem. This awareness enables people to avoid fantasies and myths about the abilities of a democratized presidency—or the potential of a reform effort, or the powers of technology, or the populist rhetoric of a new Congress—to change the nature of governance by bureaucracy.

CHAPTER REVIEW

Most American citizens possess less information and more misinformation about bureaucracy than about any other feature of government. We therefore began the chapter with an elementary definition of bureaucracy, identifying its key characteristics and demonstrating the extent to which bureaucracy is not only a phenomenon but an American phenomenon. In the second section of the chapter, we showed how all essential government services and controls are carried out by bureaucracies—or to be more objective, administrative agencies. Following a very general description of the different general types of bureaucratic agencies in the executive branch, we divided the agencies of the executive branch into four categories according to mission: the clientele agencies, the agencies for maintaining the Union, the regulatory agencies, and the agencies for redistribution. These illustrate the varieties of administrative experience in American government. Although the bureaucratic phenomenon is universal, not all the bureaucracies are the same in the way they are organized, in the degree of their responsiveness, or in the way they participate in the political process.

Finally, the chapter concluded with a review of all three of the chapters on "representative government" in order to assess how well the two political branches (the legislative and the executive) do the toughest job any government has to do: making the bureaucracy accountable to the people it serves and controls. "Bureaucracy in a Democracy" is the subtitle and theme of the chapter not because we have succeeded in democratizing bureaucracies but because it is the never-ending task of politics in a democracy.

KEY TERMS

administrative adjudication   Applying rules and precedents to specific cases to settle disputes with regulated parties.

administrative legislation   Rules made by regulatory agencies and commissions.

bureaucracy   The complex structure of offices, tasks, rules, and principles of organization that are employed by all large-scale institutions to coordinate the work of their personnel.

clientele agencies   Departments or bureaus of government whose mission is to promote, serve, or represent a particular interest.

deregulation   A policy of reducing or eliminating regulatory restraints in the conduct of individuals or private institutions.

devolution   A policy to remove a program from one level of government by delegating it or passing it down to a lower level of government, such as from the national government to the states.

Federal Reserve System (Fed)   Consisting of twelve Federal Reserve Banks, an agency that facilitates exchanges of cash, checks, and credit; it regulates member banks, and it uses monetary policies to fight inflation and deflation.

implementation   The efforts of departments and agencies to translate laws into specific bureaucratic routines.

oversight   The effort by Congress, through hearings, investigations, and other techniques, to exercise control over the activities of executive agencies.

privatization   Removing all or part of a program from the public sector to the private sector.

regulatory agencies   Departments, bureaus, or independent agencies whose primary mission is to impose limits, restrictions, or other obligations on the conduct of individuals or companies in the private sector.

rulemaking   A quasilegislative administrative process that produces regulations by government agencies.

FOR FURTHER READING

Arnold, Peri E. *Making the Managerial Presidency: Comprehensive Organization Planning.* Princeton: Princeton University Press, 1986.

Downs, Anthony. *Inside Bureaucracy.* Boston: Little, Brown, 1966.

Fesler, James W., and Donald F. Kettl. *The Politics of the Administrative Process.* Chatham, NJ: Chatham House, 1991.

Heclo, Hugh. *A Government of Strangers.* Washington, DC: Brookings Institution, 1977.

Skowronek, Stephen. *Building a New American State:* *The Expansion of National Administrative Capacities, 1877–1920.* New York: Cambridge University Press, 1982.

Wildavsky, Aaron. *The New Politics of the Budget Process,* 2nd ed. New York: HarperCollins, 1992.

Wilson, James Q. *Bureaucracy: What Government Agencies Do and Why They Do It.* New York: Basic Books, 1989.

Wood, Dan B. *Bureaucratic Dynamics: The Role of Bureaucracy in a Democracy.* Boulder, CO: Westview, 1994.

CHAPTER 8

The Federal Courts: Least Dangerous Branch or Imperial Judiciary?

How Courts Work

Originally, a "court" was the place where a sovereign ruled—where the king and his entourage governed. Settling disputes between citizens was part of governing. According to the Bible, King Solomon had to settle the dispute between two women over which of them was the mother of the child both claimed. Judging is the settling of disputes, a function that was slowly separated from the king and the king's court and made into a separate institution of government. Courts have taken over from kings the power to settle controversies by hearing the facts on both sides and deciding which side possesses the greater merit. But since judges are not kings, they must have a basis for their authority. That basis in the United States is the Constitution and the law. Courts decide cases by hearing the facts on both sides of a dispute and applying the relevant law or principle to the facts. (See the In Brief Box on page 177 for an explanation of the various types of laws and disputes.)

Courts as Political Institutions

Judges are central players in important political institutions and this makes them politicians. To understand what animates judicial behavior, we thus need to place the judge or justice in con-

CORE OF THE ANALYSIS

- The power of judicial review makes the Supreme Court more than a judicial agency; it also makes the Court a major lawmaking body.
- The dominant influences shaping Supreme Court decisions are the philosophies and attitudes of the members of the Court and the solicitor general's control over cases involving the government.
- The role and power of the federal courts, particularly the Supreme Court, have been significantly strengthened and expanded over the last fifty years.

text by briefly considering the role of the courts in the political system more generally. In doing so, we emphasize the role of courts as *dispute resolvers,* as *coordinators,* and as *interpreters of rules.*

DISPUTE RESOLUTION   So much of the productive activity that occurs within families, among friends and associates, and even between absolute strangers takes place because the participants do not have to devote substantial resources to protecting themselves and their property or monitoring compliance with agree-

CENTRAL QUESTIONS

• **How Courts Work**
  Within what broad categories of law do cases arise?
  How is the U.S. court system structured?

• **Federal Jurisdiction**
  What is the importance of the federal court system?
  What factors play a role in the appointment of federal judges?

• **Judicial Review**
  What is the basis for the Supreme Court's power of judicial review?
  How does the power of judicial review make the Supreme Court a lawmaking body?

• **The Supreme Court in Action**
  How does a case reach the Supreme Court? What shapes the flow of cases through the
     Supreme Court? Once accepted, how does a case proceed?
  What factors influence the judicial philosophy of the Supreme Court?

• **Judicial Power and Politics**
  How has the power of the federal courts been limited throughout much of American
     history?
  How have the role and power of the federal courts been transformed over the last fifty
     years?
  How has the increase in the Supreme Court's power changed its role in the political
     process?

ments.[1] For any potential violation of person or property, or defection from an agreement, all parties know in advance that an aggrieved party may take an alleged violator to court. The court, in turn, serves as a venue in which the facts of a case are established, punishment is meted out to violators, and compensation awarded to victims. The court, therefore, is an institution that engages in fact-finding and judgment.

In disputes between private parties, the court serves principally to determine whether claims of violation can be substantiated. An employee, for example, may sue her employer for allegedly violating the terms of a privately negotiated employment contract. Or a consumer may sue a producer for violating the terms of a product warranty. Or a tenant may sue a landlord for violating provisions of a lease. In all of these cases, some issue between private parties is in dispute. The court system provides the service of dispute resolution.

The examples in the preceding paragraph involve civil law. An entirely separate category of dispute, one in which the courts also have a role to play, involves criminal law. In these cases, "the public" is a party to the dispute because the alleged violation concerns not (only) something involving private parties, but (also) a public law. This brings the public agencies of justice into play as parties to a dispute. When an individual embezzles funds from his partner, he not only violates a privately negotiated agreement between them (namely, a promise of honest dealings), he also violates a public law prohibiting embezzlement generally. A court proceeding, in this case, determines not only

---

[1]Naturally, some resources are devoted to protection and monitoring. However, if extraordinary resources had to be devoted, then their rising cost would cause the frequency of the productive activities alluded to in the text to decline, according to elementary economic theory. Indeed, since the costs of negotiating, monitoring, and enforcing agreements (what political economists call *transaction costs*) can be very high, they are a serious impediment to social interaction and productive activities of all sorts. Economizing on them—by providing the services of courts and judges, for example—is one of the great contributions of the modern state to social welfare.

IN BRIEF BOX — TYPES OF LAWS AND DISPUTES

Type of law	Type of case or dispute	Form of case
Criminal law	Cases arising out of actions that violate laws protecting the health, safety, and morals of the community. The government is always the plaintiff.	*U.S. (or state) v. Jones* *Jones v. U.S. (or state)*, if Jones lost and is appealing
Civil law	"Private law," involving disputes between citizens or between government and citizen where no crime is alleged. Two general types are contract and tort. *Contract cases* are disputes that arise over voluntary actions. *Tort cases* are disputes that arise out of obligations inherent in social life. Negligence and slander are examples of torts.	*Smith v. Jones* *New York v. Jones* *U.S. v. Jones* *Jones v. New York*
Public law	All cases where the powers of government or the rights of citizens are involved. The government is the defendant. *Constitutional law* involves judicial review of the basis of a government's action in relation to specific clauses of the Constitution as interpreted in Supreme Court cases. *Administrative law* involves disputes of the statutory authority, jurisdiction, or procedures of administrative agencies.	*Jones v. U.S. (or state)* *In re Jones* *Smith v. Jones*, if a license or statute is at issue in their private dispute

whether a violation of a private arrangement has occurred but also whether the alleged perpetrator is innocent or guilty of violating a public law.

In all of these instances, the judge is responsible for managing the fact-finding and judgment phases of dispute resolution (sometimes in collaboration with a jury). Thus, a large part of the daily life of a judge involves making an independent, experienced assessment of the facts, determining whether the dispute involves a violation of a private agreement or a public law (or both), and finally rendering a judgment—a determination of which

party (if either) is liable, and what compensation is in order (to the private party victimized and, if judged a criminal activity, to the larger public). Judging is a sophisticated blend of the skills involved in reading a mystery novel, solving a crossword puzzle, and providing wise counsel.

COORDINATION   Dispute resolution occurs after the fact—that is, after a dispute has already occurred. In a manner of speaking, it represents a failure of the legal system since one function of law and its judicial institutions is to discourage such disputes in the first place. We may also think of courts and judges as before-the-fact *coordination mechanisms* inasmuch as the anticipation of what happens once their services are called upon allows private parties to form rational expectations and thereby coordinate their actions in advance of possible disputes. A prospective embezzler, estimating the odds of getting caught, prosecuted, and subsequently punished, may think twice about cheating his partner. Surely, *some* prospective embezzlers are deterred from their crimes by these prospects. Conversely, the legal system can work as an incentive: Two acquaintances, for example, may confidently entertain the possibility of going into business together, knowing that the sword of justice hangs over their collaboration.

In this sense, the court system is as important for what it doesn't do as for what it does. The system of courts and law coordinates private behavior by providing incentives and disincentives for specific actions. To the extent that these work, there are fewer disputes to resolve and thus less after-the-fact dispute resolution for courts and judges to engage in. What makes the incentives and disincentives work is their power (are the rewards and penalties big or small?), their clarity, and the consistency with which judges administer them. Clear incentives, consistently employed, provide powerful motivations for private parties to resolve disputes ahead of time. This sort of advanced coordination, encouraged by a properly functioning legal system, economizes on the transaction costs that would diminish the frequency of, and otherwise discourage, socially desirable activity.

RULE INTERPRETATION   Dispute resolution and coordination affect private behavior and the daily lives of ordinary citizens tremendously. Judges, however, are not entirely free agents (despite the fact that some of them are tyrants in their courtrooms). In matching the facts of a specific case to judicial principles and statutory guidelines, judges must engage in *interpretive* activity. They must determine what particular statutes or judicial principles mean, which of them fit the facts

of a particular case, and then, having determined all this, they must ascertain the disposition of the case at hand. Does the statute of 1927 regulating the electronic transmission of radio waves apply to television, cellular phones, ship-to-shore radios, fax machines, and e-mail? Does the law governing the transportation of dangerous substances, passed in 1937, apply to nuclear fuels, infected animals, and artificially created biological hazards? Often, the enacting legislative body has not been crystal clear about the scope of the legislation it passes. Indeed, a legislature acting in 1927 or 1937 could not have anticipated technological developments to come. Nevertheless, cases such as these come up on a regular basis, and judges must make judgment calls, so to speak, on highly complex issues.

Interpreting the rules is probably the single most important activity in which higher courts engage. This is because the court system is *hierarchical* in the sense that judgments by higher courts constrain the discretion of judges in lower courts. If the Supreme Court rules that nuclear fuels are covered by the 1937 law on transporting dangerous substances, then lower courts must render subsequent judgments in a manner consistent with this ruling. The judge in a civil or criminal trial concerning the shipment of nuclear isotopes from a laboratory to a commercial user, for example, must make sure his or her ruling complies with the legal interpretations passed down by the higher courts. Also, because of the federal principle by which the American polity is organized, federal law and interpretations thereof often trump state and local laws.

As we shall see in the following section, courts and judges engage not only in *statutory interpretation* but in *constitutional interpretation* as well. Here they interpret the provisions of the U.S. Constitution, determining their scope and content. In determining, for example, whether the act of Congress regulating the transportation of dangerous substances from one state to another is constitutional, the justices of the Supreme Court might appeal to the commerce clause of the Constitution (allowing the federal government to regulate interstate commerce) to justify the constitutionality of that act. On the other hand, a Supreme Court majority might also rule that a shipment of spent fuel rods from a nuclear reactor in Kansas City to a nuclear waste facility outside of St. Louis is *not* covered by this law since the shipment took place entirely within the boundaries of a single state and, thus, did not constitute interstate commerce.

In short, judges and justices are continually engaged in elaborating, embellishing, even rewriting the rules by which private and public life are organized. In these interpretive acts they are conscious of the fact that their rulings will affect not only the participants in a specific case before them, but also will carry interpretive weight in all similar cases that percolate down to the lower courts. Thus, statutory and constitutional interpretations have authority over subsequent deliberations (and, in turn, are themselves influenced by earlier interpretations according to *stare decisis*).

However, judicial interpretation—elaboration, embellishment, and "redrafting"—of statutes is naturally subject to review. Statutory interpretation, even if it is conducted by the highest court in the land, is exposed to legislative review. If Congress is unhappy with a specific statutory interpretation—for example, suppose the current Congress does not like the idea of federal regulation of e-mail that a federal court claimed to be permissible under the 1927 act on electronic transmission—then it may amend the legislation so as to reverse the court ruling explicitly. Of course, if the court makes a *constitutional* ruling, Congress cannot then abrogate that ruling through new legislation. But Congress can commence the process of constitutional amendment, thereby effectively reversing constitutional interpretations with which it disagrees.

In this chapter, we will first examine the judicial process, including the types of cases that the federal courts consider. Second, we will assess the organization and structure of the federal court system as well as the flow of cases through the courts. Third, we will consider judicial review and how it makes the Supreme Court a "lawmaking body." Fourth, we will examine various influences on the

Supreme Court. Finally, we will analyze the role and power of the federal courts in the American political process, looking in particular at the growth of judicial power in the United States. The framers of the American Constitution called the Court the "least dangerous branch" of American government. Today, it is not unusual to hear friends and foes of the Court alike refer to it as the "imperial judiciary."[2] Before we can understand this transformation and its consequences, however, we must look in some detail at America's judicial process.

Cases and the Law

Court cases in the United States proceed under three broad categories of law: criminal law, civil law, and public law.

Cases of **criminal law** are those in which the government charges an individual with violating a statute that has been enacted to protect the public health, safety, morals, or welfare. In criminal cases, the government is always the **plaintiff** (the party that brings charges) and alleges that a criminal violation has been committed by a named **defendant.** Most criminal cases arise in state and municipal courts and involve matters ranging from traffic offenses to robbery and murder. While the great bulk of criminal law is still a state matter, a growing body of federal criminal law deals with such matters as tax evasion, mail fraud, and the sale of narcotics. Defendants found guilty of criminal violations may be fined or sent to prison.

Cases of **civil law** involve disputes among individuals or between individuals and the government where no criminal violation is charged. But unlike criminal cases, the losers in civil cases cannot be fined or sent to prison, although they may be required to pay monetary damages for their actions. In a civil case, the one who brings a complaint is the plaintiff and the one against whom the complaint is brought is the defendant. The two most common types of civil cases involve contracts and torts. In a typical contract case, an individual or

[2]See Richard Neely, *How Courts Govern America* (New Haven: Yale University Press, 1981).

corporation charges that it has suffered because of another's violation of a specific agreement between the two. For example, the Smith Manufacturing Corporation may charge that Jones Distributors failed to honor an agreement to deliver raw materials at a specified time, causing Smith to lose business. Smith asks the court to order Jones to compensate it for the damage allegedly suffered. In a typical tort case, one individual charges that he or she has been injured by another's negligence or malfeasance. Medical malpractice suits are one example of tort cases.

Court cases in the United States proceed under three broad categories of law: criminal, civil, and public.

In deciding cases, courts apply statutes (laws) and legal *precedents* (prior decisions). State and federal statutes, for example, often govern the conditions under which contracts are and are not legally binding. Jones Distributors might argue that it was not obliged to fulfill its contract with the Smith Corporation because actions by Smith, such as the failure to make promised payments, constituted fraud under state law. Attorneys for a physician being sued for malpractice, on the other hand, may search for prior instances in which courts ruled that actions similar to those of their client did not constitute negligence. Such precedents are applied under the doctrine of *stare decisis,* a Latin phrase meaning "let the decision stand."

Courts use legal precedent to render judgments. Precedent can take the form of previous court cases, federal law, or state law.

A case becomes a matter of the third category, *public law,* when plaintiffs or defendants in a civil or criminal case seeks to show that their case involves the powers of government or rights of citizens as defined under the Constitution or by statute. One major form of public law is constitutional law, under which a court will examine the

government's actions to see if they conform to the Constitution as it has been interpreted by the judiciary. Thus, what began as an ordinary criminal case may enter the realm of public law if a defendant claims that the police violated his or her constitutional rights. Another important arena of public law is administrative law, which involves disputes over the jurisdiction, procedures, or authority of administrative agencies. Under this type of law, civil litigation between an individual and the government may become a matter of public law if the individual asserts that the government is violating a statute or abusing its power under the Constitution. For example, land owners have asserted that federal and state restrictions on land use constitute violations of the Fifth Amendment's restrictions on the government's ability to confiscate private property. Recently, the Supreme Court has been very sympathetic to such claims, which effectively transform an ordinary civil dispute into a major issue of public law.

Most of the important Supreme Court cases we will examine in this chapter involve judgments concerning the constitutional or statutory basis of the actions of government agencies. As we shall see, it is in this arena of public law that the Supreme Court's decisions can have significant consequences for American politics and society.

Types of Courts

In the United States, systems of courts have been established both by the federal government and by the governments of the individual states. Both systems have several levels, as shown in Figure 8.1. More than 99 percent of all court cases in the United States are heard in state courts. The overwhelming majority of criminal cases, for example, involves violations of state laws prohibiting such actions as murder, robbery, fraud, theft, and assault. If such a case is brought to trial, it will be heard in a state *trial court,* in front of a judge and sometimes a jury, who will determine whether the defendant violated state law. If the defendant is convicted, he or she may appeal the conviction to a higher court, such as a state *court of appeals,* and from there to a state's *supreme court.* Simi-

THE U.S. COURT SYSTEM

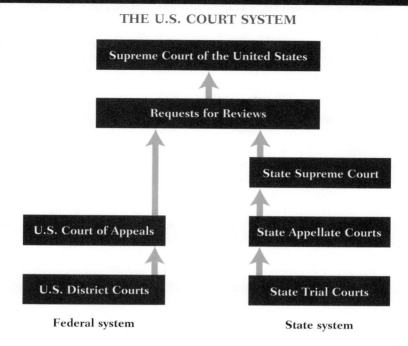

Federal system   **State system**

larly, in civil cases, most litigation is brought in the courts established by the state in which the activity in question took place. For example, a patient bringing suit against a physician for malpractice would file the suit in the appropriate court in the state where the alleged malpractice occurred. The judge hearing the case would apply state law and state precedent to the matter at hand. (It should be noted that in both criminal and civil matters, most cases are settled before trial through negotiated agreements between the parties. In criminal cases, these agreements are called *plea bargains.*)

Three types of state courts exist: trial courts, where a defendant is convicted or acquitted of violating state law; appellate courts, where a convicted defendant may appeal; and the supreme court, which is the state's highest appellate court.

Although each state has its own set of laws, these laws have much in common from state to state. Murder and robbery, obviously, are illegal in all states, although the range of possible punishments for those crimes varies from state to state. Some states, for example, provide for capital punishment (the death penalty) for murder and other serious offenses; other states do not. As we saw in Chapter 4, however, some acts that are criminal offenses in one state may be legal in another state. Prostitution, for example, is legal in some Nevada counties, although it is outlawed in all other states. Considerable similarity among the states is also found in the realm of civil law. In the case of contract law, most states have adopted the *Uniform Commercial Code* in order to reduce interstate differences. In areas such as family law, however, which covers such matters as divorce and child custody arrangements, state laws vary greatly.

Cases are heard in the federal courts if they involve federal laws, treaties with other nations, or the U.S. Constitution; these areas are the official *jurisdiction* of the federal courts. In addition, any case in which the U.S. government is a party is heard in the federal courts. If, for example, an individual is charged with violating a federal criminal statute, such as evading the payment of income taxes, a federal prosecutor would bring charges before a federal judge. Civil cases involving the citizens of more than one state and in which more than fifty thousand dollars is at stake may be heard in either the federal or the state courts, usually depending upon the preference of the plaintiff.

Federal courts serve another purpose in addition to trying cases within their jurisdiction: that of hearing appeals from state-level courts. Individuals found guilty of breaking a state criminal law, for example, can appeal their convictions to a federal court by raising a constitutional issue and asking a federal court to determine whether the state's actions were consistent with the requirements of the U.S. Constitution. An appellant might assert, for example, that the state court denied him or her the right to counsel, imposed excessive bail, or otherwise denied the appellant *due process.* Under such circumstances, an appellant can ask the federal court to overturn his or her conviction. Federal courts are not obligated to accept such appeals and will do so only if they feel that the issues raised have considerable merit and if the appellant has exhausted all possible remedies within the state courts. (This procedure is discussed in more detail later in this chapter.) The decisions of state supreme courts may also be appealed to the U.S. Supreme Court if the state court's decision has conflicted with prior U.S. Supreme Court rulings or has raised some important question of federal law. Such appeals are accepted by the U.S. Supreme Court at its discretion.

The jurisdiction of federal courts includes cases that involve federal laws, the Constitution, and treaties with other nations. Federal courts also hear appeals from state courts.

Although the federal courts hear only a small fraction of all the civil and criminal cases decided each year in the United States, their decisions are extremely important. It is in the federal courts that the Constitution and federal laws that govern all Americans are interpreted and their meaning and significance established. Moreover, it is in the federal courts that the powers and limitations of the increasingly powerful national government are tested. Finally, through their power to review the decisions of the state courts, it is ultimately the federal courts that dominate the American judicial system.

FEDERAL JURISDICTION

The overwhelming majority of court cases are tried not in federal courts but in state and local courts under state common law, state statutes, and local ordinances. Of all cases heard in the United States in 2003, federal district courts (the lowest federal level) received 323,604. Although this number is up substantially from the 87,000 cases heard in 1961, it still constitutes under 1 percent of the judiciary's business. A major reason that the case load of the federal courts has increased in recent years is that Congress has greatly expanded the number of federal crimes, particularly in the realm of drug possession and sale. Behavior that once was exclusively a state criminal question has, to some extent, come within the reach of federal law. Former Chief Justice William Rehnquist criticized Congress for federalizing too many offenses and intruding unnecessarily into areas that should be handled by the states.[3] The federal courts of appeal listened to 60,847 cases in 2003, and 9,406 cases were filed with the U.S. Supreme Court during its 2002–2003 term. Most of the cases filed with the Supreme Court are dismissed without a ruling on their merits. The Court has broad latitude to decide what cases it will hear and generally listens only to those cases it deems to raise the most important issues. Only 84 cases were given full-dress Supreme Court review (the nine justices actually sitting *en banc*—in full court—and hearing the lawyers argue the case) during the 2002–2003 term.[4]

[3]Roberto Suro, "Rehnquist: Too Many Offenses Are Becoming Federal Crimes," *Washington Post,* 1 January 1999, p. A2.

The Federal Trial Courts

The federal district courts handle most of the cases of original federal jurisdiction. These trial courts have general jurisdiction, and their cases are, in form, indistinguishable from cases in the state trial courts.

The lower federal courts are the first tier of the court system.

There are eighty-nine district courts in the fifty states, plus one in the District of Columbia and one in Puerto Rico, and three territorial courts. These courts are staffed by 665 federal district judges. District judges are assigned to district courts according to the workload; the busiest of these courts may have as many as twenty-eight judges. The routines and procedures of the federal district courts are essentially the same as those of the lower state courts, except that federal procedural requirements tend to be stricter. States, for example, do not have to provide a grand jury, a twelve-member trial jury, or a unanimous jury verdict. Federal courts must provide all these things.

Federal Appellate Courts

Roughly 20 percent of all lower court cases along with appeals from some federal agency decisions are subsequently reviewed by a federal appeals court. The country is divided into twelve judicial circuits, each of which has a U.S. Court of Appeals. A thirteenth appellate court, the U.S. Court of Appeals for the Federal Circuit, is defined by subject matter rather than geographical jurisdiction. This court accepts appeals regarding patents, copyrights, and international trade.

Except for cases selected for review by the Supreme Court, decisions made by the appeals courts are final. Because of this finality, certain safeguards have been built into the system. The most

[4]U.S. Bureau of the Census, *Statistical Abstract of the United States 1997* (Washington, DC: Government Printing Office, 1997).

important is the provision of more than one judge for every appeals case. Each court of appeals has three to twenty-eight permanent judgeships, depending on the workload of the circuit. Although normally three judges hear appealed cases, in some instances a larger number of judges sit together *en banc.*

Another safeguard is provided by the assignment of a Supreme Court justice as the circuit justice for each of the eleven circuits. The circuit justice deals with requests for special action by the Supreme Court. The most frequent and best-known action of circuit justices is that of reviewing requests for stays of execution when the full Court is unable to do so—mainly during the summer, when the Court is in recess.

The Supreme Court

The Supreme Court is America's highest court. Article III of the Constitution vests "the judicial power of the United States" in the Supreme Court, and this court is supreme in fact as well as form. The Supreme Court is made up of a chief justice and eight associate justices. The **chief justice** presides over the Court's public sessions and conferences. In the Court's actual deliberations and decisions, however, the chief justice has no more authority than his or her colleagues. Each justice casts one vote. The chief justice, though, is always the first to speak and the last to vote when the justices deliberate. In addition, if the chief justice has voted with the majority, he decides which of the justices will write the formal opinion for the court. The character of the opinion can be an important means of influencing the evolution of the law beyond the mere affirmation or denial of the appeal at hand. To some extent, the influence of the chief justice is a function of his or her own leadership ability. Some chief justices, such as the late Earl Warren, have been able to lead the court in a new direction. In other instances, a forceful associate justice, such as the late Felix Frankfurter, is the dominant figure on the Court.

The Constitution does not specify the number of justices who should sit on the Supreme Court; Congress has the authority to change the Court's size. In the early nineteenth century, there were six

Supreme Court justices; later there were seven. Congress set the number of justices at nine in 1869, and the Court has remained that size every since. In 1937, President Franklin D. Roosevelt, infuriated by several Supreme Court decisions that struck down New Deal programs, asked Congress to enlarge the court so that he could add a few sympathetic justices to the bench. Although Congress balked at Roosevelt's "court packing" plan, the Court gave in to FDR's pressure and began to take a more favorable view of his policy initiatives. The president, in turn, dropped his efforts to enlarge the Court. The Court's surrender to FDR came to be known as "the switch in time that saved nine."

Nine justices currently sit on the Supreme Court, each appointed by the president and approved by the Senate.

How Judges Are Appointed

Federal judges are appointed by the president and are generally selected from among the more prominent or politically active members of the legal profession. Many federal judges previously served as state court judges or state or local prosecutors. Before the president makes a formal nomination, however, the senators from the candidate's own state must indicate that they support the nominee. This is an informal but seldom violated practice called *senatorial courtesy*. Because the Senate will rarely approve a nominee opposed by a senator from the nominee's own state, the president will usually not bother to present such a nomination to the Senate. Through this arrangement, senators are able to exercise veto power over appointments to the federal bench in their own states. Senators often see such a nomination as a way to reward important allies and contributors in their states. If the state has no senator from the president's party, the governor or members of the state's House delegation may make suggestions. In general, presidents endeavor to appoint judges who possess legal experience and good character and whose partisan and ideological views are similar to the president's own.

During the presidencies of Ronald Reagan and George H. W. Bush, most federal judicial appointees were conservative Republicans. Bush established an advisory committee to screen judicial nominees to make certain that their legal and political philosophies were sufficiently conservative. Bill Clinton's appointees to the federal bench, on the other hand, tended to be liberal Democrats. Clinton also made a major effort to appoint women and African Americans to the federal courts. He drew nearly half of his nominees from these groups.

Once the president has formally nominated an individual, the nominee must be considered by the Senate Judiciary Committee and confirmed by a majority vote in the full Senate. In recent years, the Senate Judiciary Committee has sought to signal the president when it has had qualms about a judicial nomination. After the Republicans won control of the Senate in 1994, for example, Judiciary Committee Chair Orrin Hatch of Utah let President Clinton know that he considered two of Clinton's nominees to be too liberal. The president withdrew the nominations.

Federal appeals court nominations follow much the same pattern. Since appeals court judges preside over jurisdictions that include several states, however, senators do not have as strong a role in proposing potential candidates. Instead, the Justice Department or important members of the administration usually suggest potential appeals court candidates to the president. The senators from the nominee's own state are still consulted before the president will formally act.

During President George W. Bush's first two years in office, Democrats controlled the Senate and used their majority on the Judiciary Committee to block eight of the president's first eleven federal court nominations. After the GOP won a narrow Senate majority in the 2002 national elections, Democrats used a filibuster to block action on several other Bush federal appeals court nominees. Both Democrats and Republicans saw struggles over lower court slots as practice and preparation for all-out partisan warfare over the next Supreme Court vacancy.

If political factors play an important role in the selection of district and appellate court judges, they are decisive when it comes to Supreme Court appointments. For example, presidents Ronald Reagan and George H. W. Bush appointed five justices whom they believed to have conservative perspectives: Justices Sandra Day O'Connor, Antonin Scalia, Anthony Kennedy, David Souter, and Clarence Thomas. Reagan also elevated William Rehnquist to the position of chief justice. Reagan and Bush sought appointees who believed in reducing government intervention in the economy and who supported the moral positions taken by the Republican Party in recent years, particularly opposition to abortion. However, not all the Reagan and Bush appointees have fulfilled their sponsors' expectations. Bush appointee David Souter, for example, has been attacked by conservatives as a turncoat for his decisions on school prayer and abortion rights. Nevertheless, through their appointments, Reagan and Bush were able to create a far more conservative Supreme Court. For his part, President Bill Clinton named Ruth Bader Ginsburg and Stephen Breyer to the Court, hoping to counteract the influence of the Reagan and Bush appointees.

In 2005, President George W. Bush was presented with an opportunity to put his own stamp on the Supreme Court as Justice Sandra Day O'Connor announced her decision to retire and Chief Justice Rehnquist died of the cancer that had limited his judicial activities for the past year. Bush quickly nominated federal appeals court judge John G. Roberts, Jr., initially to replace O'Connor but then as Chief Justice when Rehnquist died while the Senate was still considering the appointment. Roberts, a moderate conservative with a brilliant legal record, provoked some Democratic opposition but won confirmation without much difficulty. Bush's next nominee, though, sparked an intense battle within the president's own party. To the surprise of most observers, the president named one of his long-time associates, White House Counsel Harriet Miers, to replace Justice O'Connor. Many Republicans viewed Miers as merely a Bush crony lacking judicial qualifications and insufficiently supportive of conservative causes. Opposition to Miers within the GOP was so intense that Democrats remained gleefully silent as the president was forced to allow her to withdraw her name from consideration. In the wake of the Miers debacle, President Bush turned to a more conventional nominee, federal appeals court

TABLE 8.1

SUPREME COURT JUSTICES, 2005 (AS OF OCTOBER*)

Name	Year of birth	Prior experience	Appointed by	Year of appointment
John G. Roberts, Jr. *Chief Justice*	1955	Federal judge	G. W. Bush	2005
John Paul Stevens	1920	Federal judge	Ford	1975
Sandra Day O'Connor	1930	State judge	Reagan	1981
Antonin Scalia	1936	Law professor, federal judge	Reagan	1986
Anthony Kennedy	1936	Federal judge	Reagan	1988
David Souter	1939	Federal judge	G. H. W. Bush	1990
Clarence Thomas	1948	Federal judge	G. H. W. Bush	1991
Ruth Bader Ginsburg	1933	Federal judge	Clinton	1993
Stephen Breyer	1938	Federal judge	Clinton	1994

*On July 1, 2005, Sandra Day O'Connor announced her retirement from the court, effective upon confirmation of her successor. As this book went to press, Samuel Alito had been nominated but not yet confirmed to replace O'Connor.

judge Samuel Alito. This nomination pleased Republican conservatives who saw Alito as cut from the same mold as arch-conservative Justice Antonin Scalia. Indeed, Alito had sometimes been called "Scalito" because of the similarities between his views and Scalia's. But while Rebuplicans were pleased, Democrats and liberal political forces promised an all-out battle to block the nomination. (Table 8.1 shows more information about the current Supreme Court justices.)

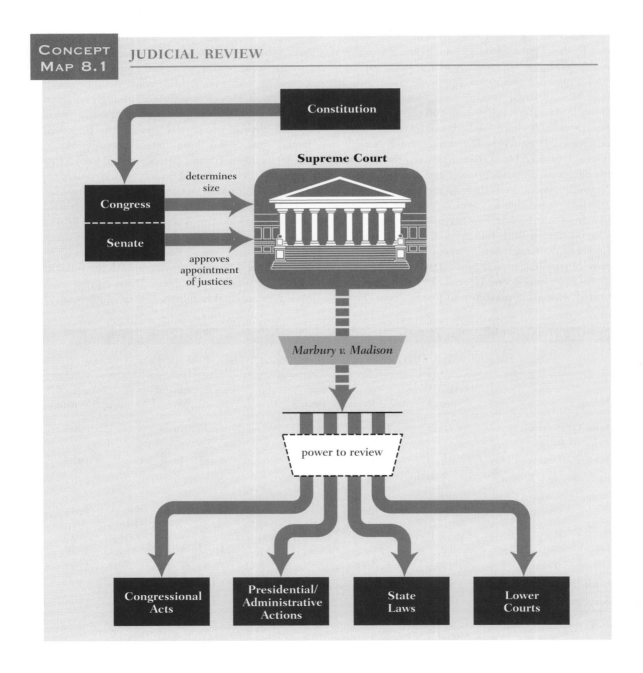

CONCEPT MAP 8.1   JUDICIAL REVIEW

Constitution

Supreme Court

Congress — determines size

Senate — approves appointment of justices

Marbury v. Madison

power to review

Congressional Acts

Presidential/ Administrative Actions

State Laws

Lower Courts

In recent years, Supreme Court nominations have come to involve intense partisan struggle. Typically, after the president has named a nominee, interest groups opposed to the nomination have mobilized opposition in the media, the public, and the Senate. When former President George H. W. Bush proposed conservative judge Clarence Thomas for the Court, for example, liberal groups launched a campaign to discredit Thomas. After extensive research into his background, opponents of the nomination were able to produce evidence suggesting that Thomas had sexually harassed a former subordinate, Anita Hill. Thomas denied the charge. After contentious Senate Judiciary Committee hearings, highlighted by testimony from both Thomas and Hill, Thomas narrowly won confirmation.

Likewise, conservative interest groups carefully scrutinized Bill Clinton's somewhat more liberal nominees, hoping to find information about them that would sabotage their appointments. During his two opportunities to name Supreme Court justices, Clinton was compelled to drop several potential appointees because of information unearthed by political opponents.

These struggles over judicial appointments indicate the growing intensity of partisan struggle in the United States today. They also indicate how much importance competing political forces attach to Supreme Court appointments. Because these contending forces see the outcome as critical, they are willing to engage in a fierce struggle when Supreme Court appointments are at stake.

JUDICIAL REVIEW

The phrase *judicial review* refers to the power of the judiciary to examine and, if necessary, invalidate actions undertaken by the legislative and executive branches (see Concept Map 8.1). The phrase is sometimes used, as well, to describe the scrutiny that appeals courts give to the actions of

---

BOX 8.1

MARBURY V. MADISON

The 1803 Supreme Court decision handed down in *Marbury v. Madison* established the power of the Court to review acts of Congress. The case arose over a suit filed by William Marbury and seven other people against Secretary of State James Madison to require him to approve their appointments as justices of the peace. These had been last-minute appointments ("midnight judges") of outgoing President John Adams. Chief Justice Marshall held that although Marbury and the others were entitled to their appointments, the Supreme Court had no power to order Madison to deliver them.

Marshall reasoned that constitutions are framed to serve as the "fundamental and paramount law of the nation." Thus, he argued, with respect to the legislative action of Congress, the Constitution is a "superior . . . law, unchangeable by ordinary means." He concluded that an act of Congress that contradicts the Constitution must be judged void.

As to the question of whether the Court was empowered to rule on the constitutionality of legislative action, Marshall responded empathically that it is "the province and duty of the judicial department to say what the law is." Since the Constitution is the supreme law of the land, he reasoned, it is clearly within the realm of the Court's responsibility to rule on the constitutionality of legislative acts and treaties. This principle has held sway ever since.

SOURCES: Gerald Gunther, *Constitutional Law* (Mineola, NY: Fountain Press, 1980), pp. 9–11; and *Marbury v. Madison*, 1 Cr. 137 (1803).

trial courts, but, strictly speaking, this is an improper usage. A higher court's examination of a lower court's decision might be called "appellate review" but it is not "judicial review."

Judicial Review of Acts of Congress

Since the Constitution does not give the Supreme Court the power of judicial review of congressional enactments, the Court's exercise of it is something of a usurpation. Though Congress and the president have often been at odds with the Court, its legal power to review acts of Congress has not been seriously questioned since 1803 and the case of *Marbury v. Madison* (see Box 8.1). One reason is that judicial power has been accepted as natural even though not specifically intended by the framers of the Constitution. Another reason is that over the course of more than two centuries, the Supreme Court has struck down only some 160 acts of Congress. When such acts do finally come up for review, the Court makes a self-conscious effort to give them an interpretation that will make them constitutional.

The Supreme Court has the power to review acts of Congress.

Judicial Review of State Actions

The power of the Supreme Court to review state legislation or other state action and to determine its constitutionality is neither granted by the Constitution nor inherent in the federal system. But the logic of the *supremacy clause* of Article VI of the Constitution, which declares it and laws made under its authority to be the supreme law of the land, is very strong. Furthermore, in the Judiciary Act of 1789, Congress conferred on the Supreme Court the power to reverse state constitutions and laws whenever they are clearly in conflict with the U.S. Constitution, federal laws, or treaties.[5] This power gives the Supreme Court jurisdiction over all of the millions of cases handled by American courts each year.

[5]This review power was affirmed by the Supreme Court in *Martin v. Hunter's Lesses,* 1 Wheaton 304 (1816).

The supremacy clause of Article VI of the Constitution allows the Supreme Court to review state laws as well as lower court decisions.

The supremacy clause of the Constitution not only established the federal Constitution, statutes, and treaties as the "supreme law of the land," but also provided that "the Judges in every State shall be bound thereby, any Thing in the Constitution or Laws of the State to the Contrary notwithstanding." Under this authority, the Supreme Court has frequently overturned state constitutional provisions or statutes and state court decisions that it feels are counter to rights or privileges guaranteed under the Constitution or federal statutes.

Judicial Review of Federal Agency Actions

Though Congress makes the law, as we saw in Chapters 5 and 7, it can hardly administer the thousands of programs it has enacted and must delegate power to the president and to a huge bureaucracy to achieve its purposes. For example, if Congress wishes to improve air quality, it cannot possibly anticipate all the conditions and circumstances that may arise with respect to that general goal. Inevitably, Congress must delegate to the executive substantial discretionary power to make judgments about the best ways to improve air quality in the face of changing circumstances. Thus, over the years, almost any congressional program will result in thousands of pages of administrative regulations developed by executive agencies nominally seeking to implement the will of the Congress.

Such delegation is inescapable in the modern era. But delegation of power to the executive poses a number of problems for the Congress and for the federal courts. If Congress delegates broad authority to the president, it risks seeing its goals subordinated to and subverted by those of the executive branch.[6] If Congress attempts to limit executive

[6]See Theodore J. Lowi, *The End of Liberalism,* 2nd ed. (New York: Norton, 1979). See also David Schoenbrod, *Power without Responsibility: How Congress Abuses the People through Delegation* (New Haven: Yale University Press, 1993).

discretion by enacting precise rules and standards to govern the conduct of the president and the executive branch, it risks writing laws that do not conform to real-world conditions and that are too rigid to be adapted to changing circumstances.[7]

The issue of delegation of power has led to a number of court decisions over the past two centuries generally revolving around the question of the scope of the delegation. Courts have also been called upon to decide whether the rules and regulations adopted by federal agencies are consistent with Congress's express or implied intent.

As presidential power expanded during the New Deal era, one measure of increased congressional subordination to the executive was the enactment of laws that contained few, if any, principles limiting executive discretion. Congress enacted legislation, often at the president's behest, that gave the executive virtually unfettered authority to address a particular concern. For example, the Emergency Price Control Act of 1942 authorized the executive to set "fair and equitable" prices without offering any indication of what those terms might mean.[8] While the Court initially challenged these delegations of power to the president during the New Deal, a confrontation with President Franklin D. Roosevelt caused the Court to retreat from its position. Perhaps as a result, no congressional delegation of power to the president has been struck down as impermissibly broad in more than six decades. In the last two decades in particular, the Supreme Court has found that as long as federal agencies developed rules and regulations "based upon a permissible construction" or "reasonable interpretation" of Congress's statute, the judiciary would accept the views of the executive branch.[9] Generally, the courts give considerable deference to administrative agencies as long as those agencies have engaged in a formal rule-making process and can show that they have carried out the conditions prescribed by the various statutes governing agency rule making. These include the 1946 Administrative Procedure Act, which requires agencies to notify parties affected by proposed rules as well as allow them ample time to comment on such rules before they go into effect.

Judicial Review and Presidential Power

The federal courts are also called on to review the actions of the president. As we saw in Chapter 6, presidents increasingly make use of unilateral executive powers rather than rely on congressional legislation to achieve their objectives. On many occasions, presidential orders and actions have been challenged in the federal courts by members of Congress and by individuals and groups opposing the president's policies. In recent years, assertions of presidential power in such realms as foreign policy, war and emergency powers, legislative power and administrative authority have, more often than not, been upheld by the federal bench. Indeed, the federal judiciary has sometimes taken extraordinary presidential claims made for limited and temporary purposes and rationalized them, that is, converted them into routine and permanent instruments of presidential government. Take, for example, Richard Nixon's sweeping claims of executive privilege. In U.S. v. Nixon, the Court, to be sure, rejected the president's refusal to turn over tapes to congressional investigators. For the first time, though, the justices also recognized the validity of the principle of executive privilege and discussed the situations in which such claims might be appropriate.[10] This judicial recognition of the principle encouraged President Bill Clinton and George W. Bush to make broad claims of executive privilege during their terms in office.[11] Executive privilege has recently been invoked to protect even the deliberations of the vice president from congressional scrutiny in the case of Dick Cheney's consultations with representatives of the energy industry.

---

[7]Kenneth Culp Davis, *Discretionary Justice: A Preliminary Inquiry* (Baton Rouge: Louisiana State University Press, 1969), pp. 15–21.
[8]56 Stat. 23 (30 January 1942).
[9]*Chevron v. Natural Resources Defense Council*, 467 U.S. 837 (1984).

[10]*U.S. v. Nixon*, 418 U.S. 683 (1974).
[11]On Clinton, see Jonathan Turley, "Paradise Lost: The Clinton Administration and the Erosion of Executive Privilege," 60 *Maryland Law Review* 205 (2001). On Bush, see Jeffrey P. Carlin, "*Walker v. Cheney*: Politics, Posturing and Executive Privilege," 76 *Southern California Law Review* 235 (November 2002).

This pattern of judicial deference to presidential authority is also manifest in the Supreme Court's recent decisions regarding President Bush's "War on Terror." In June 2004, the Supreme Court ruled in three cases involving the president's antiterror initiatives and claims of executive power and in two of the three cases appeared to place some limits on presidential authority. Indeed, the justices had clearly been influenced by revelations that U.S. troops had abused prisoners in Iraq and sought in these cases to make a statement against the absolute denial of procedural rights to individuals in the custody of American military authorities. But while the Court's decisions were widely hailed as reining in the executive branch, they actually fell far short of stopping presidential power in its tracks.

The most important case decided by the Court was *Hamdi v. Rumsfeld*.[12] Yaser Esam Hamdi, apparently a Taliban soldier, was captured by American forces in Afghanistan and brought to the United States, where he was incarcerated at the Norfolk Naval Station. Hamdi was classified as an enemy combatant and denied civil rights, including the right to counsel, despite the fact that he had been born in Louisiana and held American citizenship. A federal district court scheduled a hearing on Hamdi's *habeas corpus* petition and ordered that he be given unmonitored access to counsel. This ruling, however, was reversed by the Fourth Circuit Court of Appeals. In its opinion the court held that in the national security realm, the president wields "plenary and exclusive power." This power was even greater, said the court, when the president acted with statutory authority from Congress. The court did not indicate which statute, in particular, might have authorized the president's actions, but went on to affirm the president's constitutional power, as supported in many prior rulings, to conduct military operations, decide who is and is not an enemy combatant, and determine the rules governing the treatment of such individuals. In essence, said the court, the president had virtually unfettered discretion to deal with emergencies and it was inappropriate for the judiciary to saddle presidential decisions with

what the court called the "panoply of encumbrances associated with civil litigation."

In June 2004, the Supreme Court ruled that Hamdi was entitled to a lawyer and "a fair opportunity to rebut the government's factual assertions." However, the Supreme Court affirmed that the president possessed the authority to declare a U.S. citizen to be an enemy combatant and to order such an individual held in federal detention. Several of the justices intimated that once designated an enemy combatant, a U.S. citizen might be tried before a military tribunal and the normal presumption of innocence suspended. One government legal adviser indicated that the impact of the Court's decision was minimal. "They are basically upholding the whole enemy combatant status and tweaking the evidence test," he said.[13]

Thus, the Supreme Court did assert that presidential actions were subject to judicial scrutiny and placed some constraints on the president's unfettered power. But at the same time the Court affirmed the president's single most important claim—the unilateral power to declare individuals, including U.S. citizens, "enemy combatants" who could be detained by federal authorities under adverse legal circumstances. This hardly seems to threaten the foundations of the imperial presidency.

Judicial Review and Lawmaking

Much of the work of the courts involves the application of statutes to the particular case at hand. Over the centuries, however, judges have developed a body of rules and principles of interpretation that are not grounded in specific statutes. This body of judge-made law is called *common law*.

The appellate courts, however, are in another realm. When a court of appeals hands down its decision, it accomplishes two things. First, of course, it decides who wins—the person who won in the lower court or the person who lost in the lower court. But at the same time, it expresses its decision in a manner that provides guidance to the lower courts for

---

[12]2004 Westlaw 1431951.

[13]Charles Lane, "Justices Back Detainee Access to U.S. Courts," *Washington Post,* 29 June 2004, p. 1.

handling future cases in the same area. Appellate judges try to give their reasons and rulings in writing so the "administration of justice" can take place most of the time at the lowest judicial level. They try to make their ruling or reasoning clear, so as to avoid confusion, which can produce a surge of litigation at the lower levels. These rulings can be considered laws, but they are laws governing the behavior only of the judiciary. Decisions by appellate courts affect citizens by giving them a cause of action or by taking it away from them. That is, they open or close access to the courts.

The decisions of higher courts accomplish two ends. They decide which party wins a case, and they help set precedent for future cases, in effect establishing law.

THE SUPREME COURT IN ACTION

How Cases Reach the Supreme Court

Given the millions of disputes that arise every year, the job of the Supreme Court would be impossible if it were not able to control the flow of cases and its own case load. The Supreme Court has original jurisdiction in a limited variety of cases defined by the Constitution. The original jurisdiction includes (1) cases between the United States and one of the fifty states, (2) cases between two or more states, (3) cases involving foreign ambassadors or other ministers, and (4) cases brought by one state against citizens of another state or against a foreign country. The most important of these cases are disputes between states over land, water, or old debts. Generally, the Supreme Court deals with these cases by appointing a "special master," usually a retired judge, to actually hear the case and present a report. The Supreme Court then allows the states involved in the dispute to present arguments for or against the master's opinion.[14]

[14]Walter F. Murphy, "The Supreme Court of the United States," in *Encyclopedia of the American Judicial System*, ed. Robert J. Janosik (New York: Scribner's, 1987).

RULES OF ACCESS Over the years, the courts have developed specific rules that govern which cases within their jurisdiction they will and will not hear. To have access to the courts, cases must meet certain criteria that are initially applied by the trial court but may be reconsidered by appellate courts. These rules of access can be broken down into three major categories: case or controversy, standing, and mootness.

Article III of the Constitution and Supreme Court decisions define judicial power as extending only to "cases and controversies." This means that the case before a court must be an actual controversy, not a hypothetical one, with two truly adversarial parties. The courts have interpreted this language to mean that they do not have power to render advisory opinions to legislatures or agencies about the constitutionality of proposed laws or regulations. Furthermore, even after a law is enacted, the courts will generally refuse to consider its constitutionality until it is actually applied.

Parties to a case must also have **standing,** that is, they must show that they have a substantial stake in the outcome of the case. The traditional requirement for standing has been to show injury to oneself; that injury can be personal, economic, or even aesthetic, for example. For a group or class of people to have standing (as in class action suits), each member must show specific injury. This means that a general interest in the environment, for instance, does not provide a group with sufficient basis for standing.

To reach the Supreme Court, a case must meet three criteria: The case must be an actual controversy; parties in the case must prove a substantial stake in its outcome; and the case must be heard in such time that the dispute has not become moot.

The Supreme Court also uses a third criterion in determining whether it will hear a case: that of **mootness.** In theory, this requirement disqualifies

PROCESS
BOX 8.1

HOW CASES REACH THE SUPREME COURT

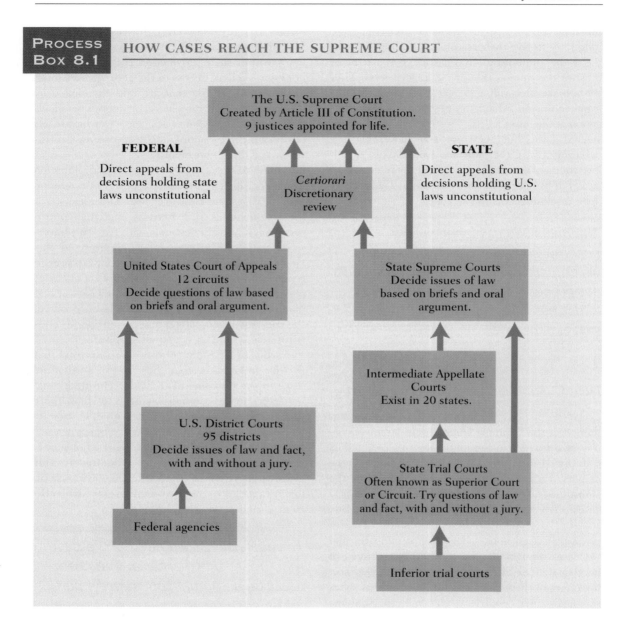

The U.S. Supreme Court
Created by Article III of Constitution.
9 justices appointed for life.

FEDERAL

Direct appeals from
decisions holding state
laws unconstitutional

Certiorari
Discretionary
review

STATE

Direct appeals from
decisions holding U.S.
laws unconstitutional

United States Court of Appeals
12 circuits
Decide questions of law based
on briefs and oral argument.

State Supreme Courts
Decide issues of law
based on briefs and oral
argument.

Intermediate Appellate
Courts
Exist in 20 states.

U.S. District Courts
95 districts
Decide issues of law and fact,
with and without a jury.

State Trial Courts
Often known as Superior Court
or Circuit. Try questions of law
and fact, with and without a jury.

Federal agencies

Inferior trial courts

cases that are brought too late—after the relevant facts have changed or the problem has been resolved by other means. The criterion of mootness, however, is subject to the discretion of the courts, which have begun to relax the rules of mootness, particularly in cases where a situation that has been resolved is likely to come up again.

In the abortion case *Roe v. Wade,* for example, the Supreme Court rejected the lower court's argument that because the pregnancy had already come to term, the case was moot. The Court agreed to hear the case because no pregnancy was likely to outlast the lengthy appeals process.

Putting aside the formal criteria, the Supreme

Court is most likely to accept cases that involve conflicting decisions by the federal circuit courts, cases that present important questions of civil rights or civil liberties, and cases in which the federal government is the appellant.[15] Ultimately, however, the question of which cases to accept can come down to the preferences and priorities of the justices. If a group of justices believes that the Court should intervene in a particular area of policy or politics, they are likely to look for a case or cases that will serve as vehicles for judicial intervention. For many years, for example, the Court was not interested in considering challenges to affirmative action or other programs designed to provide particular benefits to minorities. In recent years, however, several of the Court's more conservative justices have been eager to push back the limits of affirmative action and racial preference, and have therefore accepted a number of cases that would allow them to do so. In 1995, the Court's decision in *Adarand Constructors v. Peña, Missouri v. Jenkins,* and *Miller v. Johnson* placed new restrictions on federal affirmative action programs, school desegregation efforts, and attempts to increase minority representation in Congress through the creation of "minority districts" (see Chapter 10).[16] Similarly, because some justices have felt that the Court had gone too far in the past in restricting public support for religious ideas, the Court accepted the case of *Rosenberger v. University of Virginia.* This case was brought by a Christian student group against the University of Virginia, which had refused to provide student activities fund support for the group's magazine, *Wide Awake.* Other student publications received subsidies from the activities fund, but university policy prohibited grants to religious groups. Lower courts supported the university, finding that support for the magazine would violate the Constitution's prohibition against government support for

religion. The Supreme Court, however, ruled in favor of the students' assertion that the university's policies amounted to support for some ideas but not others. The Court said this violated the First Amendment.[17]

WRITS Most cases reach the Supreme Court through a *writ of certiorari.* Certiorari is an order to a lower court to deliver the records of a particular case to be reviewed for legal errors. The term certiorari is sometimes shortened to *cert* and cases deemed to merit certiorari are referred to as "certworthy." An individual who loses in a lower federal court or state court and wants the Supreme Court to review the decision has 90 days to file a petition for a writ of certiorari with the clerk of the U.S. Supreme Court. There are two types of petitions, paid petitions and petitions *in forma pauperis* (in the form of a pauper). The former requires payment of filing fees, submission of a certain number of copies and compliance with a variety of other rules. For *in forma pauperis* petitions, usually filed by prison inmates, the Court waives the fees and most other requirements.

Since 1972, most of the justices have participated in a "certiorari pool" in which they pool their law clerks to evaluate the petitions. Each petition is reviewed by one clerk who writes a memo for all the justices participating in the pool summarizing the facts and issues and making a recommendation. Clerks for the other justices add their comments to the memo. After they review the memos, any justice may place any case on the "Discuss List." This is a list circulated by the Chief Justice of all the petitions to be talked about and voted on at the Court's conference. If a case is not placed on the discuss list it is automatically denied certiorari. Cases placed on the discuss list are considered and voted on during the justices' closed-door conference.

For certiorari to be granted four justices must be convinced that the case satisfies Rule 10 of the Rules of the U.S. Supreme Court. Rule 10 states that certiorari is not a matter of right but is to be granted only where there are special and com-

[15]Gregory A. Caldeira and John R. Wright, "Organized Interests and Agenda Setting in the U.S. Supreme Court," *American Political Science Review,* 82 (1988):1109–27.

[16]*Adarand Constructors, Inc. v. Pena,* 115 S. Ct. 2097 (1995); *Missouri v. Jenkins,* 115 S. Ct. 2038 (1995); *Miller v. Johnson,* 115 S. Ct. 2475 (1995).

[17]*Rosenberger v. University of Virginia,* 115 S. Ct. 2510 (1995).

pelling reasons. These include conflicting decisions by two or more circuit courts; conflicts between circuit courts and state courts of last resort; conflicting decisions by two or more state courts of last resort; decisions by circuit courts on matters of federal law that should be settled by the Supreme Court; or a circuit court decision on an important question that conflicts with Supreme Court decisions. It should be clear from this list that the Court will usually take action only under the most compelling circumstances—where there are conflicts among the lower courts about what the law should be; where an important legal question has been raised in the lower courts but not definitively answered; and where a lower court deviates from the principles and precedents established by the High Court. The support of four justices is needed for certiorari and few cases are able to satisfy this requirement. In recent sessions, though thousands of petitions are filed, the Court has granted certiorari to hardly more than 80 petitioners each year—about 1 percent of those seeking a Supreme Court review.

A handful of cases reach the Supreme Court through avenues other than certiorari. One of these is the "writ of certification." This writ can be used when a U.S. Court of Appeals asks the Supreme Court for instructions on a point of law that has never been decided. A second avenue is the "writ of appeal," used to appeal the decision of a three-judge district court.

A lower court's decision may reach the Supreme Court through a writ, a document that conveys a court order. The court has almost complete discretion as to which cases it will hear.

Controlling the Flow of Cases: The Role of the Solicitor General

If any single person has greater influence than the individual justices over the work of the Supreme Court, it is the **solicitor general** of the United States. The solicitor general is third in status in the Justice Department (below the attorney general and the deputy attorney general, who serve as the government's chief prosecutors) but is the top government defense lawyer in almost all cases before the appellate courts where the government is a party. Although others can regulate the flow of cases, the solicitor general has the greatest control, with no review of his or her actions by any higher authority in the executive branch. More than half the Supreme Court's total workload consists of cases under the direct charge of the solicitor general. Even the bland description in the *U.S. Government Manual* cannot mask the extraordinary importance of this official:

> The Solicitor General is in charge of representing the Government in the Supreme Court. He decides what cases the Government should ask the Supreme Court to review and what position the Government should take in cases before the Court; he supervises the preparation of the Government's Supreme Court briefs and other legal documents and the conduct of the oral arguments in the Court and argues most of the important cases himself. The Solicitor General's duties also include deciding whether the United States should appeal in all cases it loses before the lower courts.[18]

The solicitor general exercises especially strong influence by screening cases long before they approach the Supreme Court; the justices rely on the solicitor general to "screen out undeserving litigation and furnish them with an agenda to government cases that deserve serious consideration."[19] Agency heads may lobby the president or otherwise try to circumvent the solicitor general, and a few of the independent agencies have a statutory right to make direct appeals, but without the solicitor general's support, these are seldom reviewed by the Court or, at best, doomed to

---

[18]*United States Government Organization Manual* (Washington, DC: Government Printing Office, 1985).

[19]Robert Scigliano, *The Supreme Court and the Presidency* (New York: Free Press, 1971), p. 162. For an interesting critique of the solicitor general's role during the Reagan administration, see Lincoln Caplan, "Annals of the Law," *New Yorker,* 17 August 1987, pp. 30–62.

per curiam rejection—rejection through a brief, unsigned opinion by the whole Court—if the solicitor general refuses to participate.

The solicitor general has control over the flow of cases that the Supreme Court hears.

The solicitor general can enter a case even when the federal government is not a direct litigant by writing an **amicus curiae** ("friend of the court") brief. A "friend of the court" is not a direct party to a case but has a vital interest in its outcome. Thus, when the government has such an interest, the solicitor general can file an *amicus curiae,* or the Court can invite such a brief because it wants an opinion in writing. Other interested parties may file briefs as well.

The Supreme Court's Procedures

THE PREPARATION   The Supreme Court's decision to accept a case is the beginning of what can be a lengthy and complex process (see Figure 8.2). First, the attorneys on both sides must prepare *briefs*—written documents in which the attorneys explain why the Court should rule in favor of their client. The document filed by the individual bringing the case is called the petitioner's brief. This brief summarizes the facts of the case and presents the legal basis upon which the Supreme Court is being asked to overturn the lower court's decision. The document filed by the side that prevailed in the lower court is called the respondent's brief. This brief explains why the Supreme Court should affirm the lower court's verdict. The petitioners will then file a brief answering and attempting to refute the points made in the respondent's brief. This document is called the petitioner's reply brief. Briefs are filled with referrals to precedents specifically chosen to show that other courts have frequently ruled in the same way that the Supreme Court is being asked to rule. The attorneys for both sides muster the most compelling precedents they can in support of their arguments.

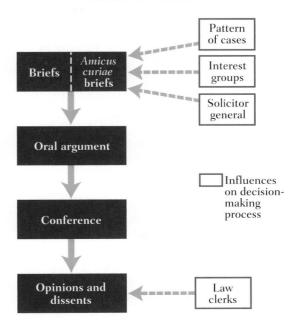

FIGURE 8.2

THE SUPREME COURT'S DECISION-MAKING PROCESS

As the attorneys prepare their briefs, they often ask sympathetic interest groups for their help. Groups are asked to file *amicus curiae* briefs that support the claims of one or the other litigant. In a case involving separation of church and state, for example, liberal groups such as the ACLU and Citizens for the American Way are likely to file *amicus* briefs in support of strict separation, whereas conservative religious groups are likely to file *amicus* briefs advocating increased public support for religious ideas. Often, dozens of briefs will be filed on each side of a major case. *Amicus* filings are one of the primary methods used by interest groups to lobby the Court. By filing these briefs, groups indicate to the Court where their group stands and signal to the justices that they believe the case to be an important one.

ORAL ARGUMENT   The next stage of a case is *oral argument,* in which attorneys for both sides appear

IN BRIEF BOX

INFLUENCES ON SUPREME COURT DECISIONS

The Justices	Controlling the Flow of Cases
The ideologies of the justices have a great influence on the decisions of the Court. These ideologies are made known through opinion writing. Dissenting opinions can be more eloquent and less guarded than majority opinions, and they indicate to lawyers that there is a sympathetic ear on the Court for such cases, thus encouraging such cases to be brought to the Court again.	The solicitor general exercises a great deal of control over what cases are heard by the Supreme Court. He or she has the power to screen cases long before they approach the Supreme Court level and can write an *amicus curiae* brief so as to enter a case, even when the federal government is not a litigant.

before the Court to present their positions and answer the justices' questions. Each attorney has only a half hour to present his or her case, and this time includes interruptions for questions. Certain members of the Court, such as Justice Antonin Scalia, are known to interrupt attorneys dozens of times. Others, such as Justice Clarence Thomas, seldom ask questions. For an attorney, the opportunity to argue a case before the Supreme Court is a singular honor and a mark of professional distinction. It can also be a harrowing experience, as justices interrupt a carefully prepared presentation. Nevertheless, oral argument can be very important to the outcome of a case. It allows justices to better understand the heart of the case and to raise questions that might not have been addressed in the opposing side's briefs. It is not uncommon for justices to go beyond the strictly legal issues and ask opposing counsel to discuss the implications of the case for the Court and the nation at large.

After filing written arguments, or briefs, attorneys present oral argument to the Supreme Court. After oral argument, the justices discuss the case and vote on a final decision.

THE CONFERENCE   Following oral argument, the Court discusses the case in its Wednesday or Friday conference. The chief justice presides over the conference and speaks first; the other justices follow in order of seniority. The Court's conference is secret, and no outsiders are permitted to attend. The justices discuss the case and eventually reach a decision on the basis of a majority vote. As the case is discussed, justices may try to influence or change one another's opinions. At times, this may result in compromise decisions.

OPINION WRITING   After a decision has been reached, one of the members of the majority is assigned to write the *opinion.* This assignment is made by the chief justice, or by the most senior justice in the majority if the chief justice is on the losing side. The assignment of the opinion can make a significant difference to the interpretation of a decision. Every opinion of the Supreme Court sets a major precedent for future cases throughout the judicial system. Lawyers and judges in the lower courts will examine the opinion carefully to ascertain the Supreme Court's meaning. Differences in wording and emphasis can have important implications for future litigation. Thus, in assigning an opinion, serious thought must be given to the impression the case will make on lawyers and on the public, as well as to the probability that one justice's opinion will be more widely accepted than another's.

One of the more dramatic instances of this tactical consideration occurred in 1944, when Chief Justice Harlan F. Stone chose Justice Felix Frankfurter to write the opinion in the "white primary" case *Smith v. Allwright*. The chief justice believed that this sensitive case, which overturned the Southern practice of prohibiting black participation in nominating primaries, required the efforts of the most brilliant and scholarly jurist on the Court. But the day after Stone made the assignment, Justice Robert H. Jackson wrote a letter to Stone urging a change of assignment. In his letter, Jackson argued that Frankfurter, a foreign-born Jew from New England, would not win the South with his opinion, regardless of its brilliance. Stone accepted the advice and substituted Justice Stanley Reed, an American-born Protestant from Kentucky and a Southern Democrat in good standing.[20]

Once the majority opinion is drafted it is circulated to the other justices. Some members of the majority may agree with both the outcome and the rationale but wish to emphasize or highlight a particular point and so will draft a concurring opinion for that purpose. In other instances, one or more justices may agree with the majority but may disagree with the rationale presented in the majority opinion. These justices may draft special concurrences, explaining their disagreements with the majority.

DISSENT   Justices who disagree with the majority decision of the Court may choose to publicize the character of their disagreement in the form of a *dissenting opinion.* The dissenting opinion is generally assigned by the senior justice among the dissenters. Dissents can be used to express irritation with an outcome or to signal to defeated political forces in the nation that at least some members of the Court support their position. Ironically, the most dependable way an individual justice can exercise a direct and clear influence on the Court is to write a dissent. Because there is no need to please a majority, dissenting opinions can be more eloquent and less guarded than majority opinions. The current Supreme Court often produces five-to-four decisions, with dissenters writing long and detailed opinions that, they hope, will help them convince a swing justice to join their side on the next round of cases dealing with a similar topic. Thus, for example, Justice Souter wrote a thirty-four-page dissent in a 2002 case upholding the use of government-funded school vouchers to pay for parochial school tuition. Souter called the decision "a dramatic departure from basic Establishment Clause principle," which he hoped a "future court will reconsider."[21]

Dissent plays a special role in the work and impact of the Court because it amounts to an appeal to lawyers all over the country to keep bringing cases of the sort at issue. Therefore, an effective dissent influences the flow of cases through the Court as well as the arguments that will be used by lawyers in later cases. Even more important, dissent emphasizes the fact that, although the Court speaks with a single opinion, it is the opinion only of the majority.

Judicial Decision Making

The judiciary is conservative in its procedures, but its impact on society can be radical. That impact depends on a variety of influences, two of which stand out above the rest. The first influence is the individual members of the Supreme Court, their attitudes, and their relationships with each other. The second is the other branches of government, particularly Congress.

THE SUPREME COURT JUSTICES   The Supreme Court explains its decisions in terms of law and precedent. But although law and precedent do have an effect on the Court's deliberations and

---

[20]*Smith v. Allwright*, 321 U.S. 649 (1944).

[21]Warren Richey, "Dissenting Opinions as a Window on Future Rulings," *Christian Science Monitor*, 1 July 2002, p. 1.

eventual decisions, it is the Supreme Court that decides what laws actually mean and what importance precedent will actually have. Throughout its history, the Court has shaped and reshaped the law. If any individual judges in the country influence the federal judiciary, they are the Supreme Court justices.

The Supreme Court always explains its decisions in terms of law and precedent.

From the 1950s to the 1980s, the Supreme Court took an activist role in such areas as civil rights, civil liberties, abortion, voting rights, and police procedures. For example, the Supreme Court was more responsible than any other governmental institution for breaking down America's system of racial segregation. The Supreme Court virtually prohibited states from interfering with the right of a woman to seek an abortion and sharply curtailed state restrictions on voting rights. And it was the Supreme Court that placed restrictions on the behavior of local police and prosecutors in criminal cases.

But since the early 1980s, resignations, deaths, and new judicial appointments have led to many shifts in the mix of philosophies and ideologies represented on the Court. In a series of decisions between 1989 and 2001, the conservative justices appointed by Ronald Reagan and George H. W. Bush were able to swing the Court to a more conservative position on civil rights, affirmative action, abortion rights, property rights, criminal procedure, voting rights, desegregation, and the power of the national government.

However, precisely because the Court has been so evenly split in recent years, the conservative bloc has not always prevailed. Among the justices serving at the beginning of 2005, Rehnquist, Scalia, and Thomas took conservative positions on most issues and were usually joined by O'Connor and Kennedy. Breyer, Ginsburg, Souter, and Stevens were reliably liberal. This produced many 5-4 splits. On some issues, though, Justice O'Connor or Justice Kennedy tended to side with the liberal

camp, producing a 5-4 and sometimes a 6-3 victory for the liberals. This pattern was very evident during the Court's 2003–2004 term. In the case of *Missouri v. Siebert,* for example, Justice Kennedy joined a 5-4 majority to strengthen Miranda rights.[22] Similarly, in *McConnell v. Federal Election Commission,* Justice O'Connor joined the liberal bloc to uphold the validity of the Bipartisan Campaign Reform Act.[23] Neither O'Connor nor Kennedy was ready to join their conservative colleagues in overturning the Court's landmark abortion decision, *Roe v. Wade.*[24] It remains to be seen, of course, how new Chief Justice John G. Roberts and the successor to Sandra Day O'Connor will rule on abortion rights.

ACTIVISM AND RESTRAINT   One element of judicial philosophy is the issue of activism versus restraint. Over the years, some justices have believed that courts should interpret the Constitution according to the stated intentions of its framers and defer to the views of Congress when interpreting federal statutes. The late justice Felix Frankfurter, for example, advocated judicial deference to legislative bodies and avoidance of the "political thicket," in which the Court would entangle itself by deciding questions that were essentially political rather than legal in character. Advocates of *judicial restraint* are sometimes called "strict constructionists," because they look strictly to the words of the Constitution in interpreting its meaning.

The alternative to restraint is *judicial activism.* Activist judges such as the former Chief Justice Earl Warren believed that the Court should go beyond the words of the Constitution or a statute to consider the broader societal implications of its decisions. Activist judges sometimes strike out in new directions, promulgating new interpretations or inventing new legal and constitutional concepts when they believe these to be socially desirable. For example, Justice Harry Blackmun's opinion in *Roe v. Wade* was based on a constitutional right to privacy that is not found in the words of the Con-

[22]02-0371 (2003).
[23]02-1674 (2003).
[24]410 U.S. 113 (1973).

stitution. Blackmun and the other members of the majority in the *Roe* case argued that other constitutional provisions implied the right to privacy. In this instance of judicial activism, the Court knew the result it wanted to achieve and was not afraid to make the law conform to the desired outcome.

Activism and restraint are sometimes confused with liberalism and conservatism. For example, conservative politicians often castigate "liberal activist" judges and call for the appointment of conservative jurists who will refrain from reinterpreting the law. To be sure, some liberal jurists are activists and some conservatives have been advocates of restraint, but the relationship is by no means one to one. Indeed, the Rehnquist Court, dominated by conservatives, was among the most activist Courts in American history, striking out in new directions in such areas as federalism and election law.

Despite the rule of precedent, the Court often reshapes law. Such changes in the interpretation of law can be explained, in part, by changes in the judicial philosophy of activism versus restraint and by changes in political ideology.

POLITICAL IDEOLOGY   The second component of judicial philosophy is political ideology. The liberal or conservative attitudes of justices play an important role in their decisions.[25] Indeed, the philosophy of activism versus restraint is, to a large extent, a smokescreen for political ideology. For the most part, liberal judges have been activists, willing to use the law to achieve social and political change, whereas conservatives have been associated with judicial restraint. Interestingly, however, in recent years some conservative justices who have long called for restraint have actu-

ally become activists in seeking to undo some of the work of liberal jurists over the past three decades.

Other Institutions of Government

CONGRESS   At both the national and state level in the United States, courts and judges are "players" in the policy game because of the separation of powers. Essentially, this means that the legislative branch formulates policy (defined constitutionally and institutionally by a legislative process); that the executive branch implements policy (according to well-defined administrative procedures, and subject to initial approval by the president or the legislative override of his veto); and that the courts, when asked, rule on the faithfulness of the legislated and executed policy either to the substance of the statute or to the Constitution itself. The courts, that is, may strike down an administrative action either because it exceeds the authority granted in the relevant statute (statutory rationale) or because the statute itself exceeds the authority granted the legislature by the Constitution (constitutional rationale).

If the court declares the administrative agent's act as outside the permissible bounds prescribed by the legislation, we suppose the court's majority opinion can declare whatever policy it wishes. If the legislature is unhappy with this judicial action, then it may either recraft the legislation (if the rationale for striking it down were statutory)[26] or initiate a constitutional amendment that would enable the stricken-down policy to pass constitutional muster (if the rationale for originally striking it down were constitutional).

In reaching their decisions, Supreme Court justices must anticipate Congress's response. As a result, judges will not always vote according to their true preferences because doing so may provoke Congress to enact legislation that moves the policy further away from what the judges prefer. By voting for a lesser preference, the justices can get

---

[25]C. Herman Pritchett, *The Roosevelt Court* (New York: Macmillan, 1948).

[26]William N. Eskridge, Jr., "Overriding Supreme Court Statutory Interpretation Decisions," *Yale Law Journal* 101(1991): 331–55.

something they prefer to the status quo without provoking congressional action to overturn their decision. The most famous example of this phenomenon is the "switch in time that saved nine," when several justices voted in favor of New Deal legislation, the constitutionality of which they doubted, in order to diminish congressional support for President Roosevelt's plan to "pack" the Court by increasing the number of justices. In short, the interactions between the Court and Congress are part of a complex strategic "game."[27]

THE PRESIDENT   The president's most direct influence on the Court is the power to nominate justices. Presidents typically nominate judges who they believe are close to their policy preferences and close enough to the preferences of a majority of senators, who must confirm the nomination.

Yet the efforts by presidents to reshape the federal judiciary are not always successful. Often in American history, judges have surprised and disappointed the presidents who named them to the bench. Justice Souter, for example, has been far less conservative than President George H. W. Bush and the Republicans who supported Souter's appointment in 1990 thought he would be. Likewise, Justices O'Connor and Kennedy have disappointed conservatives by opposing limitations on abortion.

JUDICIAL POWER AND POLITICS

One of the most important institutional changes to occur in the United States during the past half-century has been the striking transformation of the role and power of the federal courts, those of the

Supreme Court in particular. Understanding how this transformation came about is the key to understanding the contemporary role of the courts in America.

Traditional Limitations on the Federal Courts

For much of American history, the power of the federal courts was subject to five limitations.[28] First, courts were constrained by judicial rules of standing that limited access to the bench. Claimants who simply disagreed with governmental action or inaction could not obtain access. Access to the courts was limited to individuals who could show that they were directly affected by the government's behavior in some area. This limitation on access to the courts diminished the judiciary's capacity to forge links with important political and social forces. Second, courts were traditionally limited in the kind of relief they could provide. In general, courts acted only to offer relief to individuals and not to broad social classes, again inhibiting the formation of alliances between the courts and important social forces.

Third, courts lacked enforcement powers and were compelled to rely on executive or state agencies to ensure compliance. If the executive or state agencies were unwilling to assist the courts, judicial enactments could go unheeded, as was illustrated when President Andrew Jackson declined to enforce Chief Justice John Marshall's 1832 order to the state of Georgia to release two missionaries it had arrested on Cherokee lands. Marshall asserted that the state had no right to enter the lands of the Cherokees without their assent.[29] Jackson is reputed to have said, "John Marshall has made his decision, now let *him* enforce it." Congress and the president have ignored Supreme Court rulings in recent years as well. For example, in 1983 the Supreme Court declared that a practice known as the one-house legislative veto was unconstitutional. This practice entailed the enact-

---

[27]A fully strategic analysis of the maneuvering among legislative, executive, and judicial branches in the separation-of-powers arrangement choreographed by the U.S. Constitution may be found in William Eskridge and John Ferejohn, "The Article I, Section 7 Game," *Georgetown Law Review* 80 (1992):523–65. The entire issue of this journal is devoted to the theme of strategic behavior in American institutional politics.

[28]For limits on judicial power, see Alexander Bickel, *The Least Dangerous Breach* (Indianapolis: Bobbs-Merrill, 1962).
[29]*Worcester v. Georgia*, 6 Peters 515 (1832).

ment of legislation that could later be rescinded by either house of Congress if it was dissatisfied with the results. In the case of *Immigration and Naturalization Service v. Chadha,* the Court ruled that this amounted to the usurpation of executive power by the legislature.[30] Congress and the president, however, find the legislative procedure convenient and continue to use it by other names despite the Court's ruling.

Fourth, federal judges are appointed by the president (with the consent of the Senate). As a result, the president and Congress can shape the composition of the federal courts and ultimately, perhaps, the character of judicial decisions. Finally, Congress has the power to change both the size and the jurisdiction of the Supreme Court and other federal courts. In many areas, federal courts obtain their jurisdiction not from the Constitution but from the congressional statutes. On a number of occasions, Congress has threatened to take matters out of the Court's hands when it was unhappy with the Court's rulings on certain cases.[31]

Historically, the powers of the federal courts have been limited.

As a result of these five limitations on judicial power, through much of their history, the chief function of the federal courts has been to provide judicial support for executive agencies and to legitimate acts of Congress by declaring them to be consistent with constitutional principles. Only on rare occasions did the federal courts actually dare to challenge Congress or the executive.[32]

Two Judicial Revolutions

Since the Second World War, however, the role of the federal judiciary has been strengthened and expanded through two judicial revolutions in the United States. The first and most visible of these was the substantive revolution in judicial policy. In policy areas, including school desegregation, legislative apportionment, and criminal procedure, as well as obscenity, abortion, and voting rights, the Supreme Court was at the forefront of a series of sweeping changes in the role of the U.S. government and, ultimately, in the character of American society.[33]

The first judicial revolution was a revolution of policy, during which the Court made sweeping social reforms.

But at the same time that the courts were introducing important policy innovations, they were also bringing about a second, less visible revolution. During the 1960s and 1970s, the Supreme Court and other federal courts instituted a series of institutional changes in judicial procedure that had major consequences by fundamentally expanding the power of the courts in the United States. First, the federal courts liberalized the concept of standing to permit almost any group to bring its case before the federal bench. This change has given the courts a far greater role in the administrative process than ever before. Many federal judges are concerned that federal legislation in areas such as health care reform would create new rights and entitlements that would give rise to a deluge of court cases. "Any time you create a new right, you create a host of disputes and claims," warned Barbara Rothstein, chief judge of the federal district court in Seattle, Washington.[34]

Second, the federal courts broadened the scope of relief to permit action on behalf of broad categories or classes of persons in "class action" cases, rather than just on behalf of individuals.[35] A *class*

---

[30]462 U.S. 919 (1983).

[31]See Walter Murphy, *Congress and the Court* (Chicago: University of Chicago Press, 1962).

[32]Robert Dahl, "The Supreme Court and National Policy Making," *Journal of Public Law* 6 (1958), p. 279.

[33]Martin Shapiro, "The Supreme Court: From Warren to Burger," in *The New American Political System,* ed. Anthony King (Washington, DC: American Enterprise Institute, 1978).

[34]Toni Locy, "Bracing for Health Care's Caseload," *Washington Post,* 22 August 1994, p. A15.

[35]See "Developments in the Law—Class Actions," *Harvard Law Review* 89 (1976), p. 1318.

action suit permits large numbers of persons with common interests to join together under a representative party to bring or defend a lawsuit.

Third, the federal courts began to employ so-called structural remedies, in effect retaining jurisdiction of cases until the court's mandate had actually been implemented to its satisfaction.[36] The best known of these instances was Federal Judge W. Arthur Garrity's effort to operate the Boston school system from his bench in order to ensure its desegregation. Between 1974 and 1985, Judge Garrity issued fourteen decisions relating to different aspects of the Boston school desegregation plan that had been developed under his authority and put into effect under his supervision.[37] In its five-to-four decision in the 1990 case of *Missouri v. Jenkins*, the Supreme Court held that federal judges could actually order local governments to increase taxes to remedy such violations of the Constitution as school segregation.[38] This decision upheld an order by a federal district judge, Russel G. Clark, to the Kansas City, Missouri, school board to adopt a "magnet" school plan that would lessen segregation in the schools. Potentially, this decision claims for the judiciary the power to levy taxes—a power normally seen as belonging to electoral legislatures.

Through these three judicial mechanisms, the federal courts paved the way for an unprecedented expansion of national judicial power. In essence, liberalization of the rules of standing and expansion of the scope of judicial relief drew the federal courts into linkages with important social interests and classes, while the introduction of structural remedies enhanced the courts' abilities to serve these constituencies. Thus, during the 1960s and 1970s, the power of the federal courts expanded in the same way that the power of the executive expanded during the 1930s—through links with constituencies, such as civil rights, consumer, environmental, and feminist groups, that staunchly defended the Supreme Court in its battles with Congress, the executive, or other interest groups.

The second judicial revolution was procedural. It allowed many more groups to bring cases before the courts; it broadened the scope of the courts to provide relief for entire classes of persons; and it saw the courts employ structural remedies to implement decisions.

The Reagan and first Bush administrations, of course, sought to end the relationship between the Court and liberal political forces. The conservative judges appointed by these Republican presidents modified the Court's position in areas such as abortion, affirmative action, and judicial procedure—though not as completely as some conservatives had hoped. In June 2003, for example, the Court handed down a series of decisions that pleased many liberals and outraged conservative advocacy groups. Within a period of one week, the Supreme Court affirmed the validity of affirmative action, reaffirmed abortion rights, strengthened gay rights, offered new protection to individuals facing the death penalty, and issued a ruling in favor of a congressional apportionment plan that dispersed minority voters across several districts—a practice that appeared to favor the Democrats.[39] Interestingly, however, the Court has not been eager to surrender the expanded powers carved out by its liberal predecessors. In a number of decisions during the 1980s and 1990s, the Court was willing to make use of its expanded powers on behalf of interests it favored.[40]

The role and power of the federal courts, particularly the Supreme Court, was especially evident after the 2000 presidential election. The battle over the final outcome was fought not in the electoral

---

[36]See Donald Horowitz, *The Courts and Social Policy* (Washington, DC: Brookings Institution, 1977).

[37]*Moran v. McDonough*, 540 F. 2nd 527 (1 Cir., 1976; *cert denied* 429 U.S. 1042 [1977]).

[38]*Missouri v. Jenkins*, 110 S. Ct. 1651 (1990).

[39]David Van Drehle, "Court That Liberals Savage Proves to Be Less of a Target," *Washington Post*, 29 June 2003, p. A18.

arena but in the courts, in the Florida state legislature, and in the executive institutions of the Florida state government by small groups of attorneys and political activists. Some forty lawsuits were filed in the Florida circuit and Supreme courts, the U.S. District Court, U.S. Court of Appeals, and U.S. Supreme Court.[41] Together, the Bush and Gore campaigns amassed nearly $10 million in legal fees during the one month of litigation. In most of the courtroom battles, the Bush campaign prevailed. Despite two setbacks before the all-Democratic Florida Supreme Court, Bush attorneys won most circuit court cases and the ultimate clash before the U.S. Supreme Court by a narrow 5-4 vote.

During the arguments before the Supreme Court, it became clear that the conservative majority was determined to prevent a Gore victory. Conservative justices were sharply critical of the arguments presented by Gore's lawyers, while openly sympathetic to the arguments made by Bush's lawyers. Conservative Justice Antonin Scalia went so far as to intervene when Bush attorney Theodore Olson responded to a question from Justices Souter and Ginsburg. Scalia evidently sought to assure that Olson did not concede too much to the Gore argument. "It's part of your submission, I think," Scalia said, "that there is no wrong when a machine does not count those ballots that it's not supposed to count?" Scalia was reminding Olson that when voter error rendered a ballot unreadable by a tabulating machine, it was not appropriate for a court to order them counted by hand. "The voters are instructed to detach the chads entirely," Scalia said, "and the machine does not count those chads where those instructions are not followed, there isn't any wrong." Olson was happy to accept Scalia's reminder.[42]

Liberal Justice John Paul Stevens said the majority opinion smacked of partisan politics. The opinion, he said, "can only lend credence to the most cynical appraisal of the work of judges throughout the land." He concluded by saying this: "Although we may never know with complete certainty the identity of the winner of this year's presidential election, the identity of the loser is perfectly clear. It is the nation's confidence in the judge as an impartial guardian of the rule of law." Justice Stevens's eloquent dissent did not change the outcome. Throughout the nation, Democrats saw the Supreme Court majority's opinion as a blatantly partisan decision. Nevertheless, the contest was over. The next day Al Gore made a speech conceding the election and, on December 18, 2000, 271 presidential electors—the constitutionally prescribed majority—cast their votes for George W. Bush.

This battle over Florida's electoral votes shows that judges are just like other politicians—they have political goals and policy preferences and they act accordingly so that those goals are realized. While thinking of judges as "legislators in robes" is antithetical to the view that judges rule according to a well-thought-out judicial philosophy based on constitutional law, there is evidence that strategic thinking on the part of judges is also a factor in their decision-making processes. This battle also illustrates the political power that the courts now exercise. Over the past fifty years, the prominence of the courts has been heightened by the sharp increase in the number of major policy issues that have been fought and decided in the judicial realm. But since judges are not elected and accountable to the people, what does this shift in power mean for American democracy?

There can be little doubt that the contemporary Supreme Court exercises considerably more power than the framers of the Constitution intended. In the original conception of the framers, the judiciary was to be the institution that would protect individual liberty from the government. As we saw in Chapter 2, the framers believed that in a democracy, the great danger was what they termed "tyranny of the majority"—the possibility that a

[40]Mark Silverstein and Benjamin Ginsberg, "The Supreme Court and the New Politics of Judicial Power," *Political Science Quarterly* 102 (Fall 1987), pp. 371–88.
[41]"In the Courts," *San Diego Union-Tribune* 7 December 2000, p. A14.
[42]Linda Greenhouse, "U.S. Supreme Court Justices Grill Bush, Gore Lawyer in Effort to Close the Book on Presidential Race," *New Orleans Times-Picayune,* 12 December 2000, p. 1.

popular majority, "united or actuated by some common impulse or passion," would "trample on the rules of justice."[43] The framers hoped that the courts would protect liberty from the potential excesses of democracy. And for most of American history, this was precisely the role played by the federal courts. The courts' most important decisions were those that protected the freedoms—to speak, worship, publish, vote, and attend school—of groups and individuals whose political views, religious beliefs, or racial or ethnic backgrounds made them unpopular.

In recent years, however, the courts have been changing their role in the political process. Rather than serving simply as a bastion of individual liberty against the excessive power of the majority, the judiciary has tried to play an active role in helping groups and forces in American society bring about social and political change in the fight for equality. In a sense, the judiciary has entered the political process and has begun to behave more like the democratic institutions whose sometimes misdirected impulses toward tyranny the courts were supposed to keep in check.

Is this an ideal state of affairs? The answer is no. In an ideal world, public policies would be made through the democratically elected branches of our government while the courts would deal with individual problems and injustices. Ours, however, is not always an ideal world. Democratically elected legislatures sometimes enact programs that violate constitutional rights. Congress and the president sometimes become locked in political struggles that blind them to the interests of certain citizens. On such occasions, we may be grateful that our "least dangerous branch" has some teeth.

CHAPTER REVIEW

Millions of cases come to trial every year in the United States. The great majority—nearly 99 percent—are tried in state and local courts. The types of law are civil law, criminal law, and public law. Cases are heard at the state level before three types of courts: trial court, appellate court, and (state) supreme court.

There are three kinds of federal cases: (1) civil cases involving diversity of citizenship, (2) civil cases where a federal agency is seeking to enforce federal laws that provide for civil penalties, and (3) cases involving federal criminal statutes or where state criminal cases have been made issues of public law.

Each district court is in one of the twelve appellate districts, called circuits, presided over by a court of appeals. Appellate courts admit no new evidence; their rulings are based solely on the records of the court proceedings or agency hearings that led to the original decision. Appeals court rulings are final unless the Supreme Court chooses to review them.

The Supreme Court has some original jurisdiction, but its major job is to review lower court decisions involving substantial issues of public law. Congress and the state legislatures can reverse Supreme Court decisions, but seldom do. There is no explicit constitutional authority for the Supreme Court to review acts of Congress. Nonetheless, the 1803 case of *Marbury v. Madison* established the Court's right to review congressional acts. The supremacy clause of Article VI and the Judiciary Act of 1789 give the Court the power to review state constitutions and laws.

Cases reach the Court mainly through the writ of *certiorari*. The Supreme Court controls its case load by issuing few writs and by handing down clear leading opinions that enable lower courts to resolve future cases without further review.

Judge-made law is like a statute in that it articulates the law as it relates to future controversies. It differs from a statute in that it is intended to guide judges rather than the citizenry in general.

The judiciary as a whole is subject to two major influences: (1) the individual members of the Supreme Court, who have lifetime tenure; and (2) the Justice Department—particularly the solicitor general, who regulates the flow of cases.

The influence of an individual member of the

[43]Clinton Rossiter, ed., *The Federalist Papers* (New York: New American Library, 1961), No. 10, p. 78.

Supreme Court is limited when the Court is polarized, and close votes in a polarized Court impair the value of the decision rendered. Writing the majority opinion for a case gives a justice an opportunity to influence the judiciary. But the need to frame an opinion in such a way as to develop majority support on the Court may limit such opportunities. Dissenting opinions can have more impact than the majority opinion; they stimulate a continued flow of cases around that issue. The solicitor general is the most important single influence outside the Court itself because he or she controls the flow of cases brought by the Justice Department and also shapes the argument in those cases.

In recent years, the importance of the federal judiciary—the Supreme Court in particular—has increased substantially as the courts have developed new tools of judicial power and forged alliances with important forces in American society.

KEY TERMS

amicus curiae   Literally, "friend of the court"; individuals or groups who are not parties to a lawsuit but who seek to assist the court in reaching a decision by presenting additional briefs.

brief   A written document in which attorneys explain why a court should rule in favor of their client.

chief justice   Justice on the Supreme Court who presides over the Court's public sessions.

civil law   A system of jurisprudence, including private law and governmental actions, to settle disputes that do not involve criminal penalties.

class action suit   A lawsuit in which large numbers of persons with common interests join together under a representative party to bring or defend a lawsuit, such as hundreds of workers together suing a company.

court of appeals   A court that hears the appeals of trial court decisions.

criminal law   The branch of law that deals with disputes or actions involving criminal penalties (as opposed to civil law). It regulates the conduct of individuals, defines crimes, and provides punishment for criminal acts.

defendant   The individual or organization against whom a complaint is brought in criminal or civil cases.

dissenting opinion   Decision written by a justice in the minority in a particular case in which the justice wishes to express his or her reasoning in the case.

due process   To proceed according to law and with adequate protection for individual rights.

en banc   As a panel; involving all the judges on a court.

habeas corpus   A court order demanding that an individual in custody be brought into court and shown the cause for detention. *Habeas corpus* is guaranteed by the Constitution and can be suspended only in cases of rebellion or invasion.

judicial activism   Proclivity of a court to select cases because of their importance to society rather than adhere to strict legal standards of jurisdiction.

judicial restraint   Judicial deference to the views of legislatures and adherence to strict jurisdictional standards.

judicial review   Power of the courts to declare actions of the legislative and executive branches invalid or unconstitutional. The Supreme Court asserted this power in *Marbury v. Madison.*

jurisdiction   The authority of a court to consider a case initially. Distinguished from appellate jurisdiction, which is the authority to hear appeals from a lower court's decision.

mootness   A criterion used by courts to screen cases that no longer require resolution.

opinion   The written explanation of the Supreme Court's decision in a particular case.

oral argument   Oral presentations to a court made by attorneys for both sides in a dispute.

per curiam   Decision by an appellate court, without a written opinion, that refuses to review the decision of a lower court; amounts to a reaffirmation of the lower court's opinion.

plaintiff   The individual or organization who brings a complaint in court.

plea bargains Negotiated agreements in criminal cases in which a defendant agrees to plead guilty in return for the state's agreement to reduce the severity of the criminal charge the defendant is facing.

precedents Prior cases whose principles are used by judges as the bases for their decisions in present cases.

public law Cases in private law, civil law, or criminal law in which one party to the dispute argues that a license is unfair, a law is inequitable or unconstitutional, or an agency has acted unfairly, violated a procedure, or gone beyond its jurisdiction.

senatorial courtesy The practice whereby the president, before formally nominating a person for a federal judgeship, will seek approval of the nomination from the senators who represent the candidate's own state.

solicitor general The top government lawyer in all cases before the appellate courts where the government is a party.

standing The right of an individual or organization to initiate a court case.

stare decisis Literally "let the decision stand." A previous decision by a court applies as a precedent in similar cases until that decision is overruled.

supremacy clause Article VI of the Constitution, which states that laws passed by the national government and all treaties are the supreme laws of the land and superior to all laws adopted by any state or any subdivision.

supreme court The highest court in a particular state or in the United States. This court primarily serves an appellate function.

trial court The first court to hear a criminal or civil case.

Uniform Commercial Code A set of standards for contract law, recognized by all states, that greatly reduces interstate differences in the practice of contract law.

writ of *certiorari* A decision of at least four of the nine Supreme Court justices to review a decision of a lower court; from the Latin "to make more certain."

FOR FURTHER READING

Abraham, Henry. *The Judicial Process,* 6th ed. New York: Oxford University Press, 1993.

Bickel, Alexander. *The Least Dangerous Branch.* Indianapolis: Bobbs-Merrill, 1962.

Bryner, Gary, and Dennis L. Thompson. *The Constitution and the Regulation of Society.* Provo, UT: Brigham Young University Press, 1988.

Carp, Robert, and Ronald Stidham. *The Federal Courts.* Washington, DC: Congressional Quarterly Press, 1985.

Davis, Sue. *Justice Rehnquist and the Constitution.* Princeton: Princeton University Press, 1989.

Faulkner, Robert K. *The Jurisprudence of John Marshall.* Princeton: Princeton University Press, 1968.

Goldman, Sheldon, and Thomas P. Jahnige. *The Federal Courts as a Political System.* New York: Harper & Row, 1985.

Graber, Mark A. *Transforming Free Speech: The Ambiguous Legacy of Civil Libertarianism.* Berkeley: University of California Press, 1991.

McCann, Michael W. *Rights at Work.* Chicago: University of Chicago Press, 1994.

Neely, Richard. *How Courts Govern America.* New Haven: Yale University Press, 1981.

O'Brien, David M. *Storm Center: The Supreme Court in American Politics,* 5th ed. New York: Norton, 1999.

Rosenberg, Gerald. *The Hollow Hope: Can Courts Bring about Social Change?* Chicago: University of Chicago Press, 1991.

Scigliano, Robert. *The Supreme Court and the Presidency.* New York: Free Press, 1971.

Silverstein, Mark. *Judicious Choices: The New Politics of Supreme Court Confirmations.* New York: Norton, 1994.

Tribe, Laurence. *Constitutional Choices.* Cambridge: Harvard University Press, 1985.

Wolfe, Christopher. *The Rise of Modern Judicial Review.* New York: Basic Books, 1986.

PART 3

Politics and Policy

CHAPTER 9

Public Opinion and the Media

In March 2003, American and British military forces invaded Iraq with the express intent of disarming Iraq's military and driving Iraqi President Saddam Hussein from power. The invasion followed months of diplomatic wrangling and an ultimately unsuccessful effort by President George W. Bush and British Prime Minister Tony Blair to win United Nations support for military action against Iraq. Bush and Blair charged that the Iraqi regime was hiding weapons of mass destruction and had failed to cooperate with weapons inspectors sent by the UN Security Council to investigate Iraq's military programs. In the months prior to the war, many Americans were dubious about the need to attack Iraq and uncertain about President Bush's foreign policy leadership. For example, according to a CBS News poll taken during the first week in March 2003, only 50 percent of those responding thought removing Suddam Hussein from power was worth the potential costs of war, while 43 percent thought it was not worth it. The same poll reported that only 55 percent of Americans approved of the way President Bush was handling the situation with Iraq. Once the American and British invasion of Iraq began, however, popular support for U.S. military action rose by 24 points to 77 percent, with only 10 percent of respondents saying that removing Hussein from power was not worth the costs and risks of war. Support for President Bush in the same poll increased to just under 70 percent.[1]

[1] Data describing opinions on the Iraq war can be found at www.pollingreport.com/iraq.htm.

CORE OF THE ANALYSIS

- Opinions are shaped by individuals' characteristics but also by institutional, political, and governmental forces.

- Among the most important influences shaping public opinion are the media. The media have tremendous power to shape the public agenda and our images of politicians and policies.

- The political power of the media has increased considerably through the growing prominence of investigative reporting.

- In general, the government's actions are consistent with public preferences.

Many commentators attributed these shifts in opinion to a "rally 'round the flag" effect that is commonly seen when the president leads Americans into battle. Pundits predicted that support for the war and the president would drop if fighting were prolonged or inconclusive. It also quickly became apparent that support for the president and his war policy varied considerably with demographic and political factors. Men were more supportive than women of the president's policies, indicating a continuation of the gender gap that has been a persistent feature of American public opinion. Race was also a factor, with African Americans much more critical than whites of President Bush and his goals. In addition,

CENTRAL QUESTIONS

- **The Marketplace of Ideas**
  In what ways do Americans agree on fundamental values but disagree on fundamental issues?
  What do the differences between liberals and conservatives reveal about American political debate?
- **Shaping Public Opinion**
  What influences the way we form political opinions?
  How are political issues marketed and managed by the government, private groups, and the media?
- **The Media**
  How do the media shape public perceptions of events, issues, and institutions?
  What are the sources of media power?
- **Measuring Public Opinion**
  How can public opinion be measured?
  What problems arise from public opinion polling?
- **Public Opinion and Government Policy**
  How responsive is the government to public opinion?

partisanship was important. Republicans were nearly unanimous in their approval of President Bush's policies, while Democrats were closely divided on the wisdom of going to war. Partisan politics, it seemed, did not stop at the water's edge.

After American forces destroyed the Iraqi army and occupied the country, many Americans who had once supported the war began to question the administration's policies. President Bush had told the nation that Saddam Hussein had to be overthrown because he sought to produce weapons of mass destruction (WMDs) that would threaten the United States. Bush had also suggested that Hussein had been linked to the Al Qaeda terrorists responsible for the attacks of September 11, 2001. Most Americans did not know enough about Iraq to evaluate the president's assertions. Indeed, Americans know little enough about the programs and policies of their own government, much less the plans of a dictatorial regime thousands of miles from their homes.[2] And, as is so often the case, even the experts to whom Americans might have looked for guidance seemed divided, with some

pundits declaring that Iraq posed an imminent threat to the United States and others declaring that it posed little or no danger.

As American occupation forces sifted through the wreckage of Iraq's military and intelligence programs, it soon became apparent that Iraq had no active WMD program and that there was little or no evidence pointing to Iraqi cooperation with Al Qaeda. To make matters worse from the president's perspective, early in 2004 Iraqi insurgents began to inflict a steady stream of casualties on American troops so that by the end of that year more Americans had been killed and wounded during the occupation than in actual combat operations. Democrats highlighted these problems throughout the 2004 presidential campaign. Democratic presidential candidate John Kerry and his running mate, John Edwards, frequently pointed to the president's erroneous claims and lamented the unnecessary loss of American lives. Not surprisingly, by the end of 2004, popular approval of the president's policies in Iraq had dropped more than 30 points from its peak at what had seemed to be America's moment of military triumph a year earlier. By the end of 2005, Bush's standing in the polls had fallen even more precipitously.

[2]Carroll J. Glynn, Susan Herbst, Garrett J. O'Keefe, Robert Y. Shapiro, and Mark Lindeman, *Public Opinion,* 2nd ed. (New York: Westview, 2004), Chapter 8.

Even as support for his policies eroded, Bush remained steadfast. The president won reelection despite doubts about his handling of the Iraq situation and was determined to bring about the creation of a pro-American regime in that nation. He attempted to halt the erosion of popular approval for his policies by hinting that American forces might be reduced after the 2005 Iraqi elections and continually restating the need to promote democracy in the Middle East. At the same time, though, Bush made it clear that his policies would not respond to shifts in popular opinion. The president reminded Americans that he planned to do his duty as he saw it regardless of the vicissitudes of public sentiment.

These events underline many of the issues raised in this chapter. Do Americans know enough to form meaningful opinions about important policy issues? What factors account for differences in opinion? To what extent can the government manipulate popular sentiment? To what extent do—or should—the government's policies respond to public opinion?

Public opinion is the term used to denote the values and attitudes that people have about issues, events, and personalities. Although the terms are sometimes used interchangeably, it is useful to distinguish between values and beliefs on the one hand, and attitudes or opinions on the other. *Values (or beliefs)* are a person's basic orientations to politics. Values represent deep-rooted goals, aspirations, and ideals that shape an individual's perceptions of political issues and events. Liberty, equality, and democracy are basic political values that most Americans hold.

Another useful term for understanding public opinion is *ideology*. *Political ideology* refers to a complex and interrelated set of beliefs and values that, as a whole, form a general philosophy about government. As we shall see, liberalism and conservatism are important ideologies in America today. For example, many Americans believe that governmental solutions to problems are inherently inferior to solutions offered by the private sector. This general belief, in turn, may lead individuals to have negative views about specific government programs even before they know much about them.

An *attitude (or opinion)* is a specific view about a particular issue, personality, or event. An individual may have an opinion about George W. Bush or an attitude toward American policy in Iraq. The attitude or opinion may have emerged from a broad belief about Republicans or military interventions, but an attitude itself is very specific. Some attitudes may be short-lived.

In this chapter, we will examine the role of public opinion in American politics. First, we will examine the political values and beliefs that help Americans form their perceptions of the political process. After reviewing basic American political values, we will analyze how values and beliefs are formed and how certain processes and institutions influence their formation. We conclude this section by considering the ways in which values and beliefs can cumulate to comprise political ideologies. Second, we will see how general values and beliefs help to shape more specific attitudes and opinions. In this discussion we will consider the role of political knowledge and the influence of political leaders, private groups, and the media. We will see why there appear to be so many differences of opinion among Americans. Third, we will assess the science of gathering and measuring public opinion. Finally, we will assess the impact of public opinion on the government and its policies. Is the U.S. government responsive to public opinion? Should it be?

One reason that public policy and public opinion may not always coincide is that our government is a representative one, not a direct democracy. The framers of the Constitution thought that our nation would be best served by a system of government that allowed elected representatives of the people an opportunity to reflect and consider their decisions rather than bow immediately to shifts in popular sentiment. A century after the Founding, however, the Populist movement averred that government was too far removed from the people and introduced procedures for direct popular legislation through the initiative and referendum. A number of states allow policy issues to be placed on the ballot, where they are resolved by a popular vote. Some modern-day populists believe that initiative and referendum processes should be adopted at the national level as well. Whether this would lead to greater responsiveness, however, is an open question to which we shall return.

WHAT ARE THE ORIGINS OF PUBLIC OPINION?

Opinions are products of individuals' personalities, social characteristics, and interests. But opinions are also shaped by institutional, political, and governmental forces that make it more likely that citizens will hold some beliefs and less likely that they will hold others.

COMMON FUNDAMENTAL VALUES   Today most Americans share a common set of political beliefs. First, Americans generally believe in *equality of opportunity.* That is, they assume that all individuals should be allowed to seek personal and material success. Moreover, Americans generally

believe that such success should be linked to personal effort and ability rather than family, "connections," or other forms of special privilege. Second, Americans strongly believe in individual freedom. They typically support the notion that governmental interference with individuals' lives and property should be kept to the minimum consistent with the general welfare (although in recent years Americans have grown accustomed to greater levels of governmental intervention than would have been deemed appropriate by the founders of liberal theory). Third, most Americans believe in democracy. They presume that every person should have the opportunity to take part in the nation's governmental and policy-making processes and to have some "say" in determining how they are governed (see Figure 9.1).[3]

[3]For a discussion of the political beliefs of Americans, see Everett Carll Ladd, *The American Ideology* (Storrs, CT: Roper Center, 1994).

FIGURE 9.1

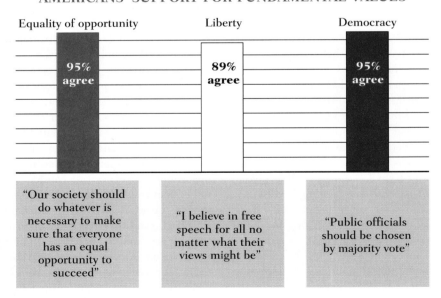

AMERICANS' SUPPORT FOR FUNDAMENTAL VALUES

Equality of opportunity — 95% agree — "Our society should do whatever is necessary to make sure that everyone has an equal opportunity to succeed"

Liberty — 89% agree — "I believe in free speech for all no matter what their views might be"

Democracy — 95% agree — "Public officials should be chosen by majority vote"

SOURCES: 1992 American National Election Studies; Herbert McCloskey and John Zaller, *The American Ethos: Public Attitudes toward Capitalism and Democracy* (Cambridge, MA: Harvard University Press, 1984), p. 25; and Robert S. Erikson, Norman R. Luttbeg, and Kent L. Tedin, *American Public Opinion: Its Origins, Content, and Impact,* 4th ed. (New York: Macmillan, 1991), p. 108.

One indication that Americans of all political stripes share these fundamental political values is the content of the acceptance speeches delivered by John Kerry and George W. Bush upon receiving their parties' presidential nominations in 2004. Kerry and Bush differed on many specific issues and policies. Yet the political visions they presented reveal an underlying similarity. A major emphasis of both candidates was equality of opportunity. Kerry referred frequently to opportunity in his speeches: "We believe that what millions want is not narrow appeals masquerading as values . . . but the shared values that unite us: family, faith, hard work, opportunity . . . so that every child, every adult, every parent, every worker in America has an equal shot at living up to their God-given potential." And, in a similar vein, Bush said, "We seek to provide not just a government program but a path to greater opportunity [and] more freedom." Thus, however much the two candidates differed in means and specifics, both seemed to share this fundamental American value.

Most Americans share a common set of political beliefs, such as a belief in equality of opportunity, individual freedom, and democracy.

Agreement on fundamental political values, though certainly not absolute, is probably more widespread in the United States than anywhere else in the Western world. During the course of Western political history, competing economic, social, and political groups put forward a variety of radically divergent views, opinions, and political philosophies. America was never socially or economically homogeneous. But two forces that were extremely powerful and important sources of ideas and beliefs elsewhere in the world were relatively weak or absent in the United States.

First, the United States never had the feudal aristocracy like the one that dominated so much of European history. Second, for reasons including America's prosperity and the early availability of political rights, no socialist movements compa-

rable to those that developed in nineteenth-century Europe were ever able to establish themselves in the United States. As a result, during the course of American history, there existed neither an aristocracy to assert the virtues of inequality, special privilege, and a rigid class structure, nor a powerful American communist or socialist party to challenge the desirability of limited government and individualism.[4]

Obviously, the principles that Americans espouse have not always been put into practice. For two hundred years, Americans were able to believe in the principles of equality of opportunity and individual liberty while denying them in practice to generations of African Americans. Yet it is important to note that the strength of the principles ultimately helped to overcome practices that deviated from those principles. Proponents of slavery and, later, of segregation were defeated in the arena of public opinion because their practices differed so sharply from the fundamental principles accepted by most Americans. Ironically, in contemporary politics, Americans' fundamental commitment to equality of opportunity has led to divisions over racial policy. In particular, both proponents and opponents of affirmative action programs cite their belief in equality of opportunity as the justification for their position. Proponents see these programs as necessary to ensure equality of opportunity, while opponents believe that affirmative action is a form of preferential treatment that violates basic American values.[5]

Political Socialization

The attitudes that individuals hold about political issues and personalities tend to be shaped by their underlying political beliefs and values. For example, someone who has basically negative feelings about government intervention into America's economy and society would probably be predis-

---

[4]See Louis Hartz, *The Liberal Tradition in America* (New York: Harcourt, Brace, 1955).
[5]Paul M. Sniderman and Edward G. Carmines, *Reaching beyond Race* (Cambridge, MA: Harvard University Press, 1997).

posed to oppose the development of new health care and social programs. Similarly, someone who distrusts the military would likely be suspicious of any call for the use of American troops. The processes through which these underlying political beliefs and values are formed are collectively called *political socialization.*

The process of political socialization is important. Probably no nation, and certainly no democracy, could survive if its citizens did not share some fundamental beliefs. If Americans had few common values or perspectives, it would be very difficult for them to reach agreement on particular issues. In contemporary America, some elements of the socialization process tend to produce differences in outlook, whereas others promote similarities. Four of the most important *agencies of socialization* that foster differences in political perspectives are the family, membership in social groups, education, and prevailing political conditions.

No inventory of agencies of socialization can fully explain the development of a given individual's basic political beliefs. In addition to the factors that are important for everyone, forces that are unique to each individual play a role in shaping political orientations. For one person, the character of an early encounter with a member of another racial group can have a lasting impact on that individual's view of the world. For another, a highly salient political event, such as the Vietnam War, can leave an indelible mark on that person's political consciousness. For a third person, some deep-seated personality characteristic, such as paranoia, for example, may strongly influence the formation of political beliefs. Nevertheless, knowing that we cannot fully explain the development of any given individual's political outlook, let us look at some of the most important agencies of socialization that do affect one's beliefs.

THE FAMILY   Most people acquire their initial orientation to politics from their families. As might be expected, differences in family background tend to produce divergent political outlooks. Although relatively few parents spend much time teaching their children about politics, political conversations occur in many households and children tend to absorb the political views of parents and other caregivers, perhaps without realizing it. Studies have suggested, for example, that party preferences are initially acquired at home. Children raised in households in which the primary caregivers are Democrats tend to become Democrats themselves, whereas children raised in homes where their caregivers are Republicans tend to favor the GOP (Grand Old Party, a traditional nickname for the Republican Party).[6] Similarly, children reared in politically liberal households are more likely than not to develop a liberal outlook, whereas children raised in politically conservative settings are prone to see the world through conservative lenses. Obviously, not all children absorb their parents' political views. Two of former conservative Republican President Ronald Reagan's three children, for instance, rejected their parents' conservative values. Moreover, even those children whose views are initially shaped by parental values may change their minds as they mature and experience political life for themselves. Nevertheless, the family is an important initial source of political orientation for everyone.

SOCIAL GROUPS   Another important source of divergent political orientations and values are the social groups to which individuals belong. Social groups include those to which individuals being involuntarily—gender and racial groups, for example—as well as those to which people belong voluntarily—such as political parties, labor unions, and educational and occupational groups. Some social groups have both voluntary and involuntary attributes. For example, individuals are born with a particular social-class background, but as a result of their own efforts people may move up—or down—the class structure.

Membership in social groups can affect political values in a variety of ways. Membership in a

[6]See Angus Campbell, Philip E. Converse, Warren E. Miller, and Donald E. Stokes, *The American Voter* (New York: Wiley, 1960), p. 147.

particular group can give individuals important experiences and perspectives that shape their view of political and social life. In American society, for example, the experiences of blacks and whites can differ significantly. Blacks are a minority and have been victims of persecution and discrimination throughout American history. Blacks and whites also have different educational and occupational opportunities, often live in separate communities, and many attend separate schools. Such differences tend to produce distinctive political outlooks. For example, in 1995 blacks and whites had very different reactions to the murder trial of former football star O. J. Simpson, who was accused of killing his ex-wife and one of her friends. Seventy percent of the white Americans surveyed believed that Simpson was guilty, based on the evidence presented by the police and prosecutors. But an identical 70 percent of the black Americans surveyed immediately after the trial believed that the police had fabricated evidence and had sought to convict Simpson of a crime he had not committed; these beliefs were presumably based on blacks' experiences with and perceptions of the criminal justice system.[7]

According to other recent surveys, blacks and whites in the United States differ on a number of issues. For example, among middle-income Americans (defined as those earning between $30,000 and $75,000 per year), 65 percent of black respondents and only 35 percent of white respondents thought racism was a major problem in the United States today. Within this same group of respondents, 63 percent of blacks and only 39 percent of whites thought the federal government should provide more services even at the cost of higher taxes.[8] Nearly three-quarters of white Americans but only one-third of black Americans favored going to war against Iraq in 2003. Other issues show a similar pattern of disagreement, reflecting the differences in experience, background, and interests between blacks and whites in America (see Figure 9.2).

Political party membership can be another factor affecting political orientations.[9] Partisans tend to rely on party leaders and spokespersons for cues on the appropriate positions to take on major political issues. In recent years, congressional redistricting and partisan realignment in the South have reduced the number of conservative Democrats and all but eliminated liberal Republicans from Congress and from positions of prominence in the party. As a result, the leadership of the Republican Party has become increasingly conservative while that of the Democratic Party has become more and more liberal. These changes in the positions of party leaders have been reflected in the views of party adherents and sympathizers in the general public. According to recent studies, differences between Democratic and Republican partisans on a variety of political and policy questions are greater today than during any other period for which data are available. On issues of national security, for example, Republicans have become very "hawkish" while Democrats have become quite "dovish." In October 2003, for instance, 85 percent of Republicans, compared to 39 percent of the Democrats surveyed, thought America's war against Iraq had been a good idea. Gaps on domestic social and economic issues were nearly as broad.[10]

Men and women have important differences of opinion as well. Reflecting differences in social roles, political experience, and occupational patterns, women tend to be less militaristic than men on issues of war and peace, more likely than men to favor measures to protect the environment, and more supportive than men of government social and health-care programs (see Table 9.1). Perhaps because of these differences on issues, women are more likely than men to vote for Democratic candidates.[11] This tendency for men's and women's opinions to differ is called the **gender gap.**

[7]Richard Morin, "Poll Reflects Division over Simpson Case," *Washington Post,* 8 October 1995, p. A31.

[8]"Middle-Class Views in Black and White," *Washington Post,* 9 October 1995, p. A22.

[9]Donald Green, Bradley Palmquist, and Eric Schickler, *Partisan Hearts and Minds: Political Parties and the Social Identities of Voters* (New Haven, CT: Yale University Press, 2002).

[10]David S. Broder, "Partisan Gap Is at a High, Poll Finds," *Washington Post,* 9 November 2003, p. A6.

[11]For data, see Rutgers University, Eagleton Institute of Politics, Center for the American Woman in Politics, "Sex Differences in Voter Turnout," August 1994.

FIGURE 9.2

DISAGREEMENT AMONG BLACKS AND WHITES

...Race relations in the U.S.

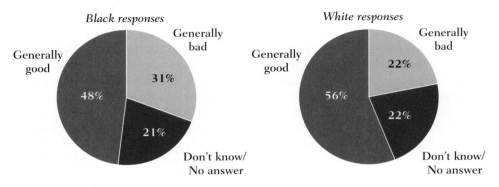

. . . Do black children have as good a chance as white children to get a good education?

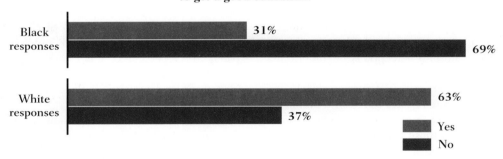

...Treatment blacks receive

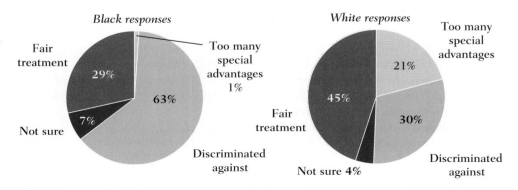

African Americans and white Americans have strong differences of opinion on certain issues.

TABLE 9.1

DISAGREEMENTS AMONG MEN AND WOMEN ON ISSUES OF WAR AND PEACE

Government Action	Percentage Approving of Action	
	Men	Women
Going to war against Iraq (2003)	78	66
Prefer cease-fire over NATO air strikes on Yugoslavia (1999)	44	51
Ending ban on homosexuals in military (1993)	34	51
Military operation against Somali warlord (1993)	72	60
Going to war against Iraq (1991)	72	53

SOURCE: Gallup Poll, 1991, 1993, 1998, 1999, 2003.

Membership in a social group can affect individuals' political orientations in another way: through the efforts of groups themselves to influence their members. Labor unions, for example, often seek to "educate" their members through meetings, rallies, and literature. These activities are designed to shape union members' understanding of politics and to make them more amenable to supporting the political positions favored by union leaders. Similarly, organization can sharpen the impact of membership in an involuntary group. Women's groups, black groups, religious groups, and the like usually endeavor to structure their members' political views through intensive educational programs. The importance of such group efforts can be seen from the impact of group membership on political opinion. Women who belong to women's organizations, for example, are likely to differ more from men in their political views than women without such group affiliation.[12] Other analysts have found that African Americans who belong to black organizations are likely to differ more from whites in their political orientations than blacks who lack such affiliations.[13]

In many cases, no particular efforts are required by groups to affect their members' beliefs and opinions. Often, individuals will consciously or unconsciously adapt their views to those of the groups with which they identify. For example, an African American who is dubious about affirmative action is likely to come under considerable peer pressure and internal pressure to modify his or her views. In this and other cases, dissenters are likely gradually to shift their own views to conform to those of the group. Political psychologist Elisabeth Noelle-Neumann has called this process the "spiral of silence."[14]

A third way that membership in social groups can affect political beliefs is through what might be called objective political interests. On many economic issues, for example, the interests of the rich and poor differ significantly. Inevitably, these differences of interest will produce differences of political outlook. James Madison and other framers of the Constitution thought that the inherent gulf between the rich and the poor would always be the most important source of conflict in political life. Certainly today, struggles over tax policy, welfare policy, health care policy, and so forth are fueled by differences of interest between wealthier and poorer Americans. In a similar vein, objective dif-

[12] Pamela Johnston Conover, "The Role of Social Groups in Political Thinking," *British Journal of Political Science* 18 (1988): 51–78.

[13] See Michael C. Dawson, "Structure and Ideology: The Shaping of Black Opinion," paper presented to the 1995 annual meeting of the Midwest Political Science Association, Chicago, Illinois, 7–9 April 1995. See also Michael C. Dawson, *Behind the Mule: Race and Class in African-American Politics* (Princeton, NJ: Princeton University Press, 1994).

[14] Elisabeth Noelle-Neumann, *The Spiral of Silence: Public Opinion, Our Social Skin* (Chicago: University of Chicago Press, 1984).

ferences of interest between "senior citizens" and younger Americans can lead to very different views on such diverse issues as health care policy, Social Security, and criminal justice. To take another example, in recent decades, major differences of opinion and political orientation have developed between American civilians and members of the armed services. Military officers, in particular, are far more conservative in their domestic and foreign policy views than the public at large and are heavily Republican in their political leanings.[15] Interestingly, support for the Republicans among military officers climbed sharply during the 1980s and 1990s, decades in which the GOP championed large military budgets. Could this be another case of objective interests swaying ideology?

It is worth pointing out again that, like the other agencies of socialization, group membership can never fully explain a given individual's political views. One's unique personality and life experiences may produce political views very different from those of the group to which one might nominally belong. This is why some African Americans are conservative Republicans, or why an occasional wealthy industrialist is also a socialist. Group membership is conducive to particular outlooks, but it is not determinative.

DIFFERENCES IN EDUCATION   A third important source of differences in political perspectives comes from a person's education. In some respects, of course, schooling is a great equalizer. Governments use public education to try to teach all children a common set of civic values. It is mainly in school that Americans acquire their basic belief in liberty, equality, and democracy. In history classes, students are taught that the founders fought for the principle of liberty. Through participation in class elections and student government, students are taught the virtues of democracy. In the course of studying such topics as the Constitution, the Civil War, and the civil

rights movement, students are taught the importance of equality. These lessons are repeated in every grade in a variety of contexts. No wonder they are such an important element in Americans' beliefs.

At the same time, however, differences in educational attainment are strongly associated with differences in political outlook. In particular, those who attend college are often exposed to philosophies and modes of thought that will forever distinguish them from their friends and neighbors who do not pursue college diplomas. Table 9.2 outlines some general differences of opinion found in one survey taken in 2000 comparing college graduates and other Americans.

In recent years, conservatives have charged that liberal college professors indoctrinate their students with liberal ideas. College does seem to have some "liberalizing" effect upon students, but, more significantly, college seems to convince students of the importance of political participation and of their own capacity to have an impact on politics and policy. Thus, one of the major differences between college graduates and other Americans can be seen in levels of political participation. College graduates vote, write "letters to the editor," join campaigns, take part in protests, and, generally, make their voices heard.

POLITICAL CONDITIONS   A fourth set of factors that shape political orientations and values are the conditions under which individuals and groups are recruited into and involved in political life. Although political beliefs are influenced by family background and group membership, the precise content and character of these views is, to a large extent, determined by political circumstances. For example, many Americans who came of political age during the Great Depression and World War II developed an intense sense of loyalty to President Franklin D. Roosevelt and became permanently attached to his Democratic Party. In a similar vein, the Vietnam War and social upheavals of the 1960s produced lasting divisions among Americans of the "baby boomer" generation. Indeed, arguments over Vietnam per-

[15]Ole R. Holsti, "A Widening Gap between the Military and Society?" in *Some Evidence, 1976–1996,* John M. Olin Institute for Strategic Studies, Harvard University, Working Paper no. 13 (October 1997).

TABLE 9.2

EDUCATION AND PUBLIC OPINION IN 2000

Issues	Education			
	Drop-out	High School	Some College	College Grad.
1. Women and men should have equal roles.	45%	72%	84%	85%
2. Abortion should never be allowed.	31	16	11	5
3. The government should adopt national health insurance.	50	43	38	37
4. The U.S. should not concern itself with other nations' problems.	27	34	27	12
5. Government should see to fair treatment in jobs for African Americans.	24	33	32	43
6. Government should provide fewer services to reduce government spending.	18	13	19	31

SOURCE: The American National Election Studies, 2000 data, provided by the Inter-University Consortium for Political and Social Research, University of Michigan.

sisted into the 2004 presidential election, some 30 years after American troops left Southeast Asia. Perhaps the 9/11 terrorist attacks and ongoing threats to America's security will have a lasting impact on the political orientations of contemporary Americans.

In a similar vein, the views held by members of a particular group can shift drastically over time, as political circumstances change. For example, American white Southerners were staunch members of the Democratic Party from the Civil War through the 1960s. As members of this political group, they became key supporters of liberal New Deal and post–New Deal social programs that greatly expanded the size and power of the American national government. Since the 1960s, however, Southern whites have shifted in large numbers to the Republican Party. Now they provide a major base of support for efforts to scale back social programs and sharply reduce the size and power of the national government. The South's

move from the Democratic to the Republican camp took place because of white Southern opposition to the Democratic Party's racial policies and because of determined Republican efforts to win white Southern support. It was not a change in the character of white Southerners but a change in the political circumstances in which they found themselves that induced this major shift in political allegiances and outlooks in the South.

The moral of this story is that a group's views cannot be inferred simply from the character of the group. College students are not inherently radical or inherently conservative. Jews are not inherently liberal. Southerners are not inherently conservative. Men are not inherently supportive of the military. Any group's political outlooks and orientations are shaped by the political circumstances in which that group finds itself, and those outlooks can change as circumstances change. Quite probably, the generation of American students now coming of political age will have a very different view of the use of American military power than their parents—members of a generation that reached political consciousness during the 1960s, when opposition to the Vietnam War and military conscription were important political phenomena.

Agreement on fundamentals, however, by no means implies that Americans do not differ with one another on a wide variety of issues. As we shall see, American political life is characterized by vigorous debate on economic, foreign policy, and social policy issues; race relations; environmental affairs; and a host of other matters.

Political Ideology

As we have seen, people's beliefs about government can vary widely. But for some individuals, this set of beliefs can fit together into a coherent philosophy about government. This set of underlying orientations, ideas, and beliefs through which we come to understand and interpret politics is called a political ideology.

In America today, people often describe themselves as liberals or conservatives. Liberalism and conservatism are political ideologies that include beliefs about the role of the government, ideas about public policies, and notions about which groups in society should properly exercise power. Historically these terms were defined somewhat differently than they are today. As recently as the nineteenth century, a liberal was an individual who favored freedom from state control, while a conservative was someone who supported the use of governmental power and favored continuation of the influence of church and aristocracy in national life.

Today, the term *liberal* has come to imply support for political and social reform; support for extensive governmental intervention in the economy; the expansion of federal social services; more vigorous efforts on behalf of the poor, minorities, and women; and greater concern for consumers and the environment. In social and cultural areas, liberals generally support abortion rights and oppose state involvement with religious institutions and religious expression. In international affairs,

liberal positions are usually seen as including support for aid to poor nations, opposition to the use of American troops to influence the domestic affairs of developing nations, and support for international organizations such as the United Nations.

Of course, liberalism is not monolithic. For example, among individuals who view themselves as liberal, many support American military intervention when it is tied to a humanitarian purpose, as in the case of America's military action in Kosovo in 1998–99. Most liberals supported President George W. Bush's war on terrorism, even when some of the president's actions seemed to curtail civil liberties.

By contrast, the term *conservative* today is used to describe those who generally support the social and economic status quo and are suspicious of efforts to introduce new political formulae and economic arrangements. Conservatives believe strongly that a large and powerful government poses a threat to citizens' freedom. Thus, in the domestic area, conservatives generally oppose the expansion of governmental activity, asserting that solutions to social and economic problems can be developed in the private sector. Conservatives particularly oppose efforts to impose government regulation on business, pointing out that such regulation is frequently economically inefficient and costly and can ultimately lower the entire nation's standard of living. As to social and cultural positions, many conservatives oppose abortion and support school prayer. In international affairs, conservatism has come to mean support for the maintenance of American military power.

Like liberalism, conservatism is far from a monolithic ideology. Some conservatives support many government social programs. George W. Bush calls himself a "compassionate conservative" to indicate that he favors programs that assist the poor and needy. Other conservatives oppose efforts to outlaw abortion, arguing that government intrusion in this area is as misguided as government intervention in the economy. Such a position is sometimes called "libertarian." In a similar vein, Pat Buchanan has angered many fellow conservatives by opposing most American military intervention in other regions. Many conservatives charge Buchanan with advocating a form of American "isolationism" that runs counter to contemporary conservative doctrine. The real political world is far too complex to be seen in terms of a simple struggle between liberals and conservatives.

To some extent, contemporary liberalism and conservatism can be seen as differences of emphasis with regard to the fundamental American political values of liberty and equality. For liberals, equality is the most important of the core values. Liberals are willing to tolerate government intervention in such areas as college admissions and business decisions when these seem to result in high levels of race, class, or gender inequality. For conservatives, on the other hand, liberty is the core value. Conservatives oppose most efforts by the government, however well intentioned, to intrude into private life or the marketplace. This simple formula for distinguishing liberalism and conservatism, however, is not always accurate, because political ideologies seldom lend themselves to neat or logical characterizations.

Liberalism and conservatism are political ideologies that include beliefs about the role of the government, ideas about public policies, and notions about which groups in society should exercise political power.

Often political observers search for logical connections among the various positions identified with liberalism or with conservatism, and they are disappointed or puzzled when they are unable to find a set of coherent philosophical principles that define and unite the several elements of either of these sets of beliefs. On the liberal side, for example, what is the logical connection between opposition to U.S. government intervention in the affairs of foreign nations and calls for greater intervention in America's economy and society? On the conservative side, what is the logical relationship between opposition to governmental regulation

of business and support for a ban on abortion? Indeed, the latter would seem to be just the sort of regulation of private conduct that conservatives claim to abhor.

Frequently, the relationships among the various elements of liberalism or the several aspects of conservatism are *political* rather than *logical*. One underlying basis of liberal views is that all or most represent criticisms of or attacks on the foreign and domestic policies and cultural values of the business and commercial strata that have been prominent in the United States for the past century. In some measure, the tents of contemporary conservatism represent this elite's defense of its positions against its enemies, who include organized labor, minority groups, and some intellectuals and professionals. Thus, liberals attack business and commercial elites by advocating more governmental regulation, including consumer protection and environmental regulation, opposition to military weapons programs, and support for expensive social programs. Conservatives counterattack by asserting that governmental regulation of the economy is ruinous and that military weapons are needed in a changing world, and they seek to stigmatize their opponents for showing no concern for the rights of "unborn" Americans.[16]

Of course, it is important to note that many people who call themselves liberals or conservatives accept only part of the liberal or conservative ideology. During the 1980s, many political commentators asserted that Americans were becoming increasingly conservative in their political orientations. Indeed, it was partly in response to this view that the Democrats in 1992 selected a presidential candidate, Bill Clinton, drawn from the party's moderate wing. Although it appears that Americans have adopted more conservative outlooks on some issues, their views in other areas have remained largely unchanged or even become more liberal in recent years. Thus, many individuals are

[16]For a discussion of this conflict, see Benjamin Ginsberg and Martin Shefter, "A Critical Realignment? The New Politics, the Reconstituted Right, and the Election of 1984," in *The Elections of 1984*, ed. Michael Nelson (Washington, DC: Congressional Quarterly Press, 1985), pp. 1–26.

liberal on social issues but conservative on economic issues. There is nothing illogical about these mixed positions. They indicate the relatively open and fluid character of American political debate.

HOW ARE POLITICAL OPINIONS FORMED?

An individual's opinions on particular issues, events, and personalities emerge as he or she evaluates these phenomena through the lenses of the beliefs and orientations that, taken together, comprise his or her political ideology. Thus, if a conservative is confronted with a plan to expand federal social programs, he or she is likely to express opposition to the endeavor without spending too much time pondering the specific plan. Similarly, if a liberal is asked to comment on former President Ronald Reagan, he or she is not likely to hesitate long before offering a negative view. Underlying beliefs and ideologies tend to automatically color people's perceptions and opinions about politics.

Opinions on particular issues, however, are seldom fully shaped by underlying ideologies. Few individuals possess ideologies so cohesive and intensely held that they will automatically shape all their opinions. Indeed, when we occasionally encounter individuals with rigid worldviews, who see everything through a particular political lens, we tend to dismiss them as "ideologues."

Although ideologies color our political perspectives, they seldom fully determine our views. This is true for a variety of reasons. First, as noted earlier, most individuals' ideologies contain internal contradictions. Take, for example, a conservative view of the issue of abortion. Should conservatives favor outlawing abortion as an appropriate means of preserving public morality, or should they oppose restrictions on abortion because these represent government intrusions into private life? In this instance, as in many others, ideology can point in different directions.

Second, individuals may have difficulty linking particular issues or personalities to their own underlying beliefs. Some issues defy ideological characterizations. Should conservatives support or oppose the formation of the Department of Homeland Security? What should liberals think about America's bombing of Iraq? Each of these policies combines a mix of issues and is too complex to be viewed through simple ideological lenses.

Finally, most people have at least some conflicting underlying attitudes. Most conservatives support *some* federal programs—defense, or tax deductions for businesses, for example—and wish to see them, and hence the government, expanded. Many liberals favor American military intervention in other nations for what they deem to be humanitarian purposes but generally oppose American military intervention in the affairs of other nations.

Thus, most individuals' attitudes on particular issues do not spring automatically from their ideological predispositions. It is true that most people have underlying beliefs that help to shape their opinions on particular issues,[17] but other factors are also important: a person's knowledge of political issues, and outside influences on that person's views.

Knowledge and Information

As we have seen, general political beliefs can guide the formation of opinions on specific issues, but an individual's beliefs and opinions are not always consistent with one another. Studies of political opinion have shown that most people don't hold specific and clearly defined opinions on every political issue.[18] As a result, they are easily influenced by others. What best explains whether citizens are generally consistent in their political views or inconsistent and open to the influence of others? The key is knowledge and information about political issues. In general, knowledgeable citizens are better able to evaluate new information and determine whether it is relevant to and consistent with their beliefs and opinions.

[17]R. Michael Alvarez and John Brehm, *Hard Choices, Easy Answers: Values, Information, and American Public Opinion* (Princeton, NJ: Princeton University Press, 2002).
[18]John R. Zaller, *The Nature and Origins of Mass Opinion* (New York: Cambridge University Press, 1992).

The average American, however, exhibits little knowledge of political institutions, processes, leaders, and policy debates. For example, in a 1996 poll, only about half of all Americans could correctly identify Newt Gingrich, who was then the speaker of the House of Representatives.[19] Some analysts have argued that political attentiveness is costly—it means spending time at the very least, but often money as well, to collect, organize, and digest political information.[20] Balanced against this cost to an individual is the very low probability that he or she will, on the basis of this costly information, take an action that would not otherwise have been taken, *and* that this departure in behavior will make a beneficial difference to him or her, *and* that difference, if it exists, will exceed the cost of acquiring the information in the first place. That is, since individuals anticipate that informed actions taken by them will rarely make much difference while the costs of informing oneself are often not trivial, it is rational to remain ignorant. A more moderate version of "rational" ignorance recognizes that some kinds of information are inexpensive to acquire, such as sound bites from the evening news, or actually pleasant, such as reading the front page of the newspaper while drinking a cup of coffee. In these cases, an individual may become partially informed, but usually not in detail. Taking cues from trusted others—the local preacher, the TV commentator or newspaper editorialist, an interest-group leader, friends, and relatives—is another "inexpensive" way to become informed.[21] Does this ignorance, no matter how rational, of key political facts matter?

Another important concern is the character of those who possess and act upon the political information that they acquire. Political knowledge, even that which is inexpensive to acquire, is not evenly distributed throughout the population. Those with higher education, income, and occupational status and who are members of social or political organizations are more likely to know about and be active in politics. An interest in politics reinforces an individual's sense of political efficacy and provides more incentive to acquire additional knowledge and information about politics. Those who don't think they can have an effect on government tend not to be interested in learning about or participating in politics. When asked for their views on political issues, they are less able than those with higher levels of education and income to form and articulate coherent and consistent opinions.[22] As a result, individuals with a disproportionate share of income and education also have a disproportionate share of knowledge and influence and are better able to get what they want from government.[23]

When individuals attempt to form opinions about particular political issues, events, and personalities, they seldom do so in isolation. Typically, they are confronted—sometimes bombarded—by the efforts of a host of individuals and groups seeking to persuade them to adopt a particular point of view. Someone trying to decide what to think about Bill Clinton, Al Gore, or George W. Bush could hardly avoid an avalanche of opinions expressed through the media, in meetings, or in conversations with friends. The **marketplace of ideas** is the interplay of opinions and views that takes place as competing forces attempt to persuade as many people as possible to accept a particular position on a particular event. Given constant exposure to the ideas of others, it is virtually impossible for most individuals to resist some modification of their own beliefs. For example, African Americans and white Americans disagree

[19]Michael X. Delli Carpini and Scott Keeter, *What Americans Know about Politics and Why It Matters* (New Haven: Yale University Press, 1996).

[20]Anthony Downs, *An Economic Theory of Democracy* (New York: Harper, 1957).

[21]For a discussion of the role of information in democratic politics in light of the cognitive limitations, restricted interest, and diminished attention span of today's voters, see Arthur Lupia and Mathew D. McCubbins, *The Democratic Dilemma: Can Citizens Learn What They Need to Know?* (New York: Cambridge University Press, 1998).

[22]Adam J. Berinsky, "Silent Voices: Social Welfare Policy Opinions and Political Equality in America," *American Journal of Political Science* 46(2002): 276–88.

[23]Steven J. Rosenstone and John Mark Hansen, *Mobilization, Participation, and Democracy in America* (New York: Macmillan, 1993).

on a number of matters. Yet, as political scientists Paul M. Sniderman and Edward G. Carmines have shown, considerable crossracial agreement has evolved on fundamental issues of race and civil rights.[24] Thus, to some extent, public opinion is subject to deliberate shaping and manipulation by *opinion leaders.* For example, in the summer of 1963, the public's attention was riveted to the dramatic struggle of nonviolent protestors attempting to win civil rights in the South. News stories and television film footage repeatedly showed peaceful demonstrators being chased and beaten by police, suffering attacks by dogs, and being sprayed with fire hoses. These scenes filled Americans with shock and outrage. Then, in August 1963, civil rights leaders staged a massive march on Washington (when Martin Luther King, Jr., delivered his famous "I Have a Dream" speech on the steps of the Lincoln Memorial). The impact on public opinion was dramatic: Between the spring and summer of that year, the percentage of Americans who considered civil rights to be "the most important issue" facing the country increased from 4 percent to 52 percent—the largest such increase ever recorded.[25] This is also an example of "agenda setting"—the ability of the media to turn the country's focus toward a particular issue (see discussion later in this chapter).

In many areas of the world, governments determine which opinions their citizens may or may not express. People who assert views that their rulers do not approve of may be subject to imprisonment—or worse. Americans and the citizens of the other Western democracies are fortunate to live in nations where freedom of opinion and expression are generally taken for granted.

Freedom of opinion, however, does not mean that all ideas and opinions flourish. Both private groups and the government itself today attempt to influence which opinions do take hold in the public imagination.

Few ideas spread spontaneously. Usually, whether they are matters of fashion, science, or

politics, ideas must be vigorously promoted to become widely known and accepted. For example, the clothing, sports, and entertainment fads that occasionally seem to appear from nowhere and sweep the country before being replaced by some new trend are almost always the product of careful marketing campaigns by some commercial interest, rather than spontaneous phenomena. Even in the sciences, generally considered *the* bastions of objectivity, new theories, procedures, and findings are not always accepted simply and immediately on their own merit. Often, the proponents of a new scientific principle or practice must campaign within the scientific community on behalf of their views. Like their counterparts in fashion and science, successful—or at least widely held—political ideas are usually the products of carefully orchestrated campaigns by government or by organized groups and interests rather than the results of spontaneous popular enthusiasm.

In general, new ideas are presented in ways that make them seem consistent with, or even logical outgrowths of, Americans' more fundamental beliefs. For example, proponents of affirmative action generally present the policy as a necessary step toward racial equality. Or opponents of a proposed government regulation will vehemently assert that the rule is inconsistent with liberty. Both supporters and opponents of campaign finance reform seek to wrap their arguments in the cloak of democracy.[26]

Three forces that play important roles in shaping opinions are the government, private groups, and the news media.

Government and Political Leaders

All governments attempt, to a greater or lesser extent, to influence, manipulate, or manage their citizens' beliefs. In the United States, some efforts have been made by every administration since the nation's founding to influence public sentiment. But efforts to shape opinion did not become a rou-

[24]Sniderman and Carmines, *Reaching beyond Race,* Chapter 4.
[25]Michael Robinson, "Television and American Politics 1956–1976," *Public Interest* 48 (Summer 1977): 23.

[26]For an interesting discussion of opinion formation, see John Zaller, *The Nature and Origins of Mass Opinion.* (New York: Cambridge University Press, 1992).

tine and formal official function until World War I, when the Wilson administration created a censorship board, enacted sedition and espionage legislation, and attempted to suppress groups that opposed the war, such as the International Workers of the World (IWW) and the Socialist Party. Eugene Debs, a prominent Socialist and a presidential candidate, was arrested and convicted of having violated the Espionage Law, and he was sentenced to ten years in prison for delivering a speech that defended the IWW.

Government attempts to shape public opinion in order to enlist the support of the people.

The extent to which public opinion is actually affected by governmental public relations efforts is probably limited. The government—despite its size and power—is only one source of information and evaluation in the United States. Very often, governmental claims are disputed by the media, by interest groups, and, at times by opposing forces within the government itself.

Often, too, governmental efforts to manipulate public opinion backfire when the public is made aware of the government's tactics. Thus, in 1971, the United States government's efforts to build popular support for the Vietnam War were hurt when CBS News aired its documentary "The Selling of the Pentagon," which revealed the extent and character of government efforts to sway popular sentiment. In this documentary, CBS demonstrated the techniques, including planted news stories and faked film footage, that the government had used to misrepresent its activities in Vietnam. These revelations, of course, had the effect of undermining popular trust in all government claims. During the 1991 Persian Gulf War, the U.S. military was much more concerned with the accuracy of its assertions.

A hallmark of the Clinton administration was the steady use of campaign techniques such as those used in election campaigns to bolster popular enthusiasm for White House initiatives. The

president established a "political war room" in the Executive Office Building similar to the one that operated in his campaign headquarters. Representatives from all departments met in the war room every day to discuss and coordinate the president's public relations efforts. Many of the same consultants and pollsters who directed the successful Clinton campaign were employed in the selling of the president's programs.[27]

Indeed, the Clinton White House made more sustained and systematic use of public opinion polling than any previous administration. For example, during his presidency Bill Clinton relied heavily on the polling firm of Penn & Schoen to help him decide which issues to emphasize and what strategies to adopt. During the 1995–1996 budget battle with Congress, the White House commissioned polls almost every night to chart changes in public perceptions about the struggle. Poll data suggested to Clinton that he should present himself as struggling to save Medicare from Republican cuts. Clinton responded by launching a media attack against what he claimed were GOP efforts to hurt the elderly. This proved to be a successful strategy and helped Clinton defeat the Republican budget.[28]

Evidence exists to support effectiveness of methods used by the Clinton White House. Political scientists Robert Shapiro and Lawrence Jacobs studied how polls are used by politicians and discovered that the ideology of political leaders, not public opinion, was the decisive influence on the formulation of a policy. They also found that the primary use of polling was to choose the language, rhetoric, and arguments for policy proposals in order to build the public's support.[29]

After he assumed office in 2001, President George W. Bush asserted that political leaders should base their programs upon their own conception of the public interest rather than the polls.

[27]Gerald F. Seib and Michael K. Frisby, "Selling Sacrifice," *Wall Street Journal*, 5 February 1993, p. 1.
[28]Michael K. Frisby, "Clinton Seeks Strategic Edge with Opinion Polls," *Wall Street Journal*, 24 June 1996, p. A16.
[29]Reported in Richard Morin, "Which Comes First, the Politician or the Poll?" *Washington Post National Weekly Edition*, 10 February 1997, p. 31.

This, however, did not mean that Bush ignored public opinion. Bush has relied on pollster Jan van Lohuizen to conduct a low-key operation, sufficiently removed from the limelight to allow the president to renounce polling while continuing to make use of survey data.[30] At the same time, the Bush White House developed an extensive public relations program, led by former presidential aide Karen P. Hughes, to bolster popular support for the president's policies. Hughes, working with conservative Republican strategist Mary Matalin, coordinated White House efforts to maintain popular support for the administration's war against terrorism. These efforts included presidential speeches, media appearances by administration officials, numerous press conferences, and thousands of press releases presenting the administration's views. The White House also made a substantial effort to sway opinion in foreign countries, even sending officials to present the administration's views on television networks serving the Arab world.

Another example of a Bush administration effort to shape public opinion is a series of commercials it produced at taxpayer expense in 2004 to promote the new Medicare prescription drug program. The commercials, prominently featuring the president, were designed to look like actual news stories and were aired in English and Spanish by hundreds of local television stations. Called a "video news release," this type of commercial is designed to give viewers the impression that they are watching a real news story. The presumption is that viewers are more likely to believe what they think is news coverage than material they know to be advertising. Democrats, of course, accused the administration of conducting a partisan propaganda campaign with public funds, but Republicans pointed out that the Clinton administration had engaged in similar practices.

Private Groups

Political issues and ideas seldom emerge spontaneously from the grass roots. We have already seen

how the government tries to shape opinion. In addition, the ideas that become prominent in political life are developed and spread by important economic and political groups searching for issues that will advance their causes. In some instances, private groups espouse values in which they truly believe in the hope of bringing others over to their side. Take, for example, the campaign against so-called partial birth abortion that resulted in the Partial Birth Abortion Ban Act of 2003. Proponents of the act believed that prohibiting particular sorts of abortions would be a first step toward eliminating all abortions—something they viewed as a moral imperative.[31] In other cases, groups will promote principles designed mainly to further hidden agendas of political and economic interests. One famous example is the campaign against cheap, imported handguns—the so-called Saturday night specials—covertly financed by domestic manufacturers of more expensive firearms. The campaign's organizers claimed that cheap handguns posed a grave risk to the public and should be outlawed. The real goal, though, was not safeguarding the public but protecting the economic well-being of the domestic gun industry. A more recent example is the campaign against the alleged "sweatshop" practices of some American companies manufacturing products in third-world countries. This campaign is mainly financed by U.S. labor unions seeking to protect their members' jobs by discouraging American firms from manufacturing products abroad.

Public opinion is also influenced by private interest groups and the news media.

Typically, ideas are best marketed by groups with access to financial resources, public or private institutional support, and sufficient skill or education to select, develop, and draft ideas that will attract interest and support. Thus, the devel-

---

[30]Joshua Green, "The Other War Room," *Washington Monthly,* April 2002.

[31]Cynthia Gorney, "Gambling with Abortion," *Harper's Magazine,* November 2004, pp. 33–46.

opment and promotion of conservative themes and ideas in recent years has been greatly facilitated by the millions of dollars that conservative corporations and business organizations, such as the Chamber of Commerce and the Public Affairs Council, spend each year on public information and what is now called in corporate circles "issues management." In addition, conservative businesses have contributed millions of dollars to such conservative institutions as the Heritage Foundation, the Hoover Institution, and the American Enterprise Institute.[32]

Although they do not usually have access to financial assets that match those available to their conservative opponents, liberal intellectuals and professionals have ample organizational skills, access to the media, and practice in creating, communicating, and using ideas. During the past three decades, the chief vehicle through which liberal intellectuals and professionals have advanced their ideas has been the "public interest group," an institution that relies heavily upon voluntary contributions of time, effort, and interest on the part of its members. Through groups such as Common Cause, the National Organization for Women, the Sierra Club, Friends of the Earth, and Physicians for Social Responsibility, intellectuals and professionals have been able to use their organizational skills and educational resources to develop and promote ideas.[33]

Journalist and author Joe Queenan correctly observed that although political ideas can erupt spontaneously, they almost never do. Instead,

. . . issues are usually manufactured by tenured professors and obscure employees of think tanks. . . . It is inconceivable that the American people, all by themselves, could independently arrive at the conclusion that the depletion of the ozone layer poses a dire threat to our national well-being, or that an immedi-

ate, across-the-board cut in the capital-gains tax is the only thing that stands between us and the economic abyss. The American people do not have that kind of sophistication. *They have to have help.*[34]

Typically, groups with the most access to financial and organizational resources have the greatest influence on public opinion.

THE MEDIA

Among the most important forces shaping public opinion are the national news media. The content and character of news and public affairs programming—what the media choose to present and how they present it—can have the most far-reaching political consequences. Media disclosures can greatly enhance—or fatally damage—the careers of public officials. Media coverage can rally support for—or intensify opposition to—national policies. The media can shape and modify, if not fully form, public perceptions of events, issues, and institutions.

Shaping Events

In recent American political history, the media have played a central role in at least three major events. First, the media were critically important factors in the Civil Rights movement of the 1950s and 1960s. Television pictures showing peaceful civil rights marchers attacked by club-swinging police helped to generate sympathy among Northern whites for the civil rights struggle and greatly increased the pressure on Congress to bring an end to segregation.[35]

Second, the media were instrumental in compelling the Johnson and Nixon administrations to

---

[32]See David Vogel, "The Power of Business in America: A Reappraisal," *British Journal of Political Science* 13 (January 1983): 19–44.

[33]See David Vogel, "The Public Interest Movement and the American Reform Tradition," *Political Science Quarterly* 96 (Winter 1980): 607–27.

[34]Joe Queenan, "Birth of a Notion," *Washington Post*, 20 September 1992, p. C1. [Emphasis in original.]

[35]David Garrow, *Protest at Selma* (New Haven, CT: Yale University Press, 1978).

negotiate an end to the Vietnam War. Beginning in 1967, the national media portrayed the war as misguided and unwinnable and, as a result, helped to turn popular sentiment against continued American involvement.[36]

Third, the media were central actors in the Watergate affair, which ultimately forced President Richard Nixon, landslide victor in the 1972 presidential election, to resign from office in disgrace. It was the relentless series of investigations launched by the *Washington Post,* the *New York Times,* and the major television networks that led to the disclosures of the various abuses of which Nixon was guilty and ultimately forced Nixon to choose between resignation and almost certain impeachment.

The Sources of Media Power

AGENDA SETTING   The power of the media stems from several sources. The first is *agenda setting,* which means the media help to set the agenda for political discussion. Groups and forces that wish to bring their ideas before the public in order to generate support for policy proposals or political candidacies must somehow secure media

[36]See Todd Gitlin, *The Whole World Is Watching* (Berkeley: University of California Press, 1980), and William Hammond, *Reporting Vietnam: Media and Military at War* (Lawrence: University of Kansas Press, 1999).

coverage. If the media are persuaded that an idea is newsworthy, then they may declare it an "issue" that must be resolved or a "problem" to be solved, thus clearing the first hurdle in the policy-making process. On the other hand, if an idea lacks or loses media appeal, its chance of resulting in new programs or policies is diminished. Some ideas seem to surface, gain media support for a time, lose media appeal, and then resurface. In most instances, the media serve as conduits for agenda-setting efforts by competing groups and forces. Occasionally, however, journalists themselves play an important role in setting the agenda of political discussion. For example, whereas many of the scandals and investigations surrounding President Clinton were initiated by his political opponents, the Watergate scandal that destroyed Nixon's presidency was in some measure initiated and driven by the *Washington Post* and the national television networks.

FRAMING   A second source of the media's power, known as *framing,* is their power to decide how political events and results are interpreted by the American people. For example, during the 1995–96 struggle between President Clinton and congressional Republicans over the nation's budget—a struggle that led to several partial shutdowns of the federal government—the media's interpretation of events forced the Republicans to back down and agree to a budget on Clinton's

IN BRIEF BOX

SOURCES OF MEDIA POWER

Setting the agenda for political discussion: Groups wishing to generate support for policy proposals or political candidacies must secure media coverage. The media must be persuaded that an item is newsworthy.

Framing: The media's interpretation of an event or political action can sometimes determine how people perceive the event or result.

Priming: Most citizens will never meet their political leaders, but will base opinions of these leaders on their media images. The media have a great deal of control over how a person is portrayed or whether an individual even receives public attention.

terms. At the beginning of the crisis, congressional Republicans, led by House Speaker Newt Gingrich, were confident that they could compel Clinton to accept their budget, which called for substantial cuts in domestic social programs. Republicans calculated that Clinton would fear being blamed for lengthy government shutdowns and would quickly accede to their demands, and that once Americans saw that life went on with government agencies closed, they would support the Republicans in asserting that the United States could get along with less government.

For the most part, however, the media did not cooperate with these plans. Media coverage of the several government shutdowns during this period emphasized the hardships imposed upon federal workers who were being furloughed in the weeks before Christmas. Indeed, Speaker Gingrich was portrayed as the villain who caused the crisis and was called the "Gin*grinch*" who stole Christmas from the children of hundreds of thousands of federal workers. Rather than suggest that the shutdown demonstrated that America could carry on with less government, media accounts focused on the difficulties encountered by Washington tourists unable to visit the capital's monuments, museums, and galleries. The woes of American travelers whose passport applications were delayed were given considerable attention. This sort of coverage eventually convinced most Americans that the government shutdown was bad for the country. In the end, Gingrich and the congressional Republicans were forced to surrender and to accept a new budget reflecting many of Clinton's priorities. The Republicans' defeat in the budget showdown contributed to the unraveling of the GOP legislative program and, ultimately, to the Republicans' poor showing in the 1996 presidential elections. The character of media coverage of an event thus had enormous repercussions for how Americans interpreted it.

Media frames were also quite important during the 2000 election. Early in the campaign, the national media presented George W. Bush as lacking in intelligence and Al Gore as somewhat dis-

honest. These characterizations were reinforced by many stories. For example, when Bush responded to a question about his favorite book from childhood by naming a well-known children's book, *The Very Hungry Caterpillar,* news accounts suggested that the book was one of his current favorites.[37] As for Gore, the media frequently played up what it deemed his tendency to exaggerate with stories poking fun at his claims of having worked on a farm in his youth and his contention that he played a role in the development of the Internet. These media frames helped to shape voters' perceptions of the two candidates. Strikingly, in one instance, a media frame shaped a candidate's perception of himself. After the first presidential debate, the news media presented Gore as overly aggressive. Not only did the public accept this characterization, but Gore himself responded to the image presented by the media by completing shifting his behavior in the second debate. While he had been extremely critical of Bush in their first encounter, Gore went out of his way to praise Bush during their second meeting.[38] In this case, a media frame affected the participants as much as the viewers.

PRIMING   A third important media power is *priming*. This occurs when media coverage affects the way the public evaluates political leaders or candidates for office. For example, nearly unanimous media praise for President George W. Bush's speeches to the nation in the wake of the September 11 terrorist attacks prepared, or "primed," the public to view Bush's subsequent response to terrorism in an extremely positive light, even though some aspects of the administration's efforts, most notably those in the realm of preventing bioterrorism, were problematic.

In the case of political candidates, the media have considerable influence over whether or not a particular individual will receive public attention, whether or not a particular individual will be taken

---

[37]Kathleen Hall Jamieson and Paul Waldman, *The Press Effect* (New York: Oxford University Press, 2003), p. 61.
[38]Jamieson and Waldman, *The Press Effect,* p. 56.

seriously as a viable contender, and whether the public will perceive a candidate's performance favorably. Thus, if the media find a candidate interesting, they may treat him or her as a serious contender even though the facts of the matter seem to suggest otherwise. In a similar vein, the media may declare that a candidate has *"momentum,"* a mythical property that the media confer upon candidates they admire. Momentum has no substantive meaning—it is simply a media prediction that a particular candidate will do even better in the future than in the past. Such media prophecies can become self-fulfilling as contributors and supporters jump on the bandwagon of the candidate possessing this "momentum." In 1992, when Bill Clinton's poll standings surged in the wake of the Democratic National Convention, the media determined that Clinton had enormous momentum. In fact, nothing that happened during the remainder of the race led the media to change their collective judgment.

Typically, media coverage of election campaigns focuses on the "horse race" to the detriment of attention to issues and candidate records. During the 2000 presidential contest, Senator John McCain of Arizona was able to use his Senate committee chairmanship to raise enough money to mount a challenge to George W. Bush. In reality, McCain had little chance of defeating the front-runner. Seeing the possibility of a "horse race," however, the media gave McCain a great deal of generally positive coverage and helped him mount a noisy, if brief, challenge to Bush. McCain's hopes were dashed, though, when he was trounced by Bush in a series of primaries, including those held in South Carolina and other GOP strongholds.

The media's power to shape images is not absolute. Throughout the last decade, politicians implemented new techniques for communicating with the public and shaping their own images. For instance, Bill Clinton pioneered the use of town meetings and television entertainment programs as a means for communicating directly with voters in the 1992 election. During the 2000 presidential race between Bush and Gore, both candidates made use of town meetings, as well as talk shows and entertainment programs such as *The Oprah Winfrey Show, The Tonight Show with Jay Leno,* and *Saturday Night Live,* to reach mass audiences. During a town meeting, talk show, or entertainment program, politicians are free to craft their own images without interference from journalists.

Political candidates try to shape their media images by appearing on talk shows and at town meetings.

In 2000, George W. Bush was also able to shape his image by effectively courting the press through informal conversation and interaction. Journalists concluded that Bush was a nice fellow, albeit inexperienced, and refrained from subjecting him to harsh criticism and close scrutiny. Al Gore, on the other hand, seemed to offend journalists by remaining aloof and giving an impression of disdain for the press. Journalists responded by portraying Gore as "stiff." The result was unusually positive coverage for the Republican candidate and unusually negative coverage for the Democratic candidate.

In the fall of 2001, President Bush had little difficulty convincing the media that terrorism and his administration's campaign to combat terrorist attacks merited a dominant place on the agenda. Some stories have such overwhelming significance that political leaders' main concern is not whether the story will receive attention, but whether they will figure prominently and positively in media accounts. The same is true of the 2003 Iraq war.

The Rise of Adversarial Journalism

The political power of the news media has greatly increased in recent years through the growing prominence of "adversarial journalism"—a form of journalism in which the media adopt a hostile posture toward the government and public officials.

During the nineteenth century, American newspapers were completely subordinate to the political parties. Newspapers depended upon official patronage—legal notices and party subsidies—for their financial survival and were controlled by party leaders. (A vestige of that era survived into the twentieth century in such newspaper names as the *Springfield Republican* and the *St. Louis Globe-Democrat.*) At the turn of the century, with the development of commercial advertising, newspapers became financially independent. This made possible the emergence of a formally nonpartisan press.

Presidents were the first national officials to see the opportunities in this development. By communicating directly to the electorate through newspapers and magazines, Theodore Roosevelt and Woodrow Wilson established political constituencies for themselves independent of party organizations and strengthened their own power relative to Congress. President Franklin Roosevelt used the radio, most notably in his famous fireside chats, to reach out to voters throughout the nation and to make himself the center of American politics. FDR was also adept at developing close personal relationships with reporters, which enabled him to obtain favorable news coverage despite the fact that in his day a majority of newspaper owners and publishers were staunch conservatives. Following Roosevelt's example, subsequent presidents have all sought to use the media to enhance their popularity and power. For example, through televised news conferences, President John F. Kennedy mobilized public support for his domestic and foreign policy initiatives.

During the 1950s and 1960s, a few members of Congress also made successful use of the media—especially television—to mobilize national support for their causes. Senator Estes Kefauver of Tennessee became a major contender for the presidency and won a place on the 1956 Democratic national ticket as a result of his dramatic televised hearings on organized crime. Senator Joseph McCarthy of Wisconsin made himself a powerful national figure through his well-publicized investigations of alleged Communist infiltration of key American institutions. These senators, however, were more exceptional than typical. Through the mid-1960s, the executive branch continued to generate the bulk of news coverage, and the media served as a cornerstone of presidential power.

The Vietnam War shattered this relationship between the press and the presidency. During the early stages of U.S. involvement, American officials in Vietnam who disapproved of the way the war was being conducted leaked information critical of administrative policy to reporters. Publication of this material infuriated the White House, which pressured publishers to block its release—on one occasion, President Kennedy went so far as to ask the *New York Times* to reassign its Saigon correspondent. The national print and broadcast media—the network news divisions, the national news weeklies, the *Washington Post,* and the *New York Times*—discovered, however, that there was an audience for critical coverage among segments of the public skeptical of administration policy.

As the Vietnam conflict dragged on, critical media coverage fanned antiwar sentiment. Moreover, growing opposition to the war among liberals encouraged some members of Congress, most notably Senator J. William Fulbright, chair of the Senate Foreign Relations Committee, to break with the president. In turn, these shifts in popular and congressional sentiment emboldened journalists and publishers to continue to present critical news reports. Through this process, journalists developed a commitment to adversarial journalism, while a constituency emerged that would rally to the defense of the media when it came under White House attack.

The political power of the news media has greatly increased because of the growing prominence of adversarial journalism.

This pattern endured through the 1970s and into the 1990s. Political forces opposed to presidential policies, many members of Congress, and the national news media began to find that their interests often overlapped.

Adversarial, or "attack," journalism has become commonplace in America, and some critics have suggested that the media have contributed to popular cynicism and the low levels of citizen participation that characterize contemporary American political processes. But before we begin to think about means of compelling the media to adopt a more positive view of politicians and political issues, we should consider the possibility that media criticism is one of the major mechanisms of political accountability in the American political process. Without aggressive media coverage, would we have known of Bill Clinton's misdeeds or, for that matter, those of Richard Nixon? Without aggressive media coverage, would important questions be raised about the conduct of American foreign and domestic policy? It is easy to criticize the media for their aggressive tactics, but would our democracy function effectively without the critical role of the press? A vigorous and critical media are needed as the "watchdogs" of American politics. Of course, in October 2001, the adversarial relationship between the government and the media was at least temporarily transformed into a much more supportive association as the media helped rally the American people for the fight against terrorism. And, indeed, some commentators have suggested that segments of the media, the more conservative media in particular, have become far less adversarial in their tone during the George W. Bush presidency than in prior years.

The adversarial relationship between the government and segments of the press, however, resumed after the early months of the Iraq war. Such newspapers as the *Washington Post* and the *New York Times* castigated President Bush for going to war without winning the support of some of America's major allies. When American forces failed to uncover evidence that Iraq possessed weapons of mass destruction—a major reason cited by the administration for launching the war—these newspapers intimated that the war had been based on intelligence failures, if not outright presidential deceptions. The president and other administration officials denounced the media for distorting his record. In a similar vein, in October 2003, President Bush accused the media of failing to report

American successes in the occupation of Iraq while dwelling only on apparent failures of U.S. policy. In 2004, an article by investigative reporter Seymour Hersh in the *New Yorker* along with a story on *60 Minutes 2* revealed that soldiers had abused Iraqi prisoners in their custody. The story prompted a televised apology from President Bush, congressional hearings, and calls for the resignation of Defense Secretary Donald Rumsfeld. As the abuse scandal widened, it became a major issue in the 2004 presidential race. Thus, after a brief interlude of post–9/11 harmony, the customary hostilities between the government and the press seemed to manifest themselves once again.

Politicians have grown increasingly dependent on the news media for favorable coverage, while the news media has grown independent of politicians for information.

MEASURING PUBLIC OPINION

As recently as fifty years ago, American political leaders gauged public opinion by people's applause or cheers and by the presence of crowds in meeting places. This direct exposure to the people's views did not necessarily produce accurate knowledge of public opinion. It did, however, give political leaders confidence in their public support—and therefore confidence in their ability to govern by consent.

Abraham Lincoln and Stephen Douglas debated each other seven times in the campaign for the Illinois Senate seat during the summer and autumn of 1858, two years before they became presidential nominees. Their debates took place before audiences in parched cornfields and courthouse squares. A century later, the presidential debates, although seen by millions, take place before a few reporters and technicians in television studios that might as well be on the moon. The public's response cannot be experienced directly. This distance between leaders and followers is one of the agonizing problems of modern democracy. The media send information to millions of people, but they are not yet as efficient at getting information back to leaders. Is government by consent possible where the scale of communication is so large and so impersonal? To compensate for the decline in their ability to experience public opinion for themselves, leaders have turned to science, in particular to the science of opinion polling.

It is no secret that politicians and public officials make extensive use of *public opinion polls* to help them decide whether to run for office, what policies to support, how to vote on important legislation, and what types of appeals to make in their campaigns. President Lyndon Johnson was famous for carrying the latest Gallup and Roper poll results in his hip pocket, and it is widely believed that he began to withdraw from politics because the polls reported losses in public support. All recent presidents and other major political figures have worked closely with polls and pollsters.

Constructing Public Opinion from Surveys

The population in which pollsters are interested is usually quite large. To conduct their polls, they choose a *sample* of the total population. The selection of this sample is important. Above all, it must be representative; the views of those in the sample must accurately and proportionately reflect the views of the whole. To a large extent, the validity of the poll's results depends on the sampling procedure used.

SAMPLING TECHNIQUES AND SELECTION BIAS
The most common techniques for choosing such a sample are probability sampling and random digit dialing. In the case of *probability sampling,* the pollster begins with a listing of the population to be surveyed. This listing is called the sampling frame. After assigning each member of the population a number, the pollster uses a table of random numbers or a computerized random selection process to select those to be surveyed. This technique is appropriate when the entire population can be identified. For example, all students registered at Texas colleges and universities can be identified from college records and a sample of them can easily be drawn. When the pollster is interested in a national sample of Americans, however, this technique is not feasible, as no complete list of Americans exists.[39] National samples are usually drawn using a technique called *random digit dialing.* A computer random number generator is used to produce a list of as many ten-digit numbers as the pollster deems necessary. Since more than 95 percent of American households have telephones, this technique usually results in a random national sample.

The importance of sampling was brought home early in the history of political polling. A 1936 *Literary Digest* poll predicted that Republican presidential candidate Alf Landon would defeat Democrat Franklin D. Roosevelt in that year's presidential election. The actual election, of course, ended in a Roosevelt landslide. The main problem with the survey had been what is called *selection bias* in drawing the sample. The pollsters relied on telephone directories and automobile registration rosters to produce a sampling frame. During the Great Depression, only wealthier Americans owned telephones and automobiles. Thus, the millions of working-class Americans who constituted Roosevelt's principal base of support were excluded from the sample.

In recent years, the issue of selection bias has been further complicated by the fact that growing numbers of individuals refuse to answer pollsters' questions or use such devices as answering machines and caller ID to screen unwanted callers. If pollsters could be certain that those who responded to their surveys simply reflected the views of those who refused to respond, there would be no problem. Some studies, however, suggest that the views of respondents and nonrespondents can differ, especially along social-class lines. Middle- and upper-middle-class individuals are more likely to be willing to respond to surveys than their working-class counterparts.[40] Thus far, "nonre-

---

[39]Herbert Asher, *Polling and the Public* (Washington, DC: CQ Press, 2001), p. 64.
[40]John Goyder, Keith Warriner, and Susan Miller, "Evaluating Socio-economic Status Bias in Survey Nonresponse," *Journal of Official Statistics* 18, no. 1 (2002).

sponse bias" has not undermined a major national survey, but the possibility of a future *Literary Digest* fiasco should not be ignored.

SAMPLE SIZE   The degree of reliability in polling is also a function of sample size. The same sample is needed to represent a small population as to represent a large population. The typical size of a sample ranges from 450 to 1,500 respondents. This number, however, reflects a trade-off between cost and degree of precision desired. The degree of accuracy that can be achieved with even a small sample can be seen from the polls' success in predicting election outcomes.

Table 9.3 shows how accurate two of the major national polling organizations have been in predicting the outcomes of presidential elections. Pollsters have mostly been correct in their predictions.

SURVEY DESIGN   Even with reliable sample procedures, surveys may fail to reflect the true distribution of opinion within a target population. One frequent source of *measurement error* is the wording of survey questions. The precise words used in a question can have an enormous impact on the answers it elicits. The validity of survey results can also be adversely affected by poor question format, faulty ordering of questions, inappropriate vocabulary, ambiguity of questions, or questions with built-in biases. In some instances, bias may be intentional. Polls conducted on behalf of interest groups or political candidates are often designed to allow the sponsors of the poll to claim that they have the support of the American people.[41] Often, seemingly minor differences in the wording of a question can convey vastly different meanings to respondents and, thus, produce quite different response patterns.

For example, for many years the University of Chicago's National Opinion Research Center has asked respondents whether they think the federal government is spending too much, too little,

or about the right amount of money on "assistance for the poor." Answering the question posed this way, about two-thirds of all respondents seem to believe that the government is spending too little. However, the same survey also asks whether the government spends too much, too little, or about the right amount for "welfare." When the word "welfare" is substituted for "assistance for the poor," about half of all respondents indicate that too much is being spent by the government.[42]

PUSH POLLING   In recent years, a new form of bias has been introduced into surveys by the use of a technique called *push polling*. This technique involves asking a respondent a loaded question about a political candidate designed to elicit the response sought by the pollster and, simultaneously, to shape the respondent's perception of the candidate in question. For example, during the 1996 New Hampshire presidential primary, push pollsters employed by the campaign of one of Lamar Alexander's rivals called thousands of voters to ask, "If you knew that Lamar Alexander had raised taxes six times in Tennessee, would you be less inclined or more inclined to support him?"[43] More than one hundred consulting firms across the nation now specialize in push polling.[44] Calling push polling the "political equivalent of a drive-by shooting," Representative Joe Barton (R-Tex.) launched a congressional investigation into the practice.[45] Push polls may be one reason that Americans are becoming increasingly skeptical about the practice of polling and increasingly unwilling to answer pollsters' questions.[46]

---

[41]August Gribbin, "Two Key Questions in Assessing Polls: 'How?' and 'Why?' " *Washington Times*, 19 October 1998, p. A10.

[42]Michael Kagay and Janet Elder, "Numbers Are No Problem for Pollsters, Words Are," *New York Times*, 9 August 1992, p. E6.

[43]Donn Tibbetts, "Draft Bill Requires Notice of Push Polling," *Manchester Union Leader*, 3 October 1996, p. A6.

[44]"Dial S. for Smear," *Memphis Commercial Appeal*, 22 September 1996, p. 6B.

[45]Amy Keller, "Subcommittee Launches Investigation of Push Polls," *Roll Call*, 3 October 1996, p. 1.

[46]For a discussion of the growing difficulty of persuading people to respond to surveys, see John Brehm, *Phantom Respondents* (Ann Arbor: University of Michigan Press, 1993).

TABLE 9.3

TWO POLLSTERS AND THEIR RECORDS (1948–2004)

		Harris	Gallup	Actual Outcome
2004	Bush	49%	49%	51%
	Kerry	48	49	48
	Nader	1	1	0
2000	Bush	47%	48%	48%
	Gore	47	46	49
	Nader	5	4	3
1996	Clinton	51%	52%	49%
	Dole	39	41	41
	Perot	9	7	8
1992	Clinton	44%	44%	43%
	Bush	38	37	38
	Perot	17	14	19
1988	Bush	51%	53%	54%
	Dukakis	47	42	46
1984	Reagan	56%	59%	59%
	Mondale	44	41	41
1980	Reagan	48%	47%	51%
	Carter	43	44	41
	Anderson		8	
1976	Carter	48%	48%	51%
	Ford	45	49	48
1972	Nixon	59%	62%	61%
	McGovern	35	38	38
1968	Nixon	40%	43%	43%
	Humphrey	43	42	43
	G. Wallace	13	15	14
1964	Johnson	62%	64%	61%
	Goldwater	33	36	39
1960	Kennedy	49%	51%	50%
	Nixon	41	49	49
1956	Eisenhower	NA	60%	58%
	Stevenson		41	42
1952	Eisenhower	47%	51%	55%
	Stevenson	42	49	44
1948	Truman	NA	44.5%	49.6%
	Dewey		49.5	45.1

All figures except those for 1948 are rounded. NA = Not asked.
SOURCES: Data from the Gallup Poll, the Harris Survey (New York: Chicago Tribune–New York News Syndicate, various press releases 1964–2004). Courtesy of the Gallup Organization and Louis Harris & Associates.

ILLUSION OF SALIENCY   In the early days of a political campaign when voters are asked which candidates they do or do not support, the answer they give often has little significance, because the choice is not yet salient to them. Their preference may change many times before the actual election. This is part of the explanation for the phenomenon of the postconvention "bounce" in the popularity of presidential candidates, which was observed after the 1992 and 1996 Democratic and Republican national conventions. Respondents' preferences reflected the amount of attention a candidate had received during the conventions rather than strongly held views.

The degree of reliability in polling is a function of sample size. The wording of the questions asked can also affect poll results.

Salient interests are interests that stand out beyond others, that are of more than ordinary concern to respondents in a survey or to voters in the electorate. Politicians, social scientists, journalists, or pollsters who assume something is important to the public when in fact it is not are creating an **illusion of saliency.** Polls can create or foster this illusion despite careful controls over sampling, interviewing, and data analysis. In fact, the illusion is strengthened by the credibility that science gives survey results.

The problem of saliency has become especially acute as a result of the proliferation of media polls. The television networks and major national newspapers all make heavy use of opinion polls. Increasingly, polls are being commissioned by local television stations and local and regional newspapers as well.[47] On the positive side, polls allow journalists to make independent assessments of political realities—assessments not influenced by the partisan claims of politicians.

Another problem with poll results is that they can create an illusion of saliency.

At the same time, however, media polls can allow journalists to make news when none really exists. Polling diminishes journalists' dependence upon news makers. A poll commissioned by a news agency can provide the basis for a good story even when candidates, politicians, and other news makers refuse to cooperate by engaging in newsworthy activities. Thus, on days when little or nothing is actually taking place in a political campaign, poll results, especially apparent changes in candidate margins, can provide voters with exciting news.

Interestingly, because rapid and dramatic shifts in candidate margins tend to take place when voters' preferences are least fully formed, horse-race news is most likely to make the headlines when it is actually least significant.[48] In other words, media interest in poll results is inversely related to the actual salience of voters' opinions and the significance of the polls' findings. However, by influencing perceptions, especially those of major contributors, media polls can influence political realities.

BANDWAGON EFFECT   The most noted, but least serious, of polling problems is the **bandwagon effect,** which occurs when polling results influence people to support the candidate marked as the probable victor. Some scholars argue that this bandwagon effect can be offset by an "underdog effect" in favor of the candidate who is trailing in the polls.[49] However, a candidate who demonstrates a lead in the polls usually finds it considerably easier to raise campaign funds than a candidate whose poll standing is poor. With these

[47]See Thomas E. Mann and Gary Orren, eds., *Media Polls in American Politics* (Washington, DC: Brookings Institution, 1992).

[48]For an excellent and reflective discussion by a journalist, see Richard Morin, "Clinton Slide in Survey Shows Perils of Polling," *Washington Post,* 29 August 1992, p. A6.

[49]See Michael Traugott, "The Impact of Media Polls on the Public," in Mann and Orren, eds., *Media Polls in American Politics,* pp. 125–49.

additional funds, poll leaders can often afford to pay for television time and other campaign activities that will cement their advantage. For example, Bill Clinton's substantial lead in the polls during much of the summer of 1992 helped the Democrats raise far more money than in any previous campaign, primarily from interests hoping to buy access to a future President Clinton. For once, the Democrats were able to outspend the usually better-heeled Republicans. Thus, the *appearance* of a lead, according to the polls, helped make Clinton's lead a reality.

PUBLIC OPINION AND GOVERNMENT POLICY

In democratic nations, leaders should pay attention to public opinion, and most evidence suggests that they do. There are many instances in which public policy and public opinion do not coincide, but in general the government's actions are consistent with citizens' preferences. One study, for example, found that between 1935 and 1979, in about two-thirds of all cases, significant changes in public opinion were followed within one year by changes in government policy consistent with the shift in the popular mood.[50] Other studies have come to similar conclusions about public opinion and government policy at the state level.[51] Do these results suggest that politicians pander to the public? The answer is no. Elected leaders don't always pander to the results of public opinion polls, but instead use polling to sell their policy proposals and shape the public's views.[52]

[50]Benjamin I. Page and Robert Y. Shapiro, "Effects of Public Opinion on Policy," *American Political Science Review* 77 (March 1983): 175–90.

[51]Robert A. Erikson, Gerald Wright, and John McIver, *Statehouse Democracy: Public Opinion and Democracy in the American States* (New York: Cambridge University Press, 1994).

[52]The results of separate studies by the political scientists Lawrence Jacobs, Robert Shapiro, and Alan Monroe were reported by Richard Morin in "Which Comes First, the Politician or the Poll?" *Washington Post National Weekly Edition*, 10 February 1997, p. 35.

> *In general, the government's policy decisions are consistent with public opinion.*

In addition, there are always areas of disagreement between opinion and policy. For example, the majority of Americans favored stricter governmental control of handguns for years before Congress finally adopted the modest restrictions on firearms purchases embodied in the 1994 Brady Bill and the Crime Control Act. Similarly, most Americans—blacks as well as whites—oppose school busing to achieve racial balance, yet such busing continues to be used extensively throughout the nation. Most Americans are far less concerned with the rights of the accused than the federal courts seem to be. Most Americans oppose U.S. military intervention in other nations' affairs, yet interventions continue to take place and often win public approval after the fact.

Several factors can contribute to a lack of consistency between opinion and governmental policy. First, the national majority on a particular issue may not be as intensely committed to its preference as the adherents of the minority viewpoint. An intensely committed minority may often be more willing to commit its time, energy, efforts, and resources to the affirmation of its opinions than an apathetic, even if large, majority. In the case of firearms, for example, although the proponents of gun control are in the majority by a wide margin, most do not regard the issue as one of critical importance to themselves and are not willing to commit much effort to advancing their cause. The opponents of gun control, by contrast, are intensely committed, well organized, and well financed, and as a result are usually able to carry the day.

A second important reason that public policy and public opinion may not coincide has to do with the character and structure of the American system of government. The framers of the American Constitution, as we saw in Chapter 2, sought to create a system of government that was based upon popular consent but that did not invariably and automatically translate shifting popular sentiments into public policies. As a result, the American governmental process includes arrangements such as an appointed judiciary that can produce policy decisions that may run contrary to prevailing popular sentiment—at least for a time.

Perhaps the inconsistencies between opinion and policy could be resolved if broader use were made of the initiative and referendum. This procedure allows propositions to be placed on the ballot and voted into law by the electorate thereby eliminating most of the normal machinery of representative government. In recent years, several important propositions sponsored by business and conservative groups have been enacted by voters in the states.[53] For example, California's Proposition 209, approved by the state's voters in 1996, prohibited the state and local government agencies in California from using race or gender preferences in the processes of hiring, contracting, or admitting university students. Responding to conservatives' success, liberal groups launched a number of ballot initiatives in 2000. For example, in Washington State, voters were asked to consider propositions sponsored by teachers' unions that would have required annual cost-of-living raises for teachers and more than $1.8 billion in additional state spending over six years.[54]

Initiatives such as these seem to provide the public with an opportunity to express its will. The major problem, however, is that government by initiative offers little opportunity for reflection and compromise. Voters are presented with a proposition, usually sponsored by a special interest group, and are asked to take it or leave it. Perhaps the true will of the people, not to mention their best interest, might lie somewhere between the positions taken by various interest groups. Perhaps, for example, California voters might have wanted affir-

mative action programs to be modified but not scrapped altogether as Proposition 209 mandated. In a representative assembly, as opposed to a referendum campaign, a compromise position might have been achieved that was more satisfactory to all the residents of the state. This is one reason the framers of the U.S. Constitution strongly favored representative government rather than direct democracy.

When all is said and done, however, there can be little doubt that in general the actions of the American government do not remain out of line with popular sentiment for very long. A major reason for this is, of course, the electoral process, to which we shall next turn.

CHAPTER REVIEW

All governments claim to obey public opinion, and in the democracies politicians and political leaders actually try to do so.

The American government does not directly regulate opinions and beliefs in the sense that dictatorial regimes often do. Opinion is regulated by an institution that the government constructed and that it maintains—the marketplace of ideas. In this marketplace, opinions and ideas compete for support. In general, opinions supported by upper-class groups have a better chance of succeeding than those views that are advanced mainly by the lower classes.

Americans share a number of values and viewpoints but often classify themselves as liberal or conservative in their basic orientations. The meaning of these terms has changed greatly over the past century. Once liberalism meant opposition to big government. Today liberals favor an expanded role for the government. Once conservatism meant support for state power and aristocratic rule. Today conservatives oppose almost all government regulation.

Although the United States relies mainly on market mechanisms, our government does intervene to influence particular opinions and, more important, the general climate of political opinion,

[53]David S. Broder, *Democracy Detailed: Initiative Campaigns and the Power of Money* (New York: Harcourt, 2000).

[54]Robert Tomsho, "Liberals Take a Cue from Conservatives: This Election, the Left Tries to Make Policy with Ballot Initiatives," *Wall Street Journal*, 6 November 2000, p. A12.

often by trying to influence media coverage of events.

Another important force shaping public opinion is the news media, which help to determine the agenda or focus of political debate and to shape popular understanding of political events. The power of the media stems from their having the freedom to present information and opinion critical of government, political leaders, and policies.

Free media are essential ingredients of popular government.

The scientific approach to learning public opinion is called polling. Through polling, elections can be accurately predicted; polls also provide information on the bases and conditions of voting decisions and make it possible to assess trends in attitudes and the influence of ideology on attitudes.

KEY TERMS

agencies of socialization   Social institutions, including families and schools, that help to shape individuals' basic political beliefs and values.

agenda setting   The power of the media to bring public attention to particular issues and problems.

attitude (or opinion)   A specific preference on a particular issue.

bandwagon effect   A situation wherein reports of voter or delegate opinion can influence the actual outcome of an election or a nominating convention.

conservative   Today this term refers to one who generally supports the social and economic status quo and is suspicious of efforts to introduce new political formulae and economic arrangements. Conservatives believe that a large and powerful government poses a threat to citizens' freedom.

equality of opportunity   A universally shared American ideal that all people should have the freedom to use whatever talents and wealth they have to reach their fullest potential.

framing   The power of the media to influence how events and issues are interpreted.

gender gap   A distinctive pattern of voting behavior reflecting the differences in views between women and men.

illusion of saliency   Impression conveyed by polls that something is important to the public when actually it is not.

liberal   A liberal today generally supports political and social reform; extensive governmental intervention in the economy; the expansion of federal social services; more vigorous efforts on behalf of the poor, minorities, and women; and greater concern for consumers and the environment.

marketplace of ideas   The public forum in which beliefs and ideas are exchanged.

measurement error   Failure to identify the true distribution of opinion within a population because of errors such as ambiguous or poorly worded questions.

momentum   A media prediction that a particular candidate will do even better in the future than in the past.

opinion leaders   Those whom other citizens turn to for political information and cues.

political ideology   A cohesive set of beliefs that form a general philosophy about the role of government.

political socialization   The induction of individuals into the political culture; learning the underlying beliefs and values upon which the political system is based.

priming   When media coverage affects public perception and evaluation of political leaders and candidates.

probability sampling   A method used by pollsters to select a representative sample in which every individual in the population has an equal probability of being selected as a respondent.

public opinion   Citizens' attitudes about political issues, personalities, institutions, and events.

public opinion polls   Scientific instruments for measuring public opinion.

push polling   A polling technique in which the questions are designed to shape the respondent's opinion.

random digit dialing   Polls in which respondents are selected at random from a list of ten-digit telephone numbers, with every effort made to avoid bias in the construction of the sample.

salient interests   Attitudes and views that are especially important to the individual holding them.

sample   A small group selected by researchers to represent the most important characteristics of an entire population.

selection bias   Polling error that arises when the sample is not representative of the population being studied, which creates errors in overrepresenting or underrepresenting some opinions.

values (or beliefs)   Basic principles that shape a person's opinions about political issues and events.

FOR FURTHER READING

Asher, Herbert. *Polling and the Public: What Every Citizen Should Know.* Washington, DC: Congressional Quarterly Press, 1988.

Erikson, Robert S., Norman Luttbeg, and Kent Tedin. *American Public Opinion: Its Origins, Content and Impact.* New York: Wiley, 1980.

Gallup, George. *The Pulse of Democracy.* New York: Simon and Schuster, 1940.

Ginsberg, Benjamin. *The Captive Public: How Mass Opinions Promotes State Power.* New York: Basic Books, 1986.

Graber, Doris. *Mass Media and American Politics.* Washington, DC: Congressional Quarterly Press, 1989.

Lippmann, Walter. *Public Opinion.* New York: Harcourt, Brace, 1922.

Lipset, Seymour M., and William Schneider. *The Confidence Gap: Business, Labor, and Government in the Public Mind,* rev. ed. Baltimore: Johns Hopkins University Press, 1987.

Mueller, John. *Policy and Opinion in the Gulf War.* Chicago: University of Chicago Press, 1994.

Neuman, W. Russell. *The Paradox of Mass Politics: Knowledge and Opinion in the American Electorate.* Cambridge: Harvard University Press, 1986.

Owen, Diana. *Media Messages in American Presidential Elections.* Westport, CT: Greenwood, 1991.

CHAPTER 10

Elections

HOW ELECTIONS WORK

*O*ver the past two centuries, elections have come to play a significant role in the political processes of most nations. The forms that elections take and the purposes they serve, however, vary greatly from nation to nation. The most important difference among national electoral systems is that some provide the opportunity for opposition while others do not. Democratic electoral systems, such as those that have evolved in the United States and western Europe, allow opposing forces to compete against and even to replace current officeholders. Authoritarian electoral systems, by contrast, do not allow the defeat of those in power. In the authoritarian context, elections are used primarily to mobilize popular enthusiasm for the government, to provide an outlet for popular discontent, and to persuade foreigners that the regime is legitimate— i.e., that it has the support of the people. In the former Soviet Union, for example, citizens were required to vote even though no opposition to Communist Party candidates was allowed.

In democracies, elections can also serve as institutions of legitimation and as safety valves for social discontent. But beyond these functions, democratic elections facilitate popular influence, promote leadership accountability, and offer groups in society a measure of protection from the abuse of governmental power. Citizens exercise influence through elections by determining who

CORE OF THE ANALYSIS

- Elections are important because they promote accountability in elected officials and facilitate popular influence in the governmental process.
- The government exerts a measure of control over the electoral process by regulating the composition of the electorate, translating voters' choices into electoral decisions, and insulating day-to-day government from the impact of those decisions.
- The strongest influences on voters' decisions are partisan loyalty, issue and policy concerns, and candidate characteristics.
- The increasing importance of money in elections has profound consequences for American democracy.
- Ordinary voters have little influence on the political process today.

should control the government (see Concept Map 10.1). The chance to decide who will govern serves as an opportunity for ordinary citizens to make choices about the policies, programs, and directions of government action. In the United States, for example, recent Democratic and Republican candidates have differed significantly on issues of taxing, social spending, and governmental regula-

CENTRAL QUESTIONS

- **How Elections Work**
  What roles do elections serve?

- **Regulating the Electoral Process**
  What rules determine who can vote in elections?
  What rules determine who wins elections?
  How does the government draw the boundaries of electoral districts?
  How is the makeup of the ballot determined?

- **How Voters Decide**
  What are the primary influences on voters' decisions?

- **The 2004 Elections**
  What is the significance of the 2004 elections?

- **Campaign Finance**
  How do candidates raise and spend campaign funds?
  How does the government regulate campaign spending?
  How does money affect the electoral outcome for certain social groups?

- **Do Elections Matter?**
  Why has participation declined over time?
  Why are elections important as institutions of democratic government?

tion. As American voters have chosen between the two parties' candidates, they have also made choices about these issues.

Elections promote leadership accountability because the threat of defeat at the polls exerts pressure on those in power to conduct themselves responsibly and to take account of popular interests and wishes when they make their decisions. As James Madison observed in the *Federalist Papers*, elected leaders are "compelled to anticipate the moment when their power is to cease, when their exercise of it is to be reviewed, and when they must descend to the level from which they were raised, there forever to remain unless a faithful discharge of their trust shall have established their title to a renewal of it."[1] It is because of this need to anticipate that elected officials constantly monitor public opinion polls as they decide what positions to take on policy issues.

Finally, the right to vote, or *suffrage,* can serve as an important source of protection for groups in American society. The passage of the 1965 Voting Rights Act, for example, enfranchised millions of African Americans in the South, paving the way for the election of thousands of new black public officials at the local, state, and national levels and ensuring that white politicians could no longer ignore the views and needs of African Americans. The Voting Rights Act was one of the chief spurs for the elimination of many overt forms of racial discrimination as well as for the diminution of racist rhetoric in American public life.

Democratic elections facilitate popular influence, promote leadership accountability, and protect groups in society from abuses of governmental power.

Although voting is an essential political and social process, actually getting voters to participate in elections has proven difficult. Voter *turnout* continued to hover around 50 percent in the 2000 presidential election, despite the expenditure of

[1]Clinton Rossiter, ed., The Federalist Papers (New York: New American Library, 1961), No. 57, p. 352.

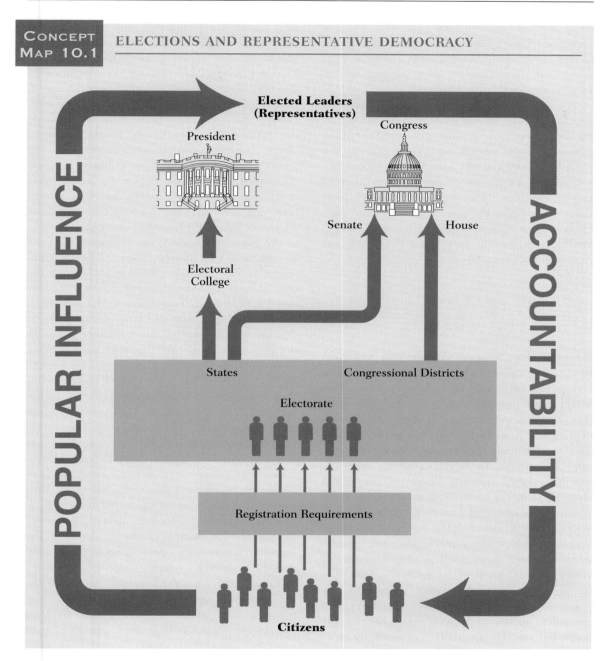

CONCEPT MAP 10.1

ELECTIONS AND REPRESENTATIVE DEMOCRACY

$3 billion by the candidates and claims by both major parties that they planned major efforts to bring voters to the polls. Voter turnout is not the only problem in our electoral process. First, the 2000 election demonstrated that the ballots used in many parts of the United States, especially those cast using the now infamous "Votomatic" machines, were prone to error. Second, the election outcome, as determined by the electoral college, produced a president who won half a million fewer popular votes than his opponent. Third, a variety of special interests pumped record amounts of money into political campaigns, renewing concerns that politicians are more accountable to wealthy donors than to mere voters.

We will examine these problems and possible solutions further in this chapter. Also, we will do the following: look at what distinguishes voting from other forms of political activity; examine the formal structure and setting of American elections; see how—and what—voters decide when they take part in elections; focus on recent national elections; and discuss the role of money in the electoral process, particularly in recent elections. Finally, we will assess the place of elections in the American political process.

REGULATING THE ELECTORAL PROCESS

While elections allow citizens a chance to participate in politics, they also allow the government a chance to exert a good deal of control over when, where, how, and which of its citizens will participate. Electoral processes are governed by a variety of rules and procedures that allow government an excellent opportunity to regulate and control popular involvement. Three general forms of regulation have played especially important roles in the electoral history of the Western democracies. First, governments often attempt to regulate who can vote in order to diminish the influence of groups they deem to be undesirable. Second, governments frequently seek to manipulate the translation of voters' choices into electoral outcomes. Third, virtually all governments attempt to insulate the policy-making process from electoral intervention through regulation of the relationship between the ballot box and the organization of government.

Electoral Composition

Perhaps the oldest and most obvious device used to regulate voting and its consequences is manipulation of the electorate's composition. In the first elections in western Europe, for example, the suffrage was generally limited to property owners and others who could be trusted to vote in a way acceptable to those in power. Property qualifications in France prior to 1848 limited the electorate to 240,000 of some 7 million men over the age of twenty-one.[2] No women were permitted to vote. During the same era, other nations manipulated the electorate's composition by assigning unequal electoral weights to different classes of voters. The 1831 Belgian constitution, for example, assigned individuals anywhere from one to three votes depending upon their property holdings, education, and position.[3] But even in the context of America's ostensibly universal and equal suffrage in the twentieth century, the composition of the electorate is still subject to manipulation. Until recent years, some states tried to manipulate the vote by the discriminatory use of *poll taxes* and literacy tests or by such practices as the placement of polls and the scheduling of voting hours to depress participation by one or another group. In the aftermath of the 2004 presidential elections, in which Ohio proved a pivotal state for George Bush's victory, it has been alleged that Republicans engaged in this sort of manipulation. In the county in which Kent State University (a Democratic stronghold) is located, very few voting machines were made available, producing long lines and up to nine-hour waiting times. Republican suburban locations, on the other hand, were more than adequately provisioned with voting machines. Similar stores about Democratic manipulations also circulated in the aftermath of the election. Today the most important example of the regulation of the American electorate's composition is the unique personal registration requirement.

Levels of voter participation in twentieth-century American elections are quite low by comparison to those of the other Western democracies (see Figure 10.1).[4] Indeed, voter participation in

[2]Stein Rokkan, *Citizens, Elections, Parties* (New York: David McKay, 1970), p. 149.
[3]John A. Hawgood, *Modern Constitutions since 1787* (New York: D. Van Nostrand, 1939), p. 148.
[4]See Walter Dean Burnham, "The Changing Shape of the American Political Universe," *American Political Science Review* 59 (1965), pp. 7–28.

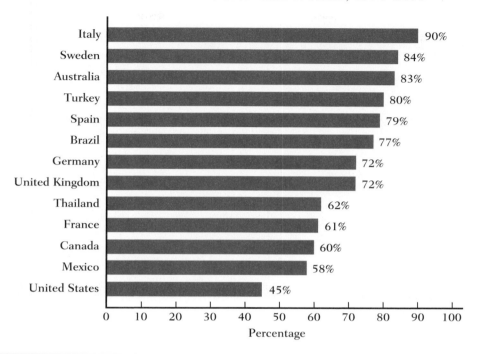

FIGURE 10.1

VOTER TURNOUT AROUND THE WORLD, 1991–2000*

Country	Percentage
Italy	90%
Sweden	84%
Australia	83%
Turkey	80%
Spain	79%
Brazil	77%
Germany	72%
United Kingdom	72%
Thailand	62%
France	61%
Canada	60%
Mexico	58%
United States	45%

*Note: Average during the 1990s.
SOURCE: Center for Voting and Democracy, www.fairvote.org/turnout.

U.S. presidential elections has barely averaged 50 percent in recent years. Turnout in the 2000 presidential election was 51 percent. In 2004, major efforts to get out the vote brought turnout to over 59 percent. This was the first significant increase in voting in recent years. During the nineteenth century, by contrast, voter turnout in the United States was extremely high. Records, in fact, indicate that in some counties as many as 105 percent of those eligible voted in presidential elections. Some proportion of this total obviously was artificial—a result of the widespread corruption that characterized American voting practices during that period. Nevertheless, it seems clear that the proportion of eligible voters actually going to the polls was considerably greater in nineteenth-century America than it is today.

Though the United States now has a system of universal suffrage, turnout in recent elections has been low.

As Figure 10.2 indicates, the critical years during which voter turnout declined across the United States were between 1890 and 1910 (see page 000). These years coincide with the adoption of laws across much of the nation requiring eligible citizens to appear personally at a registrar's office to register to vote some time prior to the actual date of an election. Personal registration was one of several "progressive" reforms initiated at the turn of the century. The ostensible purpose of registration was to discourage fraud and corruption. But

ELECTORAL COMPOSITION

Manipulation of the electorate's composition is a device used to regulate voting and its consequences.

Past methods by which voter participation was limited	Current limits on participation
Property ownership and literacy requirements Poll taxes Race and gender restrictions Placement of polls and scheduling of polling hours Voter registration rules	There are numerous restrictions on the voting rights of convicted felons that vary from state to state. Prison inmates serving a felony sentence are prohibited from voting in 48 states and the District of Columbia. There are no other official limits (other than the age requirement), except that voter must be an American citizen. However, any voter registration rules tend to depress participation on the part of the poor and uneducated.

FIGURE 10.2

VOTER TURNOUT IN PRESIDENTIAL AND MIDTERM ELECTIONS (1892–2004)

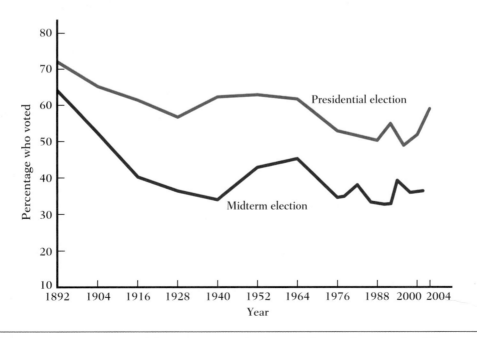

SOURCES: For 1892–1958, U.S. Bureau of the Census, Historical Statistics of the United States, Colonial Times to 1970, Pt. 2, p. 1071. For 1932–1992, U.S. Bureau of the Census, Statistical Abstract of the United States, 1993 (Washington, DC: Government Printing Office, 1993), p. 284. For 1996, 2000, and 2004, authors' update.

to many Progressive reformers, "corruption" was a code word referring to the politics practiced in large cities where political parties had organized immigrant and ethnic populations. Reformers not only objected to this corruption but also opposed the growing political power of these urban populations and their leaders.

Personal registration imposed a new burden upon potential voters and altered the format of American elections. Under the registration systems adopted after 1890, it became the duty of individual voters to secure their own eligibility. This duty could prove to be a significant burden for potential voters. During a personal appearance before the registrar, individuals seeking to vote were (and are) required to furnish proof of identity, residence, and citizenship. While the inconvenience of registration varied from state to state, usually voters could register only during business hours on weekdays. Many potential voters could not afford to lose a day's pay in order to register. Second, voters were usually required to register well before the next election, in some states up to several months earlier. Third, since most personal registration laws required a periodic purge of the election rolls to keep them up to date, voters often had to reregister to maintain their eligibility. Thus, although personal registration requirements helped to diminish the widespread electoral corruption that accompanied a completely open voting process, they also made it much more difficult for citizens to participate in the electoral process.

Registration requirements particularly depress participation on the part of those with little education and low incomes, for two reasons. First, the simple obstacle of registering on weekdays during business hours is difficult for working-class persons to overcome. Second, and more important, registration requires a greater degree of political involvement and interest than does the act of voting itself. To vote, a person need only be concerned with the particular election campaign at hand. Requiring individuals to register before the next election forces them to make a decision to participate on the basis of an abstract interest in the electoral process rather than a simple concern with a specific campaign. Such an abstract interest in electoral politics is largely a product of education. Those with relatively little education may become interested in political events because of a particular campaign, but by that time it may be too late to register. As a result, personal registration requirements not only diminish the size of the electorate but also tend to create an electorate that is, in the aggregate, better educated, higher in income and social status, and composed of fewer African Americans and other minorities than the citizenry as a whole. Presumably this is why the elimination of personal registration requirements has not always been viewed favorably by some conservatives.[5]

Registration requirements inhibit citizens, especially the poor and uneducated, from voting.

Over the years, voter registration restrictions have been modified somewhat to make registration easier. In 1993, for example, Congress approved and President Clinton signed the **Motor Voter bill** to ease voter registration by allowing individuals to register when they applied for driver's licenses as well as in public assistance and military recruitment offices.[6] In Europe, there is typically no registration burden on the individual voter; the government handles voter registration automatically. This is one reason that voter turnout rates in Europe are higher than those in the United States.

Another factor explaining low rates of voter turnout in the United States is the weakness of the American party system. During the nineteenth century, American political party machines employed hundreds of thousands of workers to organize and mobilize voters and bring them to the polls. The result was an extremely high rate of turnout, typ-

[5]See Kevin Phillips and Paul H. Blackman, *Electoral Reform and Voter Participation* (Washington, DC: American Enterprise Institute, 1975).
[6]Helen Dewar, "'Motor Voter' Agreement Is Reached," *Washington Post*, 28 April 1993, p. A6.

WHO WINS? TRANSLATING VOTERS' CHOICES INTO ELECTORAL OUTCOMES

Majority System
Winner must receive a simple majority (50 percent plus one).
Example: Formerly used in primary elections in the South.

Plurality System
Winner is the candidate who receives the most votes, regardless of the percentage.
Example: Currently used in almost all general elections throughout the country.

Proportional Representation
Winners are selected to a representative body in the proportion to the votes their party received.
Example: Used in New York City in the 1930s, resulting in several Communist seats on the City Council.

ically more than 90 percent of eligible voters.[7] But political party machines began to decline in strength in the early twentieth century and by now have largely disappeared. Without party workers to encourage them to go to the polls and even to bring them there if necessary, many eligible voters will not participate. In the absence of strong parties, participation rates drop the most among poorer and less-educated citizens. Because of the absence of strong political parties, the American electorate is smaller and skewed more toward the middle class than toward the population of all those potentially eligible to vote.

Translating Voters' Choices into Electoral Outcomes

With the exception of America's personal registration requirements, contemporary governments generally do not try to limit the composition of their electorates. Instead, they prefer to allow everyone to vote and then to manipulate the outcome of the election. This is possible because there

[7]Erik Austin and Jerome Chubb, *Political Facts of the United States since 1789* (New York: Columbia University Press, 1986), pp. 378–79.

is more than one way to decide the relationship between individual votes and electoral outcomes. Any number of possible rules can be used to determine how individual votes will be translated into collective electoral decisions. Two types of regulations are especially important: the rules that set the criteria for victory, and the rules that define electoral districts.

THE CRITERIA FOR VICTORY   In some nations, to win a seat in the parliament or other representative body, a candidate must receive a simple majority (50% + 1) of all the votes cast in the relevant district. This type of electoral system is called a *majority system* and was used in the primary elections of most Southern states until recent years. Generally, majority systems have a provision for a second or "runoff" election among the two top candidates if the initial contest drew so many contestants that none received an absolute majority of the votes cast.

In other nations, candidates for office need not receive an absolute majority of the votes cast to win an election. Instead, victory is awarded to the candidate who receives the most votes in a given election regardless of the actual percentage of votes this represents. Thus, a candidate who

REGULATING THE ELECTORAL PROCESS 249

receives 40 percent, 30 percent, or 20 percent of the votes cast may win the contest so long as no rival receives more votes. This type of electoral process is called a *plurality system,* and it is the system used in almost all general elections in the United States.

Many different electoral systems exist to determine the winners in democratic elections. The United States uses a plurality system in most general elections.

Most European states employ a third form of electoral system, called *proportional representation.* Under proportional rules, competing political parties are awarded legislative seats roughly in proportion to the percentage of the popular vote that they receive. For example, a party that won 30 percent of the votes would receive roughly 30 percent of the seats in the parliament or other representative body. In the United States, many states use proportional representation in presidential primary elections. In these primaries, candidates for the Democratic and Republican nominations are awarded convention delegates in rough proportion to the percentage of the popular vote they receive in the primary.

Despite the use of proportional representation and the occasional use of majority voting systems, most electoral contests in the United States are decided on the basis of plurality rules.

ELECTORAL DISTRICTS Congressional district boundaries in the United States are redrawn by governors and state legislatures every ten years, after the decennial census determines the number of House seats to which each state is entitled (see Process Box 10.1). Rather than seeking to manipulate the criteria for victory, American politicians have usually sought to influence electoral outcomes by manipulating the organization of electoral districts. This is called *gerrymandering* in honor of nineteenth-century Massachusetts Governor Elbridge Gerry, who was alleged to have

drawn district boundaries in the shape of a salamander to capture a disproportionate number of his party's votes within the district. The principle is simple. Different distributions of voters among districts produce different electoral outcomes; those in a position to control the arrangements of districts are also in a position to manipulate the results. For example, until recent years, gerrymandering to dilute the voting strength of racial minorities was a tactic of many state legislatures. One of the more common strategies involved redrawing congressional boundary lines in such a way as to divide and disperse a black population that otherwise would have constituted a majority within the original district.

This form of *racial gerrymandering,* sometimes called "cracking," was used in Mississippi during the 1960s and 1970s to prevent the election of an African American to Congress. Historically, the black population in Mississippi was clustered in the western half of the state, along the Mississippi Delta. From 1882 until 1966, the delta was one congressional district. Although blacks constituted a clear majority within the district (66 percent in 1960), the continuing election of white representatives was assured simply because blacks were denied the right to register and vote. With Congress's passage of the Voting Rights Act of 1965, however, the Mississippi state legislature moved swiftly to minimize the potential voting power of African Americans by redrawing congressional district lines to fragment the African American population in the delta into four of the state's five congressional districts. Mississippi's gerrymandering scheme was preserved in the state's redistricting plans in 1972 and 1981 and helped to prevent the election of any African American representative until 1986, when Mike Espy became the first African American since Reconstruction to represent Mississippi in Congress.

Politicians have sought to influence the outcomes of elections by manipulating the organization of electoral districts, a practice known as gerrymandering.

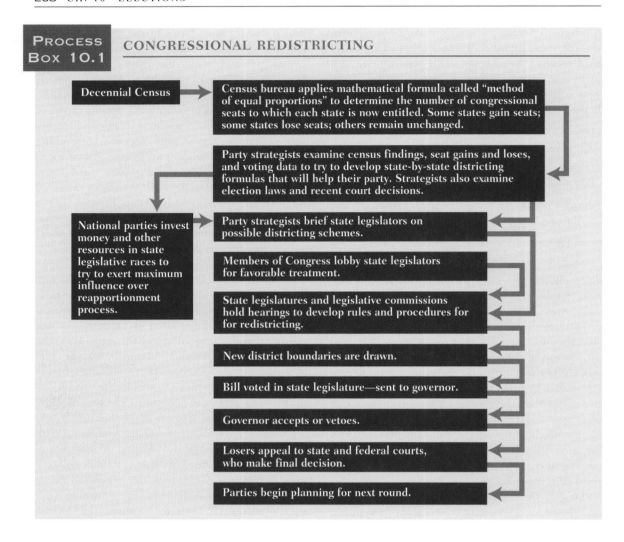

PROCESS BOX 10.1   CONGRESSIONAL REDISTRICTING

Decennial Census

Census bureau applies mathematical formula called "method of equal proportions" to determine the number of congressional seats to which each state is now entitled. Some states gain seats; some states lose seats; others remain unchanged.

Party strategists examine census findings, seat gains and loses, and voting data to try to develop state-by-state districting formulas that will help their party. Strategists also examine election laws and recent court decisions.

National parties invest money and other resources in state legislative races to try to exert maximum influence over reapportionment process.

Party strategists brief state legislators on possible districting schemes.

Members of Congress lobby state legislators for favorable treatment.

State legislatures and legislative commissions hold hearings to develop rules and procedures for for redistricting.

New district boundaries are drawn.

Bill voted in state legislature—sent to governor.

Governor accepts or vetoes.

Losers appeal to state and federal courts, who make final decision.

Parties begin planning for next round.

Recently, the federal government has encouraged what is sometimes called *"benign" gerrymandering,* designed to increase minority representation in Congress. The 1982 amendments to the Voting Rights Act of 1965 foster the creation of legislative districts with predominantly African American or Hispanic American populations by requiring states, when possible, to draw district lines that take account of concentrations of African American and Hispanic American voters. These amendments were initially supported by Democrats who assumed that minority-controlled districts would guarantee the election of Democratic members of Congress. Republicans championed them, too, hoping that if minority voters were concentrated in particular districts, Republican prospects in other districts would be enhanced.[8]

The 1993 Supreme Court in decision in *Shaw v. Reno,* however, opened the way for challenges by white voters to the drawing of these districts. In the five-to-four majority opinion, Justice San-

[8]Roberto Suro, "In Redistricting, New Rules and New Prizes," *New York Times,* 6 May 1990, sec. 4, p. 5.

dra Day O'Connor wrote that if district boundaries were so "bizarre" as to be inexplicable on any grounds other than an effort to ensure the election of minority group members to office, white voters would have reason to assert that they had been the victims of unconstitutional racial gerrymandering.[9] In the 1995 case of *Miller v. Johnson,* the Supreme Court put further limits on "benign" gerrymandering by asserting that the use of race as a "predominant factor" in creating election districts was presumptively unconstitutional. However, the Court held open the possibility that race could be *one* of the factors influencing legislative redistricting.[10]

Traditionally, district boundaries have been redrawn only once a decade, following the decennial national census. In recent years, however, the Republican Party has adopted an extremely aggressive redistricting strategy, in some instances not waiting for a new census before launching a redistricting effort that could serve its political interests. In Texas, for example, after the GOP took control of both houses of the state legislature in the 2002 elections, Republican lawmakers sought to enact a redistricting plan that promised to shift as many as five congressional seats to the Republican column. This Republican effort was masterminded by U.S. House Majority Leader at the time, Tom DeLay, who is himself a Texan. DeLay saw an opportunity to increase the Republican majority in the House and reduce Democratic prospects for regaining control of Congress. In an effort to block DeLay's plan, fifty-one Democratic legislators refused to attend state legislative sessions, leaving the Texas legislature without a quorum and unable to conduct its business. The legislature's Republican leadership ordered the state police to apprehend the missing Democrats and return them to the Capitol. The Democrats responded by escaping to Oklahoma, beyond the jurisdiction of the Texas police. Eventually, the Democrats capitulated and the GOP was able to enact its redistricting plan. A similar GOP redistricting effort in

Colorado failed when the state's supreme court ruled it unconstitutional. The court declared that the Colorado constitution permitted the legislature to redistrict the state only once every ten years.

Although governments do have the capacity to manipulate electoral outcomes, this capacity is not absolute. Electoral arrangements conceived to be illegitimate may prompt some segments of the electorate to seek other ways of participating in political life. Moreover, no electoral system that provides universal and equal suffrage can, by itself, long prevent an outcome favored by large popular majorities. Yet, faced with opposition short of an overwhelming majority, governments' ability to manipulate the translation of individual choices into collective decisions can be an important factor in preserving the established distribution of power.

Insulating Decision-Making Processes

Virtually all governments attempt at least partially to insulate decision-making processes from electoral intervention. The most obvious ways of doing this are confining popular elections to only some governmental positions, using various modes of indirect election, and setting lengthy terms of office. In the United States, the framers of the Constitution intended that only members of the House of Representatives would be subject to direct popular election. The president and senators were to be indirectly elected for longer terms to allow them, as the *Federalist Papers* put it, to avoid "an unqualified complaisance to every sudden breeze of passion, or to every transient impulse which the people may receive."[11]

THE ELECTORAL COLLEGE   In the early history of popular voting, nations often made use of indirect elections. In these elections, voters would choose the members of an intermediate body. These members would, in turn, select public officials. The assumption underlying such processes was that ordinary citizens were not really quali-

[9]*Shaw v. Reno,* 113 S. Ct. 2816 (1993); Linda Greenhouse, "Court Questions Districts Drawn to Aid Minorities," *New York Times,* 29 June 1993, p. 1.
[10]*Miller v. Johnson,* 63 USLW 4726 (1995).

[11]Rossiter, ed., *The Federalist Papers,* No. 71, p. 432.

fied to choose their leaders and could not be trusted to do so directly. The last vestige of this procedure in America is the *electoral college*, the group of electors who formally select the president of the United States.

When Americans go to the polls on election day, they are technically not voting directly for presidential candidates. Instead, voters within each state are choosing among slates of electors who have been elected or appointed to their positions some months earlier. The electors are pledged to support their own party's presidential candidate chosen in the presidential race. In each state (except for Maine and Nebraska), the slate that wins casts all the state's electoral votes for its party's candidate.[12] Each state is entitled to a number of electoral votes equal to the number of the state's senators and representatives combined, for a total of 538 electoral votes for the fifty states and the District of Columbia. Occasionally, an elector breaks his or her pledge and votes for the other party's candidate. For example, in 1976, when the Republicans carried the state of Washington, one Republican elector from that state refused to vote for Gerald Ford, the Republican presidential nominee. Many states have now enacted statutes formally binding electors to their pledges, but some constitutional authorities doubt whether such statutes are enforceable.

Americans do not vote directly for presidential candidates. Rather, they choose electors who are pledged to support a party's presidential candidate.

In each state, the electors whose slate has won proceed to the state's capital on the Monday following the second Wednesday in December and

[12]State legislatures determine the system by which electors are selected and almost all states use this "winner-take-all" system. Maine and Nebraska, however, provide that one electoral vote goes to the winner in each congressional district and two electoral votes go to the winner statewide.

formally cast their ballots. These are sent to Washington, tallied by Congress in January, and the name of the winner is formally announced. If no candidate receives a majority of all electoral votes, the names of the top three candidates are submitted to the House, where each state can cast one vote. Whether a state's vote is decided by a majority, plurality, or some other fraction of the state's delegates is determined under rules established by the House.

In 1800 and 1824, the electoral college failed to produce a majority for any candidate. In the election of 1800, Thomas Jefferson, the Jeffersonian Republican Party's presidential candidate, and Aaron Burr, that party's vice-presidential candidate, received an equal number of votes in the electoral college, throwing the election into the House of Representatives. (The Constitution at that time made no distinction between presidential and vice-presidential candidates, specifying only that the individual receiving a majority of electoral votes would be named president.) Some members of the Federalist Party in Congress suggested that they should seize the opportunity to damage the Republican cause by supporting Burr and denying Jefferson the presidency. Federalist leader Alexander Hamilton put a stop to this mischievous notion, however, and made certain that his party supported Jefferson. Hamilton's actions enraged Burr and helped lead to the infamous duel between the two men, in which Hamilton was killed. The Twelfth Amendment, ratified in 1804, was designed to prevent a repetition of such a situation by providing for separate electoral college votes for president and vice president.

In the 1824 election, four candidates—John Quincy Adams, Andrew Jackson, Henry Clay, and William H. Crawford—divided the electoral vote; no one of them received a majority. The House of Representatives eventually chose Adams over the others, even though Jackson had won more electoral and popular votes. This choice resulted from the famous "corrupt bargain" between Adams and Henry Clay. After 1824, the two major political parties had begun to dominate presidential politics to such an extent that by December of each election year, only two candidates remained for the electors to choose between, thus ensuring that one would receive a majority. This freed the parties and the candidates from having to plan their campaigns to culminate in Congress, and Congress very quickly ceased to dominate the presidential selection process.

On all but three occasions since 1824, the electoral vote has simply ratified the nationwide popular vote. Since electoral votes are won on a state-by-state basis, it is mathematically possible for a candidate who receives a nationwide popular plurality to fail to carry states whose electoral votes would add up to a majority. Thus, in 1876, Rutherford B. Hayes was the winner in the electoral college despite receiving fewer popular votes than his rival, Samuel Tilden. In 1888, Grover Cleveland received more popular votes than Benjamin Harrison, but received fewer electoral votes. And in 2000, Al Gore outpolled his opponent, George W. Bush, but narrowly lost the electoral college by a mere four electoral votes.

FREQUENCY OF ELECTIONS Less obvious are the insulating effects of electoral arrangements that permit direct, and even frequent, popular election of public officials, but tend to fragment the impact of elections upon the government's composition. In the United States, for example, the constitutional provision of staggered terms of service in the Senate was designed to diminish the impact of shifts in electoral sentiment upon the Senate as an institution. Since only one-third of its members were to be selected at any time, the composition of the institution would be partially protected from changes in electoral preferences.

SIZE OF ELECTORAL DISTRICTS The division of the nation into relatively small, geographically based constituencies for the purpose of selecting members of the House of Representatives was, in part, designed to have a similar effect. Representatives were to be chosen frequently. And although not prescribed by the Constitution, the fact that each was to be selected by a discrete constituency was thought by Madison and others to diminish

the government's vulnerability to mass popular movements.

In a sense, the House of Representatives was compartmentalized in the same way that a submarine is divided into watertight sections to confine the impact of any damage to the vessel. First, dividing the national electorate into small districts increased the importance of local issues. Second, because of the salience of local issues, a representative's electoral fortunes were more closely tied to factors peculiar to his or her own district than to national responses to issues. Third, given a geographical principle of representation, national groups were somewhat fragmented while the formation of local forces that might or might not share common underlying attitudes were encouraged. No matter how well represented individual constituencies might be, the influence of voters on national policy questions would be fragmented.

THE BALLOT Prior to the 1890s, voters cast ballots according to political parties. Each party printed its own ballots, listed only its own candidates for each office, and employed party workers to distribute its ballots at the polls. This ballot format virtually prevented split-ticket voting. Because only one party's candidates appeared on any ballot, it was very difficult for a voter to cast anything other than a *straight party vote*.

The advent of a new, neutral ballot (known as the *Australian ballot*) represented a significant change in electoral procedure. The new ballot was prepared and administered by the state rather than the parties. Each ballot was identical and included the names of all candidates for office. This ballot reform made it possible for voters to make their choices on the basis of the individual rather than the collective merits of a party's candidates. Because all candidates for the same office now appeared on the same ballot, voters were no longer forced to choose a straight party ticket. This gave rise to the phenomenon of *split-ticket voting* in American elections.

Prior to the reform of the ballot, it was not uncommon for an entire incumbent administration to be swept from office and replaced by an entirely new set of officials. In the absence of a real possibility of split-ticket voting, any desire on the part of the electorate for change could be expressed only as a vote against all candidates of the party in power. Because of this, there always existed the possibility, particularly at the state and local levels, that an insurgent slate committed to policy change could be swept into power. The party ballot thus increased the potential impact of elections upon the government's composition. Although this potential may not always have been realized, the party ballot at least increased the chance that electoral decisions could lead to policy changes. By contrast, because it permitted choice on the basis of candidates' individual appeals, ticket splitting led to increasingly divided partisan control of government.

The United States uses a party-neutral ballot, which allows voters to split their votes among candidates of different parties.

The actual ballots used by voters vary from county to county across the United States. Some counties employ paper ballots; others use mechanical voting machines. Some use punch-card systems; still others have introduced electronic and computerized systems. Not surprisingly, the controversy surrounding Florida's presidential vote in 2000 led to a closer look at the different balloting systems, and it became apparent that some of them produced unreliable results. Indeed, faulty ballots in Florida and other states may have changed the outcome of the 2000 election. Many counties moved to introduce computerized voting systems, which they hoped would lessen the chance of spoiled or incorrectly counted ballots. Some critics of computerized systems, however, warn that they may be vulnerable to unauthorized use or "hacking," which could call the result of an entire election into question.

Taken together, regulation of the electorate's composition, the translation of voters' choices into electoral decisions, and the impact of those deci-

sions upon the government's composition allow those in power a measure of control over mass participation in political life. These techniques do not necessarily have the effect of diminishing citizens' capacity to influence their rulers' conduct. Rather, these techniques are generally used to influence *electoral influence.*

Direct Democracy: The Referendum and Recall

In addition to voting for candidates, voters in some states also vote on referenda. The **referendum** process allows citizens to vote directly on proposed laws or other governmental actions. In recent years, voters in several states have voted to set limits on tax rates, to block state and local spending proposals, and to prohibit social services for illegal immigrants. Although it involves voting, a referendum is not an election. The election is an institution of representative government. Through an election, voters choose officials to act for them. The referendum, by contrast, is an institution of direct democracy; it allows voters to govern directly without intervention by government officials. The validity of referenda results, however, is subject to judicial action. If a court finds that a referendum outcome violates the state or national constitution, it can overturn the result. This happened in the case of a 1995 California referendum curtailing social services to illegal aliens.[13]

Twenty-four states permit various forms of the **initiative.** Whereas the referendum described above allows citizens to affirm or reject a policy produced by legislative action, the initiative provides citizens with a way forward in the face of legislative inaction. This is done by placing a policy proposal (legislative or state constitutional amendment) on the ballot to be approved or disapproved by the electorate. In order to reserve a place on the ballot, a petition must be accompanied by a minimum number of voter signatures—a requirement that varies from state to state—that are certified by the state's Secretary of State.

[13]*League of United Latin American Citizens v. Wilson*, CV-94-7569 (C.D. Calif.) (1995)

The initiative is also vulnerable to adverse selection. Ballot propositions involve policies the state legislature cannot (or does not want to) resolve. Like referendum issues, these are often highly emotional and, consequently, not always well-suited to resolution in the electoral arena. One of the "virtues" of the initiative is that it may be *action-forcing*. Legislative leaders can induce recalcitrant legislators to move ahead on controversial issues in the knowledge that a possibly worse outcome will result from inaction.[14]

Eighteen states also have legal provisions for *recall* elections. The recall is an electoral device introduced by turn-of-the-century Populists to allow voters to remove governors and other state officials from office prior to the expiration of their terms. Federal officials such as the president and members of Congress are not subject to recall. Generally, a recall effort begins with a petition campaign. For example, in California, the site of a tumultuous recall battle in 2003, if 12 percent of those who voted in the last general election sign petitions demanding a special recall election, the state board of elections must schedule one. Such petition campaigns are relatively common, but most fail to garner enough signatures to bring the matter to a statewide vote. In the California case, however, a conservative Republican member of Congress, Darrell Issa, led a successful effort to recall Democratic Governor Gray Davis. Voters were unhappy about the state's economy, dissatisfied with Davis's performance, and blamed Davis for the state's $38 billion budget deficit. Issa and his followers were able to secure enough signatures to force a vote, and in October 2003 Davis became the second governor in American history to be recalled by his state's electorate (the first was North Dakota Governor Lynn Frazier, who was recalled in 1921). Under California law, voters in a special recall election are also asked to choose a replacement for the official whom they dismiss. Californians in 2003 elected movie star Arnold Schwartzenegger to be their governor. While critics charged that the Davis recall had been a "political circus," the campaign had the effect of greatly increasing voter interest and involvement in the political process. More than four hundred thousand new voters registered in California in 2003, many drawn into the political arena by the opportunity to participate in the recall campaign.

HOW VOTERS DECIDE

Thus far, we have focused on the election as an institution. But, of course, the election is also a process in which millions of individuals make decisions and choices that are beyond the government's control. Whatever the capacity of those in power to organize and structure the electoral process, it is these millions of individual decisions that ultimately determine electoral outcomes. Sooner or later the choices of voters weigh more heavily than the schemes of electoral engineers.

The Bases of Electoral Choice

Three types of factors influence voters' decisions at the polls: partisan loyalty, issue and policy concerns, and candidate characteristics.

PARTISAN LOYALTY   Many studies have shown that most Americans identify more or less strongly with one or the other of the two major political parties. Partisan loyalty was considerably stronger during the 1940s and 1950s than it is today. But even now most voters feel a certain sense of identification or kinship with the Democratic or Republican party. This sense of identification is often handed down from parents to children and is reinforced by social and cultural ties. Partisan identification predisposes voters in favor of their party's candidates and against those of the opposing party. At the level of the presidential contest, issues and candidate personalities may become very important, although even here many Americans supported George Bush or John Kerry because of partisan loyalty. But partisanship is

---

[14]This point is developed in Mordon Bennedsen and Sven Fledmann, "Lobbying Legislatures," *Journal of Political Economy* 110 (2002).

more likely to assert itself in the less visible races, where issues and the candidates are not as well known. State legislative races, for example, are often decided by voters' party ties. Once formed, voters' partisan loyalties seldom change. Voters tend to keep their party affiliations unless some experience causes them to reexamine the bases of their loyalties and to conclude that they have not given their support to the appropriate party. During these relatively infrequent periods of electoral change, millions of voters can change their party ties. For example, at the beginning of the New Deal era between 1932 and 1936, millions of former Republicans transferred their allegiance to Franklin Roosevelt and the Democrats.

ISSUES   Issues and policy preferences are a second factor influencing voters' choices at the polls. Voters may cast their ballots for the candidate whose position on economic issues they believe to be closest to their own. Similarly, they may select the candidate who has what they believe to be the best record on foreign policy. Issues are more important in some races than others. If candidates actually "take issue" with one another—that is, articulate and publicize very different positions on important public questions—then voters are more likely to be able to identify and act upon whatever policy preferences they may have.

Three factors influence voters' decisions at the polls: partisan loyalty, issue and policy concerns, and candidate characteristics.

The ability of voters to make choices on the bases of issue or policy preferences is diminished if competing candidates do not differ substantially or do not focus their campaigns on policy matters. Very often, candidates deliberately take the safe course and emphasize topics that will not be offensive to any voters. Thus, candidates often trumpet their opposition to corruption, crime, and inflation. Presumably, few voters favor these things. While it may be perfectly reasonable for candidates to

take the safe course and remain as inoffensive as possible, this candidate strategy makes it extremely difficult for voters to make their issue or policy preferences the bases for their choices at the polls.

Similarly, a paucity of information during a campaign can influence the decisions of "knowledge-challenged" voters. Some analysts claimed that in 2000 Al Gore snatched defeat from the jaws of victory in just this way. In his efforts to distance himself from his scandal-plagued predecessor, he also failed to remind voters of his great successes—eight years of peace and prosperity as Clinton's vice president. Consequently, voters, such as moderate Republicans, who may have been prepared to overlook Gore's party label because of his achievements, were not given much opportunity to do so.[15]

Voters' issue choices usually involve a mix of their judgments about the past behavior of competing parties and candidates and their hopes and fears about candidates' future behavior. Political scientists call choices that focus on future behavior *prospective voting,* while those based on past performance are called *retrospective voting,* To some extent, whether prospective or retrospective evaluation is more important in a particular election depends on the strategies of competing candidates. Candidates always endeavor to define the issues of an election in terms that will serve their interests. Incumbents running during a period of prosperity will seek to take credit for the economy's happy state and define the election as revolving around their record of success. This strategy encourages voters to make retrospective judgments. By contrast, an insurgent running during a period of economic uncertainty will tell voters it is time for a change and ask them to make prospective judgments. Thus, Bill Clinton focused on change in 1992 and prosperity in 1996, and through well-crafted media campaigns was able to define voters' agenda of choices.

In 2004, President Bush emphasized his efforts to protect the nation from terrorists and his strong

[15]This argument is spelled out in Morris Fiorina, Samuel Abrams, and Jeremy Pope, "The 2000 U.S. Presidential Election: Can Retrospective Voting Be Saved?" *British Journal of Political Science* 33 (2003): 163–87.

HOW VOTERS DECIDE: THREE FACTORS INFLUENCE VOTERS' DECISIONS AT THE POLLS

Partisan loyalty—Most Americans identify with either the Democratic or Republican party and will vote for candidates accordingly. Party loyalty rarely changes and is most influential in less visible electoral contests, such as on the state or local level where issues and candidates are less well known.

Issues—Voters may choose a candidate whose views they agree with on a particular issue that is very important to them, even if they disagree with the candidate in other areas. It is easier for voters to make choices based on issues if candidates articulate very different positions and policy preferences.

Candidate characteristics—Voters are more likely to identify with and support a candidate who shares their background, views, and perspectives; therefore, race, ethnicity, religion, gender, geography, and social background are characteristics that influence how people vote. Personality characteristics such as honesty and integrity have become more important in recent years.

commitment to religious and moral values. Democratic candidate John Kerry, on the other hand, attacked Bush's decision to invade Iraq, questioned the president's leadership in the war on terror, and charged that the president's economic policies had failed to produce prosperity. When asked by exit pollsters which issue mattered most in deciding how they voted for president, 22 percent of all voters cited moral values as their chief concern. More than 80 percent of these voters supported President Bush. The economy was cited as the most important issue by 20 percent of those who voted and 80 percent of these Americans voted for Senator Kerry. Terrorism ranked third in terms of the percentage of voters who indicated it was the most important issue for them. President Bush received more than 80 percent of the votes of those Americans concerned mainly with terrorism.

A voter's choice that focuses on a candidate's future behavior is known as prospective voting, while a choice that focuses on past performance is known as retrospective voting.

CANDIDATE CHARACTERISTICS Candidates' personal attributes always influence voters' decisions. Some analysts claim that voters prefer tall candidates to short candidates, candidates with shorter names to candidates with longer names, and candidates with lighter hair to candidates with darker hair. Perhaps these rather frivolous criteria do play some role. But the more important candidate characteristics that affect voters' choices are race, ethnicity, religion, gender, geography, and social background. Voters presume that candidates with similar backgrounds to their own are likely to share their views and perspectives. Moreover, they may be proud to see someone of their ethnic, religious, or geographic background in a position of leadership. This is why for many years politicians sought to "balance the ticket," making certain that their party's ticket included members of as many important groups as possible.

Just as a candidate's personal characteristics may attract some voters, they may repel others. Many voters are prejudiced against candidates of certain ethnic, racial, or religious groups. And many voters—both men and women—continue to be reluctant to support the political candidacies of women, although this appears to be changing.

Voters also pay attention to candidates' personality characteristics, such as their "decisiveness," "honesty," and "vigor." In recent years, integrity has become a key election issue. In the 2004 presidential race, President Bush and the Republicans accused Senator Kerry of being inconsistent, a "flip-flopper" who continually changed his positions when it was expedient to do so. Bush, on the other hand, emphasized his own constancy. "I say what I mean, and I do what I say" was the president's frequent refrain. The president also pointed to his strong religious commitment as evidence of exemplary character. For their part, Democrats emphasized Senator Kerry's intelligence, empathy for ordinary Americans, and record of wartime heroism, which, they said, stood in sharp contrast to Bush's own somewhat blemished military record. In the end, the GOP's characterization of Kerry as a "flip-flopper" and Bush as an individual with deep moral and religious commitments seemed to resonate with voters. Among those who said that it was important for the president to take a clear stand on issues, 80 percent voted for President Bush; among those for whom strong religious faith was important, 90 percent voted for Bush; and among those who cited honesty as the candidate quality that mattered most, more than 70 percent gave their votes to Bush. On the other hand, among Americans who thought a president should be empathic and care about people like them, Kerry received 75 percent support, and among those who thought intelligence was the most important personal characteristic of a president, 91 percent voted for Kerry and only 9 percent for Bush.

All candidates seek, through polling and other mechanisms, to determine the best image to project to the electorate. At the same time, the communications media—television in particular—exercise a good deal of control over how voters perceive candidates. During the 1992 campaign, the candidates developed a number of techniques designed to take control of the image-making process away from the media. Among the chief instruments of this "spin control" was the candidate talk-show appearance used very effectively by both Ross Perot and Bill Clinton. And in 1996, the Republican and Democratic parties both sought to stage-manage their national conventions to control media coverage. As we saw in Chapter 9, however, no candidate was fully able to circumvent media scrutiny.

THE 2004 ELECTIONS

In 2004, President George W. Bush led the Republican Party to a solid electoral victory, winning 51 percent of the popular vote versus Senator John Kerry's 48 percent, a 286–252 majority in the Electoral College (see Figure 10.3), and helping to solidify what had been shaky Republican control of both houses of Congress. Republicans added four seats in the Senate, giving them a 55–44 majority (with one independent) and five seats in the House of Representatives, to gain a 234–200 majority in the lower chamber (with one independent). To embarrass the Democrats further, Senate Democratic leader Tom Daschle was defeated by his Republican opponent in a hard-fought South Dakota campaign.

Bush's political strategists, led by senior advisor Karl Rove, believed that three ingredients would combine to solidify the president's political strength and ensure his reelection in 2004. The first of these was an expansive economic policy. The Bush administration pursued a program of tax cuts and low interest rates that it hoped would produce a booming economy by election time. Generally, presidents who preside during times of economic decline are not returned to office. The second ingredient was money. Early in his term, President Bush embarked upon an unprecedented fund-raising effort, building a $100 million campaign chest before the Democrats were even close to nominating a candidate.

The final ingredient was the war on terror. The war on terror entailed new risks but, politically speaking, also produced new opportunities. A war of indefinite duration would mean that on a permanent and ongoing basis the American public would look to its government, especially to its pres-

FIGURE 10.3

DISTRIBUTION OF ELECTORAL VOTES IN THE 2004 PRESIDENTIAL ELECTION

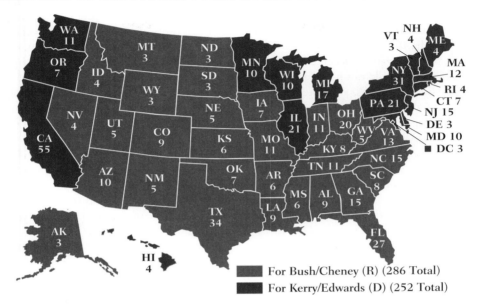

For Bush/Cheney (R) (286 Total)
For Kerry/Edwards (D) (252 Total)

ident, for protection and reassurance. So long as the public remained convinced that President Bush was making an effective effort to safeguard the nation, it would be unlikely to deprive him of office.

Democratic Opportunities

In the aftermath of 9/11, President Bush seemed to have developed a formula that virtually guaranteed political success. A new set of political circumstances, however, emerged to diminish the president's political standing and to threaten his grip on power. The first of these was the economy. Despite the administration's efforts, economic growth was slow and job growth anemic through Bush's first term in office. The sluggish economy allowed Democrats to declare that Bush was the only president in recent history to preside over a net loss of jobs during his administration. Ultimately more important than the economy was the Iraq war. Most Americans initially supported the war, and early battlefield success seemed to bolster Pres-

ident Bush's standing. It soon became apparent, however, that any Iraqi weapons of mass destruction program that might once have existed had been largely abandoned by Saddam Hussein's regime. The administration, moreover, failed to prove a connection between Hussein and terrorist threats to the U.S. Thus the president's stated war aims seemed to have been mistaken. To make matters worse, armed resistance to the American occupation of Iraq gradually stiffened, producing a steady drumbeat of American casualties. The Iraq war, though militarily successful in removing Hussein from power, suddenly made Bush politically vulnerable.

Adding to the president's problems and to the Democrats' opportunities was the effort by rich liberal activists—George Soros, for example—to form independent groups, known as 527 committees, specifically to defeat President Bush. Beyond raising millions of dollars to defeat Bush, these independent groups also registered millions of new Democratic voters. This influx of registrants posed a substantial threat to the GOP, not only at the presidential level but in congressional and local races as well.

Still, Democrats understood that to have any serious chance of defeating President Bush, they must somehow undermine the president's strongest political claim—that he responded forcefully to the 9/11 attacks and continued to protect the country from the threat of terrorism. As Bush had calculated, so long as voters accepted the president's contentions, he could not be defeated. But the 9/11 Commission's findings, announced in late July 2004, suggested that the Bush administration had not been sufficiently attentive to the terrorist threat prior to September 2001 and deeply embarrassed the president. Bush was now clearly vulnerable, and throughout the campaign Democrats charged that the president had failed to heed warnings of a terrorist attack and had subsequently focused on an imaginary threat from Iraq rather than the real danger from Al Qaeda. This was a theme emphasized by Senator Kerry during all three presidential debates.

Republican Strategies

Republicans were hardly idle while their Democratic foes enrolled voters and castigated the president. To counter the newly registered Democratic voters, the GOP began its own voter registration campaign. Operatives in every state—especially in so-called battleground states such as Ohio, Florida, Iowa, and Pennsylvania—embarked upon an ambitious effort to register millions of conservative voters. Religious conservatives were a particular target of GOP registration efforts. To ensure that the growing number of religious conservatives actually went to the polls on November 2, Republican campaign materials emphasized moral themes and the president's religious and moral commitments and the GOP launched a series of ballot initiatives on such "hot-button" issues as same-sex marriage and abortion. Republicans calculated that these initiatives in such battleground states as Ohio and Florida would bring religious conservatives to the polls. Once at their polling places, they would also vote for President Bush. This strategy seems to have been especially successful in Ohio, where religious conservatives strongly supported an initiative

to ban same-sex marriage. Ohio turned out to be essential to Bush's reelection.

Ultimately, competitive Democratic and Republican registration efforts produced the highest level of voter turnout in nearly four decades. Slightly more than 59 percent of eligible Americans went to the polls in 2004, an increase of almost 5 percentage points over 2000. Ultimately, more new voters supported Kerry than Bush but the margin was not overwhelming. The Democratic effort to overwhelm the GOP with new registrants had been blunted.

In addition to enrolling their own new voters and emphasizing the religious themes deemed important to these voters, Republicans worked to discredit Kerry as a plausible president. Bush and other Republican campaigners accused Kerry of continually "flip-flopping" on important issues. Republicans also sought to undermine one of Kerry's strongest moral claims, his record during the Vietnam War. Just as Democrats had raised questions about Bush's leadership during 9/11, so Republicans raised questions about Kerry's military record. The GOP organized a group of conservative veterans called "Swift Boat Veterans for Truth" who succeeded in airing doubts about the truth of Kerry's wartime heroism. The GOP's efforts seemed to bear fruit. Throughout the early fall 2004, President Bush maintained a solid lead in the polls despite months of Democratic attacks.

The End Game

In October, however, Bush's lead appeared to evaporate in the wake of the presidential debates. In most national elections, the first debate is crucial. Much of the nation watches or listens to the first debate while the audience diminishes in size during the ensuing debates. Most observers agreed that President Bush's performance in the first debate was a political disaster. The president appeared ill-at-ease and some commentators described him as irritable, while Senator Kerry was articulate and quite presidential in demeanor. The national news media, generally unfriendly to Bush, declared the debate a major Kerry victory. Republicans were stunned and Democrats elated. Bush rallied in the subsequent two debates, but most of the media declared Kerry the victor in each one and awarded his running mate, John Edwards, the victory in the vice-presidential clash. In the aftermath of the debates, the polls indicated that the two tickets were now running neck and neck.

As the election approached, each side realized that success would depend upon its ability to produce high levels of turnout among its most loyal partisans in the ten or so states that could swing to either party. Democrats relied upon their traditional allies such as labor unions and African American churches as well as seeking to ensure high levels of turnout among their new registrants. For example, to encourage newly registered college students to go to the polls, the Kerry campaign charged that President Bush was planning to reinstitute military conscription—a factually baseless but politically useful claim. For their part, Republicans relied heavily upon such conservative groups as the Home School Legal Defense Fund and a host of religious organizations to bring out their voters. In this so-called ground game, each party made use of enormous computer data banks to identify likely voters and volunteers.

In the end, the GOP's superior on-the-ground organization prevailed. Republicans registered and brought to the polls tens of millions of religious conservatives who gave President Bush the margin of victory in such key states as Florida, Ohio, and Missouri. The importance of religious conservatives is manifest in the exit poll data, which indicates that on a national basis 22 percent of all voters cited moral values as the issue that mattered most to them—more than cited the economy, terrorism, the Iraq war, or any other issue. Of these morally committed Americans, an astonishing 82 percent gave their votes to President Bush.

For the most part, each candidate ran well among voters who normally support his party. Kerry won the support of union members, Jews, African Americans, and women. Bush was successful among white males, upper-income wage earners, and Southerners. Neither candidate reached much beyond his political base, though Bush was somewhat more successful in 2004 than in 2000 among women, Hispanics, and Catholics. After hundreds of millions of dollars in expenditures and years of planning and maneuvering, the key to victory was old-fashioned voter turnout. After the issues had been debated, charges made and answered, and claims asserted and debunked, Bush, and the GOP prevailed because a record number of Republicans went to the polls on November 2—a democratic conclusion to an untidy but thoroughly democratic process.

CAMPAIGN FINANCE

Modern national political campaigns are fueled by enormous amounts of money. In a national race, millions of dollars are spent on media time, as well as on public opinion polls and media consultants. In 2000, political candidates and independent groups spent a total of more than $3 billion on election campaigns. The average winning candidate in a campaign for a seat in the House of Representatives spent more than $500,000; the average winner in a senatorial campaign spent $4.5 million.[16] The 2004 Democratic and Republican presidential candidates received a total of $150 million in public funds to run their campaigns.[17] Each presidential candidate was also helped by tens of millions of dollars in so-called independent expenditures by individuals and groups. As long as such political expenditures are not formally coordinated with a candidate's campaign, they are considered to be constitutionally protected free speech and are not subject to legal limitation or even reporting requirements.

[16]Jonathan Salant, "Million-Dollar Campaigns Proliferate in 105th," Congressional *Quarterly Weekly Report,* 21 December 1996, pp. 3448–51.
[17]U.S. Federal Election Commission, "Financing the 1996 Presidential Campaign," Internet release, www.fec.gov/pres96/presmstr.html, 28 April 1998.

Sources of Campaign Funds

Federal Election Commission (FEC) data suggest that approximately one-fourth of the private funds spent on political campaigns in the United States is raised through small, direct-mail contributions; about one-fourth is provided by large, individual gifts; and another fourth comes from contributions from political action committees. The remaining fourth is drawn from the political parties and from candidates' personal or family resources.[18] Another source of campaign funds, which are not required to be reported to the Federal Election Commission, are independent expenditures by interest groups and parties.

Campaign funds in the United States are provided by small, direct-mail contributions, large independent expenditures, candidates' resources, PACs, political parties' soft money, and public funding. In 1996, 1998, and 2000, some candidates also benefited from issue advocacy.

INDIVIDUAL DONORS   Direct mail serves both as a vehicle for communicating with voters and as a mechanism for raising funds. Direct-mail fundraising efforts begin with the purchase or rental of computerized mailing lists of voters deemed likely to support the candidate because of their partisan ties, interests, or ideology. Candidates send out pamphlets, letters, and brochures describing their views and appealing for funds. Tens of millions of dollars are raised by national, state, and local candidates through direct mail each year, usually in $25 and $50 contributions; in 2000, Bush and Gore collected about three-quarters of their donor contributions from individuals giving the then-maximum amount of $1,000.[19] Individual

[18]FEC reports.
[19]Ibid.

supporters of the parties and candidates are important not only as donors but also as fundraisers.

POLITICAL ACTION AND 527 COMMITTEES
Political action committees (PACs) are organizations established by corporations, labor unions, or interest groups to channel the contributions of their members into political campaigns. Under the terms of the 1971 Federal Elections Campaign Act, which governs campaign finance in the United States, PACs are permitted to make larger contributions to any given candidate than individuals are allowed to make. Individuals may donate a maximum of $2,100 to any single candidate, but a PAC may donate as much as $5,000 to each candidate. Moreover, allied or related PACs often coordinate their campaign contributions, greatly increasing the amount of money a candidate actually receives from the same interest group. More than 4,500 PACs are registered with the Federal Election Commission, which oversees campaign finance practices in the United States. Nearly two-thirds of all PACs represent corporations, trade associations, and other business and professional groups. Alliances of bankers, lawyers, doctors, and merchants all sponsor PACs. One example of a PAC is the National Beer Wholesalers' Association PAC, which for many years was known as "SixPAC." Labor unions also sponsor PACs, as do ideological, public interest, and nonprofit groups. The National Rifle Association sponsors a PAC, as does the Sierra Club. Many congressional and party leaders have established PACs, known as leadership PACs, to provide funding for their political allies.

In recent years, PACs have raised hundreds of millions of dollars for political campaigns, but while these organizations have been important fund-raising tools, the hard money from PACs has been overshadowed by so-called *soft money* contributed to the political parties and then recycled into campaigns. Soft money, or unregulated contributions to the national parties nominally to assist in party-building or voter registration efforts rather than for particular campaigns, was not subject to the limitations of the FEC act; as a result, well-heeled individuals and interests often prefer to make large, anonymous soft-money contributions rather than—or in addition to—relatively small and publicly recorded contributions to PACs. By 2000, as many as three soft-money dollars were spent for every dollar of "hard money" given directly to candidates and PACs and thus subject to FEC regulation. The 2002 campaign finance reform act (BCRA) outlawed many, albeit not all, forms of soft money and potentially will increase the importance of political action committees in the funding process. Parties and candidates, however, have been able to evade some of the act's restrictions. Thus, the importance of PACs may continue to be overshadowed by soft-money contributions.

The **527** *committees* mentioned earlier have been another important source of soft money. These nonprofit fundraising groups, which are named after the section of the tax code that defines them, have raised and spent millions of dollars attempting to influence recent elections. Expenditures by these committees are "soft" because they are not subject to FEC regulations, and technically, they are not given to or coordinated with any specific candidate's campaign. Indeed 527 advertisements cannot directly endorse a candidate. But by registering voters with serious Democratic propensities in 2004, as did the 527 committee financed by billionaire George Soros, or attacking John Kerry's Vietnam service record, as did the Swift Boat Veterans for Truth 527 committee, these soft money expenditures had clear and significant candidate- and party-specific effects.

THE CANDIDATES On the basis of the Supreme Court's 1976 decision in *Buckley v. Valeo,* the right of individuals to spend their own money to campaign for office is a constitutionally protected matter of free speech and is not subject to limitation. Thus, extremely wealthy candidates often contribute millions of dollars to their own campaigns. Jon Corzine, for example, spent approximately $60 million of his own funds in a successful New Jersey Senate bid in 2000.

INDEPENDENT SPENDING "Independent" spending is also free from regulation; private groups and wealthy individuals, engaging in what is called *issue advocacy,* may spend as much as they wish to help elect one candidate or defeat another, as long as these expenditures are not coordinated with any political campaign. Many business and ideological groups engage in such activities. Some estimates suggest that groups and individuals spent as much as $509 million on issue advocacy—generally through television advertising—during the 2000 elections.[20] The National Rifle Association, for example, spent $3 million dollars reminding voters of the importance of the right to bear arms, while the National Abortion and Reproductive Rights League spent nearly $5 million to express its support for Al Gore.

Some groups are careful not to mention particular candidates in their issues ads to avoid any suggestion that they might merely be fronts for a candidate's campaign committee. Most issue ads, however, are attacks on the opposing candidate's record or character. Organized labor spent more than $35 million in 1996 to attack a number of Republican candidates for the House of Representatives. Business groups launched their own multi-million-dollar issues campaign to defend the GOP House members targeted by labor.[21] In 2000, liberal groups ran ads bashing Bush's record on capital punishment, tax reform, and Social Security. Conservative groups attacked Gore's views on gun ownership, abortion, and environmental regulation. In 2004, pro-Republican groups sponsored a series of ads portraying President George W. Bush as protecting the nation by fighting terrorism while his political opponents tried to undermine him (and the nation) for selfish political reasons. Democratic groups, for their part, attacked Bush's economic policies and handling of the Iraq war.

PARTIES AND SOFT MONEY Before 2002, most campaign dollars took the form of soft money. The amount the national parties could accept from any individual or PAC for the support of candidates for national office was limited by law. To circum-

[20]Kathleen Hall Jamieson, "Issue Advertising in the 1999–2000 Election Cycle," Annenberg Public Policy Center, University of Pennsylvania, 1 February 2001.
[21]David Broder and Ruth Marcus, "Wielding Third Force in Politics," *Washington Post,* 20 September 1997, p. 1.

vent the limits, the national parties forwarded much of the money they raised to state and local Party organizations—again, nominally, for party-building purposes. At the state and local levels, political party units used most of these funds in thinly disguised campaign activities such as advertising campaigns that stopped just short of urging citizens to vote for or against a particular candidate. For example, in 1996, commercials sponsored by state Democratic Party organizations looked just like commercials for Bill Clinton. They praised the president's record while criticizing the GOP. However, because these ads did not specifically ask viewers to vote for Clinton or against his opponent, they were considered issue ads rather than campaign appeals and thus did not fall under the authority of the FEC. In 2000, the Democratic and Republican parties together raised nearly $1 billion in soft money mainly from corporate and professional interests.

Federal campaign finance legislation crafted by Senators John McCain and Russell Feingold and enacted in 2002 sought to ban soft money by prohibiting the national parties from soliciting and receiving contributions from corporations, unions, or individuals and prevented them from directing such funds to their affiliated state parties. The act, known as the Bipartisan Campaign Reform Act (BCRA) of 2002, also prohibited issue ads within sixty days of a national election. BCRA may have the effect of weakening political parties, but both parties have moved aggressively to circumvent the new law. Democratic and Republican activists have formed organizations that are nominally unaffiliated with the two parties—and are thus not subject to most BCRA provisions—but that plan to participate vigorously in electoral contests. These groups, sometimes called 527 committees, were heavily involved on both sides of the 2004 presidential race. For example, financier George Soros donated more than $12 million to groups working for the defeat of George W. Bush. For their part, Republican sympathizers established groups such as Americans for a Better Country to solicit funds from Republican donors and work for Bush's reelection. So long

as these efforts are not coordinated with those of a campaign, they represent constitutionally protected free speech and are not subject to BCRA limitations. Late in 2002, federal appeals court invalidated portions of BCRA. In December 2003, however, the U.S. Supreme Court overturned the lower court decision and upheld BCRA's key provisions.

PUBLIC FUNDING   The Federal Elections Campaign Act also provides for public funding of presidential campaigns. As they seek a major party presidential nomination, candidates become eligible for public funds by raising at least $5,000 in individual contributions of $250 or less in each of twenty states. Candidates who reach this threshold may apply for federal funds to match, on a dollar-for-dollar basis, all individual contributions of $250 or less they receive. The funds are drawn from the Presidential Election Campaign Fund. Taxpayers can contribute $3 to this fund, at no additional cost to themselves, by checking a box on the first page of their federal income tax returns. Major party presidential candidates receive a lump sum (currently nearly $75 million) during the summer prior to the general election. They must meet all their general expenses from this money. Third-party candidates are eligible for public funding only if they received at least 5 percent of the vote in the previous presidential race. This stipulation effectively blocks preelection funding for third-party or independent candidates, although a third party that wins more than 5 percent of the vote can receive public funding after the election. In 1980, John Anderson convinced banks to loan him money for an independent candidacy on the strength of poll data showing that he would receive more than 5 percent of the vote and thus would obtain public funds with which to repay the loans. Under current law, no candidate is required to accept public funding for either the nominating races or general presidential election. Candidates who do not accept public funding are not affected by expenditure limits. Thus, in 1992 Ross Perot financed his own presidential bid and was not bound by the $55 million limit to which

FEDERAL CAMPAIGN FINANCE REGULATION

Campaign Contributions

No individual may contribute more than $2,100 to any one candidate in any single election. Individuals may contribute as much as $25,000 to a national party committee and up to $5,000 to a political action committee. Full disclosure is required by candidates of all contributions over $100. Candidates may not accept cash contributions over $100. Contribution limits are raised for individuals facing "millionaire" opponents.

Political Action Committees

Any corporation, labor union, trade association, or other organization may establish a political action committee (PAC). PACs must contribute to the campaigns of at least five different candidates and may contribute as much as $5,000 per candidate in any given election.

Soft Money

Contributions to state party committees are limited to $10,000 and must be used for get-out-the-vote and registration efforts. National party committees are blocked from most campaign-related expenditures.

Broadcast Advertising

Unions, corporations, and nonprofit agencies may not broadcast "issue ads" mentioning federal candidates within sixty days of a general election and thirty days of a primary election.

Presidential Elections

Candidates in presidential primaries may receive federal matching funds if they raise at least $5,000 in each of twenty states. The money raised must come in contributions of $250 or less. The amount raised by candidates in this way is matched by the federal government, dollar for dollar, up to a limit of $5 million. In the general election, major-party candidates' campaigns are fully funded by the federal government. Candidates may spend no money beyond their federal funding. Independent groups may spend money on behalf of a candidate as long as their efforts are not directly tied to the official campaign. Minor-party candidates may get partial federal funding.

Federal Election Commission (FEC)

The six-member FEC supervises federal elections, collects and publicizes campaign finance records, and investigates violations of federal campaign finance law.

the Democrat and Republican candidates were held. Perot accepted public funding in 1996. In 2000, George W. Bush refused public funding and raised enough money to finance his own primary campaign. Eventually, Bush raised and spent nearly $200 million—twice as much as he could have if he had accepted matching funds. Al Gore accepted funding and was nominally bound by the associated spending limitations. However, soft money and independent spending, not limited by election law, allowed Gore to close the gap with his Republican opponent.

In 2004, neither President Bush nor Senator John Kerry accepted public funding prior to receiving the Republican and Democratic presidential nominations. Thus, Kerry raised private funds to compete in the lengthy Democratic primary process. Both candidates accepted public funding for their general election campaigns, each receiving approximately $75 million. In addition, private groups spent hundreds of millions more on behalf of the two candidates.

Implications for Democracy

The important role played by private funds in American politics affects the balance of power among contending social groups. Politicians need large amounts of money to campaign successfully for major offices. This fact inevitably ties their interests to the interests of the groups and forces that can provide this money. In a nation as large and diverse as the United States, to be sure, campaign contributors represent many different groups and often represent clashing interests. Business groups, labor groups, environmental groups, and pro-choice and right-to-life forces all contribute millions of dollars to political campaigns. Through such PACs as EMILY's List, women's groups contribute millions of dollars to women running for political office. One set of trade associations may contribute millions to win politicians' support for telecommunications reform, while another set may contribute just as much to block the same reform efforts. Insurance companies may contribute millions of dollars to Democrats to win their support for changes in the health care system, while physicians may contribute equal amounts to prevent the same changes from becoming law.

Interests that donate large amounts of money to campaigns expect, and often receive, favorable treatment from the beneficiaries of their largesse. For example, in 2000 a number of major interests

groups with specific policy goals made substantial donations to the Bush presidential campaign. These interests included airlines, energy producers, banks, tobacco companies, and a number of others.

After Bush's election, these interests pressed the new president to promote their legislative and regulatory agendas. For example, MBNA America was a major donor to the 2000 Bush campaign. The bank and its executives gave Bush $1.3 million. The bank's president helped raise millions more for Bush and personally gave an additional $100,000 to the president's inaugural committee after the election. All told, MBNA and other banking companies donated $26 million to the GOP in 2000. Within weeks of his election, President Bush signed legislation providing MBNA and the others with something they had sought for years: bankruptcy laws making it more difficult for consumers to escape credit-card debts. Such laws could potentially enhance the earnings of large credit-card issuers such as MBNA by tens of millions of dollars every year.

In a similar vein, a coalition of manufacturers led by the U.S. Chamber of Commerce and the National Association of Manufacturers also provided considerable support for Bush's 2000 campaign. This coalition sought, among other things, the repeal of federal rules, promulgated in 2000 by the federal Occupational Safety and Health Administration (OSHA), that were designed to protect workers from repetitive-motion injuries. Again, within weeks of his election, the president approved a resolution rejecting the rules. In March 2001, the House and Senate both voted to kill the ergonomic regulations.

Despite this diversity of contributors, however, not all interests play a role in financing political campaigns. Only those interests that have a good deal of money to spend can make their interests known in this way. These interests are not monolithic, but they do not completely reflect the diversity of American society. The poor, the destitute, and the downtrodden also live in America and have an interest in the outcome of political campaigns. Who is to speak for them?

DO ELECTIONS MATTER?

What is the place of elections in the American political process? Unfortunately, recent political trends raise real questions about the continuing ability of ordinary Americans to influence their government through electoral politics.

Why Is There a Decline in Voter Turnout?

Despite the sound and fury of contemporary American politics, one very important fact stands out: Participation in the American political process is abysmally low. Politicians in recent years have been locked in intense struggles. As we saw in Chapter 5, partisan division in Congress has reached its highest level of intensity since the nineteenth century. Nevertheless, millions of citizens have remained uninvolved. For every registered voter who voted in the 2000 races, for example, one stayed home.

COMPETITION AND VOTER TURNOUT Throughout much of American history, the major parties have been the principal agents responsible for giving citizens the motivation and incentive to vote. One of the most interesting pieces of testimony to the lengths to which parties have been willing to go to induce citizens to vote is a list of Chicago precinct captains' activities in the 1920s and 1930s. Among other matters, these party workers helped constituents obtain food, coal, and money for rent; gave advice in dealing with juvenile and domestic problems; helped constituents obtain government and private jobs; adjusted taxes; aided with permits, zoning, and building-code problems; served as liaisons with social, relief, and medical agencies; provided legal assistance and help in dealing with government agencies; handed out Christmas baskets; and attended weddings and funerals.[22] Obviously, all these services were provided in the hope of winning voters' support at election time.

Party competition has long been known to be a key factor in stimulating voting. As political scientists Stanley Kelley, Richard Ayres, and William Bowen note, competition gives citizens an incentive to vote and politicians an incentive to get them to vote.[23] The origins of the American national electorate can be traced to the competitive organizing activities of the Jeffersonian Republicans and the Federalists. According to historian David Fischer:

> During the 1790s the Jeffersonians revolutionized electioneering. . . . Their opponents complained bitterly of endless "dinings," "drinkings," and celebrations; of handbills "industriously posted along every road"; of convoys of vehicles which brought voters to the polls by the carload; of candidates "in perpetual motion."[24]

The Federalists, although initially reluctant, soon learned the techniques of mobilizing voters: "mass meetings, barbecues, stump-speaking, festivals of many kinds, processions and parades, runners and riders, door-to-door canvassing, the distribution of tickets and ballots, electioneering tours by candidates, free transportation to the polls, outright bribery and corruption of other kinds."[25] The result of this competition for votes was described by historian Henry Jones Ford in his clas-

---

[22]Harold F. Gosnell, *Machine Politics, Chicago Model*, rev. ed. (Chicago: University of Chicago Press, 1968), Chapter 4.

[23]Stanley Kelley, Jr., Richard E. Ayres, and William G. Bowen, "Registration and Voting: Putting First Things First," *American Political Science Review* 61 (June 1967): 359–70.

[24]David H. Fischer, *The Revolution of American Conservatism: The Federalist Party in the Era of Jeffersonian Democracy* (New York: Harper & Row, 1965), p. 93. For a full account of parties as agents both of candidate selection and of mass mobilization, see John H. Aldrich, *Why Parties? The Origin and Transformation of Political Parties in America* (Chicago: University of Chicago Press, 1995).

[25]Ibid., p. 109. With various forms of the secret ballot, it was often difficult to know exactly how a citizen voted—and thus chancy to bribe him if you couldn't know you were getting what you paid for. Because of this, it was often the case that buying votes was transformed into buying *non*participation— paying, that is, for those who opposed your candidates to "go fishing" on Election Day. For evidence of this in rural New York, see Gary Cox and Morgan Kousser, "Turnout and Rural Corruption in New York as a Test Case," *American Journal of Political Science* 25 (November 1981): 646–63.

sic *Rise and Growth of American Politics.*[26] Ford examined the popular clamor against John Adams and Federalist policies in the 1790s that made government a "weak, shakey affair" and appeared to contemporary observers to mark the beginnings of a popular insurrection against the government.[27] Attempts by the Federalists initially to suppress mass discontent, Ford observed, might have "caused an explosion of force which would have blown up the government."[28] What intervened to prevent rebellion was Jefferson's "great unconscious achievement," the creation of an opposition party that served to "open constitutional channels of political agitation."[29] The creation of the Jeffersonian party diverted opposition to the administration into electoral channels. Party competition gave citizens a sense that their votes were valuable and that it was thus not necessary to take to the streets to have an impact upon political affairs. Whether or not Ford was correct in crediting party competition with an ability to curb civil unrest, it is clear that competition between the parties promoted voting.

The parties' competitive efforts to attract citizens to the polls are not their only influence on voting. Individual voters tend to form psychological ties with parties. Although the strength of partisan ties in the United States has declined in recent years, a majority of Americans continue to identify with either the Republican or Democratic party. Party loyalty gives citizens a stake in election outcomes that encourages them to take part with considerably greater regularity than those lacking partisan ties.[30] Even where both legal facilitation and competitiveness are weak, party loyalists vote with great regularity.

In recent decades, as we will see in Chapter 11, the importance of party as a political force in the United States has diminished considerably. The decline of party influence is undoubtedly one of the factors responsible for the relatively low rates of voter turnout that characterize American national elections. To an extent, the federal and state governments have directly assumed some of the burden of voter mobilization once assigned to the parties. For example, the 1993 Motor Voter bill was a step, though a hesitant one, in the direction of expanded voter participation. This act requires all states to allow voters to register by mail when they renew their driver's licenses (twenty-eight states already had similar mail-in procedures) and provides for the placement of voter registration forms in motor vehicle, public assistance, and military recruitment offices. Motor Voter did result in some increases in voter registration. Thus far, however, few of these newly registered individuals have actually gone to the polls to cast their ballots. In 1996, the percentage of newly registered voters who appeared at the polls actually dropped.[31]

A number of other simple institutional reforms could increase voter turnout. Same-day registration, currently used in several states including Minnesota, could boost turnout. Making Election Day a federal holiday would make it easier for Americans to go to the polls. Weekend voting in a number of European nations has increased turnout by as much as 10 percentage points. One reform that has been suggested, but should not be adopted at this point, is Internet voting. Computer use and Internet access remains highly correlated with income and education. This method of voting would reinforce the existing class bias in the voting process as well as introduce computer security problems. Imagine hackers changing the results of a presidential election! Even with America's personal registration rules, higher levels of political participation could be achieved if competing political forces made a serious effort to mobilize voters. Unfortunately, however, contending political forces in the United States have found ways of

[26]Henry Jones Ford, *The Rise and Growth of American Politics: A Sketch of Constitutional Development* (New York: Da Capo Press, 1967 reprint of 1898 edition), Chapter 9.

[27]Ibid., p. 125.

[28]Ibid.

[29]Ibid., p. 126.

[30]See Angus Campbell et al., *The American Voter* (New York: Wiley, 1960).

[31]Peter Baker, "Motor Voter Apparently Didn't Drive Up Turnout," *Washington Post,* 6 November 1996, p. B7.

DO ELECTIONS MATTER? 269
]]

attacking their opponents that do not require them to engage in voter mobilization, and many prefer to use these methods than to endeavor to bring more voters to the polls. The low levels of popular mobilization that are typical of contemporary American politics are very much a function of the way that politics is conducted in the United States today.

The quasidemocratic character of American elections is underscored by the electoral college. This eighteenth-century device may have seemed reasonable to the Constitution's framers as a check on the judgment of a largely illiterate and uneducated electorate. Today, however, this institution undermines respect for and the legitimacy of electoral results. Abolition of the electoral college would impact campaigning and the two-party system. Candidates would be compelled to campaign throughout the nation rather than in the small number of states they currently see as the key "battlegrounds" for electoral college victory. This would be a welcome development. The abolition of the electoral college might also make way for new parties which might breathe new life into the political process, add to the confusion of presidential elections, or both. Time would tell. What is critical, however, is that we reinvigorate and enhance the legitimacy of popular politics. For that reason the electoral college should be replaced by a direct popular presidential choice.

WHY SHOULD CITIZENS VOTE? Compared to that of other democracies, voter turnout in national elections is extremely low in the United States. It is usually around 50 percent for presidential elections and between 30 percent and 40 percent for midterm elections. In other Western democracies, turnout regularly exceeds 80 percent. In defense of American citizens, it should be pointed out that occasions for voting as a form of civic activity occur more frequently in the United States than in other democracies. There are more offices filled by election in the United States than elsewhere—indeed, more offices per capita, which is somewhat startling given how large a democracy the United States

is. Many of these are posts that are filled by appointment in other democracies. Especially unusual in this respect are elected judges in many jurisdictions and elected local "bureaucrats" (like the local sheriff and the proverbial town dog catcher). In addition, there are primaries as well as general elections, and, in many states, there are initiatives and referenda to vote on, too. It is a wonder that American citizens don't suffer from some form of democratic fatigue! Though many scholars have tried to answer the question "Why is turnout so low?" others have argued that the real question should be "Why is turnout so high?" That is, why does anyone turn out to vote at all?

There are many costs to voting. People must take time out of their busy schedules, possibly incurring a loss of wages, in order to show up at the polls. In many states, voters have to overcome numerous hurdles just to register. If an individual wants to cast an informed vote, he or she must also spend time learning about the candidates and their positions.

Voters must bear these costs no matter what the outcome of the election, yet it is extremely unlikely that an individual's vote will actually affect the outcome, unless the vote makes or breaks a tie. Just making a close election one vote closer by voting for the loser, or the winner one vote more secure by voting for her, doesn't matter much. As the old saw has it, "Closeness only counts in horseshoes and dancing." It is almost certain that if an individual did not incur the costs of voting and stayed home instead, the election results would be the same. The probability of a single vote being decisive in a presidential election is about one in 10 million.[32]

One possible solution to this puzzle is that people are motivated by more than just their preferences for electing a particular candidate—they are,

[32]Andrew Gelman, Gary King, and John Boscardin, "Estimating the Probability of Events That Have Never Occurred: When Is Your Vote Decisive?" *Journal of the American Statistical Association* 93, no. 441 (March 1998): 1–9.
]]

in fact, satisfying their duty as citizens, and this benefit exceeds the costs of voting.[33]

John Aldrich offers another possible solution: he looks at the question from the politician's point of view.[34] Candidates calculate how much to invest in campaigns based on their probability of winning. In the unlikely event that an incumbent appears beatable, the challengers often invest heavily in their own campaigns because they believe the investment has a good chance of paying off. In response to these strong challenges, incumbents will not only work harder to raise campaign funds but also spend more of what they raise.[35] Parties seeking to maximize the number of positions in the government they control may also shift resources to help out the candidates in these close races.

More vigorous campaigns will generally lead to increased turnout. The increase is not necessarily due to citizens reacting to the closeness of the race (that is, the perception that their vote may affect the outcome) but to the greater effort and resources that candidates put into close races, which, in turn, reduce the costs of voting. Candidates share some of the costs of voting by helping citizens register and by getting them to the polls on Election Day. Heated advertising campaigns reduce the voters' costs of becoming informed (since candidates flood the public with information about themselves). This decrease in costs to individual voters in what strategic politicians perceive to be a close race at least partially explains why citizens would turn out to vote.

[33]In effect, there is an experiential as well as an instrumental rationale for voting. In more economic terms, this is the view that voting is a form of consumption as much as it is a type of investment. For a brief and user-friendly development of this logic, see Kenneth A. Shepsle and Mark S. Bonchek, Analyzing Politics: *Rationality, Behavior, and Institutions* (New York: Norton, 1997) pp. 251–59.

[34]John H. Aldrich, "Rational Choice and Turnout," *American Journal of Political Science* 37 (February 1993): 246–78.

[35]Gary C. Jacobson and Samuel Kernell, *Strategy and Choice in Congressional Elections*, 2nd ed. (New Haven: Yale University Press, 1983).

Why Do Elections Matter as Political Institutions?

Voting choices and electoral outcomes can be extremely important in the United States. Yet, to observe that there can be relationships among voters' choices, leadership composition, and policy outputs is only to begin to understand the significance of democratic elections, rather than to exhaust the possibilities. Important as they are, voters' choices and electoral results may still be less consequential for government and politics than the simple fact of voting itself. The impact of electoral decisions upon the governmental process is, in some respects, analogous to the impact made upon organized religion by individuals' being able to worship at the church of their choice. The fact of worship can be more important than the particular choice. Similarly, the fact of mass electoral participation can be more significant than what or how the citizens decide once they participate. Thus, electoral participation has important consequences in that it socializes and institutionalizes political action.

First, democratic elections socialize political activity. Voting is not a natural or spontaneous phenomenon. It is an institutionalized form of mass political involvement. That individuals vote rather than engage in some other form of political behavior is a result of national policies than create the opportunity to vote and discourage other political activities relative to voting. Elections transform what might otherwise consist of sporadic, citizen-initiated acts into a routine public function. This transformation expands and democratizes mass political involvement. At the same time, however, elections help to preserve the government's stability by containing and channeling away potentially more disruptive or dangerous forms of mass political activity. By establishing formal avenues for mass participation and accustoming citizens to their use, government reduces the threat that volatile, unorganized involvement can pose to the established order.

Second, elections bolster the government's power and authority. Elections help to increase popular support for political leaders and for the regime itself. The formal opportunity to participate in elections serves to convince citizens that the government is responsive to their needs and wishes. Moreover, elections help to persuade citizens to obey. Electoral participation increases popular acceptance of taxes and military service upon which the government depends. Even if popular voting can influence the behavior of those in power, voting serves simultaneously as a form of cooptation. Elections—particularly democratic elections—substitute consent for coercion as the foundation of governmental power.

Finally, elections institutionalize mass influence in politics. Democratic elections permit citizens to select and depose public officials routinely, and elections can serve to promote popular influence over officials' conduct. But however effective this electoral sanction may be, it is hardly the only means through which citizens can reward or punish public officials for their actions. Spontaneous or privately organized forms of political activity, or even the threat of their occurrence, can also induce those in power to heed the public's wishes. The alternative to democratic elections is not clearly and simply the absence of popular influence; it can be unregulated and unconstrained popular intervention into government. It is often precisely because spontaneous forms of mass political activity can have too great an impact upon the actions of government that elections are introduced. Walter Lippmann, a journalist who helped to pioneer the idea of public opinion voicing itself through the press via the "opinion-editorial," or op-ed, page, once observed that "new numbers were enfranchised because they had power, and giving them the vote was the least disturbing way of letting them exercise their power."[36] The vote can provide the "least disturbing way" of allowing ordinary people to exercise power. If the people had been powerless to begin with, elections would never have been introduced.

[36]Walter Lippmann, *The Essential Lippmann,* eds. Clinton Rossiter and James Lare (New York: Random House, 1965), p. 12.

Thus, although citizens can secure enormous benefits from their right to vote, government secures equally significant benefits from allowing them to do so.

Elections are important as an institution of democratic government because they socialize political activity, help support the government's power and authority, and provide citizens with a means to influence government.

CHAPTER REVIEW

Allowing citizens to vote represents a calculated risk on the part of power holders. On the one hand, popular participation can generate consent and support for the government. On the other hand, the right to vote may give ordinary citizens more influence in the governmental process than political elites would like.

Voting is only one of the many possible types of political participation. The significance of voting is that it is an institutional and formal mode of political activity. Voting is organized and subsidized by the government. This makes voting both more limited and more democratic than other forms of participation.

All governments regulate voting to influence its effects. The most important forms of regulation include regulation of the electorate's composition, regulation of the translation of voters' choices into electoral outcomes, and insulation of policy-making processes from electoral intervention.

Voters' choices are based on partisanship, issues, and candidates' personalities. Which of these criteria will be most important varies over time and depends upon the factors and issues that opposing candidates choose to emphasize in their campaigns.

Whatever voters decide, elections are important because they socialize political activity, increase governmental authority, and institutionalize popular influence in political life.

KEY TERMS

Australian ballot An electoral format that presents the names of all the candidates for any given office on the same ballot. Introduced at the turn of the twentieth century, the Australian ballot replaced the partisan ballot and facilitated split-ticket voting.

benign gerrymandering Attempts to draw districts so as to create districts made up primarily of disadvantaged or underrepresented minorities.

electoral college The presidential electors from each state who meet in their respective state capitals after the popular election to cast ballots for president and vice president.

527 committees Nonprofit independent groups that receive and disburse funds to influence the nomination, election, or defeat of candidates. Named after Section 527 of the Internal Revenue Code, which defines and provides tax-exempt status for nonprofit advocacy groups.

gerrymandering Apportionment of voters in districts in such a way as to give unfair advantage to one political party.

initiative The process that allows citizens to propose new laws and submit them for approval by the state's voters.

issue advocacy Independent spending by individuals or interest groups on a campaign issue but not directly tied to a particular candidate.

majority system Type of electoral system in which, to win a seat in the parliament or other representative body, a candidate must receive a majority of all the votes cast in the relevant district.

Motor Voter bill A legislative act passed in 1993 that requires all states to allow voters to register by mail when they renew their drivers' licenses and provides for the placement of voter registration forms in motor vehicle, public assistance, and military recruitment offices.

plurality system Type of electoral system in which, to win a seat in the parliament or other representative body, a candidate need only receive the most votes in the election, not necessarily a majority of votes cast.

political action committee (PAC) A private group that raises and distributes funds for use in election campaigns.

poll tax A state-imposed tax upon voters as a prerequisite for registration. Poll taxes were rendered unconstitutional in national elections by the Twenty-fourth Amendment, and in state elections by the Supreme Court in 1966.

proportional representation A multiple-member district system that awards seats based on the percentage of the vote won by each candidate. By contrast, the "winner-take-all" system of elections awards the seat to the one candidate who wins the most votes.

prospective voting Voting based on the imagined future performance of a candidate.

racial gerrymandering Redrawing congressional boundary lines in such a way as to divide and disperse a racial minority population that otherwise would constitute a majority within the original district.

recall Procedure to allow voters an opportunity to remove state officials from office before their terms expire.

referendum The practice of referring a measure proposed by a legislature to the vote of the electorate for approval or rejection.

retrospective voting Voting based on the past performance of a candidate.

soft money Money contributed directly to political parties for voter registration and organization.

split-ticket voting The practice of casting ballots for the candidates of at least two different political parties in the same election. Voters who support only one party's candidates are said to vote a straight party ticket.

straight party vote The practice of casting ballots for candidates of only one party.

suffrage The right to vote; also called franchise.

turnout The percentage of eligible individuals who actually vote.

FOR FURTHER READING

Andersen, Kristi. *The Creation of a Democratic Majority: 1928–1936*. Chicago: University of Chicago Press, 1979.

Black, Earl, and Merle Black. *The Vital South: How Presidents Are Elected*. Cambridge: Harvard University Press, 1992.

Brady, David. *Critical Elections and Congressional Policymaking*. Stanford: Stanford University Press, 1988.

Carmines, Edward G., and James Stimson. *Issue Evolution: The Racial Transformation of American Politics*. Princeton: Princeton University Press, 1988.

Conway, M. Margaret. *Political Participation in the United States*. Washigton, DC: Congressional Quarterly Press, 1985.

Fowler, Linda. *Candidates, Congress, and the American Democracy*. Ann Arbor: University of Michigan Press, 1994.

Fowler, Linda, and Robert D. McClure. *Political Ambition: Who Decides to Run for Congress*. New Haven: Yale University Press, 1989.

Ginsberg, Benjamin, and Martin Shefter. *Politics by Other Means: Institutional Conflict and the Declining Significance of Elections in America*, rev. and updated ed. New York: Norton, 1999.

Niemi, Richard, and Herbert Weisberg. *Controversies in American Voting Behavior*. Washington, DC: Congressional Quarterly Press, 1984.

Piven, Frances Fox, and Richard A. Cloward. *Why Americans Don't Vote*. New York: Pantheon, 1988.

Sorauf, Frank. *Inside Campaign Finance: Myths and Realities*. New Haven: Yale University Press, 1992.

Tate, Katherine. *From Protest to Politics: The New Black Voters in American Elections*. Cambridge: Harvard University Press, 1994.

Witt, Linda, Karen Paget, and Glenna Matthews. *Running as a Woman: Gender and Power in American Politics*. New York: Free Press, 1994.

CHAPTER 11

Political Parties

HOW PARTIES WORK

$\mathcal{W}$e often refer to the United States as a nation with a "two-party system." By this we mean that in the United States the Democratic and Republican parties compete for office and power. Most Americans believe that party competition contributes to the health of the democratic process.

In recent years, however, electoral politics has become a "candidate-centered" affair in which individual candidates for office build their own campaign organizations, while voters make choices based more upon their reactions to the candidates than upon loyalty to the parties. Party organization, as we saw in Chapter 5, continues to be an important factor within Congress. Even in Congress, however, the influence of party leaders is based more upon ideological affinity than any real power over party members. The weakness of the party system is an important factor in understanding contemporary American political patterns.[1]

We will examine the realities underlying changing conceptions of *political parties*. As we shall see, parties expand popular political participation, promote more effective choice, and smooth the flow of public business in Congress. Today the

---

[1]For an excellent discussion of the fluctuating role of political parties in the United States and the influence of government on that role, see John J. Coleman, *Party Decline in America: Policy, Politics, and the Fiscal State* (Princeton: Princeton University Press, 1996).

CORE OF THE ANALYSIS

- Today the Democratic and Republican parties dominate the American two-party political system.

- The most important functions of American political parties are facilitating nominations and elections and organizing the institutions of national government.

- The role of parties in electoral politics has declined in the United States over the last thirty years.

- New political technology has strengthened the advantage of wealthier political groups.

problem is not that political life is too partisan, but that the parties are not strong enough to function effectively. This is one reason that America has such low levels of popular political involvement. Unfortunately, reforms enacted in 2002 such as the elimination of soft money, will likely further erode party strength in America.

Political parties as they are known today developed along with the expansion of suffrage and can be understood only in the context of elections. The two are so intertwined that American parties actually take their shape from the electoral process. They were formed because there were elections to run. The shape of party organization in the United

CENTRAL QUESTIONS	• **Functions of the Parties** What are the important electoral functions of parties? How do the differences between Democrats and Republicans affect Congress, the president, and the policy-making process? • **The Two-Party System in America** How have political parties developed in the United States? What are the historical origins of today's Democratic and Republican parties? What is the history of party politics in America? What has been the historical role of third parties in the United States? • **Weakening of Party Organization** What factors led to the diminishment of party strength in America? How has this development affected election campaigns? How are parties important to contemporary politics?

States has followed a simple rule: For every district where an election is held, there should be some kind of party unit (see Figure 11.1).

Political parties are organizations that try to win control over government through elections.

Party organization is generally an essential ingredient for effective electoral competition by groups lacking substantial economic or institutional resources. Party building has typically been the strategy pursued by groups that must organize the collective energies of large numbers of individuals to counter their opponents' superior material means or institutional standing. Historically, disciplined and coherent party organizations were generally developed first by groups representing the political aspirations of the working class. Parties, French political scientist Maurice Duverger notes, "are always more developed on the Left than on the Right because they are always more necessary on the Left than on the Right."[2]

Compared to political parties in Europe, parties in the United States have always seemed weak. They have no criteria for party membership—no cards for

their members to carry, no obligatory participation in any activity, no notion of exclusiveness. And today, they seem weaker than ever: They inspire less loyalty and are less able to control nominations. Some people are even talking about a "crisis of political parties," as though party politics were being abandoned. But there continues to be at least some substance to party organizations in the United States.

Political parties are also essential elements in the process of making policy. Within the government, parties are coalitions of individuals with shared or overlapping interests who, as a rule, will support one another's programs and initiatives. Even though there may be areas of disagreement within each party, a common party label in and of itself gives party members a reason to cooperate. Because they are permanent coalitions, parties greatly facilitate the policy-making process. If alliances had to be formed from scratch for each legislative proposal, the business of government would slow to a crawl or would halt altogether. Parties create a basis for coalition and thus sharply reduce the time, energy, and effort needed to advance a legislative proposal. For example, in 2001 when President George W. Bush considered a series of new policy initiatives, he met first with the House and Senate leaders of the Republican party. Although some congressional Republicans disagreed with the president's approach to a number of issues, all felt they had a stake in cooperat-

[2] Maurice Duverger, *Political Parties* (New York: Wiley, 1954), p. 426.

FIGURE 11.1

HOW AMERICAN PARTIES ARE ORGANIZED

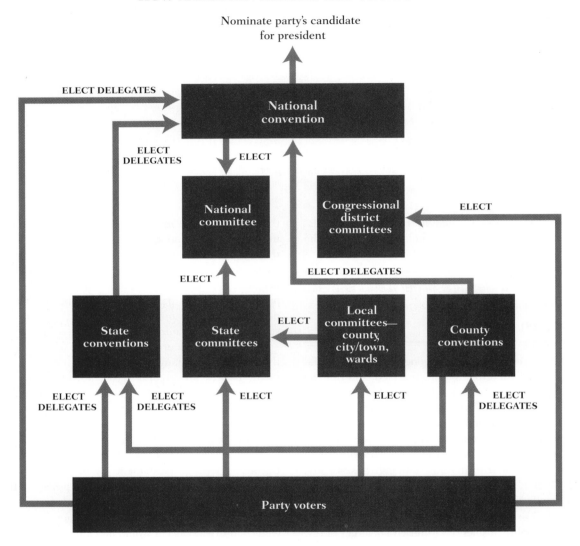

FUNCTIONS OF THE PARTIES

ing with him to burnish the party's image in preparation for the next round of national elections. Without the support of a party, the president would be compelled to undertake the daunting and probably impossible task of forming a completely new coalition for each and every policy proposal—a virtually impossible task.

Parties perform a wide variety of functions. They are mainly involved in nominations and elections—providing the candidates for office, getting out the vote, and facilitating mass electoral choice. They also influence the institutions of government—

providing the leadership and organization of the various congressional committees.

Recruiting Candidates

One of the most important but least noticed party activities is the recruitment of candidates for local, state, and national office. Each election year, candidates must be found for thousands of state and local offices as well as congressional seats. Where they do not have an incumbent running for reelection, party leaders attempt to identify strong candidates and to interest them in entering the campaign.

An ideal candidate will have an unblemished record and the capacity to raise enough money to mount a serious campaign. Party leaders are usually not willing to provide financial backing to candidates who are unable to raise substantial funds on their own. For a House seat, this can mean several hundred thousand dollars; for a Senate seat, a serious candidate must be able to raise several million dollars. Often, party leaders have difficulty finding attractive candidates and persuading them to run. Candidate recruitment is problematic in an era when political campaigns often involve mudslinging, and candidates must assume that their personal lives will be intensely scrutinized in the press.[3]

Nominations

Nomination is the process of selecting one party candidate to run for each elective office. The nominating process can precede the election by many months, as it does when the many candidates for the presidency are eliminated from consideration through a grueling series of debates and state primaries until there is only one survivor in each party—the party's nominee. Nomination is the parties' most serious and difficult business.

> *Parties are important in the electoral process for recruiting and nominating candidates.*

NOMINATION BY CONVENTION A nominating convention is a formal caucus bound by a number of rules that govern participation and nominating procedures. Conventions are meetings of delegates elected by party members from the relevant county (county convention) or state (state convention). Delegates to each party's national convention (which nominates the party's presidential candidate) are chosen by party members on a state-by-state basis; there is no single national delegate selection process.

NOMINATION BY PRIMARY ELECTION In primary elections, party members select the party's nominees directly rather than selecting convention delegates who then select the nominees. Primaries are far from perfect replacements for conventions, since it is rare that more than 25 percent of the enrolled voters participate in them. Nevertheless, they are replacing conventions as the dominant method of nomination.[4] Currently, only a few states, including Connecticut, Delaware, and Utah, provide for state conventions to nominate candidates for statewide offices, and even these states combine them with primaries whenever a substantial minority of delegates vote for one of the defeated aspirants.

Primary elections are of two types: closed and open. In a **closed primary,** participation is limited to individuals who have declared their affiliation by registering with the party. In an **open primary,** individuals declare their party affiliation on the actual day of the primary election—they simply go to the polling place and ask for the ballot of a par-

---

[3]For an excellent analysis of the parties' role in recruitment, see Paul Herrnson, *Congressional Elections: Campaigning at Home and in Washington* (Washington, DC: Congressional Quarterly Press, 1995).

[4]For a discussion of some of the effects of primary elections, see Peter F. Galderisi and Benjamin Ginsberg, "Primary Elections and the Evanescence of Third Party Activity in the United States," in *Do Elections Matter?* eds. Benjamin Ginsberg and Alan Stone (Armonk, NY: M. E. Sharpe, 1986), pp. 115–30.

ticular party. The open primary allows each voter an opportunity to consider candidates and issues before deciding whether to participate and in which party's contest to participate. Open primaries, therefore, are less conducive than closed contests to strong political parties. But in either case, primaries are more open then conventions or caucuses to new issues and new candidates.

Getting Out the Vote

The actual election period begins immediately after the nominations. Historically, this has been a time of glory for the political parties, whose popular base of support is fully displayed. All the paraphernalia of party committees and all the committee members are activated into local party work forces.

The first step in the electoral process involves voter registration. This aspect of the process takes place all year round. There was a time when party workers were responsible for virtually all of this kind of electoral activity, but they have been supplemented (and in many states virtually displaced) by civic groups such as the League of Women Voters, unions, and chambers of commerce.

Those who have registered have to decide on Election Day whether to go to the polling place, stand in line, and actually vote for the various candidates and referenda on the ballot. Political parties, candidates, and campaigning can make a big difference in convincing the voters to vote.

Traditionally, parties are responsible for getting out the vote for their candidates and providing voters with information about candidates and policies.

In recent years, each of the two parties has developed extensive data files on hundreds of millions of potential voters. The GOP has called its archive "Voter Vault," while the Democratic file has been designated "Demzilla." Democrats claim their files contain the names, addresses, voting preferences, contribution history, ethnic backgrounds, and other information on some 165 million Americans. Republican files contain similar data on nearly 200 million individuals. These elaborate data files allow the two parties to bring their search for votes, contributions, and campaign help down to named individuals. Voter mobilization, once an art, has now become a science.

Facilitation of Mass Electoral Choice

Parties facilitate mass electoral choice. As the late Harvard political scientist V. O. Key pointed out long ago, the persistence over time of competition between groups possessing a measure of identity and continuity is a necessary condition for electoral control.[5] *Party identity* increases the electorate's capacity to recognize its options. Consistent party division organizes voters in a way necessary to sustain any popular influence in the governmental process. In the absence of party division, the voter is, in Key's words, confronted constantly by "new faces, new choices."[6]

Parties are important to the electoral process because they help voters recognize their options and also encourage electoral competition.

While political parties continue to be significant in the United States, the role of party organizations in electoral politics has clearly declined over the past three decades. This decline, and the partial replacement of the party by new forms of electoral technology, is one of the most important developments in twentieth-century American politics.

Influence on National Government

The ultimate test of the party system is its relationship to and influence on the institutions of

[5]V. O. Key, *Southern Politics* (New York: Random House, 1949), Chapter 14.
[6]Ibid.

national government and the policy-making process. Thus, it is important to examine the party system in relation to Congress and the president.

PARTIES AND POLICY One of the most familiar observations about American politics is that the two major parties try to be all things to all people and are therefore indistinguishable from each other. Data and experience give some support to this observation. Parties in the United States are not programmatic or ideological, as they have sometimes been in Britain or in other parts of Europe. But this does not mean there are no differences between them. During the Reagan era, important differences emerged between the positions of Democratic and Republican party leaders on a number of key issues, and these differences are still apparent today. For example, the national leadership of the Republican Party supports maintaining high levels of military spending, cuts in social programs, tax relief for middle- and upper-income voters, tax incentives to businesses, and the "social agenda" backed by members of conservative religious denominations. The national Democratic leadership, on the other hand, supports expanded social welfare spending, cuts in military spending, increased regulation of business, and a variety of consumer and environmental programs.

These differences reflect differences in philosophy as well as differences in the core constituencies to which the parties seek to appeal. The Democratic Party at the national level seeks to unite organized labor, the poor, members of racial minorities, and liberal upper-middle-class professionals. The Republicans, by contrast, appeal to business, upper-middle- and upper-class groups in the private sector, and social conservatives. Often, party leaders will seek to develop issues they hope will add new groups to their party's constituent base. During the 1980s, for example, under the leadership of Ronald Reagan, the Republicans devised a series of "social issues," including support for school prayer, opposition to abortion, and opposition to affirmative action, designed to culti-

vate the support of white Southerners. This effort was extremely successful in increasing Republican strength in the once solidly Democratic South. In the 1990s, under the leadership of Bill Clinton, who called himself a "new Democrat," the Democratic Party sought to develop new social programs designed to solidify the party's base among working-class and poor voters, and new, somewhat more conservative economic programs aimed at attracting the votes of middle- and upper-middle-class voters.

As these examples suggest, parties do not always support policies because they are favored by their constituents. Instead, party leaders can play the role of *policy entrepreneurs,* seeding ideas and programs that will expand their party's base of support while eroding that of the opposition. It is one of the essential characteristics of party politics in America that a party's programs and policies often lead, rather than follow, public opinion. Like their counterparts in the business world, party leaders seek to identify and develop "products" (programs and policies) that will appeal to the public. The public, of course, has the ultimate voice. With its votes it decides whether or not to "buy" new policy offerings.

Through members elected to office, both parties have made efforts to translate their general goals into concrete policies. Republicans, for example, implemented tax cuts, increased defense spending, cut social spending, and enacted restrictions on abortion during the 1980s and 1990s. Democrats were able to defend consumer and environmental programs against GOP attacks and sought to expand domestic social programs in the late 1990s. During his two terms in office, President George W. Bush sought substantial cuts in federal taxes, "privatization" of the social security system, and a larger role for faith-based organizations allied with the Republican party in the administration of federal social programs. In the context of the nation's campaign against terrorism, Bush also sought to shift America's defense posture from an emphasis on deterrence to a doctrine of preemptive strikes against perceived threats.

The differences between the two parties reflect not only a general difference in philosophy but also an attempt to appeal to core constituencies. The party's policy agenda often reflects these differences.

THE PARTIES AND CONGRESS   Congress, in particular, depends more on the party system than is generally recognized. First, the speakership of the House is a party office. All the members of the House take part in the election of the speaker. But the actual selection is made by the *majority party.* When the majority party caucus presents a nominee to the entire House, its choice is then invariably ratified in a straight party-line vote.

The committee system of both houses of Congress is also a product of the two-party system. Although the rules organizing committees and the rules defining the jurisdiction of each committee are adopted like ordinary legislation by the whole membership, parties shape all other features of the committees. For example, each party is assigned a quota of members for each committee, depending upon the percentage of total seats held by the party. On the rare occasions when an independent or third-party candidate is elected, the leaders of the two parties must agree against whose quota this member's committee assignments will count.

The assignment of individual members to committees is a party decision. Each party has a "committee on committees" to make such decisions. Permission to transfer from one committee to another is also a party decision. Moreover, advancement up the committee ladder toward the chair is a party decision. Since the late nineteenth century, most advancements have been automatic—based upon the length of continual service on the committee. This seniority system has existed only because of the support of the two parties, and

each party can depart from it by a simple vote. During the 1970s, both parties reinstituted the practice of reviewing each chair—voting anew every two years on whether each chair would be continued. In 2001, Republicans lived up to their 1995 pledge to limit House committee chairs to three terms. Existing chairpersons were forced to step down, but were replaced generally by the most senior Republican member of each committee.

Party leadership in Congress determines a policy agenda and pressures party members to vote uniformly.

President and Party

As we saw earlier, the party that wins the White House is always led, in title anyway, by the president. The president normally depends upon fellow party members in Congress to support legislative initiatives. At the same time, members of the party in Congress hope that the president's programs and personal prestige will help them raise campaign funds and secure reelection. During his two terms in office, President Bill Clinton had a mixed record as party leader. In the realm of trade policy, Clinton sometimes found more support among Republicans than among Democrats. In addition, although Clinton proved to be an extremely successful fund-raiser, congressional Democrats often complained that he failed to share his largesse with them. At the same time, however, a number of Clinton's policy initiatives seemed calculated to strengthen the Democratic Party as a whole. Clinton's early health care initiative would have linked millions of voters to the Democrats for years to come, much as FDR's Social Security program had done in a previous era. But by the middle of Clinton's second term, the president's acknowledgment of his sexual affair with a White House intern threatened his position as party leader. Initially, Democratic candidates nationwide feared that the scandal would undermine their own chances for election, and many moved to distance themselves from the president. The Democrats' surprisingly good showing in the 1998 elections, however, strengthened Clinton's position and gave him another chance to shape the Democratic agenda.

Between the 1998 and 2000 elections, however, the president's initiatives on Social Security and nuclear disarmament failed to make much headway in a Republican-controlled Congress. The GOP was not prepared to give Clinton anything for which Democrats would claim credit in the 2000 elections. Lacking strong congressional leadership, however, the GOP did agree to many of Clinton's budgetary proposals in 1999 and dropped its own plan for large-scale cuts in federal taxes.

When he assumed office in 2001, President George W. Bush called for a new era of bipartisan cooperation, and the new president did receive the support of some Democratic conservatives. Generally, however, Bush depended upon near-unanimous backing from his own party in Congress to implement his plans for cutting taxes as well as other elements of his program.

The president serves as an informal party head by seeking support from congressional members of the party and by supporting their bids for reelection.

THE TWO-PARTY SYSTEM IN AMERICA

Although George Washington deplored partisan politics, the two-party system emerged early in the history of the new Republic. Beginning with the Federalists and the Jeffersonian Republicans in the early 1800s, two major parties would dominate national politics, although which particular two parties they were would change with the times and issues. This two-party system has cul-

minated in today's Demo-crats and Republicans. The evolution of American political parties is shown in Process Box 11.1.

The Democrats

When the Jeffersonian party splintered in 1824, Andrew Jackson emerged as the leader of one of its four factions. In 1830, Jackson's group became the Democratic Party. This new party had the strongest national organization of its time and presented itself as the party of the common man. Jacksonians supported reductions in the price of public lands and a policy of cheaper money and credit. Laborers, immigrants, and settlers west of the Alleghenies were quickly attracted to it.

From 1828, when Jackson was elected president, to 1860, the Democratic Party was the dominant force in American politics. For all but eight of those years, the Democrats held the White House. In addition, a Democratic majority controlled the Senate for twenty-six years and the House for twenty-four years during the same time period. Nineteenth-century Democrats emphasized the importance of interpreting the Constitution literally, upholding states' rights, and limiting federal spending.

In 1860, the issue of slavery split the Democrats along geographic lines. In the South, many Democrats served in the Confederate government. In the North, one faction of the party (the Copperheads) opposed the war and advocated negotiating a peace with the South. Thus, for years after the war, Republicans denounced the Democrats as the "party of treason."

The Democratic Party was not fully able to regain its political strength until the Great Depression. In 1933, Democrat Franklin D. Roosevelt entered the White House, and the Democrats won control of Congress as well. Roosevelt's New Deal coalition, composed of Catholics, Jews, African Americans, farmers, intellectuals, and members of organized labor, dominated American politics until the 1970s and served as the basis for the party's expansion of federal power and efforts to remedy social problems.

PROCESS BOX 11.1

HOW THE U.S. PARTY SYSTEM EVOLVED

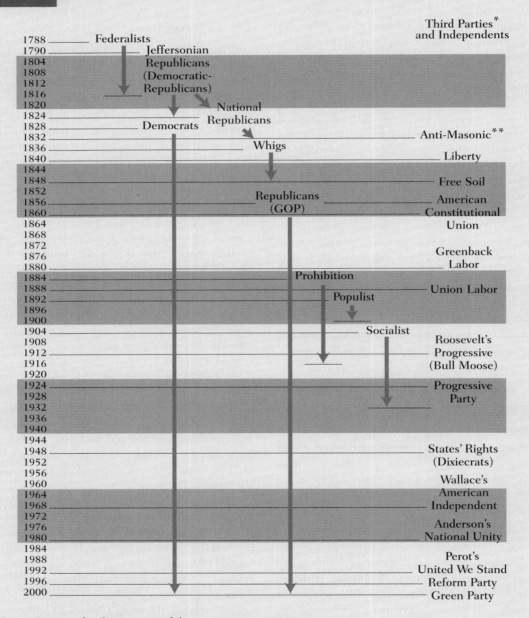

*Or in some cases, fourth party; most of these are one-term parties.

**The Anti-Masonics not only had the distinction of being the first third party, but it was also the first party to hold a national nominating convention and the first to announce a party platform.

The Democrats were never fully united. In Congress, Southern Democrats often aligned with Republicans in the "conservative coalition" rather than with members of their own party. But the Democratic Party remained America's majority party, usually controlling Congress and the White House, for nearly four decades after 1932. By the 1980s, the Democratic coalition faced serious problems. The once-solid South often voted for the Republicans, along with many blue-collar Northern voters. On the other hand, the Democrats increased their strength among African American voters and women. The Democrats maintained a strong base in the bureaucracies of the federal government and the states, in labor unions, and in the not-for-profit sector of the economy. During the 1980s and 1990s, moderate Democrats were able to take control of the party nominating process and sought to broaden middle-class support for the party. This helped the Democrats elect a president in 1992. In 1994, however, the unpopularity of Democratic President Bill Clinton led to the loss of the Democrats' control of both houses of Congress for the first time since 1946. In 1996, Clinton was able to win reelection to a second term over the weak opposition of Republican candidate Robert Dole. Democrats were, however, unable to dislodge their GOP rivals from the leadership of either house of Congress. During the 2000 national presidential elections, Vice President Al Gore won the nomination despite a serious challenge from former New Jersey Senator Bill Bradley. In the general presidential election, Gore outpolled Republican candidate George W. Bush but lost the electoral vote after Bush won a long battle over Florida's votes.

Disagreements between the two wings of the party were evident during the campaign for the Democratic presidential nomination in 2003 and 2004. Moderate Democrat Joseph Lieberman, for example, supported President Bush's decision to launch a war against Iraq, while liberal Democrats such as Howard Dean and Al Sharpton strongly criticized the president's military policies. The party's eventual nominee, Senator John Kerry of Massachusetts, had originally supported the war but sought to stake out a position in opposition to Bush's policies that would satisfy liberal Democrats but not appear to be indecisive.

The Republicans

The 1854 Kansas-Nebraska Act overturned the Missouri Compromise of 1820 and the Compromise of 1850, which had both barred the expansion of slavery in the American territories. The Kansas-Nebraska Act gave each territory the right to decide whether or not to permit slavery. Opposition to this policy galvanized antislavery groups and led them to create a new party, the Republicans. It drew its membership from existing political groups—former Whigs, Know-Nothings, Free Soilers, and antislavery Democrats. In 1856, the party's first presidential candidate, John C. Frémont, won one-third of the popular vote and carried eleven states.

The early Republican platforms appealed to commercial as well as antislavery interests. The Republicans favored homesteading, internal improvements, the construction of a transcontinental railroad, and protective tariffs, as well as the containment of slavery. In 1858, the Republican Party won control of the House; in 1860, the Republican presidential candidate, Abraham Lincoln, was victorious.

From the Civil War to the Great Depression, the Republicans were America's dominant political party, especially after 1896. In the seventy-two years between 1860 and 1932, Republicans occupied the White House for fifty-six years, controlled the Senate for sixty years, and controlled the House for fifty. During these years, the Republicans came to be closely associated with big business. The party of Lincoln became the party of Wall Street.

The Great Depression, however, ended Republican supremacy. The voters held Republican President Herbert Hoover responsible for the economic catastrophe, and by 1936 the party's popularity was so low that Republicans won only eighty-nine seats in the House and seventeen in the Senate. The Republican presidential candidate, Governor Alfred M. Landon of Kansas, carried only two states. The Republicans won only four presidential elections between 1932 and 1980, and they controlled Congress for only four of those years (1947–1949 and 1953–1955).

The Republican Party has widened its appeal over the last four decades. Groups previously associated with the Democratic Party—particularly blue-collar workers and Southern Democrats—have been increasingly attracted to Republican presidential candidates (for example, Dwight D. Eisenhower, Richard Nixon, Ronald Reagan, and George Bush). But Republicans generally did not do as well at the state and local levels and had little chance of capturing a majority in either the House or Senate. Yet in 1994, the Republican Party finally won a majority in both houses of Congress, in large part because of the party's growing strength in the South.

During the 1990s, conservative religious groups, who had been attracted to the Republican camp by its opposition to abortion and support for school prayer, made a concerted effort to expand their influence within the party. This effort led to conflict between these members of the "religious Right" and more traditional "country-club" Republicans, whose major concerns were matters such as taxes and federal regulation of business. This coalition swept the polls in 1994 and maintained its control of both houses of Congress in 1996, despite President Clinton's reelection. In 1998, however, severe strains began to show in the GOP coalition. In 2000, George W. Bush sought to unite the party's centrist and right wings behind a program of tax cuts, education reform, military strength, and family values. Bush avoided issues that divided the GOP camp, like abortion. In 2004, he adopted a similar strategy. Bush's candidacy boded well for the future of the GOP insofar as he was able to find a political formula that could unite the party. Republicans hoped that future candidates might apply this formula to restore the GOP to its glory years.

Electoral Alignments and Realignments

In the United States, party politics has followed a fascinating pattern (see Figure 11.2). Typically, during the course of American political history, the national electoral arena has been dominated by one party for a period of roughly thirty years. At the conclusion of this period, a new party has supplanted the dominant party in what political scientists call an *electoral realignment.* The realignment is typically followed by a long period in which the new party is the dominant political force in the United States—not necessarily winning every election but generally maintaining control of the Congress and usually of the White House as well.[7]

Although there are some disputes among scholars about the precise timing of these critical realignments, there is general agreement that at least five have occurred since the founding of the American Republic. The first took place around 1800 when the Jeffersonian Republicans defeated the Federalists and became the dominant force in American politics. The second realignment occurred in about 1828, when the Jacksonian Democrats took control of the White House and the Congress. The third period of realignment centered on 1860. During this period, the newly founded Republican Party led by Abraham Lincoln won power, in the process destroying the Whig Party, which had been one of the nation's two major parties since the 1830s. During the fourth critical period, centered on the election of 1896, the Republicans reasserted their dominance of the national government, which had been weakening since the 1880s. The fifth realignment took place during the period 1932–1936 when the Democrats, led by Franklin Delano Roosevelt, took control of the White House and Congress and, despite sporadic interruptions, maintained control of both through the 1960s. Since that time, American party politics has been characterized primarily by *divided government*, wherein one party controls the presidency while the other party controls one or both houses of Congress.

---

[7]See Walter Dean Burnham, *Critical Elections and the Mainsprings of American Electoral Politics* (New York: Norton, 1970). See also James L. Sundquist, *Dynamics of the Party System* (Washington, DC: Brookings Institution, 1983).

FIGURE 11.2

ELECTORAL REALIGNMENTS

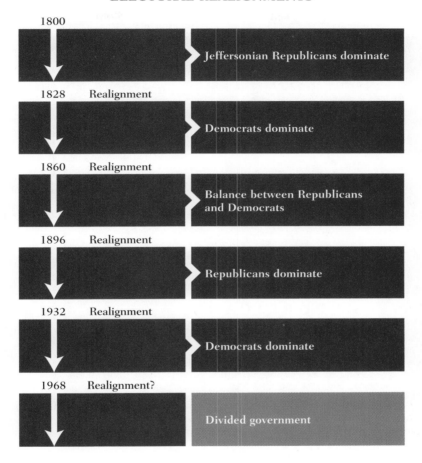

1800

Jeffersonian Republicans dominate

1828   Realignment

Democrats dominate

1860   Realignment

Balance between Republicans and Democrats

1896   Realignment

Republicans dominate

1932   Realignment

Democrats dominate

1968   Realignment?

Divided government

Historically, realignments occur when new issues combined with economic or political crises persuade large numbers of voters to reexamine their traditional partisan loyalties and permanently shift their support from one party to another (see Concept Map 11.1). For example, in the 1850s, diverse regional, income, and business groups supported one of the two major parties, the Democrats or the Whigs, on the basis of their positions on various economic issues, such as internal improvements, the tariff, monetary policy, and

banking. This economic alignment was shattered during the 1850s. The newly formed Republican Party campaigned on the basis of opposition to slavery and, in particular, opposition to the expansion of slavery into the territories. The issues of slavery and sectionalism produced divisions within both the Democratic and the Whig parties, ultimately leading to the dissolution of the latter, and these issues compelled voters to reexamine their partisan allegiances. Many Northern voters who had supported the Whigs or the Democrats on the

CONCEPT
MAP 11.1
ELECTORAL REALIGNMENT IN THE 1930s

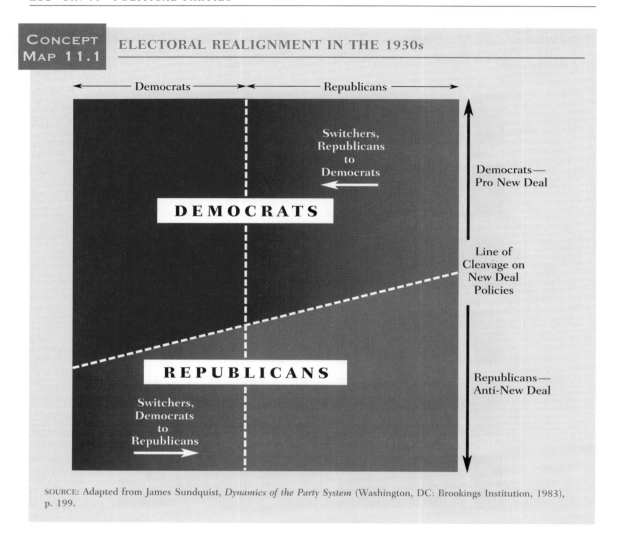

← Democrats →│← Republicans →

Switchers,
Republicans
to
Democrats
←

DEMOCRATS

Democrats—
Pro New Deal

Line of
Cleavage on
New Deal
Policies

REPUBLICANS

Republicans—
Anti-New Deal

Switchers,
Democrats
to
Republicans
→

SOURCE: Adapted from James Sundquist, *Dynamics of the Party System* (Washington, DC: Brookings Institution, 1983), p. 199.

basis of their economic stands shifted their support to the Republicans as slavery replaced tariffs and economic concerns as the central item on the nation's political agenda. Many Southern Whigs shifted their support to the Democrats. The new sectional alignment of forces that emerged was solidified by the trauma of the Civil War and persisted almost to the turn of the century.

In 1896, this sectional alignment was at least partially supplanted by an alignment of political forces based on economic and cultural factors. During the economic crises of the 1880s and 1890s, the Democrats forged a coalition consisting of economically hard-pressed Midwestern and Southern farmers, as well as small-town and rural economic interests. These groups tended to be descendants of British Isles, Dutch, and Hessian fundamentalist Protestants. The Republicans, on the other hand, put together a coalition comprising most of the business community, industrial workers, and city dwellers. In the election of 1896, Republican candidate William McKinley, emphasizing business, industry, and urban interests, decisively defeated Democrat William Jennings Bryan, who spoke for sectional interests, farmers, and fundamentalism. Republican dominance lasted until 1932.

Such periods of critical realignment in American politics have had extremely important institutional and policy results. Realignments occur when new issue concerns coupled with economic or political crises weaken the established political elite and permit new groups of politicians to create coalitions of forces capable of capturing and holding the reins of governmental power. The construction of new governing coalitions during these realigning periods has effected major changes in American governmental institutions and policies. Each period of realignment represents a turning point in American politics. The choices made by the national electorate during these periods have helped shape the course of American political history for generations.[8]

Electoral realignments occur when new issues or events cause a shift in partisan loyalty. The new electoral coalitions resulting from realignments have effected major change on governmental policy and institutions.

Third Parties

The United States is always said to have a two-party system, and Americans usually assume that only the candidates nominated by one of the two major parties have any chance of winning. Voters who would prefer a *third-party* candidate may feel compelled, nonetheless, to vote for the major-party candidate whom they regard as the "lesser of the two evils," to avoid wasting their vote in a futile

[8]Benjamin Ginsberg, *The Consequences of Consent* (New York: Random House, 1982), Chapter 4.

gesture. Third-party candidates must struggle—usually without success—to overcome the perception that they cannot win.

Table 11.1 shows a listing of all the parties that offered candidates in one or more states in the presidential election of 2004, as well as independent candidates who ran. With the exception of Ralph Nader, the third-party and independent candidates together polled only 7.23 million votes. They gained no electoral votes for president, and most of them disappeared immediately after the presidential election. The significance of Table 11.1 is that it demonstrates the large number of third parties running candidates and appealing to voters. Third-party candidacies also arise at the state and local levels. In New York, the Liberal and Conservative parties have been on the ballot for decades. In 1998, Minnesota elected a third-party governor, former professional wrestler Jesse Ventura.

Although the Republican Party was only the third American political party ever to make itself permanent (by replacing the Whigs), other third parties have enjoyed an influence far beyond their electoral size. This was because large parts of their programs were adopted by one or both of the major parties, who sought to appeal to the voters mobilized by the new party, and so to expand their own electoral strength. The Democratic Party, for example, became a great deal more liberal when it adopted most of the Progressive program early in the twentieth century. Many Socialists felt that President Roosevelt's New Deal had adopted most of their party's program, including old-age pensions, unemployment compensation, an agricultural marketing program, and laws guaranteeing workers the right to organize into unions.

This kind of influence explains the short lives of third parties. Their causes are usually eliminated by the ability of the major parties to absorb their programs and to draw their supporters into the mainstream. There are, of course, additional reasons that most third parties are short-lived. One is the usual limitation of their electoral support to one or two regions. Populist support, for example, was primarily Midwestern. The 1948 Progressive

TABLE 11.1

PARTIES AND CANDIDATES IN 2004

In the 2004 presidential election, in addition to the Democratic and Republican nominees, at least fifteen candidates appeared on the ballot in one or more states. Ralph Nader came the closest to challenging the major-party candidates. The remaining fourteen candidates shared about .6 percent of the votes cast with numerous write-ins.

Candidate	Party	Vote Total	Percentage of Vote
George W. Bush	Republican	62,040,610	51%
John F. Kerry	Democrat	59,028,444	48%
Ralph Nader	Independent	465,650	0%
Michael Badnarik	Libertarian	397,265	0%
Michael A. Peroutka	Constitution	143,630	0%
David Cobb	Green	119,859	0%
Leonard Peltier	Peace and Freedom	27,607	0%
Walter F. Brown	Socialist/Natural Law	10,837	0%
James Harris	Socialist Workers	7,102	0%
Róger Calero	Socialist Workers	3,689	0%
Thomas J. Harens	Christian Freedom	2,387	0%
Bill Van Auken	Socialist Equality	1,944	0%
Gene Amondson	Concerns of People/Prohibition	1,857	0%
John Parker	Liberty Union	1,646	0%
Charles Jay	Personal Choice	946	0%
Stanford "Andy" E. Andress	Unaffiliated	804	0%
Earl F. Dodge	Prohibition	140	0%
None of the above	—	3,688	0%

SOURCE: www.fec.gov/pubrec/fe2004/federalelections2004.pdf

Party, with Henry Wallace as its candidate, drew nearly half its votes from the state of New York. The American Independent Party polled nearly 10 million popular votes and 45 electoral votes for George Wallace in 1968—the most electoral votes ever polled by a third-party candidate. But all of Wallace's electoral votes and the majority of his popular vote came from the states of the Deep South.

Americans usually assume that only the candidates nominated by one of the two major parties have any chance of winning an election. Thus, a vote cast for a third-party or independent candidate is often seen as a wasted vote. Thus, in 1996, many voters who favored Ross Perot gave their votes to Bob Dole or Bill Clinton on the presumption that Perot was not really electable.

As many scholars have pointed out, third-party prospects are also hampered by America's *single-member-district* plurality election system. In many other nations, several individuals can be elected to represent each legislative district. This is called a system of **multiple-member districts.** With this type of system, the candidates of weaker parties have a better chance of winning at least some seats. For their part, voters are less concerned about wasting ballots and usually more willing to support minor-party candidates.

Reinforcing the effects of the single-member district, plurality voting rules (as was noted in Chapter 10) generally have the effect of setting what could be called a high threshold for victory. To win a plurality race, candidates usually must secure many more votes than they would need under most European systems of proportional representation. For example, to win an American plurality election in a single-member district where there are only two candidates, a politician must win more than 50 percent of the votes cast. To win a seat from a European multiple-member district under proportional rules, a candidate may need to win only 15 or 20 percent of the votes cast. This high American threshold discourages minor parties and encourages the various political factions that might otherwise form minor parties to minimize their differences and remain within the major-party coalitions.

Voters tend to view support for a third-party candidate as a wasted vote. As a result, third-party candidates usually cannot muster the high number of votes required to win a single-member-district plurality system.

It would nevertheless be incorrect to assert (as some scholars have maintained) that America's single-member plurality election system is the major cause of our historical two-party pattern. All that can be said is that American election law depresses the number of parties likely to survive over long periods of time in the United States. There is no requirement that there be even two strong parties. Indeed, the single-member plurality system of election can also discourage second parties. After all, if one party consistently receives

a large plurality of the vote, people may eventually come to see their vote *even for the second party* as a wasted effort. This happened to the Republican Party in the Deep South before World War II.

Despite these obstacles, every presidential election brings out a host of minor-party hopefuls (see Table 11.1). Few survive until the next contest.

HOW STRONG ARE POLITICAL PARTIES TODAY?

Opposition to party politics was the basis for a number of the institutional reforms of the American political process at the turn of the twentieth century during the so-called Progressive Era. Many Progressive reformers were motivated by a sincere desire to rid politics of corruption and to improve the quality and efficiency of government in the United States. But simultaneously, from the perspective of middle- and upper-class Progressives and the financial, commercial, and industrial elites with which they were often associated, the weakening or elimination of party organization would also mean that power could more readily be acquired and retained by those with wealth, position, and education.

The list of antiparty reforms of the Progressive Era is a lengthy one. Ballot reform took away the parties' privilege of printing and distributing ballots and thus introduced the possibility of split-ticket voting. The introduction of nonpartisan local elections eroded grassroots party organization. The extension of "merit systems" for administrative appointments stripped party organizations of their vitally important access to patronage and thus reduced their ability to recruit workers. The development of the direct primary reduced party leaders' capacity to control candidate nominations. These reforms obviously did not destroy political parties as entities, but taken together they did substantially weaken party organizations in the United States.

After the turn of the century, the organizational strength of American political parties gradually diminished. Between the two world wars, organization remained the major tool available to contending electoral forces, but in most areas of the country the "reformed" state and local parties that survived the Progressive Era gradually lost their organizational vitality and coherence, and they became less effective campaign tools. While most areas of the nation continued to boast Democratic and Republican party groupings, reform meant the elimination of the long-running mass organizations that had been the parties' principal campaign weapons.

High-Tech Politics

As a result of Progressive reform, American party organizations entered the twentieth century with rickety substructures. As the use of civil service, primary elections, and other Progressive innovations spread, the strength of party organizations eroded. By the end of World War II, political scientists were already bemoaning the absence of party discipline and "party responsibility" in the United States. This erosion of the parties' organizational strength set the stage for the introduction of new political techniques that represented radical departures from the campaign practices perfected during the nineteenth century. In place of workers and organization, contending forces began to employ intricate electronic communications techniques to attract supporters. This new political technology includes six basic elements.

1. *Polling.* Surveys of voter opinion provide the information that candidates and their staffs use to craft campaign strategies. Candidates use polls to select issues, to assess their own strengths and weaknesses (as well as those of the opposition), to check voter response to the campaign, and to determine the degree to which various constituent groups are susceptible to campaign appeals. Virtually all contemporary campaigns for national and statewide office, as well as many local campaigns, make extensive use of opinion surveys. As we saw in Chapter 9, President Clinton used polling extensively both during and after the 1996 presidential election, using the results to shape his rhetoric and to guide his policy initiatives.

2. *The broadcast media.* Extensive use of the electronic media, television in particular, has become the hallmark of the modern political campaign. Generally, media campaigns attempt to follow the guidelines indicated by a candidate's polls, emphasizing issues and personal characteristics that appear important in the poll data.

The broadcast media are now so central to modern campaigns that most candidates' activities are tied to their media strategies.[9] Candidate activities are designed expressly to stimulate television news coverage. For instance, members of Congress running for reelection or for president almost always sponsor committee or subcommittee hearings to generate publicity.

3. *Phone banks.* Through the broadcast media, candidates communicate with voters en masse and impersonally. Phone banks, on the other hand, allow campaign workers to make personal contact with hundreds of thousands of voters. Personal contacts of this sort are thought to be extremely effective. Again, poll data serve to identify the groups that will be targeted for phone calls. Computers select phone numbers from areas in which members of these groups are concentrated. Staffs of paid or volunteer callers, using computer-assisted dialing systems and prepared scripts, place calls to deliver the candidate's message. The targeted groups are generally those identified by polls as either uncommitted or weakly committed to the candidate, or they may be strong supporters of the candidate who are contacted simply to encourage them to vote.

4. *Direct mail.* Direct mail serves both as a vehicle for communicating with voters and as a mechanism for raising funds. The first step in any direct-mail campaign is the purchase or rental of a computerized mailing list of voters deemed to have some particular perspective or social characteristic. Often sets of magazine subscription lists or lists of donors to various causes are employed. For example, a candidate interested in reaching conservative voters might rent subscription lists from the *National Review,* a candidate interested

---

[9]Larry J. Sabato, *The Rise of Political Consultants* (New York: Basic Books, 1981).

in appealing to liberals might rent subscription lists from the *New York Review of Books* or the *New Republic*. Considerable fine-tuning is possible. After obtaining the appropriate mailing lists, candidates usually send pamphlets, letters, and brochures describing themselves and their views to voters believed to be sympathetic. Different types of mail appeals are made to different electoral subgroups.

In addition to its use as a political advertising medium, direct mail has also become an important source of campaign funds. Computerized mailing lists permit campaign strategists to pinpoint individuals whose interests, background, and activities suggest that they may be potential donors to the campaign. Letters of solicitation are sent to these potential donors. Some of the money raised is then used to purchase additional mailing lists. Direct-mail solicitation can be enormously effective.[10]

5. *Professional public relations.* Modern campaigns and the complex technology upon which they rely are typically directed by professional public relations consultants. Virtually all serious contenders for national and statewide office retain the services of professional campaign consultants. Increasingly, candidates for local office, too, have come to rely upon professional campaign managers. Consultants offer candidates the expertise necessary to conduct accurate opinion polls, produce effective television commercials, organize direct-mail campaigns, and make use of sophisticated computer analyses.

6. *The Internet.* A more recent form of new technology has been the Internet. Most candidates for office set up a Web site as an inexpensive means to establish a public presence. The 1998 election saw increased use of the Internet by political candidates. Virtually all statewide candidates, as well as many candidates for Congress and local offices, developed Web sites providing contact information, press releases, speeches, photos, and information on how to volunteer, contact the candidate, or donate money to the campaign. During his campaign, Florida Governor Jeb Bush sold "Jebware,"

articles of clothing emblazoned with his name, through his Web site.

In 2000, the politician who made the most extensive use of the Internet was John McCain. McCain used his Web site to mobilize volunteers and to raise hundreds of thousands of dollars for his bid for the Republican presidential nomination. In the future, all politicians will use the Web to collect information about potential voters and supporters; this will, in turn, allow them to personalize direct mailings and telephone calls and develop direct e-mail advertising. One consultant now refers to politics on the Internet as "netwar," and asserts that "small, smart attackers" can defeat more powerful opponents in the new, information-age "battlespace."[11]

Thus far, the political impact of the Internet has been limited by the fact that, unlike a TV commercial that comes to viewers without any action on their part, a Web site requires citizens to take the initiative to visit it. In general, this means that only those already supporting a candidate are likely to visit the site, limiting its political utility. However, it may be possible to lure voters to Web sites through television advertising or through other online media. During the 2004 presidential primaries, Democratic hopeful Howard Dean made extensive use of the Internet as a communication and fund-raising tool. Thousands of bloggers maintained discussion forums that promoted Dean's candidacy and solicited funds. By the end of 2003, Dean had amassed a war chest of more than $15 million, much of it raised on the Internet, for his presidential bid. Dean Internet guru Joe Trippi hoped to persuade 2 million Americans to each give "one hundred dollars online," to match the funds President Bush was expected to accumulate through traditional fund-raising methods. In the general election, both Kerry and Bush used the Internet to raise money and mobilize voters. Liberal advocacy groups tied to the Democratic party, like Americans Coming Together, also made use of the Internet to boost voter registration among

[11]Dana Milbanks, "Virtual Politics," *New Republic*, 5 July 1999, p. 22.

HIGH-TECH POLITICS

Polling—Candidates use polls to select issues, to assess their own strengths and weaknesses, and to check voter response.

Broadcast media—Television spot ads are the most common use of television by candidates. Ads establish name recognition, communicate the candidate's stand on issues, and link the candidate to desirable groups in the community. The televised debate is another long-standing use of the media. New media techniques include the talk-show interview, the "electronic town hall" meeting, and the "infomercial."

Phone banks—Through phone banks, campaign workers make personal contact with hundreds of thousands of voters.

Direct mail—Direct mail serves as a fund-raising tool and as a means of communicating a candidate's ideas. The choice of mailing lists is very important.

Professional public relations—Professional campaign consultants offer expertise in how best to utilize the above-mentioned methods. Virtually all national and statewide candidates and more and more local political candidates rely on consultants.

Internet—Candidates use Web sites as a point of contact with voters.

young people and others thought to have Democratic leanings.

In recent years, the introduction of high-tech campaign techniques, including polls, broadcast media, phone banks, direct mail, professional public relations, and the Internet has transformed the role of the parties during the general campaign.

The number of technologically oriented campaigns increased greatly after 1971. The Federal Elections Campaign Act of 1972 prompted the creation of large numbers of political action committees (PACs) by a host of corporate and ideological groups. This development increased the availability of funds to political candidates, which meant in turn that the new technology could be used more extensively.

Initially, the new techniques were employed mainly by individual candidates who often made little or no effort to coordinate their campaigns with those of other political aspirants sharing the same party label. For this reason, campaigns employing the new technology sometimes came to be called "candidate-centered" efforts, as distinguished from the traditional party-coordinated campaign. Nothing about technology, however, precluded its use by political party leaders seeking to coordinate a number of campaigns. In recent years, party leaders—Republicans in particular—have learned to make good use of modern campaign technology. The difference between the old and new political methods is not that the latter is inherently candidate-centered while the former is strictly a party tool. Rather, the difference is a matter of the types of political resources upon which each method depends.

With the new political techniques, the party organization became less important, resulting in a shift from labor-intensive to capital-intensive campaigns. Campaign tasks once performed by masses of party workers and moderate funding now require fewer personnel but a great deal more money. The new political campaign depends on polls, computers, and other electronic paraphernalia. Nevertheless, parties remain important as providers of money, resources, and expertise.

The enormous cost of new political techniques means that modern campaigns depend heavily upon money.

Contemporary Party Organizations

In the United States, party organizations exist at virtually every level of government (see Figure 11.3). These organizations are usually committees made up of a number of active party members.

State law and party rules prescribe how such committees are constituted. Usually, committee members are elected at local party meetings—called *caucuses*—or as part of the regular primary election. The best-known examples of these committees are at the national level—the Democratic National Committee and the Republican National Committee.

NATIONAL CONVENTION   At the national level, the party's most important institution is the quadrennial national convention. The convention is attended by delegates from each of the states; as a group, they nominate the party's presidential and vice-presidential candidates, draft the party's campaign platform for the presidential race, and approve changes in the rules and regulations gov-

FIGURE 11.3

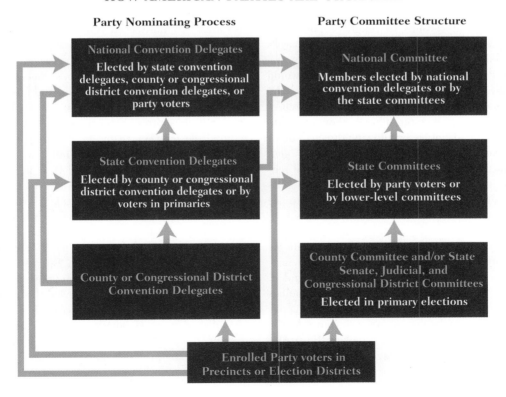

HOW AMERICAN PARTIES ARE ORGANIZED

Party Nominating Process	Party Committee Structure
National Convention Delegates Elected by state convention delegates, county or congressional district convention delegates, or party voters	**National Committee** Members elected by national convention delegates or by the state committees
State Convention Delegates Elected by county or congressional district convention delegates or by voters in primaries	**State Committees** Elected by party voters or by lower-level committees
County or Congressional District Convention Delegates	**County Committee and/or State Senate, Judicial, and Congressional District Committees** Elected in primary elections

Enrolled Party voters in Precincts or Election Districts

erning party procedures. Before World War II, presidential nominations occupied most of the time, energy, and effort expended at the national convention. The nomination process required days of negotiation and compromise among state party leaders and often required many ballots before a nominee was selected. In recent years, however, presidential candidates have essentially nominated themselves by winning enough delegate support in primary elections to win the official nomination on the first ballot. The actual convention has played little or no role in selecting the candidates.

The convention's other two tasks, establishing the party's rules and platform, remain important. Party rules can determine the relative influence of competing factions within the party and can also increase or decrease the party's chances for electoral success. In 1972, for example, the Democratic National Convention adopted a new set of rules favored by the party's liberal wing. Under these rules, state delegations to the Democratic convention were required to include women and members of minority groups in rough proportion to those groups' representation among the party's membership in that state. Liberals correctly calculated that women and African Americans would generally support liberal ideas and candidates. The rules also called for the use of proportional representation—a voting system liberals thought would give them an advantage by allowing the election of more women and minority delegates. (Although Republican rules do not require proportional representation for selecting delegates, some state legislatures have moved to compel both parties to use this system in all their presidential primaries.)

The convention also approves the party platform. Platforms are often dismissed as documents filled with platitudes that are seldom read by voters. To some extent this criticism is well founded. Not one voter in a thousand so much as glances at the party platform, and even the news media pay little attention to the documents. Furthermore, the parties' presidential candidates make little use of the platforms in their campaigns; usually they prefer to develop and promote their own themes.

Occasionally, nominees even disavow their party's platform. In 1864, for example, Democratic presidential nominee General George McClellan repudiated his party's peace platform. Nonetheless, the platform can be an important document. The platform should be understood as a contract in which the various party factions attending the convention state their terms for supporting the ticket. For one faction, welfare reform may be a key issue. For another faction, tax reduction may be more important. For a third, the critical issue may be deficit reduction. When one of these "planks" is included in the platform, its promoters are asserting that this is what they want in exchange for their support of the ticket, while other party factions are agreeing that the position seems reasonable and appropriate.

NATIONAL COMMITTEE   Between conventions, each national political party is technically headed by its national committee. For the Democrats and Republicans, these are called the Democratic National Committee (DNC) and the Republican National Committee (RNC), respectively. These national committees raise campaign funds, head off factional disputes within the party, and endeavor to enhance the party's media image. Since 1972, the size of staff and the amount of money raised have increased substantially for both national committees. The work of each national committee is overseen by its chairperson. Other committee members are generally major party contributors or fund-raisers and serve in a largely ceremonial capacity. Prior to the enactment of campaign finance reforms in 2002, during every election cycle the DNC and RNC each raised tens of millions of dollars of so-called soft money that could be used to support party candidates throughout the nation. The 2002 Bipartisan Campaign Reform Act (BCRA), sometimes known as the McCain-Feingold Act, outlawed this practice. To circumvent BCRA, however, each party has established a set of "shadow parties." These are groups nominally unaffiliated with parties and organized to promote and publicize political issues. As such, they can claim tax-exempt status under Section 527 of the Internal Revenue Code, which defines and provides tax-exempt status for nonprofit political advocacy groups. Such groups are sometimes called **527 *committees*** because of this provision of the tax code.

Under the law, 527 committees can raise and spend unlimited amounts of money as long as their activities are not coordinated with those of the formal party organizations. While some 527 committees are actually independent, many are directed by former Republican and Democratic party officials and run shadow campaigns on behalf of the parties. On the Republican side, a major shadow is the Republican Club for Growth, which raises and spends millions of dollars for GOP television ads. Democratic shadows include such groups as Americans Coming Together (ACT) and the Media Fund, which together raised tens of millions of dollars in support of Senator John Kerry's presidential bid. In a recent decision, the Federal Election Commission (FEC) affirmed the legality of unlimited spending by 527 committees.[12]

For the party that controls the White House, the national committee chair is appointed by the president. Typically, this means that that party's national committee becomes little more than an adjunct to the White House staff. For a first-term president, the committee devotes the bulk of its energy to the re-election campaign. The national committee chair of the party not in control of the White House is selected by the committee itself and usually takes a broader view of the party's needs, raising money and performing other activities on behalf of the party's members in Congress and in the state legislatures.

CONGRESSIONAL CAMPAIGN COMMITTEES Each party forms House and Senate campaign committees to raise funds for House and Senate election campaigns. Their efforts may or may not be coordinated with the activities of the national committees. For the party that controls the White

House, the national committee and the congressional campaign committees are often rivals since both groups are seeking donations from the same people but for different candidates: The national committee seeks funds for the presidential race while the congressional campaign committees approach the same contributors for support for the congressional contests. In recent years, the Republican Party has attempted to coordinate the fund-raising activities of all its committees. Republicans have sought to give the GOP's national institutions the capacity to invest funds in those close congressional, state, and local races where they can do the most good. The Democrats have been slower to coordinate their various committee activities, and this may have placed them at a disadvantage in recent congressional and local races. The efforts of the parties to centralize and coordinate fund-raising activities have helped bring about greater party unity in Congress. As members have come to rely upon the leadership for campaign funds, they have become more likely to vote with the leadership on major issues.

All in all, campaign committees have begun to resemble large-scale campaign consulting firms, hiring full-time political operatives and evolving into professional organizations.

STATE AND LOCAL PARTY ORGANIZATIONS Each of the two major parties has a central committee in each state. The parties traditionally also have county committees and, in some instances, state senate district committees, judicial district committees, and, in the case of larger cities, citywide party committees and local assembly district "ward" committees as well. Congressional districts also may have party committees.

Some cities also have precinct committees. Precincts are not districts from which any representative is elected but instead are legally defined subdivisions of wards that are used to register voters and set up ballot boxes or voting machines. A precinct is typically composed of three hundred to six hundred voters. Well-organized political parties—especially the famous old machines of New York, Chicago, and Boston—provide for

---

[12]Glen Justice, "F.E.C. Declines to Curb Independent Fund Raisers," *New York Times,* 14 May 2004, p. A16.

"precinct captains" and a fairly tight group of party members around them. Precinct captains were usually members of long standing in neighborhood party clubhouses, which were important social centers as well as places for distributing favors to constituents. But few, if any, machines are left today.

Nevertheless, state and local party organizations are very active in recruiting candidates and conducting voter registration drives. Under current federal law, state and local party organizations can spend unlimited amounts of money on "party-building" activities such as voter registration and get-out-the-vote drives (though in some states such practices are limited by state law). As a result, for many years the national party organizations, which have enormous fund-raising abilities but were restricted by law in how much they could spend on candidates, transferred millions of dollars to the state and local organizations. The state and local parties, in turn, spent these funds, sometimes called soft money, to promote the candidacies of national, as well as state and local, candidates. In this process, as local organizations have become linked financially to the national parties, American political parties became somewhat more integrated and nationalized than ever before. At the same time, the state and local party organizations came to control large financial resources and play important roles in elections despite the collapse of the old patronage machines.[13]

THE CONTEMPORARY PARTY AS SERVICE PROVIDER TO CANDIDATES   Party leaders have adapted parties to the modern age. Parties as organizations are more professional, better financed, and more organized than ever before.[14] Political scientists argue that parties have evolved into "service organizations," which, though they

no longer hold a monopoly over campaigns, still provide services to candidates, without which it would be extremely difficult for candidates to win and hold office. Parties have not declined but have simply adapted to serve the interests of political actors.[15]

Many politicians, however, are able to raise funds, attract volunteers, and win office without much help from local party organizations. Once in office, these politicians often refuse to submit to party discipline; instead they steer independent courses. They are often supported by voters who see independence as a virtue and party discipline as "boss rule." Analysts refer to this pattern as a "candidate-centered" politics to distinguish it from a political process in which parties are the dominant forces. The problem with a candidate-centered politics is that it tends to be associated with low turnout, high levels of special-interest influence, and a lack of effective decision making. In short, many of the problems that have plagued American politics in recent years can be traced directly to the independence of American voters and politicians and the candidate-centered nature of American national politics.

The Role of the Parties in Contemporary Politics

Political parties make democratic government possible. We often do not appreciate that democratic government is a contradiction in terms. Government implies policies, programs, and decisive action. Democracy, on the other hand, implies an opportunity for all citizens to participate fully in the governmental process. The contradiction is that full participation by everyone is often inconsistent with getting anything done. At what point should participation stop and governance begin? How can we make certain that popular participation will result in a government capable of making decisions and developing needed policies? The problem of democratic government is especially

[13]For a useful discussion, see John Bibby and Thomas Holbrook, "Parties and Elections," in *Politics in the American States: A Comparative Analysis*, eds. Virginia Gray and Herbert Jacob, 6th ed. (Washington, DC: Congressional Quarterly Press, 1996), pp. 78–121.

[14]See John H. Aldrich, *Why Parties? The Origin and Transformation of Party Politics in America* (Chicago: University of Chicago Press, 1995), Chapter 8.

[15]See Paul S. Herrnson, *Party Campaigning in the 1980s* (Cambridge: Harvard University Press, 1988).

acute in the United States because of the system of separated powers bequeathed to us by the Constitution's framers. Our system of separated powers means that it is very difficult to link popular participation and effective decision making. Often, after the citizens have spoken and the dust has settled, no single set of political forces has been able to win control of enough of the scattered levers of power to actually do anything. Instead of government, we have a continual political struggle.

Strong political parties are a partial antidote to the inherent contradiction between participation and government. Strong parties can both encourage popular involvement and convert participation into effective government. More than fifty years ago, a committee of the academic American Political Science Association (APSA) called for the development of a more "responsible" party government. By *responsible party government,* the committee meant political parties that mobilized voters and were sufficiently well organized to develop and implement coherent programs and policies after the election. Strong parties can link democratic participation and government.

Although they are significant factors in politics and government, American political parties today are not as strong as the "responsible parties" advocated by the APSA. Can political parties be strengthened? The answer is, in principle, yes. For example, political parties could be strengthened if the rules governing campaign finance were revised to make candidates more dependent financially upon state and local party organizations rather than on personal resources or private contributors. Such a reform, to be sure, would require more strict regulation of party fund-raising practices to prevent soft money abuses. The potential benefit, however, of a greater party role in political finance could be substantial. If parties controlled the bulk of the campaign funds, they would become more coherent and disciplined, and might come to resemble the responsible parties envisioned by the APSA. In 2002, Congress enacted campaign finance reforms that diminished the role of the national party organizations in financing campaigns. Time will tell what consequences will be brought about by this change. Political parties have

been such important features of American democratic politics that we need to think long and hard about how to preserve and strengthen them.

Political parties make democratic government possible. Parties could be strengthened through effective campaign finance reform.

CHAPTER REVIEW

Political parties seek to control government by controlling its personnel. Elections are their means to this end. Thus, parties take shape from the electoral process. The formal principle of party organization is this: For every district in which an election is held—from the entire nation to the local county or precinct—there should be some kind of party unit.

The two-party system dominates U.S. politics. Today, on individual issues, the two parties differ little from each other. In general, however, Democrats lean more to the left on issues and Republicans lean more to the right. Even though party affiliation means less to Americans than it once did, partisanship remains important. What ticket-splitting there is occurs mainly at the national level between Congress and the presidency.

Voters' choices have had particularly significant consequences during periods of critical electoral realignment. During these periods, which have occurred roughly every thirty years, new electoral coalitions have formed, new groups have come to power, and important institutional and policy changes have occurred. The last such critical period was associated with Franklin Roosevelt's New Deal.

Third parties are short-lived for several reasons. They have limited electoral support, the tradition of the two-party system is strong, and a major party often adopts their platforms. Single-member districts with two competing parties also discourage third parties.

Nominating and electing are the basic functions of parties. Originally nominations were made in party caucuses, and individuals who ran as independents had a difficult time getting on the ballot. In the 1830s, dissatisfaction with the cliquish caucuses led to nominating conventions. In 2002, Congress enacted campaign finance reforms that diminished the role of the national party organizations in financing campaigns. Time will tell what consequences will be brought about by this change. Although these ended the "King Caucus" that controlled the nomination of the presidential candidates, and thereby gave the presidency a popular base, they too proved unsatisfactory. Primaries have now more or less replaced the conventions. There are both closed and open primaries. Closed primaries are more supportive of strong political parties than open primaries. Contested primaries sap party strength and financial resources, but they nonetheless serve to resolve important social conflicts and recognize new interest groups. Winning at the top of a party ticket usually depends on the party regulars at the bottom getting out the vote.

At all levels, the mass communications media are important. Mass mailings, too, are vital in campaigning. Thus, campaign funds are crucial to success.

Congress is organized around the two-party system. The House speakership is a party office. Parties determine the makeup of congressional committees, including their chairs, which are no longer based entirely on seniority.

In recent years, the role of parties in political campaigns has been partially supplanted by the use of new political technologies. These include polling, the broadcast media, phone banks, direct-mail fund-raising and advertising, professional public relations, and the Internet. These techniques are enormously expensive and have led to a shift from labor-intensive to capital-intensive politics. This shift works to the advantage of political forces representing the well-to-do. The parties currently have also entrenched themselves in government agencies and sectors of the national economy.

KEY TERMS

caucus (political)   A normally closed meeting of a political or legislative group to select candidates, plan strategy, or make decisions regarding legislative matters.

closed primary   A primary election in which voters can participate in the nomination of candidates, but only of the party in which they are enrolled for a period of time prior to primary day.

divided government   The condition in American government wherein the presidency is controlled by one party while the opposing party controls one or both houses of Congress.

electoral realignment   The point in history when a new party supplants the ruling party, becoming in turn the dominant political force. In the United States, this has tended to occur roughly every thirty years.

527 committees   Nonprofit independent groups that receive and disburse funds to influence the nomination, election, or defeat of candidates. Named after Section 527 of the Internal Revenue Code, which defines and provides tax-exempt status for nonprofit advocacy groups.

majority party   The party that holds the majority of legislative seats in either the House or the Senate.

multiple-member district   An electorate that selects all candidates at large from the whole district; each voter is given the number of votes equivalent to the number of seats to be filled.

nomination   The process through which political parties select their candidate for election to public office.

open primary   A primary election in which the voter can wait until the day of the primary to choose which party to enroll in to select candidates for the general election.

party identity   An individual voter's psychological ties to one party or another.

policy entrepreneur   An individual who identifies a problem as a political issue and brings a policy proposal into the political agenda.

political parties   Organized groups that attempt to influence the government by electing their members to important government offices.

responsible party government A set of principles that idealizes a strong role for parties in defining their stance on issues, mobilizing voters, and fulfilling their campaign promises once in office.

single-member district An electorate that is allowed to elect only one representative from each district; the normal method of representation in the United States.

third parties Parties that organize to compete against the two major American political parties.

FOR FURTHER READING

Aldrich, John H. *Why Parties?: The Origin and Transformation of Party Politics in America*. Chicago: University of Chicago Press, 1995.

Chambers, William N., and Walter Dean Burnham. *The American Party Systems: Stages of Political Development*. New York: Oxford University Press, 1975.

Coleman, John J. *Party Decline in America: Policy, Politics, and the Fiscal State*. Princeton: Princeton University Press, 1996.

Hofstadter, Richard. *The Idea of a Party System: The Rise of Legitimate Opposition in the United States, 1780–1840*. Berkeley: University of California Press, 1969.

Kayden, Xandra, and Eddie Mahe, Jr. *The Party Goes On: The Persistence of the Two-Party System in the United States*. New York: Basic Books, 1985.

Lawson, Kay, and Peter Merkl. *When Parties Fail: Emerging Alternative Organizations*. Princeton: Princeton University Press, 1988.

Milkis, Sidney. *The Presidency and the Parties: The Transformation of the American Party System since the New Deal*. New York: Oxford University Press, 1993.

Polsby, Nelson W. *Consequences of Party Reform*. New York: Oxford University Press, 1983.

Sabato, Larry. *PAC Power*. New York: Norton, 1984.

Sabato, Larry. *The Rise of Political Consultants*. New York: Basic Books, 1981.

Shafer, Byron, ed. *Beyond Realignment: Interpreting American Electoral Eras*. Madison: University of Wisconsin Press, 1991.

Sorauf, Frank J. *Party Politics in America*. Boston: Little, Brown, 1984.

Sundquist, James. *Dynamics of the Party System*. Washington, DC: Brookings Institution, 1983.

Wattenberg, Martin. *The Decline in American Political Parties, 1952–1988*. Cambridge: Harvard University Press, 1989.

CHAPTER 12

Groups and Interests

HOW DO INTEREST GROUPS WORK?

*F*or more than two decades, lobbyists for senior citizens, led by the AARP (formerly called the American Association of Retired Persons), have sought to add a prescription drug benefit to the Medicare program on which most seniors depend for their health care. Many members of Congress have opposed such a benefit because it would cost hundreds of billions of dollars. The pharmaceutical industry also feared that such a Medicare prescription plan would open the way for government regulation of drug prices as well as other aspects of the industry. Through its political arm, the Pharmaceutical Research and Manufacturers of America (PhRMA), the pharmaceutical industry is one of the most powerful lobby groups in Washington. Drug company executives and corporate PACs have contributed more than $60 million to political campaigns since 2000, and a number of drug industry lobbyists and executives were major donors to and fund-raisers for George W. Bush's presidential campaign. The drug industry's political clout was, for years, an enormous impediment to the enactment of a Medicare prescription drug plan.

By the early 2000s, however, the industry had begun to face a number of economic and political problems. To begin with, the high prices charged for prescription drugs were producing enormous pressure in Congress to reduce the patent protection enjoyed by drug company products; this would allow

CORE OF THE ANALYSIS

- Interest groups are organized to influence government decisions.
- Interest groups have proliferated over the last thirty years as a result of the expansion of the federal government and the "New Politics" movement.
- Interest groups use various strategies to promote their goals, including lobbying, gaining access to key decision makers, using the courts, going public, and influencing electoral politics.
- Though interest groups sometimes promote public concerns, they more often represent narrow interests.

cheaper generic drugs to enter the marketplace more rapidly. Second, many consumers had discovered that they could purchase drugs in Canada and Europe for as much as 75 percent less than what they cost in the United States. These foreign purchases, while illegal, are difficult to monitor and are costing the drug companies millions of dollars in profits. Finally, growing numbers of senior citizens were not able to afford their prescription drugs at all and so were simply not buying medicine—another source of lost profit for the industry.

In the face of these problems, PhRMA changed its lobbying strategy. Rather than continue to resist a Medicare drug plan, the industry moved to craft a plan of its own. In 2002, the pharmaceutical

CENTRAL QUESTIONS

- **The Character of Interest Groups**
  Why do interest groups form?
  What interests are represented by these groups?
  What are the organizational components of interest groups?
  What are the benefits of interest-group membership?
  What are the characteristics of interest-group members?

- **The Proliferation of Groups**
  Why has the number of interest groups grown in recent years?
  What is the "New Politics" movement?

- **Strategies: The Quest for Political Power**
  What are some of the strategies interest groups use to gain influence?
  What are the purposes of these strategies?

- **Do Interest Groups Work?**
  What are the problems involved in curbing the influence of interest groups?

industry formed an alliance with several other health industry groups, including nursing home and hospital interests, to develop a new Medicare bill. The AARP had a number of misgivings about the bill but lent its support, calculating that once a law was enacted, the "senior lobby" could secure favorable amendments over the ensuing years. The resulting legislation, enacted by Congress in November 2003, after the drug industry spent nearly $40 million lobbying on its behalf, appeared to be perfectly tailored to suit the industry's needs. Under the new plan, Medicare will subsidize drug purchases for all seniors who agree to pay a modest monthly fee. The plan prohibits the government from attempting to force the companies to lower drug prices, leaves in place the ban on imported drugs, and does not address the issue of generic drugs. Once in place in 2006, the Medicare prescription plan is expected to lead to substantially higher drug purchases and to increase industry profits by as much as $13 billion a year at a cost of tens of billions of dollars a year to the federal treasury.[1] PhRMA's nursing home and hospital allies also won favorable treatment under the plan.[2] Seniors at long last will get their drug plan but in a form that will cost the nation an enormous amount of money, funds that will be transferred from the pockets of taxpayers into the coffers of an already fabulously wealthy industry.

The framers of the Constitution feared the power that could be wielded by organized interests. Yet they believed that interest groups thrived because of freedom—the freedom that all Americans enjoyed to organize and express their views. To the framers, this problem presented a dilemma—indeed, the dilemma of freedom versus power that is central to our text. If the government were given the power to regulate or in any way to forbid efforts by organized interests to interfere in the political process, the government would in effect have been given the power to suppress freedom. The solution to this dilemma was presented by James Madison:

> . . . Take in a greater variety of parties and interest [and] you make it less probable that a majority of the whole will have a common motive to invade the rights of other citizens. . . . [Hence the advantage] enjoyed by a large over a small republic.[3]

According to Madisonian theory, a good constitution encourages multitudes of interests so that no single interest can ever tyrannize the others. The

[1]Ceci Connolly, "Drugmakers Protect Their Turf," *Washington Post,* 21 November 2003, p. A4.
[2]Thomas B. Edsall, "2 Bills Would Benefit Top Bush Fundraisers," *Washington Post,* 22 November 2003, p. 1.

[3]Clinton Rossiter, ed., *The Federalist Papers* (New York: New American Library, 1961), No. 10, p. 83.

basic assumption is that competition among interests will produce balance and compromise, with all the interests regulating each other.[4] Today, this Madisonian principle is called *pluralism.*

Madison's theory of pluralism holds that free competition among interest groups results in balance and compromise.

There are tens of thousands of organized groups in the United States, ranging from civic associations to huge nationwide groups such as the National Rifle Association, whose chief cause is opposition to restrictions on gun ownership, or Common Cause, a public interest group that advocates a variety of liberal political reforms. The huge number of interest groups competing for influence in the United States, however, does not mean that all *interests* are fully and equally represented in the American political process. As we shall see, the political deck is heavily stacked in favor of those interests able to organize and to wield substantial economic, social, and institutional resources on behalf of their cause. This means that within the universe of interest-group politics it is political power—not some abstract conception of the public good—that is likely to prevail. Moreover, this means that interest-group politics, taken as a whole, is a political format that works more to the advantage of some types of interests than others. In general, politics in which interest groups predominate is politics with a distinctly upper-class bias (see Concept Map 12.1).

In this chapter, we will examine some of the antecedents and consequences of interest-group politics in the United States. First, we will seek to understand the character of the interests promoted by interest groups. Second, we will assess the growth of interest-group activity in recent American political history, including the emergence of "public interest" groups. Finally, we will review and evaluate the strategies that competing groups use in their struggle for influence.

[4]Ibid.

THE CHARACTER OF INTEREST GROUPS

An *interest group* is an organized group of people that makes policy-related appeals to government. This definition of interest groups includes membership organizations but also businesses, corporations, universities, and other institutions that do not accept members. Individuals form groups in order to increase the chance that their views will be heard and their interests treated favorably by the government. Interest groups are organized to influence governmental decisions.

Interest groups are groups of individuals that share a common set of goals and have joined together in an effort to persuade the government to adopt policies that will help them.

Interest groups are sometimes referred to as "lobbies." Interest groups are also sometimes confused with political action committees, which are actually groups that focus on influencing elections rather than trying to influence the elected. One final distinction that we should make is that interest groups are also different from political parties: interest groups tend to concern themselves with the *policies* of government; parties tend to concern themselves with the *personnel* of government.

There are an enormous number of interest groups in the United States, and millions of Americans are members of one or more groups, at least to the extent of paying dues or attending an occasional meeting. By representing the interests of such large numbers of people and encouraging political participation, organized groups can and do enhance American democracy. Organized groups educate their members about issues that affect them. Groups lobby members of Congress and the executive, engage in litigation, and generally represent their members' interests in the political

INTEREST GROUP PLURALISM

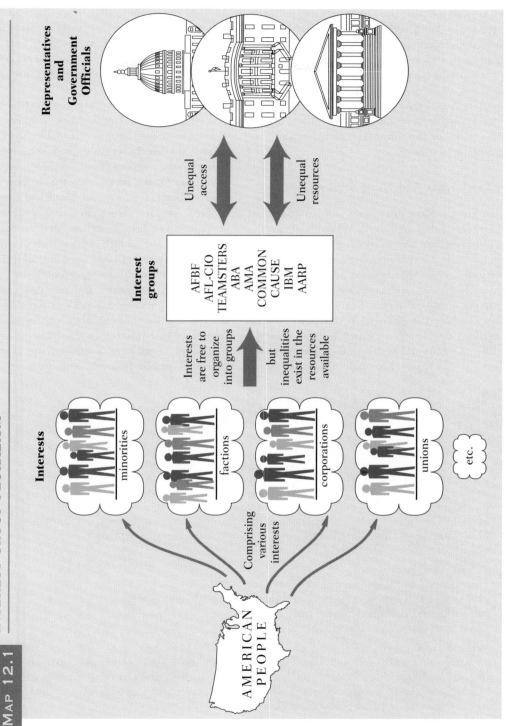

Interests

minorities

factions

corporations

unions

etc.

AMERICAN PEOPLE

Comprising various interests

Interests are free to organize into groups

but inequalities exist in the resources available

Interest groups

AFBF
AFL-CIO
TEAMSTERS
ABA
AMA
COMMON CAUSE
IBM
AARP

Unequal access

Unequal resources

Representatives and Government Officials

arena. Groups mobilize their members for elections and grassroots lobbying efforts, thus encouraging participation. Interest groups also monitor government programs to make certain that their members are not adversely affected by these programs. In all these ways, organized interests can be said to promote democratic policies. But because not all interests are represented equally, interest-group politics works to the advantage of some and the disadvantage of others.

What Interests Are Represented

Interest groups come in as many shapes and sizes as the interests they represent. When most people think about interest groups, they immediately think of groups with a direct economic interest in governmental actions. These groups are generally supported by groups of producers or manufacturers in a particular economic sector. Examples of this type of group include the National Petroleum Refiners Association, the American Farm Bureau Federation, and the National Federation of Independent Business, which represents small business owners.

At the same time that broadly representative groups like these are active in Washington, specific companies, like Disney, Shell Oil, International Business Machines, and General Motors, may be active on certain issues that are of particular concern to them.

Labor organizations are equally active lobbyists. The AFL-CIO, the United Mine Workers, and the Teamsters are all groups that lobby on behalf of organized labor. In recent years, lobbies have arisen to further the interests of public employees, the most significant among these being the American Federation of State, County, and Municipal Employees.

Professional lobbies like the American Bar Association and the American Medical Association have been particularly successful in furthering their own interests in state and federal legislatures. Financial institutions, represented by organizations like the American Bankers Association and the National Savings & Loan League, although frequently less visible than other lobbies, also play an important role in shaping legislative policy.

Recent years have witnessed the growth of a powerful *"**public interest**"* lobby purporting to rep-

---

IN BRIEF BOX

THE CHARACTER OF INTEREST GROUPS

What Interests Are Represented
   Economic interests—American Farm Bureau Federation
   Labor organizations—AFL-CIO, United Mine Workers, Teamsters
   Professional lobbies—American Bar Association, American Medical Association
   Financial institutions—American Bankers Association, National Savings & Loan League
   Public interest groups—Common Cause, Union of Concerned Scientists
   Public sector lobby—National League of Cities

Organizational Components
   Attracting and keeping members
   Fund-raising to support their infrastructure and their lobbying efforts
   Leadership and decision-making structure
   Agency that carries out the group's tasks

Characteristics of Members
   Interest groups tend to attract members from the middle and upper-middle classes because these people are more likely to have the time, the money, and the inclination to take part in such associations. People from less advantaged socioeconomic groups need to be organized on the massive scale of political parties.

resent interests whose concerns are not likely to be addressed by traditional lobbies. These groups have been most visible in the consumer protection and environmental policy areas, although public interest groups cover a broad range of issues. The National Resources Defense Council, the Union of Concerned Scientists, and Common Cause are all examples of public interest groups.

The perceived need for representation on Capitol Hill has generated a public sector lobby in the past several years, including the National League of Cities and the "research" lobby. The latter group comprises think tanks and universities that have an interest in obtaining government funds for research and support, and it includes such prestigious institutions as Harvard University, the Brookings Institution, and the American Enterprise Institute. Indeed, many universities have expanded their lobbying efforts even as they have reduced faculty positions and course offerings and increased tuition.[5]

Many different kinds of interest groups exist, representing a diverse set of issues.

Organizational Components

Although there are many interest groups, most share certain key organizational components. First and most important, all groups must attract and keep members. Somehow, groups must persuade individuals to invest the money, time, energy, or effort required to take part in the group's activities. Members play a larger role in some groups than in others. In *membership associations*, group members actually serve on committees and engage in projects. In the case of labor unions, members may march on picket lines, and in the case of political or ideological groups, members may participate in demonstrations and protests. In another set of groups, *staff organizations,* a professional staff conducts most of the group's activities; members

are called on only to pay dues and make other contributions. Among the well-known public interest groups, some—such as the National Organization for Women (NOW)—are membership groups; others—such as Defenders of Wildlife and the Children's Defense Fund—are staff organizations.

Usually, groups appeal to members not only by promoting political goals or policies they favor but also by offering them direct *informational, material,* or *social benefits* (see Table 12.1). Thus, for example, the AARP, which promotes the interests of senior citizens, offers members information, insurance benefits, and commercial discounts. In many organizations information is provided through conferences, training programs, and newsletters and other periodicals sent automatically to those who have paid membership dues. Material benefits can be discount purchasing, shared advertising, and perhaps most valuable of all, health and retirement insurance. Another benefit that can attract members is social interaction, networking, and good fellowship. Thus, the local chapters of many national groups provide their members with a congenial social environment while collecting dues that finance the national office's political efforts. Among these social benefits is one that has become extremely important: "consciousness-raising." Many women's organizations claim that active participation conveys to each member of the organization an enhanced sense of her own value and a stronger ability to advance individual as well as collective civil rights. A similar psychological benefit has been an important appeal to African Americans in groups of particular interest to them.

Another kind of benefit involves the appeal of an interest group's purpose. The best examples of such *purposive benefits* are those of religious interest groups. The Christian Right is made up of a number of interest groups that offer virtually no material benefits to their members, depending almost entirely on the religious identifications and affirmations of their members. Many religion-based interest groups have arisen throughout American history, such as those that drove abolition and prohibition.

The second component shared by all groups is that every one must build a financial structure capa-

[5]Betsy Wagner and David Bowermaster, "B.S. Economics," *Washington Monthly* (November 1992), pp. 19–22.

TABLE 12.1	

SELECTIVE BENEFITS OF INTEREST GROUP MEMBERSHIP

Category	Benefits
Informational benefits	Conferences Professional contacts Training programs Publications Coordination among organizations Research Legal help Professional codes Collective bargaining
Material benefits	Travel packages Insurance Discounts on consumer goods
Social benefits	Friendship Networking opportunities
Purposive benefits	Advocacy Representation before government Participation in public affairs

SOURCE: Adapted from Jack Walker, Jr., *Mobilizing Interest Groups in America: Patrons, Professions, and Social Movements* (Ann Arbor: University of Michigan Press, 1991), p. 86.

ble of sustaining an organization and funding the group's activities. Most interest groups rely on annual membership dues and voluntary contributions from sympathizers. Many also sell some ancillary services, such as insurance and vacation tours, to members.

Third, every group must have a leadership and decision-making structure. For some groups, this structure is very simple. For others, it can be quite elaborate and involve hundreds of local chapters that are melded into a national apparatus.

Last, most groups include an agency that actually carries out the group's tasks. This may be a research organization, a public relations office, or a lobbying office in Washington or a state capital.

The "Free Rider" Problem

Whether organizations need individuals to volunteer or merely to write checks, all must recruit and retain members. Yet many groups find this difficult, even with regards to those who agree strongly with the group's goals. The reason is because, as economist Mancur Olson explains, the benefits of a group's success are often broadly available and cannot be denied to nonmembers.[6] Such benefits can be called **collective goods.** This term is usually associated with certain government benefits, but it can also be applied to beneficial outcomes of interest-group activity.

Following Olson's theory, suppose a number of private property owners live near a mosquito-infested swamp. Each owner wants this swamp cleared. But if one or a few of the owners were to clear the swamp alone, their actions would benefit all the other owners as well, without any effort on the part of those other owners. Each of the inac-

[6]Mancur Olson, *The Logic of Collective Action* (Cambridge, MA: Harvard University Press, 1971).

tive owners would be a *free rider* on the efforts of the ones who cleared the swamp. Thus, there is a disincentive for any of the owners to undertake the job alone.

Since the number of concerned owners is small in this particular case, they might eventually be able to organize themselves to share the costs as well as enjoy the benefits of clearing the swamp. But suppose the numbers of interested people are increased. Suppose the common concern is not the neighborhood swamp but polluted air or groundwater involving thousands of residents in a region, or in fact millions of residents in a whole nation. National defense is the most obvious collective good whose benefits are shared by every resident, regardless of the taxes they pay or the support they provide. As the number of involved persons increases, or as the size of the group increases, the free rider phenomenon becomes more of a problem. Individuals do not have much incentive to become active members and supporters of a group that is already working more or less on their behalf. The group would no doubt be more influential if all concerned individuals were active members—if there were no free riders. But groups will not reduce their efforts just because free riders get the same benefits as dues-paying activists. In fact, groups may try even harder precisely because there are free riders, with the hope that the free riders will be encouraged to join in.

The Characteristics of Members

Membership in interest groups is not randomly distributed in the population. People with higher incomes, higher levels of education, and management or professional occupations are much more likely to become members of groups than those who occupy lower rungs on the socioeconomic ladder.[7] Well-educated, upper-income business and professional people are more likely to have the time and the money, and to have acquired through the educational process the concerns and skills needed

to play a role in a group or association. Moreover, for business and professional people, group membership may provide personal contacts and access to information that can help advance their careers. At the same time, of course, corporate entities—businesses and the like—usually have ample resources to form or participate in groups that seek to advance their causes.

The result is that interest-group politics in the United States tends to have a very pronounced upper-class bias. Certainly, there are many interest groups and political associations that have a working-class or lower-class membership—labor organizations or welfare-rights organizations, for example—but the great majority of interest groups and their members are drawn from the middle and upper-middle classes. In general, the "interests" served by interest groups are the interests of society's "haves." Even when interest groups take opposing positions on issues and policies, the conflicting positions they espouse usually reflect divisions among upper-income strata rather than conflicts between the upper and lower classes.

Interest groups tend to be composed of people with higher incomes and higher levels of education.

In general, to obtain adequate political representation, forces from the bottom rungs of the socioeconomic ladder must be organized on the massive scale associated with political parties. Parties can organize and mobilize the collective energies of large numbers of people who, as individuals, may have very limited resources. Interest groups, on the other hand, generally organize smaller numbers of the better-to-do. Thus, the relative importance of political parties and interest groups in American politics has far-ranging implications for the distribution of political power in the United States. As we saw in Chapter 11, political parties have declined in influence in recent years. Interest groups, on the other hand, as we shall see shortly, have become much more numerous, active, and influential.

[7]Kay Lehman Schlozman and John T. Tierney, *Organized Interests and American Democracy* (New York: Harper & Row, 1986), p. 60.

THE PROLIFERATION OF GROUPS

Interest groups and our concerns about them are not a new phenomenon. As long as there is government, as long as government makes policies that add value or impose costs, and as long as there is liberty to organize interest groups will abound; and if government expands so will interest groups. There was, for example, a spurt of growth in the national government during the 1880s and 1890s, arising largely from the first government efforts at economic intervention to fight large monopolies and to regulate some aspects of interstate commerce. In the latter decade, a parallel spurt of growth occurred in national interest groups, including the imposing National Association of Manufacturers (NAM) and numerous other trade associations. Many groups organized around specific agricultural commodities, as well. This period also marked the beginning of the expansion of trade unions as interest groups. Later, in the 1930s, interest groups with headquarters and representation in Washington began to grow significantly, concurrent with that decade's historic and sustained expansion within the national government (see Chapter 3).

Over the past thirty years, there has been an enormous increase both in the number of interest groups seeking to play a role in the American political process and in the extent of their opportunity to influence that process. The explosion of interest-group activity during the past quarter century has three basic origins: first, the expansion of the role of government during this period; second, the coming of age of the New Politics movement, a dynamic set of political forces in the United States that has relied heavily on public interest groups to advance its causes; and third, a revival of grassroots conservatism in American politics.

The Expansion of Government

Modern governments' extensive economic and social programs have powerful politicizing effects, often sparking the organization of new groups and interests. The activities of organized groups are usually viewed in terms of their effects on governmental action. But interest-group activity is often as much a consequence as an antecedent of governmental programs. Even when national policies are initially responses to the appeals of pressure groups, government involvement in any area can be a powerful stimulus for political organization and action by those whose interests are affected. A *New York Times* report, for example, noted that during the 1970s, expanded federal regulation of the automobile, oil, gas, education, and health care industries impelled each of these interests to increase substantially its efforts to influence the government's behavior. These efforts, in turn, had the effect of spurring the organization of other groups to augment or counter the activities of the first.[8]

Similarly, federal social programs have occasionally sparked political organization and action on the part of clientele groups seeking to influence the distribution of benefits and, in turn, the organization of groups opposed to the programs or to their cost. In the same vein, federal programs and court decisions in such areas as abortion and school prayer were the stimuli for political action and organization by fundamentalist religious groups. Thus, the expansion of government in recent decades has also stimulated increased group activity and organization.

The expansion of government has contributed to the enormous increase in the number of groups seeking to influence the American political system.

The New Politics Movement and Public Interest Groups

The second factor accounting for the explosion of interest group activity in recent years was the emer-

---

[8]John Herbers, "Special Interests Gaining Power as Voter Disillusionment Grows," *New York Times,* 14 November 1978.

gence of a new set of forces in American politics that can collectively be called the "New Politics movement."

The **New Politics movement** is a coalition of upper-middle-class professionals and intellectuals that formed during the 1960s in opposition to the Vietnam War and racial inequality. In more recent years, the forces of New Politics have focused their attention on such issues as environmental protection, women's rights, and nuclear disarmament. This movement was spearheaded by young members of the upper middle class for whom the civil rights and antiwar movements were formative experiences, just as the Great Depression and World War II had been for their parents. The crusade against racial discrimination and the Vietnam War led these young men and women to become conscious of themselves, and to define themselves, as a political force in opposition to the public policies and politicians associated with the nation's postwar regime.

Members of the New Politics movement constructed or strengthened "public interest" groups such as Common Cause, the Sierra Club, the Environmental Defense Fund, Physicians for Social Responsibility, the National Organization for Women, and the various organizations formed by consumer activist Ralph Nader. Through these groups, New Politics forces were able to influence the media, Congress, and even the judiciary, and to enjoy a remarkable degree of success during the late 1960s and early 1970s in securing the enactment of policies they favored. New Politics activists also played a major role in securing the enactment of environmental, consumer, and occupational health and safety legislation.

A second factor accounting for the explosion of interest-group activity in recent year has been the emergence of the New Politics movement.

Among the factors contributing to the rise and success of New Politics forces was technology. In the 1970s and 1980s, use of computers to organize direct mail campaigns allowed public interest groups to reach hundreds of thousands of potential sympathizers and contributors. Today, the Internet and e-mail serve the same function. Electronic communication allows relatively small groups to efficiently identify and mobilize their adherents throughout the nation. Individuals with perspectives that might be in the minority can become conscious of one another and mobilize for national action through the many developing political uses for new technology.

New Politics groups sought to distinguish themselves from other interest groups—business groups, in particular—by styling themselves as "public interest" organizations to suggest that they served the general good rather than their own selfish interest. These groups' claims to represent *only* the public interest should be viewed with caution, however. Quite often, goals that are said to be in the general or public interest are also primarily in the particular interest of those who espouse them.

STRATEGIES: THE QUEST FOR POLITICAL POWER

Interest groups work to improve the probability that they and their policy interests will be heard and treated favorably by all branches and levels of the government. The quest for political influence or power takes many forms. Insider strategies include access to key decision makers and using the courts. Outsider strategies include going public and using electoral politics. These strategies do not exhaust all the possibilities, but they paint a broad picture of ways that groups utilize their resources in the fierce competition for power (see Process Box 12.1).

Many groups employ a mix of insider and outsider strategies. For example, environmental groups like the Sierra Club lobby members of Congress and key congressional staff members, participate in bureaucratic rule making by offering comments and suggestions to agencies on new environmental rules, and bring lawsuits under various environmental acts like the Endangered Species Act, which authorizes groups and citizens to come to court if they believe the act is being vio-

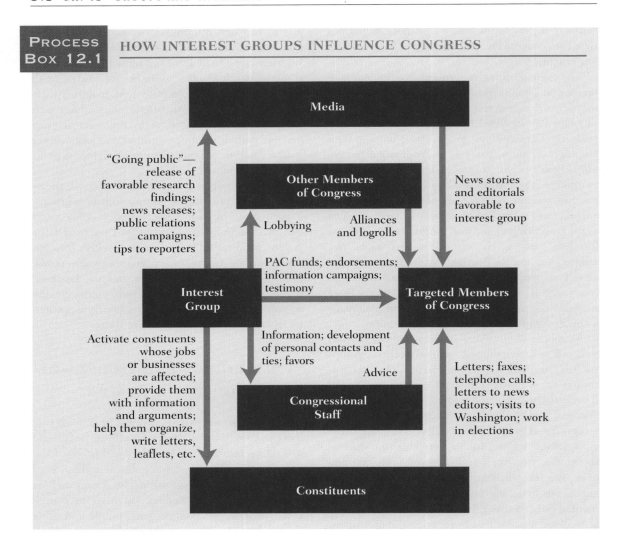

PROCESS BOX 12.1   HOW INTEREST GROUPS INFLUENCE CONGRESS

Media

"Going public"— release of favorable research findings; news releases; public relations campaigns; tips to reporters

News stories and editorials favorable to interest group

Other Members of Congress

Lobbying

Alliances and logrolls

Interest Group

PAC funds; endorsements; information campaigns; testimony

Targeted Members of Congress

Activate constituents whose jobs or businesses are affected; provide them with information and arguments; help them organize, write letters, leaflets, etc.

Information; development of personal contacts and ties; favors

Advice

Congressional Staff

Letters; faxes; telephone calls; letters to news editors; visits to Washington; work in elections

Constituents

lated. At the same time, the Sierra Club attempts to influence public opinion through media campaigns and to influence electoral politics by supporting candidates whom they believe share their environmental views and opposing candidates whom they view as foes of environmentalism.

Lobbying

Lobbying is an attempt by an individual or a group to influence the passage of legislation by exerting direct pressure on members of the legislature. The First Amendment to the Constitution provides for the right to "petition the Government for a redress of grievances." But as early as the 1870s, "lobbying" became the common term for petitioning— and it is an accurate one. Petitioning cannot take place on the floor of the House or Senate. Therefore, petitioners must confront members of Congress in the lobbies, giving rise to the term "lobbying."

The Federal Regulation of Lobbying Act defines

a lobbyist as "any person who shall engage himself for pay or any consideration for the purpose of attempting to influence the passage or defeat of any legislation to the Congress of the United States." The Lobbying Disclosure Act requires all organizations employing lobbyists to register with Congress and to disclose whom they represent, whom they lobby, what they are lobbying for, and how much they are paid. More than 7,000 organizations, collectively employing many thousands of lobbyists, are currently registered.

Lobbying involves a great deal of activity on the part of someone speaking for an interest. Lobbyists badger and buttonhole legislators, administrators, and committee staff members with facts about pertinent issues and facts or claims about public support of them.[9] Lobbyists can serve a useful purpose in the legislative and administrative process by providing this kind of information. In 1978, during debate on a bill to expand the requirement for lobbying disclosures, Democratic Senators Edward Kennedy of Massachusetts and Dick Clark of Iowa joined with Republican Senator Robert Stafford of Vermont to issue the following statement: "Government without lobbying could not function. The flow of information to Congress and to every federal agency is a vital part of our democratic system."[10]

LOBBYING CONGRESS   Today, lobbyists attempt to influence the policy process in a variety of ways.[11] Traditionally, however, the term *lobbyist* referred mainly to individuals who sought to influence the passage of legislation in the Congress.

In many instances, the influence of lobbyists is based on networks of personal relationships and behind-the-scenes services that they are able to perform for lawmakers. For example, one of Washington's most successful lobbyists is J. Steven Hart,

a senior partner at Williams & Jensen, a well-known Washington, D.C., lobbying and law firm. Hart's roster of clients includes such firms as Dell Inc. and Bass Enterprises. What does Hart offer such clients? The most important service Hart provides is direct access to the leadership of Congress. Hart, as it happens, served as the personal attorney for former House majority leader Tom DeLay as well as a number of other members of the House leadership. Often, this legal work is performed at a nominal fee, as a "loss leader."[12] As a result of this personal relationship with the majority leader, Hart is able to promise clients that their case will be heard by the nation's most important officials. Hart, for example, organized a meeting at DeLay's office in September 2001 in which airline executives were able to convince congressional leaders of the need for an airline bailout package in the wake of September 11. On the whole, about 50 percent of Washington lobbyists have prior government experience.

Interest groups also have substantial influence in setting the legislative agenda and in helping to craft specific language in legislation. Today, sophisticated lobbyists win influence by providing information about policies to busy members of Congress. As one lobbyist noted, "You can't get *access* without knowledge. . . . I can go in to see [former Energy and Commerce Committee chair] John Dingell, but if I have nothing to offer or nothing to say, he's not going to want to see me.[13] In recent years, interest groups have also begun to build broader coalitions and comprehensive campaigns around particular policy issues.[14] These coalitions do not rise from the grass roots but instead are put together by Washington lobbyists who launch comprehensive lobbying campaigns

[9]For discussions of lobbying, see Allan J. Cigler and Burdett A. Loomis, eds., *Interest Group Politics* (Washington, DC: Congressional Quarterly Press, 1983). See also Jeffrey M. Berry, *Lobbying for the People* (Princeton: Princeton University Press, 1977).

[10]"The Swarming Lobbyists," *Time*, 7 August 1978, p. 15.

[11]See Frank Baumgartner and Beth Leech, *Basic Interests* (Princeton, NJ: Princeton University Press, 1998).

[12]Steven Brill, *After: How America Confronted the September 12 Era* (New York: Simon & Schuster, 2003).

[13]Daniel Franklin, "Tommy Boggs and the Death of Health Care Reform," *Washington Monthly* (April 1995), p. 36.

[14]Marie Hojnacki, "Interest Groups' Decisions to join Alliances or Work Alone," *American Journal of Political Science* 41 (1997) pp. 61–87; Kevin W. Hula, *Lobbying Together: Interest Groups Coalitions in Legislative Politics* (Washington, DC: Georgetown University Press, 1999).

that combine stimulated grassroots activity with information and campaign funding for members of Congress. In recent years, the Republican leadership worked so closely with lobbyists that critics charged that the boundaries between lobbyists and legislators had been erased, and that lobbyists had become "adjunct staff to the Republican leadership."[15]

Groups attempt to influence legislators directly through lobbying. Lobbyists are key sources of information for members of Congress and for federal agencies.

Lobbyists also often testify on behalf of their clients at congressional committee and agency hearings. Lobbyists talk to reporters, place ads in newspapers, and organize letter-writing, e-mail, and telegram campaigns. Lobbyists also play an important role in fund-raising, helping to direct clients' contributions to members of Congress and presidential candidates.

What happens to interests that do not engage in extensive lobbying? They often find themselves "Microsofted." In 1998, the software giant was facing antitrust action from the Justice Department and had few friends in Congress. One former member of the House, Representative Billy Tauzin, told Microsoft chairman Bill Gates that without an extensive investment in lobbying, the corporation would continue to be "demonized." Gates responded by quadrupling Microsoft's lobbying expenditures and hiring a group of lobbyists with strong ties to Congress. The result was congressional pressure on the Justice Department resulting in a settlement of the Microsoft suit on terms favorable to the company. Similarly, in 1999, a member of Congress advised Wal-Mart that its efforts to win approval to operate savings and loans in its stores were doomed to failure if the retailer did not greatly increase its lobbying

efforts. "They don't give money. They don't have congressional representation—so nobody here cares about them," said one influential member of Congress. Like Microsoft, Wal-Mart learned its lesson, hired more lobbyists, and got what it wanted.[16]

LOBBYING THE PRESIDENT   So many individuals and groups clamor for the president's time and attention that only the most skilled and well-connected members of the lobbying community can hope to influence presidential decisions. One Washington lobbyist who fills this bill is Tom Kuhn, president of the Edison Electric Institute, a lobbying organization representing the electric power industry. Kuhn is a friend and former college classmate of President George W. Bush. In 2000, Kuhn was among the leading "Pioneers"—individuals who raised at least $100,000 for the Bush election campaign. Later, the electric power companies represented by Kuhn gave nearly $20 million to congressional candidates in the 2001–2002 election cycle. Kuhn's close relationship with the president and his efforts on behalf of the president's election have given Kuhn enormous leverage with the White House. During the 2000 transition, candidates for a presidential nomination to head the EPA felt compelled to pay "courtesy calls" to Kuhn. Subsequently, Kuhn led a successful effort to delay and weaken proposed new EPA controls on electric-power-plant emissions of mercury, a toxic substance linked to neurological damage, especially in children.[17] This was a victory for the electric power industry that promised to save the industry hundreds of millions of dollars a year and illustrates the influence that can be brought to bear by a powerful lobbyist.

LOBBYING   THE   EXECUTIVE   BRANCH   Even when an interest group is very successful at getting its bill passed by Congress and signed by the

[15]Peter H. Stone, "Follow the Leaders," *National Journal*, 24 June 1995, p. 1641.

[16]www.commoncause.org, "The Microsoft Playbook: A Report from Common Cause," 25 September 2000.
[17]"Edison Electric Institute Lobbying to Weaken Toxic Mercury Standards," http://tristatenews.com, 28 February 2003.

president, the prospect of full and faithful implementation of that law is not guaranteed. Often, a group and its allies do not pack up and go home as soon as the president turns their lobbied-for new law over to the appropriate agency. On average, 40 percent of interest-group representatives regularly contact both legislative and executive branch organizations, while 13 percent contact only the legislature and 16 percent only the executive branch.[18]

In some respects, interest-group access to the executive branch is promoted by federal law. The Administrative Procedure Act, first enacted in 1946 and frequently amended in subsequent years, requires most federal agencies to provide notice and an opportunity for comment before implementing proposed new rules and regulations. So-called "notice and comment rule-making" is designed to allow interests an opportunity to make their views known and to participate in the implementation of federal legislation that affects them. In 1990, Congress enacted the Negotiated Rule-making Act to encourage administrative agencies to engage in direct and open negotiations with affected interests when developing new regulations. These two pieces of legislation—which have been strongly enforced by the federal courts—have played an important role in opening the bureaucratic process to interest-group influence. Today, few federal agencies would consider attempting to implement a new rule without consulting affected interests.[19]

Cultivating Access

Lobbying is an effort by outsiders to exert influence on Congress or government agencies by providing them with information about issues, with support, and even with threats of retaliation. *Access* is actual involvement in the decision-making process. It may be the outcome of long years of lobbying, but it should not be confused with lob-

bying. If lobbying has to do with "influence on" a government, access has to do with "influence within" it. Many interest groups resort to lobbying because they have insufficient access or insufficient time to develop access.

Exerting influence on Congress or government agencies by providing them with information about issues, support, and even threats of retaliation requires easy and constant access to decision makers. Figure 12.1 is a sketch of one of the most important access patterns in recent American political history: that of the defense industry. Each of these patterns is almost literally a triangular shape, with one point in an executive branch program, another point in a Senate or House legislative committee or subcommittee, and a third point in some highly stable and well-organized interest group. The points in the *"iron triangle"* are mutually supporting; they count as access only if they last over a long period of time. For example, access to a legislative committee or subcommittee requires that at least one member of it support the interest group in question. This member also must have built up considerable seniority in Congress. An interest group cannot feel comfortable about its access to Congress until it has one or more of its "own" people with ten or more years of continuous service on the relevant committee or subcommittee.

The pattern of access among interest groups, congressional committees, and executive agencies is called an "iron triangle."

A number of important policy domains, such as the environmental and welfare arenas, are controlled, not by highly structured and unified iron triangles, but by rival *issue networks*. These networks consist of like-minded politicians, consultants, public officials, political activists, and interest groups who have some concern with the issue in question. Activists and interest groups recognized as being involved in the area are sometimes called "stakeholders" and are customarily invited to testify before congressional committees or give their

---

[18]John P. Heinz et al., *The Hollow Core: Private Interests in National Policy Making* (Cambridge, MA: Harvard University Press, 1993).

[19]For an excellent discussion of the political origins of the Administrative Procedure Act, see Martin Shapiro, "APA: Past, Present, Future," 72 *Virginia Law Review* 377 (March 1986), pp. 447–92.

FIGURE 12.1

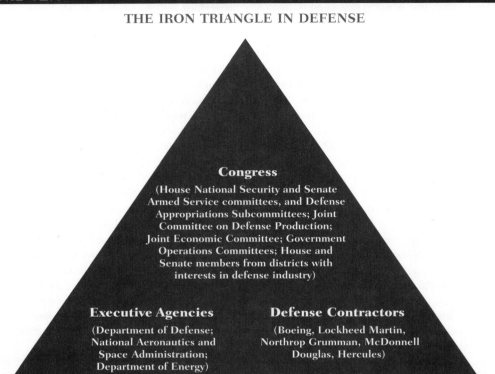

THE IRON TRIANGLE IN DEFENSE

Congress
(House National Security and Senate
Armed Service committees, and Defense
Appropriations Subcommittees; Joint
Committee on Defense Production;
Joint Economic Committee; Government
Operations Committees; House and
Senate members from districts with
interests in defense industry)

Executive Agencies
(Department of Defense;
National Aeronautics and
Space Administration;
Department of Energy)

Defense Contractors
(Boeing, Lockheed Martin,
Northrop Grumman, McDonnell
Douglas, Hercules)

views to government agencies considering action in their domain.

With the growing influence of the lobbying industry, stricter guidelines regulating the actions of lobbyists have been adopted in the last decade. For example, as of 1993, businesses may no longer deduct lobbying costs as a business expense. Trade associations must report to members the proportion of their dues that goes to lobbying, and that proportion of the dues may not be reported as a business expense either. The most important attempt to limit the influence of lobbyists was the 1995 Lobbying Disclosure Act, which significantly broadened the definition of people and organizations that must register as lobbyists. According to the filings under the Lobbying Disclosure Act of

1995, there were almost 11,500 lobbyists working the halls of Congress.

In 1996, Congress passed legislation limiting the size of gifts to its own members: no gift could be worth more than $50, and no member could receive more than $100 from a single source. It also banned the practice of honoraria for giving speeches, which had been used by special interests to supplement congressional salaries. But Congress did not limit payment by lobby groups for travel of representatives, senators, their spouses, or congressional staff members. Interest groups can pay for congressional travel as long as a trip is related to legislative business and is disclosed on congressional reports within 30 days. On these trips, meals and entertainment expenses are not limited to $50 per event and $100 annually. The rules of Congress allow its members to travel on corporate jets as long as they pay an amount equal to first-class airfare.

Using the Courts (Litigation)

Interest groups sometimes turn to litigation when they lack access or when they are dissatisfied with government in general or with a specific government program and feel they have insufficient influence to change the situation. They can use the courts to affect public policy in at least three ways: (1) by bringing suit directly on behalf of the group itself, (2) by financing suits brought by individuals, or (3) by filing a companion brief as *amicus curiae* (literally "friend of the court") to an existing court case.

Among the most significant modern illustrations of the use of the courts as a strategy for political influence are those that accompanied the "sexual revolution" of the 1960s and the emergence of the movement for women's rights. Beginning in the mid-sixties, a series of cases was brought into the federal courts in an effort to force definition of a right to privacy in sexual matters. The case began with a challenge to state restrictions on obtaining contraceptives for nonmedical purposes, a challenge that was effectively made in *Griswold v. Connecticut,* where the Supreme Court held that states could neither prohibit the dissemination of information about nor prohibit the actual use of contraceptives by married couples. That case was soon followed by *Eisenstadt v. Baird,* in which the Court held that the states could not prohibit the use of contraceptives by single persons any more than they could prohibit their use by married couples. One year later, the Court held, in the 1973 case of *Roe v. Wade,* that states could not impose an absolute ban on voluntary abortions. Each of these cases, as well as others, was part of the Court's enunciation of a constitutional doctrine of privacy.[20]

The 1973 abortion case sparked a controversy that brought conservatives to the fore on a national level. These conservative groups made extensive use of the courts to whittle away the scope of the privacy doctrine. They obtained rulings, for example, that prohibit the use of federal funds to pay for voluntary abortions. And in 1989, right-to-life groups used a strategy of litigation that significantly undermined the *Roe v. Wade* decision in the case of *Webster v. Reproductive Health Services* (see Chapter 4), which restored the right of states to place restrictions on abortion.[21]

Another extremely significant set of contemporary illustrations of the use of the courts as a strategy for political influence is found in the history of the NAACP. The most important of these court cases was, of course, *Brown v. Board of Education of Topeka,* in which the U.S. Supreme Court held that legal segregation of the schools was unconstitutional.[22]

Business groups are also frequent users of the courts because of the number of government programs applied to them. Litigation involving large businesses is most mountainous in such areas as taxation, antitrust, interstate transportation, patents, and product quality and standardization.

Major corporations and their trade associations pay tremendous amounts of money each year in fees to the most prestigious Washington law firms. Some of this money is expended in gaining access. A great proportion of it, however, is used to keep the best and most experienced lawyers prepared to represent the corporations in court or before administrative agencies when necessary.

New Politics forces made significant use of the courts during the 1970s and 1980s, and judicial decisions were instrumental in advancing their goals. Facilitated by changes in the rules governing access to the courts (these rules of standing were discussed in Chapter 9), the New Politics agenda was clearly visible in court decisions

---

[20]*Griswold v. Connecticut,* 381 U.S. 479 (1965); *Eisenstadt v. Baird,* 405 U.S. 438 (1972); *Roe v. Wade,* 410 U.S. 133 (1973).

[21]*Webster v. Reproductive Health Services,* 109 S. Ct. 3040 (1989).
[22]*Brown v. Board of Education of Topeka,* 347 U.S. 483 (1954).

handed down in several key policy areas. In the environmental policy area, New Politics groups were able to force federal agencies to pay attention to environmental issues, even when the agency was not directly involved in activities related to environmental quality. For example, the Federal Trade Commission (FTC) became very responsive to the demands of New Politics activists during the 1970s and 1980s. The FTC stepped up its activities considerably, litigating a series of claims arising under regulations prohibiting deceptive advertising in cases ranging from false claims for over-the-counter drugs to inflated claims about the nutritional value of children's cereal.

Interest groups often turn to litigation when they lack access or believe that they have insufficient influence over the formulation and implementation of public policy.

Mobilizing Public Opinion

Going public is a strategy that attempts to mobilize the widest and most favorable climate of opinion. Many groups consider it imperative to maintain this climate at all times, even when they have no issue to fight about. An increased use of this kind of strategy is usually associated with modern advertising. As early as the 1930s, political analysts were distinguishing between the "old lobby" of direct group representation before Congress and the "new lobby" of public relations professionals addressing the public at large to reach Congress.[23]

One of the best-known ways of going public is the use of institutional advertising. A casual scanning of important mass circulation magazines and newspapers will provide numerous examples of expensive and well-designed ads by the major oil companies, automobile and steel companies, other large corporations, and trade associations. The ads

show how much these organizations are doing for the country, for the protection of the environment, or for the defense of the American way of life. Their purpose is to create and maintain a strongly positive association between the organization and the community at large in the hope that these favorable feelings can be drawn on as needed for specific political campaigns later on.

Another form of going public is the *grassroots lobbying* campaign. In such a campaign, a lobby group mobilizes ordinary citizens to write to their representatives in support of the group's position. A grassroots campaign can cost anywhere from $40,000 to sway the votes of one or two crucial members of a committee or subcommittee, to millions of dollars to mount a national effort aimed at the Congress as a whole.

During the past several years, grassroots lobbying campaigns have played an important role in battles over presidential appointments. In 2005, President George W. Bush was presented with an opportunity to fill two Supreme Court vacancies occasioned by the death of Chief Justice William Rehnquist and the retirement of Justice Sandra Day O'Connor. Immediately, liberal and conservative advocacy groups mobilized their members for battle. In particular, pro-choice and pro-life groups saw the two Supreme Court appointments as a decisive point in the long-standing national struggle over abortion. Pro-choice groups feared that Bush would appoint justices hostile to abortion rights while pro-life groups feared that he would not. As each side urged its members to pressure the Congress, hundreds of thousands of calls, letters, telegrams, and emails flooded Capitol Hill. These campaigns had a major impact upon the appointment process, forcing President Bush to withdraw the name of one nominee, Harriet Miers, and very nearly derailing a second Bush nominee, Judge Samuel Alito.

Among the most effective users of the grassroots lobby effort in contemporary American politics is the religious Right. Networks of evangelical churches have the capacity to generate hundreds of thousands of letters and phone calls to Congress and the White House. For example, the religious Right was outraged when President Clinton an-

[23]E. Pendleton Herring, *Group Representation before Congress* (New York: McGraw-Hill, 1936).

nounced soon after taking office that he planned to end the military's ban on gay and lesbian soldiers. The Reverend Jerry Falwell, an evangelist leader, called upon viewers of his television program to dial a telephone number that would add their names to a petition urging Clinton to retain the ban on gays in the military. Within a few hours, 24,000 people had called to support the petition.[24]

Grassroots lobbying campaigns have been so effective in recent years that a number of Washington consulting firms have begun to specialize in this area. Firms such as Bonner and Associates or Direct Impact, for example, will work to generate grassroots telephone campaigns on behalf of or in opposition to important legislative proposals. Such efforts can be very expensive. Reportedly, one trade association recently paid the Bonner firm $3 million to generate and sustain a grassroots effort to defeat a bill on the Senate floor.[25] The annual tab for grassroots lobbying has been estimated at $1 billion.

Grassroots lobbying has become more prevalent in Washington over the last couple of decades because the adoption of congressional rules limiting gifts to members has made traditional lobbying more difficult. This circumstance makes all the more compelling the question of whether grassroots campaigning has reached an intolerable extreme. One case in particular may have tipped it over: in 1992, ten giant companies in the financial services, manufacturing, and high-tech industries began a grassroots campaign and spent millions of dollars over the next three years to influence a decision in Congress to limit the ability of investors to sue for fraud. Retaining an expensive consulting firm, these corporations paid for the use of specialized computer software to persuade Congress that there was "an outpouring of popular support for the proposal." Thousands of letters from individuals flooded Capitol Hill. Many of those letters were written and sent by people who sincerely believed that investor lawsuits are often frivolous and should be curtailed. But much

of the mail was phony, generated by the Washington-based campaign consultants; the letters came from people who had no strong feelings or even no opinion at all about the issue. More and more people, including leading members of Congress, are becoming quite skeptical of such methods, charging that these are not genuine grassroots campaigns but instead represent "*Astroturf lobbying*" (a play on the name of an artificial grass used on many sports fields). Such "Astroturf" campaigns have increased in frequency in recent years as members of Congress grow more skeptical of Washington lobbyists and far more concerned about demonstrations of support for a particular issue by their constituents. But after the firms mentioned above spent millions of dollars and generated thousands of letters to members of Congress, they came to the somber conclusion that "it's more effective to have 100 letters from your district where constituents took the time to write and understand the issue," because "Congress is sophisticated enough to know the difference."[26]

Using Electoral Politics

In addition to attempting to influence members of Congress and other government officials, interest groups also seek to use the electoral process to elect the right legislators in the first place and to ensure that those who are elected will owe them a debt of gratitude for their support. To put matters into perspective, groups invest far more resources in lobbying than in electoral politics. Nevertheless, financial support and campaign activism can be important tools for organized interests.

POLITICAL ACTION COMMITTEES   By far the most common electoral strategy employed by interest groups is that of giving financial support to the parties or to particular candidates. But such support can easily cross the threshold into outright bribery. Therefore, Congress has occasionally made an effort to regulate this strategy. A

[24]Michael Weisskopf, "Energized by Pulpit or Passion, the Public Is Calling," *Washington Post,* 1 February 1993, p. 1.

[25]Stephen Engelberg, "A New Breed of Hired Hands Cultivates Grass-Roots Anger," *New York Times,* 17 March 1993, p. A1.

[26]Jane Fritsch, "The Grass Roots, Just a Free Phone Call Away," *New York Times,* 23 June 1995, pp. A1, A22.

INTEREST GROUP STRATEGIES

Lobbying
Influencing the passage or defeat of legislation.
Three types of lobbyists:
Amateur—loyal members of a group seeking passage of legislation that is currently under scrutiny.
Paid—often lawyers or professionals without a personal interest in the legislation who are not lobbyists full time.
Staff—employed by a specific interest group full-time for the express purpose of influencing or drafting legislation.

Access
Development of close ties to decision makers on Capitol Hill and bureaucratic agencies.

Litigation
Taking action through the courts, usually in one of three ways:
Filing suit against a specific government agency or program.
Financing suits brought against the government by individuals.
Filing companion briefs as *amicus curiae* (friend of the court) to existing court cases.

Going Public
Especially via advertising; also through boycotts, strikes, rallies, marches, and sit-ins, generating positive news coverage.

Electoral Politics
Giving financial support to a particular party or candidate.
Congress passed the Federal Election Campaign Act of 1971 to try to regulate this practice by limiting the amount of funding interest groups can contribute to campaigns.

recent effort was the Federal Election Campaign Act of 1971 (amended in 1974), which we discussed in Chapter 10. This act limits campaign contributions and requires that each candidate or campaign committee itemize the full name and address, occupation, and principal business of each person who contributes more than $100. These provisions have been effective up to a point, considering the rather large number of embarrassments, indictments, resignations, and criminal convictions in the aftermath of the Watergate scandal.

The Watergate scandal, itself, was triggered by the illegal entry of Republican workers into the office of the Democratic National Committee in the Watergate apartment building. But an investigation quickly revealed numerous violations of campaign finance laws, involving millions of dollars in unregistered cash from corporate executives to President Nixon's reelection committee. Many of these revelations were made by the famous Ervin committee, whose official name was the Senate Select Committee to Investigate the 1972 Presidential Campaign Activities.

Reaction to Watergate produced further legislation on campaign finance in 1974 and 1976, but the effect has been to restrict individual rather than interest group campaign activity. Individuals may now contribute no more than $2,100 to any candidate for federal office in any primary or general election. A *political action committee (PAC)*, however, can contribute $2,000, provided it contributes to at least five different federal candidates each year. Beyond this, the laws permit corporations, unions, and other interest groups to form

PACs and to pay the costs of soliciting funds from private citizens for the PACs.

Electoral spending by interest groups has been increasing steadily despite the flurry of reform following Watergate. Table 12.2 presents a dramatic picture of the growth of PACs as the source of campaign contributions. The dollar amounts for each year indicate the growth in electoral spending. The number of PACs has also increased significantly—from 480 in 1972 to almost 4,000 in 2004 (see Figure 12.2). Although the reform legislation of the early and mid-1970s attempted to reduce the influence of special interests over elections, the effect has been almost the exact opposite. Opportunities for legally influencing campaigns with large donations are now widespread.

Given the enormous costs of television commercials, polls, computers, and other elements of the new political technology, most politicians are eager to receive PAC contributions and are at least willing to give a friendly hearing to the needs and interests of contributors. Most politicians probably will not simply sell their services to the interests that fund their campaigns, but there is some evidence that interest groups' campaign contributions do influence the overall pattern of political behavior in Congress and in the state legislatures.

Indeed, PACs and campaign contributions provide organized interests with such a useful tool for gaining access to the political process that calls to abolish PACs have been quite frequent among political reformers. Concern about PACs grew through the 1980s and 1990s, creating a constant drumbeat for reform of federal election laws. Proposals were introduced in Congress on many occasions, perhaps the most celebrated being the McCain-Feingold bill, which became the Bipartisan Campaign Reform Act (BCRA) of 2002. When originally proposed in 1996, McCain-Feingold was aimed at reducing or eliminating PACs. But in a stunning about-face, when campaign finance reform was adopted in 2002, it did not restrict PACs in any significant way. Rather, it eliminated unrestricted *soft money* donations to the national political parties (see Chapter 10). One consequence of this reform, as we saw in Chapters 10 and 11, was the creation of a host of new organizations known as 527 committees. These are often directed by former party officials but nominally unaffiliated with the two parties. This change probably will continue strengthening interest groups and weakening parties.

The campaign spending of activist groups is carefully kept separate from party and candidate organizations to avoid the restrictions of federal campaign finance laws. As long as a group's campaign expenditures are not coordinated with those of a candidate's own campaign, the group is free to spend as much money as it wishes. Such expenditures are viewed as "issue advocacy" and are protected by the First Amendment. This view was recently reaffirmed by the Federal Election Commission, which ruled in May 2004 that spending by 527 committees was not limited by BCRA.

TABLE 12.2

PAC SPENDING

Years	Contributions
1977–1978 (est.)	$ 77,800,000
1979–1980	131,153,384
1981–1982	190,173,539
1983–1984	266,822,476
1985–1986	339,954,416
1987–1988	364,201,275
1989–1990	357,648,557
1991–1992	394,785,896
1993–1994	388,102,643
1995–1996	429,887,819
1997–1998	470,830,847
1999–2000	579,358,330
2001–2002	685,305,553
2003–2004	915,723,383

SOURCE: Federal Election Commission.

Interest groups often contribute heavily to political action committees (PACs) to support their candidate's campaign.

FIGURE 12.2

GROWTH OF POLITICAL ACTION COMMITTEES, 1977–1998

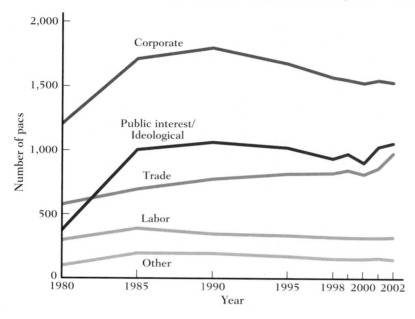

SOURCE: Federal Election Commission

CAMPAIGN ACTIVISM   Financial support is not the only way that organized groups seek influence through electoral politics. Sometimes, activism can be even more important than campaign contributions. Campaign activism on the part of conservative groups played a crucial role in bringing about the Republican capture of both houses of Congress in the 1994 congressional elections. For example, Christian Coalition activists played a role in many races, including ones in which Republican candidates were not overly identified with the religious Right. One postelection study suggested that more than 60 percent of the over 600 candidates supported by the Christian Right were successful in state, local, and congressional races in 1994.[27] The efforts of conservative Republican activists to bring voters to the polls was one major reason that turnout among Republicans exceeded

Democratic turnout in a midterm election for the first time since 1970. This increased turnout was especially marked in the South, where the Christian Coalition was most active. In many congressional districts, Christian Coalition efforts on behalf of the Republicans were augmented by grassroots campaigns launched by the National Rifle Association (NRA) and the National Federation of Independent Business (NFIB). The NRA had been outraged by Democratic support for gun control legislation, while the NFIB had been energized by its campaign against employer mandates in the failed Clinton health care reform initiative. Both groups are well organized at the local level and were able to mobilize their members across the country to participate in congressional races.

Groups also support their candidates through campaign activism.

[27]Richard L. Burke, "Religious-Right Candidates Gain as GOP Turnout Rises," *New York Times,* 12 November 1994, p. 10.

In 2004, a number of advocacy groups supporting the Democratic Party made a concerted effort to register and mobilize millions of new voters they hoped would support Democratic candidates. Organized labor, of course, targeted union households. Civil rights groups worked to register African Americans. And a number of new groups, including MoveOn.org labored to reach young people via the Internet. Their presumption was that young voters would tend to favor the Democrats.

Republicans, for their part, worked with church groups and such advocates of conservative causes as the National Rifle Association and the National Federation of Independent Business to register and mobilize voters likely to support the GOP. Ultimately, Republicans were more successful than their Democratic counterparts. In such key states as Ohio and Florida, hundreds of thousands of religious conservatives, motivated by strong opinions on social issues like gay marriage and abortion, trooped to the polls and helped hand the GOP a solid victory.

THE INITIATIVE   Another political tactic sometimes used by interest groups is sponsorship of ballot initiatives at the state level. The initiative, a device adopted by a number of states around 1900, allows laws proposed by citizens to be placed on the general election ballot and submitted directly to the state's voters. This procedure bypasses the state legislature and governor. The initiative was originally promoted by late-nineteenth-century Populists as a mechanism that would allow the people to govern directly. Populists saw the initiative as an antidote to interest group influence in the legislative process.

Ironically, many studies have suggested that most initiative campaigns today are actually sponsored by interest groups seeking to circumvent legislative opposition to their goals. In recent years, for example, initiative campaigns have been sponsored by the insurance industry, trial lawyers' associations, and tobacco companies.[28] The role of interest groups in initiative campaigns should come as no surprise since such campaigns can cost millions of dollars.

DO INTEREST GROUPS WORK?

Do interest groups have an impact upon government and policy? The short answer is yes, certainly they do. One of the best academic studies of the impact of lobbying was conducted in 2001 by John M. De Figueiredo of MIT and Brian Silverman of the University of Toronto.[29] Figueiredo and Silverman focused on a particular form of lobbying: efforts by lobbyists for colleges and universities to obtain "earmarks," special, often disguised, congressional appropriations for their institutions. Millions of dollars in earmarks are written into law every year.

The authors discovered that lobbying had an impact. The more money schools spent on lobbying activities, the larger the total quantity of earmarked funds they received. The extent of lobbying's impact, however, varied with institutional factors. Schools whose state's senator served on the Senate Appropriations Committee, received $18 to $29 in earmarks for every dollar spent on lobbying. Schools located in congressional districts whose representative served on the House Appropriations Committee received between $49 and $55 for every dollar spent on lobbying. Schools lacking such representation, however, averaged only about $1.09 for every dollar spent on lobbying—hardly worth the effort.

These results suggest, as is so often the case, that institutions and politics are profoundly related. Schools without access to members of Congress in a position to help them cannot gain much from lobbying. Schools with such access still need to lobby to take advantage of the potential that representation on the Senate and House Appropriations committees can give them. But, if

---

[28]Elisabeth R. Gerber, *The Populist Paradox* (Princeton, NJ: Princeton University Press, 1999).

[29]de Figueiredo, John M. P., and Silverman, Brian S., "Academic Earmarks and the Returns to Lobbying" (May 2002). Harvard Law and Economics Discussion Paper no. 370; MIT Sloan Working Paper no. 4245-02.

they do so, the potential return from lobbying is substantial.

Do Interest Groups Foster or Impede Democracy?

We would like to think that policies are products of legislators' concepts of the public interest. Yet the truth of the matter is that few programs and policies ever reach the public agenda without the vigorous support of important national interest groups. In the realm of economic policy, social policy, international trade policy, and even such seemingly interest-free areas as criminal justice policy—where, in fact, private prison corporations lobby for longer sentences for law breakers—interest-group activity is a central feature. Of course, before we throw up our hands in dismay, we should remember that the untidy process and sometimes undesirable outcomes of interest-group politics are virtually inherent aspects of democratic politics.

James Madison wrote that "liberty is to faction what air is to fire."[30] By this he meant that the organization and proliferation of interests were inevitable in a free society. To seek to place limits on the organization of interests, in Madison's view, would be to limit liberty itself. Madison believed that interests should be permitted to regulate themselves by competing with one another. So long as competition among interests was free, open, and vigorous, there would be some balance of power among them and none would be able to dominate the political or governmental process.

There is considerable competition among organized groups in the United States. For example, pro-choice and anti-abortion forces continue to be locked in a bitter struggle. Nevertheless, interest-group politics is not as free of bias as Madisonian theory might suggest. Though the weak and poor do occasionally organize to assert their rights, interest-group politics is generally a form of political competition in which the wealthy and powerful are best able to engage.

Moreover, though groups sometimes organize to promote broad public concerns, interest groups more often represent relatively narrow, selfish interests. Small, self-interested groups can be organized much more easily than large and more diffuse collectives. For one thing, the members of a relatively small group—say, bankers or hunting enthusiasts—are usually able to recognize their shared interests and the need to pursue focused goals in the political arena. Members of large and more diffuse groups—say, consumers or potential victims of firearms—often find it difficult to recognize their shared interests or the need to engage in collective action to achieve them.[31] This is why causes presented as public interests by their proponents often turn out, upon examination, to be private interests wrapped in a public mantle.

The responsiveness of government agencies to interest groups is a challenge to democracy. Groups seem to have a greater impact than voters upon the government's policies and programs. Yet, before we decide that we should do away with interest groups, we should think carefully: if there were no organized interests, would the government pay more attention to ordinary voters, or would the government simply pay no attention to anyone? In his great work *Democracy in America*, Alexis de Tocqueville argued that the proliferation of groups promoted democracy by encouraging governmental responsiveness. Does group politics foster democracy or impede democracy? It does both.

The organization of private interests into groups is inevitable, but the results are biased in favor of the wealthy and the powerful, who have superior education, opportunity, and resources with which to organize.

Thus, we have a dilemma to which there is no ideal answer. To regulate interest-group politics is, as Madison warned, to limit freedom and to expand

---

[30]Rossiter, ed., *The Federalist Papers,* No. 10, p. 78.

[31]Mancur Olson, Jr., *The Logic of Collective Action* (Cambridge: Harvard University Press, 1971).

governmental power. Not to regulate interest-group politics, on the other hand, may be to ignore justice. Those who believe that there are simple solutions to the problems of political life would do well to ponder this problem.

CHAPTER REVIEW

Efforts by organized groups to influence government and policy are becoming an increasingly important part of American politics. The expansion of government over the past several decades has fueled an expansion of interest-group activity. In recent years upper-middle-class Americans have organized public interest groups to vie with more specialized interests. All groups use a number of strategies to gain power.

Lobbying is the act of petitioning legislators. Lobbyists—individuals who receive some form of compensation for lobbying—are required to register in the House and the Senate. In spite of an undeserved reputation for corruption, they serve a useful function, providing members of Congress with a vital flow of information.

Access is participation in government. Groups with access have less need for lobbying. Most groups build up access through great effort. They work for years to get their members into positions of influence on congressional committees.

Litigation sometimes serves interest groups when other strategies fail. Groups may bring suit on their own behalf, finance suits brought by individuals, or file *amicus curiae* briefs.

Going public is an effort to mobilize the widest and most favorable climate of opinion. Advertising is a common technique in this strategy.

Groups engage in electoral politics either by embracing one of the major parties, usually through financial support, or through a nonpartisan strategy. Interest groups' campaign contributions now seem to be flowing into the coffers of candidates at a faster rate than ever before.

KEY TERMS

access   The actual involvement of interest groups in the decision-making process.

Astroturf lobbying   A negative term used to describe group-directed and exaggerated grassroots lobbying.

collective goods   Benefits, sought by groups, that are broadly available and cannot be denied to nonmembers.

free riders   Those who enjoy the benefits of collective goods but did not participate in acquiring them.

going public   A strategy that attempts to mobilize the widest and most favorable climate of opinion.

grassroots lobbying   A lobbying campaign in which a group mobilizes its membership to contact government officials in support of the group's position.

informational benefits   Special newsletters, periodicals, training programs, conferences, and other information provided to members of groups to entice others to join.

interest group   A group of people organized around a shared belief or mutual concern who try to influence the government to make policies promoting their belief or concerns.

iron triangle   The stable and cooperative relationships that often develop between a congressional committee, an administrative agency, and one or more supportive interest groups. Not all of these relationships are triangular, but the iron triangle is the most typical.

issue network   A loose network of elected leaders, public officials, activists, and interest groups drawn together by a specific policy issue.

lobbying   Strategy by which organized interests seek to influence the passage of legislation by exerting direct pressure on members of the legislature; this term is derived from having to wait in the lobbies just outside the floor of the legislature, where outsiders are not permitted.

material benefits   Special goods, services, or money provided to members of groups to entice others to join.

membership association   An organized group in which members actually play a substantial role, sitting on committees and engaging in group projects.

New Politics movement   Political movement that began in the 1960s and 1970s, made up of professionals and intellectuals for whom the civil rights and antiwar movements were formative experiences. The New Politics movement strengthened public-interest groups.

pluralism   The theory that all interests are and should be free to compete for influence in the government. The outcome of this competition is balance and compromise.

political action committee (PAC)   A private group that raises and distributes funds for use in election campaigns.

public interest groups   Lobbies that claim they serve the general good rather than their own particular interest, such as consumer protection or environmental lobbies.

purposive benefits   Selective benefits of group membership that emphasize the purpose and accomplishments of the group.

social benefits   Selective benefits of a group membership that emphasize friendship, networking, and consciousness-raising.

soft money   Money contributed directly to political parties for voter registration and organization.

staff organization   A type of membership group in which a professional staff conducts most of the group's activities.

FOR FURTHER READING

Cigler, Allan J., and Burdett A. Loomis, eds. *Interest Group Politics.* Washington, DC: Congressional Quarterly Press, 1983.

Clawson, Dan, Alan Neustadtl, and Denise Scott. *Money Talks: Corporate PACs and Political Influence.* New York: Basic Books, 1992.

Costain, Anne. *Inviting Women's Rebellion: A Political Process Interpretation of the Women's Movement.* Baltimore: Johns Hopkins University Press, 1992.

Hansen, John Mark. *Gaining Access: Congress and the Farm Lobby, 1919–1981.* Chicago: University of Chicago Press, 1991.

Heinz, John P., et al. *The Hollow Core: Private Interests in National Policy Making.* Cambridge: Harvard University Press, 1993.

Lowi, Theodore J. *The End of Liberalism.* New York: Norton, 1979.

Moe, Terry M. *The Organization of Interests.* Chicago: University of Chicago Press, 1980.

Olson, Mancur, Jr. *The Logic of Collective Action: Public Goods and the Theory of Groups.* Cambridge: Harvard University Press, 1971.

Petracca, Mark, ed. *The Politics of Interests: Interest Groups Transformed.* Boulder, CO: Westview, 1992.

Schlozman, Kay Lehman, and John T. Tierney. *Organized Interests and American Democracy.* New York: Harper & Row, 1986.

Truman, David. *The Governmental Process: Political Interests and Public Opinion.* New York: Alfred A. Knopf, 1951.

CHAPTER 13

Introduction to Public Policy

HOW DOES PUBLIC POLICY WORK?

Public policy is an officially expressed intention backed by a sanction, and that sanction can be a reward or a punishment. A public policy may also be called a law, a rule, a statute, an edict, a regulation, an order. Today, *public policy* is the preferred term, probably because it conveys more of an impression of flexibility and compassion than other terms. But citizens, especially students of political science, should never forget that "policy" and "police" have common origins. Both derive from *polis* and *polity,* which refer to the political community, and "political community" is another, more positive term for public order. A public policy is thus composed of two parts—(1) one or more goals; and (2) some kind of a sanction. The first has to do with the purposes of government. The second is concerned with the means of achieving those purposes. Governments adopt many policies to pursue many goals, which is why Congress is so busy all the time. In contrast, there are very few types of sanctions to provide government with the means of fulfilling those purposes. We call these sanctions "techniques of control" to indicate the coercive aspect of policy. But we will first look at the substantive goals and uses of economic and social policies.

CORE OF THE ANALYSIS

- Governments are essential to the creation and maintenance of a capitalist economy and a national market.

- The Social Security Act of 1935 distinguished between two kinds of welfare policies: contributory programs, generally called "social security," to which people must pay in order to receive benefits; and noncontributory programs, also called "welfare" or "public assistance," for which eligibility is determined by means testing.

- Governments establish order by using three techniques of control: promotional, regulatory, and redistributive policies.

- Promotional techniques bestow benefits, regulatory techniques directly control individual conduct, and redistributive techniques manipulate the entire economy.

Public policy is defined as an officially expressed intention backed by a sanction that can be either a reward or a punishment.

CENTRAL QUESTIONS

- **Substantive Uses of Public Policies**
  How is the national government fundamental in promoting a national market economy?
  What goals influence government adoption of regulatory policies?
  What forms of economic policy help encourage a capitalist economy?
  What are some important examples of contributory and noncontributory welfare policies?
  Has welfare reform been successful? Why or why not?
- **Implementing Public Policies: The Techniques of Control**
  What categories of techniques of control does the government use to form public policy?
  What are some examples of each?

SUBSTANTIVE USES OF PUBLIC POLICIES

Until 1929, most Americans believed that the government had little role to play in managing the economy or in helping those at the bottom of the economic ladder. The world was guided by Adam Smith's theory that the economy, if left to its own devices, would produce full employment and maximum production. This traditional view of the relationship between government and the economy crumbled in 1929 before the stark reality of the Great Depression of 1929–1933. Some misfortune befell nearly everyone. Around 20 percent of the workforce became unemployed, and few of these individuals had any monetary resources or the old family farm to fall back upon. Banks failed, wiping out the savings of millions who had been prudent enough or fortunate enough to have any. Thousands of businesses failed, throwing middle-class Americans onto the bread lines alongside unemployed laborers and dispossessed farmers. The Great Depression had finally proven to Americans that imperfections in the economic system could exist.

Demands mounted for the federal government to take action. In Congress, some Democrats proposed that the federal government finance public works to aid the economy and put people back to work. Other members of Congress introduced legislation to provide federal grants to the states to assist them in their relief efforts.

When President Franklin D. Roosevelt took office in 1933, he energetically threw the federal government into the business of fighting the Depression. He proposed a variety of temporary measures to provide federal relief and work programs. Most of the programs he proposed were to be financed by the federal government but administered by the states. In addition to these temporary measures, Roosevelt presided over the creation of several important federal programs designed to provide future economic security for Americans. Since that time, the government has been instrumental in ensuring that the economy will never again collapse as it did during the Depression and that Americans will not suffer from the devastating consequences that widespread economic hardship can produce.

Managing the Economy

Let's begin with an examination of the substantive uses of economy policy by looking at how governments implement public policies and achieve their economic goals. By maintaining public order throughout the history of the United States, both the national and the state governments have fostered a market economy that has enabled individuals and companies to function and has encouraged both private ownership and government intervention. The U.S. economy is no accident; it is the result of specific policies that have sustained massive economic growth.

As you read this section and encounter the many ways in which government intervenes in the economy, keep in mind two important questions: "In confronting a particular economic goal, what should government do?" and "What would be different without government and its policies?" Although economic growth or low inflation are economic goals that everyone can agree on, the public policies designed to achieve these goals are open to debate. Indeed, one area of heated debate in recent years has been over whether the national government should be involved in the nation's economy at all. In response to this question, many have cited the long-held American belief that at one time the economy was unregulated and operated on its own without government support. In our view, this belief is a myth. As we will see, a capitalist economy is highly dependent on governmental actions that make it possible for an economy to develop.

One of the main policy goals of the national government is making and maintaining a market economy.

PROMOTING THE MARKET   During the nineteenth century, the national government was almost exclusively a promoter of markets. National roads and canals were built to tie states and regions together. National tariff policies promoted domestic markets by restricting imported goods; a tax on an import raised its price and weakened its ability to compete with similar domestic products. The national government also heavily subsidized the railroad. Until the 1840s, railroads were thought to be of limited commercial value. But between 1850 and 1872, Congress granted over 100 million acres of public domain land to railroad interests, and state and local governments pitched in an estimated $280 million in cash and credit. Before the end of the century, 35,000 miles of track existed—almost half the world's total.

Railroads were not the only clients of federal support aimed at fostering the expansion of private markets. Many sectors of agriculture received federal subsidies during the nineteenth century, and some still receive federal subsidies today. Despite significant cuts in the agriculture budget in the 1980s, federal subsidies still cost the government nearly $10 billion per year, including $1.4 billion for sugar and $2 billion for the agriculture market in general, through programs such as rural electrification.

In the twentieth century traditional forms of promoting the market were expanded and some new ones were invented. For example, a great proportion of the promotional activities of the national government are now done indirectly through categorical grants-in-aid (see Chapter 3). The national government offers grants to states on the condition that the state (or local) government undertake a particular activity. Thus, in order to use motor transportation to improve national markets, a national highway system of 900,000 miles was built during the 1930s, based on a formula whereby the national government would pay 50 percent of the cost if the state would provide the other 50 percent. And then for over twenty years, beginning in the late 1950s, the federal government constructed over 45,000 miles of interstate highways. This was brought about through a program whereby the national government agreed to pay 90 percent of the construction costs on the condition that each state provide for 10 percent of the costs of any portion of a highway built within its boundaries.[1] There are examples of U.S. government promotional policy in each of the country's major industrial sectors.

The national government predominantly uses categorical grants-in-aid to promote markets.

---

[1] The Federal-Aid Highway Act of 1956 officially designated the interstate highways the National System of Interstate and Defense Highways. It was indirectly a major part of President Eisenhower's defense program. But it was just as obviously a "pork barrel" policy as any rivers and harbors legislation.

REGULATING THE MARKET   As the American economy prospered throughout the nineteenth century, some companies grew so large that they were recognized as possessing "market power." This meant that they were powerful enough to eliminate competitors and to impose conditions on consumers rather than cater to consumer demand. The growth of billion-dollar corporations led to collusion among companies to control prices, much to the dismay of smaller businesses and ordinary consumers. Moreover, the expanding economy was more mechanized and this involved greater dangers to employees as well as to consumers.

Small businesses, laborers, farmers, and consumers all began to clamor for protective regulation. Although the states had been regulating businesses in one way or another all along, interest groups turned toward Washington as economic problems appeared to be beyond the reach of the individual state governments. If markets were national, there would have to be national regulation.[2]

The first national regulatory policy was the Interstate Commerce Act of 1887, which created the first national independent regulatory commission, the Interstate Commerce Commission (ICC), designed to control the monopolistic practices of the railroads. Three years later, the Sherman Antitrust Act extended regulatory power to cover all monopolistic practices, including "trusts" or any other agreement between companies to eliminate competition. These policies were strengthened in 1914 with the enactment of the Federal Trade Act (creating the Federal Trade Commission, or FTC) and the Clayton Act. The only significant addition of national regulatory policy beyond interstate regulation of trade, however, was the establishment of the *Federal Reserve System* in 1913, which was given powers to regulate the banking industry along with its general monetary powers.

The modern epoch of comprehensive national regulation began in the 1930s. Most of the regulatory programs of the 1930s were established to regulate the conduct of companies within specifically designated sectors of American industry. For example, the jurisdiction of one agency was the securities industry; the jurisdiction of another was the radio (and eventually television) industry. Another was banking. Another was coal mining; still another was agriculture. When Congress turned once again toward regulatory policies in the 1970s, it became still more bold, moving beyond the effort to regulate specific sectors of industry toward regulating some aspect of the entire economy. The scope or jurisdiction of such agencies as the Occupational Safety and Health Administration (OSHA), the Consumer Product Safety Commission (CPSC), and the Environmental Protection Agency (EPA) is as broad and as wide as the entire economy, indeed the entire society.

Initially, attempts by the national government to regulate the market focused on organizing agencies to regulate a specialized sector, but recently Congress began regulating broader aspects of the entire economy.

DEREGULATION   Economic conservatives are in principle opposed to virtually any sort of government intervention in the economy.[3] As President Reagan once put it, they see government not as part of the solution, but as part of the problem. They adamantly oppose intervention by techniques of promoting commerce and are even more opposed to intervention through techniques of

---

[2]For an account of the relationship between mechanization and law, see Lawrence Friedman, *A History of American Law* (New Simon & Schuster, 1973), pp. 409–29.

[3]Actually, this point of view is better understood as nineteenth-century liberalism, or free-market liberalism, following the theories of Adam Smith. However, after the New Deal appropriated "liberal" for their pro-government point of view, the Republican antigovernment wing got tagged with the conservative label. With Reagan, the conservative label took on more popular connotations, while "liberal" became stigmatized as the "L-word."

regulation. They believe that markets would be bigger and healthier if not regulated at all.

President George W. Bush's support of deregulation suggests that the antiregulation spirit will stay alive awhile longer. Substantial deregulation in the telecommunications industry and in agriculture, and officially supported relaxation of regulatory activity in civil rights, pollution control, and protection of endangered species and natural resources, also tend to support that expectation.

Maintaining a Capitalist Economy

Government and capitalism are not inherent foes; they depend on each other. The study of government policies toward our capitalist economy will thus enrich our understanding of capitalism and strengthen our grasp of the relation between freedom and power.

The Constitution provides that Congress shall have the power

> To lay and collect Taxes . . . to pay the Debts and provide for the common Defense and general Welfare . . . to borrow Money . . . to coin Money and regulate the Value thereof. . . .

These clauses of Article I, Section 8, are the constitutional sources of the fiscal and monetary policies of the national government. Nothing is said, however, about *how* these powers can be used, although the way they are used shapes the economy. Most of the policies in the history of the United States have been distinctly capitalistic, that is, they have aimed at promoting investment and ownership by individuals and corporations in the private sector. That was true even during the first half of the nineteenth century, before anyone had a firm understanding of what capitalism was really all about.[4]

MONETARY POLICIES *Monetary policies* manipulate the growth of the entire economy by con-

trolling the availability of money to banks. With a very few exceptions cited below, banks in the United States are privately owned and locally operated. Until well into the twentieth century, banks were regulated, if at all, by state legislatures. Each bank was granted a charter, giving it permission to make loans, hold deposits, and make investments. Although more than 25,000 banks continue to be state-chartered, they are less important than they used to be in the overall financial picture, as the most important banks now are members of the "federal system."

Congress established the Federal Reserve System in 1913 to integrate private banks into a single system. Yet even the "Fed" was not permitted to become a central bank. The "Fed" is a banker's bank. It charters national banks and regulates them in important respects.[5] The major advantage of belonging to the federal system is that each member bank can borrow money from the Fed, using as collateral the notes on loans already made. This enables them to expand their loan operations continually, as long as there is demand for new loans. This ability of a member bank to borrow money from the Fed is a profoundly important monetary policy. The Fed charges interest, called a discount rate, on its loans to member banks.

If the Fed significantly decreases the discount rate—that is, the interest it charges member banks when they come for new credit—that can be a very good shot in the arm of a sagging economy. If the Fed adopts a policy of higher discount rates, that will serve as a brake on the economy if it is expanding too fast, because the higher rate pushes up the interest rates charged by leading private banks to their prime customers (called the "prime rate").

The federal government also provides insurance to foster credit and encourage private capital investment. The Federal Deposit Insurance Corporation (FDIC) protects bank deposits up to $100,000. Another important promoter of investment is the federal insurance of home mortgages

---

[4]The word "capitalism" did not come into common usage, according to the *Oxford English Dictionary*, until 1854. Words like "capital" and "capitalist" were around earlier, but a concept of *capitalism* as an economic system really came to the forefront with the writings of Karl Marx.

[5]Banks can choose between a state or a national charter. Under the state system, they are less stringently regulated and avoid the fees charged members of the Fed. But they also miss out on the advantages of belonging to the Federal Reserve System.

through the Department of Housing and Urban Development (HUD). By federally guaranteeing mortgages, the government reduces the risks that banks run in making such loans, thus allowing banks to lower their interest rates and make such loans more affordable to middle- and lower-income families. These programs have enabled millions of families who could not have otherwise afforded it to finance the purchase of a home.

These examples illustrate the influence of the national government on the private economy. Most of these monetary policies are aimed at encouraging a maximum of property ownership and a maximum of capital investment by individuals and corporations in the private sector. And all of these policies are illustrative of the interdependence of government and capitalism.

Monetary policies are aimed at encouraging capital investment and property ownership by individuals and corporations in the private sector.

FISCAL POLICIES *Fiscal policies* include the government's taxing and spending powers to manipulate the economy. All taxes discriminate. The public policy question is: How to raise revenue with a tax that provides the *desired* discrimination? The tariff was the most important tax policy of the nineteenth century. But the most important choice Congress ever made about taxation (and one of the most important policy choices it ever made about anything) was the decision to raise revenue by taxing personal and corporate incomes—the "income tax."[6] And the

[6]The U.S. government imposed an income tax during the Civil War that remained in effect until 1872. In 1894, Congress enacted a modest 2 percent tax upon all incomes over $4,000. This $4,000 exemption was in fact fairly high, excluding all working-class people. But in 1895, the Supreme Court declared it unconstitutional, citing the provision of Article I, Section 9, that any direct tax would have to be proportional to the population in each state. See *Pollock v. Farmers' Loan and Trust Company,* 158 U.S. 601 (1895). In 1913, the Sixteenth Amendment was ʳ⁻ᵈ, effectively reversing the *Pollock* case.

second most important choice Congress made was that the income tax be "progressive" or "graduated," with the heaviest burden carried by those most able to pay. A tax is called *progressive* if the rate of taxation goes up with each higher income bracket. A tax is called *regressive* if people in lower income brackets pay a higher proportion of their income toward the tax than people in higher income brackets. For example, a sales tax is deemed regressive because everybody pays at the same rate, so that the proportion of total income paid in taxes goes down as the total income goes up (assuming, as is generally the case, that as total income goes up the amount spent on sales-taxable purchases increases at a lower rate). The Social Security tax is another example of a regressive tax. In 2005, Social Security law applied a tax of 6.2 percent on the first $90,000 of income for the retirement program and an additional 1.45 percent on all income (without limit) for Medicare benefits, for a total of 7.65 percent in Social Security taxes. This means that a person earning an income of $90,000 pays $6,885 in Social Security taxes, a rate of 7.65 percent. But someone earning twice that income, $180,000, pays a total of $8,190 in Social Security taxes, a rate of 4.55 percent. As income continues to rise, the amount of Social Security taxes also rises, but the *rate,* or the percentage of income that goes to taxes, declines.

Although the primary purpose of the graduated income tax is, of course, to raise revenue, an important second objective is to collect revenue in such a way as to reduce the disparities of wealth between the lowest and the highest income brackets. We call this a *policy of redistribution.*

Redistribution of wealth is not the *only* policy behind the income tax. Another important secondary policy is the encouragement of the capitalist economy. When the tax law allows individuals or companies to deduct from their taxable income any money they can justify as an investment or as a "business expense," that is an incentive to individuals and companies to spend money to expand their production, their advertising, or their staff, and it reduces the income taxes they pay. These kinds of deductions are called incentives or "equity" by those who support them. For others, they might be called "loopholes." The tax laws of 1981 actually closed a number of important loopholes. But others still exist—on home mortgages, including second homes, and on business expenses, for example—and others will return, because there is a strong consensus among members of Congress that businesses often need such incentives. They may differ on which incentives are best, but there is almost universal agreement in government that some incentives are justifiable.[7] There is, however, no absolutely fair way to impose taxation. The only absolute rules should be (1) that government benefits not be hidden in the tax code and (2) that all other tax policies be made explicit to the public so that tax policy is the result of a genuine public choice.

Although the primary purpose of the income tax is to raise revenue, two other important objectives are the redistribution of wealth and the encouragement of the capitalist economy.

GOVERNMENT SPENDING   Most people associate the policy of government spending with the New Deal period of the 1930s. But government spending is as old as any government policy, and older than most. As Chapter 3 demonstrated, government spending was favored by the national government from the beginning. Today's government has more money to spend, but nineteenth-century governments spent money at a relatively high

degree for the economy of the times—on highways, canals, postal services, surveys, protection of settlers, and other services; the difference today is that we recognize that the *aggregate amount* of government expenditure is even more important as *policy* than are the particular purposes and projects for which the public monies are spent—a system of thinking attributed to the great English theorist John Maynard Keynes. Keynes reasoned that governments had become such a significant economic force that they could use their power to compensate for the imperfections in the capitalist system. He contended that government expenditures should be used as part of a "countercyclical" policy, in which, on the one hand, spending would be significantly increased (with significant "deficit spending" where necessary) to fight the deflationary side of the business cycle. On the other hand, spending should be reduced and tax rates kept high to produce budget surpluses when the problem was to fight the inflationary side of the business cycle.[8]

Government spending is another technique for influencing the economy and redistributing wealth.

At least three serious weaknesses in the Keynesian approach to fiscal policy were exposed during the 1970s. First, although public spending can supplement private spending to produce higher demand and thereby heat up the economy, there is no guarantee that the public money will be spent on things that help produce higher productivity, higher employment, and prosperity. Public expenditure can merely inflate the economy.

Second, governments may not be able to increase spending quickly enough to reverse the declining employment or the pessimistic psychology among consumers and investors. New public works take time, arriving perhaps too late to boost the economy, perhaps just in time to inflate it.

[7]For a systematic account of the role of government in providing incentives and inducements to business, see C. E. Lindblom, *Politics and Markets* (New York: Basic Books, 1997), Chapter 13. For a detailed account of the dramatic Reagan tax cuts and reforms, see Jeffrey Birnbaum and Alan Murray, *Showdown at Gucci Gulch: Lawmakers, Lobbyists, and the Unlikely Triumph of Tax Reform* (New York: Random House, 1987).

[8]John Maynard Keynes, *The General Theory of Employment Interest and Money* (New York: Harcourt, Brace, 1936).

Third, a very large and growing proportion of the annual federal budget is mandated or, in the words of OMB, "relatively uncontrollable." Interest payments on the national debt, for example, are determined by the actual size of the national debt and prevailing interest rates. Legislation has mandated payment rates for such programs as retirement under Social Security, retirement for federal employees, unemployment assistance, Medicare, and farm price supports. These payments go up with the cost of living; they go up as the average age of the population goes up; they go up as national and world agricultural surpluses go up.

In an effort to hold down mandatory spending, Congress has directed the Bureau of Labor Statistics to adopt a series of technical changes in calculating the Consumer Price Index (CPI), on which automatic *cost of living adjustments (COLAs)* are based. In other words, as the CPI goes up, reflecting inflation, the law mandates increases in Social Security and other types of benefits to the same degree. In 2003, mandatory spending accounted for around 61.7 percent of the budget. This means that the national government now has very little discretionary spending that will allow it to counteract fluctuations in the business cycle.

The Welfare System as Fiscal and Social Policy

Government involvement in the relief of poverty and dependency was insignificant until the twentieth century because of Americans' antipathy to government and because of their confidence that all of the deserving poor could be cared for by private efforts alone. This traditional approach crumbled in 1929 in the wake of the Great Depression, when some misfortune befell nearly everyone. Americans finally confronted the fact that poverty and dependency could be the result of imperfections of the economic system itself, rather than a result of individual irresponsibility. Americans held to their distinction between the deserving and undeserving poor but significantly altered these ....ards regarding who was deserving and who

was not. And once the idea of an imperfect system was established, a large-scale public approach became practical not only to alleviate poverty but also to redistribute wealth and to manipulate economy activity through fiscal policy.

The architects of the original Social Security system in the 1930s were probably well aware that a large welfare system can be good *fiscal* policy. When the economy is declining and more people are losing their jobs or are retiring early, welfare payments go up automatically, thus maintaining consumer demand and making the "downside" of the business cycle shorter and shallower. Conversely, during periods of full employment or high levels of government spending, when inflationary pressures can mount, welfare taxes take an extra bite out of consumer dollars, tending to dampen inflation, flattening the "upside" of the economy.

However, the authors of Social Security were more aware of the *social* policy significance of the welfare system. They recognized that a large proportion of the unemployment, dependency, and misery of the 1930s was due to the imperfections of a large, industrial society and occurred through no fault of the victims of these imperfections. They also recognized that opportunities to achieve security, let alone prosperity, were unevenly distributed in our society. This helps explain how the original Social Security laws came to be called—both by supporters and by critics—"the welfare state." The 1935 Social Security Act provided for two separate categories of *welfare—contributory* and *noncontributory*. Table 13.1 outlines the key programs in each of these categories.

Government's welfare programs serve as both fiscal and social policies.

SOCIAL SECURITY   *Contributory programs* are financed by taxation in a way that can be called "forced savings." These programs are what most people have in mind when they refer to Social Security or social insurance. Under the original old-age insurance program, the employer and the

TABLE 13.1

PUBLIC WELFARE PROGRAMS

Type of Program	Year enacted	Federal outlays in 2005 (in billions)
Contributory (Insurance) System		
Old Age, Survivors, and Disability Insurance	1935	510.2
Medicare	1965	325.4
Unemployment Compensation	1935	41.1
Noncontributory (Public Assistance) System		
Medicaid	1965	182.1
Food Stamps	1964	30.7
Supplemental Security Income (cash assistance for aged, blind, disabled)	1974	35.4
Housing Assistance to low-income families	1937	31.1
School Lunch Program	1946	11.6
Temporary Assistance to Needy Families*	1996	22.6

*Replaced Aid to Families with Dependent Children, which was enacted in 1935.
SOURCE: Office of Management and Budget, *Budget of the United States Government, Fiscal Year 2005* (Washington, DC: Government Printing Office, 2004), chapters 8, 10–15.

employee were each required to pay equal amounts, which in 1937 were set at 1 percent of the first $3,000 of wages, to be deducted from the paycheck of each employee and matched by the same amount from the employer. This percentage has increased over the years; the total contribution is now 7.65 percent subdivided as follows: 6.20 percent on the first $90,000 of income for the Social Security benefits and an additional 1.45 percent on all earnings for Medicare.[9]

[9]The figures cited are for 2005. Although on paper the employer is taxed, this is all part of "forced savings," because in reality the employer's contribution is nothing more than a mandatory wage supplement that the employee never sees or touches before it goes into the trust fund held exclusively for the contributory programs.

Social Security is a rather conservative approach to welfare. In effect, the Social Security (FICA) tax is a message that people cannot be trusted to save voluntarily in order to take care of their own needs. But in another sense, it is quite radical. Social Security is not real insurance; workers' contributions do not accumulate in a personal account like an annuity. Consequently, contributors do not receive benefits in proportion to their own contributions, and this means that there is a redistribution of wealth occurring. In brief, contributory Social Security mildly redistributes wealth from higher- to lower-income people, and it quite significantly redistributes wealth from young to old people and from younger workers to older retirees.

REFORMING SOCIAL SECURITY Since its creation in 1935, the Social Security system has provided retirement, survivor, and disability benefits to millions of Americans. Up until now, the system has run "in the black"—that is, it has collected more money than it has given out. In 2004, almost 48 million Americans received a total of $506 billion in Social Security benefits, given to 40 million retirees, dependents, and survivors of deceased workers, and to 8 million disabled workers. Even today, more than half of all American workers do not have a private pension plan; they will have to rely solely on Social Security for their retirement. If there were no Social Security, half of all senior citizens would be living below the poverty line. Thus, Social Security guarantees a measure of equality.

Nearly all wage earners and self-employed individuals pay into Social Security. Yet many fear that the system cannot sustain itself. When the baby boomer generation—a relatively large percentage of Americans, born between 1946 and 1964—reaches retirement age, their large numbers and longer life expectancies may place too great a demand on the system, forcing today's young people to pay ever more into a system that may be bankrupt by the time they retire.

Those who argue for a major change in Social Security point out that Social Security benefits are not drawn from an interest-bearing account; rather, they are paid for from taxes collected from current workers. Therefore, current workers carry the primary financial burden for the system. When baby boomers retire, their political and economic clout will be so great that they will be able to push aside any effort to limit benefits or relieve the financial burden on a much smaller number of younger wage earners. For Social Security to continue, it may have to borrow, or draw money from the federal Treasury, leaving younger generations with a staggering debt. If no changes are made in the current system, the Social Security Trust Fund (the account where surplus monies are held) will, according to projections, experience a shortfall beginning in 2042.

Contrary to popular impressions, Social Security benefits are not a simple repayment, plus interest, of money contributed by workers. The average retiree receives back the equivalent of all the money he or she contributed over a lifetime of work, plus interest, in the space of four to eight years. Most retirees receive far more than they put in. Why should today's student-age population provide subsidies to retirees who do not need the extra income?

In 2004, the debate about Social Security's future had heated up when Federal Reserve Chairman Alan Greenspan warned Congress that growing federal deficits would require Social Security and Medicare benefits to be reduced in the future. The large generation of baby boomers expected to retire by the end of 2010, combined with federal deficits, would put too much pressure on the program. Greenspan recommended that the retirement age for Social Security benefits be raised above 67 and that adjustments for inflation be slowed. In an election year, few politicians, including the president, wanted to be associated with remarks that could be interpreted as undermining Social Security.

President George W. Bush came to office supporting Social Security reforms, including the creation of private retirement accounts. Given the politically volatile character of debates about Social Security, President Bush waited until his second term to propose changes in the program. Bush advocated a reform plan that offered workers the choice of contributing a portion of the payroll tax to an individual account. The worker's traditional benefits would be reduced by the amount diverted to the individual account. According to Bush's vision for an "ownership society," individual plans would create a better system because they would allow workers to accumulate assets and build wealth, wealth that could be passed on to their children.

Supporters of the current Social Security system contend that the system's financial troubles are exaggerated. They dispute arguments, such as Greenspan's, that deficits require cuts in Social Security. They point out that Social Security taxes were raised in 1983—on the recommendation of a commission that Greenspan himself chaired—so that the program would be prepared to serve the aging baby boomer generation. Instead of saving that money, however, the federal government cut taxes on the wealthy and used Social Security taxes to finance the deficit. Advocates of the current system believe that many of Social Security's troubles could be solved by raising income taxes on the wealthy and eliminating the cap on payroll taxes. In 2005, only the first $90,000 of income was subject to the payroll tax. If this cap were lifted, these critics argue, the resulting revenues would cover more than 75 percent of the expected shortfall in the Social Security Trust Fund.

While nearly all observers agree that reforming Social Security is necessary for its long-term existence, there are debates on how to accomplish this.

Supporters of the current system are also deeply skeptical about the benefits of individual accounts. They charge the president with presenting a rosy scenario that overestimates likely gains through the stock market. When more realistic assumptions are adopted and the costs of the private accounts are considered, they argue, individual accounts do not provide higher benefits than the current system. Moreover, these critics note that the reforms would still not solve the budget crisis that Social Security will face.[10]

Finally, supporters of the present system emphasize that Social Security is not just a retirement account; it is a social insurance program that provides "income protection to workers and their families if the wage earner retires, becomes disabled or dies."[11] Because it provides this social insurance protection, supporters argue, Social Security's returns should not be compared to those of a private retirement account.

In 1972, Congress decided to end the grind of biennial legislation by establishing *indexing,* whereby benefits paid out under contributory programs would be modified annually by *cost of living adjustments (COLAs)* based on changes in the Consumer Price Index, so that benefits would increase automatically as the cost of living rose. But, of course, Social Security taxes (contributions) also increased after almost every benefit increase. This made Social Security, in the words of one observer, "a politically ideal program. It bridged partisan conflict by providing liberal benefits under conservative financial auspices."[12]

MEDICARE   The biggest single expansion in contributory programs since 1935 was the establishment in 1965 of *Medicare,* which provides substantial medical services to elderly persons who are already eligible to receive old-age, survivors', and disability insurance under the original Social Security system. Medicare provides hospital insurance but allows beneficiaries to choose whether or not to participate in a government-assisted insurance program to cover doctors' fees. A major role is guaranteed to the private health-care industry by essentially limiting Medicare to a financing system. Program recipients purchase all their health services in the free market. The government's involvement is primarily payment for these services. As a result, there is little government control over the quality of the services provided and the fees that health-care providers charge.

Like Social Security, Medicare is not means-tested. The benefits are available to all former workers and their spouses over the age of sixty-five—over 40 million people today—whether they are poor or not. Spending on Medicare has proved difficult to control in recent years, in part because of the growing numbers of people eligible for the programs but also because of rising health-care costs. Health-care expenditures, especially the cost of prescription drugs, have risen much more sharply than inflation in recent years.

---

[10]*Goldberg v. Kelly,* 397 U.S. 254 (1970).

[11]See U.S. House of Representatives, Committee on Ways and Means, *Where Your Money Goes: The 1994–95 Green Book* (Washington, DC: Brassey's, 1994), pp. 325, 802.

[12]Edward J. Harpham, "Fiscal Crisis and the Politics of Social Security Reform," in *The Attack on the Welfare State,* ed. Anthony Champagne and Edward Harpham (Prospect Heights, IL: Waveland Press, 1984), p. 13.

Between the 1970s and the 1990s, there was mounting concern among policy makers about the rising costs of Medicare, and cost containment was a constant theme. The start of the Medicare prescription-drug benefit debate in the mid-1990s, stemming from the exorbitant medication costs being borne by people with Medicare, coupled with worries about the impending retirement of the baby-boom generation, led to the birth of a full-fledged movement to "overhaul" Medicare. Proponents of this effort propagated the idea that the Medicare program needed to be "saved," claiming Medicare was out-of-date and on the brink of bankruptcy.

In 2003, Congress enacted a major reform of the Medicare program, which has provided health care to seniors since 1964. Most notably, Congress added a prescription drug benefit to the package of health benefits for the elderly. The high cost of prescription drugs is an issue of growing concern to millions of older Americans.

Contributory programs such as Social Security and Medicare are financed by taxpayers as a form of social insurance for the elderly.

PUBLIC ASSISTANCE PROGRAMS Programs to which beneficiaries do not have to contribute—*noncontributory programs*—are also known as public assistance programs, or, derisively, as welfare. Until 1996, the most important noncontributory program was *Aid to Families with Dependent Children* (*AFDC,* originally called Aid to Dependent Children, or ADC), which was founded in 1935 by the original Social Security Act. In 1996, Congress abolished AFDC and replaced it with the *Temporary Assistance to Needy Families* (*TANF*) block grant (see also page 338). Eligibility for public assistance is determined by *means testing,* a procedure that requires applicants to show a financial need for assistance. Between 1935 and 1965, the government created programs to provide housing assistance, school lunches, and food stamps to other needy Americans.

As with contributory programs, the noncontributory public assistance programs also made their most significant advances in the 1960s and 1970s. The largest single category of expansion was the establishment in 1965 of *Medicaid,* a program that provides extended medical services to all low-income persons who have already established eligibility through means testing under AFDC or TANF. Noncontributory programs underwent another major transformation in the 1970s in the level of benefits they provide. Besides being means tested, noncontributory programs are federal rather than national; grants-in-aid are provided by

---

IN BRIEF BOX

THE WELFARE STATE AS FISCAL AND SOCIAL POLICY

Fiscal policy—When the economy is declining and more and more people have less money to spend, welfare payments increase, which helps maintain consumer spending, thus shortening the "downside" of the business cycle. On the other hand, if inflation is threatening, then welfare taxes absorb some consumer dollars, having a (desired) dampening effect on an economy that is growing too quickly.

Social policy—Contributory programs were established in recognition of the fact that not all people have the means to establish financial security, that is, to save for the future. These programs are financed by taxation and can be considered "forced savings." Noncontributory programs provide assistance to those who cannot provide for themselves.

the national government to the states as incentives to establish the programs (see Chapter 3). Thus, from the beginning there were considerable disparities in benefits from state to state. The national government sought to rectify the disparities in levels of old-age benefits in 1974 by creating the **Supplemental Security Income (SSI)** program to augment benefits for the aged, the blind, and the disabled. SSI provides uniform minimum benefits across the entire nation and includes mandatory COLAs. States are allowed to be more generous if they wish, but no state is permitted to provide benefits below the minimum level set by the national government. As a result, twenty-five states increased their own SSI benefits to the mandated level.

The new TANF program is also administered by the states and, like the old-age benefits just discussed, benefit levels vary widely from state to state

(see Figure 13.1). For example, although the median national "standard of need" for a family of three was $1306 per month (55 percent of the poverty-line income) in 2004, the states' monthly TANF benefits varied from $170 in Mississippi to $923 in Alaska.[13]

The number of people receiving AFDC benefits expanded in the 1970s, in part because new welfare programs had been established in the mid-1960s: Medicaid (discussed earlier) and **food stamps,** which are coupons that can be exchanged for food at most grocery stores. These programs provide what are called **in-kind benefits**—noncash goods and services that would otherwise have to

[13]Ways and Means Committee Print, WMCP: 108–6, *2003 Green Book,* from U.S. GPO Online via GPO Access at waysandmeans.house.gov/media/pdf/greenbook2003/section7.pdf.

FIGURE 13.1

VARIATIONS IN STATE SPENDING ON AVERAGE MONTHLY TANF BENEFITS

■ Below $300   ■ $300 to $399 $400 to $499 $500 and above

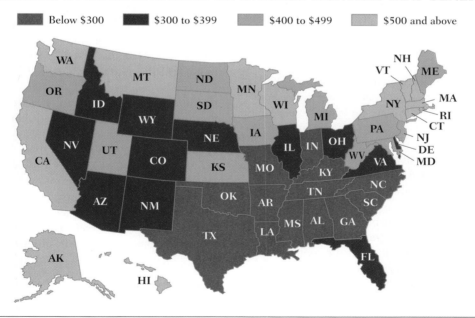

SOURCE: Ways and Means Committee Print, WMCP: 108–6, *2003 Green Book*, at waysandmeans.house.gov/media/pdf/greenbook2003/section7.pdf.

be paid for in cash by the beneficiary. In addition to simply adding on the cost of medical services and food to the level of benefits given to AFDC recipients, the possibility of receiving Medicaid benefits provided an incentive for poor Americans to establish their eligibility for AFDC, which would also establish their eligibility to receive Medicaid. At the same time, the government significantly expanded its publicity efforts to encourage the dependent unemployed to establish their eligibility for these various programs.

Noncontributory programs, including Temporary Assistance to Needy Families (TANF), Medicaid, and food stamps, provide assistance through means testing.

Another more complex reason for the growth of AFDC in the 1970s was that it became more difficult for the government to terminate people's AFDC benefits for lack of eligibility. In the 1970 case of *Goldberg v. Kelly*, the Supreme Court held that the financial benefits of AFDC could not be revoked without due process—that is, a hearing at which evidence is presented, and so on.[14] This ruling inaugurated the concept of the **entitlement**, a class of government benefits with a status similar to that of property (which, according to the Fourteenth Amendment, cannot be taken from people "without due process of law"). *Goldberg v. Kelly* did not provide that the beneficiary had a "right" to government benefits; it provided that once a person's eligibility for AFDC was established, and as long as the program was still in effect, that person could not be denied benefits without due process. The decision left open the possibility that Congress could terminate the program and its benefits by passing a piece of legislation. If the welfare benefit were truly a property right, Congress would have no authority to deny it by a mere majority vote.

Thus the establishment of in-kind benefit programs and the legal obstacles involved in terminating benefits contributed to the growth of the welfare state. But it is important to note that real federal spending on AFDC itself did not rise after the mid-1970s. Unlike Social Security, AFDC was not indexed to inflation; without cost of living adjustments, the value of AFDC benefits fell by more than one-third. Moreover, the largest noncontributory welfare program, Medicaid (as shown by Table 13.1), actually devotes less than one-third of its expenditures to poor families; the rest goes to the disabled and the elderly in nursing homes.[15] Together, these programs have significantly increased the security of the poor and the vulnerable and must be included in a genuine assessment of the redistributive influence and the cost of the welfare state today.

WELFARE REFORM   During the 1992 presidential campaign, President Clinton promised to "end welfare as we know it," but not until the approach of the 1996 presidential campaign was the Personal Responsibility and Work Opportunity Act (PRA) signed into law.

The new law replaced the sixty-one-year-old program of AFDC and its education/work training program, known as JOBS, with block grants to the states over a five-year period for *Temporary Assistance to Needy Families (TANF)*. The Act not only imposed the five-year time limit on the TANF benefits but also required work after two years of benefits. It also required community service after two months of benefits, unless the state administrators agree to an exemption of the rule. Many additional requirements for eligibility were spelled out in the law. And the states are under severe obligation to impose all these requirements on the threat of losing their TANF federal grants.

Since this new welfare law was enacted, the number of families receiving assistance has dropped by 58 percent.[16] Some observers take this

---

[15]See U.S. House of Representatives, Committee on Ways and Means, *Where Your Money Goes: The 1994–95 Green Book* (Washington, DC: Brassey's, 1994) pp. 325, 802.

[16]Ways and Means Committee Print, WMCP:105-7, *1998 Green Book*, from U.S. GPO Online via GPO Access at www.access.gpo.gov/congress/wm001.html (accessed June 1998).

---

erg v. Kelly, 397 U.S. 254 (1970).

as a sign that welfare reform is working; indeed, former welfare recipients have been more successful at finding and keeping jobs than many critics of the new law predicted.

The Personal Responsibility and Work Opportunity Act (PRA) implemented welfare reform by abolishing AFDC and replacing it with block grants to the states through TANF.

Other additional evidence suggests more caution in declaring welfare reform a success. Early studies show that welfare recipients are not paid enough to pull their families out of poverty and that child care and transportation continue to cause many problems for people seeking to leave welfare.[17] Moreover, one big question remains unanswered: What will happen to former welfare recipients and other low-income workers when there is an economic downturn and fewer jobs are available? Welfare reform was implemented in a time of record low unemployment levels; when employers are less desperate for workers, welfare recipients are more likely to have difficulty finding jobs. These concerns suggest that the 1996 law may not mark the end of welfare reform but may be a prelude to a round of future reforms.

IMPLEMENTING PUBLIC POLICIES: THE TECHNIQUES OF CONTROL

Up to this point, our introduction to public policy has focused on the substance and goals of policies, particularly economic policies. But underlying each substantive policy issue and each policy goal are means and methods for satisfying the substantive demands and for implementing the goals.

[17]See National Conference of State Legislatures, "Tracking Recipients after They Leave Welfare," at www.ncsl.org/statefed/welfare/followup.htm (accessed June 1998).

These are called *techniques of control*. Techniques of control are to policy makers roughly what tools are to a carpenter. There are a limited number of techniques; there is a logic or an orderliness to each of them; and there is an accumulation of experience that helps us know if a certain technique is likely to work. There is no unanimous agreement on technique, just as carpenters will disagree about the best tool for a task. But we offer here a workable elementary handbook of techniques that will be useful for analyzing all policies.

The In Brief Box on page 340 lists important techniques of control available to policy makers. They are grouped into three categories—promotional, regulatory, and redistributive techniques. In this section, the specifics of each will be discussed and explained. Each category of policy is associated with a different kind of politics. In other words, since these techniques are different ways of using government, each type is likely to develop a distinctive pattern of power.

Techniques of control—promotional, regulatory, and redistributive—are the "tools" of making public policy.

Promotional Techniques

Promotional techniques are the carrots of public policy. Their purpose is to encourage people to do something they might not otherwise do, or to get people to do more of what they are already doing. Sometimes the purpose is merely to compensate people for something done in the past. As the In Brief Box demonstrates, promotional techniques can be classified into at least three separate types—subsidies, contracts, and licenses.

SUBSIDIES   **Subsidies** are simply government grants of cash, goods, services, or land. Although subsidies are often denounced as "giveaways," they have played a fundamental role in the history of government in the United States. As we discussed in Chapter 3, subsidies were the dominant form of public policy of the national government throughout the

IN BRIEF BOX

TECHNIQUES OF PUBLIC CONTROL

Types of Techniques	Techniques	Definitions and Examples
Promotional techniques	Subsidies and grants of cash, land, etc.	"Patronage" is the promotion of private activity through what recipients consider "benefits" (example: in the nineteenth century the government encouraged westward settlement by granting land to those who went West)
	Contracting	Agreements with individuals or firms in the "private sector" to purchase goods or services
	Licensing	Unconditional permission to do something that is otherwise illegal (franchise, permit)
Regulatory techniques	Criminal penalties	Heavy fines or imprisonment; loss of citizenship
	Civil penalties	Less onerous fines, probation, exposure, restitution
	Administrative regulation	Setting interest rats, maintaining standards of health, investigating and publicizing wrongdoing
	Subsidies, contracting, and licensing	Regulatory techniques when certain conditions are attached (example: the government refuses to award a contract to firms that show no evidence of affirmative action in hiring)
	Regulatory taxation	Taxes that keep consumption or production down (liquor, gas, cigarette taxes)
	Expropriation	"Eminent domain"—the power to take private property for public use
Redistributive techniques	Fiscal use of taxes	Altering the distribution of money by changing taxes or tax rules
	Fiscal use of budgeting	Deficit spending to pump money into the economy when it needs a boost; creating a budget surplus through taxes to discourage consumption in inflationary times
	Fiscal use of credit and interest (monetary techniques)	Changing interest rates to affect both demand for money and consumption. When rates are low it is easy to borrow and thus invest and consume

nineteenth century. They continue to be an important category of public policy at all levels of government. The first planning document ever written for the national government, Alexander Hamilton's *Report on Manufactures,* was based almost entirely on Hamilton's assumption that American industry could be encouraged by federal subsidies and that these were not only desirable but constitutional.

The thrust of Hamilton's plan was not lost on later policy makers. Subsidies in the form of land grants were given to farmers and to railroad companies to encourage western settlement. Substantial cash subsidies have traditionally been given to commercial shipbuilders to help build the commercial fleet and to guarantee the use of the ships as military personnel carriers in time of war.

The government grants subsidies of money, goods, services, or land in order to encourage commerce.

Subsidies have always been a technique favored by politicians because subsidies can be treated as "benefits" that can be doled out in response to many demands that might otherwise produce profound conflict. Subsidies can, in other words, be used to buy off the opposition.

So widespread is the use of the subsidy technique in government that it takes encyclopedias to keep track of them all. Indeed, for a number of years, one company published an annual *Encyclopedia of U.S. Government Benefits,* a thousand-page guide to benefits

> for every American—from all walks of life . . . [R]ight now, there are thousands of other American Taxpayers who are missing out on valuable Government Services, simply because they do not know about them. . . . Start your own business. . . . Take an extra vacation. . . . Here are all the opportunities your tax dollars have made possible.[18]

Another secret of the popularity of subsidies is that those who receive the benefits do not perceive the controls inherent in them. In the first place, most of the resources available for subsidies come from taxation. (In the nineteenth century, there was a lot of public land to distribute, but that is no longer the case.) Second, the effect of any subsidy has to be measured in terms of what people *would be doing* if the subsidy had not been available. For example, many thousands of people settled in lands west of the Mississippi only

because land subsidies were available. Hundreds of research laboratories exist in universities and corporations only because certain types of research subsidies from the government are available. And finally, once subsidies exist, the threat of their removal becomes a very significant technique of control.

CONTRACTING Like any corporation, a government agency must purchase goods and services by contract. The law requires open bidding for a substantial proportion of these contracts because government contracts are extremely valuable to businesses in the private sector and because the opportunities for abuse are great. But contracting is more than a method of buying goods and services. Contracting is also an important technique of policy because government agencies are often authorized to use their **contracting power** as a means of encouraging corporations to improve themselves, as a means of helping to build up whole sectors of the economy, and as a means of encouraging certain desirable goals or behavior, such as equal employment opportunity.

For example, the infant airline industry of the 1930s was nurtured by the national government's lucrative contracts to carry airmail. A more recent example is the use of contracting to encourage industries, universities, and others to engage in research and development.

Contracting allows government to use its power to build up sectors of the economy and to encourage certain desirable goals or behavior.

The power of contracting was of great significance for administrations like those of Reagan and Bush because of their commitment to "privatization." When a presidential administration wants to turn over as much government as possible to the private sector, it may seek to terminate a government program and leave the activity to private companies to pick up. That would be true privatization. But in most instances, true privatization is neither sought nor achieved. Instead, the government

---

[18]Roy A. Grisham and Paul McConaughty, eds., *Encyclopedia of U.S. Government Benefits* (Union City, NJ: William H. Wise, 1972). The quote is taken from the dust jacket. A comparable guide published by the *New York Times* is called *Federal Aid for Cities and Towns* (New York: Quadranble Books, 1972). It contains 1,312 pages of federal government benefits that cities and towns, rather than individuals, can apply for.

program is transferred to a private company to provide the service *under a contract with the government,* paid for by the government, and supervised by a government agency. In this case, privatization is only a euphemism. Government by contract has been around for a long time and has always been seen by business as a major source of economic opportunity.

LICENSING   A *license* is a privilege granted by a government to do something that it otherwise considers to be illegal. For example, state laws make practicing medicine or driving a taxi illegal without a license. The states then create a board of doctors and a "hack bureau" to grant licenses for the practice of medicine or for the operation of a cab to all persons who have met the particular qualifications specified in the statute or by the agency.

Like subsidies and contracting, licensing has two sides. One is the giveaway side, making the license a desirable object of patronage. The other side of licensing is the control or regulatory side.

Regulatory Techniques

If promotional techniques are the carrots of public policy, **regulatory techniques** are the sticks. Regulation comes in several forms, but every regulatory technique share a common trait—direct government control of conduct. The conduct—such as drunk driving or false advertising—may be regulated because people feel it is harmful or threatens to be. Or the conduct—such as prostitution, gambling, or drinking—may be regulated because people think it's just plain immoral, whether it's harming anybody or not. Because there are many forms of regulation, we subdivide them here: (1) police regulation, through civil and criminal penalties, (2) administration regulation, and (3) regulatory taxation.

POLICE REGULATION   "Police regulation" is not a technical term, but we use it for this category because these techniques come closest to the traditional exercise of *police power.* After a person's arrest and conviction, these techniques are administered by courts and, where necessary, penal institutions. They are regulatory techniques.

Civil penalties usually refer to fines or some other form of material restitution (such as public service) as a sanction for violating civil laws or such common law principles as negligence. Civil penalties can range from a $5 fine for a parking violation to a heavier penalty for late payment of income taxes to the much more onerous penalties for violating antitrust laws against unfair competition or environmental protection laws against pollution. *Criminal penalties* usually refer to imprisonment but can also involve heavy fines and the loss of certain civil rights and liberties, such as the right to vote or the freedom of speech.

Police regulation consists of civil and criminal penalties to those who violate the law.

ADMINISTRATIVE REGULATION   Police regulation addresses conduct considered immoral. In order to eliminate such conduct, strict laws have been passed and severe sanctions enacted. But what about conduct that is not considered morally wrong but has harmful consequences? There is, for example, nothing morally wrong with radio or television broadcasting. But broadcasting on a particular frequency or channel is regulated by government because there would be virtual chaos if everybody could broadcast on any frequency at any time.

This kind of conduct is thought of less as *policed* conduct and more as *regulated* conduct. When conduct is said to be regulated, the purpose is rarely to eliminate the conduct but rather to influence it toward more appropriate channels, toward more appropriate locations, or toward certain qualified types of persons, all for the purpose of minimizing injuries or inconveniences. This type of regulated conduct is sometimes called **administrative regulation** because the controls are given over to administrative agencies rather than to the

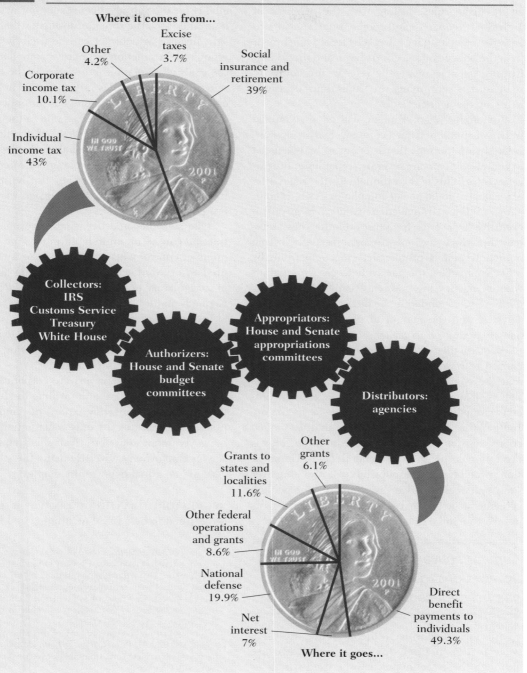

PROCESS BOX 13.1

THE FEDERAL DOLLAR: WHERE IT COMES FROM, WHERE IT GOES, AND HOW (FISCAL YEAR 2004)

Where it comes from...

Other 4.2%

Excise taxes 3.7%

Social insurance and retirement 39%

Corporate income tax 10.1%

Individual income tax 43%

Collectors:
IRS
Customs Service
Treasury
White House

Authorizers:
House and Senate budget committees

Appropriators:
House and Senate appropriations committees

Distributors:
agencies

Grants to states and localities 11.6%

Other grants 6.1%

Other federal operations and grants 8.6%

National defense 19.9%

Net interest 7%

Direct benefit payments to individuals 49.3%

Where it goes...

police. Each regulatory agency in the executive branch has extensive powers to keep a sector of the economy under surveillance and also has powers to make rules dealing with the behavior of individual companies and people. But these administrative agencies have fewer powers of punishment than the police and the courts have, and the administrative agencies generally rely on the courts to issue orders enforcing the rules and decisions made by the agencies.

Sometimes a government will adopt administrative regulation if an economic activity is considered so important that it is not to be entrusted to competition among several companies in the private sector. This is the rationale for the regulation of local or regional power companies. A single company, traditionally called a "utility," is given an exclusive license (or franchise) to offer these services, but since the one company is made a legal monopoly and is protected from competition by other companies, the government gives an administrative agency the power to regulate the quality of the services rendered, the rates charged for those services, and the margin of profit that the company is permitted to make.

At other times, administrative regulation is the chosen technique because the legislature decides that the economy needs protection from itself—that is, it may set up a regulatory agency to protect companies from destructive or predatory competition, on the assumption that economic competition is not always its own solution. This is the rationale behind the Federal Trade Commission, which has the responsibility of watching over such practices as price discrimination or pooling agreements between companies when their purpose is to eliminate competitors.

Administrative regulation allows government to control conduct that has harmful consequences.

Subsidies, licensing, and contracting are listed twice in the In Brief Box on page 340 because although these techniques can be used strictly as promotional policies, they can also be used as techniques of administrative regulation. It all depends on whether the law sets serious conditions on eligibility for the subsidy, license, or contract. To put it another way, the threat of losing a valuable subsidy, license, or contract can be used by the government as a sanction to improve compliance with the goals of regulation. For example, the threat of removal of the subsidies called "federal aid to education" has had a very significant influence on the willingness of schools to cooperate in the desegregation of their student bodies and faculties. For another example, social welfare subsidies (benefits) can be lowered to encourage or force people to take low-paying jobs, or they can be increased to placate people when they engage in political protest.[19]

Like subsidies and licensing, government contracting can be an entirely different kind of technique of control when the contract or its denial is used as a reward or punishment to gain obedience in a regulatory program. For example, Presidents Kennedy and Johnson initiated the widespread use of executive orders, administered by the Office of Federal Contract Compliance in the Department of Labor, to prohibit racial discrimination by firms receiving government contracts.[20] The value of these contracts to many private corporations was so great that they were quite willing to alter if not eliminate racial discrimination in employment practices if that was the only way to qualify to bid for government contracts. Today it is common to see on employment advertisements the statement, "We are an equal opportunity employer."

REGULATORY TAXATION   Taxation is generally understood to be a fiscal technique, and it will be

---

[19]For an evaluation of the policy of withholding subsidies to carry out desegregation laws, see Gary Orfield, *Must We Bus?* (Washington, DC: Brookings Institution, 1978). For an evaluation of the use of subsidies to encourage work or to calm political unrest, see Frances Fox Piven and Richard Cloward, *Regulating the Poor: The Functions of Public Welfare* (New York: Random House, 1971).

[20]For an evaluation of Kennedy's use of this kind of executive power, see Carl M. Brauer, *John F. Kennedy and the Second Reconstruction* (New York: Columbia University Press, 1977), especially Chapter 3.

discussed as such below. But in many instances, the primary purpose of the tax is not to raise revenue but to discourage or eliminate an activity altogether by making it too expensive for most people. For example, since the end of Prohibition, although there has been no penalty for the production or sale of alcoholic beverages, the alcohol industry has not been free from regulation. First, all alcoholic beverages have to be licensed, allowing only those companies that are "bonded" to put their product on the market. Federal and state taxes on alcohol are also made disproportionately high, on the theory that, in addition to the revenue gained, less alcohol will be consumed.

The government uses regulatory taxation to discourage or eliminate certain activities by making them too expensive for most people.

We may be seeing a great deal more regulation by taxation in the future for at least the following reasons. First, it is a kind of hidden regulation, acceptable to people who in principle are against regulation. Second, it permits a certain amount of choice. For example, a heavy tax on gasoline or on smokestack and chemical industries (called an "effluent tax") will encourage drivers and these companies to regulate their own activities by permitting them to decide how much pollution they can afford. Third, advocates of regulatory taxation believe it to be more efficient than other forms of regulation, requiring less bureaucracy and less supervision.

EXPROPRIATION *Expropriation*—seizing private property for a public use—is a widely used technique of control in the United States, especially in land-use regulation. Almost all public works, from highways to parks to government office buildings, involve the forceful taking of some private property in order to assemble sufficient land and the correct distribution of land for the necessary construction. The vast Interstate Highway Program required expropriation of thou-

sands of narrow strips of private land. "Urban redevelopment" projects often require city governments to use the powers of seizure in the service of private developers, who actually build the urban projects on land that would be far too expensive if purchased on the open market. Private utilities that supply electricity and gas to individual subscribers are given powers to take private property whenever a new facility or a right-of-way is needed.

We generally call the power to expropriate *eminent domain.*[21] The Fifth Amendment of the U.S. Constitution surrounds this expropriation power with important safeguards against abuse, so that government agencies in the United States are not permitted to use that power except through a strict due process, and they must offer "fair market value" for the land sought. Another form of expropriation is forcing individuals to work for a public purpose—for example, drafting people for service in the armed forces.

Government can use the constitutional power of eminent domain to expropriate resources for public use.

Redistributive Techniques

Redistributive techniques are usually of two types—fiscal and monetary—but they have a common purpose: to control people by manipulating the entire economy rather than by regulating people directly. As observed earlier, regulatory techniques focus on individual conduct. The regulatory rule may be written to apply to the whole economy: "Walking on the grass is not permitted," or "Membership in a union may not be used to deny employment, nor may a worker be fired for promoting union membership." Nevertheless, the regulation focuses on individual strollers or individual

---

[21]For an evaluation of the politics of eminent domain, see Theodore Lowi, Benjamin Ginsberg, et al., *Poliscide* (New York: Macmillan, 1976 and 1990), especially Chapters 11 and 12, written by Julia and Thomas Vitullo-Martin.

employers who might walk on the grass or discriminate against a trade union member. In contrast, techniques are redistributive if they seek to control conduct more indirectly by altering the conditions of conduct or manipulating the environment of conduct.

FISCAL TECHNIQUES　*Fiscal techniques* of control are the government's taxing and spending powers. Personal and corporate income taxes, which raise most government revenues, are the most prominent examples. While the direct purpose of taxes is to raise revenue, each type of tax has a different impact on the economy, and government can plan for that impact. For example, although the main reason given for increasing the Social Security tax (which is an income tax) under President Carter was to keep Social Security solvent, a big reason for it in the minds of many legislators was that it would reduce inflation by shrinking the amount of money people could spend on goods and services.

Likewise, President Clinton's commitment in his 1992 campaign to a "middle-class tax cut" was motivated by the goal of encouraging economic growth through increased consumption. Soon after the election, upon learning that the deficit was far larger than had earlier been reported, he had to break his promise of such a tax cut. Nevertheless, the idea of a middle-class tax cut is still an example of a fiscal policy aimed at increased consumption, because of the theory that people in middle-income brackets will tend to spend a high proportion of unexpected earnings or windfalls, rather than saving or investing them.[22]

MONETARY TECHNIQUES　*Monetary techniques* also seek to influence conduct by manipulating the entire economy through the supply or availability of money. The **Federal Reserve Board**

---

[22]For a fascinating behind-the-scenes look at how and why President Clinton abandoned his campaign commitment to tax cuts and economic stimulus, and instead accepted the fiscal conservatism advocated by the Federal Reserve and its chair, Alan Greenspan, see Bob Woodward, *The Agenda: Inside the Clinton White House* (New York: Simon & Schuster, 1994).

(the Fed) can adopt what is called a "hard money policy" by increasing the interest rate it charges member banks (called the **discount rate**). Another monetary policy is one of increasing or decreasing the **reserve requirement,** which sets the actual proportion of deposited money that a bank must keep "on demand" as it makes all the rest of the deposits available as new loans. A third important technique used by the Fed is **open market operations**—the buying and selling of Treasury securities to absorb excess dollars or to release more dollars into the economy.

Redistributive techniques are used to control the economy as a whole. The two types are fiscal, which represents government's taxing and spending power, and monetary, which controls the supply and availability of money.

SPENDING POWER AS FISCAL POLICY　Perhaps the most important redistributive technique of all is the most familiar one—the *"spending power"*—which is a combination of subsidies and contracts. These techniques can be used for policy goals far beyond the goods and services bought and the individual conduct regulated.

One of the most important examples of the national government's use of purchasing power as a fiscal or redistributive technique is found in another of the everyday activities of the Federal Reserve Board. As mentioned above, the Fed goes into the "open market" to buy and sell government bonds in order to increase or decrease the amount of money in circulation. By doing so, the Fed can raise or lower the prices paid for goods and the interest rate paid on loans.

CHAPTER REVIEW

Madison set the tone for this chapter in *The Federalist*, No. 51, in three sentences of prose that have more the character of poetry:

Justice is the end of government.
  It is the end of civil society.
  It ever has been and ever will be
    pursued
    Until it be obtained,
  Or until liberty be lost in the pursuit.

Our economic system is the most productive ever developed, but it is not perfect—and many policies have been adopted over the years to deal with its imperfections. Policy is the purposive and deliberate aspect of government in action. But if a policy is to come anywhere near obtaining its stated goal (clean air, stable prices, equal employment opportunity), it must be backed up by some kind of sanction—the ability to reward or punish—coupled with some ability to administer or implement those sanctions. These "techniques of control" were presented in three categories—promotional techniques, regulatory techniques, and redistributive techniques. These techniques are found in the multitude of actual policies adopted by legislatures and implemented by administrative agencies. Good policy analysis consists largely of identifying the techniques of control and choosing the policies that seek to manipulate "the economy as a system."

Promotional techniques are thought to be the carrots of public policy. Government subsidies, government contracts, and licensing are examples of incentives available to government to get people to do things they might not otherwise do, or to do more of what they are already doing. The first part of this chapter examined how promotional techniques are used to promote and maintain the national market economy.

Regulatory techniques seek to control conduct by imposing restrictions and obligations directly on individuals. Although many people complain about regulatory policies, the purpose of most such policies is to benefit the economy by imposing restrictions on companies thought to be engaging in activities harmful to the economy. For example, antitrust policies are intended to benefit economic competition by restricting monopolistic practices. Less popular reg-

ulatory policies seek to protect the consumer even if the regulation is an intervention in the economy that reduces competition or efficiency. Laws requiring companies to reduce air and water pollution, laws keeping new drugs off the market, and laws requiring the full labeling of the contents of foods and drugs are examples of such regulatory policies.

Redistributive techniques fall into two groups: fiscal and monetary policies. The government uses redistributive techniques to influence the entire economy, largely in a capitalistic direction. Currency, banks, and credit are heavily shaped by national monetary policies. Taxation, the most important fiscal policy, exists for far more than raising revenue. Taxation is a redistributive policy, which can be either progressive (with higher taxes for upper than for lower incomes) or regressive (applying one rate to all and therefore taking a higher percentage tax from the lowest brackets). Various exemptions, deductions, and investment credits are written into taxes to encourage desired behavior, such as more investment or more saving versus more consumption.

The capitalist system is the most productive type of economy on earth, but it is not perfect. Poverty amidst plenty continues. Many policies have emerged to deal with these imperfections. A part of this chapter discussed the welfare state and gave an account of how Americans came to recognize extremes of poverty and dependency and how Congress then attempted to reduce these extremes with policies that moderately redistribute resources.

Welfare state policies are subdivided into several categories. First there are the contributory programs. Virtually all employed persons are required to contribute a portion of their wages into welfare trust funds, and later on, when they retire or are disabled, they have a right, or entitlement, to draw on those contributions. Another category of welfare is composed of noncontributory programs, also called public assistance. These programs provide benefits for people who can demonstrate need by passing a means test. Assistance from contributory and noncontributory programs can involve either cash benefits or in-kind benefits.

KEY TERMS

administrative regulation   Rules made by regulatory agencies and commissions.

Aid to Families with Dependent Children (AFDC)   Federal funds, administered by the states, for children living with persons or relatives who fall below state standards of need. Abolished in 1996 and replaced with TANF.

contracting power   The power of government to set conditions on companies seeking to sell goods or services to government agencies.

contributory programs   Social programs financed in whole or in part by taxation or other mandatory contributions by their present or future recipients. The most important example is Social Security, which is financed by a payroll tax.

cost of living adjustments (COLAs)   Changes made to the level of benefits based on the rate of inflation.

discount rate   The interest rate charged by the Federal Reserve when commercial banks borrow in order to expand their lending operations; an effective tool of monetary policy.

eminent domain   The right of government to take private property for public use, with reasonable compensation awarded for the property.

entitlement   Eligibility for benefits by virtue of a category of benefits defined by legislation.

expropriation   Confiscation of property with or without compensation.

Federal Reserve Board   The governing board of the Federal Reserve System comprising a chair and six other members, appointed by the president with the consent of the Senate.

Federal Reserve System   A system of twelve Federal Reserve Banks that facilitates exchanges of cash, checks, and credit; regulates member banks; and uses monetary policies to fight inflation and deflation.

fiscal policies (techniques)   The government's use of taxing, monetary, and spending powers to manipulate the economy.

food stamps   Coupons that can be exchanged for food at most grocery stores; the largest in-kind benefits program.

indexing   Periodic adjustments of welfare payments, wages, or taxes, tied to the cost of living.

in-kind benefits   Goods and services provided to needy individuals and families by the federal government.

license   Permission to engage in some activity that is otherwise illegal, such as hunting or practicing medicine.

means testing   Procedure by which potential beneficiaries of a public assistance program establish their eligibility by demonstrating a genuine need for the assistance.

Medicaid   A federally financed, state-operated program providing medical services to low-income people.

Medicare   National health insurance for the elderly and for the disabled.

monetary policies (techniques)   Efforts to regulate the economy through manipulation of the supply of money and credit. America's most powerful institution in the area of monetary policy is the Federal Reserve Board.

noncontributory programs   Social programs that provide assistance to people based on demonstrated need rather than any contribution they have made.

open market operations   The buying and selling of government securities to help finance government operations and to loosen or tighten the total amount of credit circulating in the economy.

police power   Power reserved to the state to regulate the health, safety, and morals of its citizens.

policy of redistribution   A policy whose objective is to tax or spend in such a way as to reduce the disparities of wealth between the lowest and the highest income brackets.

progressive/regressive taxation   Taxation that hits the upper income brackets more heavily (progressive) or the lower income brackets more heavily (regressive).

promotional technique   A technique of control that encourages people to do something they might not otherwise do, or to continue an action or behavior. Three types of promotional techniques are subsidies, contracts, and licenses.

public policy   A law, rule, statute, or edict that expresses the government's goals and provides for rewards and punishments to promote their attainment.

redistributive techniques   Techniques—fiscal or monetary—designed to control people by manipulating the entire economy rather than by regulating people directly.

regulatory techniques   Techniques that government uses to control the conduct of the people.

reserve requirement The amount of liquid assets and ready cash that the Federal Reserve requires banks to hold to meet depositors' demands for their money.

Social Security A contributory welfare program into which working Americans contribute a percentage of their wages, and from which they receive cash benefits after retirement.

spending power A combination of subsidies and contracts that the government can use to redistribute income.

subsidies Government grants of cash or other valuable commodities, such as land, to individuals or organizations; used to promote activities desired by the government, to reward political support, or to buy off political opposition.

Supplemental Security Income (SSI) A program providing a minimum monthly income to people who pass a "means test" and who are sixty-five or older, blind, or disabled. Financed from general revenues rather than from Social Security contributions.

Temporary Assistance to Needy Families (TANF) A policy by which states are given block grants by the federal government in order to create their own programs for public assistance.

FOR FURTHER READING

Derthick, Martha. *Agency under Stress: The Social Security Administration in American Government*. Washington, DC: Brookings Institution, 1990.

Foreman, Christopher. *Signals from the Hill: Congressional Oversight and the Challenge of Social Regulation*. New Haven: Yale University Press, 1988.

Gutmann, Amy. *Democracy and the Welfare State*. Princeton: Princeton University Press, 1988.

Heilbroner, Robert. *The Nature and Logic of Capitalism*. New York: Norton, 1985.

Holmes, Stephen and Cass R. Sunstein. *The Cost of Rights: Why Liberty Depends on Taxes*. New York: Norton, 1999.

Lemann, Nicholas. *The Promised Land: The Great Black Migration and How It Shaped America*. New York: Alfred A. Knopf, 1991.

Lenno, Rhonda F. *Class Struggle and the New Deal: Industrial Labor, Industrial Capital, and the State*. Lawrence: University Press of Kansas, 1988.

Levi, Margaret. *Of Rule and Revenue*. Berkeley: University of California Press, 1988.

Levy, Frank. *The New Dollars and Dreams*. New York: Russell Sage Foundation, 1998.

Marmor, Theodore R., Jerry L. Mashaw, and Phillip L. Harvey. *America's Misunderstood Welfare State*. New York: Basic Books, 1990.

Mink, Gwendolyn. *Welfare's End*. Ithaca, NY: Cornell University Press, 1998.

Piven, Frances Fox, and Richard A. Cloward. *Regulating the Poor*. New York: Random House, 1971.

Rubin, Irene S. *The Politics of Public Budgeting: Getting and Spending, Borrowing and Balancing*. Chatham, NJ: Chatham House, 1990.

Self, Peter. *Government by the Market? The Politics of Public Choice*. Boulder, CO: Westview, 1994.

Weir, Margaret, Ann Orloff, and Theda Skocpol. *The Politics of Social Policy in the United States*. Princeton: Princeton University Press, 1988.

CHAPTER 14

Foreign Policy and Democracy

HOW DOES FOREIGN POLICY WORK?

*T*his chapter will explore American foreign policy, the changing attitudes of presidents and other Americans toward world politics, and the place of America in world affairs. Although modern presidents cannot escape the demands of foreign policy and world politics, this has not always been the case, as we shall see in this chapter.

We will begin with the players, those who make and shape foreign policy. From there, we will cover American values: What does the United States want? What are its national interests, if any? What counts as success? Then we will identify and evaluate the six basic instruments of American foreign policy. Finally, we will look at actual roles the United States has attempted to play in world affairs.

As in domestic policy, foreign policy making is a highly pluralistic arena. First there are the official players, those who make up the "foreign policy establishment"; these players and the agencies they head can be called the actual "makers" of foreign policy. But there are other major players, less official but still influential. We call these the "shapers."

Who Makes Foreign Policy?

THE PRESIDENT   The terrorist attacks of September 11, 2001, accentuated the president's role

CORE OF THE ANALYSIS

- All foreign policies must be made and implemented in the name of the president.

- Certain values—fear of centralized power and of foreign entanglements—have traditionally shaped American foreign policy; today these values find expression in the intermingling of domestic and foreign policy institutions and the tendency toward unilateralism.

- American foreign policy is carried out through certain instruments, including diplomacy, the United Nations, the international monetary structure, economic aid, collective security, and military deterrence.

- In the conduct of foreign policy, nations can play one of several roles: the Napoleonic role, the Holy Alliance role, the balance-of-power role, and the economic expansionist role.

- The United States plays different roles in foreign affairs, depending on what it seeks to achieve in a particular situation; the Holy Alliance role seems to be the most typical American role in the post–cold war era.

and place in foreign policy immensely. Congress's first action after the attacks was to approve virtually unanimously in both the House and Senate

CENTRAL QUESTIONS

- **How Does Foreign Policy Work?**
  What institutions make up the foreign policy establishment?
  What groups help shape foreign policy? Among these players, which are most influential?

- **The Values in American Foreign Policy**
  What are the legacies of the traditional system of foreign policy?
  When and why did the traditional system of foreign policy end?
  What new values guided U.S. foreign policy after World War II?

- **The Instruments of Modern American Foreign Policy**
  What are the six primary instruments of modern American foreign policy?
  How does each instrument reflect a balance between the values of the traditional system of foreign policy and the values of cold war politics?

- **Roles Nations Play**
  What four traditional foreign policy roles has the United States adopted throughout its history?
  Since the end of World War II, how has the role of the United States in world affairs evolved?

an authorization for the president to use "all necessary and appropriate force," coupled with a $40 billion emergency appropriation bill for home defense and reconstruction. Significant as this was, however, it only emphasized what was already true—that the president is our head of state and the epicenter of foreign policy (see Concept Map 14.1). Although many foreign policy decisions can be made without the president's approval, these decisions must be made and implemented in the name of the president. This is not simply a matter of American preference. It is in the nature of international relations that all foreign policies must come from the president as head of state.

THE BUREAUCRACY The major foreign policy players in the bureaucracy are the secretaries of the departments of state, defense, and the treasury; the Joint Chiefs of Staff (JCOS), especially the chair of the JCOS; and the director of the Central Intelligence Agency (CIA). A separate unit in the bureaucracy comprising these people and a few others is the National Security Council (NSC), whose main purpose is to iron out the differences among the key players and to integrate their positions in order to confirm or reinforce a

decision the president wants to make in foreign policy or military policy. The secretary of commerce has also become an increasingly important foreign policy maker, with the rise and spread of economic globalization.

The key foreign players in the bureaucracy are the secretaries of state, defense, and treasury; the Joint Chiefs of Staff (especially the chair); and the CIA director.

To this group another has been added: the Department of Homeland Security. The department has four main divisions: Border and Transportation Security; Emergency Preparedness and Response; Chemical, Biological, Radiological, and Nuclear Countermeasures; and Information Analysis and Infrastructure Protection.

Coordinating the diverse missions of a single agency is a challenge; coordinating the efforts of multiple agencies is especially problematic. The National Security Council and now the Department of Homeland Security attempt to keep the

CONCEPT MAP 14.1   MAKING FOREIGN POLICY

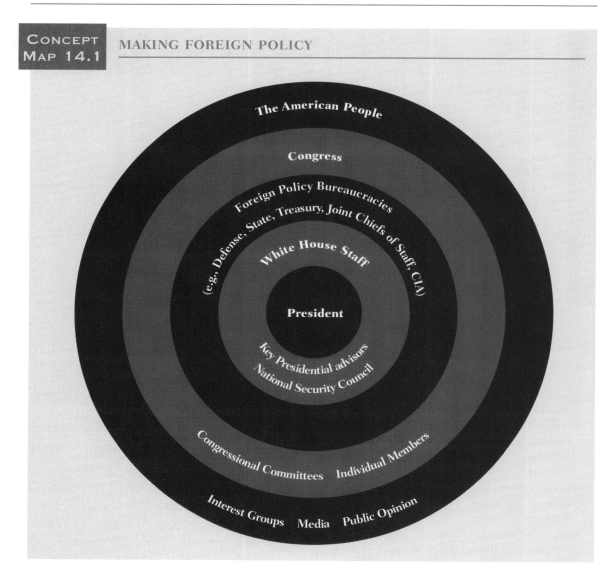

The American People

Congress

Foreign Policy Bureaucracies

(e.g. Defense, State, Treasury, Joint Chiefs of Staff, CIA)

White House Staff

President

Key Presidential advisors
National Security Council

Congressional Committees   Individual Members

Interest Groups   Media   Public Opinion

various players on the same page. But will these agencies—each with their own authority, interests, and priorities—follow the same protocol?

In addition to top cabinet-level officials, key lower-level staff members have policy-making influence as strong as that of the cabinet secretaries—some may occasionally exceed cabinet influence. These include the two or three specialized national security advisors in the White House,

the staff of the NSC (headed by the national security advisor), and a few other career bureaucrats in the departments of state and defense whose influence varies according to their specialty and to the foreign policy issue at hand.

CONGRESS   In foreign policy, Congress has to be subdivided into three parts. The first part is the Senate. For most of American history, the Senate was the only important congressional foreign policy player because of its constitutional role in reviewing and approving treaties. The treaty power is still the primary entrée of the Senate into foreign policy making. But since World War II and the continual involvement of the United States in international security and foreign aid, Congress as a whole has become a major foreign policy maker because most modern foreign policies require financing, which requires approval from both the House of Representatives and the Senate. Congress has also become increasingly involved in foreign policy making because of the increasing use by the president of *executive agreements* to conduct foreign policy. Executive agreements have the force of treaties but do not require prior approval by the Senate. They can, however, be revoked by action of both chambers of Congress.

The third congressional player is the foreign policy and military policy committees: in the Senate these are the Foreign Relations Committee and the Armed Services Committee; in the House, these are the International Affairs Committee and the Armed Services Committee. Usually, a few members of these committees who have spent years specializing in foreign affairs become trusted members of the foreign policy establishment and are actually makers rather than mere shapers of foreign policy. In fact, several members of Congress have left to become key foreign affairs cabinet members.[1]

Although the Senate traditionally has more foreign policy power than the House, since World War II both the House and the Senate have been important players in foreign policy.

Who Shapes Foreign Policy?

The shapers of foreign policy are the nonofficial, informal players, but they are typically people or groups that have great influence in the making of foreign policy. Of course, the influence of any given group varies according to the party and the ideology that is dominant at a given moment.

INTEREST GROUPS Far and away the most important category of nonofficial player is the interest group—that is, the interest groups to whom one or more foreign policy issues are of long-standing and vital relevance. The type of interest group with the reputation for the most influence is the economic interest group. Yet the heft of the myths about their influence far outweighs the reality. The influence of organized economic interest groups in foreign policy varies enormously from issue to issue and year to year. Most of these groups are "single-issue" groups and are therefore most active when their particular issue is on the agenda. On many of the broader and more sustained policy issues, such as the *North American Free Trade Agreement (NAFTA)* or the general question of American involvement in international trade, the larger interest groups find it difficult to maintain tight enough control of their many members to speak with a single voice. The most systematic study of international trade policies and their interest groups concluded that the leaders of these large, economic interest groups spend more time maintaining consensus among their members than lobbying Congress or pressuring major players in the executive branch.[2] The economic interest groups more successful in influencing foreign policy are the narrower, single-issue groups such as the tobacco industry, which over the years has successfully kept American foreign policy from putting heavy restrictions on international trade in and advertising of tobacco products. Likewise, computer hardware and software industries have successfully hardened the American attitude toward Chinese piracy of intellectual property rights.

[1] For example, under President Clinton, Senator Lloyd Bentsen and Representative Les Aspin left Congress to become the secretaries of the treasury and defense, respectively.

[2] Raymond A. Bauer, Ithiel de Sola Pool, and Lewis Anthony Dexter, *American Business and Public Policy: The Politics of Foreign Trade,* 2nd ed. (Chicago: Aldine-Atherton, 1972).

MAKERS AND SHAPERS OF FOREIGN POLICY

Makers
  the president
  the bureaucracy (secretaries of state, defense, and the treasury; the Joint Chiefs of Staff, and the director of the Central Intelligence Agency)
  Congress (Senate approves treaties; both chambers vote on financing; foreign policy and military policy committees in each chamber)
Shapers
  interest groups (economic, cultural/ethnic groups, human rights groups, environmental groups)
  the media

Another type of interest groups with a well-founded reputation for influence in foreign policy is made up of people with strong attachments and identifications to their country of origin. The interest group with the reputation for greatest influence is Jewish Americans, some of whom maintain family and emotional ties to Israel that may make them particularly concerned with U.S. policies toward Israel. Similarly, some Americans of Irish heritage, despite having resided in the United States for two, three, or four generations, still maintain a vigilance about American policies toward Ireland and Northern Ireland. Many other ethnic and national interest groups wield similar influence over American foreign policy.

A third type of interest group, one with a reputation that has been growing in the past two decades, is the human rights interest group. Such groups are made up of people who, instead of having self-serving economic or ethnic interests in foreign policy, are genuinely concerned for the welfare and treatment of people throughout the world—particularly those who suffer under harsh political regimes. A relatively small but often quite influential example is Amnesty International, whose exposés of human rights abuses have altered the practices of many regimes around the world. In recent years, the Christian Right has also

been a vocal advocate for the human rights of Christians who are persecuted in other parts of the world, most notably in China, for their religious beliefs. For example, the Christian Coalition joined groups like Amnesty International in lobbying Congress to cut trade with countries that permit attacks against religious believers.

Many types of interest groups help shape foreign policy. These groups include economic interest groups, ethnic or national interest groups, and human rights interest groups.

A related type of group with a fast-growing influence is the ecological or environmental group, sometimes called the "greens." Groups of this nature often depend more on demonstrations than on the usual forms and strategies of influence in Washington—lobbying and using electoral politics, for example. Demonstrations in strategically located areas can have significant influence on American foreign policy. Recent important examples were the demonstrations against the World Trade Organization (WTO) and its authority to impose limits and restrictions on sovereign nations, even in the United States, such as the 1999 protests in Seattle, Washington, and the 2001 protest in Genoa, Italy.

THE MEDIA   The most important element of the policy influence of the media is the speed and scale with which the media can spread political communications. In that factor alone, the media's influence is growing—more news reaches more people faster, and people's reaction times are therefore shorter than ever before. When we combine this ability to communicate faster with the "feedback" medium of public opinion polling, it becomes clear how the media have become so influential—they enable the American people to reach the president and the other official makers of foreign policy.[3]

The media links the public and the makers of foreign policy.

Putting It Together

What can we say about who really makes American foreign policy? First, except for the president, the influence of players and shapers varies from case to case—this is a good reason to look with some care at each example of foreign policy in this chapter. Second, since the one constant influence is the centrality of the president in foreign policy making, it is best to evaluate other actors and factors as they interact with the president.[4] Third, the reason influence varies from case to case is that each case arises under different conditions and with vastly different constraints: for issues that arise and are resolved quickly, the opportunity for influence is limited. Fourth, foreign policy experts will usually disagree about the level of influence any player or type of player has on policy making.

But just to get started, let's make a few tentative generalizations and then put them to the test with the substance and experience reported in the remainder of this chapter. First, when an important foreign policy decision has to be made under conditions of crisis—where "time is of the essence"—the influence of the presidency is at its strongest. Second, under those time constraints, access to the decision-making process is limited almost exclusively to the narrowest definition of the "foreign policy establishment." The arena for participation is tiny; any discussion at all is limited to the officially and constitutionally designated players. To put this another way, in a crisis, the foreign policy establishment works as it is supposed to.[5] As time becomes less restricted, even when the decision to be made is of great importance, the arena of participation expands to include more government players and more nonofficial, informal players—the most concerned interest groups and the most important journalists. In other words, the arena becomes more pluralistic, and therefore less distinguishable from the politics of domestic policy making. Third, because there are so many other countries with power and interests on any given issue, there are severe limits on the choices the United States can make. As one author concludes, in foreign affairs, "policy takes precedence over politics."[6] Thus, even though foreign policy mak-

---

[3]For further discussion of the vulnerability of modern presidents to the people through the media, see Theodore Lowi, *The Personal President: Power Invested, Promise Unfulfilled* (Ithaca, NY: Cornell University Press, 1985); Jeffrey K. Tulis, *The Rhetorical Presidency* (Princeton: Princeton University Press, 1987); Samuel Kernell, *Going Public: New Strategies of Presidential Leadership* (Washington, DC: Congressional Quarterly Press, 1986); Richard Rose, *The Postmodern President: The White House Meets the World* (Chatham, NJ: Chatham House, 1988); and George C. Edwards, *The Public Presidency: The Pursuit of Popular Support* (New York: St. Martin's, 1983).
[4]A very good brief outline of the centrality of the president in foreign policy will be found in Paul E. Peterson, "The President's Dominance in Foreign Policy Making," *Political Science Quarterly* 109, no. 2 (Summer 1994), pp. 215, 234.

[5]One confirmation of this will be found in Theodore Lowi, *The End of Liberalism,* 2nd ed. (New York: Norton, 1979), pp. 127–30; another will be found in Stephen Krasner, "Are Bureaucracies Important?" *Foreign Policy* 7 (Summer 1972), pp. 159–79. However, it should be added that Krasner was writing his article in disagreement with Graham T. Allison, "Conceptual Models and the Cuban Missile Crisis," *American Political Science Review* 63, no. 3 (September 1969), pp. 689–718.
[6]Peterson, "The President's Dominance in Foreign Policy Making," p. 232.

ing in noncrisis situations may more closely resemble the pluralistic politics of domestic policy making, foreign policy making is still a narrower arena with few participants.

The one constant influence on foreign policy making is the president.

THE VALUES IN AMERICAN FOREIGN POLICY

When President Washington was preparing to leave office in 1796, he crafted with great care, and with the help of Alexander Hamilton and James Madison, a farewell address that is one of the most memorable documents in American history. In it, one of Washington's greater concern was to warn the nation against foreign influence:

> History and experience prove that foreign influence is one of the most baneful foes of republican government. . . . The great rule of conduct for us in regard to foreign nations is, in extending our commercial relations to have with them as little political connection as possible. So far as we have already formed engagements let them be fulfilled with perfect good faith. Here let us stop. . . . There can be no greater error than to expect or calculate upon real favors from nation to nation. . . . Trust to temporary alliances for extraordinary emergencies, [but in all other instances] steer clear of permanent alliances with any portion of the foreign world. . . . Such an attachment of a small or weak toward a great and powerful nation dooms the former to be the satellite of the latter.[7]

With the exception of a few leaders such as Thomas Jefferson and Thomas Paine, who were

eager to take sides with the French against all others, Washington was probably expressing sentiments shared by most Americans. In fact, during most of the nineteenth century, American foreign policy was to a large extent no foreign policy. But Americans were never isolationist, if isolationism means the refusal to have any associations with the outside world. Americans were eager for trade and for treaties and contracts facilitating trade. Americans were also expansionists, but their vision of expansionism was limited to filling up the North American continent only.

Three familiar historical factors help explain why Washington's sentiments became the tradition and the source of American foreign policy values. The first was the deep antistatist ideology shared by most Americans in the nineteenth century and into the twentieth century. Although we witness widespread antistatism today, in the form of calls for tax cuts, deregulation, privatization, and other efforts to "get the government off our backs," such sentiments were far more intense in the past, when many Americans opposed foreign entanglements, a professional military, and secret diplomacy. The second factor was federalism. The third was the position of the United States in the world as a *client state* (a state that has the capacity to carry out its own foreign policy most of the time but still depends on the interests of one or more of the major powers). Most nineteenth-century Americans recognized that if the United States became entangled in foreign affairs, national power would naturally grow at the expense of the states, and so would the presidency at the expense of Congress. Why? Because foreign policy meant having a professional diplomatic corps, professional armed forces with a general staff—and secrets. This meant professionalism, elitism, and remoteness from citizens. Being a client state gave Americans the luxury of being able to keep its foreign policy to a minimum. Moreover, maintaining American sovereignty was in the interest of the European powers, because it prevented any one of them from gaining an advantage over the others in the Western Hemisphere.

---

[7]A full version of the text of the farewell address, along with a discussion of the contribution to it made by Hamilton and Madison, will be found in Daniel J. Boorstin, ed., *An American Primer* (Chicago: University of Chicago Press, 1966), vol. 1, pp. 192–210. This editing is by Richard B. Morris.

Americans have traditionally been skeptical of other nations' influence on their own foreign policy.

Legacies of the Traditional System

Two identifiable legacies flowed from the long tradition based on antistatism, federalism, and client status. One is the intermingling of domestic and foreign policy institutions. The second is unilateralism—America's willingness to go it alone. Each of these reveals a great deal about the values behind today's conduct of foreign policy.

INTERMINGLING OF DOMESTIC AND FOREIGN POLICY   Because the major European powers once policed the world, American political leaders could treat foreign policy as a mere extension of domestic policy. The *tariff* is the best example. A tax on one category of imported goods as a favor to interests in one section of the country would directly cause friction elsewhere in the country. But the demands of those adversely affected could be met without directly compromising the original tariff, by adding a tariff to still other goods that would placate those who were complaining about the original tariff. In this manner, Congress was continually adding and adjusting tariffs on more and more classes of commodities.

An important aspect of the treatment of foreign affairs as an extension of domestic policy was amateurism. Unlike many other countries, Americans refused to develop a tradition of a separate foreign service composed of professional people who spent much of their adult lives in foreign countries, learning foreign languages, absorbing foreign cultures, and developing a sympathy for foreign points of view. Instead, Americans have tended to be highly suspicious of any American diplomat or entrepreneur who spoke sympathetically of any such foreign viewpoints.[8] No systematic progress was made

[8]E. E. Schattschneider, *Politics, Pressures, and the Tariff* (Englewood Cliffs, NJ: Prentice-Hall, 1935).

to create a professional diplomatic corps until after the passage of the Foreign Service Act of 1946.

UNILATERALISM   Unilateralism, not isolationism, was the American posture toward the world until the middle of the twentieth century. Isolationism means to try to cut off contacts with the outside, to be a self-sufficient fortress. America was never isolationist; it preferred *unilateralism,* or "going it alone." Americans have always been more likely to rally around the president in support of direct action rather than sustained, diplomatic involvement.

Unilateralism and the intermingling of domestic and foreign policies are two identifiable legacies from America's traditional system of conducting foreign policy.

The Great Leap to World Power

The traditional era of U.S. foreign policy came to an end with World War I for several important reasons. First, the "balance of power" system[9] that had kept the major European powers from world war for a hundred years had collapsed.[10] In fact, the great powers themselves had collapsed internally. The most devastating of all wars up to that time had ruined their economies, their empires, and, in most cases, their political systems. Second, the United States was no longer a client state but in fact one of the great powers. Third, as we saw in earlier chapters, the United States was soon to shed its traditional domestic system of federalism

[9]"Balance of power" was the primary foreign policy role played by the major European powers during the nineteenth century, and it is a role available to the United States in contemporary foreign affairs, a role occasionally adopted but not on a world scale. This is the third of the four roles identified and discussed later in this chapter.
[10]The best analysis of what he calls the "100 years' peace" will be found in Karl Polanyi, *The Great Transformation* (New York: Rinehart, 1944; Beacon paperback ed., 1957), pp. 5ff.

with its national government of almost pure promotional policy. Thus, virtually all the conditions that contributed to the traditional system of American foreign policy had disappeared. Yet there was no discernible change in America's approach to foreign policy in the period between World War I and World War II. After World War I, as one foreign policy analyst put it, "the United States withdrew once more into its insularity. Since America was unwilling to use its power, that power, for purposes of foreign policy, did not really exist."[11]

The Great Leap in foreign policy was finally made thirty years after conditions demanded it and only after another world war. Following World War II, pressure for a new tradition came into direct conflict with the old. The new tradition required foreign entanglements; the old tradition feared them deeply. The new tradition required diplomacy; the old distrusted it. The new tradition required acceptance of antagonistic political systems; the old embraced democracy and was aloof from all else.

The values of the new tradition were all apparent during the *cold war.* Instead of unilateralism, the United States pursued *multilateralism,* entering into treaties with other nations to achieve its foreign policy goals. The most notable of these treaties is the one that formed the **North Atlantic Treaty Organization (NATO)** in 1949, which allied the United States, Canada, and most of Western Europe. With its NATO allies, the United States practiced a two-pronged policy in dealing with its rival, the Soviet Union: *containment* and *deterrence.* Fearing that the Soviet Union was bent on world domination, the United States fought wars in Korea and Vietnam to "contain" Soviet power. And in order to deter a direct attack against itself or its NATO allies, the United States developed a multibillion-dollar nuclear arsenal capable of destroying the Soviet Union many times over.

A new tradition for conducting foreign policy, which involved the pursuit of multilateralism, containment, and deterrence, was born during the cold war.

An arms race between the United States and the Soviet Union was extremely difficult if not impossible to resist because there was no way for either side to know when they had enough deterrent power to continue preventing aggression by the other side. The cold war ended abruptly in 1989 after the Soviet Union had spent itself into oblivion and allowed its empire to collapse. Many observers called the end of the cold war a victory for democracy. But more important, it was a victory for capitalism over communism, a vindication of the free market as the best way to produce the greatest wealth of nations. Furthering capitalism has long been one of the values guiding American foreign policy and this might be more true at the beginning of the twenty-first century than at any time before.

THE INSTRUMENTS OF MODERN AMERICAN FOREIGN POLICY

Any nation-state has at hand certain instruments, or tools, to use in implementing its foreign policy. Any instrument is neutral, capable of serving many goals. There have been many instruments of American foreign policy, and we can deal here only with those instruments we deem to be most important in the modern epoch: diplomacy, the United Nations, the international monetary structure, economic aid, collective security, and military deterrence. Each of these instruments will be evaluated in this section for its utility in the conduct of American foreign policy, and each will be assessed in light of the history and development of American values.

[11]John G. Stoessinger, *Crusaders and Pragmatists: Movers of Modern American Foreign Policy* (New York: Norton, 1985), pp. 21, 34.

Diplomacy

We begin this treatment of instruments with diplomacy because it is the instrument to which all other instruments should be subordinated, although they seldom are. **Diplomacy** is the representation of a government to other foreign governments. Its purpose is to promote national values or interests by peaceful means. According to Hans Morgenthau, "a diplomacy that ends in war has failed in its primary objective."[12]

The first effort to create a modern diplomatic service in the United States was made through the Rogers Act of 1924, which established the initial framework for a professional foreign service staff. But it took World War II and the Foreign Service Act of 1946 to forge the foreign service into a fully professional diplomatic corps.

Diplomacy, by its very nature, is overshadowed by spectacular international events, dramatic initiatives, and meetings among heads of state or their direct personal representatives. The traditional American distrust of diplomacy continues today, albeit in weaker form. Impatience with or downright distrust of diplomacy has been built not only into all the other instruments of foreign policy but also into the modern presidential system itself.[13] So much personal responsibility has been heaped upon the presidency that it is difficult for presidents to entrust any of their authority or responsibility in foreign policy to professional diplomats in the state department and other bureaucracies. And the American practice of appointing political friends and campaign donors to major ambassadorial positions does not inspire trust.

> Diplomacy's purpose is to protect national interests through peaceful means.

Distrust of diplomacy has also produced a tendency among all recent presidents to turn frequently to military and civilian personnel outside the state department to take on a special diplomatic role as direct personal representatives of the president. As discouraging as it is to those who have dedicated their careers to foreign service to have political hacks appointed over their heads, it is probably even more discouraging when they are displaced from a foreign policy issue as soon as relations with the country they are posted in begin to heat up. When a special personal representative is sent abroad to represent the president, that envoy holds a status higher than that of the local ambassador, and the embassy becomes the envoy's temporary residence and base of operation. Despite the impressive professionalization of the American foreign service—with advanced training, competitive exams, language requirements, and career commitment—this practice of displacing career ambassadors with political appointees and special personal presidential representatives continues.

For instance, when President Clinton in 1998 sought to boost the peace process in Northern Ireland, he called upon former senator George Mitchell. Mitchell received almost unanimous praise for his skill and patience in chairing the Northern Ireland peace talks. The caliber of his work in Northern Ireland led to Senator Mitchell's becoming involved in another of the world's apparently unsolvable conflicts, that between the Israelis and the Palestinians.

Despite the United States' track record of distrusting diplomacy, immediately following September 11, 2001, questions arose about how the United States could go after terrorist networks without the active cooperation of dozens of governments. Getting access to terrorists in various countries, plus assembling and keeping together the worldwide alliance of governments necessary to fight terrorism was a diplomatic, not a military, chore. In calls to more than eighty nations, then-Secretary of State Colin Powell helped to extract dozens of pledges that would have been more difficult to get months later, when worldwide sympathy for America would have waned. In short, global unity and success fighting terrorism required

[12]Hans Morgenthau, *Politics among Nations*, 2nd ed. (New York: Knopf, 1956), p. 505.
[13]See Lowi, *The Personal President*, pp. 167–69.

constant diplomatic efforts, not only on the part of Powell but also Secretary of Defense Donald Rumsfeld, then-National Security Advisor Condoleezza Rice, and even President George W. Bush.

The significance of diplomacy and its vulnerability to domestic politics may be better appreciated as we proceed to the other instruments. Diplomacy was an instrument more or less imposed on Americans as the prevailing method of dealing among nation-states in the nineteenth century. The other instruments to be identified and assessed below are instruments that Americans self-consciously crafted for themselves to take care of their own chosen place in the world affairs of the second half of the twentieth century. They are, therefore, more reflective of American culture and values than is diplomacy.

The United Nations

The utility of the **United Nations (UN)** to the United States as an instrument of foreign policy can too easily be underestimated. During the first decade or more after its founding in 1945, the United Nations was a direct servant of American interests. The most spectacular example of the use of the United Nations as an instrument of American foreign policy was the official UN authorization and sponsorship of intervention in Korea with an international "peacekeeping force" in 1950. Thanks to the Soviet boycott of the United Nations at that time, which deprived the U.S.S.R. of its ability to use its veto in the Security Council of the UN, the United States was able to conduct the Korean War under the auspices of the United Nations.

As the cold war intensified with the Bay of Pigs, the Cuban Missile Crisis, and then the Vietnam War, the UN became more of a domestic political issue. For example, in 1960, over 60 percent of the American public, when polled, were of the opinion that the UN was "doing a good job." By 1970, this positive support had dropped to just over 30 percent. And although positive opinion was climbing for a while in the 1990s, negative opinion (that the UN was doing a poor job) had climbed from a low of 10 percent in 1960 to highs of 50 percent in the '70s and '80s, fluctuating around the 40-plus percent level in the '90s. The main factor behind those variations in public opinion support was probably the involvement of U.S. armed forces in peace*keeping* missions and (especially) peace *enforcing* missions, including instances where our troops were under foreign command. This does not sit well with many Americans or their representatives in Congress, even though U.S. troops have served under foreign command in World War I, World War II, and some earlier cold war involvements. These were some of the reasons for Congress's decision in 1993 to refuse to pay our UN dues until the UN "met certain conditions." The precise amount of our UN debt is in dispute, but most estimates put it close to $1.5 billion in 1999—making us, according to the *New York Times,* the world's "biggest deadbeat."[14]

In 1999, Congress authorized payment of $926 million of its acknowledged debt to the UN in three installments, whenever the Secretary of State determines that the UN has met various conditions, including reform of UN management and reduction of our annual dues. In addition to the $926 million, Congress agreed to forgive $107 million the UN allegedly owes the United States. Regular U.S. dues for the UN organization budget, which had been 40 percent in 1946 (the first full year of operation), were reduced in 2001 from 25 percent to 22 percent. U.S. dues for peacekeeping were reduced from over 30 percent to 25 percent.[15]

The United Nations gained a new lease on life in the post–cold war era, first with its performance in the 1991 Gulf War. Although President Bush's immediate reaction to Iraq's invasion of Kuwait

---

[14]This paragraph owes a great deal to Bruce Jentleson, *American Foreign Policy—The Dynamics of Choice in the 21st Century* (New York: Norton, 2000), pp. 237–245.

[15]In 1997, the next five biggest dues payers were Japan (16.0%), Germany (9.0%), France (6.7%), the United Kingdom (5.6%), and the Russian Federation (4.4%). These figures are neither up-to-date nor precise, but they do give an accurate impression of the relative contribution made to the financing of the United Nations and its various commissions, committees, and diplomatic peacekeeping activities.

was unilateral, he quickly turned to the UN for sponsorship. The UN General Assembly immediately adopted resolutions condemning the invasion and approving the full blockade of Iraq. Once the blockade was seen as having failed to achieve the unconditional withdrawal demanded by the UN, the General Assembly adopted further resolutions authorizing the twenty-nine-nation coalition to use force if, by January 15, 1991, the resolutions were not observed. The Gulf War victory was a genuine UN victory. The cost of the operation was estimated at $61.6 billion. First authorized by Congress, actual U.S. outlays were offset by pledges from the other participants—the largest shares coming from Saudi Arabia ($15.6 billion), Kuwait ($16 billion), Japan ($10 billion), and Germany ($6.5 billion). The final U.S. costs were estimated at a maximum of $8 billion.[16]

The United Nations helps to support U.S. foreign policy goals by allowing the United States to rely upon another institution for peacekeeping.

Whether or not the UN is able to maintain its central position in future border and trade disputes, demands for self-determination, and other provocations to war depend entirely upon the character of each dispute. The Gulf War was a special case because it was a clear instance of invasion of one country by another that also threatened the control of oil, which is of vital interest to the industrial countries of the world. But in the case of the former Yugoslavia, although the Bosnian conflict violated the world's conscience, it did not threaten vital national interests outside the country's region.

When Yugoslavia's communist regime collapsed in the early 1990s, the country broke apart into historically ethnically distinct regions. In one of

these, Bosnia, a fierce war broke out among Muslims, Croatians, and Serbians. From the outset, all outside parties urged peace, and United Nations troops were deployed to create "safe havens" in several Bosnian cities and towns. But faced with resistance from NATO allies and from Russia, and with the unwillingness of the American people to risk the lives of U.S. soldiers over an issue not vital to U.S. interests, President Clinton gave up his stern warnings and accepted the outcome: the international community's failure to prevent Serbs from waging a war of aggression and genocide.

Not until November 1995, after still another year of frustration and with UN peacekeeping troops in increasingly serious danger from both sides in the Yugoslav civil war, was President Clinton able to achieve a ceasefire and a peace agreement in Dayton, Ohio, among the heads of the warring factions. (UN peacekeepers and aid workers were again present in Kosovo immediately following the pullout of hostile Serbian troops in 1999.) Despite the difficulty of restoring peace, the UN and its peacekeeping troops did an extraordinary job in the former Yugoslavia, dealing both with the intransigence of the warring parties and with the disagreement among the European powers about how to deal with a vicious and destructive civil war in their own neighborhood.

The 2001 terrorist attacks also implicated the United Nations. Less than three weeks after September 11, the UN Security Council unanimously (15–0) approved a U.S.-sponsored resolution requiring all countries to deny safe haven to anyone financing or committing a terrorist act. The resolution actually criminalized the financing of terrorist activity and extended its coverage beyond countries to individuals and "entities" within countries. The United Nations also created a committee of the Security Council members to monitor implementation of the resolution, which included the freezing of all monetary assets available to terrorists and the passage of tougher laws to detain suspected terrorists as well as to share information regarding terrorism. Moreover, although this resolution stresses economic rather than military means, it does not prohibit "use of force," which

---

[16]There was, in fact, an angry dispute over a "surplus" of at least $2.2 billion, on the basis of which Japan and others demanded a rebate. *Report of the Secretary of Defense to the President and Congress* (Washington, DC: Government Printing Office, 1992), p. 26.

the UN Charter allows as long as force is used for self-defense and not for "armed reprisals" after the fact.

The UN Security Council was central in the debate over the United States' potential invasion of Iraq during the fall of 2002. At first, President Bush was reluctant to seek UN approval because he believed that he already had enough UN authority based on past Security Council resolutions that Saddam Hussein had so egregiously disregarded. But growing opposition to unilateral U.S. action against Iraq on the part of several Security Council members produced second thoughts and led Bush to appear at the United Nations and request a renewed and more authoritative, unconditional resolution. In response to this renewed U.S. cooperativeness, the Security Council unanimously adopted a resolution, calling on Iraq's president Saddam Hussein to disarm and to allow weapons inspectors into Iraq.

Following authorization for weapons inspections, the Bush administration in early 2003 pressured the UN Security Council to support military action in Iraq, but met resistance from France, Russia, Germany, and others. Knowing they faced a veto by France and possibly Russia, the Bush administration ultimately decided to go to war without another UN Security Council vote. These recent UN interventions show the promise and the limits of the United Nations in the post–cold war era. Although the United States can no longer control UN decisions, as it could in the United Nations' early days, the UN continues to function as a useful instrument of American foreign policy.[17]

The International Monetary Structure

Fear of a repeat of the economic devastation that followed World War I brought the United States together with its allies (except the U.S.S.R.) to Bretton Woods, New Hampshire, in 1944 to create a new international economic structure for the postwar world. The result was two institutions: the International Bank for Reconstruction and Development (commonly called the World Bank) and the International Monetary Fund.

The World Bank was set up to finance long-term capital. Leading nations took on the obligation of contributing funds to enable the World Bank to make loans to capital-hungry countries. (The U.S. quota has been about one-third of the total.)

The *International Monetary Fund (IMF)* was set up to provide for the short-term flow of money. After the war, the dollar, instead of gold, was the chief means by which the currencies of one country would be "changed into" currencies of another country for purposes of making international transactions. To permit debtor countries with no international balances to make purchases and investments, the IMF was set up to lend dollars or other appropriate currencies to needy member countries to help them overcome temporary trade deficits. For many years after World War II, the IMF, along with U.S. foreign aid, in effect constituted the only international medium of exchange.

The World Bank and the IMF were created to prevent economic devastation in countries with struggling economies.

The IMF, with $93 billion, has more money to lend poor countries than the United States, Europe, or Japan (the three leading IMF shareholders) do individually and it makes its policy decisions in ways that are generally consonant with the interests of the leading shareholders.[18] Not surprisingly, the IMF immediately became

---

[17]Not all American policy makers agree that the UN is a worthy instrument of American foreign policy. The UN is on the verge of bankruptcy. For a review, see Barbara Crossette, "U.N., Facing Bankruptcy, Plans to Cut Payroll by Ten Percent," *New York Times*, February 6, 1996, p. A3.

[18]James Dao and Patrick E. Tyler, "U.S. Says Military Strikes Are Just a Part of Big Plan," *The Alliance,* 27 September 2001; and Joseph Kahn, "A Nation Challenged: Global Dollars," *New York Times*, 20 September 2001.

involved in the crises following September 11. Within two weeks it had approved a $135 million loan to economically troubled Pakistan, a strategic player in the war against the Taliban government of Afghanistan because of its location. Turkey, with its proximity to relevant areas in the Middle East, was also put back in the IMF pipeline.[19]

Economic Aid

Commitment to rebuilding war-torn countries came as early as commitment to the basic postwar international monetary structure. This is the way President Franklin Roosevelt put the case in a press conference in November 1942, less than one year after the United States entered World War II:

> Sure, we are going to rehabilitate [other nations after the war]. Why? . . . Not only from the humanitarian point of view . . . but from the viewpoint of our own pocketbooks, and our safety from future war.[20]

The particular form and timing for enacting American foreign aid was heavily influenced by Great Britain's sudden decision in 1947 that it would no longer be able to maintain its commitments to Greece and Turkey (full proof that America would now have to *have* clients rather than *be* one). Within three weeks of that announcement, President Truman recommended a $400 million direct aid program for Greece and Turkey, and by mid-May of 1947, Congress approved it. Since President Truman had placed the Greece-Turkey action within the larger context of a commitment to help rebuild and defend all countries the world over, wherever the leadership wished to develop democratic systems or to ward off communism, the Greek-Turkish aid was followed quickly by the historically unprecedented program that came to

be known as the Marshall Plan, named in honor of Secretary of State (and former five-star general) George C. Marshall.[21]

The *Marshall Plan*—officially known as the European Recovery Plan (ERP)—was essential for the rebuilding of war-torn Europe. By 1952, the United States had spent over $34 billion for the relief, reconstruction, and economic recovery of Western Europe. The emphasis was shifted in 1951, with passage of the Mutual Security Act, to building up European military capacity. Of the $48 billion appropriated between 1952 and 1961, over half went for military assistance, the rest for continuing economic aid. Over those years, the geographic emphasis of U.S. aid also shifted toward South Korea, Taiwan, the Philippines, Vietnam, Iran, Greece, and Turkey—that is, toward the rim of communism. In the 1960s, the emphasis shifted once again, toward what became known as the Third World. From 1962 to 1975, over $100 billion was sent, mainly to Latin America for economic assistance. Other countries of Africa and Asia were also brought in.[22]

Many critics have argued that foreign aid is really aid for political and economic elites, not for the people. Although this is to a large extent true, it needs to be understood in a broader context. If a country's leaders oppose distributing food or any other form of assistance to its people, there is little the United States, or any aid organization, can do, short of terminating the assistance. Goods have to be exchanged across national borders before they can reach the people who need them. Needy people would probably be worse off if the United States cut off aid altogether. The lines of international communication must be kept open. That is why diplomacy exists, and foreign aid can facilitate diplomacy, just as diplomacy is needed to help get foreign aid where it is most needed.

Another important criticism of U.S. foreign aid policy is that it has not been tied closely enough

---

[19]Turkey was desperate for help to extricate its economy from its worst recession since 1945. The Afghanistan crisis was going to hurt Turkey all the more, and its strategic location helped its case with the IMF. *New York Times,* 6 October 2001, p. A7.

[20]Quoted in John Lewis Gaddis, *The United States and the Origins of the Cold War* (New York: Columbia University Press, 1972), p. 21.

[21]The best account of the decision and its purposes will be found in Joseph Jones, *The Fifteen Weeks* (New York: Viking, 1955).

[22]Robert A. Pastor, *Congress and the Politics of U.S. Foreign Economic Policy* (Berkeley: University of California Press, 1980), pp. 256–80.

to U.S. diplomacy. The original Marshall Plan was set up as an independent program outside the state department and had its own separate missions in each participating country. Essentially, "ERP became a Second State Department."[23] This did not change until the program was reorganized as the Agency for International Development (AID) in the early 1960s. Meanwhile, the defense department has always had principal jurisdiction over that substantial proportion of economic aid that goes to military assistance. The department of agriculture administers the commodity aid programs, such as Food for Peace. Each department has in effect been able to conduct its own foreign policy, leaving many foreign diplomats to ask, "Who's in charge here?"

That brings us back to the history of U.S. efforts to balance traditional values with the modern needs of world leadership. Economic assistance is an instrument of American foreign policy, but it has been less effective than it might have been because of the inability of American politics to overcome its traditional opposition to foreign entanglements and build a unified foreign policy—something that the older nation-states would call a foreign ministry. The United States has undoubtedly made progress, but those outside its borders still often wonder who is in charge.

Economic aid such as the Marshall Plan has been an important tool of U.S. foreign policy, but it has had limitations.

Collective Security

In 1947, most Americans hoped that the United States could meet its world obligations through the United Nations and economic structures alone. But most foreign policy makers recognized this as a vain hope even as they were permitting and encouraging Americans to believe it. They had anticipated the need for military entanglements at the time of drafting the original UN charter by insisting upon language that recognized the right of all nations to provide for their mutual defense independently of the United Nations. And almost immediately after enactment of the Marshall Plan, the White House and a parade of state and defense department officials followed up with an urgent request to the Senate to ratify mutual defense alliances and to Congress to finance them.

At first quite reluctant to approve treaties providing for national security alliances, the Senate ultimately agreed with the executive branch. The first collective security agreement was the Rio Treaty (ratified by the Senate in September 1947), which created the Organization of American States (OAS). This was the model treaty, anticipating all succeeding collective security treaties by providing that an armed attack against any of its members "shall be considered as an attack against all the American States," including the United States. A more significant break with U.S. tradition against peacetime entanglements came with the North Atlantic Treaty (signed in April 1949), which created the North Atlantic Treaty Organization (NATO). ANZUS, a treaty tying Australia and New Zealand to the United States, was signed in September 1951. Three years later, the Southeast Asia Treaty created the Southeast Asia Treaty Organization (SEATO).

In addition to these multilateral treaties, the United States entered into a number of bilateral treaties—treaties between two countries. As one author has observed, the United States has been a *producer* of security while most of its allies have been *consumers* of security.[24] Figure 14.1 demonstrates that the United States has constantly devoted a greater percentage of its gross domestic product (GDP) to defense than have its NATO allies and Japan.

This pattern has continued in the post–cold war era, and its best illustration is in the Persian Gulf War, where the United States provided the initia-

---

[23]Quoted in Lowi, *The End of Liberalism*, 2nd ed., p. 162.

[24]George Quester, *The Continuing Problem of International Politics* (Hinsdale, IL: Dryden Press, 1974), p. 229.

FIGURE 14.1

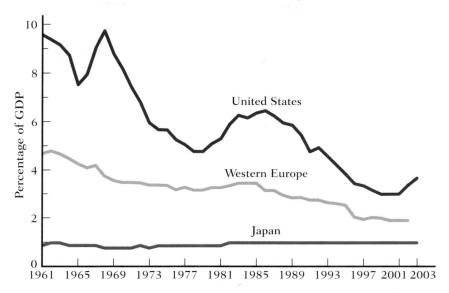

DEFENSE SPENDING AS A PERCENTAGE OF GROSS DOMESTIC PRODUCT, 1961–2003

SOURCES: Office of Management and Budget, *Budget of the United States Government, Fiscal Year 2005, Historical Tables* (Washington, DC: Government Printing Office, 1994); Stockholm International Peace Research Institute, (SIPRI).

tive, the leadership, and most of the armed forces, even though its allies were obliged to reimburse over 90 percent of the cost.

It is difficult to evaluate collective security and its treaties, because the purpose of collective security as an instrument of foreign policy is prevention, and success of this kind has to be measured according to what did *not* happen. The critics have argued that U.S. collective security treaties posed a threat of encirclement to the Soviet Union, forcing it to produce its own collective security, particularly the Warsaw Pact.[25] Nevertheless, no one can deny the counterargument that the world has enjoyed more than forty-five years without world war.

[25]The Warsaw Pact was signed in 1955 by the Soviet Union, the German Democratic Republic (East Germany), Poland, Hungary, Czechoslovakia, Romania, Bulgaria, and Albania. Albania later dropped out. The Warsaw Pact was terminated in 1991.

The cold war was marked by a dramatic increase in collective security treaties, including the creation of the North Atlantic Treaty Organization. These treaties have caused tension between great powers but have generally helped to maintain peace.

Although the Soviet Union has collapsed, Russia has emerged from a period of confusion and consolidation signaling its determination to play once again an active role in regional and world politics. The challenge for the United States and NATO in coming years will be how to broaden membership in the alliance to include the nations of Eastern Europe and some of the former Soviet republics without antagonizing Russia, which might see such an expansion of NATO as a new era of encirclement.

In 1998 the expansion of NATO took its first steps, extending membership to Poland, Hungary, and the Czech Republic. Most of Washington embraced this expansion as the true and fitting end of the cold war, and the U.S. Senate echoed this support with a resounding 80 to 19 vote to induct these three former Soviet satellites into NATO. The expansion was also welcomed among European member nations, who quickly approved the move, which was hailed as the final closing of the book on Yalta, the 1945 treaty that divided Europe into Western and Soviet spheres of influence after the defeat of Germany. But some strong voices did not support NATO expansion. George Kennan, architect of the United States' containment policy, predicted that NATO expansion was "the beginning of a new Cold War . . . a tragic mistake. . . . Our differences in the Cold War were with the Soviet Communist regime. And now we are turning our backs on the very people [Russia's current leaders] who mounted the greatest bloodless revolution in history to remove that Soviet Regime."[26]

NATO's ability to assist in implementing the uncertain peace in the former Yugoslavia was a genuine test of the viability of NATO, and collective security in general, now that the cold war is over. Efforts to halt the "ethnic cleansing" in Kosovo by the Serbs included months of a relentless bombing campaign, and while NATO prevailed, Kosovo's future seemed uncertain.

The September 11 attack on the United States was the first time in its fifty-plus year history that Article 5 of the North Atlantic Treaty had to be invoked; it provides that an attack on one country is an attack on all the member countries. The global coalition initially forged after September 11 numbered over 170 countries. Not all joined the war effort in Afghanistan, but most if not all provided some form of support for some aspect of the

war on terrorism, such as economic sanctions and intelligence. The war in Iraq, however, put the "coalition of the willing" to a test. The Bush administration was determined not to make its decision to go to war subject to the UN or NATO or any other international organization. The breadth of the United States' coalition was deemed secondary to its being nonconstraining. As a result, other than the British government, no major power supported the United States' actions.

NATO and the other mutual security organizations throughout the world are likely to survive. But these organizations are going to be less like military alliances and more like economic associations to advance technology, reduce trade barriers, and protect the world environment or diplomatic associations to fight terrorism. Another form of collective security may well have emerged from the 1991 Persian Gulf War, with nations forming temporary coalitions under UN sponsorship to check a particularly aggressive nation.

Military Deterrence

For the first century and a half of its existence as an independent republic, the United States held strongly to a "Minuteman" theory of defense: Maintain a small corps of professional officers, a few flagships, and a small contingent of marines; leave the rest of defense to the state militias. In case of war, mobilize as quickly as possible, taking advantage of the country's immense size and its separation from Europe to gain time to mobilize.

The United States applied this policy as recently as the post–World War I years and was beginning to apply it after World War II, until the new policy of preparedness won out. The cycle of demobilization-remobilization was broken, and in its place the United States adopted a new policy of constant mobilization and preparedness: deterrence, or the development and maintenance of military strength as a means of discouraging attack. After World War II, military deterrence against the Soviet Union became the fundamental American foreign policy objective, requiring a vast commitment of national resources. With preparedness as

---

[26]Quoted in Thomas Friedman, "NATO Expansion Starting New Cold War?" *Times-Picayune,* 5 May 1998, p. B5. See also *Baltimore Sun,* 2 May 1998, p. 12A.

the goal, peacetime defense expenditures grew steadily over the course of the cold war.

The United States maintains an active and strong military in hopes of deterring other nations from attack.

The end of the cold war raised public expectations for a "peace dividend" at last, after nearly a decade of the largest peacetime defense budget increases in U.S. history. Many defense experts, liberal and conservative, feared what they called a budget "free-fall," not only because deterrence was still needed but also because severe and abrupt cuts could endanger private industry in many friendly foreign countries as well as in the United States.

The Persian Gulf War brought both points dramatically into focus. First, the Iraqi invasion of Kuwait revealed the size, strength, and advanced modern technological base not only of the Iraqi armed forces but of other countries—Arab and non-Arab—including their capability, then or soon, to make atomic weapons and other weapons of massive destructive power. Moreover, the demand for advanced weaponry was intensifying. The decisive victory of the United States and its allies in the Gulf War, far from discouraging the international arms trade, gave it fresh impetus. Following the Gulf War victory, *Newsweek* reported that "industry reps quickly realized that foreign customers would now be beating a path to their doors, seeking to buy the winning weaponry." The Soviet Union at one time led the list of major world arms sellers, and Russia and several other republics of the former Soviet Union have continued to make international arms sales, particularly since now there are "no ideological limitations" in the competition for customers.[27] The United States now leads the list of military weapons exporters, followed by Russia, France, Great Britain, and China. Thus, some shrinkage of defense expenditure has

been desirable, but Democrats and Republicans alike agree that this reduction must be guided by the continuing need to maintain U.S. and allied credibility as a deterrent to post–cold war arms races.

As to the second point, domestic pressures join international demands to fuel post–cold war defense spending. Each cut in military production and each closing of a military base or plant translates into a significant loss of jobs. Moreover, the conversion of defense industries to domestic uses is not a problem faced by the United States alone. Figure 14.2 conveys a dramatic picture of the "international relations" of the production of one single weapons system, the F-16 fighter airplane.

While we no longer have a conventional arms race toward some kind of balance—as was the case during the cold war when it was called Mutual Assured Destruction (MAD)—there is greater awareness, post–September 11, that one small nuclear, biological, or chemical device delivered in a suitcase, a shipping carton, or a suicide bomber's waistband might be sufficient to bring a powerful nation-state to its knees. Here is deterrence put to its ultimate test.

Indeed, it's this new political reality that served as the impetus for the **Bush doctrine** of preemptive use of force. Preemption means striking first based on credible evidence that the adversary is likely to attack you. Deterrence is based on striking back, on the logic that the threat of second-strike capacity will stop an adversary from striking first. Although deterrence held up well during the Cold War, the nature of the enemy and of the threat has changed in the war on terrorism, requiring, at least according to the Bush doctrine, a different kind of response. Preemption might not be used often, but proponents argue that it needs to be an option if deterrence fails. The war in Iraq was the first major application of the Bush doctrine. Some allegations were made of Iraqi connections to Al Qaeda, but the main contention was that if Saddam Hussein was not disarmed of his weapons of mass destruction, and if he was not removed from power, the threat he posed to the U.S. would escalate from potential to actual.

---

[27]"Arms for Sale," *Newsweek*, 8 April 1991, pp. 22–27.

FIGURE 14.2

HOW THE F-16 IS PRODUCED:
THE INTERNATIONAL RELATIONS OF DEFENSE

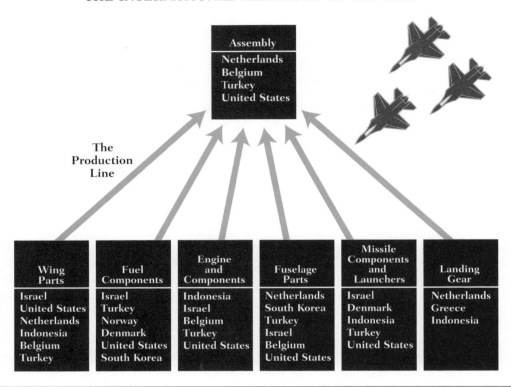

Assembly
Netherlands
Belgium
Turkey
United States

The
Production
Line

Wing Parts	Fuel Components	Engine and Components	Fuselage Parts	Missile Components and Launchers	Landing Gear
Israel	Israel	Indonesia	Netherlands	Israel	Netherlands
United States	Turkey	Israel	South Korea	Denmark	Greece
Netherlands	Norway	Belgium	Turkey	Indonesia	Indonesia
Indonesia	Denmark	Turkey	Israel	Turkey	
Belgium	United States	United States	Belgium	United States	
Turkey	South Korea		United States		

SOURCES: U.S. Congress, Office of Technology Assessment, *Arming Our Allies: Cooperation and Competition in Defense Technology,* Series OTA-ICS-449 (Washington, DC: Government Printing Office, May 1990), pp. 42–43. Information provided by the primary manufacturer, General Dynamics Corporation.

Before and during the war in Iraq, debate over whether Iraq actually possessed weapons of mass destruction has continued. In addition to questioning the basis of war, critics also questioned the strategy of the Bush doctrine. Preemptive force requires careful planning for enemy countermoves and other contingencies, including the enemy's own possible decision to act "pre-preemptively" and strike first. These critics further added that if the United States can take preemptive action in the name of its own security, what will stop other countries from doing so? These are all legitimate criticisms that will continue to be debated. And two other questions will persist: Does the Bush doctrine make the world a safer place? Is there a substitute for war?

ROLES NATIONS PLAY

Although each president has hundreds of small foreign fires to fight and can choose whichever instruments of policy best fit each particular situation, the primary foreign policy problem any president faces is choosing an overall role for the country in foreign affairs. Roles help us to define a situation in order to control the element of surprise in inter-

THE ROLES NATIONS PLAY

Napoleonic role—A country feels that in order to safeguard its form of government (i.e., democracy), it must ensure (by force if necessary) that other countries adopt the same form of government.

Holy Alliance role—Using every political instrument available to keep existing governments in power, whatever form those governments may take; keeping peace is more important than promoting one particular form of government.

Balance-of-power role—Major powers play off each other so that no one power or combination of powers can impose conditions on others.

Economic expansionist role—Being primarily concerned with what other countries have to buy or to sell and with their dependability in honoring contracts, regardless of their form of government.

national relations. Surprise is in fact the most dangerous aspect of international relations, especially in a world made smaller and more fragile by advances in and the proliferation of military technology.

Choosing a Role

The problem of choosing a role can be understood by identifying a limited number of roles played by nation-states in the past. Four such roles will be drawn from history—the Napoleonic, the Holy Alliance, the balance-of-power, and the economic expansionist roles. Although the definitions given here will be exaggerations of the real world, they do capture in broad outline the basic choices available.

THE NAPOLEONIC ROLE   The *Napoleonic role* takes its name from the role played by postrevolutionary France under Napoleon. The French at that time felt not only that their new democratic system of government was the best on earth but also that France would not be safe until democracy was adopted universally. If this meant intervention in the internal affairs of France's neighbors, and if that meant warlike reactions, then so be it. President Woodrow Wilson expressed a similar viewpoint when he supported the U.S. declaration of war in 1917 with his argu-

ment that "the world must be made safe for democracy." Obviously such a position can be adopted by any powerful nation as a rationalization for intervening at its convenience in the internal affairs of another country. But it can also be sincerely espoused, and in the United States it has from time to time enjoyed broad popular consensus. The United States played the Napoleonic role recently in ousting Philippine dictator Ferdinand Marcos (February 1986), Panamanian leader Manuel Noriega (December 1989), the Sandinista government of Nicaragua (February 1990), the military rulers of Haiti (September 1994), and Iraqi dictator Saddam Hussein (April 2003).

THE HOLY ALLIANCE ROLE   The concept of the *Holy Alliance role* emerged out of the defeat of Napoleon and the agreement by the leaders of Great Britain, Russia, Austria, and Prussia to preserve the social order against *all* revolution, including democratic revolution, at whatever cost. (Post–Napoleonic France also joined it.) The Holy Alliance made use of every kind of political instrument available—including political suppression, espionage, sabotage, and outright military intervention—to keep existing governments in power. The Holy Alliance role is comparable to the Napoleonic role in that each operates on the assumption that intervention in the internal affairs of other countries is justified for the maintenance of peace. But Napoleonic intervention is motivated by fear of dictatorship, and it can accept and even encourage revolution. In contrast, Holy Alliance intervention is antagonistic to any form of political change, even when this means supporting an existing dictatorship.[28] Because the Holy Alliance role became more important after the cold war ended, illustrations of this role will be given later in the chapter.

THE BALANCE-OF-POWER ROLE   The *balance-of-power role* is basically an effort by the major powers to play off each other so that no great power or combination of great and lesser powers can impose conditions on others. The most relevant example of the use of this strategy is found in the nineteenth century, especially the latter half. The feature of the balance-of-power role that is most distinct from the two previously identified roles is that this role accepts the political system of each country, asking no questions except whether the country will join an alliance and will use its resources to ensure that each country will respect the borders and interests of all the others.[29]

THE ECONOMIC EXPANSIONIST ROLE   The *economic expansionist role,* also called the capitalist role, shares with the balance-of-power role the attitude that the political system or ideology of a country is irrelevant; the only question is whether a country has anything to buy or sell and whether its entrepreneurs, corporations, and government agencies will honor their contracts. Governments and their armies are occasionally drawn into economic expansionist relationships in order to establish, reopen, or expand trade relationships, and to keep the lines of commerce open. But the role is political, too. The point can be made that the economic expansionist role was the role consistently played by the United States in Latin and Central America, until the cold war (perhaps in the 1960s and beyond) pushed us toward the Holy Alliance role with most of those countries.

Economic expansion does not happen spontaneously, however. In the past, economic expansion owed a great deal to military backing, because contracts do not enforce themselves, trade deficits are not paid automatically, and new regimes do not always honor the commitments made by regimes they replace. The only way to expand economic relationships is through diplomacy.

There are four roles that nations can choose when conducting foreign policy: the Napoleonic role, the Holy Alliance role, the balance-of-power role, and the economic expansionist role.

Roles for America Today

Although "making the world safe for democracy" was used to justify the U.S. entry into World War I, it was taken more seriously after World War II, when at last the United States was willing to play a more sustained part in world affairs. The Napoleonic role was most suited to America's view of the postwar world. To create the world's ruling regimes in the American image would indeed give Americans the opportunity to return to their private pursuits, for if all or even most of the world's countries were governed by democratic constitutions, there would be no more war, since no democracy would ever attack another democracy— or so it has been assumed.[30]

[28]For a thorough and instructive exposition of the original Holy Alliance Pattern, see Paul M. Kennedy, *The Rise and Fall of the Great Powers: Economic Change and Military Conflict from 1500 to 2000* (New York: Random House, 1987), pp. 159–60. And for a comparison of the Holy Alliance role with the balance-of-power role, to be discussed next, see Polanyi, *The Great Transformation,* pp. 5–11 and 259–62.

[29]Felix Gilbert et al., *The Norton History of Modern Europe* (New York: Norton, 1971), pp. 1222–24.

[30]For a summary of the entire literature about the "democratic peace," see Henry S. Farber and Joanne Gowa, "Politics and Peace," *International Security* 20, no. 2 (Fall 1995), pp. 123–46. See also Jack Levi, "Domestic Politics and War," *Journal of Interdisciplinary History* 18, no. 4 (Spring 1988), pp. 653–73.

MAKING THE WORLD SAFE FOR DEMOCRACY
The emergence of the Soviet Union as a super-power was the overwhelming influence on American foreign policy thinking in the post–World War II era. The distribution of power in the world was "bipolar," and Americans saw the world separated in two, with an "iron curtain" dividing the communist world from the free world. Immediately after the war, America's foreign policy goal had been "pro-democracy," a Napoleonic role dominated by the Marshall Plan and the genuine hope for a democratic world. This quickly shifted toward a Holy Alliance role, with "containment" as the primary foreign policy criterion.[31] Containment was fundamentally a Holy Alliance concept. According to foreign policy expert Richard Barnet, during the 1950s and 1960s, "the United States used its military or paramilitary power on an average of once every eighteen months either to prevent a government deemed undesirable from coming to power or to overthrow a revolutionary or reformist government considered inimical to America's interest."[32] Although Barnet did not refer to Holy Alliance, his description fits the model perfectly.

During the 1970s, the United States played the Holy Alliance role less frequently, not so much because of the outcome of the Vietnam War as because of the emergence of a multipolar world. In 1972, the United States accepted (and later recognized) the communist government of the People's Republic of China and broke forever its pure bipolar, cold war view of world power distribution. Other powers became politically important as well, including Japan, the European Economic Community (now the European Union), India, and, depending on their own resolve, the countries making up the Organization of Petroleum Exporting Countries (OPEC). The United States experimented with all four of the previously identified

roles, depending on which was appropriate to a specific region of the world. In the Middle East, America tended to play an almost classic balance-of-power role, by appearing sometimes cool in its relations with Israel and by playing one Arab country against another. The United States has been able to do this despite the fact that every country in the Middle East recognizes that for cultural, domestic, and geostrategic reasons, the United States has always considered Israel its most durable and important ally in the region and has unwaveringly committed itself to Israel's survival in a very hostile environment. President Nixon introduced balance-of-power considerations in the Far East by "playing the China card." In other parts of the world, particularly in Latin America, America tended to hold to the Holy Alliance and Napoleonic roles.

During the cold war, the United States experimented with all four foreign policy roles, depending on which one was appropriate to that region of the world.

This multipolar phase ended after 1989, with the collapse of the Soviet Union and the end of the cold war. Soon thereafter the Warsaw Pact collapsed too, ending armed confrontation in Europe. With almost equal suddenness, the popular demand for "self-determination" produced several new nation-states and the demand for still more. On the one hand, it is indeed good to witness the reemergence of some twenty-five major nationalities after anywhere from forty-five to seventy-five years of suppression. On the other hand, policy makers with a sense of history are aware that this new world order bears a strong resemblance to the world of 1914. Then, the trend was known as "Balkanization." Balkanization meant nationhood and self-determination, but it also meant war. The Soviet Union after World War I and Yugoslavia after World War II kept more than twenty nationalities from making war against each other for several decades. In 1989 and the years that followed,

[31]The original theory of containment was articulated by former ambassador and scholar George Kennan in a famous article published under the pseudonym Mr. X, "The Sources of Soviet Conduct," *Foreign Affairs* 25 (1947), p. 556.
[32]Richard Barnet, "Reflections," *New Yorker*, 9 March 1987, p. 82.

the world was caught unprepared for the dangers of a new disorder that the reemergence of these nationalities produced.

Note also that the demand for nationhood emerged with new vigor in many other parts of the world—the Middle East, South and Southeast Asia, and South Africa. Perhaps we are seeing worldwide Balkanization; we should not overlook the spirit of nationhood among ethnic minorities in Canada and the United States.

MAKING THE WORLD SAFE FOR DEMOCRACY AND MARKETS The abrupt end of the cold war unleashed another dynamic factor, the globalization of markets; one could call it the globalization of capitalism. This is good news, but it has its problematic side because the free market can disrupt nationhood. Although the globalization of markets is enormously productive, countries like to enjoy its benefits while attempting at the same time to prevent international economic influences from affecting local jobs, local families, and established class and tribal relationships.

This struggle between capitalism and nationhood produces a new kind of bipolarity in the world. The old world order was shaped by *external bipolarity*—of West versus East. This seems to have been replaced by *internal bipolarity*, wherein each country is struggling to make its own hard policy choices to preserve its cultural uniqueness while competing effectively in the global marketplace.

Approval of the North American Free Trade Agreement (NAFTA) serves as the best example of this struggle within the United States. NAFTA was supported by a majority of Democrats and Republicans on the grounds that a freer, global market was in America's national interest. But even as NAFTA was being embraced by large bipartisan majorities in Congress, three important factions were rising to fight it. Former presidential candidate Pat Buchanan led a large segment of conservative Americans to fight NAFTA because, he argued, communities and families would be threatened by job losses and by competition from legal and illegal immigrant workers. Another large faction, led by Ross Perot, opposed NAFTA largely on

the theory that American companies would move their operations to Mexico, where labor costs are lower. Organized labor also joined the fight against NAFTA.

Another form of internal bipolarity became evident in 1999 over the World Trade Organization (WTO) and its authority to impose limits and restrictions on sovereign nations, even the United States. The WTO had been around since 1994, when it was set up by the major trading nations to facilitate implementation of treaties made under the General Agreement on Tariffs and Trade (GATT). But protestors in Seattle saw the WTO as a threat to local ways of life and a contributor to job loss, environmental degradation, and violation of human rights.

In the new global marketplace, nations continually undergo internal debates in an attempt to balance their national identities with their developing roles in international capitalism. The United States has adopted a policy, through diplomacy and force, to promote a stable marketplace with democratic ideals.

The global market is here to stay and American values have changed enough to incorporate it, despite the toll it may take on community and family tradition. Meanwhile, many of the elements of foreign policy created during the cold war still exist because they turned out to be good adjustments to the modern era. The Marshall Plan and the various forms of international economic aid that succeeded it continue to this day. Although appropriations for foreign aid have been shrinking, only a small minority of members of the Senate and the House favor the outright abolition of foreign aid programs. NATO and other collective security arrangements continue, as do some aspects of containment even though there is no longer a Soviet Union, because collective security arrangements have, as we shall see, proven useful in dealing with new democracies and other nations seeking to join the global market. Even though the former Soviet Union is now more often an ally than an adversary, the United States still quite frequently uses unilateral and multilateral means of keeping civil wars contained within their own borders, so that conflict does not spread into neighboring states. America is practicing a new form of containment, but one that is based on the values and institutions of cold war containment.

The quest for a global market is more than a search for world prosperity. Economic globalization carries with it the hope that economic competition will displace armed conflict, perhaps even reducing if not eliminating the need for traditional diplomacy. But since there are too many instances in world history when economic competition actually led to war rather than avoided it, the United States has added democratization to the recipe of globalization because of the fairly well-supported hypothesis that democracies never go to war against each other. Thus democratization is a genuine and strongly committed goal of U.S. foreign policy, even if it is secondary to economic expansion. Meanwhile, we play the economic card in hopes that capitalism will contribute not only to world prosperity but also to the expansion of democratization.

One of the first indications of the post–cold war American foreign policy was former President George H. W. Bush's conciliatory approach to the dictatorial regime of the People's Republic of China after its brutal military suppression of the democratic student movement in Tiananmen Square in June 1989. Subsequently, President Clinton also maintained friendly relations with the dictatorial regimen, and both presidents continued to grant the Chinese "normal trade relations" status. Their policy was to separate China's trade status from its human rights record, arguing that economic growth provided the only effective means to bring about political reform in a country as large and as powerful as China.

THE HOLY ALLIANCE ROLE IN THE POST–COLD WAR ERA   During the cold war era, the purpose

of the Holy Alliance role was to keep regimes in power as long as they did not espouse Soviet foreign policy goals. In the post–cold war world, the purpose of the Holy Alliance role is still to keep regimes in power, but only as long as they maintain general stability, keep their nationalities contained within their own borders, and encourage their economies to attain some level of participation in the global market. If countries fail to satisfy these conditions, the United States has shown signs of reverting to its Napoleonic role. The United States has also continued to confront unfriendly dictators by adopting a Napoleonic strategy of intervention.

We have already dealt with the first case of the Holy Alliance role in the post–cold war era, Iraq's invasion of Kuwait and our Desert Storm response to it. (It was used earlier in this chapter to illustrate the renewed importance of the UN) Desert Storm is in fact a very dramatic case of the Holy Alliance role. Iraq's invasion of Kuwait occurred in July 1990, and Desert Storm was not undertaken until January 1991. In the interim, President George H. W. Bush was mobilizing Congress and the American people, not only in case the United States had to intervene militarily, but also in hopes that the possibility of such action might convince Saddam Hussein to withdraw voluntarily. President Bush also put together a worldwide alliance of twenty-nine nations—he had no intention of leading the United States into Desert Storm without this alliance, even though most of its members did not send troops but instead sent political approval plus what amounted to a monetary subscription. Bush had initially taken a Napoleonic position, urging the people of Iraq to "take matters into their own hands" and to force Hussein to "step aside." But after America withdrew its troops, and uprisings inside Iraq began to emerge, President Bush backed away, thus revealing his real intent of leaving the existing dictatorship in power, with or without Hussein. It was enough that the Iraqis stayed within their borders.

Bosnia was another clear case of America playing the Holy Alliance role. At first, the United States refused to exert leadership, and it deferred to the European nations when civil war erupted after Croatia and Bosnia-Herzegovina declared independence from Yugoslavia. When Europe failed to address the problem adequately, the United States and the United Kingdom stepped in, again to no avail. Although our surprise bombing in 1995 to drive the warring factions to the negotiating table was virtually unilateral, what emerged was a new alliance of twenty-five nations acting "in concert" to separate the warring factions from one another. And, although one-third of the sixty thousand occupying troops and virtually all the navy and air force units were American, twenty-four other nations established and maintained a physical presence in the field, all in order to maintain the status quo. Almost everything about the Bos-nian operation was an acting out of the traditional Holy Alliance role.

Kosovo in 1999 is another case of post–cold war Holy Alliance policy—although history may prove that the United States and virtually the entire Western world stumbled into this war.[33] Throughout 1998 and early 1999, ethnic cleansing was proceeding in Kosovo, but the United States would not go it alone, and the NATO nations (except for Great Britain) were not willing to intervene in Kosovo. European leaders ultimately reconsidered but only if the United States took the lead and promised to limit the assault to an air war only, which guaranteed a minimum of casualties on the allied side.

So the United States got its alliance—and a precedent-setting one—but without any ground troops. President Clinton deserves some blame for the delays and for the artificial restrictions that allowed Slobodan Milosevic to make the eventual intervention by the alliance all the more dangerous for the Kosovars, whom the United States wanted to defend and protect. The charge that Clinton's impeachment delayed action on Kosovo seems to have had some basis to it. But there are inherent limits to multinational coalitions, which President Clinton had to confront no matter what his domestic political distractions were at the time. NATO is simply a more formalized version of any multicoun-

try alliance with the same fundamental problem of any such alliance: *The power of decision tends toward the weakest member.* This was undoubtedly in the mind of Admiral Leighton Smith, commander of NATO forces in southern Europe, 1994–1996, when he observed of Kosovo: "The lesson we've learned is that coalitions aren't good ways to fight a war."[34] Opposition within the NATO alliance to intervene in Kosovo came mostly from the weaker and more internally divided Italy and Greece than from Britain, France, or Germany.

The Kosovo campaign validates what we have been observing throughout this chapter: Holy Alliance politics is the prevailing American role in the world today, and the United States draws virtually all its allies and potential allies into that role at one point or another. As the *Washington Post* put it in 1999:

> Whatever the shortcomings, fighting in coalition arrangements appears to be an unavoidable fact of post–Cold War life. . . . "We need partners both for political legitimacy and for risk-sharing," says . . . a senior Pentagon planner earlier in the Clinton administration.[35]

The *Economist* magazine goes even further:

> The one-superpower world will not last. [China, Russia, and the Muslim world will all become geopolitical competitors.]
>   . . . This is why the alliance of the democracies needs not only new members but also a new purpose. The alliance can no longer be just a protective American arm around Europe's shoulder; it also has to be a way for Europe and America to work together in other parts of the world. . . . This must be done—if it can be done at all—in partnership with America. . . . [36]

[33]See, for example, the cover story of the *Economist,* "Stumbling into War," 27 March–2 April 1999, pp. 17, 27, 49, 50.

[34]Bradley Graham and Dana Priest, "'No Way to Fight a War': The Limits of Coalitions," *Washington Post National Weekly Edition,* 14 June 1999, p. 8.

[35]Quoted in Graham and Priest, "'No Way to Fight a War,'" p. 8.

[36]Editorial, "Leaders: When the Snarling's Over," the *Economist,* 13 March 1999, p. 17.

A new alliance with a new purpose was developed in response to the terrorist attacks of September 11. Such an international alliance has not been seen since the mid-nineteenth century, when the threat came from middle-class revolutionaries rather than religious extremists. But even though the enemies are different, the goals and strategies are about the same. All countries in the West are vulnerable because Al Qaeda and its associated groups are anti-West. All capitalist and developing countries are susceptible because terrorism is intensely anticapitalist. And all moderate Arab regimes are vulnerable because they are seen by Al Qaeda as traitors and collaborators with the West. All of these vulnerable nation-states need each other to deprive terrorists of the turf they need for safe havens, headquarters, training, and communication, not to mention financing. Even though the war against the Taliban regime was almost entirely conducted by the United States, there was no hope for a sustained campaign without the substantial cooperation and participation of many other countries.

Yet once the Afghan phase of the war on world terrorism began quieting down, the United States confronted a new challenge: the resurgence of Iraq and the possibility that the weapons of mass destruction Saddam Hussein was thought to possess would be used against the United States or one of its allies. President Bush's response, the "Bush doctrine," as already alluded to, was a significant departure from the Holy Alliance model and movement toward a Napoleonic role.

In the post-cold war era, the Holy Alliance role seems to be more prominent than ever for the United States.

No foreign policy role—however the roles are categorized—can ever relieve the United States of the need for sustained diplomacy. In fact, diplomacy has become all the more important because despotic regimes eventually fail and in their fail-

ures create instability. Since September 11, it is also quite clear that failing regimes can become the breeding grounds for world terrorism. This is not to argue that war is never justifiable or that peace can always be achieved through discussions among professional diplomats. It is only to argue that there are limits to any role a country chooses to play and that failure will come faster and will be more serious if the choice of role is not made with patience, deliberation, rationality, and most important, a sense of history.

DOES FOREIGN POLICY WORK?

The American people are too large and diffuse a nation to participate in making foreign policy in any truly democratic way. A people, even a free and mature people, can at best set limits or broadly define national interests within which policy makers and policy shapers can operate. A people can constrain power but cannot guide or direct the powerful.

If the whole American people is too broad to conduct foreign policy, the American presidency is too narrow. We need a "vital middle" player to form foreign policy in our democracy. This "vital middle" is in fact provided by the Constitution. Foreign policy was always supposed to involve the president and Congress, and now that the cold war has ended, no time is more appropriate to revive that principle. During the cold war, a genuine foreign policy debate was carried out in Congress about once every decade. Each time it happened, it was a great moment of renewal of the Constitution and redirection and revitalization of public policy. The "Cooper/Church" debate in 1970 over the continuation of military activity in Cambodia did very little to alter the course of the Vietnam War, but in focusing on the constitutionality of the war and the legality of the U.S. incursion into Cambodia, the debate revived the strength of constitutionalism in the United States and brought America to its senses about the difference between democracy and tyranny. Almost exactly twenty years later, the Persian Gulf War did the same thing. Anticipating opposition in Congress, President Bush sought and got UN support and multilateral cooperation. When he took the issue to Congress in January 1991, he was supported by a narrow margin, but he got from the debate an enlightened and guided support that no opinion poll could have provided. Success in the Gulf War brought Bush a 90 percent popular approval rating. But that was not the true measure of his political base; Congress was.

The end of the cold war has opened Congress to opportunities in foreign policy debates that it has not had since before the Great Depression. During the cold war, following as it did a world war and a long domestic economic crisis, Congress developed what one expert has called "a culture of deference"—a bipartisan culture of defeat that can be summed up by a maxim shared by most influential members of the House and Senate: "We shouldn't make foreign policy."[37] But this doesn't make any sense any more. Foreign policy making in the United States will remain the president's domain. But public deliberation and debate, in an ongoing search for the national interest, is the domain of Congress. Congress is the vital middle between a hopeless isolationist rejection of foreign policy altogether and an equally hopeless delegation of total power to the chief executive.

CHAPTER REVIEW

This chapter began by raising some dilemmas about forming foreign policy in a democracy like the United States. Skepticism about foreign entanglements and the secrecy surrounding many foreign policy issues form the basis of these dilemmas. Although we cannot provide solutions to the foreign policy issues that the United States faces, we can provide a well-balanced analysis of the problems of foreign policy.

[37]Stephen R. Weissman, *A Culture of Deference* (New York: Basic Books, 1995), p. 17.

The first section of this chapter looked at the players in foreign policy: the makers and the shapers. The influence of institutions and groups historically has varied from case to case, with the important exception of the president. Since the president is central to all foreign policy, it is best to assess how other actors interact with the president. In most instances, this interaction involves only the narrowest element of the foreign policy establishment. The American people have an opportunity to influence foreign policy, but primarily through Congress or interest groups.

The next section, on values, traced the history of American values that had a particular relevance to American perspectives on the outside world. We found that the American fear of a big government applied to foreign as well as domestic governmental powers. The founders and the active public of the founding period all recognized that foreign policy was special, that the national government had special powers in its dealings with foreigners, and that presidential supremacy was justified in the conduct of foreign affairs. The only way to avoid the big national government and presidential supremacy was to avoid the foreign entanglements that made foreign policy, diplomacy, secrecy, and presidential discretion necessary. Americans held on to their "antistatist" tradition until World War II, long after world conditions cried out for American involvement. And even as it became involved in world affairs, the United States held on tightly to the legacies of one hundred fifty years of tradition: the intermingling of domestic and foreign policy institutions, and unilateralism, the tendency to "go it alone" when confronted with foreign conflicts.

We then looked at the instruments—that is, the tools—of American foreign policy. These are the basic statutes and the institutions by which foreign policy has been conducted since World War II: diplomacy, the United Nations, the international monetary structure, economic aid, collective security, and military deterrence. Although Republicans and Democrats look at the world somewhat differently, and although each president has tried to impose a distinctive flavor on foreign policy, they have all made use of these basic instruments, and that has given foreign policies a certain continuity. When Congress created these instruments after World War II, the old tradition was still so strong that it moved Congress to try to create instruments that would do their international work with a minimum of diplomacy—a minimum of human involvement. This is what we called power without diplomacy.

The next section concentrated on the role or roles the president and Congress have sought to play in the world. To help simplify the tremendous variety of tactics and strategies that foreign policy leaders can select, we narrowed the field down to four categories of roles nations play, suggesting that there is a certain amount of consistency and stability in the conduct of a nation-state in its dealings with other nation-states. These were labeled according to actual roles that diplomatic historians have identified in the history of major Western nation-states: the Napoleonic, Holy Alliance, balance-of-power, and economic expansionist roles.

We also attempted to identify and assess the role of the United States in the post–cold war era, essentially the Holy Alliance role. But whatever its advantages may be, the Holy Alliance approach will never allow the United States to conduct foreign policy without diplomacy. America is tied inextricably to the perils and ambiguities of international relationships, and diplomacy is still the monarch of all available instruments of foreign policy.

We concluded by returning to the dilemma we raised in the chapter's introduction: In a democracy like the United States, who should make foreign policy? The chapter provided numerous case studies to seek an answer to this question. We believe that between the extremes of isolationism and total power resting with the president resides a middle ground where the American people can express their will through the members of Congress. The national interest can be defined only through debate and deliberation, which we hope will serve as the foundations for the formation of foreign policy in the American democracy.

KEY TERMS

balance-of-power rule   The strategy whereby many countries form alliances with one or more other countries in order to counterbalance the behavior of other, usually more powerful, nation-states.

Bush doctrine   Foreign policy based on the idea that the United States should take preemptive action against threats to its national security.

client state   A nation-state dependent upon a more powerful nation-state but still with enough power and resources to be able to conduct its own foreign policy up to a point.

cold war   The period of struggle between the United States and the former Soviet Union between the late 1940s and 1990.

containment   The policy used by the United States during the cold war to restrict the expansion of communism and limit the influence of the Soviet Union.

deterrence   The development and maintenance of military strength as a means of discouraging attack.

diplomacy   The representation of a government to other foreign governments.

economic expansionist role   The strategy often pursued by capitalist countries to adopt foreign policies that will maximize the success of domestic corporations in their dealings with other countries.

executive agreement   An agreement between the president and another country, which has the force of a treaty but does not require the Senate's "advice and consent."

Holy Alliance role   A strategy pursued by a superpower to prevent any change in the existing distribution of power among nation-states, even if this requires intervention into the internal affairs of another country in order to keep a ruler from being overthrown.

International Monetary Fund (IMF)   An institution established in 1944 at Bretton Woods, New Hampshire, to provide loans to needy member countries and to facilitate international monetary exchange.

Marshall Plan   The U.S. European Recovery Plan, in which over $34 billion was spent for relief, reconstruction, and economic recovery of Western Europe after World War II.

multilateralism A foreign policy that seeks to encourage the involvement of several nation-states in coordinated action, usually in relation to a common adversary, with terms and conditions usually specified in a multicountry treaty, such as NATO.

Napoleonic role Strategy pursued by a powerful nation to prevent aggressive actions against itself by improving the internal state of affairs of a particular country, even if this means encouraging revolution in that country.

North American Free Trade Agreement (NAFTA) An agreement among Canada, the United States, and Mexico that promotes economic cooperation and abolishes many trade restrictions between the three countries.

North Atlantic Treaty Organization (NATO) A treaty organization comprising the United States, Canada, and most of Western Europe, formed in 1948 to counter the perceived threat from the Soviet Union.

tariff A tax placed on imported goods.

unilateralism A foreign policy that seeks to avoid international alliances, entanglements, and permanent commitments in favor of independence, neutrality, and freedom of action.

United Nations (UN) The organization of nations founded in 1945, mainly to serve as a channel for negotiation and a means of settling international disputes peaceably. It has had frequent successes in providing a forum for negotiation and on some occasions a means of preventing international conflicts from spreading. On a number of occasions, the UN has been a convenient cover for U.S. foreign policy goals.

FOR FURTHER READING

Crabb, Cecil V., and Kevin V. Mulcahy. *Presidents and Foreign Policymaking: From FDR to Reagan.* Baton Rouge: Louisiana State University Press, 1986.

Gilpin, Robert. *The Political Economy of International Relations.* Princeton: Princeton University Press, 1987.

Graubard, Stephen, ed. "The Exit from Communism." *Daedalus* 121, no. 2 (Spring 1992).

Graubard, Stephen, ed. "The Quest for World Order." *Daedalus* 124, no. 3 (Summer 1995).

Greenfield, Liah. *Nationalism: Five Roads to Modernity.* Cambridge: Harvard University Press, 1993.

Keller, William W. *Arm in Arm: The Political Economy of the Global Arms Race.* New York: Basic Books, 1995.

Kennan, George F. *Around the Cragged Hill: A Personal and Political Philosophy.* New York: Norton, 1993.

Kennedy, Paul M. *The Rise and Fall of the Great Powers: Economic Change and Military Conflict from 1500 to 2000.* New York: Random House, 1987.

LaFeber, Walter. *The American Age: United States Foreign Policy at Home and Abroad since 1750.* New York: Norton, 1989.

Smist, Frank J., Jr. *Congress Oversees the U.S. Intelligence Community, 1947–1994,* 2nd ed. Knoxville: University of Tennessee Press, 1994.

U.S. Congress. *Report of the Congressional Committees Investigating the Iran-Contra Affair.* New York: Random House, 1988.

Wirls, Daniel. *Buildup: The Politics of Defense in the Reagan Era.* Ithaca, NY: Cornell University Press, 1992.

EPILOGUE

Governance

Now that we have reviewed America's politics, political institutions, and public policies, let us conclude by reflecting on the question of governance. Are we well governed? The answer involves at least three issues: (1) the size and scope of government, (2) how reasonably and effectively the government does what it does, and (3) whether the government generally does the right thing.

BIG GOVERNMENT

At one time Americans vigorously debated the proper size and scope of government. Since Franklin Roosevelt's New Deal, Democrats have been advocates of "big government" to solve the nation's problems. Until recently, though, Republicans agreed with Ronald Reagan's assertion that government was a problem rather than a solution. This debate is virtually at an end. The Republican Party, led by George W. Bush, has become firmly committed to the use of the governmental power it once excoriated.

President Bush, of course, is no ordinary Republican. He is the third generation of a powerful Republican family—through his father, former President George H. W. Bush, and his grandfather, Prescott Bush, a distinguished Republican U.S. senator from Connecticut. President Bush's father, the first President Bush, held a number of important government posts as well

CORE OF THE ANALYSIS

- To decide whether we are well governed we must look at three major issues: the size and scope of government; how reasonably and effectively government does what it does; whether the government generally does the right thing.

- The once-vigorous debate over the proper size of government is virtually at an end. Republicans and Democrats are now both firmly committed to "big government."

- The effectiveness of government action can be analyzed according to four criteria: appropriateness, rationality, responsiveness, and significance.

- Whether government generally does the right thing is the most important question to ask and the hardest to answer. It is the job of each citizen to see that government does the right thing.

as the top position in the Republican National Committee, and George W. Bush learned national campaign politics during the Reagan administration. You can hardly be more Republican than that. And any thoroughgoing Republican will be for capitalism, and that means singing in the free-market, laissez-faire choir.

George W. Bush made a much more concerted and, some would say, sincere effort than his father to hold the Republican Party together by making stronger and more specific appeals to the Christian Right and the secular Right factions of the party because they had been vital to Republican victories at least since 1994. But no one doubted that George W. would remain first and foremost a strong antigovernment, free-market ideologue and that he would continue opposing the expansion of the national government. This would be accomplished primarily by lightening the tax burden with deep cuts in taxes, by lowering the tax rates of those classes most likely to invest, and then supporting those policies with the Reagan "supply-side" argument that the revenue lost from tax cuts would be recouped by the upsurge of revenues due to the net growth of this less-taxed economy, and by the additional Reagan argument that we would have had less of a deficit had there been cuts in federal expenditures, especially in "discretionary spending." And besides, every Republican is supposed to believe that most of the tax money in the government coffers actually belongs to the people and should be returned.

But that is far from the whole story. During the 2000 campaign, Bush had continually referred to himself as a "compassionate conservative," conveying to most people that he did not want to be rigidly ideological in his opposition to government. At first he gave the impression that he would follow his father and President Reagan and make a few symbolic gestures toward his right-wing factions that would keep them from rebellion. He set up an office of faith-based initiatives in the White House; and he regularly espoused certain conservative causes that were more symbolic than expensive, such as opposition to *Roe v. Wade* and "late-term" abortion; and he made promises to nominate more orthodox conservatives as federal judges.

It soon became clear that he would stray so far from the traditional Republican camp that the *Economist*, the most ideologically consistent free-market publication in the world, became hostile enough to play President Bush's own game of attaching nicknames to people to suit their character. The nickname the *Economist* chose for President Bush was "Red George." Why? What had made his erstwhile friends at the *Economist* so hostile? The editors were all too eager to explain:

Why has the self-proclaimed party of small government turned itself into the party of unlimited spending? Republicans invariably bring up two excuses—the war on terrorism and the need to prime the pump . . . ; and then they talk vaguely about Ronald Reagan. . . .

None of this makes much sense. The war on terrorism accounts for only around half the increase in spending. The prescription-drug entitlement will continue to drain the budget long after the current recession has faded. As for Mr. Reagan, closer inspection only makes the comparison less favourable for Mr. Bush. The Gipper cut non-defence spending sharply in his first two years in office, and he vetoed 22 spending bills in his first three years in office. Mr. Bush has yet to veto one. [As of July 5, 2003.]

The real reasons for the profligacy are more depressing. Mr. Bush seems to have no real problem with big government; it is just big Democratic government he can't take. . . . Bill Clinton was not only better at balancing the budget than Mr. Bush. He was better at keeping spending under control, increasing total government spending by a mere 3.5 percent in his first three years in office [compared to 13.5 percent in the first three of the Bush administration].[1]

Later in the chapter, we will look more closely at President George W. Bush's use of government. Many of his policies differ from those that might have been pursued by a Democratic president. He is, nevertheless, every bit as committed as the most liberal Democrat to the use of government to address what he perceives to be the nation's problems and needs.

[1]Editorial, "Lexington/Red George," *Economist*, 3 July 2003, p. 30.

CAN THE GOVERNMENT GOVERN?

The New Deal initiated the era of big government and, after a period of resistance, Republicans have embraced the concept. But because government does a lot certainly does not mean that it does it well. Indeed, many commentators seem to think that the government is inept and inefficient and that many public policies and programs make little sense. To properly address this question, we need to develop analytic criteria that are independent of particular policy preferences. We do not wish to praise the government simply for undertaking programs with which we agree, or attack it for engaging in efforts we deplore. Instead, we will follow the example of the corporate auditor who employs criteria that allow an objective evaluation of the company's books regardless of whether the auditor personally likes the company's products.

Table 15.1 presents four criteria for evaluating governmental programs and then gives a quick sketch of each and how it might be applied to specific cases. The criteria are appropriateness, rationality, responsiveness, and significance. On the basis of these criteria, America's recent presidential administrations have not governed badly at all. We may or may not agree with every president's preferences and priorities, but for the most part, their policies made sense given each administration's goals and the nature of the problems each one faced.

With *appropriateness*, item 1 in Table 15.1, we seek judgments about whether and to what extent the particular government decision or policy was suitable for the government action for which it was designed. Some policies have so little integrity that they give almost no direction to the administrator who must implement the law or to the citizen who must obey it. When the ordinary citizen cannot read and understand a law, the law is at fault, not the citizen. Thus, how much of a connection is there between the stated goal (or goals) of government and the authority and power designed to meet that goal? These are the kinds of questions that would help guide a judgment of "*appropriateness.*"

Rationality is surely related to *appropriateness*, but at a higher level. The *rationality* of a policy and the government activity it produces is rated on the policy's clarity of purpose and its having been selected after serious consideration of all the available and practical alternatives for reaching the same goal. Our government's current policies toward terrorism may be appropriate but may not be the best available alternatives. A policy gains a still higher rating if there is a demonstrable, logical, symbiotic, synergistic relation to other government activities. Designing policies and programs for symbiosis and synergy with a maximum number of other government activities is called planning, even though planning got a bad reputation from its use by social governments.

TABLE 15.1

SELECTED CRITERIA FOR JUDGING THE CAPACITY OF GOVERNMENT TO GOVERN

Appropriateness:	timeliness; adequacy of authority and resources; likelihood of reaching the stated goal
Responsiveness:	consonance with electoral outcomes; consonance with party and public opinion; consonant with hegemonic agenda
Rationality:	clarity of stated purpose (legal integrity); logical and functional relation to other, functionally related programs; demonstrably superior to policy alternatives not chosen
Significance:	longer run judgment as to impact on society, on electoral/party alignments, and on reinforcement of existing agenda or change to new agenda

Responsiveness ordinarily refers to the relationship between the members of the legislature and their districts because that is a vital element of accountability in representative government. However, a more aggregate concept of *responsiveness* is needed here to capture the extent to which presidents and their party in Congress demonstrate some cooperative relationship to or consonance with public opinion—or, the "climate of opinion."

Significance is the most discretionary of judgment calls because, even after a government activity has been in place for as long as twenty years, no one can be sure whether the changes in the desired direction of the policy were truly attributable to the policy itself. Supporters cannot, for example, claim beyond reasonable doubt that the decline in the spread of AIDS is attributable to massive, worldwide public health efforts rather than to a natural decline of the virus; or that the decline in the incidence of crime is attributable to new crime control policies rather than to the aging of the most violent population: young people.

Keeping these criteria in mind, let us examine the recent history of U.S. public policies, beginning with the first real post–New Deal administration, that of Republican President Dwight D. Eisenhower, who held office from 1952 to 1960. Our focus, like the text more generally, will be on the domestic policies through which the nation is governed. Students, though, are encouraged to apply these criteria for policy evaluation to some of the major foreign and international policies of the several presidential eras. These might include U.S. policy in Southeast Asia during the 1960s and in the Middle East today.

The Eisenhower Administration

Turn now to Table 15.2. We will go step by step through the items on the table, touching briefly on the policy items and also on the president, the prevailing party breakdown in Congress, and the climate of opinion. Beginning our brief history with President Eisenhower, we have two items that alone say a tremendous amount about his administration and how effectively it governed. On

domestic issues, Eisenhower campaigned in 1952 on a classic, Republican pro–free market and antigovernment platform, emphasizing this theme with a charge that the Democrats had presided over twenty years of "creeping socialism." Yet, except for some tax reform, Ike's only important policy initiative was the 1956 Interstate and Defense Highway Act. When Congress adopted his plan for 41,000 toll-free miles of interstate, limited access roads, with the national government paying 90 percent of the total costs of construction, Eisenhower would be able to take credit (or blame) for the biggest public works project in our nation's history—outstripping even the Works Progress Administration (WPA), the key public works project Franklin Roosevelt used to battle the Depression. The projected cost of the interstate highway system was $41 billion (in 1958 dollars), and the estimated final cost was $329 billion (in 1996 dollars).[2] The second of Eisenhower's decisions about government was not a single policy but a broad and implicit policy of *non*-action, a choice *not to terminate a single major New Deal program*—programs that were the very heart of "creeping socialism."

Because no one in the Eisenhower administration ever gave a rationalization or justification for the highway program—other than the somewhat misleading claim that highway construction would contribute to the nation's defense—or even for the decision to leave the New Deal in place, we have to make some educated guesses about them. Political scientists agree widely that public works and "pork barrel" are virtually synonymous. However, attributing ignoble political motives to a party twenty years out of power does not demean or disqualify all other possible motives, and two such motives for Eisenhower are clear: that limited access highways were both logical and essential for the already mature "automobile culture," and they were important also as the third domestic com-

[2]Wendell Cox and Jean Love, "40 Years of the U.S. Interstate Highway System: An Analysis of the Best Investment a Nation Ever Made," in *Highway and Motorway Fact Book,* American Highway Users Alliance, June 1996.

TABLE 15.2

SOME SIGNIFICANT MOMENTS IN AMERICAN GOVERNMENT, 1953–2003

President	Date	Event
Eisenhower	1954–60	no termination of New Deal programs
	1956	Interstate Highway System
Kennedy/Johnson	1961	Investment Tax Credit
	1964	Civil Rights Act
	1964	Equal Opportunity (War on Poverty Act)
	1965	Civil Rights Act
	1965	Medicare/Medicaid
Nixon/Ford	1968–76	no termination of New Deal programs
	1970–73	wage and price controls
	1972	revenue sharing
	1972	indexing Social Security Benefits to cost of living
Carter	1978	Civil Service Reform Act
Reagan	1981	tax cuts
	1982–88	no terminations of existing programs
	1982	deregulation by oversight
	1986	comprehensive tax reform
G. H. W. Bush	1989–93	no terminations and no new programs
	1990	tax increase
Clinton	1993	deficit reduction
	1993	Omnibus Crime Control Amendments
	1996	welfare reform
	1996	Defense of Marriage Act
G. W. Bush	2001	tax cuts
	2002–03	tax cuts and reforms
	2002	Homeland Security Act
	2002	USA PATRIOT Act
	2003	Leave No Child Behind (Education) Act
	2001–04	no terminations of existing programs

mercial artery, an equal to rail and air that was eventually to become more vital than either one.

Thus, the interstate highway program must be rated quite high on at least three of the four criteria: *appropriateness*, *responsiveness*, and *significance*. Such an enormous federal subsidy to an already enormous automobile industry, coupled with a use of federal grants-in-aid to force the states and local governments to cooperate by following national guidelines, had to be a shock, indeed a slap in the face, to orthodox Republicans.

Even so, the high ratings still stand. *Rationality*, however, must be graded much lower. It is so typical of America's diffuse democracy with poorly disciplined political parties to enter a new government venture with a sense of urgency, a "crash program" mentality with a sense that this is a "war on . . . " whatever problem there is to be solved. Typically in that state of mind, there is a tendency to oversell the value of the solution and to overdo beyond all proportion the size of the commitment. And due to its exaggerated claims and hopes, the highway program killed off any chance of creating a balanced transportation system. By devolving most of the design and placement to states and cities, the interstate highway system fell very far short of being an integral part of the national defense. For the same reasons, it failed to alleviate urban congestion even in peacetime as it did not foster better urban circulation or contribute to mass public transit.[3] Thus, when the criteria are applied one at a time and in absolute terms, the interstate highway program fails the test of *rationality* because of "suboptimal" use of human, natural, and technological resources.

Finally, the implicit policy of leaving the New Deal in place was above all a recognition by the Republican Party that the consensus favoring a larger and more positive government was not merely a moment of madness in the 1930s but had become a genuine collective preference. Moreover, Republicans approached the New Deal shrewdly, thinking that the Democrats in their urgency had simply established all these programs and had merely thrown money at them; the Republicans now could tighten up all the programs and get more results with less expenditure. This idea was neatly summed by the administration's characterization of its defense program as providing "a bigger bang for the buck"—and this approach raises the rationality assessment of Eisenhower's administration. Thus, as a consequence of Republican tacit acceptance of the New Deal, serious observers of American political parties during that epoch were suggesting, with some justification, that the big difference between the two parties lay between the Democratic Party as the party of innovation and the Republican Party as the party of consolidation.[4]

The Kennedy and Johnson Years

Kennedy and Johnson are presented together in Table 15.2 because with the exception of a signif

[3]James J. Flink, *The Car Culture* (Cambridge, MA: MIT Press, 1975), pp. 213–15.
[4]See, for example, Clinton Rossiter, *Parties and Politics in America* (Ithaca, NY: Cornell University Press, 1960), Chapter 3, "Democrats and Republicans: Who Are They?"

icant tax cut initiative by JFK in 1961, the Kennedy New Frontier program became part of the Johnson Great Society accomplishments. The Civil Rights Acts of 1964 and 1965 equaled the Social Security Act of 1935 as innovations of deep constitutional *significance*. However, the civil rights laws, along with Medicare and Medicaid, were logical extensions of the New Deal, in effect completing the unfinished business of the New Deal by reaching out to people on the basis of race, class, and gender. In the 1930s, to keep the southern conservative wing of the party in the New Deal coalition, the northern liberal Democrats had offered the southern Democrats a "Faustian bargain": The northern Democrats could have their welfare state and their regulatory state—and thus their "constitutional revolution"—but they would abandon any thought of a "social revolution" by leaving race, class, and gender alone as part of "states' rights." This meant designing the Social Security and labor policies of the 1930s with a minimum coverage of occupations filled primarily by blacks of both sexes and women of any race. This bargain was broken in the mid-1960s with the civil rights laws and the extension of welfare through Medicare and Medicaid to people virtually outside the economic system altogether: the indigent elderly (Medicare) and the structurally unemployed (Medicaid), giving benefits as an entitlement to all who could demonstrate need, regardless of race, gender, or marital status.

All of the Kennedy-Johnson programs should be given the highest ratings on *appropriateness* and *responsiveness,* with moderately high ratings on *significance.* Black men and women came out of World War II with a sense of collective self that would then be certified and validated by a unanimous Supreme Court in its 1954 *Brown v. Board of Education* ruling. This produced the vast civil rights movement culminating in the March on Washington in August 1963. The assassination of President Kennedy the following November ensured that the entire social democratic agenda of the Democratic Party would be adopted. These actions were indeed consonant with the postwar public spirit and were appropriate to the extent that they could meet the unmet needs that the New Deal had deliberately resisted, for reasons given.

Thus, although these four great acts were obviously deserving of the highest ratings on the scales of government *appropriateness* and *responsiveness,* they have to be rated a good deal lower on *significance* because of the compromises that still had to be made, not only to keep the southern senators from total obstruction through filibuster but also to solidify the support of a relatively substantial number of liberal northern, midwestern, and western Republicans. Their votes were needed, but even more important was the need to show the same national consensus demonstrated by the unanimity of the 1954 Supreme Court. The compromises that reduced the *significance* of the Civil Rights Acts of 1964 and 1965 were primarily in the enforcement provisions against discrimination, which were softened, making implementation a longer and more complex process. The *significance* of Medicare and Medicaid was probably reduced by the provision that basically turned over implementation of the medical services to private insurance corporations as third-party payers with power to set conditions on coverage and extent of reimbursement.

What of *rationality?* The civil rights laws should be rated very high on *rationality* as the various titles of the statutes covered virtually all areas of life and work, public and private, whose prejudicial access had so impaired the prospects of the victims. Moreover, the clarity of the legal provisions restricting discriminatory treatment served as genuine public education for the entire middle-class white population. The law, coupled with educational programs, began the process of converting Americans to racial and gender tolerance. The voting rights provisions of the 1965 Civil Rights Act should probably be rated even higher on *rationality* and on *significance.* The enforcement provisions were stronger than those in the 1964 act, and the subsequent increases in black voter turnout and black office holding were undeniably attributable to those laws. Such laws should be rated still higher on *rationality* precisely because they generated the democratic forces in favor of changing the system to a more just one.

Medicare and Medicaid should receive a much lower rating for *rationality* mainly because of their financing provisions. Because reimbursements for services were made by third parties, restraints were removed from doctor and patient, unleashing a strong, built-in inflationary force that would expand costs until the large public consensus favoring these medical services began a steep downward slide. The government's capacity to govern in these highly volatile social areas has been proven, but limits on that capacity require wisdom that succeeding Congresses and presidents have not been able to find—however hard they've tried.

Presidents Nixon and Ford

The eight Republican years of Nixon and Ford were really over with the end of Nixon's first term. If Nixon had retired then, his administration would probably stand as one of the most effective presidencies ever. Despite his victory in 1968, the Democratic Party was still hegemonic, and the social democratic phase of the New Deal was still the national policy agenda. President Nixon had a keen enough sense of history to recognize that he could not govern on any other terms. Thus, numerous late New Deal programs were adopted by the Democratic Congress, and although he often grumbled, Nixon vetoed none of them. Moreover, he made a few of his own genuine contributions to the inventory.[5]

The first of these is the same implicit policy decision that President Eisenhower made: to leave in place the basic government of the New Deal. This included not only the programs of the 1930s but also the more recent and far more bold pro-

---

[5]For a more thorough account of the policy activity of those Nixon years, see Lowi, *The End of the Republican Era,* pp. 51–59. However, Nixon's boldest contribution, his Family Assistance Plan of 1969, was never enacted. It was adopted in the House but bottled up in the Senate by a combination of conservatives who were shocked that it looked like communism and liberal Democrats who were suspicious that the work requirement was a hidden effort to sabotage welfare altogether. In light of the draconian 1996 welfare reforms, Nixon's Family Assistance Plan looks enlightened and quite moderate in its restrictions on the poor. Cf. Nixon, *The Memoirs of Richard Nixon* (New York: Grosset & Dunlap, 1978), pp. 424–28.

grams adopted between 1964 and 1968. The Nixon scheme was the Republican one of "governing" these policies by making them do the same work with a much smaller budget. But to this he added a second policy, a genuine innovation that he called revenue sharing, whose principle was to take the annual congressional appropriations and to turn them over in large block grants to the states to deal with according to their own discretion. Accepting the welfare and urban policy programs of the late New Deal and subjecting them to revenue sharing can be considered a "policy bundle" that has to be rated quite high in *responsiveness, appropriateness,* and *rationality.* Revenue sharing enabled Nixon to stay within the New Deal consensus while using broad and permissive grants to the states to allow the more conservative states to continue discriminating on the basis of race and gender. This was a major factor in Nixon's "southern strategy" that was to pay off handsomely in southern party realignment in the 1970s and beyond.

Two other innovations during the Nixon epoch deserve attention: "indexing" Social Security benefits and wage/price regulation. "Indexing" meant "pegging" or adjusting benefits to the cost of living, so that people on Social Security would not see their benefits deteriorating because of inflation. Indexing was appropriate and responsive policy, as indicated by the overwhelming bipartisan support for it. And it seemed like a rational policy choice as it took away the politics of annual inflation adjustments by legislation. However, in the larger context, *rationality* drops away because no one, from the president and the Council of Economic Advisors on down, had any inkling that the United States would soon enter the worst decade of inflation in its history. Moreover, they did not look closely enough at the indexing itself to see that it would make its own contribution to the upward spiral of inflation.[6] And its *significance* was lost in the unintended consequences of their effort at "automatic government."

Finally, wage/price controls: The Economic Stabilization Act of 1970 was the most ambitious, sweeping, open-ended regulatory policy ever imposed on America in peacetime. And nothing since 1970 equals it. The Democratic Congress imposed this on Nixon. Nixon did not veto it but vowed he would not use it. Yet, as inflationary forces mounted, he not only reversed course but seized the initiative with a new economic policy that imposed a ninety-day national "wage-price freeze" prohibiting increases in wages and prices; under a second Economic Stabilization Act of 1971, this was extended through 1973. To implement this "income policy" to the fullest, Nixon assigned the responsibility to the one agency with the size, the local organization, and the expertise and stature to put millions of people (employers, banks, landlords, wholesalers, small business owners) under surveillance: the Internal Revenue Service! *Appropriate?* Arguably yes; inflation was rampant, and the steep incline in the price of oil alone was a grievous enemy. *Responsive?* Support for the program was strongly bipartisan, and this enormously ambitious effort to put a dent in inflation surely gave the impression that government was at least trying its best to cope. But the superficiality of that effort was revealed when a few days after his second term began, President Nixon surprised everyone with an executive order immediately ending some of the controls and phasing out the rest. The lasting *significance* of this policy was probably in the lesson it taught against overly ambitious use of regulatory power.[7]

Jimmy Carter

With President Ford overshadowed more by the great innovations of Nixon's first term than by the Watergate scandal itself, history skips a beat to

---

[6]A good and brief account of indexing and revenue sharing will be found in Bruce Jansson, *The Reluctant Welfare State* (Pacific Grove, CA: Brooks/Cole, 1997), pp. 243–47.

[7]A balanced account will be found in James E. Anderson, *Public Policy and Politics in America* (Belmont, CA: Wadsworth, 1978), pp. 182–86. The lessons of wage/price control may be disappearing, and that is a great pity. In a later edition, Anderson reduces his treatment to part of one paragraph: Anderson, *Public Policymaking* (New York: Houghton Mifflin, 2000), p. 57. And the most intense critique, by Lowi, *The End of Liberalism* (New York: Norton, 1979), pp. 119–24, is twenty-five years old.

President Carter, whose moment was also insignificant—with one interesting exception: civil service reform. Every president takes office with fierce determination to control or tame "the bureaucracy," but he hardly makes a dent, largely because a serious effort would use too many of his political resources. To his great credit, therefore, Carter proved willing to use a great part of his unusually meager political resources to gain passage of the Civil Service Reform Act (CSRA) of 1978, abolishing the century-old Civil Service Commission and creating three agencies in its place. The Office of Personnel Management (OPM) retained the classic job of enforcing the civil service laws, administering competitive exams, and so forth. The Merit System Protection Board was set up to act as a judiciary to deal with employee rights, questions of promotion, and grievances against adverse decisions. The Federal Labor Relations Board was established to cover employee rights to organize and bargain as well as to deal with unfair labor practices, including all forms of discrimination. Civil servants gained significantly with the organization and bargaining provisions; they also gained significantly from the extension, through the New Senior Executive Service, of the number of senior offices to which careerists could hope to rise. The chief executive also gained by acquiring additional power to remove not only incompetent employees but also the under-performing, mediocre employees by outright removal or transfer, without all the traditional requirements of a dossier resembling the brief of a prosecution in court for a major crime. It is still difficult to remove civil servants— it is easier to promote or transfer than to remove. But at the top, in the Senior Executive Service (not to mention the political appointees), the 1978 reforms did make it a lot easier to reward for outstanding service and to reassign and remove without weighty personnel protection procedures.[8]

Appropriate? Responsive? Such boring enterprises are never considered responsive; and there is rarely a groundswell of popular demand to respond to or build on for civil service reform. For all that, Carter deserves high marks for persevering. *Rationality* also rates fairly high, but, along with *significance,* only time will tell how much, and we are still waiting after twenty-five years. Lack of satisfaction is reflected in the gestures each president has made since Carter to impose further reforms toward greater efficiency at less cost, with more power in the hands of the chief executive. Let it be dismissed with a brief look ahead, to the first President Bush and President Clinton. President George H. W. Bush set up a "blue ribbon" committee, the National Commission on the Public Service, appointing the highly prestigious Paul Volcker as chair. Publications appropriate for use in a very good course in public administration were produced by the Volcker Commission, but little of significance was left in administrative reform. President Clinton made an equally prominent public effort to "reinvent government" by assigning Vice President Al Gore to the task; the administration's National Performance Review and such principles as Total Quality Management, plus the newly coined e-government principles borrowed from the private corporate sphere, figured prominently in the very strong commitment that Gore made to this effort. Big claims were put forward for how many millions of dollars were saved in greater efficiency, but the only measurable result was a modest reduction in the total number of employees working for the federal government.

Ronald Reagan and George H. W. Bush

Although the Reagan presidency would prove to be extremely important for the reconstruction of the Republican Party and, through that, the American two-party system, it pales in significance in comparison to Nixon's. (And of even less significance is the presidency of George H. W. Bush.) Reagan was far more explicit than his Republican predecessors in his campaign pledges to treat "government as the problem, not the solution," by pledging to "deregulate" and "privatize" in general and to

[8]Philip Cooper, *Public Law and Public Administration* (Itasca, IL: Peacock, 2000), pp. 497–500; and Fesler and Kettl, *The Politics of the Administrative Process* (Washington, DC: Congressional Quarterly Press, 2005) pp. 114–34, and 150–68.

eliminate the Departments of Education and Energy in particular. Within a few weeks in office, he put this plan on the back burner "for further discussion," and by the end of his first year, the Department of Energy had not only survived but had actually grown by almost 18,000 new employees. He succeeded better with deregulation, but not by abolishing *any* of the regulatory agencies or their programs. (Actually President Carter had succeeded better than that, with abolition of the Civil Aeronautics Board that had regulated the airlines since the 1930s.) Reagan accomplished his deregulation not by efforts to terminate agencies but by a flanking move, through executive review and oversight of the rules that regulatory agencies were proposing.

Since Reagan was a true-to-form Republican, he basically favored a "policy of no policies"—that is, doing less rather than more. This makes his two substantive policy initiatives stand out even more prominently: the across-the-board tax cuts of 1981 and the Tax Reform Act of 1986. As two careful observers put the case:

> As dramatic as Reagan's successes were in his first year, they were not followed up by comparable domestic policy successes during the remainder of his administration. With the exception of the Tax Reform Act of 1986, . . . Reagan spent the remainder of his term fighting an increasingly animated congressional opposition.[9]

Taking the two tax initiatives as the primary legacy of Reagan's domestic policies, we are able to make some assessments. First, we again witness the government of the New Deal essentially still in place—older, a bit tattered, less legitimate in both major parties—yet still in place. Some would say that President Reagan tried to starve it out of existence with what he called "supply-side" economics. That concept was first used to ration-

alize the tax cuts in economic terms, the argument being that deep tax cuts would so stimulate the economy that it would produce revenues even larger from a tax base far smaller than what was produced earlier by the larger tax base. But when that theory was shown to be what George H. W. Bush had called "voodoo economics," Reagan used "supply-side" instead to defend the deficit as a way to keep the Democrats from adding new "spending programs." In any event, the deficits during the Reagan years exceeded "by any measure" those of every president since FDR's deep Depression years.[10] We can also include the first President Bush here because he followed Reagan with a "policy of no policies." He probably killed his own reelection chances in 1992 by promising "no new taxes" and then having to renege on his promise. But this brings to nineteen (Ford's three plus Carter's four plus Reagan's eight plus Bush's four) the years continuing a government basically created by the New Deal and the JFK–LBJ "Great Society" years.

The Reagan/Bush "policy of no policies" was surely responsive to the prevailing political forces of the 1980s. Large tax cuts are generally popular, but coupled with the rhetoric of opposition to big government, the idea of "no policies" became irresistible and would soon enthrall the centralist core of the Democratic Party, with formation of the Democratic Leadership Council, led by such Democratic leaders as Governor Bill Clinton of Arkansas. The "policy of no policies" was strengthened by the mounting deficits that would be used as a stick to stir the opposition to any new federal programs. This Reagan posture toward government was also appropriate, appearing to be precisely what *globalization* seemed to require: lowering if not destroying all of the barriers to free trade, free markets, and worldwide competition. Both parties would join in preparing America to take the lead in the globalization of capitalism with sound currency, tariff reduction, and deregulation of the

[9]Paul E. Peterson and Mark Rom, "Lower Taxes, More Spending, and Budget Deficits," in Charles O. Jones, ed., *The Reagan Legacy: Promise and Performance* (Chatham, NJ: Chatham House, 1988), p. 214.

[10]Peterson and Rom, "Lower Taxes," p. 215.

economy, permitting corporations greater freedom to get larger by merger, and freedom to export manufacturing and jobs to the least expensive countries and regions. From a purely economic viewpoint, such reductions in the size of the national government by deficits and deregulation have to be considered quite rational. They are conducive to the expansion of international trade and direct foreign investment. It was also rational to have a military force strong enough to defend America's interests everywhere, even if that contributed to still larger deficits. And it was also rational to beef up local police forces to maintain social order as expansion in some areas and "deindustrialization" in other areas were both going to cause some degree of social disruption.

Finally, was this posture of smaller government in this larger universe a significant change in governance? All the economic indicators for the Reagan eight years and the ensuing twelve or even sixteen years showed development upward and outward, an expansion of capitalism that is beginning to equal the original globalization of 1880–1914.

But at this point, *significance* can be on a collision course with *rationality* as capitalism expanded from the Western countries toward the eastern and southern directions of the globe. Although there may be no natural limit to economic expansion, *rationality* imposes some degree of proportionality in its insistence on looking at the costs and risks as well as the advantages of expansion. The first stages of globalization ended in 1914, with the outbreak of the most expensive war in the history of the world up to that time. It is quite possible that the course of globalization was significantly altered by 9/11 and its violent rejection of what appear to be Western forms of economic enterprise as well as democracy.

Free trade and economic opportunity are not life's only ideals. Competing ideals require balance, and that means policies that take balance and proportion into account. What James Madison said of government applies across the board to government in the economic realm: "You must first

enable the government to control the governed; and in the next place oblige it to control itself." (*Federalist,* No. 51)

William Jefferson Clinton

To review Clinton's record, we see that Table 15.2 provides only four of a much larger number of policy cases, since, as a Democrat—even a "centrist" Democratic founder of the Democratic Leadership Council—Clinton was inevitably more ambitious in desiring to have "a policy of *more* policies." But even the few policies here are sufficient to reveal the shape of governing at the dawn of the third American century. Clinton's first policy was as Republican as any policy the Republicans had come forward with during the previous twelve years: a genuine antideficit policy. Abandoning his own campaign promises, Clinton proposed and got a first-year budget devoted to *deficit reduction*, with a commitment to keep future deficits on a downward trend well below those of his Republican predecessors. That first budget brought the deficit down by $72 billion; it continued to drop, then to become a surplus. To make this possible the Democrats raised taxes on the wealthier income brackets and on gasoline, and also put a cap on increases of spending levels except where specific legislation mandated it.

The second key policy initiative bore the awkward label of "To Amend the Omnibus Crime Control and Safe Streets Act of 1968." Its popular name was the "Crime Bill of 1994." This was another arrow taken right out of the conservative Republican quiver. The 1993 Brady Handgun Violence Prevention Act mandating gun registration was a tiny liberal overture to the grand anticrime opera of 1994. The 1994 Act provided, among other things, for distinctly conservative policies, such as authorization of the death penalty for dozens of existing and new federal crimes; adopting the "three strikes and you're out" rule, mandating life imprisonment for the third violent felony, no matter how small; a provision allowing juveniles thirteen and older to be tried as adults in federal court for certain violent crimes; and a "truth in sentencing" provision that all violent offenders serve at least 85 percent of their sentences. The Act also appropriated over $30 billion for "crime prevention" including provision for 100,000 new police officers, expanded state and local prisons, illegal alien imprisonment, and the general discretionary category of "crime prevention." All of this is federal involvement in inherently local matters.

The third, and most important by any measure, was welfare reform, which, as Clinton promised, would "end welfare as we know it." The record will show that almost the entire package was filched from the Republican "Contract with America," which had arisen out of the "Gingrich Revolution" of 1994 but had failed in a Congress run by what appeared to be the radicalism of then-Speaker Newt Gingrich and his newly elected followers. The distinct conservatism of the bill—distinctly right wing even within the Republican Party tradition—is best conveyed by its official title, the Personal Responsibility and Work Opportunity Act of 1996 (PRA for short). The main thrust of PRA was to put an end to Aid to Families with Dependent Children (AFDC) and the entitlement to benefits that it had provided. This was replaced by the Temporary Assistance for Needy Families (TANF) program, requiring the parents of dependent children to work outside the home or show evidence of seeking such work; strictly limiting *lifetime* eligibility for benefits to five years; and denying all federal funds to those who failed to find work within two years of being on public assistance. The federal funds were converted to block grants to the states, permitting each state to develop its own approach to dependency, including the power and discretion to deny benefits to women who had additional children while on welfare, and the same denial to unmarried people under eighteen unless they were living with an adult and in school. And each state was permitted to be more restrictive than the restrictions in the federal provisions.

Assessment of the Clinton approach requires some context. Clinton had entered office aware of two enormous burdens: The first was his election

with only a 43 percent plurality of the popular vote. Second was his "discovery" that the federal deficit was going to be far, far larger than the estimate he had employed during the campaign.[11] This put an end to the prospects of a return to the Democratic Party of the 1960s. Clinton, like Nixon, recognizing that the Democratic Party and its Democratic president were now in the minority, abandoned his campaign commitment to a "middle-class tax cut" and made only one effort to extend the national government: health care reform. His pursuit of a bold approach to this important and controversial policy area ended in a grossly embarrassing failure in Congress in 1993. Following that fiasco, and then the addition of a third and still larger constraint—the loss of Congress in the 1994 midterm election—Clinton became as much a Republican as Nixon had become a Democrat, both having had the political acumen to recognize they could not govern in defiance of what appeared to be the hegemony of the other party and its approach to government and governing.

From that standpoint, we must conclude that virtually all of Clinton's initiatives were *appropriate* and *responsive*—that is, without regard to partisan or ideological views, Clinton's posture toward governing in these and related policy positions was in accord with "political time," as political scientist Stephen Skowronek would put it.[12] The country had been turning decisively rightward, and this had been expressed not only in the takeover of the Republican Party in Congress by the right-wing faction of the party but also by the rightward tack of the Democratic Party. The Democratic Party's rightward shift had been spearheaded by the Democratic Leadership Council, popularly known

[11]Bob Woodward, *The Agenda: Inside the Clinton White House* (New York: Simon & Schuster, 1994), p. 165. "Discovery" is put in quotes here because the insider account reported in the Woodward book was virtually staged to make it seem as though the larger deficit had come as a surprise that forced Clinton to conduct his presidency "just to please the bond market." Woodward also quotes Clinton as saying "We've all become Eisenhower Republicans!"
[12]Stephen Skowronek, *The Politics Presidents Make: Leadership from John Adams to George Bush* (Cambridge, MA: Harvard University Press, 1993).

as the "new Democrats," in which Clinton had played the prominent role during the 1980s and through which he had achieved sufficient exposure to be credible as a presidential candidate. These policies, coupled with NAFTA and other trade-related policies, were also not only in tune with the rightward trend but in tune with globalization, which required such adjustments. Even the severe shrinkage of the American welfare state—the first genuine revision of any of the major provisions of the New Deal in over sixty years—was consonant with what appeared to be the economic requirements of globalization, because social programs of that sort are "protective" legislation comparable to protective tariffs on agricultural goods. Moreover, whether we were following or leading, these practices were in line with the "third way" approach of Tony Blair's Labour Party in Great Britain, as well as other center-right governments. *Appropriateness* and *responsiveness* rate quite high in the Clinton presidency.

The *significance* of Clinton's initiatives also has to be rated fairly high, especially from the purely economic point of view. Welfare reform was a deep commitment to imposing more severe work requirements on all layers and classes of society. Beefing up crime controls in the cities met the need for keeping local peace while cities adjusted to world competition and wage pressure. And tax cuts, with more to come, provided incentives to "grow the economy." But what of *rationality*? The antideficit programs actually contributed to results that were the opposite of those claimed for it. As deficits shrank, interest rates went up rather than down, in defiance of all the prevailing economic models of the time. This included the long-term bond rate, on which so much domestic and international investment hinges.[13] And, as the budget went into balance and then surplus after 1996, this upward shift proved to be an artifact of the surpluses produced by the Social Security taxes supposedly being accumulated for the coming retirement of the enormous "baby boom" generation rather than a result of Clinton's policy decisions.[14]

Rationality also comes up lacking in welfare reform. Whatever new work ethic, plus reduction of government spending, may result from eliminating support for single parents with dependent children could be far more than counterbalanced by the added costs of providing care for the children as the primary caregiver leaves home for work.[15] Moreover, work may not be available during periods of high unemployment (unlike the years when PRA was implemented) and competition for unskilled jobs would tend under those conditions to keep wages down toward or possibly below subsistence in some regions of the country. As for the *rationality* of the "Crime Act," there are too many provisions to make a single judgment. However, since all the provisions share the same goal—to prevent crime—we can make at least one judgment about that: It is impossible to make a judgment as to *rationality* or *significance*. Why? Because there's no way to actually measure prevention, which has to be defined as the number and rate of occurrences *that do not happen*. Nonhappenings defy science. As with the cold war and its goal of deterring use of the atom bomb and preventing communist expansion, we can only judge *rationality* and *significance* in theory: How many of the unwanted acts would have occurred if we had not added those new crimes as punishable, upgraded those punishments, and beefed up those local police forces? As a good case *for* the new and more conservative policies, the number of criminals in prison went up (to 2 million) as the crime rate in almost all American cities actually went down. As a good case *against* the new policies, the crime rate went down as the populous baby boom generation aged, and most violent crimes are committed by young people between the ages of eighteen and twenty-five. When fears of threats such as communism, terrorism, crime, or inflation are mount-

[13]William Greider, *One World, Ready or Not* (New York: Simon & Schuster, 1997), p. 289, and *passim.*

[14]Ibid., p. 308.
[15]Gwendolyn Mink, *Welfare's End* (Ithaca, NY: Cornell University Press, 1998), esp. Chapter 4.

ing—whether due to real evidence or to rhetoric—then any amount of government expansion is justified, and our criteria go out the window.

George W. Bush

This neatly links to the still unfinished tenure of President George W. Bush. Bush's proud self-designation as a "compassionate conservative" indicates to most sensitive ears that he was going to be "pro-active," with a "policy of policies" rather than following his father, George H. W. Bush, and his godfather Reagan. The listing in Table 15.2 tends to confirm that expectation. Although it is too soon to assess the *significance* or the *rationality* of Bush's approach to governance, these items are indicative of how far the Republican Party of the new millenium has departed from almost a century of pure laissez-faire, free-market liberalism (except for Nixon's tilt toward the New Deal approach).

The nickname invented by the *Economist* for the second President Bush, "Red George," was not meant to convey the Bolshevik Red but the Red of El Greco's Cardinal or the royal crimson of traditional rule according to divine inspiration. George W. Bush is committed to the use of government, but not the Democratic Party way. The Democratic Party way was to reduce risk by taking some of the freedom out of free enterprise. The conservative way is equally statist but is committed to using the state to impose moral standards. George Will provided a succinct definition of pro-government conservatism, or "statism of the right," in the very title of his important book, *Statecraft as Soulcraft*. This is directly contradictory to the spirit of the traditional Republican Party liberalism of free enterprise, as best articulated in recent decades by Ronald Reagan: "I've always thought that the best thing government can do is nothing."[16] And Will responded to that quote with "the one thing government cannot do is 'nothing.'" And his evidence—as a conservative—is the welfare state

itself. Will pointed out that the welfare state was necessary to preserve the stability of a capitalist economy:

> Two conservatives (Disraeli and Bismarck) pioneered the welfare state, and did so for impeccable conservative reasons: to reconcile the masses to the vicissitudes and hazards of a dynamic and hierarchical industrial economy . . . indispensable to social cohesion.[17]

All of this defines George W. Bush as an innovator equal to Reagan, but in the opposite direction. Reagan revived the Republican traditional form of "least government"—hallmark of the authentic Republican Party going all the way back to Lincoln. George W. took Reagan's Republican Party and made it into an American version of the British Conservative Party, embracing a strong state, but a statism with an opening to the right. This is Red George and his new statism. Examples are abundant: education policies in the 2003 Leave No Child Behind Act establishing national policy imposed by national examinations, with national sanctions punishing schools and school systems that fall below the mandatory national standards; a faith-based White House office, plus the Department of Health and Human Services charged with enforcing the Defense of Marriage Act, providing $300 million annually of additional funds to support marriage with welfare benefits (including teaching "relationship skills" to expectant but unmarried couples); and tax cuts to be used, just as the liberal Democrats did, as a fiscal device to "stimulate the economy." (But unlike the liberal Democrats, Republicans cut the taxes at the top of the income brackets to stimulate the economy through investment rather than through the liberal Keynesian "aggregate demand" approach, cutting taxes for the middle and lower brackets.) Then there is a still more vast expansion of the pro-active state with passage in 2002 of the Homeland Security Act and the USA PATRIOT Act, which together beefed up national

---

[16]Quoted in George Will, *Statecraft as Soulcraft* (New York: Simon & Schuster, 1983), p. 123.

[17]Ibid., pp. 126–27.

powers far beyond any national security programs associated with previous war periods. The PATRIOT Act provided for surveillance and police control of suspicious persons and for the mixing of domestic and international intelligence forces (once illegal) plus the mixing of civilian and military systems of justice into one national police force that is not only unusual in war emergencies but may have been institutionalized and perpetuated in the gigantic new bureaucracy, the Department of Homeland Security. This is a form of statism far exceeding the liberal Democratic statism. And it has not gone unnoticed by the traditional liberal Republicans who once *were* the party elite, and who now fear the direction toward governance of this Bush administration, with its undoubted dominance by the party's right wing thanks to the midterm elections of 2002. Not bothering to hide its own laissez-faire, pro-Republican ideology, the *Economist* concluded in mid-2003:

> Under Mr. Bush [George W.] the leave-us-alone bunch has been losing ground to what might be called the 'neo-paternalists'. . . . Mr. Bush is not only presiding over a huge increase in the size of government. He is also encouraging the beast to poke its nose into the nooks and crannies of people's private lives. For him politics is not just about shrinking government. . . . It is about prodding behavior in a conservative direction.[18]

The purpose here is not to take a position in a three-cornered debate between Bush's "neo-"conservatism, Reagan's Republican liberalism (which includes many of the "new Democrats"), and the old New Deal brand of liberalism. The purpose rather is to characterize Bush's approach to government. And there is a still larger purpose, which is to use Bush's record to confirm the argument that government is not something a party or an election can choose to do *without*. The New Deal

Democrats gave us more of it than we had ever had before, and government was highly responsive to the American sense of danger as the capitalist revolution showed signs of failure in the 1920s and 1930s. The Eisenhower/Reagan Republican Party, descending from Adam Smith and Abraham Lincoln—as the party of opportunity and enterprise—did not shut big government down or attempt to turn the clock back but accepted it and attempted to make it govern better, more cheaply, and, if possible, more rationally. The "George W. Bush round" lifts the veil on the Republican Party's traditional ideology and the false hope that government is expendable and gives us a proper debate: not "whether" government but "which" government. For the first time in a century or more, Americans are going to have a genuine liberal-conservative debate. For most of the twentieth century, we had two liberal parties fighting over differences of the degree to which capitalism would be free and on its own to develop, expand, and collapse. Europeans appreciated better than Americans that there were two liberal, pro-capitalist parties in America, fighting, often bitterly, over how much and how free capitalism would be: two liberal parties separated by a common problem. Now, as the twenty-first century begins, the debate deepens and thickens, forcing us to be more philosophical. The debate is finally between fundamentally different conceptions of government: a liberal, secular, utilitarian government aimed at reducing risk and expanding the pursuit of happiness *versus* a conservative, morality-driven government aimed at improving character and community within a transcendent conception of virtue. One side argues for a government judged as appropriate, responsive, rational, and significant because its policies foster a civic culture giving each individual the freedom to "do what thou wilt." The other side argues for an equally strong government whose policies are judged high on *appropriateness, responsiveness, rationality,* and *significance* because it is a government that seeks to foster a civic culture equally respectful of the individual but an individual operating within a

[18]Lexington (editorial), "Get Thee to the Church on Time," *Economist*, 12 July 2003, p. 29; and Lexington, "Philosophers and Kings," *Economist*, 21 June 2003, p. 29.

moral code that follows the dictum attributed to Lord Acton, who said essentially that freedom is not the power to do what you want, but rather the right to do what you ought.

DOING WHAT IS RIGHT

Today, America's government does a great deal and, through the last several presidencies, presents a reasonable record of developing policies and programs calculated to accomplish its goals and objectives. In other words, what the government does, it does fairly sensibly. These observations may seem forms of faint praise but they fly in the face of the views of the many commentators and pundits who seem determined to prove that the government cannot accomplish anything. America's government can and does accomplish a great deal.

And yet, these observations still do not answer the last question posed at the start of this epilogue. Does the government generally do the right thing? This is our most important question and also the hardest one to answer. What is the right thing? Do most Americans agree on the general shape of the nation's programs and priorities?

As we saw in Chapter 9, Americans are in general agreement on certain basic values, particularly equality of opportunity, liberty, and democracy. We expect the government's policies to be consistent with these values. Sooner or later, programs demonstrably at odds with Americans' basic beliefs cannot be sustained.

At the same time, though, Americans disagree on a myriad of issues and priorities. Should we increase defense spending or shift our resources to domestic priorities? Is the USA PATRIOT Act a necessary effort to protect the nation or an unnecessary affront to civil liberties? Should the federal government spend more on education or leave it to the states and localities? Is abortion a legalized form of murder or a matter of women's rights? These and thousands of other issues are debated every day by political parties, candidates, interest groups, and just plain citizens. So, let us end with two questions. With regard to the issues you care about, do you think the government is doing the right thing? If not, what are you doing about it? The ancient Greeks distinguished between the *citizen*, who could answer these questions appropriately, and the *idiote* who could not. Be a citizen. In our democracy it is your job, not someone else's, to see to it that the government does the right thing.

APPENDIX

THE DECLARATION OF INDEPENDENCE

In Congress, July 4, 1776

When in the course of human events, it becomes necessary for one people to dissolve the political bands which have connected them with another, and to assume among the Powers of the earth, the separate and equal station to which the Laws of Nature and of Nature's God entitle them, a decent respect to the opinions of mankind requires that they should declare the causes which impel them to the separation.

We hold these truths to be self-evident, that all men are created equal, that they are endowed by their Creator with certain unalienable rights, that among these are Life, Liberty, and the pursuit of Happiness. That to secure these rights, Governments are instituted among Men, deriving their just powers from the consent of the governed. That whenever any Form of Government becomes destructive of these ends, it is the Right of the People to alter or to abolish it, and to institute new Government, laying its foundation on such principles and organizing its powers in such form, as to them shall seem most likely to effect their Safety and Happiness. Prudence, indeed, will dictate that Governments long established should not be changed for light and transient causes; and accordingly all experience hath shown, that mankind are more disposed to suffer, while evils are sufferable, than to right themselves by abolishing the forms to which they are accustomed. But when a long train of abuses and usurpations, pursuing invariably the same Object evinces a design to reduce them under absolute Despotism, it is their right, it is their duty, to throw off such Government, and to provide new Guards for their future security.— Such has been the patient sufferance of these Colonies; and such is now the necessity which constrains them to alter their former Systems of Government. The history of the present King of Great Britain is a history of repeated injuries and usurpations, all having in direct object the establishment of an absolute Tyranny over these States. To prove this, let Facts be submitted to a candid world.

He has refused his Assent to Laws, the most wholesome and necessary for the public good.

He has forbidden his Governors to pass Laws of immediate and pressing importance, unless suspended in their operation till his Assent should be obtained; and when so suspended, he has utterly neglected to attend to them.

He has refused to pass other Laws for the accommodation of large districts of people, unless those people would relinquish the right of Representation in the Legislature, a right inestimable to them and formidable to tyrants only.

He has called together legislative bodies at places unusual, uncomfortable, and distant from the depository of their public Records, for the sole purpose of fatiguing them into compliance with his measures.

He has dissolved Representative Houses repeatedly, for opposing with manly firmness his invasions on the rights of the people.

He has refused for a long time, after such dissolutions, to cause others to be elected; whereby the Legislative powers, incapable of Annihilation, have returned to the People at large for their exercise; the State remaining in the mean time exposed to all dangers of invasion from without, and convulsions within.

He has endeavored to prevent the population of these States; for that purpose obstructing the Laws of Naturalization of Foreigners; refusing to pass others to encourage their migrations hither, and raising the conditions of new Appropriations of Lands.

He has obstructed the Administration of Justice, by refusing his Assent to Laws for establishing Judiciary powers.

He has made Judges dependent on his Will alone, for the tenure of their offices, and the amount and payment of their salaries.

He has erected a multitude of New Offices, and sent hither swarms of Officers to harass our People, and eat out their substance.

He has kept among us, in times of peace, Standing Armies without the Consent of our legislature.

He has affected to render the Military independent of and superior to the Civil Power.

He has combined with others to subject us to a jurisdiction foreign to our constitution, and unacknowledged by our laws; giving his Assent to their Acts of pretended Legislation:

For quartering large bodies of armed troops among us:

For protecting them, by a mock Trial, from Punishment for any Murders which they should commit on the Inhabitants of these States:

For cutting off our Trade with all parts of the world:

For imposing taxes on us without our Consent:

For depriving us in many cases, of the benefits of Trial by jury:

For transporting us beyond Seas to be tried for pretended offences:

For abolishing the free System of English Laws in a neighboring Province, establishing therein an Arbitrary government, and enlarging its Boundaries so as to render it at once an example and fit instrument for introducing the same absolute rule into these Colonies:

For taking away our Charters, abolishing our most valuable Laws, and altering fundamentally the Forms of our Governments:

For suspending our own Legislatures, and declaring themselves invested with Power to legislate for us in all cases whatsoever.

He has abdicated Government here, by declaring us out of his Protection and waging War against us.

He has plundered our seas, ravaged our Coasts, burnt our towns, and destroyed the lives of our people.

He is at this time transporting large armies of foreign mercenaries to compleat the works of death, desolation, and tyranny, already begun with circumstances of Cruelty & perfidy scarcely paralleled in the most barbarous ages, and totally unworthy the Head of a civilized nation.

He has constrained our fellow Citizens taken Captive on the high Seas to bear Arms against their Country, to become the executioners of their friends and Brethren, or to fall themselves by their Hands.

He has excited domestic insurrections amongst us, and has endeavored to bring on the inhabitants of our frontiers, the merciless Indian Savages, whose known rule of warfare, is an undistinguished destruction of all ages, sexes, and conditions.

In every stage of these Oppressions We have Petitioned for Redress in the most humble terms: Our repeated Petitions have been answered only by repeated injury. A Prince, whose character is thus marked by every act which may define a Tyrant, is unfit to be the ruler of a free people.

Nor have We been wanting in attention to our British brethren. We have warned them from time to time of attempts by their legislature to extend an unwarrantable jurisdiction over us. We have reminded them of the circumstances of our emigration and settlement here. We have appealed to their native justice and magnanimity, and we have conjured them by the ties of our common kindred to disavow these usurpations, which would inevitably interrupt our connections and correspondence. They too must have been deaf to the voice of justice and of consanguinity. We must, therefore, acquiesce in the necessity, which denounces our Separation, and hold them, as we hold the rest of mankind, Enemies in War, in Peace Friends.

WE, THEREFORE, the Representatives of the UNITED STATES OF AMERICA, in General Congress, Assembled, appealing to the Supreme Judge of the world for the rectitude of our intentions, do, in the Name, and by Authority of the good People of these Colonies, solemnly publish and declare, That these United Colonies are, and of Right ought to be FREE AND INDEPENDENT STATES; that they are Absolved from all Allegiance to the British Crown, and that all political connection between them and the State of Great Britain, is and ought to be totally dissolved; and that as Free and Independent States, they have full Power to levy War, conclude Peace, contract Alliances, establish Commerce, and to do all other Acts and Things which Independent States may of right do. And for the support of this Declaration, with a firm reliance on the Protection of Divine Providence, we mutually pledge to each other our Lives, our Fortunes, and our sacred Honor.

The foregoing Declaration was, by order of Congress, engrossed, and signed by the following members:

John Hancock

NEW HAMPSHIRE
Josiah Bartlett
William Whipple
Matthew Thornton

MASSACHUSETTS BAY
Samuel Adams
John Adams
Robert Treat Paine
Elbridge Gerry

NEW YORK
William Floyd
Philip Livingston
Francis Lewis
Lewis Morris

NEW JERSEY
Richard Stockton
John Witherspoon
Francis Hopkinson
John Hart
Abraham Clark

RHODE ISLAND
Stephen Hopkins
William Ellery

CONNECTICUT
Roger Sherman
Samuel Huntington
William Williams
Oliver Wolcott

DELAWARE
Caesar Rodney
George Read
Thomas M'Kean

MARYLAND
Samuel Chase
William Paca
Thomas Stone
Charles Carroll,
  of Carrollton

VIRGINIA
George Wyth
Richard Henry Lee
Thomas Jefferson
Benjamin Harrison
Thomas Nelson, Jr.
Francis Lightfoot Lee
Carter Braxton

PENNSYLVANIA
Robert Morris
Benjamin Rush
Benjamin Franklin
John Morton
George Clymer
James Smith
George Taylor
James Wilson
George Ross

NORTH CAROLINA
William Hooper
Joseph Hewes
John Penn

SOUTH CAROLINA
Edward Rutledge
Thomas Heyward, Jr.
Thomas Lynch, Jr.
Arthur Middleton

GEORGIA
Button Gwinnett
Lyman Hall
George Walton

Resolved, That copies of the Declaration be sent to the several assemblies, conventions, and committees, or councils of safety, and to the several commanding officers of the continental troops; that it be proclaimed in each of the United States, at the head of the army.

THE CONSTITUTION OF THE UNITED STATES OF AMERICA

Annotated with references to the *Federalist Papers*

Federalist Paper Number and Author

[PREAMBLE]

We the People of the United States, in Order to form a more perfect Union, establish Justice, insure domestic Tranquility, provide for the common defence, promote the general Welfare, and secure the Blessings of Liberty to ourselves and our Posterity, do ordain and establish this Constitution for the United States of America.

84
(Hamilton)

ARTICLE I

Section 1

[LEGISLATIVE POWERS]

10, 45
(Madison)

All legislative Powers herein granted shall be vested in a Congress of the United States, which shall consist of a Senate and House of Representatives.

Section 2

[HOUSE OF REPRESENTATIVES, HOW CONSTITUTED, POWER OF IMPEACHMENT]

39
(Madison)
45
(Madison)
52–53, 57
(Madison)
52
(Madison)
60
(Hamilton)

The House of Representatives shall be composed of Members chosen every second Year by the People of the several States, and the Electors in each State shall have the Qualifications requisite for Electors of the most numerous Branch of the State Legislature.

No Person shall be a Representative who shall not have attained to the Age of twenty-five Years, and been seven Years a Citizen of the United States, and who shall not, when elected, be an inhabitant of that State in which he shall be chosen.

54
(Madison)

Representatives and *direct Taxes*[1] shall be apportioned among the several States which may be included within this Union, according to their respective Numbers, *which shall be determined by adding to the whole Number of free Persons, including those bound to Service for a Term of Years,*

54
(Madison)

and excluding Indians not taxed, *three-fifths of all other Persons.*[2] The actual Enu-

58
(Madison)

meration shall be made within three Years after the first Meeting of the Congress of the United States, and within every subsequent Term of ten Years, in such Manner as they shall be Law direct. The Number of Representatives shall not exceed one for every thirty Thousand, but

55–56
(Madison)

each State shall have at Least one Representative; *and until such enumeration shall be made, the State of New Hampshire shall be entitled to chuse three, Massachusetts eight, Rhode-Island and Providence Plantations one, Connecticut five, New-York six, New Jersey four, Pennsylvania eight, Delaware one, Maryland six, Virginia ten, North Carolina five, South Carolina five, and Georgia three.*[3]

[1] Modified by Sixteenth Amendment.
[2] Modified by Fourteenth Amendment.
[3] Temporary provision.

A6

When vacancies happen in the Representation from any State, the Executive Authority thereof shall issue Writs of Election to fill such Vacancies.

79 (Hamilton)

The House of Representatives shall chuse their Speaker and other Officers; and shall have the sole Power of Impeachment.

Section 3
[THE SENATE, HOW CONSTITUTED, IMPEACHMENT TRIALS]

39, 45 (Madison) 60 (Hamilton)

62–63 (Madison) 59 (Hamilton)

The Senate of the United States shall be composed of two Senators from each State, *chosen by the Legislature thereof,*[4] for six Years; and each Senator shall have one Vote.

68 (Hamilton)

Immediately after they shall be assembled in Consequence of the first Election, they shall be divided as equally as may be into three Classes. The Seats of the Senators of the first Class shall be vacated at the Expiration of the second Year, of the second Class at the Expiration of the fourth Year, and of the third Class at the Expiration of the sixth Year, so that one third may be chosen every second Year; *and if vacancies happen by Resignation, or otherwise, during the Recess of the Legislature of any State, the Executive thereof may make temporary Appointments until the next Meeting of the Legislature, which shall then fill such Vacancies.*[5]

62 (Hamilton)

No person shall be a Senator who shall not have attained to the Age of thirty Years, and been nine Years a Citizen of the United States, and who shall not, when elected, be an Inhabitant of that State for which he shall be chosen.

The Vice-President of the United States shall be President of the Senate, but shall have no Vote, unless they be equally divided.

The Senate shall chuse their other Officers, and also a President pro tempore, in the Absence of the Vice-Presi-

dent, or when he shall exercise the Office of President of the United States.

39 (Madison) 65–67, 79 (Hamilton) 65 (Hamilton)

The Senate shall have the sole Power to try all Impeachments. When sitting for that Purpose, they shall be on Oath or Affirmation. When the President of the United States is tried, the Chief Justice shall preside: And no Person shall be convicted without the Concurrence of two-thirds of the Members present.

84 (Hamilton)

Judgment in Cases of Impeachment shall not extend further than to removal from Office, and disqualification to hold and enjoy any Office of honor, Trust or Profit under the United States: but the Party convicted shall nevertheless be liable and subject to Indictment, Trial, Judgment and Punishment, according to Law.

Section 4
[ELECTION OF SENATORS AND REPRESENTATIVES]

59–61 (Hamilton)

The Times, Places and Manner of holding Elections for Senators and Representatives, shall be prescribed in each State by the Legislature thereof: but the Congress may at any time by Law make or alter such Regulations, except as to the Places of chusing Senators.

The Congress shall assemble at least once in every Year, and such meeting shall be on the first Monday in December, unless they shall by Law appoint a different Day.[6]

Section 5
[QUORUM, JOURNALS, MEETINGS, ADJOURNMENTS]

Each House shall be the Judge of the Elections, Returns and Qualifications of its own Members, and a Majority of each shall constitute a Quorum to do Business; but a smaller Number may adjourn from day to day, and may be authorized to compel the Attendance of absent Members, in such Manner, and under the Penalties as each House may provide.

[4]Modified by Seventeenth Amendment.
[5]Modified by Seventeenth Amendment.

[6]Modified by Twentieth Amendment.

Each House may determine the Rules of its Proceedings, punish its Members for disorderly Behavior, and, with the Concurrence of two-thirds, expel a Member.

Each House shall keep a Journal of its Proceedings, and from time to time publish the same, excepting such Parts as may in their Judgment require Secrecy; and the Yeas and Nays of the Members of either House on any questions shall, at the Desire of one-fifth of the present, be entered on the Journal.

Neither House, during the Session of Congress, shall, without the Consent of the other, adjourn for more than three days, nor to any other Place than that in which the two Houses shall be sitting.

Section 6
[COMPENSATION, PRIVILEGES, DISABILITIES]

The Senators and Representatives shall receive a Compensation for their Services, to be ascertained by Law, and paid out of the Treasury of the United States. They shall in all Cases, except Treason, Felony and Breach of the Peace, be privileged from Arrest during their Attendance at the Session of their respective Houses, and in going to and returning from the same; and for any Speech or Debate in either House, they shall not be questioned in any other Place.

55
(Madison)
76
(Hamilton)

No Senator or Representative shall, during the time for which he was elected, be appointed to any civil Office under the authority of the United States, which shall have been created, or the Emoluments whereof shall have been encreased during such time; and no Person holding any Office under the United States, shall be a Member of either House during his Continuance in Office.

Section 7
[PROCEDURE IN PASSING BILLS AND RESOLUTIONS]

66
(Hamilton)

All Bills for raising Revenue shall originate in the House of Representatives; but the Senate may propose or concur with Amendments as on other Bills.

69, 73
(Hamilton)

Every Bill which shall have passed the House of Representatives and the Senate, shall, before it become a Law, be presented to the President of the United States; if he approve he shall sign it, but if not he shall return it, with his Objections to that House in which it shall have originated, who shall enter the Objections at large on their Journal, and proceed to reconsider it. If after such Reconsideration two-thirds of that House shall agree to pass the Bill, it shall be sent, together with the Objections, to the other House, by which it shall likewise be reconsidered, and if approved by two-thirds of that House it shall become a Law. But in all such Cases the Votes of both Houses shall be determined by Yeas and Nays, and the Names of the Persons voting for and against the Bill shall be entered on the Journal of each House respectively. If any Bill shall not be returned by the President within ten Days (Sundays excepted) after it shall have been presented to him, the Same shall be a Law, in like Manner as if he had signed it, unless the Congress by their Adjournment prevent its Return, in which Case it shall not be a Law.

69, 73
(Hamilton)

Every Order, Resolution, or Vote to which the Concurrence of the Senate and House of Representatives may be necessary (except on a question of Adjournment) shall be presented to the President of the United States; and before the Same shall take Effect, shall be approved by him, or being disapproved by him, shall be repassed by two-thirds of the Senate and House of Representatives, according to the Rules and Limitations prescribed in the Case of a Bill.

Section 8
[POWERS OF CONGRESS]

The Congress shall have Power

30–36
(Hamilton)

To lay and collect Taxes, Duties, Imposts and Excises, to pay the Debts and

41
(Madison)
56
(Madison)

provide for the common Defence and general Welfare of the United States; but all Duties, Imposts and Excises shall be uniform throughout the United States;

42, 45, 56
(Madison)

To borrow Money on the Credit of the United States;

To regulate Commerce with foreign Nations, and among the several States, and with the Indian Tribes;

32
(Hamilton)

To establish an uniform Rule of Naturalization, and uniform Laws on the subject of Bankruptcies throughout the United States;

42
(Madison)

42
(Madison)

To coin Money, regulate the Value thereof, and of foreign Coin, and fix the Standard of Weights and Measures;

42
(Madison)

To provide for the Punishment of counterfeiting the Securities and current Coin of the United States;

42
(Madison)
43
(Madison)

To establish Post Offices and post Roads;

To promote the Progress of Science and useful Arts, by securing for limited Times to Authors and Inventors the exclusive Right to their respective Writings and Discoveries;

81
(Hamilton)
42
(Madison)

To constitute Tribunals inferior to the supreme Court;

To define and Punish Piracies and Felonies committed on the high Seas, and Offences against the Law of Nations;

41
(Madison)

To declare War, grant Letters of Marque and Reprisal, and make Rules concerning Captures on Land and Water;

23, 24, 26
(Hamilton)

To raise and support Armies, but no Appropriation of Money to that Use shall be for a longer Term than two Years;

41
(Madison)

To provide and maintain a Navy;

To make Rules for the Government and Regulation of the land and naval forces;

29
(Hamilton)

To provide for calling for the Militia to execute the Laws of the Union, suppress Insurrections and repel Invasions;

29
(Hamilton)
56
(Madison)

To provide for organizing, arming, and disciplining, the Militia, and for governing such Part of them as may be employed in the Service of the United States, reserv-

ing to the States respectively, the Appointment of the Officers, and the Authority of training the Militia according to the discipline prescribed by Congress;

32
(Hamilton)

43
(Madison)
43
(Madison)

To exercise exclusive Legislation in all Cases whatsoever, over such District (not exceeding ten Miles square) as may, by Cession of particular States, and the Acceptance of Congress, become the Seat of the Government of the United States, and to exercise like Authority over all Places purchased by the Consent of the Legislature of the State in which the Same shall be, for the Erection of Forts, Magazines, Arsenals, dock-Yards, and other needful Buildings;—And

29, 33
(Hamilton)
44
(Madison)

To make all Laws which shall be necessary and proper for carrying into Execution the foregoing Powers, and all other Powers vested by this Constitution in the Government of the United States, or in any Department or Officer thereof.

Section 9

42
(Madison)

[SOME RESTRICTIONS ON FEDERAL POWER]

The Migration or Importation of such Persons as any of the States now existing shall think proper to admit, shall not be prohibited by the Congress prior to the Year one thousand eight hundred and eight, but a Tax or Duty may be imposed on such Importation, not exceeding ten dollars for each Person.[7]

83, 84
(Hamilton)

The privilege of the Writ of *Habeas Corpus* shall not be suspended, unless when in Cases of Rebellion or Invasion the public Safety may require it.

84
(Hamilton)

No Bill of Attainder or ex post facto Law shall be passed.

No Capitation, or other direct, Tax shall be laid, unless in Proportion to the Census or Enumeration herein before directed to be taken.[8]

No Tax or Duty shall be laid on Articles exported from any State.

[7]Temporary provision.
[8]Modified by Sixteenth Amendment.

32
(Hamilton)

No Preference shall be given by any Regulation of Commerce or Revenue to the Ports of one State over those of another; nor shall vessels bound to, or from, one State, be obliged to enter, clear, or pay Duties in another.

No Money shall be drawn from the Treasury, but in Consequence of Appropriations made by Law; and a regular Statement and Account of the Receipts and Expenditures of all public Money shall be published from time to time.

39
(Madison)
84
(Hamilton)

No Title of Nobility shall be granted by the United States: And no Person holding any Office or Profit or Trust under them, shall, without the Consent of the Congress, accept of any present, Emolument, Office or Title, of any kind whatever, from any King, Prince, or foreign State.

Section 10
[RESTRICTIONS UPON POWERS OF STATES]

33
(Hamilton)
44
(Madison)

No State shall enter into any Treaty, Alliance, or Confederation; grant Letters of Marque and Reprisal; coin Money; emit Bills of Credit; make any Thing but gold and silver Coin a Tender in Payment of Debts; pass any Bill of Attainder, ex post facto Law, or Law impairing the Obligation of Contracts, or grant any Title of Nobility.

32
(Hamilton)
44
(Madison)

No State shall, without the Consent of the Congress, lay any Imposts or Duties on Imports or Exports, except what may be absolutely necessary for executing its inspection Laws: and the net Produce of all Duties and Imposts, laid by any State on Imports or Exports, shall be for the Use of the Treasury of the United States; and all such Laws shall be subject to the Revision and Control of the Congress.

No State shall, without the Consent of Congress, lay any Duty of Tonnage, keep Troops, or Ships of War in time of Peace, enter into any Agreement or Compact with another State, or with a foreign Power, or engage in War, unless actually invaded, or in such imminent Danger as will not admit of Delay.

ARTICLE II

Section 1
[EXECUTIVE POWER, ELECTION, QUALIFICATIONS OF THE PRESIDENT]

39
(Madison)
70, 71, 84
(Hamilton)
69, 71
(Hamilton)
39, 45
(Madison)
68, 77
(Hamilton)

The executive Power shall be vested in a President of the United States of America. *He shall hold his Office during the Term of four years and, together with the Vice-President, chosen for the same Term, be elected, as follows:*[9]

Each State shall appoint, in such Manner as the Legislature thereof may direct, a Number of Electors, equal to the whole Number of Senators and Representatives to which the State may be entitled in the Congress: but no Senator or Representative, or Person holding an Office of Trust or Profit under the United States, shall be appointed an Elector.

66
(Hamilton)

The electors shall meet in their respective States, and vote by ballot for two Persons, of whom one at least shall not be an Inhabitant of the same State with themselves. And they shall make a List of all the Persons voted for, and of the Number of Votes for each; which List they shall sign and certify, and transmit sealed to the Seat of the Government of the United States, directed to the President of the Senate. The President of the Senate shall, in the Presence of the Senate and House of Representatives, open all the Certificates, and the Votes shall then be counted. The Person having the greatest Number of Votes shall be the President, if such Number be a Majority of the whole Number of Electors appointed; and if there be more than one who have such Majority and have an equal Number of Votes, then

[9]Number of terms limited to two by Twenty-second Amendment.

the House of Representatives shall immediately chuse by Ballot one of them for President; and if no person have a Majority, then from the five highest on the List the said House shall in like Manner chuse the President. But in chusing the President, the Votes shall be taken by States, the Representation from each State having one Vote; A quorum for this Purpose shall consist of a Member or Members from two-thirds of the States, and a Majority of all the States shall be necessary to a Choice. In every Case, after the Choice of the President, the person having the greatest Number of Votes of the Electors shall be the Vice-President. But if there should remain two or more who have equal vote, the Senate shall chuse from them by Ballot the Vice-President.[10]

64 (Jay)

The Congress may determine the Time of chusing the Electors, and the Day on which they shall give their Votes; which Day shall be the same throughout the United States.

No Person except a natural born Citizen, or a Citizen of the United States, at the time of the Adoption of this Constitution, shall be eligible to the Office of President; neither shall any Person be eligible to that Office who shall not have attained to the Age of thirty-five Years, and been fourteen Years a Resident within the United States.

In Case of the Removal of the President from Office, or his Death, Resignation, or Inability to discharge the Powers and Duties of the said Office, the same shall devolve on the Vice-President, and the Congress may by Law provide for the Case of Removal, Death, Resignation, or Inability, both of the President and Vice-President, declaring what Officer shall then act as President, and such Officer shall act accordingly, until the Disability be removed, or a President shall be elected.

[10]Modified by Twelfth and Twentieth Amendments.

73, 79 (Hamilton)

The President shall, at stated Times, receive for his Services, a Compensation, which shall neither be encreased nor diminished during the Period for which he shall have been elected, and he shall not receive within that Period any other Emolument from the United States, or any of them.

Before he enter on the Execution of his Office, he shall take the following Oath or Affirmation:—"I do solemnly swear (or affirm) that I will faithfully execute the Office of President of the United States, and will to the best of my Ability, preserve, protect and defend the Constitution of the United States."

Section 2
[POWERS OF THE PRESIDENT]

69, 74 (Hamilton)

74 (Hamilton)

69 (Hamilton)
74 (Hamilton)
42 (Madison)
64 (Jay)

66 (Hamilton)
42 (Madison)
66, 69, 76, 77 (Hamilton)

The President shall be Commander in Chief of the Army and Navy of the United States, and of the Militia of the several States, when called into the actual Service of the United States; he may require the Opinion, in writing, of the principal Officer in each of the executive Departments, upon any Subject relating to the Duties of the respective Offices, and he shall have Power to grant Reprieves and Pardons for Offences against the United States, except in Cases of Impeachment.

He shall have Power, by and with the Advice and Consent of the Senate, to make Treaties, provided two-thirds of the Senators present concur; and he shall nominate, and by and with the Advice and Consent of the Senate, shall appoint Ambassadors, other public Ministers and Consuls, Judges of the Superior Court, and all other Officers of the United States, whose Appointments are not herein otherwise provided for, and which shall be established by Law: but the Congress may by Law vest the Appointment of such inferior Officers, as they think proper, in the President alone, in the

Courts of Law, or in the Heads of Departments.

67, 76
(Hamilton)

The President shall have Power to fill up all Vacancies that may happen during the Recess of the Senate, by granting Commissions which shall expire at the End of their next Session.

Section 3
[POWERS AND DUTIES OF THE PRESIDENT]

77
(Hamilton)
69, 77
(Hamilton)
77
(Hamilton)
69, 77
(Hamilton)
42
(Madison)
69, 77
(Hamilton)
78
(Hamilton)

He shall from time to time give to the Congress Information of the State of the Union, and recommend to their Consideration such Measures as he shall judge necessary and expedient; he may, on extraordinary Occasions, convene both Houses, or either of them, and in Case of Disagreement between them, with Respect to the Time of Adjournment, he may adjourn them to such Time as he shall think proper; he shall receive Ambassadors and other public Ministers; he shall take Care that the Laws be faithfully executed, and shall Commission all the Officers of the United States.

Section 4
[IMPEACHMENT]

39
(Madison)
69
(Hamilton)

The President, Vice-President and all civil Officers of the United States shall be removed from Office on Impeachment for, and Conviction of, Treason, Bribery, or other high Crimes and Misdemeanors.

ARTICLE III
Section 1
[JUDICIAL POWER, TENURE OF OFFICE]

81, 82
(Hamilton)
65
(Hamilton)
78, 79
(Hamilton)

The judicial Power of the United States, shall be vested in one supreme Court, and in such inferior Courts as the Congress may from time to time ordain and establish. The Judges, both of the supreme and inferior Courts, shall hold their Offices during good Behavior, and shall, at stated Times, receive for their Services, a Compensation, which shall not be diminished during their Continuance in Office.

Section 2
[JURISDICTION]

80
(Hamilton)

The judicial Power shall extend to all Cases, in Law and Equity, arising under this Constitution, the Laws of the United States, and Treaties made, or which shall be made, under their Authority;—to all Cases affecting Ambassadors, other public Ministers and Consuls;—to all Cases of admiralty and maritime Jurisdiction;—to Controversies to which the United States shall be a party;—to Controversies between two or more States;—*between a State and Citizens of another States*;—between Citizens of different States,—between Citizens of the same State claiming Lands under Grants of different States, and between a State, or the Citizens thereof, *and foreign States, Citizens or Subjects.*[11]

81
(Hamilton)

In all Cases affecting Ambassadors, other public Ministers and Consuls, and those in which a State shall be Party, the supreme Court shall have original Jurisdiction. In all the other Cases before mentioned, the supreme Court shall have appellate Jurisdiction, both as to Law and Fact, with such Exceptions, and under such Regulations as Congress shall make.

83, 84
(Hamilton)

The Trial of all Crimes, except in Cases of Impeachment, shall be by Jury; and such Trial shall be held in the State where the said Crimes shall have been committed; but when not committed within any State, the Trial shall be at such Place or Places as the Congress may by Law have directed.

Section 3
[TREASON, PROOF, AND PUNISHMENT]

43
(Madison)
84
(Hamilton)

Treason against the United States, shall consist only in levying War against them, or in adhering to their Enemies, giving them Aid and Comfort. No Persons shall be convicted of Treason unless on the Testimony of two Witnesses to the same overt Act, or on Confession in open Court.

[11]Modified by Eleventh Amendment.

43
(Madison)
84
(Hamilton)

The Congress shall have Power to declare the Punishment of Treason, but no Attainder of Treason shall work Corruption of Blood, or Forfeiture except during the Life of the Person attained.

ARTICLE IV

Section 1

[FAITH AND CREDIT AMONG STATES]

42
(Madison)

Full Faith and Credit shall be given in each State to the public Acts, Records, and judicial Proceedings of every other State. And the Congress may by general Laws prescribe the Manner in which such Acts, Records and Proceedings shall be proved, and the Effect thereof.

Section 2

[PRIVILEGES AND IMMUNITIES, FUGITIVES]

80
(Hamilton)

The Citizens of each State shall be entitled to all Privileges and Immunities of Citizens in the several States.

A person charged in any State with Treason, Felony or other Crime, who shall flee from Justice, and be found in another State, shall on Demand of the executive Authority of the State from which he fled, be delivered up to be removed to the State having Jurisdiction of the Crime.

No person held to Service or Labour in one State, under the Laws thereof, escaping into another, shall, in Consequence of any Law or Regulation therein, be discharged from such Service or Labour, but shall be delivered up on Claim of the Party to whom such Service or Labour may be due.[12]

Section 3

[ADMISSION OF NEW STATES]

43
(Madison)

New States may be admitted by the Congress into this Union; but no new State shall be formed or erected within the Jurisdiction of any other States; nor any State be formed by the Junction of two or more States, or Parts of States, without the Con-

43
(Madison)

sent of the Legislatures of the States concerned as well as of the Congress.

The Congress shall have Power to dispose of and make all needful Rules and Regulations respecting the Territory or other Property belonging to the United States; and nothing in this Constitution shall be so construed as to Prejudice any Claims of the United States, or of any particular State.

Section 4

[GUARANTEE OF REPUBLICAN GOVERNMENT]

39, 43
(Madison)

The United States shall guarantee to every State in this Union a Republican Form of Government, and shall protect each of them against Invasion; and on Application of the Legislature, or of the Executive (when the Legislature cannot be convened) against domestic Violence.

ARTICLE V

[AMENDMENT OF THE CONSTITUTION]

39, 43
(Madison)
85
(Hamilton)

The Congress, whenever two-thirds of both Houses shall deem it necessary, shall propose Amendments to this Constitution, or, on the Application of the Legislatures of two-thirds of the several States, shall call a Convention for proposing Amendments, which, in either Case, shall be valid to all Intents and Purposes, as Part of this Constitution, when ratified by the Legislatures of three-fourths of the several States, or by Conventions in three-fourths thereof, as the one or the other Mode of Ratification may be proposed by the Congress; *Provided that no Amendment which may be made prior to the Year One thousand eight hundred and eight shall in any Manner affect the first and*

43
(Madison)

fourth Clauses in the Ninth Section of the first Article;[13] and that no State, without its Consent, shall be deprived of its equal Suffrage in the Senate.

[12]Repealed by the Thirteenth Amendment.

[13]Temporary provision.

ARTICLE VI

[DEBTS, SUPREMACY, OATH]

43
(Madison)

All Debts contracted and Engagements entered into, before the Adoption of this Constitution, shall be as valid against the United States under this Constitution, as under the Confederation.

27, 33
(Hamilton)

39, 44

This Constitution, and the Laws of the United States which shall be made in Pursuance thereof; and all Treaties made, or which shall be made, under the Authority of the United States, shall be the supreme Law of the Land; and the Judges in every State shall be bound thereby, any Thing in the Constitution or Laws of any State to the Contrary notwithstanding.

27
(Hamilton)

44

The Senators and Representatives before mentioned, and the Members of the several State Legislatures, and all executive and judicial Officers, both of the United States and of the several States, shall be bound by Oath or Affirmation, to support this Constitution; but no religious Test shall be required as a Qualification to any Office or public Trust under the United States.

ARTICLE VII

[RATIFICATION AND ESTABLISHMENT]

39, 40, 43
(Madison)

The Ratification of the Conventions of nine States, shall be sufficient for the Establishment of this Constitution between the States so ratifying the Same.[14]

Done in Convention by the Unanimous Consent of the States present the Seventeenth Day of September in the Year of our Lord one thousand seven hundred and Eighty seven and of the Independence of the United States of American the Twelfth. *In Witness* whereof We have hereunto subscribed our Names,

[14]The Constitution was submitted on September 17, 1787, by the Constitutional Convention, was ratified by the conventions of several states at various dates up to May 29, 1790, and became effective on March 4, 1789.

G:º WASHINGTON—
*Presidt, and Deputy
from Virginia*

New Hampshire	JOHN LANGDON
	NICHOLAS GILMAN
Massachusetts	NATHANIEL GORHAM
	RUFUS KING
Connecticut	WM SAML JOHNSON
	ROGER SHERMAN
New York	ALEXANDER HAMILTON
New Jersey	WIL: LIVINGSTON
	DAVID BREARLY
	WM PATERSON
	JONA: DAYTON
Pennsylvania	B FRANKLIN
	THOMAS MIFFLIN
	ROBT MORRIS
	GEO. CLYMER
	THOS. FITZSIMONS
	JARED INGERSOLL
	JAMES WILSON
	GOUV MORRIS
Delaware	GEO READ
	GUNNING BEDFOR JUN
	JOHN DICKINSON
	RICHARD BASSETT
	JACO: BROOM
Maryland	JAMES MCHENRY
	DAN OF ST. THOS. JENIFER
	DANL CARROLL
Virginia	JOHN BLAIR—
	JAMES MADISON JR.
North Carolina	WM BLOUNT
	RICHD DOBBS SPAIGHT
	HU WILLIAMSON
South Carolina	J. RUTLEDGE
	CHARLES COTESWORTH PINCKNEY
	PIERCE BUTLER
Georgia	WILLIAM FEW
	ABR BALDWIN

AMENDMENTS TO THE CONSTITUTION

Proposed by Congress and Ratified by the Legislatures of the Several States, Pursuant to Article V of the Original Constitution

Amendments I–X, known as the Bill of Rights, were proposed by Congress on September 25, 1789, and ratified on December 15, 1791. *Federalist Papers* **comments, mainly in opposition to a Bill of Rights, can be found in #84 (Hamilton).**

AMENDMENT I

[FREEDOM OF RELIGION, OF SPEECH, AND OF THE PRESS]

Congress shall make no law respecting an establishment of religion, or prohibiting the free exercise thereof; or abridging the freedom of speech, or of the press; or the right of the people peaceably to assemble, and to petition the Government for a redress of grievances.

AMENDMENT II

[RIGHT TO KEEP AND BEAR ARMS]

A well regulated Militia, being necessary to the security of a free State, the right of the people to keep and bear Arms, shall not be infringed.

AMENDMENT III

[QUARTERING OF SOLDIERS]

No Soldier shall, in time of peace be quartered in any house, without the consent of the Owner, nor in time of war, but in a manner to be prescribed by law.

AMENDMENT IV

[SECURITY FROM UNWARRANTABLE SEARCH AND SEIZURE]

The right of the people to be secure in their persons, houses, papers, and effects, against unreasonable searches and seizures, shall not be violated, and no Warrants shall issue, but upon probable cause, supported by Oath or affirmation, and particularly describing the place to be searched, and the persons or things to be seized.

AMENDMENT V

[RIGHTS OF ACCUSED PERSONS IN CRIMINAL PROCEEDINGS]

No person shall be held to answer for a capital, or otherwise infamous crime, unless on a presentment or indictment of a Grand Jury, except in cases arising in the land of naval forces, or in the Militia, when in actual service in time of War or in public danger; nor shall any person be subject for the same offence to be twice put in jeopardy of life or limb; nor shall be compelled in any Criminal Case to be a witness against himself, nor be deprived of life, liberty, or property, without due process of law; nor shall private property be taken for public use, without just compensation.

AMENDMENT VI

[RIGHT TO SPEEDY TRIAL, WITNESSES, ETC.]

In all criminal prosecutions, the accused shall enjoy the right to a speedy and public trial, by an impartial jury of the State and district wherein the crime shall have been committed, which district shall have been previously ascertained by law, and to be informed of the nature and cause of the accusation; to be confronted with the witnesses against him; to have compulsory process for obtaining witnesses in his favor, and to have the Assistance of Counsel for his defence.

AMENDMENT VII
[TRIAL BY JURY IN CIVIL CASES]

In suits at common law, where the value in controversy shall exceed twenty dollars, the right of trial by jury shall be preserved, and no fact tried by a jury shall be otherwise reexamined in any Court of the United States, than according to the rules of the common law.

AMENDMENT VIII
[BAILS, FINES, PUNISHMENTS]

Excessive bail shall not be required, nor excessive fines imposed, nor cruel and unusual punishments inflicted.

AMENDMENT IX
[RESERVATION OF RIGHTS OF PEOPLE]

The enumeration in the Constitution, of certain rights, shall not be construed to deny or disparage others retained by the people.

AMENDMENT X
[POWERS RESERVED TO STATES OR PEOPLE]

The powers not delegated to the United States by the Constitution, nor prohibited by it to the States, are reserved to the States respectively, or to the people.

AMENDMENT XI
[Proposed by Congress on March 4, 1794; declared ratified on January 8, 1798.]

[RESTRICTION OF JUDICIAL POWER]

The Judicial power of the United States shall not be construed to extend to any suit in law or equity, commenced or prosecuted against one of the United States by Citizens of another State, or by Citizens or Subjects of any Foreign State.

AMENDMENT XII
[Proposed by Congress on December 9, 1803; declared ratified on September 25, 1804.]

[ELECTION OF PRESIDENT AND VICE-PRESIDENT]

The Electors shall meet in their respective states, and vote by ballot for President and Vice-President, one of whom, at least, shall not be an inhabitant of the same state with themselves; they shall name in their ballots the person voted for as President, and in distinct ballots the person voted for as Vice-President, and they shall make distinct lists of all persons voted for as President, and of all persons voted for as Vice-President, and of the number of votes for each, which lists they shall sign and certify, and transmit sealed to the seat of the government of the United States, directed to the President of the Senate;—The President of the Senate shall, in presence of the Senate and House of Representatives, open all the certificates and the votes shall then be counted;—The person having the greatest number of votes for President, shall be the President, if such number be a majority of the whole number of Electors appointed; and if no person have such majority, then from the persons having the highest numbers not exceeding three on the list of those voted for as President, the House of Representatives shall choose immediately, by ballot, the President. But in choosing the President, the votes shall be taken by states, the representation from each state having one vote; a quorum for this purpose shall consist of a member or members from two-thirds of the states, and a majority of all states shall be necessary to a choice. And if the House of Representatives shall not choose a President whenever the right of choice shall devolve upon them, before the fourth day of March next following, then the Vice-President, shall act as President, as in the case of the death or other constitutional disability of the President. The person having the greatest number of votes as Vice-President, shall be the Vice-President, if such a number be a majority of the whole number of Electors appointed, and if no person have a majority, then from the two highest numbers on the list, the Senate shall choose the Vice-President; a quorum for the purpose shall consist of two-thirds of the whole number of Senators, and a majority of the whole number shall be necessary to a choice. But no person constitutionally ineligible to the office of President shall be eligible to that of Vice-President of the United States.

AMENDMENT XIII

[Proposed by Congress on January 31, 1865; declared ratified on December 18, 1865.]

Section 1
[ABOLITION OF SLAVERY]

Neither slavery nor involuntary servitude, except as a punishment for crime whereof the party shall have been duly convicted, shall exist within the United States, or any place subject to their jurisdiction.

Section 2
[POWER TO ENFORCE THIS ARTICLE]

Congress shall have power to enforce this article by appropriate legislation.

AMENDMENT XIV

[Proposed by Congress on June 13, 1866, declared ratified on July 28, 1868.]

Section I
[CITIZENSHIP RIGHTS NOT TO BE ABRIDGED BY STATES]

All persons born or naturalized in the United States, and subject to the jurisdiction thereof, are citizens of the United States and of the State wherein they reside. No state shall make or enforce any law which shall abridge the privileges or immunities of citizens of the United States; nor shall any State deprive any person of life, liberty, or property, without due process of law; nor deny to any person within its jurisdiction the equal protection of the laws.

Section 2
[APPORTIONMENT OF REPRESENTATIVES IN CONGRESS]

Representatives shall be apportioned among the several States according to their respective numbers, counting the whole number of persons in each State, excluding Indians not taxed. But when the right to vote at any election for the choice of electors for President and Vice-President of the United States, Representatives in Congress, the Executive and Judicial officers of a State, or the members of the Legislature thereof, is denied to any of the male inhabitants of such State, being twenty-one years of age, and citizens of the United States, or in any way abridged, except for participation in rebellion, or other crime, the basis of representation therein shall be reduced in the proportion which the number of such male citizens shall bear to the whole number of male citizens twenty-one years of age in such State.

Section 3
[PERSONS DISQUALIFIED FROM HOLDING OFFICE]

No person shall be a Senator or Representative in Congress, or elector of President and Vice-President, or hold any office, civil or military, under the United States, or under any State, who, having previously taken an oath, as a member of Congress, or as an officer of the United States, or as a member of any State legislature, or as an executive or judicial officer of any State, to support the Constitution of the United States, shall have engaged in insurrection or rebellion against the same, or given aid or comfort to the enemies thereof. But Congress may by a vote of two-thirds of each House, remove such disability.

Section 4
[WHAT PUBLIC DEBTS ARE VALID]

The validity of the public debt of the United States, authorized by law, including debts incurred for payment of pensions and bounties for services in suppressing insurrection or rebellion, shall not be questioned. But neither the United States nor any State shall assume or pay any debt or obligation incurred in aid of insurrection or rebellion against the United States, or any claim for the loss or emancipation of any slave; but all such debts, obligations and claims shall be held illegal and void.

Section 5
[POWER TO ENFORCE THIS ARTICLE]

The Congress shall have power to enforce, by appropriate legislation, the provisions of this article.

AMENDMENT XV

[*Proposed by Congress on February 26, 1869; declared ratified on March 30, 1870.*]

Section 1
[NEGRO SUFFRAGE]

The right of citizens of the United States to vote shall not be denied or abridged by the United States or by any State on account of race, color, or previous condition of servitude.

Section 2
[POWER TO ENFORCE THIS ARTICLE]

The Congress shall have power to enforce this article by appropriate legislation.

AMENDMENT XVI

[*Proposed by Congress on July 12, 1909; declared ratified on February 25, 1913.*]

[AUTHORIZING INCOME TAXES]

The Congress shall have power to lay and collect taxes on incomes, from whatever source derived, without apportionment among the several States, and without regard to any census or enumeration.

AMENDMENT XVII

[*Proposed by Congress on May 13, 1912; declared ratified on May 31, 1913.*]

[POPULAR ELECTION OF SENATORS]

The Senate of the United States shall be composed of two Senators from each State, elected by the people thereof, for six years; and each Senator shall have one vote. The electors in each State shall have the qualifications requisite for electors of the most numerous branch of the State Legislature.

When vacancies happen in the representation of any State in the Senate, the executive authority of such State shall issue writs of election to fill such vacancies: Provided, That the Legislature of any State may empower the executive thereof to make temporary appointment until the people fill the vacancies by election as the Legislature may direct.

This amendment shall not be so construed as to affect the election or term of any Senator chosen before it becomes valid as part of the Constitution.

AMENDMENT XVIII

[*Proposed by Congress December 18, 1917; declared ratified on January 29, 1919.*]

Section 1
[NATIONAL LIQUOR PROHIBITION]

After one year from the ratification of this article the manufacture, sale, or transportation of intoxicating liquors within, the importation thereof into, or the exportation thereof from the United States and all territory subject to the jurisdiction thereof for beverage purposes is hereby prohibited.

Section 2
[POWER TO ENFORCE THIS ARTICLE]

The Congress and the several states shall have concurrent power to enforce this article by appropriate legislation.

Section 3
[RATIFICATION WITHIN SEVEN YEARS]

This article shall be inoperative unless it shall have been ratified as an amendment to the Constitution by the legislatures of the several states, as provided in the Constitution, within seven years from the date of the submission hereof to the states by the Congress.[15]

AMENDMENT XIX

[*Proposed by Congress on June 4, 1919; declared ratified on August 26, 1920.*]

[WOMAN SUFFRAGE]

The right of the citizens of the United States to vote shall not be denied or abridged by the United States or by any State on account of sex.

Congress shall have power to enforce this article by appropriate legislation.

AMENDMENT XX

[*Proposed by Congress on March 2, 1932; declared ratified on February 6, 1933.*]

---

[15]Repealed by the Twenty-first Amendment.

Section 1
[TERMS OF OFFICE]

The terms of the President and Vice-President shall end at noon on the 20th day of January, and the terms of the Senators and Representatives at noon on the 3rd day of January, of the years in which such terms would have ended if this article had not been ratified; and the terms of their successors shall then begin.

Section 2
[TIME OF CONVENING CONGRESS]

The Congress shall assemble at least once in every year, and such meeting shall begin at noon on the 3rd day of January, unless they shall by law appoint a different day.

Section 3
[DEATH OF PRESIDENT-ELECT]

If, at the time fixed for the beginning of the term of the President, the President-elect shall have died, the Vice-President-elect shall become President. If a President shall not have been chosen before the time fixed for the beginning of his term, or if the President-elect shall have failed to qualify, then the Vice-President-elect shall act as President until a President shall have qualified; and the Congress may by law provide for the case wherein neither a President-elect nor a Vice-President-elect shall have qualified, declaring who shall then act as President, or the manner in which one who is to act shall be selected, and such person shall act accordingly until a President or Vice President shall have qualified.

Section 4
[ELECTION OF THE PRESIDENT]

The Congress may by law provide for the case of the death of any of the persons from whom the House of Representatives may choose a President whenever the right of choice shall have devolved upon them, and for the case of the death of any of the persons from whom the Senate may choose a Vice-President whenever the right of choice shall have devolved upon them.

Section 5
[AMENDMENT TAKES EFFECT]

Sections 1 and 2 shall take effect on the 5th day of October following ratification of this article.

Section 6
[RATIFICATION WITHIN SEVEN YEARS]

This article shall be inoperative unless it shall have been ratified as an amendment to the Constitution by the legislatures of three-fourths of the several States within seven years from the date of its submission.

AMENDMENT XXI
[*Proposed by Congress on February 20, 1933; declared ratified on December 5, 1933.*]

Section 1
[NATIONAL LIQUOR PROHIBITION REPEALED]

The eighteenth article of amendment to the Constitution of the United States is hereby repealed.

Section 2
[TRANSPORTATION OF LIQUOR INTO "DRY" STATES]

The transportation or importation into any State, Territory, or Possession of the United States for delivery or use therein of intoxicating liquors, in violation of the laws thereof, is hereby prohibited.

Section 3
[RATIFICATION WITHIN SEVEN YEARS]

This article shall be inoperative unless it shall have been ratified as an amendment to the Constitution by conventions in the several States, as provided in the Constitution, within seven years from the date of the submission hereof to the States by the Congress.

AMENDMENT XXII
[*Proposed by Congress on March 21, 1947; declared ratified on February 26, 1951.*]

Section 1
[TENURE OF PRESIDENT LIMITED]

No person shall be elected to the office of President more than twice, and no person who has held the office of President or acted as President for more than two years of a term to which some other person was elected President shall be elected to the Office of the President more than once. But this Article shall not apply to any person holding the office of President when this Article was proposed by the Congress, and shall not prevent any person who may be holding the office of President, or acting as President, during the term within which this Article becomes operative from holding the office of President or acting as President during the remainder of such term.

Section 2
[RATIFICATION WITHIN SEVEN YEARS]

This Article shall be inoperative unless it shall have been ratified as an amendment to the Constitution by the legislatures of three-fourths of the several states within seven years from the date of its submission to the States by the Congress.

AMENDMENT XXIII
[*Proposed by Congress on June 21, 1960; declared ratified on March 29, 1961.*]

Section 1
[ELECTORAL COLLEGE VOTES FOR THE DISTRICT OF COLUMBIA]

The District constituting the seat of Government of the United States shall appoint in such manner as the Congress may direct:

A number of electors of President and Vice-President equal to the whole number of Senators and Representatives in Congress to which the District would be entitled if it were a State, but in no event more than the least populous State; they shall be in addition to those appointed by the States, but they shall be considered, for the purposes of the election of President and Vice-President, to be electors appointed by a State; and they shall meet in the District and perform such duties as provided by the twelfth article of amendment.

Section 2
[POWER TO ENFORCE THIS ARTICLE]

The Congress shall have power to enforce this article by appropriate legislation.

AMENDMENT XXIV
[*Proposed by Congress on August 27, 1963; declared ratified on January 23, 1964.*]

Section 1
[ANTI-POLL TAX]

The right of citizens of the United States to vote in any primary or other election for President or Vice-President, for electors for President or Vice-President, or for Senator or Representative of Congress, shall not be denied or abridged by the United States or any State by reasons of failure to pay any poll tax or other tax.

Section 2
[POWER TO ENFORCE THIS ARTICLE]

The Congress shall have power to enforce this article by appropriate legislation.

AMENDMENT XXV
[*Proposed by Congress on July 7, 1965; declared ratified on February 10, 1967.*]

Section 1
[VICE-PRESIDENT TO BECOME PRESIDENT]

In case of the removal of the President from office or his death or resignation, the Vice-President shall become President.

Section 2
[CHOICE OF A NEW VICE-PRESIDENT]

Whenever there is a vacancy in the office of the Vice-President, the President shall nominate a Vice-President who shall take the office upon confirmation by a majority vote of both houses of Congress.

Section 3
[PRESIDENT MAY DECLARE OWN DISABILITY]

Whenever the President transmits to the President pro tempore of the Senate and the Speaker of the House of Representatives his written declaration that he is unable to discharge the powers and duties of his office, and until he transmits to them a written declaration to the contrary, such powers and duties shall be discharged by the Vice-President as Acting President.

Section 4

[ALTERNATE PROCEDURES TO DECLARE AND TO END PRESIDENTIAL DISABILITY]

Whenever the Vice-President and a majority of either the principal officers of the executive departments, or of such other body as Congress may by law provide, transmit to the President pro tempore of the Senate and the Speaker of the House of Representatives their written declaration that the President is unable to discharge the powers and duties of his office, the Vice-President shall immediately assume the powers and duties of the office as Acting President.

Thereafter, when the President transmits to the President pro tempore of the Senate and the Speaker of the House of Representatives his written declaration that no inability exists, he shall resume the powers and duties of his office unless the Vice-President and a majority of either the principal officers of the executive departments, or of such other body as Congress may by law provide, transmit within four days to the President pro tempore of the Senate and the Speaker of the House of Representatives their written declaration that the President is unable to discharge the powers and duties of his office. Thereupon Congress shall decide the issue, assembling within forty-eight hours for that purpose if not in session. If the Congress, within twenty-one days after receipt of the latter written declaration, or, if Congress is not in session, within twenty-one days after Congress is required to assemble, determines by two-thirds vote of both houses that the President is unable to discharge the powers and duties of his office, the Vice-President shall continue to discharge the same as Acting President; otherwise, the President shall resume the powers and duties of his office.

AMENDMENT XXVI

[*Proposed by Congress on March 23, 1971; declared ratified on June 30, 1971.*]

Section 1

[EIGHTEEN-YEAR-OLD VOTE]

The right of citizens of the United States, who are eighteen years of age or older, to vote shall not be denied or abridged by the United States or by any State on account of age.

Section 2

[POWER TO ENFORCE THIS ARTICLE]

The Congress shall have power to enforce this article by appropriate legislation.

AMENDMENT XXVII

[*Proposed by Congress on September 25, 1789; ratified on May 7, 1992.*]

[CONGRESSIONAL PAY RAISES]

No law varying the compensation for the services of the Senators and Representatives shall take effect until an election of Representatives shall have intervened.

No. 10: Madison

Among the numerous advantages promised by a well-constructed Union, none deserves to be more accurately developed than its tendency to break and control the violence of faction. The friend of popular governments never finds himself so much alarmed for their character and fate as when he contemplates their propensity to this dangerous vice. He will not fail, therefore, to set a due value on any plan which, without violating the principles to which he is attached, provides a proper cure for it. The instability, injustice, and confusion introduced into the public councils have, in truth, been the mortal diseases under which popular governments have everywhere perished, as they continue to be the favorite and fruitful topics from which the adversaries to liberty derive their most specious declamations. The valuable improvements made by the American constitutions on the popular models, both ancient and modern, cannot certainly be too much admired; but it would be an unwarrantable partiality to contend that they have as effectually obviated the danger on this side, as was wished and expected. Complaints are everywhere heard from our most considerate and virtuous citizens, equally the friends of public and private faith and of public and personal liberty, that our governments are too unstable, that the public good is disregarded in the conflicts of rival parties, and that measures are too often decided, not according to the rules of justice and the rights of the minor party, but by the superior force of an interested and overbearing majority. However anxiously we may wish that these complaints had no foundation, the evidence of known facts will not permit us to deny that they are in some degree true. It will be found, indeed, on a candid review of our situation, that some of the distresses under which we labor have been erroneously charged on the operation of our governments; but it will be found, at the same time, that other causes will not alone account for many of our heaviest misfortunes; and, particularly, for that prevailing and increasing distrust of public engagements and alarm for private rights which are echoed from one end of the continent to the other. These must be chiefly, if not wholly, effects of the unsteadiness and injustice with which a factious spirit has tainted our public administration.

By a faction I understand a number of citizens, whether amounting to a majority or minority of the whole, who are united and actuated by some common impulse of passion, or of interest, adverse to the rights of other citizens, or to the permanent and aggregate interests of the community.

There are two methods of curing the mischiefs of faction: the one, by removing its causes; the other, by controlling its effects.

There are again two methods of removing the causes of faction: the one, by destroying the liberty which is essential to its existence; the other, by giving to every citizen the same opinions, the same passions, and the same interests.

It could never be more truly said than of the first remedy that it was worse than the disease. Liberty is to faction what air is to fire, an aliment without which it instantly expires. But it could not be a less folly to abolish liberty, which is essential to political life, because it nourishes faction than it would be to wish the annihilation of air, which is essential to animal life, because it imparts to fire its destructive agency.

The second expedient is as impracticable as the first would be unwise. As long as the reason of man continues fallible, and he is at liberty to exercise it, different opinions will be formed. As long as the connection subsists between his reason and his self-love, his opinions and his passions will have a reciprocal influence on each other; and the former will be objects to which the latter will attach themselves. The diversity in the faculties of men, from which the rights of property originate, is not less an insuperable obstacle to a uniformity of interests. The protection of these faculties is the first object of government. From the protection of different and unequal faculties of acquiring property, the possession of different degrees and kinds of property immediately results; and from the influence of these on the sentiments and views of the respective proprietors ensues a division of the society into different interests and parties.

The latent causes of faction are thus sown in the nature of man; and we see them everywhere brought into different degrees of activity, according to the different circumstances of civil society. A zeal for different opinions concerning religion, concerning government, and many other points, as well of speculation as of practice; an attachment to different leaders ambitiously contending for preeminence and power; or to persons of other descriptions whose fortunes have been interesting to the human passions, have, in turn, divided mankind into parties, inflamed them with mutual animosity, and rendered them much more disposed to vex and oppress each other than to co-operate for their common good. So strong is the propensity of mankind to fall into mutual animosities that where no substantial occasion presents itself the most frivolous and fanciful distinctions have been

sufficient to kindle their unfriendly passions and excite their most violent conflicts. But the most common and durable source of factions has been the various and unequal distribution of property. Those who hold and those who are without property have ever formed distinct interests in society. Those who are creditors, and those who are debtors, fall under a like discrimination. A landed interest, a manufacturing interest, a mercantile interest, a moneyed interest, with many lesser interests, grow up of necessity in civilized nations, and divide them into different classes, actuated by different sentiments and views. The regulation of these various and interfering interests forms the principal task of modern legislation and involves the spirit of party and faction in the necessary and ordinary operations of government.

No man is allowed to be judge in his own cause, because his interest would certainly bias his judgment and, not improbably, corrupt his integrity. With equal, nay with greater reason, a body of men are unfit to be both judges and parties at the same time; yet what are many of the most important acts of legislation but so many judicial determinations, not indeed concerning the rights of single persons, but concerning the rights of large bodies of citizens? And what are the different classes of legislators but advocates and parties to the causes which they determine? Is a law proposed concerning private debts? It is a question to which the creditors are parties on one side and the debtors on the other. Justice ought to hold the balance between them. Yet the parties are, and must be, themselves the judges; and the most numerous party, or in other words, the most powerful faction must be expected to prevail. Shall domestic manufacturers be encouraged, and in what degree, by restrictions on foreign manufacturers? are questions which would be differently decided by the landed and the manufacturing classes, and probably by neither with a sole regard to justice and the public good. The apportionment of taxes on the various descriptions of property is an act which seems to require the most exact impartiality; yet there is, perhaps, no legislative act in which greater opportunity and temptation are given to a predominant party to trample on the rules of justice. Every shilling with which they overburden the inferior number is a shilling saved to their own pockets.

It is in vain to say that enlightened statesmen will be able to adjust these clashing interests and render them all subservient to the public good. Enlightened statesmen will not always be at the helm. Nor, in many cases, can such an adjustment be made at all without taking into view indirect and remote considerations, which will rarely prevail over the immediate interest which one party may find in disregarding the rights of another or the good of the whole.

The inference to which we are brought is that the *causes* of faction cannot be removed and that relief is only to be sought in the means of controlling its *effects*.

If a faction consists of less than a majority, relief is supplied by the republican principle, which enables the majority to defeat its sinister views by regular vote. It may clog the administration, it may convulse the society; but it will be unable to execute and mask its violence under the forms of the Constitution. When a majority is included in a faction, the form of popular government, on the other hand, enables it to sacrifice to its ruling passion or interest both the public good and the rights of other citizens. To secure the public good and private rights against the danger of such a faction, and at the same time to preserve the spirit and the form of popular government, is then the great object to which our inquiries are directed. Let me add that it is the great desideratum by which alone this form of government can be rescued from the opprobrium under which it has so long labored and be recommended to the esteem and adoption of mankind.

By what means is this object attainable? Evidently by one of two only. Either the existence of the same passion or interest in a majority at the same time must be prevented, or the majority, having such coexistent passion or interest, must be rendered, by their number and local situation, unable to concert and carry into effect schemes of oppression. If the impulse and the opportunity be

suffered to coincide, we well know that neither moral nor religious motives can be relied on as an adequate control. They are not found to be such on the injustice and violence of individuals, and lose their efficacy in proportion to the number combined together, that is, in proportion as their efficacy becomes needful.

From this view of the subject it may be concluded that a pure democracy, by which I mean a society consisting of a small number of citizens, who assemble and administer the government in person, can admit of no cure for the mischiefs of faction. A common passion or interest will, in almost every case, be felt by a majority of the whole; a communication and concert results from the form of government itself; and there is nothing to check the inducements to sacrifice the weaker party or an obnoxious individual. Hence it is that such democracies have ever been spectacles of turbulence and contention; have ever been found incompatible with personal security or the rights of property; and have in general been as short in their lives as they have been violent in their deaths. Theoretic politicians, who have patronized this species of government, have erroneously supposed that by reducing mankind to a perfect equality in their political rights, they would at the same time be perfectly equalized and assimilated in their possessions, their opinions, and their passions.

A republic, by which I mean a government in which the scheme of representation takes place, opens a different prospect and promises the cure for which we are seeking. Let us examine the points in which it varies from pure democracy, and we shall comprehend both the nature of the cure and the efficacy which it must derive from the Union.

The two great points of difference between a democracy and a republic are: first, the delegation of the government, in the latter, to a small number of citizens elected by the rest; secondly, the greater number of citizens and greater sphere of country over which the latter may be extended.

The effect of the first difference is, on the one hand, to refine and enlarge the public views by passing them through the medium of a chosen body of citizens, whose wisdom may best discern the true interest of their country and whose patriotism and love of justice will be least likely to sacrifice it to temporary or partial considerations. Under such a regulation it may well happen that the public voice, pronounced by the representatives of the people, will be more consonant to the public good than if pronounced by the people themselves, convened for the purpose. On the other hand, the effect may be inverted. Men of factious tempers, of local prejudices, or of sinister designs, may, by intrigue, by corruption, or by other means, first obtain the suffrages, and then betray the interests of the people. The question resulting is, whether small or extensive republics are most favorable to the election of proper guardians of the public weal; and it is clearly decided in favor of the latter by two obvious considerations.

In the first place it is to be remarked that however small the republic may be the representatives must be raised to a certain number in order to guard against the cabals of a few; and that however large it may be they must be limited to a certain number in order to guard against the confusion of a multitude. Hence, the number of representatives in the two cases not being in proportion to that of the constituents, and being proportionally greatest in the small republic, it follows that if the proportion of fit characters be not less in the large than in the small republic, the former will present a greater option, and consequently a greater probability of a fit choice.

In the next place, as each representative will be chosen by a greater number of citizens in the large than in the small republic, it will be more difficult for unworthy candidates to practice with success the viscous arts by which elections are too often carried; and the suffrages of the people being more free, will be more likely to center on men who possess the most attractive merit and the most diffusive and established characters.

It must be confessed that in this, as in most other cases, there is a mean, on both sides of which inconveniencies will be found to lie. By enlarging too much the number of electors, you render the representative too little acquainted with all their local circumstances and lesser interests; as by reducing it too much, you render him unduly attached to these, and too little fit to comprehend and puruse great and national objects. The federal Constitution forms a happy combination in this respect; the great and aggregate interests being referred to the national, the local and particular to the State legislatures.

The other point of difference is the greater number of citizens and extent of territory which may be brought within the compass of republican than of democratic government; and it is this circumstance principally which renders factious combinations less to be dreaded in the former than in the latter. The smaller the society, the fewer probably will be the distinct parties and interests composing it; the fewer the distinct parties and interests, the most frequently will be majority be found of the same party; and the smaller the number of individuals composing a majority, and the smaller the compass within which they are placed, the more easily will they concert and execute their plans of oppression. Extend the sphere and you take in a greater variety of parties and interests; you make it less probable that a majority of the whole will have a common motive to invade the rights of other citizens; or if such a common motive exists, it will be more difficult for all who feel it to discover their own strength and to act in unison with each other. Besides other impediments, it may be remarked that, where there is a consciousness of unjust or dishonorable purposes, communication is always checked by distrust in proportion to the number whose concurrence is necessary.

Hence, it clearly appears that the same advantage which a republic has over a democracy in controlling the effects of faction is enjoyed by a large over a small republic—is enjoyed by the Union over the States composing it. Does this advantage consist in the substitution of representatives whose enlightened views and virtuous sentiments render them superior to local prejudices and to schemes of injustice? It will not be denied that the representation of the Union will be most likely to possess these requisite endowments. Does it consist in the greater security afforded by a greater variety of parties, against the events of any one party being able to outnumber and oppress the rest? In an equal degree does the increased variety of parties comprised within the Union increase this security? Does it, in fine, consist in the greater obstacles opposed to the concert and accomplishment of the secret wishes of an unjust and interested majority? Here again the extent of the Union gives it the most palpable advantage.

The influence of factious leaders may kindle a flame within their particular States but will be unable to spread a general conflagration through the other States. A religious sect may degenerate into a political faction in a part of the Confederacy; but the variety of sects dispersed over the entire face of it must secure the national councils against any danger from that source. A rage for paper money, for an abolition of debts, for an equal division of property, or for any other improper or wicked project, will be less apt to pervade the whole body of the Union than a particular member of it, in the same proportion as such a malady is more likely to taint a particular county or district than an entire State.

In the extent and proper structure of the Union, therefore, we behold a republican remedy for the diseases most incident to republican government. And according to the degree of pleasure and pride we feel in being republicans ought to be our zeal in cherishing the spirit and supporting the character of Federalists.

PUBLIUS

NO. 51: MADISON

To what expedient, then, shall we finally resort, for maintaining in practice the necessary partition of power among the several departments as laid down in the Constitution? The only answer that can be given is that as all these exterior provisions are found to be inadequate the defect must be supplied, by so contriving the interior structure of the government as that its several constituent parts may, by their mutual relations, be the means of keeping each other in their proper places. Without presuming to undertake a full development of this important idea I will hazard a few general observations which may perhaps place it in a clearer light, and enable us to form a more correct judgment of the principles and structure of the government planned by the convention.

In order to lay a due foundation for that separate and distinct exercise of the different powers of government, which to a certain extent is admitted on all hands to be essential to the preservation of liberty, it is evident that each department should have a will of its own; and consequently should be so constituted that the members of each should have as little agency as possible in the appointment of the members of the others. Were this principle rigorously adhered to, it would require that all the appointments for the supreme executive, legislative, and judiciary magistracies should be drawn from the same fountain of authority, the people, through channels having no communication whatever with one another. Perhaps such a plan of constructing the several departments would be less difficult in practice than it may in contemplation appear. Some difficulties, however, and some additional expense would attend the execution of it. Some deviations, therefore, from the principle must be admitted. In the constitution of the judiciary department in particular, it might be inexpedient to insist rigorously on the principle: first, because peculiar qualifications being essential in the members, the primary consideration ought to be to select that mode of choice which best secures these qualifications; second, because the permanent tenure by which the appointments are held in that department must soon destroy all sense of dependence on the authority conferring them.

It is equally evident that the members of each department should be as little dependent as possible on those of the others for the emoluments annexed to their offices. Were the executive magistrate, or the judges, not independent of the legislature in this particular, their independence in every other would be merely nominal.

But the great security against a gradual concentration of the several powers in the same department consists in giving to those who administer each department the necessary constitutional means and personal motives to resist encroachments of the others. The provision for defense must in this, as in all other cases, be made commensurate to the danger of attack. Ambition must be made to counteract ambition. The interest of the man must be connected with the constitutional rights of the place. It may be a reflection on human nature that such devices should be necessary to control the abuses of government. But what is government itself but the greatest of all reflections on human nature? If men were angels, no government would be necessary. If angels were to govern men, neither external nor internal controls on government would be necessary. In framing a government which is to be administered by men over men, the great difficulty lies in this: you must first enable the government to control the governed; and in the next place oblige it to control itself. A dependence on the people is, no doubt, the primary control on the government; but experience has taught mankind the necessity of auxiliary precautions.

This policy of supplying, by opposite and rival interests, the defect of better motives, might be traced through the whole system of human affairs, private as well as public. We see it particularly displayed in all the subordinate distributions of power, where the constant aim is to divide and arrange the several offices in such a manner as that each may be a check on the other—that the private interest of every individual may be a sentinel over the public rights. These inventions of prudence cannot be less requisite in the distribution of the supreme powers of the State.

But it is not possible to give to each department an equal power of self-defense. In republican government, the legislative authority necessarily predominates. The remedy for this inconveniency is to divide the legislature into different branches; and to render them, by different modes of election and different principles of action, as little connected with each other as the nature of their common functions and their common dependence on the society will admit. It may even be necessary to guard against dangerous encroachments by still further precautions. As the weight of the legislative authority requires that it should be thus divided, the weakness of the executive may require,

on the other hand, that it should be fortified. An absolute negative on the legislature appears, at first view, to be the natural defense with which the executive magistrate should be armed. But perhaps it would be neither altogether safe nor alone sufficient. On ordinary occasions it might not be exerted with the requisite firmness, and on extraordinary occasions it might be perfidiously abused. May not this defect of an absolute negative be supplied by some qualified connection between this weaker branch of the stronger department, by which the latter may be led to support the constitutional rights of the former, without being too much detached from the rights of its own department?

If the principles on which these observations are founded be just, as I persuade myself they are, and they be applied as a criterion to the several State constitutions, and to the federal Constitution, it will be found that if the latter does not perfectly correspond with them, the former are infinitely less able to bear such a test.

There are, moreover, two considerations particularly applicable to the federal system of America, which place that system in a very interesting point of view.

First. In a single republic, all the power surrendered by the people is submitted to the administration of a single government; and the usurpations are guarded against by a division of the government into distinct and separate departments. In the compound republic of America, the power surrendered by the people is first divided between two distinct governments, and then the portion allotted to each subdivided among distinct and separate departments. Hence a double security arises to the rights of the people. The different governments will control each other, at the same time that each will be controlled by itself.

Second. It is of great importance in a republic not only to guard the society against the oppression of its rulers, but to guard one part of the society against the injustice of the other part. Different interests necessarily exist in different classes of citizens. If a majority be united by a common interest, the rights of the minority will be insecure. There are but two methods of providing against this evil: the one by creating a will in the community independent of the majority—that is, of the society itself; the other, by comprehending in the society so many separate descriptions of citizens as will render an unjust combination of a majority of the whole very improbable, if not impracticable. The first method prevails in all governments possessing an hereditary or self-appointed authority. This, at best, is but a precarious security; because a power independent of the society may as well espouse the unjust views of the major as the rightful interests of the minor party, and may possibly be turned against both parties. The second method will be exemplified in the federal republic of the United States. Whilst all authority in it will be derived from and dependent on the society, the society itself will be broken into so many parts, interests and classes of citizens, that the rights of individuals, or of the minority, will be in little danger from interested combinations of the majority. In a free government the security for civil rights must be the same as that for religious rights. It consists in the one case in the multiplicity of interests, and in the other in the multiplicity of sects. The degree of security in both cases will depend on the number of interests and sects; and this may be presumed to depend on the extent of country and number of people comprehended under the same government. This view of the subject must particularly recommend a proper federal system to all the sincere and considerate friends of republican government, since it shows that in exact proportion as the territory of the Union may be formed into more circumscribed Confederacies, or States, oppressive combinations of a majority will be facilitated; the best security, under the republican forms, for the rights of every class of citizens, will be diminished; and consequently the stability and independence of some member of the government, the only other security, must be proportionally increased. Justice is the end of government. It is the end of civil society. It ever has been and ever will be pursued until it be obtained, or until liberty be lost in the pursuit. In a society under the forms of which the stronger faction can readily unite and oppress the weaker, anarchy may be truly be said to reign as in a state of nature, where the weaker individual is not secured against the violence of the stronger; and as, in the latter state, even the stronger individuals are prompted, by the uncertainty of their condition, to submit to a government which may protect the weak as well as themselves; so, in the former state, will the more powerful factions or parties be gradually induced, by a like motive, to wish for a government which will protect all parties, the weaker as well as the more powerful. It can be little doubted that if the State of Rhode Island was separated from the Confederacy and left to itself, the insecurity of rights under the popular form of government within such narrow limits would be displayed by such reiterated oppressions of factious majorities that some power altogether independent of the people would soon be called for by the voice of the very factions whose misrule had proved the necessity of it. In the extended republic of the United States, and among the great variety of interests, parties, and sects which it embraces, a coalition of a majority of the whole society could seldom take place on any other principles than those of justice and the general good; whilst there being thus less danger to a minor from the will of a major party, there must be less pretext, also, to provide for the security of the former, by introducing into the government a will not dependent on the latter, or, in other words, a will independent of the society itself. It is no less certain than it is important, notwithstanding the contrary opinions which have been entertained, that the larger the society, provided it lie within a practicable sphere, the more duly capable it will be of self-government. And happily for the *republican cause*, the practicable sphere may be carried to a very great extent by a judicious modification and mixture of the *federal principle*.

PUBLIUS

GLOSSARY OF TERMS

access The actual involvement of interest groups in the decision-making process.

accountability The obligation to justify the discharge of duties in the fulfillment of responsibilities to a person or persons in higher authority; to be answerable to that authority for failing to fulfill the assigned duties and responsibilities.

administrative regulation Rules made by *regulatory agencies* and commissions.

affirmative action A policy or program designed to redress historic injustices committed against specified groups by actively promoting equal access to educational and employment opportunities.

agenda setting The power of the media to bring public attention to particular issues and problems.

Aid to Families with Dependent Children (AFDC) Federal funds, administered by the states, for children living with parents or relatives who fall below state standards of need. Abolished in 1996 and replaced with *TANF*.

amicus curiae Literally, "friend of the court"; individuals or groups who are not parties to a lawsuit but who seek to assist the court in reaching a decision by presenting additional briefs.

Antifederalists Those who favored strong state governments and a weak national government and who were opponents of the constitution proposed at the American Constitutional Convention of 1787.

appellate court A court that hears the appeals of trial court decisions.

appropriations The amounts approved by Congress in statutes (bills) that each unit or agency of government can spend.

area sampling A polling technique used for large cities, states, or the whole nation when a high level of accuracy is desired. The population is broken down into small, homogeneous units, such as counties; then several units are randomly selected to serve as the sample.

Articles of Confederation America's first written constitution. Adopted by the Continental Congress in 1777, the Articles of Confederation and Perpetual Union was the formal basis for America's national government until 1789, when it was supplanted by the Constitution.

Astroturf lobbying A negative term used to describe group-directed and exaggerated grass-roots lobbying.

attitude (or opinion) A specific preference on a particular issue.

Australian ballot An electoral format that presents the names of all the candidates for any given office on the same ballot. Introduced at the turn of the nineteenth century, the Australian ballot replaced the partisan ballot and facilitated *split-ticket voting*.

authoritarian government A system of rule in which the government recognizes no formal limits but may, nevertheless, be restrained by the power of other social institutions.

authorization The process by which Congress enacts or rejects proposed statutes (bills) embodying the positive laws of government.

autocracy A form of government in which a single individual—a monarch or dictator—rules.

balance of power A system of political alignments by which stability can be achieved.

balance-of-power role The strategy whereby many countries form alliances with one or more other countries in order to counterbalance the behavior of other, usually more powerful, *nation-states*.

bandwagon effect A situation wherein reports of voter or delegate opinion can influence the actual outcome of an election or a nominating convention.

bellwether district A town or district that is a microcosm of the whole population or that has been found to be a good predictor of electoral outcomes.

benign gerrymandering Attempts to draw election districts so as to create districts made up primarily of disadvantaged or underrepresented minorities.

bicameralism Division of a legislative body into two chambers, houses, or branches.

bilateral treaty Treaty made between two nations; contrast with *multilateral treaty*.

bill of attainder A legislative act that inflicts guilt and punishment without a judicial hearing or trial; it is proscribed by Article I, Section 10, of the Constitution.

Bill of Rights The first ten amendments to the U.S. Constitution, ratified in 1791. They ensure certain rights and liberties to the people.

bipartisanship Close cooperation between two parties; usually an effort by the two major parties in Congress to cooperate with the president in making foreign policy.

block grants Federal *grants-in-aid* that allow states considerable discretion in how the funds should be spent.

bureaucracy The complex structure of offices, tasks, rules, and principles of organization that are employed by all large-scale institutions to coordinate the work of their personnel.

cabinet The secretaries, or chief administrators, of the major departments of the federal government. Cabinet secretaries are appointed by the president with the consent of the State.

capitalism An economic state in which most of the means of production and distribution are privately owned and operated for profit.

capture An interest's acquisitions of substantial influence over the government agency charged with regulating its activities.

categorical grants-in-aid Grants by Congress to states and localities, given with the condition that expenditures be limited to a problem or group specified by the national government.

caucus (congressional) An association of members of Congress based on party, interest, or social group such as gender or race.

caucus (political) A normally closed meeting of a political or legislative group to select candidates, plan strategy, or make decisions regarding legislative matters.

checks and balances Mechanisms through which each branch of government is able to participate in and influence the activities of the other branches. Major examples include the presidential veto power over congressional legislation, the power of the Senate to approve presidential appointments, and judicial review of congressional enactments.

chief justice Justice on the Supreme Court who presides over the Court's public sessions.

citizenship The duties, rights, and privileges of being a citizen of a political unit.

civil law A system of jurisprudence, including private law and governmental actions, to settle disputes that do not involve criminal penalties.

civil liberties Areas of personal freedom with which governments are constrained from interfering.

civil penalties Regulatory techniques in which fines or another form of material restitution is imposed for violating civil laws or common law principles, such as negligence.

civil rights Legal or moral claims that citizens are entitled to make upon the government to protect them from the illegal actions of other citizens and government agencies.

class action suit A lawsuit in which large numbers of persons with common interests join together under a representative party to bring or defend a lawsuit, such as hundreds of workers together suing a company.

client state A *nation-state* dependent upon a more powerful nation-state but still with enough power and resources to be able to conduct its own foreign policy up to a point.

closed primary A primary election in which voters can participate in the nomination of candidates, but only of the party in which they are enrolled for a period of time prior to primary day. Contrast with *open primary*.

closed rule   Provision by the House Rules Committee limiting or prohibiting the introduction of amendments during debate.

cloture   Rule allowing a majority of two-thirds or three-fifths of the members in a legislative body to set a time limit on debate over a given bill.

coattail effect   Result of voters casting their ballot for president or governor and "automatically" voting for the remainder of the party's ticket.

coercion   Forcing a person to do something by threats or pressure.

cold war   The period of struggle between the United States and the former Soviet Union between the late 1940s and 1990.

commander in chief   The position of the president as commander of the national military and the state National Guard units (when they are called into service).

commerce power   Power of Congress to regulate trade among the states and with foreign countries.

common law   Law common to the realm in Anglo-Saxon history; judge-made law based on the precedents of previous lower-court decisions.

concurrent power   Authority possessed by both state and national governments, such as the power to levy taxes.

confederation   A system of government in which states retain sovereign authority except for the powers expressly delegated to the national government.

conference committee   A joint committee created to work out a compromise on House and Senate versions of a piece of legislation.

conscription   An aspect of *coercion* whereby the government requires certain involuntary services of citizens, such as compulsory military service, known as "the draft."

conservative   Today this term refers to those who generally support the social and economic status quo and are suspicious of efforts to introduce new political formulae and economic arrangements. Many conservatives also believe that a large and powerful government poses a threat to citizens' freedoms.

constituents   Members of the district from which an official is elected.

constitutional government   A system of rule in which formal and effective limits are placed on the powers of the government.

constitutionalism   An approach to legitimacy in which the rulers give up a certain amount of power in return for their right to utilize the remaining powers.

containment   The policy used by the United States during the cold war to restrict the spread of communism and limit the influence of the Soviet Union.

contract model   A theory asserting that governments originate from general agreements among members of the public about the necessity of dealing with common problems.

contracting power   The power of government to set conditions on companies seeking to sell goods or services to government agencies.

contributory programs   Social programs financed in whole or in part by taxation or other mandatory contributions by their present or future recipients. The most important example if *Social Security*, which is financed by a payroll tax.

cooperative federalism   A type of federalism existing since the New Deal era in which *grants-in-aid* have been used strategically to encourage states and localities (without commanding them) to pursue nationally defined goals. Also known as intergovernmental cooperation.

corridoring   Working to gain influence in an executive agency.

cost of living adjustments (COLAs)   See *indexing*.

criminal law   The branch of law that deals with disputes or actions involving criminal penalties (as opposed to civil law). It regulates the conduct of individuals, defines crimes, and provides punishment for criminal acts.

criminal penalties   Regulatory techniques in which imprisonment or heavy fines and the loss of certain civil rights and liberties are imposed.

debt   The cumulative total amount of money owed due to yearly operating *deficits*.

de facto segregation   Racial segregation that is not a direct result of law or government policy but is, instead, a reflection of residential patterns, income distributions, or other social factors.

defendant   The individual or organization against whom a complaint is brought in criminal or civil cases.

deficit   An annual debt incurred when the government spends more than it collects. Each yearly deficit adds to the nation's total *debt*.

de jure segregation   Racial segregation that is a direct result of law or official policy.

delegated powers   Constitutional powers that are assigned to one governmental agency but that are exercised by another agency with the express permission of the first.

democracy   A system of rule that permits citizens to play a significant part in the governmental process, usually through the election of key public officials.

deregulation   A policy of reducing or eliminating regulatory restraints on the conduct of individuals or private institutions.

deterrence   The development and maintenance of military strength as a means of discouraging attack.

devolution   A strategy in which the national government would grant the states more authority over a range of policies currently under national government authority.

diplomacy   The representation of a government to other foreign governments.

discount rate   The interest rate charged by the *Federal Reserve Board* when commercial banks borrow in order to expand their lending operations. An effective tool of monetary policy.

dissenting opinion   Decision written by a justice in the minority in a particular case in which the justice wishes to express his or her reasoning in the case.

divided government   The condition in American government wherein the presidency is controlled by one party while the opposing party controls one or both houses of Congress.

double jeopardy   Trial more than once for the same crime. The Constitution guarantees that no one shall be subjected to double jeopardy.

dual federalism   The system of government that prevailed in the United States from 1789 to 1937 in which most fundamental governmental powers were shared between the federal and state governments. Compare with *cooperative federalism*.

due process   To proceed according to law and with adequate protection for individual rights.

economic expansionist role   The strategy often pursued by capitalist countries to adopt foreign policies that will maximize the success of domestic corporations in their dealings with other countries.

elastic clause   See *necessary and proper clause*.

electoral college   The presidential electors from each state who meet in their respective state capitals after the popular election to cost ballots for president and vice president.

electoral realignment   The point in history when a new party supplants the ruling party, becoming in turn the dominant political force. In the United States, this has tended to occur roughly every thirty years.

electorate   All of the eligible voters in a legally designated area.

eminent domain   The right of government to take private property for public use, with reasonable compensation awarded for the property.

en banc   When a larger number of judges than the required minimum of three on a circuit court of appeals hear a case.

entitlement   Eligibility for benefits by virtue of a category of benefits defined by legislation.

equal protection clause   A clause in the Fourteenth Amendment that requires that states provide citizens "equal protection of the laws."

equal time rule   A Federal Communications Commission requirement that broadcasters provide candidates for the same political office an equal opportunity to communicate their messages to the public.

equality of opportunity   A universally shared American ideal that all people should have the freedom to use whatever talents and wealth they have to reach their fullest potential.

equity   Judicial process providing a remedy to a dispute where common law does not apply.

exclusionary rule   The ability of the court to exclude evidence obtained in violation of the Fourth Amendment.

exclusive powers   All the powers that the states are in effect forbidden to exercise by the Constitution rest exclusively with the national government.

executive agreement   An agreement between the president and another country, which has the force of a treaty but does not require the Senate's "advice and consent."

executive privilege   The claim that confidential communications between a president and close advisers should not be revealed without the consent of the president.

ex post facto law   "After the fact" law; law that is retroactive and that has an adverse effect on someone accused of a crime. Under Article I, Sections 9 and 10, of the Constitution, neither the state nor the national government can enact such laws; this provision does not apply, however, to civil laws.

expressed power The notion that the Constitution grants to the federal government only those powers specifically named in its text.

expressed powers (Congress) Specific powers granted to Congress under Article I, Section 8, of the Constitution.

expressed powers (president) Specific powers granted to the president under Article II, Sections 2 and 3, of the Constitution.

expropriation Confiscation of property with or without compensation.

faction Group of people with common interests, usually in opposition to the aims or principles of a larger group or the public.

fairness doctrine A Federal Communications Commission requirement for broadcasters who air programs on controversial issues to provide time for opposing views.

Federal Reserve Board The governing board of the *Federal Reserve System* is comprised of a chair and six other members, appointed by the president with the consent of the Senate.

Federal Reserve System (Fed) Consisting of twelve Federal Reserve Banks, the Fed facilitates exchanges of cash, checks, and credit; it regulates member banks; and it uses monetary policies to fight inflation and deflation.

federalism System of government in which power is divided by a constitution between a central government and regional governments.

Federalists Those who favored a strong national government and supported the constitution proposed at the American Constitutional Convention of 1787.

filibuster A tactic used by members of the Senate to prevent action on legislation they oppose by continuously holding the floor and speaking until the majority backs down. Once given the floor, senators have unlimited time to speak, and it requires a *cloture* vote of three-fifths of the Senate to end the filibuster.

fiscal policies (techniques) The government's use of taxing, monetary, and spending powers to manipulate the economy.

fiscal year The yearly accounting period, which for the national government is October 1–September 30. The actual fiscal year is designated by the year in which it ends.

food stamps The largest *in-kind benefits* program, administered by the Department of Agriculture, providing coupons to individuals and families who satisfy a "needs test"; the food stamps can be exchanged for food at most grocery stores.

formula grants Grants-in-aid in which a formula is used to determine the amount of federal funds a state or local government will receive.

framing The power of the media to influence how events and issues are interpreted.

franchise The right to vote; see *license, suffrage*.

full faith and credit clause Article IV, Section 1, of the Constitution provides that each state must accord the same respect to the laws and judicial decisions of other states that it accords to its own.

gender gap A distinctive pattern of voting behavior reflecting the differences in views between women and men.

gerrymandering Apportionment of voters in districts in such a way as to give unfair advantage to one political party.

going public A strategy that attempts to mobilize the widest and most favorable climate of opinion.

government Institutions and procedures through which a territory and its people are ruled.

grants-in-aid A general term for funds given by Congress to state and local governments.

grassroots lobbying A lobbying campaign in which a group mobilizes its membership to contact government officials in support of the group's position.

Great Compromise Agreement reached at the Constitutional Convention of 1787 that gave each state an equal number of senators regardless of its population, but linked representation in the House of Representatives to population.

gridlock Term used to describe the state of affairs when the executive and legislative branches cannot agree on major legislation and neither side will compromise.

Gross Domestic Product (GDP) An index of the total output of goods and services. A very imperfect measure of prosperity, productivity, inflation, or deflation, but its regular publication both reflects and influences business conditions.

habeas corpus A court order demanding that an individual in custody be brought into court and shown the cause for detention. *Habeas corpus* is guaranteed by the Constitution and can be suspended only in cases of rebellion or invasion.

haphazard sampling A type of sampling of public opinion that is an unsystematic choice of respondents.

Holy Alliance role A strategy pursued by a superpower to prevent any change in the existing distribution of power among *nation-states*, even if this requires intervention into the internal affairs of another country in order to keep a ruler from being overthrown.

home rule Power delegated by the state to a local unit of government to manage its own affairs.

homesteading A national policy that permits people to gain ownership of property by occupying public or unclaimed lands, living on the land for a specified period of time, and making certain minimal improvements on that land. Also known as squatting.

ideology The combined doctrines, assertions, and intentions of a social or political group that justify its behavior.

illusion of central tendency The assumption that opinions are "normally distributed"—that responses to opinion questions are heavily distributed toward the center, as in a bell-shaped curve.

illusion of saliency Impression conveyed by polls that something is important to the public when actually it is not.

impeachment To charge a government official (president or otherwise) with "Treason, Bribery, or other high Crimes and Misdemeanors" and bring him or her before Congress to determine guilt.

implementation The efforts of departments and agencies to translate laws into specific bureaucratic routines.

impoundment Efforts by presidents to thwart congressional programs that they cannot otherwise defeat by refusing to spend the funds that Congress has appropriated for them. Congress placed limits on impoundment in the Budget and Impoundment Control Act of 1974.

independent agencies Agencies set up by Congress to be independent of direct presidential authority. Congress usually accomplishes this by providing the head or heads of the agency with a set term of office rather than allowing their removal at the pleasure of the president.

independent counsel A prosecutor appointed under the terms of the Ethics in Government Act to investigate criminal misconduct by members of the executive branch.

indexing Periodic adjustments of welfare payments, wages, or taxes, tied to the cost of living.

indirect election Provision for election of an official where the voters first select the delegates or "electors," who are in turn charged with making the final choice. The presidential election is an indirect election.

inflation A consistent increase in the general level of prices.

inherent powers Powers claimed by a president that are not expressed in the Constitution, but are inferred from it.

initiative The process that allows citizens to propose new laws and submit them for approval by the state's voters.

in-kind benefits Goods and services provided to needy individuals and families by the federal government, as contrasted with cash benefits. The largest in-kind federal welfare program is *food stamps.*

interest group A group of people organized around a shared belief or mutual concern who try to influence the government to make policies promoting their belief or concerns.

interest-group liberalism The theory of governance that, in principle, all claims on government resources and actions are equally valid, and that all interests are equally entitled to participation in and benefits from the government.

International Monetary Fund (IMF) An institution established in 1944 at Bretton Woods, New Hampshire, to provide loans to needy member countries and to facilitate international monetary exchange.

interpretation Process wherein bureaucrats implement ambiguous statutes, requiring agencies to make educated guesses as to what Congress or higher administrative authorities intended.

iron triangle The stable and cooperative relationships that often develop between a congressional committee or subcommittee, an administrative agency, and one or more supportive interest groups. Not all of these relationships are triangular, but the iron triangle formulation is perhaps the most typical.

issue network A loose network of elected leaders, public officials, activists, and interest groups drawn together by a specific policy issue.

issues advocacy Independent spending by individuals or interest groups on a campaign issue but not directly tied to a particular candidate.

judicial review Power of the courts to declare actions of the legislative and executive branches invalid or unconstitutional. The Supreme Court asserted this power in *Marbury v. Madison*.

jurisdiction The authority of a court to initially consider a case. Distinguished from appellate jurisdiction, which is the authority to hear appeals from a lower court's decision.

laissez-faire An economic theory first advanced by Adam Smith, it calls for a "hands off" policy by government toward the economy, in an effort to leave business enterprises free to act in their own self-interest.

legislative clearance A process that enables the president to require all agencies of the executive branch to submit through the budget director all requests for new legislation along with estimates of their budgetary needs.

legislative supremacy The preeminence of Congress among the three branches of government, as established by the Constitution.

legislative veto A provision in a statute permitting Congress (or a congressional committee) to review and approve actions undertaken by the executive under authority of the statute. Although the U.S. Supreme Court held the legislative veto unconstitutional in the 1983 case of *Immigration and Naturalization Service v. Chadha*, Congress continues to enact legislation incorporating such a veto.

legitimacy Popular acceptance of a government and its decisions.

liberal A liberal today generally supports political and social reform; extensive governmental intervention in the economy; the expansion of federal social services; more vigorous efforts on behalf of the poor, minorities, and women; and greater concern for consumers and the environment.

license Permission to engage in some activity that is otherwise illegal, such as hunting or practicing medicine. Synonymous with *franchise*, permit, certificate of convenience and necessity.

line-item veto Power that allows a governor (or the president) to strike out specific provisions (lines) of bills that the legislature passes. Without a line-item veto, a governor (or the president) must accept or reject an entire bill.

lobbying Strategy by which organized interests seek to influence the passage of legislation by exerting direct pressure on members of the legislature.

logrolling A legislative practice wherein reciprocal agreements are made between legislators, usually in voting for or against a bill. In contrast to bargaining, logrolling unites parties that have nothing in common but their desire to exchange support.

majority leader The elected leader of the party holding a majority of the seats in the House of Representatives or in the Senate. In the House, the majority leader is subordinate in the party hierarchy to the *Speaker of the House*.

majority party The party that holds the majority of legislative seats in either the House or the Senate.

majority rule Rule by at least one vote more than half of those voting.

majority system A type of electoral system in which, to win a seat in the parliament or other representative body, a candidate must receive a majority of all the votes cast in the relevant district.

mandate (electoral) A claim made by a victorious candidate that the electorate has given him or her special authority to carry out campaign promises.

marketplace of ideas The public forum in which beliefs and ideas are exchanged and compete.

Marshall Plan The U.S. European Recovery Plan, in which over $34 billion was spent for relief, reconstruction, and economic recovery of Western Europe after World War II.

means testing Procedure by which potential beneficiaries of a public assistance program establish their eligibility by demonstrating a genuine need for the assistance.

Medicaid A federally financed, state-operated program for medical services to low-income people.

Medicare National health insurance for the elderly and for the disabled.

military-industrial complex A concept coined by President Eisenhower in his farewell address, in which he referred to the threats to American democracy that may arise from too close a friendship between major corporations in the defense industry and the Pentagon. This is one example of the larger political phenomenon of the *iron triangle*.

minority leader The elected leader of the party holding less than a majority of the seats in the House or Senate.

Miranda rule Principles developed by the Supreme Court in the 1966 case of *Miranda v. Arizona* requiring that persons under arrest be informed of their legal rights, including their right to counsel, prior to police interrogation.

momentum A media prediction that a particular candidate will do even better in the future than in the past.

monetary policies (techniques) Efforts to regulate the economy through manipulation of the supply of money and credit. America's most powerful institution in the area of monetary policy is the *Federal Reserve Board*.

monopoly The existence of a single firm in a market that divides all the goods and services of that market. Absence of competition.

mootness A criterion used by courts to screen cases that no longer require resolution.

Motor Voter bill A legislative act passed in 1993 that requires all states to allow voters to register by mail when they renew their drivers' licenses and provides for the placement of voter registration forms in motor vehicle, public assistance, and military recruitment offices.

multilateral treaty A treaty among more than two nations.

multilateralism A foreign policy that seeks to encourage the involvement of several nation-states in coordinated action, usually in relation to a common adversary, with terms and conditions usually specified in a multicountry treaty, such as NATO.

multiple-member constituency Electorate that selects all candidates at large from the whole district; each voter is given the number of votes equivalent to the number of seats to be filled.

multiple-member district See *multiple-member constituency*.

Napoleonic role Strategy pursued by a powerful nation to prevent aggressive actions against itself by improving the internal state of affairs of a particular country, even if this means encouraging revolution in that country. Based on the assumption that countries with comparable political systems will never go to war against each other.

nation-state A political entity consisting of a people with some common cultural experience (nation), who also share a common political authority (state), recognized by other sovereignties (nation-states).

National Security Council (NSC) A presidential foreign policy advisory council composed of the president, the vice president, the secretaries of state, defense, and the treasury, the attorney general, and other officials invited by the president. The NSC has a staff of foreign-policy specialists.

national supremacy A principle that asserts that national law is superior to all other law.

nationalism The widely held belief that the people who occupy the same territory have something in common, that the nation is a single community.

necessary and proper clause Article I, Section 8, of the Constitution, which enumerates the powers of Congress and provides Congress with the authority to make all laws "necessary and proper" to carry them out; also referred to as the "elastic clause."

new federalism Attempts by Presidents Nixon and Reagan to return power to the states through block grants.

New Jersey Plan A framework for the Constitution, introduced by William Paterson, which called for equal representation in the national legislature regardless of a state's population.

New Politics movement Political movement that began in the 1960s and 1970s, made up of professionals and intellectuals for whom the Civil Rights and antiwar movements were formative experiences. The New Politics movement strengthened public-interest groups.

nomination The process through which political parties select their candidates for election to public office.

noncontributory programs Social programs that provide assistance to people based on demonstrated need rather than any contribution they have made.

North American Free Trade Agreement (NAFTA) An agreement among Canada, the United States, and Mexico that promotes economic cooperation and abolishes many trade restrictions between the three countries.

North Atlantic Treaty Organization (NATO) A treaty organization, comprising the United States, Canada, and most of Western Europe, formed in 1948 to counter the perceived threat from the Soviet Union.

oligarchy A form of government in which a small group—landowners, military officers, or wealthy merchants—controls most of the governing decisions.

oligopoly The existence of two or more competing firms in a given market, where price competition is usually avoided because they know all would lose from such competition. Rather, competition is usually through other forms, such as advertising, innovation, and obsolescence.

open market operations The buying and selling of government securities, etc., to help finance government operations and to loosen or tighten the total amount of credit circulating in the economy.

open primary A primary election in which the voter can wait until the day of the primary to choose which party to enroll in to select candidates for the general election. Contrast with *closed primary*.

opinion The written explanation of the Supreme Court's decision in a particular case.

oversight The effort by Congress, through hearings, investigations, and other techniques, to exercise control over the activities of executive agencies.

paper trail Written accounts by which the process of decision making and the participants in a decision can, if desired, be later reconstructed. Often called "red tape."

partisanship Loyalty to a particular political party.

party identity An individual voter's psychological ties to one party or another.

party machines Local party organizations that control urban politics by mobilizing voters to elect the machines' candidates.

party vote A *roll-call vote* in the House or Senate in which at least 50 percent of the members of one party take a particular position and are opposed by at least 50 percent of the members of the other party. Party votes are rare today, although they were fairly common in the nineteenth century.

patronage The resources available to higher officials, usually opportunities to make partisan appointments to offices and to confer grants, licenses, or special favors to supporters.

per curiam Decision by an appellate court, without a written opinion, that refuses to review the decision of a lower court; amounts to a reaffirmation of the lower court's opinion.

petition Right granted by the First Amendment to citizens to inform representatives of their opinions and to make pleas before government agencies.

plaintiff The individual or organization who brings a complaint in court.

plea bargains Negotiated agreements in criminal cases in which a defendant pleads guilty in return for the state's agreement to reduce the severity of the criminal charge the defendant is facing.

pluralism The theory that all interests are and should be free to compete for influence in the government. The outcome of this competition is balance and compromise.

plurality system Type of electoral system in which, to win a seat in the parliament or other representative body, a candidate need only receive the most votes in the election, not necessarily a majority of votes cast.

pocket veto A presidential veto of legislation wherein the president takes no formal action on a bill. If Congress adjourns within ten days of passing a bill, and the president does not sign it, the bill is considered to be vetoed.

police power Power reserved to the state to regulate the health, safety, and morals of its citizens.

policy entrepreneur An individual who identifies a problem as a political issue and brings a policy proposal into the political agenda.

policy of redistribution An objective of the graduated income tax—to raise revenue in such a way as to reduce the disparities of wealth between the lowest and the highest income brackets.

political action committee (PAC) A private group that raises and distributes funds for use in election campaigns.

political ideology A cohesive set of beliefs that form a general philosophy about the role of government.

political parties Organized groups that attempt to influence the government by electing their members to important government offices.

political socialization Induction of individuals into the political culture; learning how to accept authority; learning what is legitimate and what is not.

politics Conflicts over the character, membership, and policies of any organization to which people belong.

polity A society with an organized government; the "political system."

poll tax A state-imposed tax upon the voters as a prerequisite to registration. It was rendered unconstitutional in national elections by the Twenty-fourth Amendment and in state elections by the Supreme Court in 1966.

populism A late 1870s political and social movement of Western and Southern farmers that protested Eastern business interests.

pork barrel legislation Appropriations made by legislative bodies for local projects that are often not needed but that are created so that local representatives can win reelection in their home district.

power Influence over a government's leadership, organization, or policies.

power elite The group that is said to make the most important decisions in a particular community.

power without diplomacy Post–World War II foreign policy in which the goal was to use American power to create an international structure that could be run with a minimum of regular diplomatic involvement.

precedents Prior cases whose principles are used by judges as the bases for their decisions in present cases.

prior restraint An effort by a governmental agency to block the publication of material it deems libelous or harmful in some other way; cen-

sorship. In the United States, the courts forbid prior restraint except under the most extraordinary circumstances.

private bill A proposal in Congress to provide a specific person with some kind of relief, such as a special exemption from immigration quotas.

privileges and immunities clause Article IV of the Constitution, which provides that the citizens of any one state are guaranteed the "privileges and immunities" of every other state, as though they were citizens of that state.

probability sampling A method used by pollsters to select a sample in which every individual in the population has a known (usually equal) probability of being selected as a respondent so that the correct weight can be given to all segments of the population.

procedural due process The Supreme Court's efforts to forbid any procedure that shocks the conscience or that makes impossible a fair judicial system. See also *due process*.

progressive/regressive taxes Taxation that hits the upper brackets more heavily (progressive) or the lower brackets more heavily (regressive).

project grants Grant proposals in which state and local governments submit proposals to federal agencies and for which funding is provided on a competitive basis.

promotional technique A technique of control that encourages people to do something they might not otherwise do, or continue an action or behavior. There are three types; *subsidies*, contracts, and *licenses*.

proportional representation A multiple-member district system that allows each political party representation in proportion to its percentage of the vote.

prospective voting Voting based on the imagined future performance of a candidate.

protective tariff A tariff intended to give an advantage to a domestic manufacturer's product by increasing the cost of a competing imported product.

public assistance program A noncontributory social program providing assistance for the aged, poor, or disabled. Major examples include *Aid to Families with Dependent Children* (AFDC) and *Supplemental Security Income* (SSI).

public corporation An agency set up by a government but permitted to finance its own operations by charging for its services or by selling bonds.

public interest groups Lobbies that claim they serve the general good rather than their own particular interest, such as consumer protection or environmental lobbies.

public law Cases in private law, civil law, or criminal law in which one party to the dispute argues that a license is unfair, a law is inequitable or unconstitutional, or an agency has acted unfairly, violated a procedure, or gone beyond its jurisdiction.

public opinion Citizens' attitudes about political issues, personalities, institutions, and events.

public opinion polls Scientific instruments for measuring public opinion.

public policy A law, rule, statute, or edict that expresses the government's goals and provides for rewards and punishments to promote their attainment.

push polling A polling technique in which the questions are designed to shape the respondent's opinion.

quota sampling A type of sampling of public opinion that is used by most commercial polls. Respondents are selected whose characteristics closely match those of the general population along several significant dimensions, such as geographic region, sex, age, and race.

racial gerrymandering Redrawing congressional boundary lines in such a way as to divide and disperse a minority population that otherwise would constitute a majority within the original district.

rallying effect The generally favorable reaction of the public to presidential actions taken in foreign policy or, more precisely, decisions made during international crises.

random sampling Polls in which respondents are chosen mathematically, at random, with every effort made to avoid bias in the construction of the sample.

realigning eras Periods during which major groups in the electorate shift their political party affiliations. Realigning eras have often been associated with long-term shifts in partisan control of the government and with major changes in public policy. One of the most important realigning eras was the period of the New Deal in the 1930s when President Franklin Roosevelt led the Democrats to a position of power that they held for more than thirty years.

reapportionment The redrawing of election districts and the redistribution of legislative representatives due to shifts in population.

redistributive techniques Techniques—fiscal or monetary—designed to control people by manipulating the entire economy rather than by regulating people directly.

referendum The practice of referring a measure proposed or passed by a legislature to the vote of the electorate for approval or rejection.

regulated federalism A form of federalism in which Congress imposes legislation on the states and localities requiring them to meet national standards.

regulation A particular use of government power, a "technique of control" in which the government adopts rules imposing restrictions on the conduct of private citizens.

regulatory agencies Departments, bureaus, or independent agencies whose primary mission is to eliminate or restrict certain behaviors defined as being evil in themselves or evil in their consequences.

regulatory tax A tax whose primary purpose is not to raise revenue but to influence conduct—e.g., a heavy tax on gasoline to discourage recreational driving.

regulatory techniques Techniques that government uses to control the conduct of the people.

representative democracy A system of government that provides the populace with the opportunity to make the government responsive to its views through the selection of representatives, who, in turn, play a significant role in governmental decision making.

reserve requirement The amount of liquid assets and ready cash that the *Federal Reserve Board* requires banks to hold to meet depositors' demands for their money.

responsible party government A set of principles that idealizes a strong role for parties in defining their stance on issues, mobilizing voters, and fulfilling their campaign promises once in office.

retrospective voting Voting based on the past performance of a candidate.

revenue sharing A scheme to allocate national

resources to the states according to a population and income formula.

right of rebuttal A Federal Communications Commission regulation giving individuals the right to have the opportunity to respond to personal attacks made on a radio or TV broadcast.

roll-call vote Vote in which each legislator's yes or no vote is recorded as the clerk calls the names of the members alphabetically.

salient interests Attitudes and views that are especially important to the individual holding them.

sample A small group selected by researchers to represent the most important characteristics of an entire population.

satellites *Nation-states* that are militarily, economically, and politically subordinate to other nations.

select committee A legislative committee established for a limited period of time and for a special purpose; not a standing committee.

selective polling A sample drawn deliberately to reconstruct meaningful distributions of an entire constituency; not a random sample.

seniority Priority or status ranking given to an individual on the basis of length of continuous service in a committee in Congress.

separate but equal rule Doctrine that public accommodations could be segregated by race but still be equal.

separation of powers The division of governmental power among several institutions that must cooperate in decision making.

single-member constituency An electorate that is allowed to elect only one representative from each district; the normal method of representation in the United States.

single-member district See *single-member constituency*.

Social Security A contributory welfare program into which working Americans contribute a percentage of their wages, and from which they receive cash benefits after retirement.

soft money Money contributed directly to political parties for voter registration and organization.

solicitor general The top government lawyer in all cases before the appellate courts where the government is a party.

sovereignty Supreme and independent political authority.

Speaker of the House The chief presiding officer of the House of Representatives. The Speaker is elected at the beginning of every Congress on a straight *party vote*. The Speaker is the most important party and House leader, and can influence the legislative agenda, the fate of individual pieces of legislation, and members' positions within the House.

spending power A combination of *subsidies* and *contracts* that the government can use to redistribute income.

split-ticket voting The practice of casting ballots for the candidates of at least two different political parties in the same election. Voters who support only one party's candidates are said to vote a straight party ticket.

standing The right of an individual or organization to initiate a court case.

standing committee A permanent committee with the power to propose and write legislation that covers a particular subject such as finance or appropriations.

stare decisis Literally "let the decision stand." A previous decision by a court applies as a precedent in similar cases until that decision is overruled.

state A community that claims the monopoly of legitimate use of physical force within a given territory; the ultimate political authority; sovereign.

statute A law enacted by a state legislature or by Congress.

straight party vote The practice of casting ballots for candidates of only one party.

strict scrutiny Higher standard of judicial protection for speech cases and other civil liberties and civil rights cases, in which the burden of proof shifts from the complainant to the government.

subsidies Governmental grants of cash or other valuable commodities, such as land, to individuals or organizations. Subsidies can be used to promote activities desired by the government, to reward political support, or to buy off political opposition.

substantive due process A judicial doctrine used by the appellate courts, primarily before 1937, to strike down economic legislation the courts felt was arbitrary or unreasonable.

suffrage The right to vote; see also *franchise*.

Supplemental Security Income (SSI) A program providing a minimum monthly income to people who pass a "needs test" and who are sixty-five years or older, blind, or disabled. Financed from general revenues rather than from Social Security contributions.

supremacy clause   Article VI of the Constitution, which states that all laws passed by the national government and all treaties are the supreme laws of the land and superior to all laws adopted by any state or any subdivision.

Supreme Court   The highest court in a particular state or in the United States. This court primarily serves an appellate function.

systematic sampling   A method used in probability sampling to ensure that every individual in the population has a known probability of being chosen as a respondent—by choosing every ninth name from a list, for example.

tariff   A tax placed on imported goods.

Temporary Assistance to Needy Families (TANF)   A policy by which states are given *block grants* by the federal government in order to create their own programs for public assistance.

third parties   Parties that organize to compete against the two major American political parties.

Three-fifths Compromise   Agreement reached at the Constitutional Convention of 1787 that stipulated that for purposes of the apportionment of congressional seats, every slave would be counted as three-fifths of a person.

totalitarian government   A system of rule in which the government recognizes no formal limits on its power and seeks to absorb or eliminate other social institutions that might challenge it.

treaty   A formal agreement between sovereign nations to create or restrict rights and responsibilities. In the United States, all treaties must be approved by a two-thirds vote in the Senate. See also *executive agreement*.

trial court   The first court to hear a criminal or civil case.

turnout   The percentage of eligible individuals who actually vote.

tyranny   Oppressive and unjust government that employs cruel and unjust use of power and authority.

uncontrollables   A term applied to budgetary items that are beyond the control of budgetary committees and can only be controlled by substantive legislative action by Congress itself. Some uncontrollables are actually beyond the power of Congress, because the terms of payment are set in contracts, such as interest on the public *debt*.

unfunded mandates   Regulations or conditions for receiving grants that impose costs on state and local governments for which they are not reimbursed by the federal government.

unilateralism   A foreign policy that seeks to avoid international alliances, entanglements, and permanent commitments in favor of independence, neutrality, and freedom of action.

United Nations   The organization of nations founded in 1945, mainly to serve as a channel for negotiation and a means of settling international disputes peaceably. It has had frequent successes in providing a forum for negotiation and on some occasions a means of preventing international conflicts from spreading. On a number of occasions, the U.N. has been a convenient cover for U.S. foreign policy goals.

Universal Commercial Code   A set of standards for contract law recognized by all states that greatly reduces interstate differences in the practice of contract law.

universalization of rights   The recognition that any group—whether defined by sex, religion, race, ethnicity, or gender—has the right not to be discriminated against.

values (or beliefs)   Basic principles that shape a person's opinions about political issues and events.

veto   The president's constitutional power to turn down acts of Congress. A presidential veto may be overridden by a two-thirds vote of each house of Congress.

Virginia Plan   A framework for the Constitution, introduced by Edmund Randolph, which called for representation in the national legislature based upon the population of each state.

whip system   Primarily a communications network in each house of Congress, whips take polls of the membership in order to learn their intentions on specific legislative issues and to assist the majority and minority leaders in various tasks.

writ of *certiorari*   A decision of at least four of the nine Supreme Court justices to review a decision of a lower court; from the Latin "to make more certain."

INDEX

Page numbers in *italics* refer to illustrations.

AARP (American Association of Retired Persons), 300–301, 305
Abernathy, David, 103
abortion, 67, 68, 76–77, 185, 198, 201, 202, 220, 222, 279, 284, 316, 321
Abu Ghraib prison, 115
ACLU (American Civil Liberties Union), 195
ACT (America Coming Together), 295
action-forcing, 255
Acton, Lord, 394
Adams, John, 17, 19, 187, 268
Adams, John Quincy, 252
Adams, Samuel, 17
Adarand Constructors v. Peña, 87, 89, 193
ADC (Aid to Dependent Children), 336
administrative adjudication, 157
administrative law, 180
administrative legislation, 162
Administrative Procedure Act (1946), 189, 313
administrative regulation, 342, 344
Advanced Research Projects Agency, 152
Advisory Council on Intergovernmental Relations, 168
AFDC (Aid to Families with Dependent Children), 56, 336, 337–38, 390

affirmative action, 85–90, 193, 198, 202, 213, 217, 238, 279
Afghanistan, 128, 147, 190, 363, 366, 375
AFL-CIO, 304
Africa, 363
African Americans, 112, 215, *216,* 217, 261
 Civil Rights Act (1964) and, 385
 civil rights groups for, 321
 election registration and, 247
 gerrymandering in Mississippi of, 249
 interest groups of, 305
 Iraq war and, 209, 215
 as judicial nominees, 184
 move to Democrat camp by, 283
 as Republicans, 218
 Voting Rights Act and, 242
 whites' agreement with, 223–24
Agency for International Development (AID), 364
agency representations, 118
Agostini v. Felton, 76
agriculture:
 federal subsidies to, 327
 national regulation of, 328
 tariffs on, 391
Agriculture Department, U.S., 129, 158, *159,* 160, 162
 Extension Service of, 160
AID (Agency for International Development), 364
AIDS, 382
Aid to Dependent Children (ADC),

336
Aid to Families with Dependent Children (AFDC), 56, 336, 337–38, 390
Air Force Department, U.S., 161
Alabama, 47
 privacy rights in, 75
 same-sex marriage and, 47
Alaska, 47
 bridge project in, 117
 same-sex marriage banned in, 85
Aldrich, John, 270
Alexander, Lamar, 234
Alien and Sedition Acts (1798), 10
Alito, Samuel, 186, 316
allocation, 155
Al Qaeda, 210, 260, 367, 375
America Coming Together (ACT), 291, 295
American Association of Retired Persons (AARP), 300–301, 305
American Bankers Association, 304
American Bar Association, 304
American Civil Liberties Union (ACLU), 195
American Enterprise Institute, 227, 305
American Farm Bureau Federation, 304
American Federation of State, County, and Municipal Employees, 304
American Independent Party, 288

American Medical Association, 304
American Political Science Association (APSA), 297
American Revolution, 9, 17, 19
Americans for a Better Country, 264
Americans with Disabilities Act (1990), 84
amicus curiae, 195
Amnesty International, 354
Amtrak, 158
Anderson, John, 264
Animal and Plant Health and Inspection Service (APHIS), 162
Annapolis Convention, 44
Anti-Federalists, 32, 33, 39, 45
antistatism, 356, 357, 376
ANZUS Treaty, 364
APHIS (Animal and Plant Health and Inspection Service), 162
appropriations, 114
APSA (American Political Science Association), 297
Armey, Dick, 100
Army Corps of Engineers, 129
Articles of Confederation, 16, 18–19, 27, 29, 32, 38, 44
    adoption of, 41
    flaws of, 19, 21
    versus Constitution, 22, 28
Astroturf lobbying, 317
attitudes, 211
Australian ballot, 253
authoritarian government, 7
autocracy, 7
Ayres, Richard, 267

Baker, James, 141
Bakke, Allan, 85
Bakke case, 85–86, 88
"balance of power" system, 357, 370, 377
Balkanization, 371–72
bandwagon effect, 236–37
Bank of the United States, 24
banks, 328, 329–30
    Federal Reserve, 163
    see also World Bank
Barnet, Richard, 371
Barron v. Baltimore, 70, 71–73, 77, 90

Barton, Joe, 234
Base Closing Commission, 162
Bass Enterprises, 311
Bay of Pigs invasion, 360
BCRA (Bipartisan Campaign Reform Act) (2002), 198, 263, 264, 294, 298, 319
Belgium, elections in, 244
beliefs, 211
"benign" gerrymandering, 250
Benton v. Maryland, 74
Bible, 175
bicameralism, 21, 96–98
Bill of Rights, 21, 24, 29, 32, 34, 36, *36*, 40, 45, 67–68, 70, 76, 90
    denationalization of, 76–77, *77*
    nationalization of, 90
    state v. national, 69–73
    see also specific amendments
bills, 104–5, *106,* 107
    see also specific bills
Bipartisan Campaign Reform Act (BCRA) (2002), 198, 263, 264, 294, 298, 319
Bismark, Otto von, 392
Blackmun, Harry, 198–99
blacks, *see* African Americans
Blair, Tony, 209
    "third way" of, 391
block grants, 56
BoB (Bureau of the Budget), 142, 149, 165
Bonner and Associates, 317
Border and Transportation Security, 351
Bosnia, 128, 360, 373–74
Boston Tea Party, 16, 17
bourgeoisie, 9, 10
Bowen, William, 267
Bowers v. Hardwick, 84
Bradley, Bill, 283
Brady Handgun Violence Prevention Act (1993), 58, 237, 389–90
Bretton Woods, N.H., 362
Breyer, Stephen, 77, 185, 198
Brookings Institution, 63, 305
Brown, Linda, 79
Brown, Oliver, 79
Brown v. Board of Education, 68, 74, 79–80, 90, 315
Bryan, William Jennings, 287

Buchanan, James, 148
Buchanan, Pat, 220–21, 372
Buckley v. Valeo, 263
Budget and Impoundment Control Act (1974), 131*n,* 140, 149
Bud Shuster Byway, 116
bureaucracy, 152–56
    Congress and, 156–57, 165–67
    control of, 163–67
    credibility of, 156
    efficiency of, 156, 171–73
    of executive branch, 158, 160–63
    possible reduction of, 167–71
Bureau of Labor Statistics, 332
Bureau of the Budget (BoB), 142, 149, 165
Burger, Warren, 76, 83
Burr, Aaron, 252
Bush, George H. W., 35, 56, 88
    Cheney as secretary of defense for, 141
    China's relations with, 373
    civil service reform by, 387
    Desert Storm ordered by, 373, 376
    as G. W. Bush's father, 379, 392
    Joint Chiefs of Staff and, 140
    judicial appointees of, 184, 185–86, 187, 198, 202
    NSC staff of, 139
    OMB under, 140
    overview of, 387–89
    Panama invasion ordered by, 128
    public appearances of, 146
    on "supply-side" economics, 388
    as vice president, 141
    Weinberger pardoned by, 129
Bush, George W., 284
    ads for, 263
    appeals court appointments of, 120
    appointments by, 137
    approval ratings, 147
    bipartisanship requested by, 281
    cabinet of, 139
    central management control by, 142
    Cheney as vice president of, 141
    as "compassionate conservative", 220, 380, 392
    Congress and, 121

congressional party squabbling and, 109–10
Democratic oversight of, 115
deregulation supported by, 329
drug company funding of, 300
election of, 142, 253
executive privilege claimed by, 189
federalism of, 57
government power used by, 379
hurricanes and, 129
Internet as campaign tool of, 291
Iraq war and, 128, 148–49, 209–11, 362
judicial appointees of, 184
Kerry's debates with, 260–61
Kuhn as friend of, 312
McCain's challenge to, 230
media portrayal of, 229, 230, 232
Miers nomination and, 185, 316
national protection and, 127
overview of, 392–94
partisan loyalty and, 255
policies of, 279
public appearances of, 146
public opinion and, 225–26
reelection of, 211, 258–60
regulatory review and, 4
Republican leaders' meeting with, 275–76
same-sex marriage and, 47
Social Security reforms supported by, 334
Soros's donations against, 264
tax cuts of, 110
town meetings of, 230
2000 campaign funds of, 265
2000 election and, 202–3
2004 campaign of, 256–57, 266
2004 nomination speech, 213, 258–60
War on Terror of, 190, 220
White House staff of, 139
Bush, Jeb, 291
Bush, Prescott, 379
Bush (G.H.W.) administration, contracting and, 341
Bush doctrine, 367, 375
business, 4

cabinet, 3, 4, 137, 158, 164–65
California:
    illegal alien referendum in, 254
    Proposition 209 in, 238
    recall election in, 255
    same-sex marriage and, 47
California Civil Rights Initiative, 89
Cambodia, 375
Cameron, Charles M., 132
campaign finance, 261–66
canals, 327
Cannon, "Uncle" Joe, 149
Carmines, Edward G., 224
Carter, Jimmy:
    civil service reform of, 387, 388
    draft evaders pardoned by, 129
    election of, 142
    overview of, 386–87
    presidential batting average of, 144
    Social Security tax and, 346
    television addresses of, 144
Case Act (1972), 115
categorical grants-in-aid, 52
caucuses, 103–4, 120, 293
CBO (Congressional Budget Office), 55, 103
CBS News, 225
Center for Disease Control (CDC), 153
Central Intelligence Agency (CIA), 127, 158, 165, 351
Chamber of Commerce, 227
checks and balances, 13, 21, 30, 31, 38, 39, 43, 60, 61, 116, 130
Chemical, Biological, Radiological, and Nuclear Countermeasures, 351
Cheney, Dick, 139, 141, 189
Cherokees, 200
China, 353, 354, 367, 371, 373
Christian Coalition, 146, 320, 354
Christian Right, 305, 320, 354, 380
    see also religious Right
CIA (Central Intelligence Agency), 127, 158, 165, 351
Citizens for the American Way, 195
City of Boerne v. Flores, 58
Civil Aeronautics Board, 388
civil law, 176, 177, 179–80
civil liberties, 39, 76
    Brown v. Board of Education, 74
    definition of, 67, 90
    nationalization of, 71
    right to privacy as, 74–75
civil penalties, 342
civil rights, 53, 78–91, 82, 198, 218
    Brown v. Board of Education, 74
    controversies regarding, 69
    definition of, 68, 90
    Fourteenth Amendment and, 77–78
    media and, 227
Civil Rights Act (1875), 78
Civil Rights Act (1964), 63, 81, 385
    Title VII, 81, 83–84
Civil Rights Act (1965), 385
Civil Rights Act (1991), 87
Civil Rights Commission, 81
Civil Service Commission, 387
Civil Service Reform Act (1978), 387
Civil War, 7, 43, 68, 71, 127, 218
Clark, Dick, 311
Clark, Russel G., 202
class action suit, 201–2
Clay, Henry, 252
Clayton Act (1914), 328
Cleveland, Grover, 253
clientele agency, 160
client state, U.S. as, 356
Clinton, Bill, 288
    affirmative action and, 87, 88
    approval ratings of, 125, 146
    bipartisan strategy of, 144–45
    Bosnia and, 361, 374
    budget negotiations of, 109, 228–29
    campaigns of, 256
    central management control by, 142
    China's relations with, 373
    civil service reform by, 387
    Congress and, 121
    crime bill of, 112–13
    deficit reduction plan of, 389
    in Democratic political ads, 264
    on Democratic Leadership Council, 388, 389
    "Don't ask, don't tell" policy of, 84, 132, 316–17
    elections of, 142
    executive privilege claimed by, 189

Clinton, Bill (*continued*)
  Gore as vice president of, 141
  health care plan of, 108, 280, 320
  impeachment of, 60, 98, 116, 124–25, 374
  increased defense spending and, 162
  judicial nominees of, 184, 187
  line-item veto used by, 131
  military base closings proposed by, 161
  as moderate Democrat, 221
  "momentum" of, 230
  Motor Voter bill signed by, 247
  as "new Democrat," 279, 391
  new federalism and, 56
  1992 polls on, 237
  Northern Ireland and, 359
  NPR and, 165, 173
  OMB under, 140
  overview of, 389–92
  partial-birth abortion and, 107
  as party leader, 280
  polls taken by, 290
  popularity loss of, 283
  radio addresses of, 144
  regulatory review and, 4
  scandals of, 62, 131, 228, 232
  Supreme Court appointments of, 77
  talk-show appearances of, 230, 258
  tax cut promise of, 346
  town meetings of, 230
  welfare reform of, 338–39, 391
Clinton, George, 32
Clinton, Hillary, 57
Clinton administration, public relations efforts of, 225
closed primary, 277
closed rule, 105
cloture, 105, 121
Coast Guard, 4, 129
Cochran, Thad, 108
coercion, 5, 6, 46
  liberty and, 12–13
coinage, 44, 45
COLAs (cost of living adjustments), 332, 337
Cold War, 358, 367
collective goods, 306
Colorado, attempted redistricting in, 251

commander in chief, 127–28
commerce, 51
  in Constitution, 45
  state power and, 25, 41
Commerce and Labor Department, U.S., 160
Commerce Department, U.S., 129
committee assignments, 111
committee system, 101–3, 104–5
Common Cause, 227, 302, 305, 309
common law, 190
Communist Party, 241
Compromise of 1850, 283
Concerned Senators for the Arts, 104
Concord, battle of, 16
concurrent powers, 46
conference committee, 105, 107
Congress, U.S., 45, 126, *164*, 168
  affirmative action strengthened by, 87
  under Articles of Confederation, 18
  budget and, 140
  bureaucracy and, 156–57, 165–67, 172–73
  caucus system in, 103–4
  Cheney in, 141
  civil rights movement and, 227
  Clinton's proposed military base closings and, 161
  Committee on Committees in, 99, 102, 280
  committee system in, 101–3, 104–5, 120
  in Connecticut Plan, 20
  Constitutional amendments and, 35
  Contract with America and, 55–56
  delegated powers and, 126–27
  economic policy and, 136
  effectiveness of, 117–20
  electoral votes and, 252
  Fed created by, 163
  First Amendment and, 36
  foreign policy and, 95, 350–51, 352–53
  government complexity and, 3–4
  grassroots campaigns and, 316–17
  Great Depression and, 326

  impeachment and, 116
  influences on, 107–14
  initiative in, 142
  interest groups and, 302, *310*, 313–15
  Iraq war and, 148–49
  judicial review and, 179, 188
  lobbying of, 311–12
  loss of power by, 137
  mutual defense alliances financed by, 364
  Nixon, Richard and, 130–31
  organization of, 96–104, 117–20
  oversight and, 114–15
  partisan division in, 267
  party organization in, 274
  party system and, 120, 280
  political struggles in, 4
  presidency and, 125
  presidential batting average and, 144
  presidential nomination by, 135
  railroads and, 327
  as representative organization, 148
  Social Security and, 334, 335
  staff system in, 103, 120
  Steering and Policy Committee of, 99
  Supreme Court size decided by, 183–84
  Supreme Court's relationship with, 199–200, 201
  Supreme Court's review of, 198
  treaties and, 115
  2004 election and, 258
  U.N. and, 360
  veto points of, 120
  war powers of, 128
Congressional Black Caucus, 104, 112–13
Congressional Budget Office (CBO), 55, 103
Congressional Caucus for Women's Issues, 104
Congressional Government (Wilson), 134
Congressional Research Service, 103
Connecticut:
  Constitution ratified by, 32
  privacy rights in, 75
  Virginia Plan opposition of, 20

Connecticut Compromise, 20
conscription, 7
Conservative Party, 287
Conservative Party, British, 392
conservatives, conservatism, 211,
    220–21, 238
  on college professors, 218
  "Contract with America" and, 39
  as Democratic base, 279
  Tenth Amendment and, 57
  voter registration and, 247
constituency, 107, 108
Constitution, U.S., 15, 25, 29, 41,
    175, 237–38, 301
  amendments to, 29, 33–38, *34,
    37,* 38, 47, 199
  Article I, 23, 24–25, 29, 36, 41,
    48, 50, 51, 74, 95, 98, 131,
    134, 329
  Article II, 26, 29, 41, 115, 126,
    127, 130, 131
  Article III, 26–27, 29, 36, 41,
    191
  Article IV, 27, 41, 46, 47, 48,
    128
  Article V, 29, 33, 34–35, 41
  Article VI, 27, 41, 45, 187
  Article VII, 29, 41
  Articles of Confederation versus,
    20, 28
  congressional term lengths in,
    97
  constitutional review by, 180
  contradictions in, 12
  courts' interpretation of,
    178–79, 182
  debts and, 27, 29
  Democratic Party and, 281
  direct elections in, 251
  economic and political forces
    and, 17
  electoral college in, 269
  enduring strength of, 15
  equality and, 218
  executive branch in, 26, 126–28,
    132, 148, 375
  federalism in, 45–48
  foreign policy in, 375
  House of Representatives in, 98
  judicial branch in, 26–27,
    183–84, 188, 191
  jurisdictional arrangement, 44
  legislative branch in, 23–24, 95,

    125, 128, 329, 375
  legislative supremacy in, 64
  national government restrained
    by, 62
  new states and, 27
  power in, 16
  ratification of, 32–33
  Section 9, 24
  Senate in, 114
  slavery in, 20–21, 27
  state powers in, 3, 24–26
  supremacy clause, 27, 188
  treaties in, 114
  viability of, 38–40
  vice presidency in, 141
  war powers in, 128, 149
  see also Bill of Rights
constitutional amendments:
  First, 35, 69, 73, 74, 76, 90,
    193, 310, 319
  Second, 36, 69
  Third, 36, 75
  Fourth, 36, 74, 75
  Fifth, 36, 67–68, 69, 70, 72, 74,
    75, 180, 345
  Sixth, 36
  Seventh, 36
  Eighth, 36
  Ninth, 75
  Tenth, 45–46, 57, 58
  Eleventh, 37, 58
  Twelfth, 252
  Thirteenth, 27, 34, 37, 38, 68
  Fourteenth, 34, 37, 68, 71–73,
    74, 75, 77–78, 79, 90, 338
  Fifteenth, 34, 68
  Sixteenth, 37, 38
  Seventeenth, 23, 60
  Eighteenth, 34, 35, 38
  Twenty-first, 34, 35
  Twenty-seventh, 37
Constitutional Convention, 15, 24,
    32, 38
constitutional government, 7, 9
constitutional interpretation, 178
Consumer Price Index (CPI), 332
Consumer Product Safety
    Commission (CPSC), 157,
    328
containment, 358
Continental Congress, First, 17
Continental Congress, Second,
    17–18

contract cases, 179–80
Contract with America, 39, 55–56,
    99, 390
conventions, national, 293–94
  see also Democratic National
    Conventions; Republican
    National Conventions
Coolidge, Calvin, 148
cooperative federalism, 51–54
"Cooper/Church" debate, 375
Copperheads, 281
"corrupt bargain," 252
Corzine, Jon, 263
cost of living adjustments
    (COLAs), 332, 337
Council of Economic advisors,
    386
court appeals, 180
Court of Appeals, U.S., 183, 194,
    203
Court of Appeals for the Fifth
    Circuit, U.S., 87
courts, 4
  interest groups and, 315–16
  political struggles in, 4
  see also judicial branch
court system, 180–82, *181*
CPI (Consumer Price Index), 332
CPSC (Consumer Product Safety
    Commission), 157, 328
Crawford, William H., 252
"Crime Bill of 1994," 389, 391
Crime Control Act (1994), 237
criminal law, *177,* 179, 198
criminal penalties, 342
Croatia, 374
Cuban Missile Crisis, 360
Customs Service, 4
Czech Republic, 366

Daschle, Tom, 109, 258
Davis, Gray, 255
Dayton, Ohio, Bosnia peace
    agreement signed in, 361
Dean, Howard, 283, 291
Debs, Eugene, 225
debts, Constitution and, 27, 29
Declaration of Independence,
    17–18, 40
defendants, 179
Defense Base Closure and
    Realignment Commission,
    169

Defense Department, U.S., 160, 161
    creation of, 4
Defense of Marriage Act (1996), 46–47, 392
De Figueiredo, John M., 321
Delaware:
    Constitution ratified by, 32
    school segregation in, 79
    Virginia Plan opposition of, 20
DeLay, Tom, 154, 251, 311
delegated powers, 126–27
delegates, 118
Dell, Inc., 311
democracy, 7, 9
    expansion of, 10–12
    representative, 12
Democracy in America (Tocqueville), 322
Democratic Forum, 104
Democratic Leadership Council, 388
Democratic National Committee (DNC), 293, 294, 318
Democratic National Conventions:
    of 1972, 294
    of 1992, 230, 236
    of 1996, 236
Democratic Party:
    ads for, 264
    advocacy groups for, 321
    airport security and, 110
    "benign" gerrymandering and, 250
    as caucus chair, 99
    Clinton as moderate in, 221
    Clinton's crime bill and, 112
    Clinton's impeachment and, 116
    coalitions of, 145–46
    "Demzilla" of, 278
    divisions within, 285
    as dominant political force, 281
    1864 peace platform of, 294
    in electoral realignments, 284–87, 285, 286
    foreign policy and, 376–77
    funding of, 261
    Great Depression and, 326
    GWB's court appointees and, 120, 184, 186
    history of, 281, 283
    Iraq war and, 110, 115, 210

Jackson's founding of, 134, 281
    liberalization of, 287
    loyalty to, 218
    New Deal and, 384
    "new Democrats" in, 279
    1998 election and, 281
    registration efforts of, 260
    Republicans' differences with, 241–42, 279
    Southern redistricting and, 215
    2004 election and, 258–60
    white southerners in, 219
Democratic Study Group, 104
democratization, 373
"Demzilla," 278
Depression, Great, 218, 233, 281, 309, 326, 332, 376
deregulation, 169–70, 328–29
deterrence, 358
devolution, 56–57, 63, 170–71
DHS, *see* Homeland Security Department, U.S.
Dingell, John, 311
diplomacy, 358, 359–60
Direct Impact, 317
direct mail, 290–91
discrimination, 78
Disney, 304
Disraeli, Benjamin, 392
distributive tendency, 118–19
District Court, U.S., 203, 204
divided government, 64, 284
division of labor, 155
DNC (Democratic National Committee), 293, 294, 318
DOE, *see* Energy Department, U.S.
Dole, Bob, 58, 283, 288
DOT, *see* Transportation Department, U.S.
double jeopardy, 74
Douglas, Stephen, 232
Douglas, William O., 75
drafts, 7
Dred Scott case, 61
dual federalism, 48
due process of law, 67, 72, 182
duties, 95
Duverger, Maurice, 275

earmarks, 117, 321
East Europe, 11
East India Company, 17
economic aid, 363–64

economic expansionist role, 370, 377
economics, economy, 326–27, 343
    Congress and, 136
    Constitution and, 17
    executive branch and, 136
    supply side, 380, 388
    see also taxes
Economic Stabilization Act (1970), 386
Economic Stabilization Act (1971), 386
Economist, 374, 380, 392, 393
Edison Electric Institute, 312
education, 7, 218, *219,* 308
Education Department, U.S., 152, 160, 388
Edwards, John, 141, 210, 261
Eighteenth Amendment, 34, 35, 38
Eighth Amendment, 36
Eisenhower, Dwight D., 80, 129, 284
    presidential batting average of, 144
    press conferences of, 144
Eisenhower Administration, overview of, 382–84
Eisenstadt v. Baird, 315
elastic clause, 23
election, campaign finance in, 261–66
Election Day, 268, 270, 278
elections, 13, 141–42, 241–71, 277
    of 1800, 252
    of 1824, 252–53
    of 1828, 281, 284
    of 1858, 283
    of 1860, 283
    of 1864, 294
    of 1876, 253
    of 1888, 253
    of 1896, 284, 287
    of 1936, 233, 283
    of 1948, 287–88
    of 1968, 288
    of 1992, 283
    of 1994, 114, 283, 528
    of 1996, 283, 284
    of 1998, 100, 281, 291
    of 2000, 202–3, 253, 258–61, 283, 291, 380

of 2004, 283, 291
complexity of, 4
criteria for victory in, 248–49
electoral composition and, 244–45, 247–48
frequency of, 253
funding for, 261–66
issues, 256
midterm, 269
nominations for, 277–78
partisan loyalty in, 255–56
primary, 277–78
registration for, 245, 247
turnout of, 242–45, *245*, 247–48
voters' decisions in, 255–58
see also voting rights
electoral college, 126, 251–52, 258, 269
electoral influence, 254
electoral realignment, 284–87, *285, 286*
Eleventh Amendment, 37, 58
Emergency Preparedness and Response, 351
Emergency Price Control Act (1942), 189
EMILY's List, 266
eminent domain, 345
employment, discrimination in, 81
Encyclopedia of U.S. Government Benefits, 341
Endangered Species Act, 309
Energy Department, U.S., 129, 160, 388
England, 29, 137
Enron, 166
entitlement, 338
Environmental Defense Fund, 309
Environmental Impact Statement, 132
environmental protection, 53, 263
Environmental Protection Agency (EPA), 132, 152, 312, 328
EOP (Executive Office of the President), 139, 140, 142, 149
EPA (Environmental Protection Agency), 132, 152, 312, 328
equality, in Constitution, 40
equality of opportunity, 212
equal protection clause, 68
Equal Rights Amendment (ERA), 35

ERP (European Recovery Plan), 363, 364
Ervin committee, 318
Espionage Law, 225
Espy, Mike, 249
Establishment Clause, 197
European Economic Community, 37
European Recovery Plan (ERP), 363, 364
European Union, 371
exclusionary rule, 74
exclusive powers, 26
executive agreements, 115, 130, 353
executive branch, 152–73, *164*
in Constitution, 26, 126–28, 132, 148
economy and, 136
lobbying of, 313
organization of, 158, 160–63
political struggles in, 4
see also presidency
Executive Office of the President (EOP), 139, 140, 142, 149
Executive Order No. 8248, 132
Executive Order No. 12291, 132
executive orders, 132
executive privilege, 62
expressed powers, 24, 45, 126
expropriation, 345

F-16 fighter airplanes, 367, 368
Falwell, Jerry, 317
farmers, 4, 17, 328
Faubus, Orval, 80, 129
FBI (Federal Bureau of Investigation), 127, 158, 161, 165
September 11 and, 152–53
FDA (Food and Drug Administration), 63, 152, 162
FDIC (Federal Deposit Insurance Corporation), 329
FEC (Federal Election Commission), 158, 262, 263, 264, 295, 319
federal appellate courts, 183
Federal Aviation Administration, 152
Federal Bureau of Investigation (FBI), 127, 158, 161, 165
September 11 and, 152–53

Federal Communication Commission, 156
Federal Deposit Insurance Corporation (FDIC), 329
Federal Election Campaign Act (1971), 262, 318
Federal Election Commission (FEC), 158, 262, 263, 264, 295, 319
Federal Elections Campaign Act (1972), 264, 292
Federal Emergency Management Agency (FEMA), 4, 129
federalism, 29, 32, 39, 43, 44, 45, 48–51, *49, 54,* 62–64, 134
in Constitution, 45–48
cooperative, 51–54
dual, 48
foreign policy and, 356
grants-in-aid, 51–54
layer cake v. marble cake, 52–53
legacies of, 357
new, 56–57
regulated, 53–56
Supreme Court and, 57–59, 74
Federalist Papers, 32, 33, 242, 251
No. 3, 16
No. 51, 134, 346–47
Federalist Party, 10–11, 24, 252, 268, 281, 284
Federalists, 32, *33,* 45–46
federal jurisdiction, 182–87
Federal Labor Relations Board, 387
Federal Occupation Safety and Health, 56
Federal Register, 157
Federal Regulation of Lobbying Act, 310–11
Federal Reserve banks, 163
Federal Reserve Board, 163, 346
discount rate and, 346
open market operations of, 346
reserve requirement and, 346
Federal Reserve System, 163, 328, 329
federal service, 167
Federal Trade Act (1914), 328
Federal Trade Commission (FTC), 158, 162, 316, 328
federal trial courts, 183
FEMA (Federal Emergency Management Agency), 4, 129

Fifteenth Amendment, 34, 68
Fifth Amendment, 36, 67–68, 69, 70, 72, 74, 75, 180, 345
filibuster, 105, 121
First Amendment, 35, 69, 73, 74, 90, 193, 310, 319
    establishment clause of, 76
First Hundred Days, 135
fiscal policies, 330–31
Fischer, David, 267
Fisher, Louis, 149
527 committees, 263, 264, 295, 319
Florida, 254
    storms in, 129
    in 2004 election, 260
Florida legislature, 203
FOIA (Freedom of Information Act) (1966), 157
Food and Drug Administration (FDA), 63, 152, 162
Food for Peace, 364
Food Safety and Inspection Service, 158
food stamps, 337
Ford, Gerald, 129, 252
    overview of, 385–86
    presidential batting average of, 144
Ford, Henry Jones, 267–68
foreign aid, 363–64
foreign policy, 350–51, 375–77
    bureaucracy and, 351–52
    Congress and, 352–53
    domestic policy intermingled with, 357
    Great Leap to world power in, 357–58
    instruments of, 358–68
    interest groups and, 353–55
    media and, 355
    roles of, 368–75
    September 11 and, 350–51
    unilateralism in, 357
    values in, 356–58
Foreign Service Act (1946), 357, 359
Forest Service, 158
formula grants, 52
401(k), 166
Fourteenth Amendment, 34, 37, 68, 71–73, 74, 75, 77–78, 79, 90, 338
Fourth Amendment, 36, 74, 75

Fourth Circuit Court of Appeals, 190
France, 29, 48, 130, 362, 367, 369, 374
    elections in, 244
Frankfurter, Felix, 183, 197, 198
Franklin, Benjamin, 17
Frazier, Lynn, 255
freedom from arbitrary search and seizure, 9
freedom of assembly, 9
    Supreme Court and, 72
Freedom of Information Act (FOIA) (1966), 157
freedom of religion, 67, 69
freedom of speech, 9, 39, 67, 73
    Supreme Court and, 72
    see also First Amendment
freedom of the press, Supreme Court and, 72
free riders, 305–6
Free-Soilers, 283
Frémont, John C., 283
French Revolution, 11
Friends of the Earth, 227
FTC (Federal Trade Commission), 158, 162, 316, 328
Fulbright, J. William, 231
full faith and credit clause, 27, 46
Fulton, Robert, 50

Gallup polls, 233, 235
Garrity, W. Arthur, 202
Gates, Bill, 312
GATT (General Agreement on Tariffs and Trade), 372
gay and lesbian movement, 84, 202, 321
gender discrimination, 83
gender gap, 215
General Accounting Office, 103
General Agreement on Tariffs and Trade (GATT), 372
General Motors, 47, 304
General Services Administration, 129
Genêt, Edmond, 130
Genoa, WTO protest in, 355
Georgia:
    Constitution ratified by, 32
    same-sex marriage and, 47
    slavery in, 21
    Virginia Plan and, 20

Gephardt, Richard, 103, 114
Gephardt health care reform bill, 103
Germany, 361, 362, 366, 374
Gerry, Elbridge, 249
gerrymandering, 249
Gibbons v. Ogden, 50–51
Gideon v. Wainwright, 74
Gingrich, Newt, 100, 168, 223, 229, 390
Ginsburg, Ruth Bader, 77, 185, 198, 203
globalization, 373, 388, 391
going public strategy, 316–17
Goldberg, Arthur, 75
Goldberg v. Kelly, 338
Gore, Al, 141, 202–3, 229, 230, 253, 256, 263, 265–66, 283, 387
government:
    American skepticism about, 8
    capacity of, 381–94
    coercion by, 5, 6, 7
    complexities of, 3–4
    contradictions of, 12
    definition of, 5
    forms of, 7
    foundations of, 5, 7
    influence of politics on, 8–9
    limits of, 10
    media's disputes with, 225
    powers and, 4–5
    Reagan on, 328, 379, 392
    responsible party, 297
    as restrained by Constitution, 62
    revenue collection by, 5, 7
    spending by, 331–32
    state v. national, 44
    see also bureaucracy; federalism; specific branches
grants-in-aid, 51–54, 62, 64, 383
grassroots lobbying, 316–17
Gratz v. Bollinger, 88
Great Britain, 363, 366, 367, 374
Great Compromise, 20–21
Great Depression, 218, 233, 281, 309, 326, 332, 376
Greece, 363, 374
Greenspan, Alan, 334
gridlock, 64
Griswold, Estelle, 75
Griswold v. Connecticut, 75, 315
Grodzins, Morton, 52

Grutter v. Bollinger, 88–89
Gulf War, *see* Persian Gulf War
gun laws, 125, 226, 237, 263
   see also Second Amendment

habeas corpus, 24, 127, 190
Haiti, 369
Hamdi, Yaser Esam, 190
Hamdi v. Rumsfeld, 190
Hamilton, Alexander, 10, 26, 32,
   252, 340, 356
Harrison, Benjamin, 253
Harris polls, 235
Hart, J. Steven, 311
Harvard University, 305
Hatch, Orrin, 184
Hatfield, Mark, 116
Hawaii, same-sex marriage banned
   in, 85
Hawaii Supreme Court, 46
Hayes, Rutherford B., 253
Health and Human Services
   Department, U.S., 129, 160,
   162, 163, 392
Henry, Patrick, 32
Heritage Foundation, 227
Hersh, Seymour, 232
highway bills, 117
Hill, Anita, 187
Hispanic Caucus, 104
Holy Alliance role, 369–70,
   373–75, 377
Homeland Security Act (2002),
   392
Homeland Security Department,
   U.S., 129, 160, 222, 351, 393
   creation of, 4, 152
home rule, 48
Home School Legal Defense Fund,
   261
Hoover, Herbert, 283
Hoover, J. Edgar, 161
Hoover Institution, 227
Hopwood case, 87
House of Commons, 17
House of Representatives, U.S., 11
   Agricultural Committee of, 99
   airport security and, 110
   Appropriations Committee of,
     99, 102, 321
   Armed Services Committee of,
     353
   bicameralism and, 96–98

Budget Committee of, 99
   campaign committees of, 295
   campaign costs in, 261, 277
   checks and balances and, 60
   committees of, 102
   in Connecticut Plan, 20
   in Constitution, 23
   Constitutional amendments and,
     34, 35
   debate in, 105
   Democrat control of, 281
   elections and, 36, 251
   electoral college and, 252
   electoral districts of, 253
   ergonomics regulations and, 266
   foreign policy and, 376
   impeachment and, 116
   interest groups and, 113
   International Affairs Committee
     of, 353
   organization of, 97–98
   organized labor and, 263
   oversight and, 114, 166
   partisanship in, 98, 105
   party leadership in, 98–100,
     109, 120
   party unity in, 109
   presidential elections and, 126
   presidential veto and, 107
   Rules Committee of, 101, 102,
     104–5, 121
   salary of, 96
   September 11 and, 350–51
   Supreme Court judges and, 184
   terms of, 23
   2004 election to, 258
   veto overridden by, 131
   Washington's refusal of request
     by, 130
   Ways and Means Committee of,
     99, 103, 140, 161
   whip system in, 112
   see also speaker of the House
Housing and Urban Development
   (HUD), 160, 330
HUD (Housing and Urban
   Development), 160, 330
Hughes, Charles Evans, 44
Hughes, Karen P., 226
Human Rights Campaign Fund, 84
Hungary, 366
Hussein, Saddam, 108, 128, 209,
   259, 362, 369, 373

ICC (Interstate Commerce Commission), 158, 328
Idaho, 170
"I Have a Dream" speech (King),
   224
illusion of saliency, 236
Immigration and Naturalization
   Service, 129
*Immigration and Naturalization
   Service v. Chadha,* 201
impeachment, 116
implementation, 156
implied powers, 45
India, 371
Industrial Revolution, 11
Information Analysis and
   Infrastructure Protection,
   351
inherent powers, 127
initiative, 142–43, 254
in-kind benefits, 337–38
interest groups, 108–9, 302–23
   access cultivated by, 313–15
   of African Americans, 305
   benefits of, *306*
   Congress and, 302, *310,* 313–15
   courts and, 315–16
   foreign policy and, 353–55
   "free riders" of, 306–7
   members of, 307
   organization of, 305–6
   PACs and, 317–19
   parties v., 307
   pluralism of, *303*
   political struggles and, 4
   proliferation of, 308–9
   pros and cons of, 322–23
   of women, 305
   see also lobbies, lobbying
Interior Department, U.S., 160
internal bipolarity, 372
Internal Revenue Code, 295
Internal Revenue Service (IRS),
   160–61, 386
International Bank for
   Reconstruction and
   Development, 362
International Business Machines,
   304
International Monetary Fund,
   362–63
International Workers of the
   World (IWW), 225

Internet, 39, 291, 298, 309
Internet voting, 268
Interstate and Defense Highway
    Act (1956), 382
Interstate Commerce Act (1887),
    328
Interstate Commerce Commission
    (ICC), 158, 328
Interstate Highway Program, 345,
    382–84
interstate highways, 54
Iowa, as battle ground state, 260
Iran, 363
Iran-Contra affair, 129, 131
Iraq, 369
    Clinton's air war with, 124
    Kuwait invaded by, 360–61, 373
Iraq war, 14–19, 108, 128, 147,
    209–11, 222, 259, 261, 283,
    362, 366, 367–68
    bureaucracy and, 167
    Bush's popularity boosted by,
        147, 209
    Congressional oversight of,
        115
    Kerry on, 257
    media and, 230
    party division over, 110, 210,
        263, 283
    race and, 209, 215
    WMDs and, 210, 259, 362,
        368
Ireland, 354
iron triangle, 313, 314
IRS (Internal Revenue Service),
    160–61, 386
isolationism, 221
Israel, 354, 359, 371
Issa, Darrell, 255
issue advocacy, 263
issue networks, 313
Italy, 274
IWW (International Workers of
    the World), 225

Jackson, Andrew, 252
    Democratic Party founded by,
        134, 281
    Marshall's ruling and, 200
    as strong president, 134
Jackson, Robert, 197
Jacksonian period, 40
Jacobs, Lawrence, 225

Japan, 361, 364, 371
Jay, John, 16, 32
JCOS (Joint Chiefs of Staff), 140,
    351
Jebware, 291
Jefferson, Thomas, 10, 17–18
    electoral college and, 252
    executive branch under, 134
    francophilia of, 356
    opposition party created by, 268
Jeffersonian period, 40
Jewish Americans, 261, 354
JOBS (Job Opportunities and Basic
    Skills), 338
Johnson, Andrew:
    Confederate amnesty given by,
        129
    impeachment of, 124
Johnson, Lyndon:
    affirmative action implemented
        by, 85
    election of, 142
    integration and, 150
    polls and, 232
    presidential batting average of,
        144
    racial discrimination and, 344
    vice presidency of, 141
Johnson administration:
    overview of, 384
    Vietnam War and, 227–28
Joint Chiefs of Staff (JCOS), 140,
    351
Jones, Charles, 146
Jones & Laughlin Steel
    Corporation, 136
judges, 175
    appointment of, 184
judicial activism, 198
judicial branch, 175–205
    in Constitution, 26–27, 183–84,
        188, 191
judicial restraint, 198
judicial review, 27, 62, 178–79,
    186, 187–91
    of Congress, 188
    of federal agency action, 188–89
    lawmaking, 190–91
    presidential power and, 189–90
Judiciary Act (1789), 188, 204
juries, 7
jurisdiction, 181
jurisdictional arrangements, 44

Justice Department, U.S., 88, 129,
    158, 160, 161, 166, 184, 194,
    204–5
    creation of, 4
    Microsoft antitrust suits and,
        312
    Tax Division of, 161

Kammen, Michael, 15
Kansas, school segregation in, 79
Kansas-Nebraska Act (1854), 283
Katrina, Hurricane, 4, 129
Kefauver, Estes, 231
Kelley, Stanley, 267
Kennan, George, 366
Kennedy, Anthony, 185, 198, 200
Kennedy, Edward, 311
Kennedy, John:
    election of, 141, 142
    New York Times and, 231
    presidential batting average of,
        144
    press conferences of, 144, 231
    racial discrimination and, 344
Kennedy administration, overview
    of, 384–85
Kent State University, 244
Kentucky, same-sex marriage and,
    47
Kernell, Samuel, 134
Kerry, John, 141, 210, 213, 255,
    257, 258, 260–61, 263, 266,
    283, 291, 295
Kettl, Donald, 171
Key, V. O., 278
Keynes, John Maynard, 331
King, Martin Luther, Jr., 224
King Caucus, 135
Kissinger, Henry, 139
Kitchen Cabinet, 139
Know-Nothings, 283
Korean War, 7, 128, 358, 360
Korematsu v. United States, 89
Kosovo, 124, 220, 361, 366
Kuhn, Tom, 312
Kuwait, 360–61, 367, 373

Labor Department, U.S., 162, 344
labor unions, 4, 217, 226, 261,
    279, 283, 287, 318, 372
Lambda Legal Defense and
    Education Fund, 84
Landon, Alfred M., 233, 283

Lasswell, Harold, 8
Latin America, 363, 370
Lawrence v. Texas, 84–85
lawsuits, 176
League of Women Voters, 278
Lee, Richard Henry, 32
legislative branch, 4
  in Constitution, 23
  from 1800–1933, 134–35
legislative clearance, 142
legislative service organizations
    (LSOs), 103–4
legislative supremacy, 60, 134
Lewinsky, Monica, 116, 124
Lexington, battle of, 16
Liberal Party, 287
liberals, liberalism, 211, 220–21,
    238
  civil rights movement and, 39
  in college, 218
  as Democratic base, 279
libertarians, 220
liberty:
  coercion and, 12–13
  Constitution and, 16, 40
  limitations of, 40
  see also specific freedoms
Lieberman, Joseph, 283
Lincoln, Abraham:
  Douglas's debates with, 232
  election of, 283, 284
  executive orders of, 127
  as strong president, 134, 148
line-item veto, 131, 149
Line-Item Veto Act (1996), 62
Lippmann, Walter, 271
Literary Digest poll (1936), 233–34
Little Rock, Ark., 80, 129
Livingston, Robert, 17
Livingston, Robert (Congressmen),
    99
lobbies, lobbying, 310–13
  of Congress, 311–12
  of executive branch, 313
  going public strategy of,
    316–17
  grassroots, 316–17
  of president, 312
  see also interest groups
Lobbying Disclosure Act (1995),
    311, 314
logrolling, 112
Los Angeles, Calif., riots in, 129

Louisiana:
  affirmative action in, 87
  same-sex marriage banned in, 85
LSOs (legislative service
    organizations), 103–4

McCain, John, 230, 264, 291
McCain-Feingold Act (2002), *see*
    Bipartisan Campaign Reform
    Act (BCRA) (2002)
McCarthy, Joseph, 231
McClellan, George, 294
*McConnell v. Federal Election
    Commission,* 198
McCulloch V. Maryland, 24, 50,
    51
McKinley, William, 287
Mack v. United States, 58
MAD (Mutual Assured
    Destruction), 367
Madison, James, 20–21, 32, 134,
    163–64, 242, 253, 346–47,
    389
  on class conflict, 217
  on constitutional amendments,
    33–34
  on factions, 40, 322
  on legislative branch, 134
  on liberty, 40, 322
  on pluralism, 301–2
  on separation of powers, 59–60
  Washington's farewell address
    and, 356
  see also Marbury v. Madison
Maine, electoral college in, 252
majority leader, 98
majority party, 280
majority rule, instability of, 13
majority system, 248
mandates, 62, 142
Mapp v. Ohio, 74
Marbury, William, 187
Marbury v. Madison, 61, 187, 188,
    204
Marcos, Ferdinand, 369
marketplace of ideas, 223
markets, 327, 328
Mark Hatfield Marine Science
    Center, 116
marriage, same-sex, 46–47
Marshall, John, 24, 50, 51, 60–61,
    70, 76, 187, 200
Marshall Plan, 363–64, 371, 372

Maryland:
  Bank of U.S. and, 24
  Constitution ratified by, 32
  slavery in, 21
Massachusetts:
  Constitution ratified by, 32
  same-sex marriage in, 47, 85
  Virginia Plan and, 20
mass popularity, 146–47
Matalin, Mary, 226
MBNA America, 266
means testing, 336
media, 227–32
  adversarial journalism and,
    230–32
  agenda setting by, 228
  foreign policy and, 355
  framing, 228–29
  government's disputes with, 225
  "momentum" predictions of, 230
  political campaigns and, 290
  political struggles and, 4 4
  power of, 228–30
  and presidency, 143–44
  priming by, 228–29
Media Fund, 295
Medicaid, 336, 338, 385
Medicare, 47, 124, 125, 225, 226,
    300–301, 330, 332, 333, 334,
    335–36, 385
membership associations, 305
merchants, 17, 19, 21, 29, 39
Merit System Projection Board,
    387
Michigan, same-sex marriage and,
    47
Microsoft, 312
Middle East, 371, 372, 382
Miers, Harriet, 185, 316
Mildred and Claude Pepper
    fountain, 116
military forces, 95
Miller v. Johnson, 251
Milosevic, Slobodan, 374
minimum wage, 56
minority leader, 98
Miranda rule, 74
Mississippi:
  affirmative action in, 87
  racial gerrymandering in, 249
Missouri, 47
  same-sex marriage banned in, 85
  in 2004 election, 261

Missouri Compromise (1820), 283
Missouri v. Jenkins, 193, 202
Missouri v. Siebert, 198
Mitchell, George, 359
Mondale, Walter, 144
monetary policies, 329
Montana, same-sex marriage and, 47
Montesquieu, Baron, 29
Motor Voter bill (1993), 247, 268
MoveOn.org, 321
multilateralism, 358
multiple-member-district, 289
Mushroom Caucus, 104
Mutual Assured Destruction (MAD), 367
Mutual Security Act (1951), 363

NAACP (National Association for the Advancement of Colored People), 75, 79, 315
Nader, Ralph, 287, 309
NAFTA (North American Free Trade Agreement), 353, 372, 391
NAM (National Association of Manufactures), 308
Napoleonic role, 369, 373, 377
National Abortion and Reproductive Rights League, 263
National Aeronautics and Space Administration (NASA), 158
National Association for the Advancement of Colored People (NAACP), 75, 79, 315
National Association of Manufactures (NAM), 308
National Beer Wholesalers' Association, 262
National Commission on the Public Service, 387
National Endowment for the Arts, 113
National Federation of Independent Business (NFIB), 304, 320, 321
National Guard, Arkansas, 129
national highway system, 327
National Labor Relations Act (1935), 135
National Labor Relations Board (NLRB), 136

National Labor Relations Board v. Jones & Laughlin Steel Corporation, 135–36
National League of Cities, 305
National Organization for Women (NOW), 227, 305, 309
National Performance Review (NPR), 141, 165, 166, 173, 387
National Petroleum Refiners Association, 304
National Resources Defense Council, 305
National Review, 290
National Rifle Association (NRA), 112, 262, 263, 302, 320, 321
National Savings & Loan League, 304
National Security Council (NSC), 127, 139, 351, 352
nation-states, 11
Native Americans, 58
NATO (North Atlantic Treaty Organization), 358, 361, 364, 365–66, 372, 374
Navy Department, U.S., 161
Nebraska:
   electoral college in, 252
   same-sex marriage banned in, 85
necessary and proper clause, 23, 45
Negotiated Rulemaking Act (1990), 313
Neumann, Mark, 99
Nevada, same-sex marriage banned in, 85
New Deal, 62, 99, 135–36, 145–46, 150, 189, 200, 256, 281, 287, 297, 331, 379, 381, 384–86
new federalism, 56–57
New Hampshire, Constitution ratified by, 32
New Jersey:
   Constitution ratified by, 32
   Virginia Plan opposition of, 20
New Jersey Plan, 20
New Politics movement, 308–9, 315–16
New Republic, 291
New Senior Executive Service, 387
Newsweek, 367

New York:
   Constitution ratified by, 32
   Virginia Plan opposition, 20
New Yorker, 232
New York Review of Books, 291
New York Times, 228, 231, 232, 308, 360
NFIB (National Federation of Independent Business, 304, 320, 321
Nicaragua, 369
9/11 Commission, 260
Ninth Amendment, 75
Nixon, Richard, 58, 62, 128, 284, 371
   congress and, 130–31, 144, 149
   election of, 142
   Environmental Protection Agency created by, 132
   executive privilege claimed by, 189
   government bureaucracy and, 165
   media coverage of, 232
   NSC staff of, 139
   overview of, 385–86
   pardon of, 129
   presidential batting average of, 144
   resignation of, 148, 228
   southern strategy of, 386
   television addresses of, 144
Nixon administration, Vietnam War and, 227–28
NLRB (National Labor Relations Board), 136
No Child Left Behind Act (2003), 57, 392
Noelle-Neumann, Elisabeth, 217
Noriega, Manuel, 369
North American Free Trade Agreement (NAFTA), 353, 372, 391
North Atlantic Treaty Organization (NATO), 358, 361, 364, 365–66, 372, 374
North Carolina:
   Constitution ratified by, 32
   slavery in, 21
   Virginia Plan, 20
North Dakota, same-sex marriage and, 47
Northern Ireland, 354, 359
North Korea, 128

NOW (National Organization for Women), 227, 305, 309
NPR (National Performance Review), 141, 165, 166, 173, 387
NRA (National Rifle Association), 112, 262, 263, 302, 320, 321
NSC (National Security Council), 127, 139, 351, 352

OAS (Organization of American States), 364
O'Brien, David M., 76
Occupational Safety and Health Administration (OSHA), 157, 162, 266, 328
O'Connor, Sandra Day, 77, 185, 198, 200, 250–51, 316
Office of Federal Contract Compliance, 344
Office of Information and Regulatory Assessment (OIRA), 4–5
Office of Management and Budget (OMB), 5, 140, 142, 165, 332
Office of Personnel Management (OPM), 387
Office of Technology Assessment, 168
Ohio:
   same-sex marriage and, 47
   in 2000 election, 260, 261
Oklahoma, same-sex marriage and, 47
oligarchy, 7
Olson, Mancur, 306
Olson, Theodore, 203
OPEC (Organization of Petroleum Exporting Countries), 371
op-ed page, 271
open market operations, 346
open primary, 277–78
open rule, 105
opinion leader, 224
Oprah Winfrey Show, The, 230
Organization of American States (OAS), 364
Organization of Petroleum Exporting Countries (OPEC), 371
OSHA (Occupational Safety and Health Administration), 157, 162, 266, 328
oversight, 114–15, 166

PAC (political action committees), 84, 108, 262, 263, 266, 292, 300, 302, 317–19, 319
Paine, Thomas, 356
Pakistan, 363
Palestinians, 359
Panama, 128, 369
Parliament, British, 149
parliaments, 9
Partial Birth Abortion Ban Act (2003), 226
parties, political see political parties
party caucus, 98
party discipline, 109
party identity, 278
party vote, 109
Paterson, William, 20
Patriot Act, see USA PATRIOT Act (2002)
patronage, 116, 137
Penn & Schoen, 225
Pennsylvania:
   as battle ground state, 260
   Constitution ratified by, 32
   radical control of, 19
   Virginia Plan and, 20
Pentagon, 154
Pepper, Claude, 116
per curiam rejection, 195
permanent campaign, 146
Perot, Ross, 258, 264–65, 288, 372
Persian Gulf War, 225, 360–61, 364–65, 366, 367, 373, 376
Personal Responsibility and Work Opportunity Reconciliation Act (PRA), 56, 163, 338, 390, 391
Pharmaceutical Research and Manufactures of America (PhRMA), 300–301
Philippines, 363, 369
phone banks, 290
Physicians for Social Responsibility, 227, 309
"Pioneers," 312
plaintiffs, 179
Planned Parenthood League of Connecticut, 75
Planned Parenthood v. Casey, 77
planters, 17, 19, 21, 39
plea bargains, 181
Plessy v. Ferguson, 78

pluralism, 302, 303
plurality system, 249
pocket veto, 107, 131
Poland, 366
police power, 46, 342
policy entrepreneurs, 279
policy-making powers, 136
policy of redistribution, 330–31
political action committees (PAC), 84, 108, 262, 263, 266, 292, 300, 302, 317–19, 319
political ideology, 211, 222
political knowledge, 22–23
political opinions, formation of, 222–27
political parties, 281–90, 296–98
   candidate recruitment by, 277
   and Congress, 120, 280
   development, 274–76
   evolution of, 282
   functions of, 276–81
   interest groups v., 307
   nomination for, 277–78
   organization of, 276, 293–96, 293
   policy entrepreneurs of, 279
   strength of, 289–97
   technology used by, 290–93
   third parties and, 287–89
political socialization, 213–20
politics:
   complexity of, 4–5
   definition of, 8
   government's influence on, 8–9
polls, 233–37, 239, 257–58
   design of, 234
   measurement error of, 234
   probability sampling in, 233
   push polling and, 234
   random digital dialing in, 233
   sample size of, 234
   selection bias in, 233
poll tax, 244
popular sovereignty, 12, 13
Populist movement, 211, 321
pork barrel, 116–17, 161–62
Postal Service, U.S., 152, 158
poverty programs, 53
Powell, Colin, 140, 359
Powell, Lewis, 88
PRA (Personal Responsibility and Work Opportunity Reconciliation Act, 56, 163, 338, 390, 391

precedents, legal, 180
precinct captains, 296
presidency, 120, 133–34, *138*
  bills and, 107
  congressional influence of, 113
  in Constitution, 125, 126–27
  1800–1933, 134–35
  elections and, 251
  expressed powers of, 127–32
  formal resources of power by,
    137, 139–47
  lobbying of, 312
  post-New Deal power gain by,
    137, 148–50
  and Supreme Court judges, 26
  Supreme Court's relationship
    with, 200
  see also executive branch
Presidential Election Campaign
  Fund, 264
presidential power, 136
President's Committee on
  Administrative Management,
  164
primary elections, 277–78
Printz v. United States, 58
private bill, 117
privatization, 170–71, 341
privileges and immunities clause,
  27, 47
procedural liberties, 67
Progressive Era, 289–90
Progressive Party, 287–88
Progressive reformers, 245, 247,
  287
Prohibition, 35, 38, 41, 345
project grants, 52
proportional representation, 249
Proposition 22, 47
Proposition 209, 89, 238
prospective voting, 256
Public Affairs Council, 227
public assistance programs, 336–37
  noncontributory, 336
public interest groups, 302, 304–5
public law, *177,* 180
public opinion, 146–47, 211,
  222–27
  origins of, 212–13
  political ideology and, 220–22
  political socialization and,
    213–20
  polls of, 233–37

public policy, 325–47
  contracts and, 341–42, 344, 347
  control techniques of, 339–42,
    340, 344–46
  fiscal techniques and, 346
  licensing and, 342, 344, 347
  monetary techniques and, 346
  promotional techniques of,
    339–42, *340*
  redistributive techniques of,
    340, 345–46, 347
  regulatory techniques of, *340,*
    342, 344–45
  spending power of, 346
  subsidies and, 339–41, 344, 347
Publius, 32

Quayle, Dan, 141
Queenan, Joe, 227

racial gerrymandering, 249
racism, 215
railroads, 327
rallying effect, 147
Randolph, Edmund, 19–20
Reagan, Ronald, 35, 58, 99, 184,
  392
  Bush as vice president of, 141
  central management control by,
    143
  children of, 214
  Congress and, 121, 149
  deregulation by, 132
  election of, 142
  on government, 328, 379, 392
  judicial appointees of, 184, 185,
    198, 202
  OMB under, 140
  overview of, 387–89
  public appearances of, 146
  regulatory review and, 4
  social issues and, 279
  "supply-side" economics of, 380,
    388
  tax cuts of, 388
  television and radio addresses of,
    144
Reagan administration, contracting
  and, 341
recall elections, 254, 255
Reed, Stanley, 197
referendum, 254
regulated federalism, 53–56

regulatory agencies, 162
regulatory review, 4
Rehnquist, William H., 62, 76,
  182, 185, 198, 318
Rehnquist Court, 199
religious Right, 284, 316–17, 320
  see also Christian Right
Report on Manufactures
  (Hamilton), 340
representative democracy, 12
Republican Club for Growth, 295
Republican National Committee
  (RNC), 293, 294, 379
Republican National Conventions:
  of 1992, 236
  of 1996, 236
Republican Party:
  African Americans as, 218
  airport security and, 110
  "benign" gerrymandering and,
    250
  big government embraced by,
    381
  Bush's meeting with leaders of,
    275–76
  campaign technology and, 292
  Clinton's budget struggle with,
    109, 228
  Clinton's crime bill and, 112–13
  Clinton's impeachment and,
    116, 124
  Clinton supported by, 280
  coalitions of, 146
  committee staff reduction policy
    of, 103
  as conference chair, 99
  and Contract with America, 99
  Democrats' differences with,
    241–42, 278
  in electoral realignments,
    284–87, *285, 286*
  foreign policy and, 376–77
  funding of, 261, 295
  Gingrich in, 100
  GWB's judicial nominees and,
    184–86
  GWB's strengthening of, 380
  history of, 283–84
  House committee pledge of, 280
  increased defense spending of,
    162
  interstate highway program and,
    383

Iraq war and, 115, 210
Lincoln's leadership of, 134
lobbyists and, 312
military officers' support for, 218
New Deal, 384
1994 victory of, 114
partial-birth abortion and, 107
registration efforts of, 260
religious right and, 284, 320
social issues of, 279
Southern redistricting and, 215
Texas redistricting by, 251
2004 election and, 258–60
"Voter Vault" of, 278
voting manipulation allegations
    against, 244
white southerners in, 219
Republican Party (Jeffersonian),
    10–11, 281, 284
Republican Wednesday Group,
    104
reserved powers amendment, 46
responsible party government, 297
retrospective voting, 256
revenue sharing, 56, 386
Rhode Island, 29
    Constitution ratified by, 33
    radical control of, 19, 21
Rice, Condoleezza, 360
right to privacy, 75
Rio Treaty (1947), 364
Rise and Growth of American
    Politics (Ford), 268
Rita, Hurricane, 129
RNC (Republican National
    Committee), 293, 294, 379
roads, 327
Roberts, John G., 77, 185
Robinson, Donald, 21
Roe v. Wade, 35, 75, 77, 192,
    198–99, 315, 380
Rogers Act (1924), 359
roll-call votes, 109
Romer v. Evans, 84
Roosevelt, Franklin D., 164
    BoB and, 149
    court packing plan of, 184, 189,
        200
    on economic aid, 363
    election of, 284
    "fireside chats" of, 144, 231
    loyalty towards, 218
    national protection and, 127

New Deal coalition of, 145–46
New Deal of, 135, 287, 297,
    326, 379
1936 poll and, 233
press conferences of, 144
proposals for legislative action
    by, 131
Republican support for, 256
Social Security, 280
as strong president, 148
White House staff of, 139
Roosevelt, Theodore, 231
Roper polls, 233
Rosenberger v. University of
    Virginia, 76, 193
Rothstein, Barbara, 201
Rove, Karl, 258
royalists, 17
Rule 10, 193–94
rulemaking, 157
Rumsfeld, Donald, 139, 232, 360
Russia, 361, 362, 365–66, 367
    see also Soviet Union

St. Louis Globe-Democrat, 231
salient interests, 236
same-sex marriage, 46–47
Sandinistas, 369
San Francisco, Calif., same-sex
    marriage in, 85
San Francisco Superior Court, 47
Saturday Night Live, 230
Saudi Arabia, 361
Scalia, Antonin, 185, 186, 196,
    198, 203
school prayer amendment, 35
Schumer, Charles, 57
Schwarzenegger, Arnold, 255
SEATO (Southeast Asia Treaty
    Organization), 364
Seattle, Wash., WTO protest in, 355
secession, 71
Second Amendment, 36, 69
Securities and Exchange
    Commission, 166
segregation, 78, 79–81, 198, 201,
    213, 315
"Selling of the Pentagon, The"
    (documentary), 225
Seminoles, 58
Senate, U.S.:
    Appropriations Committee of,
        99, 102, 117, 321

Armed Services Committee of,
    353
bicameralism, 96–98
cabinet approved by, 137
campaign committees of, 295
campaign costs in, 277
checks and balances and, 60
committees of, 102
compromises in, 98
in Connecticut Plan, 20
in Constitution, 23
Constitutional amendments and,
    34, 35
Democrat control of, 281
elections and, 36, 251
ergonomics regulations and, 266
executive appointments
    approved by, 130
Finance Committee of, 140, 161
floor debate in, 105
foreign policy and, 350–51,
    352–53, 376
Foreign Relations Committee of,
    231, 353
impeachment and, 116
interest groups and, 113
Judiciary Committee of, 184, 187
mutual defense alliances ratified
    by, 364
organization of, 97
oversight and, 114–15, 166
partisanship in, 105
party leadership in, 98–100,
    109, 121
party unity in, 109
presidential veto and, 107
September 11 and, 350–51
special powers of, 115
Supreme Court judges and, 26,
    184
terms of, 23
treaties and, 26, 95, 115
2004 election to, 258
veto overridden by, 131
vice president and, 141
Senate majority leader, 105, 112
Senate Select Committee to
    Investigate the 1972
    Presidential Campaign
    Activities, 318
senatorial courtesy, 184
Senior Executive Service (SES),
    137, 387

seniority, 102–3
separation of powers, 29, *30,* 43, 59–60, 62, 64
September 11, 2001, terrorist attacks of, 13, 63, 68, 129, 142, 210, 259, 260
  airline bailout for, 311
  alliance created by, 375
  bureaucracy and, 152, 154
  Bush's reaction to, 229
  congressional party squabbling and, 109–10
  diplomacy and, 359
  foreign policy and, 350–51
  globalization and, 389
  NATO and, 366
  possible impact of, 219
  UN and, 361–62
Serbia, 128, 366
SES (Senior Executive Service), 137, 387
Seventeenth Amendment, 23, 60
Seventh Amendment, 36
sexual revolution, 315
Shapiro, Robert, 225
Sharpton, Al, 283
Shaw v. Reno, 250–51
Shays, Christopher, 115
Shays, Daniel, 19
Shays's Rebellion, 19, 44
Shelley v. Kraemer, 79
Shell Oil, 304
Sherman, Roger, 17
Sherman Antitrust Act (1890), 328
shopkeepers, 17
Shuster, Bud, 116
Sierra Club, 39, 227, 262, 309–10
Silverman, Brian, 321
Simpson, O. J., 215
single-member-district, 288–89
SixPAC, 262
Sixteenth Amendment, 37, 38
Sixth Amendment, 36
60 Minutes 2, 232
Skowronek, Stephen, 390
slavery:
  abolition of, 38, 68
  in Constitution, 20–21, 27, 43
  Democrats split by, 281, 285
  Kansas-Nebraska Act and, 283
  as political issue, 281, 285–86
  public opinion and, 213
  as state law, 71

Smith, Adam, 326, 393
Smith, Leighton, 374
Smith v. Allwright, 197
Sniderman, Paul M., 224
Socialist Party, 225
socialization:
  agencies of, 214–20
  political, 213–14
Social Security, 56, 218, 280, 332–35, 338
  bureaucracy, 167
  Bush and, 263, 334
  Clinton and, 124, 125, 281
  contributory programs of, 332–33
  same-sex marriage and, 47
  indexing of, 386
  reforming of, 334
Social Security Act (1935), 332, 336
Social Security Administration (SSA), 163
Social Security reform, 120
Social Security tax, 330, 333, 334, 346, 391
Social Security Trust Fund, 334, 335
soft money, 262–64, 319
solicitor general, 194
Solomon, King, 175
Soros, George, 259, 262, 264
Souter, David, 185, 197, 198, 200, 203
South:
  American Independent Party in, 288
  move to Republican camp by, 219, 283
  redistricting in, 215
  religious Right in, 320
South Africa, 372
South Carolina:
  Constitution ratified by, 32
  McCain's defeat in, 230
  school segregation in, 79
  slavery in, 21
South Dakota, 258
Southeast Asia Treaty Organization (SEATO), 364
southern strategy, 386
South Korea, 128, 363
Soviet Union, 11, 169, 358, 362, 365–66, 371, 372–73

  arms sold by, 367
  elections in, 241
  Korean War and, 358, 360
  totalitarianism in, 7
  see also Russia
speaker of the House, 98, 105, 112, 280
Spirit of the Laws, The (Montesquieu), 29
split-ticket voting, 253–54
Springfield Republican, 231
SSA (Social Security Administration), 163
SSI (Supplemental Security Income), 337
Stafford, Robert, 311
staff organizations, 305
staff system, 103
stakeholders, 313–14
Stalin, Joseph, 7
standing committee, 101, 102
stare decisis, 180
Statecraft as Soulcraft (Will), 392
State Department, U.S., 160, 161
  creation of, 4
State of the Union, 131
state sovereign immunity, 58
states' power, 24–26, 27, 39, 45–46
  see also federalism
states' rights, 57, 281
statutory interpretation, 178
Steel Caucus, 104
Steel Seizure, 62
Stevens, John Paul, 198, 203
Stevens, Ted, 117
Stone, Harlan Fiske, 57, 197
straight party vote, 253
strict scrutiny, 74
substantive liberties, 67
suffrage, *see* voting rights
Supplement Security Income (SSI), 337
"supply-side" economics, 380, 388
Supreme Court, Hawaii, 46
supreme court, state, 180
Supreme Court, U.S.:
  abortion rights and, 75
  affirmative action in, 85–90
  Bill of Rights and, 70–71
  briefs of, 195
  cases heard by, 191–200, *192*
  chief justice of, 183

Congress's relationship with, 199–200, 201
in Constitution, 26–27
Constitution interpreted by, 178–79
criticism of, 75
denationalizing trend of, 76–77
dissenting opinion in, 197
on executive agreements, 115
FDR's court packing plan and, 184, 189
federalism and, 50–51, 58
Fourteenth Amendment and, 71–72, 90
gay rights and, 84
gender discrimination and, 83
interstate commerce and, 136
judicial arrangement and, 44
justices, *185*
limitations of, 200–201
line-item veto struck down by, 131
nationalized rights and, 71–73
nomination to, 132
opinion writing by, 196–97
oral arguments in, 195–96
presidential nominees to, 183–87
president's relationship with, 200
revolutions of, 201–4
right to privacy and, 75
Rules of, 193
segregation and, 78–79, 81, 315
separation of powers and, 60–62
state powers and, 3
Tenth Amendment and, 57
2000 presidential election decided by, 203
War on Terror and, 190
see also judicial review; *specific cases*
Supreme Court, Vermont, 46
Supreme Judicial Court, Massachusetts, 85
"Swift Boat Veterans for Truth," 260, 263

Taiwan, 363
Taliban, 128, 147, 190, 363, 375
TANF (Temporary Assistance to Needy Families), 56, 163, 337, 337, 338, 390

tariffs, 285, 286, 330, 357, 391
Tauzin, Billy, 312
taxes, 7, 281, 330
GWB and, 263, 279
in Constitution, 23, 45, 95
discrimination of, 330
growth of, 7
income, 37, 335, 346
liberty and, 13
progressive, 330
regressive, 330
regulatory, 344–45
Social Security, 330, 333, 334, 346, 391
between states, 44
Tax Reform Act (1986), 388
Tea Act (1773), 17
Teamsters, 304
Temporary Assistance to Needy Families (TANF), 56, 163, 337, 337, 338, 390
Tenth Amendment, 45–46, 57, 58
terrorism, 171, 257
Bush's response to, 229
DHS and, 4
see also War on Terror
Texas:
affirmative action in, 87
redistricting in, 251
Third Amendment, 36, 75
third parties, 287–89
Thirteenth Amendment, 27, 34, 37, 38, 68
Thomas, Clarence, 185, 187, 196, 198
Three-fifths Compromise, 20–21
Tiananmen Square, 373
Tilden, Samuel, 253
"To Amend the Omnibus Crime Control and Safe Streets Act of 1968" (1994), 389, 391
tobacco industry, 353
Tocqueville, Alexis de, 322
Tonight Show with Jay Leno, The, 230
tort cases, 180
totalitarian government, 7
Total Quality Management, 387
trade tariffs, 44
Transportation Department, U.S., 129, 152, 153, 160
Transportation Safety Administration, 129

Transportation Security Administration, 153
Travel and Tourism Caucus, 104
Treasury Department, U.S., 142, 160, 163, 165
creation of, 4
September 11 and, 153
Social Security and, 334
trial court, 180
Trippi, Joe, 291
Truman, Harry S., 62, 113, 128, 130, 363
trustees, 118
Turkey, 363
Twelfth Amendment, 252
Twenty-first Amendment, 34, 35
Twenty-seventh Amendment, 37

Underfunded Management Reform Act (UMRA), 55–56
underfunded mandates, 55
Uniform Commercial Code, 181
unilateralism, 357
Union of Concerned Scientists, 304
unions, 4, 217, 226, 261, 279, 283, 287, 318
United Mine Workers, 304
United Nations, 110, 209, 220, 358, 360–62, 364
United States v. Lopez, 58
United States v. Morrison, 58
United States v. Nixon, 62, 131, 189
universalization of rights, 83
University of California, 85
University of Chicago, National Opinion Research Center, 234
urban redevelopment projects, 345
USA PATRIOT Act (2002), 129, 392–93, 394
U.S. Government Manual, 194
Utah, same-sex marriage and, 47

Valley Forge, Pa., 16
values, 211
van Lohuizen, Jan, 226
Ventura, Jesse, 287
Vermont Supreme Court, 46
Very Hungry Caterpillar, The (Carle), 229
veto, 107, 132, *133*
vice presidency, 141
Vietnam, 363

Vietnam War, 115, 128, 130, 167,
      358, 360, 371
   "Cooper/Church" debate and,
      375
   draft evaders of, 129
   draft in, 7
   Kerry and, 260
   media and, 225, 227–28, 231
   New Politics and, 309
   social upheaval caused by,
      218–19, 220
Violence against Women Act
      (1994), 58, 83
Virginia:
   Constitution ratified by, 32
   school segregation in, 79
   slavery in, 21
Virginia, University of, 193
Virginia, Virginia Plan and, 20
Virginia Military Institute, 83
Virginia Plan, 20
Volcker, Paul, 387
Volcker Commission, 387
"Voter Vault," 278
voting, see elections
voting rights, 23, 81, 198, 201,
      242, 274
Voting Rights Act (1965), 242,
      249, 250
"Votomatic" machines, 243

Wagner Act (1935), 135
Wallace, George, 288
Wallace, Henry, 288
Wal-Mart, 312
war, 375
   declaration of, 44, 45
   see also specific wars

War Department, U.S., 161
Wards Cove v. Atonio, 86
War on Terror, 190, 220, 258
   see also Afghanistan; Iraq war
War Powers Resolution (1973),
      128, 149
Warren, Earl, 76, 183, 198
Warsaw Pact (1955), 365, 371
Washington, George, 15
   farewell address of, 356
   Genàt received by, 130
   House request refused by,
      130
   parties deplored by, 281
Washington Post, 228, 231, 232,
      374
Washington State, 238
Watergate scandal, 131, 131n,
      228, 318–19
weapons of mass destruction
      (WMDs), 210, 232, 259,
      367–68, 375
Weather Service, 152
Webster v. Reproductive Health
      Services, 76, 315
Weinberger, Caspar, 129
welfare, 163, 332, 333, 347
   in polls, 234
   reform plan of 1996, 63,
      338–39, 391
   see also Personal Responsibility
      and Work Opportunity
      Reconciliation Act
welfare reform, 170
Whig party, 283, 284, 285, 286,
      287
whip system, 112
White House staff, 139, 140

whites, 215, 216
   African Americans' disagreement
      with, 223–24
   Iraq War and, 209
Wide Awake (magazine), 193
Will, George, 392
Williams & Jensen, 311
Wilson, Pete, 89
Wilson, Woodrow, 134, 225, 231
Wisconsin, 170
WMDs (weapons of mass
      destruction), 210, 232, 259,
      367–68, 375
women:
   interest groups of, 305
   New Politics and, 305
   see also gender discrimination;
      gender gap; League of
      Women Voters; Violence
      against Women Act
      (1994)
Works Progress Administration
      (WPA), 382
World Bank, 362
World Trade Organization (WTO),
      354–55, 372
World War, I, 7, 225, 370
World War, I, II, 7, 218, 309, 360,
      370, 376
WPA (Works Progress
      Administration), 382
writ of certiori, 193, 204
WTO (World Trade Organization),
      354–55, 372

Y2K problem, 124
Young, Don, 117
Yugoslavia, 361, 371, 374